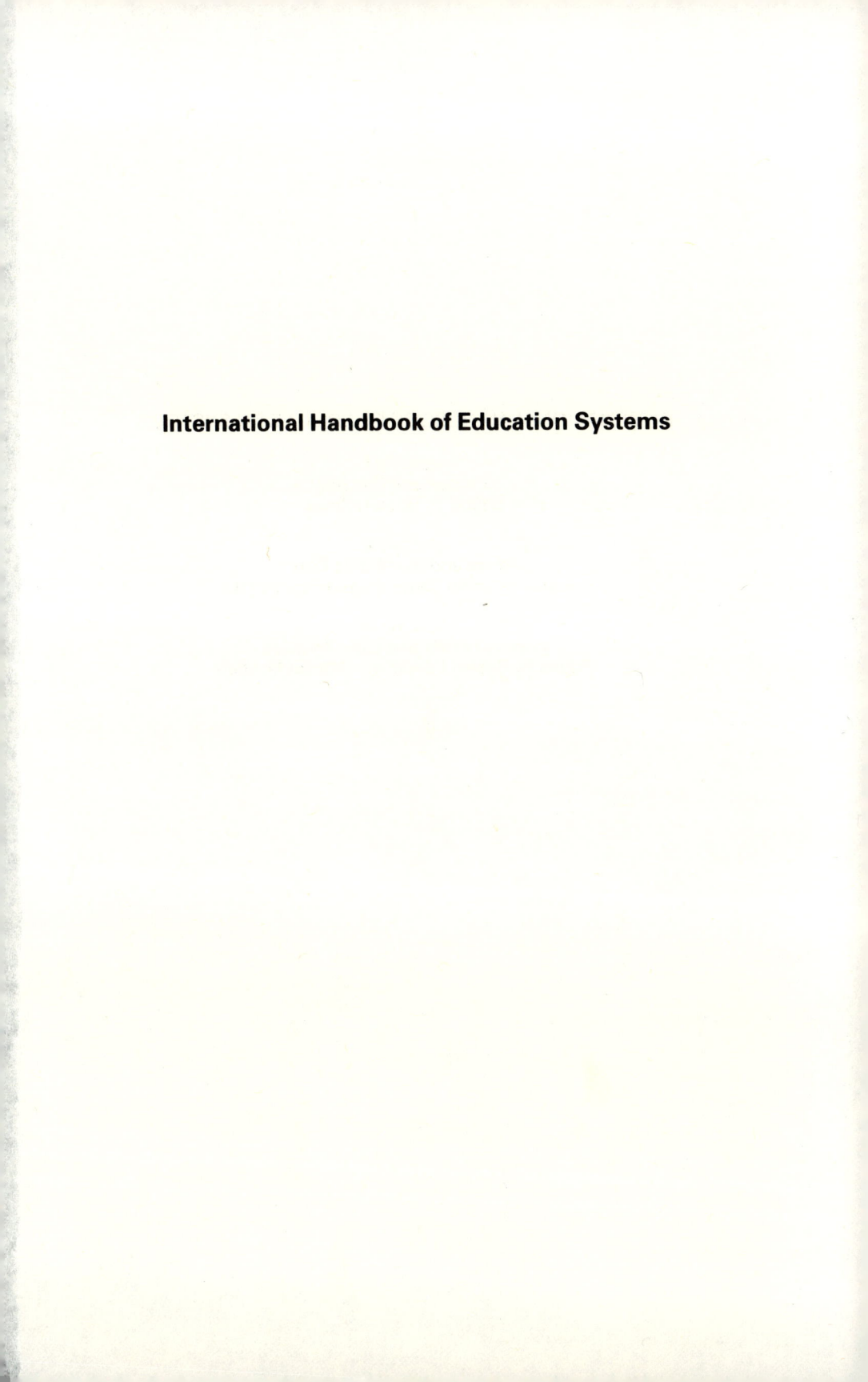

International Handbook of Education Systems

INTERNATIONAL HANDBOOK OF EDUCATION SYSTEMS

Volume I
Europe and Canada
Edited by Brian Holmes

Volume II
Africa and the Middle East
Edited by John Cameron *and* Paul Hurst

Volume III
Asia, Australia and Latin America
Edited by Robert Cowan *and* Martin McLean

International Handbook of Education Systems

Editors: J Cameron, R Cowan, B Holmes, P Hurst and M McLean

Volume I

Europe and Canada

Edited by

Brian Holmes

Institute of Education, University of London

JOHN WILEY & SONS
Chichester · New York · Brisbane · Toronto · Singapore

Copyright © 1983 by John Wiley & Sons Ltd.

Reprinted August 1985.

All rights reserved.

No part of this book may be reproduced by any means, nor transmitted, nor translated into a machine language without the written permission of the publisher.

British Library Cataloguing in Publication Data:

International handbook of education systems.
   Vol. 1: Europe and Canada
   1. Comparative education
   I. Holmes, Brian
   370.19'5   LA132

   ISBN 0 471 90078 8

Printed in Great Britain

Contents

Preface
Introduction 1
Austria 35
Belgium 75
Canada 103
Cyprus 145
Czechoslovakia 171
Denmark 195
Federal Republic of Germany 223
Finland 259
France 299
Greece 341
Hungary 371
Israel 397
Italy 423
Luxembourg 457
Malta 483
Netherlands 503
Norway 537
Poland 565
Spain 589
Sweden 615
Switzerland 641
Turkey 667
Yugoslavia 695

Preface

The need for this Handbook of Educational Systems was suggested by the success and usefulness of the profiles of educational systems compiled over the last ten years by the British Council, which is the major organisation supported by the British Government to promote the knowledge of British life and culture worldwide through cultural and educational activities.

The main headings under which data have been classified and the sequence in which the headings have been placed are the same in each of the national profiles. Sub-headings in general follow the same pattern in each case but where appropriate the headings have been changed to meet the particular circumstances of the national system described. Diagrams giving a simplified picture of the structure of each educational system have been standardised (and taken from the IBE/Unesco International Yearbook of Education, XXXII, 1980) but simplified diagrams showing how education in each country is administered have not been standardised. Statistics have been drawn from the latest Unesco Statistical Yearbook and standardised to facilitate comparisons; more detailed information about any of the systems can be obtained from the Unesco Yearbook itself. Further more detailed information about the organisation of educational administration can usually be obtained from national Ministries of Education; the address of each Ministry of Education and the address of the national documentation centre are given in the previously mentioned IBE/Unesco International Yearbook of Education, XXXII, Paris, Unesco, 1980.

The Editors of this Handbook have adopted the framework or headings of the British Council profiles for all the profiles included here, as far as the content will allow, and the Editors have drawn upon a variety of sources for information, data and first-hand experience. Although no such Handbook can hope to be entirely comprehensive it is hoped that future editions will include more countries as well as revising and updating the profiles of countries included here.

Although every effort has been made to ensure the accuracy of the information in the Handbook, no responsibility is implied or accepted by the Editors, the British Council or the Publishers for any errors or omissions. The British Council, in particular, is not associated with any opinions or interpretations which may be expressed or implied in the Handbook.

The Editors and Publishers also wish to express their thanks to those who have helped in the compilation of this Handbook:

Introduction

NATION STATES

The nations of Europe are the product of history. Wars, invasions, political alliances and the free movement of people have changed frontiers, reduced or enlarged territories leaving the present political maps of Europe distinctly different from those drawn in the recent and distant past. The physical features of the land mass with its surrounding seas that we know as Europe remains the same. The great rivers of Europe and its mountains have provided natural barriers and still, in many cases, help us even now to identify sovereign territories. To the north of Italy the Alps form a natural border. The Pyrenees separate France from Spain. The Carpathian mountains serve as a guide to the border between Poland and Czechoslovakia. Less protected boundaries have been the subject of dispute. Thus some of the great rivers of Europe, the Rhine, the Danube and the Oder are both natural boundaries, the object of innumerable disputes, and identification of the location of many great cities.

The Channel as a natural barrier to easy communication has helped to keep the United Kingdom at some distance politically, economically and culturally from the rest of Europe. These and other considerations help us to identify several major regions in Europe. The countries bordering the Mediterranean contain characteristics, so do the Scandinavian nations to the north, Denmark, Sweden, Norway and Finland. The Balkans too represent an identifiable region and the broad plains of northern Europe include nations whose peoples are differentiated less by the difficulties of communicating with each other and more by cultural differences represented by language, religion and genealogy.

From a political perspective some knowledge of the geographical conditions which helped to force people to live together in communities is necessary if we are to examine the diversity which is to be found in many of the nation states of Europe. Cultural diversity has been identified in no fewer than seventeen autonomous sovereign states in Europe. The educational problems arising from these geo-political influences are matters of present day concern in many European countries.

Geographical conditions influence education in other ways. Temperature extremes, the differences between winter and summer have some bearing on the accessibility of schools to young children, the time at which schools can reasonably begin in the morning and end in the early or late afternoon. Continental climates make a difference to the severity of winters and the heat of summers. Notable comparative educationists have, for example, pointed out that there is a correlation between the age at which children are first expected to attend school and latitude. In the northern latitudes the age at which children first attend school tends to be older than in the southern latitudes. Again, the hard winters in Moscow contrast sharply with those experienced by people living in Edinburgh on the same latitude. It is difficult to see how, even now, young children living in isolated homesteads could easily reach school when snow and ice make inadequate roads impassable.

A further possible influence of latitude may be mentioned. In the far north the days are very short in winter, in summer they are very long. The incentives, particularly in rural areas in the north of Sweden, to learn to read and write, and to acquire self-entertainment skills must still be very great. Certainly there is evidence to justify the view that long winters and short days encouraged among the rural population the growth of adult education and the Folk High School movement in the Scandinavian countries. High noon temperatures, warm evenings and smaller differences between the lengths of day and night in the Mediterranean countries certainly facilitate different lifestyles. A noonday siesta is not only culturally desired but for climatic reasons necessary.

Climatic conditions in most parts of the British Isles undoubtedly make it possible for legislators to insist that all children should attend school from the age of five. In the rural areas of the European parts of the USSR it would not be possible; in the isolated Norwegian villages it would be difficult. It is not surprising, therefore, to find that the age at which compulsory attendance commences in the northern European countries is seven, in the southern and central European nations it is six. The UK is unique in expecting children to enter school at five.

Urbanisation, improved communications and the greater involvement of women in industry and commerce have, of course, created pressures, regardless of geographical conditions for nursery schools and other pre-school institutions. In many European countries including the USSR, the earlier access of children to schools has received priority in recent years. The age at which children may attend nursery schools and other institutions, almost always on a voluntary basis, varies from one nation to another: so too does the percentage of children whose parents take advantage of these facilities as Table I shows:

Table I

Country	Year	Pre-school age range	5 year olds %	4 year olds %	3 year olds %
Belgium	1970	2½ - 6	100	95	90
France	1970			84	55
UK	1970	3 - 5	100	30	3
Greece	1975	3½ - 5½			
Austria		3 - 6			
Norway	1971	3 - 6		29% Rising	

14.87% of 3 - 6 year olds

The fact that pre-school enrolments are rising faster in the urban areas suggests that industrialisation and urban growth have greatly influenced parental pressure for pre-school provision. Climatic conditions, in spite of improvements in communication, may account for slower rates of growth in rural areas.

Physical conditions are also related to density of population. Clearly, people settled in those parts of Europe where living conditions were easier - that is on the plains near or on the rivers. On the other hand mountainous countries, like Japan, may possess very large populations. The area on which houses can be built and industries developed may be densely populated, the mountainous regions sparsely populated. Correlation between topographical features, population density and industrial development point to the geographical aspects of a nation which may have some bearing on educational provision. The educational problems associated with high and increasing density of population are different from those linked with low and declining population density.

Within nation states the geographical features and the distribution of population still influence access to schools and the equality of educational provision. These should, however, be seen in the light of population movements, the growth of urban areas and conurbations and economic differences between the centres of political and economic power and the peripheral regions. A major feature in a national analysis of conditions which bear on educational provision should be a description of urban-rural differences and the physical conditions which have contributed to the growth of large cities and industrial areas. The unplanned movement of people can be explained to a considerable extent by analysing the attraction of living near rivers and on plains rather than in the rugged mountains of, let us say, Montenegro in Yugoslavia or Norway.

Table II

Country	Date	Area sq. miles	Population	Density of population	Cities over 1,000,000
Austria	1978	32,376	7,508,400	231.9	Vienna
Belgium	1979	11,781	9,855,000	836.5	Greater Brussels
Canada	1981	3,851,809	24,088,500	6.25	Toronto, Vancouver, Montreal
Czechoslovakia	1978	49,400	15,138,188	306.4	Prague
Cyprus	1978	3,572	618,300	173.1	
Denmark	1979	17,000	5,111,534	300.6	Greater Copenhagen
Finland	1979	130,165	4,771,098	36.6	
France	1979	213,000	53,371,000	250.5	Paris
Fed. Rep. of Germany	1979	96,011	61,439,300	639.9	Berlin, Hamburg
Greece	1971	51,182	8,768,641	171.3	Athens
Malta	1979	94.9	314,500	33.1	
Poland	1978	121,000	35,000,000	289.2	Warsaw
Luxembourg	1978	999	355,400	355.7	
Yugoslavia	1979	98,725	22,111,000	223.9	Belgrade
United Kingdom	1978	93,051	55,836,000	600.0	London
Hungary	1980	36,000	19,710,000	547.5	Budapest
Italy	1975	131,000	56,024,000	427.6	Rome, Milan, Naples, Turin

Israel	1981	7,942	3,836,000	479.9	Greater Tel Aviv
Netherlands	1978	13,500	13,897,000	1,029.4	Rotterdam
Norway	1979	154,520	4,078,900	26.4	
Portugal	1977	34,000	9,774,000	287.4	Lisbon, Oporto
Spain	1978	196,700	36,958,000	187.9	Madrid, Barcelona
Sweden	1977	173,436	8,267,116	47.7	
Switzerland	1978	15,950	6,298,000	394.0	Stockholm
Turkey	1979		43,000,000		Istanbul, Ankara
USSR	1979	8,620,822	262,442,000	3.0	Baku, Dnepropetorvsk, Kharkov, Donetsk, Odessa, Gorky, Novosibirsk, Kuibyshev, Sverdlovsk, Omsk, Chelyabinks, Moscow, Leningrad, Kiev, Tashkent, Tbilisi, Erevan

Natural barriers within nation states also help to maintain and foster group cultural identity, by isolating one group from another and thus reducing social contacts and communication. The maintenance of English, Scottish, Welsh and Irish differences is in part a reflection of geographical conditions. The differences between Croats and Serbs in Yugoslavia and between the peoples of the five Republics are certainly the result of history, but that history has been influenced by the geographical conditions which make Montenegro vastly different from Croatia or Serbia.

Each of the profiles is introduced by a brief account of the topography, climate and population of the nation whose educational system is described. The extent to which these features influence educational provision can be interpreted in terms of some of the suggestions made here. A crucial point, however, is that natural boundaries, mountains and rivers, no longer play the same role as previously in the maintenance of distinctive cultural groups. Moreover, nation states have been created which ignore former natural and historical boundaries. They have incorporated peoples who, once living in relative isolation, are expected to abandon their previous identity to merge into the ethos of the nation state. Two things contribute to make such integration problematic. The geographical isolation of minority groups helps them to maintain unique cultural traits. Secondly the strength of traditions, their economic and political power determine the potential of a minority group to gain concessions from a central government in the provision of education in accordance with its minority group interests.

HISTORICAL DEVELOPMENTS

For the purposes of this survey a distinction can be usefully drawn between those periods of European history when, on balance, attempts to unify groups within the geographical boundaries set by the Atlantic seaboard to the west, the Mediterranean to the south, the Arctic circle to the north and the Urals to the east met with success, and those periods in which nationalism and small group interests prevailed.

In brief, what we now know as European civilisation may be said to have had its origins in the south-east, in the days of the Roman Empire which incorporated into its culture much of the Greek spirit and Christianity. Hellenism and Christianity, and the Judaic traditions from which it was derived, indeed constitute the intellectual core round which European systems of education have been erected. Roman institutions spread over the Mediterranean seaboard and to the coasts of the Atlantic. During the Middle Ages Roman influence penetrated central Europe and later at the beginning of the eighteenth century into Russia. The concept of Europe is, however, in the language of diplomacy, a nineteenth century innovation.

1 Religion

Early unifying tendencies were associated not only with the military success achieved by Roman generals but with the spread of Christianity and the power of the Roman Catholic Church. A succession of barbarian invasions ended after the successful raids of Scandinavian warriors who, in the ninth century, ravaged the whole of Western Europe, including northern Germany, Britain, France, Spain and Italy. Permanent settlements were established in England and France. These invasions failed to check the spread of Christianity or the emergence of identifiable kingdoms in the eleventh century. Frequently tribal chiefs, on their conversion to Christianity, took the title of king. Thus Christianity, adopted by political leaders throughout Europe, constituted a powerful unifying force politically and culturally. Europe became Christian and its systems of education were influenced profoundly by its ethos. The initiatives taken by the Christian churches to extend education and their power to control its development explain many of the common elements which can be discerned in modern European schools everywhere. Common organisational features have their origin in Roman and Christian practices; common cultural features stem from Greek and Christian-Judaic philosophies.

During the early period of Roman influence political and clerical power were closely allied. Conflicts between Popes and Emperors during the period of the Holy Roman Empire resulted finally in the emergence of a host of independent princes, dukes and lords whose political relationships with churchmen varied greatly. The growth of secular power served to break down the political unity that had been established in Western Europe by Emperor and Pope. In few countries in North Western Europe, the partial exceptions being Sweden and England, did the close alliance of Church and State survive the Reformation.

The Romans also influenced Eastern Europe where the establishment of Christianity as the official religion was approved by the State. The disintegration of the Holy Roman Empire resulted finally in the division of the Church into its Eastern and Western branches which was finalised officially in 1054. After that the Greek Orthodox and Roman Catholic Churches went their separate ways, thus dividing Christian Europe. The Eastern Church remained true to its traditional character throughout the Middle Ages. The Western Church was, as mentioned, profoundly influenced by the rise of independent kingdoms. This, followed by the Reformation, gave rise to diversity within the Western Church. Roman Catholic and Protestant churches now command the allegiance of peoples in the different nations of Western Europe. Indeed, the population in some countries such as Italy, Spain, Poland and France are still predominantly Catholic in outlook. Anti-clericalism informs political movements, however. In other countries such as the Scandinavian countries, Protestant beliefs of Luther or Calvin dominate the outlook of most people. In other nations such as the Netherlands and the Federal Republic of Germany, populations are divided more evenly.

Thus in European religious growth there exists diversity among Christians. The Western and Eastern Churches differ in some respects and there are differences of outlook, belief and organisation between the Roman Catholic Church and the Protestant Churches. In the West these differences have profoundly influenced the provision of education. Everywhere Roman Catholic leaders have insisted that the schools should be controlled by the clergy and that a Catholic ethos should inform all aspects of provision. Where they have not been able directly or vicariously to control publicly maintained schools, as in France, the Roman Catholic authorities have endeavoured to maintain, at great cost and where they have been allowed to do so, a system of instruction from primary through higher education.

National policies relating to religious education vary. Soviet law prohibits religious schools. French law prevents the teaching of religion in State schools and makes provision for circumscribed support for Roman Catholic schools. Under the 1944 Education Act Church schools in England and Wales received all their running costs and a proportion of their capital costs. Under this scheme the Roman Catholic authorities have attempted to provide primary and secondary schools and teacher training colleges for the children of their members. In the Netherlands generous public finance supports the Protestant, Catholic and non-sectarian systems of schooling.

Religious diversity in Europe consequently continues to create problems of policy for national governments. To historical differences between Christians have been added those arising from the movement of Christian and non-Christian parents and their children into Europe since 1945 and particularly during the 1950s and 1960s. Catholic Poles remained in Britain after the Second World War, Catholic Italians and Orthodox Cypriots have also settled there. In addition, Moslems from Pakistan and East Africa have settled in appreciable numbers in parts of Britain as have Hindus from India and Chinese principally from Hong Kong. Into France have moved Moslems from North Africa, and into the Federal Republic of Germany many Turkish workers. This religious diversity has created new problems associated with educational provision. The desire through the schools to maintain religious identity is strong among the leaders of recent arrivals. In a certain sense Europe is no longer Christian and to the diversity created by differences between Catholics and Protestants have been added cultural differences linked with world religions other than Christianity in a great many countries.

Some indication of the religious composition of the populations of European countries is given in Table III. It does not, of course, provide a comprehensive picture either because statistics are not collected or because recent non-Christian arrivals are not clearly identified in national statistics. Some idea of religious diversity can be gained from the brief details given. Particular problems arise in Communist countries where large numbers of Roman Catholics live. The conflict between Communist governments and branches of the Orthodox church seems less serious. Generally speaking religious schools and teaching are prohibited in countries under Communist governments.

Table III
Religion

Austria	The predominant religion is Roman Catholic.
Belgium	Nearly all Belgians are Catholic.
Czechoslovakia	
Denmark	Lutheran (90% officially)
Finland	Lutheran (90%)
France	The majority of French people are Catholics, a strong anti-clericalism informs politics and the small proportion of Huguenots have influenced education considerably.
Fed. Rep. Germany	The balance between Protestants (nearly 30,000,000) and Roman Catholics in the Republic is fairly even. Bavaria's population is heavily Catholic. A small number of Jews remain.
GDR	In old Prussia a high proportion of the population was Protestant.
Greece	Over 97% of the population belongs to the Greek Orthodox church, which is a State religion.
Hungary	About two-thirds of the population are Roman Catholics, most of the rest are Calvinists.
Italy	The majority of the population is Roman Catholic, but politically anti-clericalism is a powerful motivating force.
Netherlands	Roughly a third of the population are Catholic, another third are members of the Dutch Reform Church and a third are humanists.

Table III (contd.)

Norway	Lutheran.
Poland	The majority of people are Roman Catholics.
Portugal	Roman Catholic.
Spain	Roman Catholic is the established Church.
Sweden	The State religion is Lutheran, and over 95% of the population officially subscribe to this form of Christianity.
Switzerland	Protestant (48%); Roman Catholic (49%).
Turkey	Almost all the population are Moslems. Of the 230,000 Christians some are Orthodox (107,000), Armenian (71,000), Catholic (25,000) and Protestant (17,000). Since 1928 Islam has not been the State religion.
USSR	Freedom to profess or not profess any religion is provided for in the Constitution. The Russian Orthodox Church dominated Czarist Russia. Protestants and Moslems constitute minority groups.
Yugoslavia	The Orthodox, Roman Catholic, Protestant, Islamic and Jewish faiths are recognised. There are nearly 7,000,000 Orthodox, over 5,000,000 Catholics and about 2,000,000 Moslems. Over 2,000,000 claim to be without religion.

2 Language

Latin, the language of the Romans, had a unifying influence in Western Europe, in that it became the language of the Church and the language of scholars. People who had received no formal schooling spoke their own vernacular or a vulgar form of Latin. The Romance languages such as Italian, Provençal, French, Portuguese, Castilian, Catalan and Romanian had their origins in Latin. Ancient Greek survives as a working language only in Greece. The Germanic group includes the Scandinavian languages (Swedish, Danish, Norwegian) and the West Germanic languages (German, Dutch and English). Among the Slavonic languages are Lithuanian and Latvian in the north, Bulgarian, Macedonian, Serbo-Croat and Slovene in the south, Czech, Slovak and Polish in the west and Ukrainian and Russian in the east. Celtic languages include Irish, Welsh and Breton. Hungarian, Finnish and Estonian are related. One of the Semitic languages, Hebrew, has been revived for special purposes.

When we consider that within this simplified pattern of the main languages are innumerable dialects and modern modifications the complexity of the European language map can be appreciated.

Minority groups speaking one or other of the Indian, African (including Arabic), and Chinese languages have added in small or large numbers to linguistic diversity in Europe. History and recent immigration patterns contribute to diversity within European nations. Since language is a vehicle through which groups of people seek to maintain their identity, linguistic diversity creates many problems of educational policy.

Several language policies can be identified. In some countries, as in France, every effort has been made to create a national language and promote its acceptance through the schools. Where two major languages are spoken, as in Belgium and England and Wales, bilingual policies may be adopted; each group of children being taught in its own mother tongue. Where, as in the USSR, a multiplicity of languages exists, each child may be taught in its own mother tongue but a national language (Russian in the USSR) may be taught as a foreign language to all those who do not speak it at home.

The diversity of language within Europe and within the nations of Europe create major problems which did not exist when only a small proportion of any population went to school and learned how to read, write and speak the scholars' language, Latin. The development of vernaculars as media of instruction and the language of scholars has its origins in the seventeenth century and the rise of nationalism. Mass literacy campaigns in the vernaculars and the development of national systems of universal elementary schooling in the nineteenth century served to differentiate European systems of education as they moved from elitist to mass education. The retention of Latin and Greek as subjects for those selected for academic secondary schools and subsequently universities has helped to maintain a common culture in Western Europe. The relatively rapid decline of Latin and Greek as compulsory subjects in English grammar schools and the relative weakness of their position in nineteenth century Czarist Russian schools sets these two systems apart from the rest.

The willingness to include modern foreign languages in the curricula of schools and the enthusiasm with which they are taught and learned differs from one country to another. Parents speaking a minority language such as Dutch, Danish and Swedish usually encourage their children to learn English, French or German. English has become the most popular foreign language. French, English and Spanish speaking parents are perhaps less anxious that their children should learn another language, since their own language is widely known throughout the world.

Some indication of linguistic diversity can be gained from the summaries given in Table IV.

Table IV
Language Diversity

Austria	The national language is German but there are Slovene and Croat speaking minorities whose rights are protected.

Table IV (contd.)

Belgium	Dutch and French are official languages. The former is recognised in the northern areas, e.g. Antwerp, West and East Flanders. French is the official language in the southern, Walloon area e.g. Liege. Brussels is officially bi-lingual. The media of instruction in schools reflect the linguistic border between north and south.
Czechoslovakia	There are two official languages, Czech and Slovak, each with its own literature.
Denmark	One of the Scandinavian languages. Danish language and literature was used in the nineteenth century to unite the Danes against the threat of German domination. A small language group, its members readily learn and speak English.
Finland	More than 90% of the people speak Finnish, a small proportion, 6%, are Swedish speaking and a tiny number of Lapps, 0.2%, speak other languages. Both major languages are used in education.
France	French is the universal language. Attempts were made after the Revolution to suppress regional languages, e.g. Breton, and one task of the French Academy is to ensure the purity of the language is maintained.
Fed. Republic of Germany	Modern German as a literary language is a product of the Reformation. There are dialectical differences among the German speaking population of the Federal Republic, Austria, Alsace and some Cantons in Switzerland. German is the official language.
Greece	A distinction should be drawn between Classical, common and a conservative literary dialect evolved in the nineteenth century. Debates about the kind of languages, including a progressive literary dialect, which should be used in the schools continue.
Hungary	Magyar or Hungarian is affiliated with Finnish and Estonian.
Italy	Italian is derived from Latin, spoken in a pure form in Tuscany; there are many dialects, one of which, spoken in Sardinia, is sometimes regarded as a distinct Romance language.

Table IV (contd.)

Luxembourg	French is the official language, Letzeburgisch the spoken language although nearly everyone speaks German and many speak English.
Netherlands	Dutch, spoken by all pupils, is akin to Old English and Low German. While spoken elsewhere only a small number use the language, which may explain the readiness of the Dutch to learn and speak German, French and particularly English.
Norway	"New Norwegian", an outcome of nationalism after the country gained independence from Denmark, now has the same official standing as *bokmål* which was formed at the time of the Reformation and shows strong Danish influences.
Poland	Polish is a western Slavonic language but cf Russia, the Latin alphabet is used. Several parts of modern Poland were formerly administered by Germany and some German speaking inhabitants remain in the border areas.
Portugal	Portuguese is the national language, one of the Romance languages.
Romania	Romanian is a Romance language which shows the influence of Slavonic, Turkish, Magyar and French.
Spain	Many languages are spoken in Spain. Castilian is the language of threequarters of the population. Basque is spoken in some rural areas; Catalan in Provençal Spain; and Galician in the northwestern provinces. Since the death of Franco linguistic differences have created potential difficulties with secession movements re-emerging.
Sweden	The majority of the people speak Swedish; in the far north the Lapps possess their own language. A small linguistic group, its members once learned German but now use English as an international medium of communication.
Switzerland	French, German and Italian are all official languages. Romanisch is a national, but not an official, language. German dominates in 19 of the 26 Cantons. Language differences find expression in politics and culture.

Table IV (contd.)

Turkey	Turkish, once written in the Arabic script, now uses the Roman or Latin alphabet. The change in 1926 reflected a desire on the part of the authorities to modernise Turkey. French influence remains strong.
USSR	There are more than fifty spoken languages, Russian being the mother tongue of more than 50% of the population. Ukrainian is spoken by a large number of people and in the Baltic republics of Latvia and Estonia and Lithuania the mother tongue is not Russian. All children are taught in their mother tongue and learn Russian, and the majority now also learn English.
Yugoslavia	Serbo-Croat, Slovenian and Macedonian, the languages of the country, are all South Slavonic languages. Serbo-Croat is the language of the Federal government. The Cyrillic script is used in some parts of the country, Latin elsewhere. Minorities speak Hungarian, Turkish, Romanian, Albanian, Italian, Slovak and Ruthenian.

THE SOCIO-ECONOMIC AND POLITICAL CONTEXT

The operation of present day systems of education can only be adequately understood and compared by reference to the national context of which they are a part. The political system of a country, for example, influences the extent to which educational policies are the subject of party political debate. If they are it is necessary to draw a distinction between those which are debated by members of the political parties, whether in or out of government, and those which are not. In one-party systems the influence of the political party usually varies in accordance with the aspect of policy under consideration

In Western European countries more than one political party competes for office. On the whole it is possible to identify a pattern of educational policies favoured by left wing parties and to compare it with a pattern supported by right wing politicians. One issue which has been the subject of political debate since 1945 is the re-organisation of secondary education. Left wing spokesmen have advocated the abolition of selective secondary schools of the kind which existed in most European countries and the introduction of secondary schools designed to accept all young adolescents.

Thus the Labour Party in England has since 1946, both in and out of office, consistently supported the introduction of comprehensive schools. Paul Langevin and Henri Wallon, both Communists, chaired a committee in France which recommended the creation of *écoles uniques*. A Socialist government in Sweden pioneered the introduction of a common nine year *Grundskola*, Socialist parties in the German *Länder*, for example Lower Saxony pioneered reforms intended to introduce *Einheitschulen*. Inevitably since the Soviet model included a basic or common eight year school post-war Communist governments in Poland, the German Democratic Republic, Romania and Hungary set about with all speed to introduce some kind of comprehensive school. Against these moves throughout Europe, right wing politicians, frequently supported by academic secondary schools teachers, fought against these changes with some, little or no success.

On the other hand the reform of curricula has been less subject to party political debate and certainly the implementation or rejection of reform in practice can best be examined through the activities of teachers and the organisations to which they belong. Particular issues such as religion in the schools may spark off party political debates and conflict.

Attitudes to the centralisation or devolution of power, to levels of finance, and to the development of higher and teacher education may be the subject of political debate and conflict. It would be unwise to state categorically, however, that the political systems in Western Europe allow for debate about all aspects of educational policy while the political systems in Eastern Europe prevent debate and promote only the views of the Communist Party. This is simply to say that what takes place overtly in some countries occurs in most countries at least covertly.

Changes in some aspects of educational policy can nevertheless be related to the political complexion of the new governments and in one-party systems to the shifts in the balance within the party.

Associated with political elected members of government are appointed bureaucrats on whom considerable responsibility for policy matters rests. A major distinction has been drawn between the power of bureaucrats (and indeed elected members) of the national or central government and those working at regional or local levels. The structure of administrative systems is consequently of considerable comparative interest. Within that structure the inter-relationships between bureaucrats working in national organisations and those in regional and local organisations are not easily discovered from static organograms. If an analysis of where power lies in an educational system is to be made some understanding of these relationships is essential. Again, it should not be supposed that on every issue of policy the power of central, regional and local officials is the same or that relationships between them are similar. It should also be remembered that in most administrative systems distinctions are drawn between officials whose main duties lie in the allocation of resources – capital, equipment and personnel – and those whose concern is with matters of academic policy. The latter are frequently called 'inspectors' in English and in translation.

Nevertheless a broad distinction can be made between those systems in Europe in which a high proportion of decisions are made and implemented by personnel in the national organisations and those systems where power is delegated or is possessed by regional and local officials. The first of these two systems of administration are termed 'centralised'; the second type is usually referred to as 'decentralised' systems.

The existence in Europe of one or other type of administration is less a matter of clear ideology - although that has its influence - and much more a matter of history. The centralised national system of administration, and the principles on which it was run, established in France during Napoleon Boneparte's period of leadership, set a model of administration which was widely accepted, partly as a consequence of Napoleon's military successes, through Western and Eastern Europe. A careful study of the system in Poland, in Belgium and Austria will reveal similarities. A distinction should, however, be made between those nations like France in which a great deal of power resides in the national government and those nations, like the Federal Republic of Germany, in which control of education in most of its aspects is a provincial responsibility. Within the provinces administrative structures which replicate national structures may well exist.

An exception to a rule which applies rather generally in continental European nations is the United Kingdom, where not only is there separate legislation for England and Wales, Scotland and Northern Ireland, but such legislation as there is clearly limits the power of the central government and the regional formal organisations responsible for education.

Present debates encompass proposals to include in policy formulation a wider range of people - including parents and representatives of local communities. In short a trend towards the devolution of decision making power can be discussed in spite of the fact that the structure of administrative systems throughout Europe has not noticeably changed. In pointing to structures of government and administration we are here suggesting that it is through these that the political context in which educational systems operate can be analysed and compared. It is through an analysis of how formal organisations of government work that the influence of politicians and officials in schools can be judged and evaluated.

Political and administrative systems in Europe vary. Vienna was liberated in 1945 and in 1955 the sovereign, independent and democratic state of Austria was established within its former 1938 frontiers. In a National Assembly created in 1975 of 193 Deputies, 95 were members of the Socialist Party and 77 were members of the People's Party. As a Federal Republic the country is divided into nine provinces. The Federal government through national legislation influences educational policy. According to the Constitution of 1831 Belgium has a Senate, a Chamber of Representatives and a monarch. Representatives in the Chamber are from ten political parties. Some members of the Senate are elected on party lines, others are elected by Provincial Councils and a third group of members are co-opted. A government was formed in 1980 from a coalition of members from the three national parties, the Social Christians, the Socialists and the

Liberals. Flemish nationalists and Walloon Regionalists reflect a major division in the country.

In the Kingdom of Denmark there is one chamber the *Folketing*. The President of France is elected. Parliamentary elections were held in 1978 and at least eight parties were represented in the National Assembly; the three with most members were the Gaullists (RPR), the Giscardians (UDF) and the Socialists. Bills, other than money bills, may be presented in either the National Assembly or the Senate. The Prime Minister is appointed by the President. Educational policy has been the subject of parliamentary debate for many years.

In the Federal Republic of Germany the President is elected for five years, members of a Lower House are elected by direct suffrage for four years and members of the Upper House are delegates of the *Länder* with no fixed term of office. In 1976 the Social Democrats had 214 members, the Christian Democratic Union 190, the Christian-Social Union 53 and the Free Democrats 39. Education is for the most part a responsibility of each of the eleven *Länder*, some of which have traditionally persuaded progressives, others more conservative policies. Greece has had several changes in the type of government. In 1967 a military coup suspended parliamentary government. A referendum in 1973 ratified a presidential Constitution after the abolition of the monarchy. In 1974 it was announced that the 1957 Constitution would be re-introduced. In that year in an election 54.3% of the votes went to the New Democracy Party and gained 220 seats out of 300. Elections in 1977 reduced its majority. The Pan Hellenic Socialist Movement became the official opposition. Educational policy has, in spite of these changes, remained rather stable although reforms have been debated. Political changes in Italy, which is a Republic, have had less effect on education than might be supposed. A new Constitution, adopted in 1947, provided for an elected President, a Chamber of Deputies and a Senate. Several distinct regions can be identified – Rome and Central Italy, Lombardy and Milan, Turin and Piedmont, Genoa and the Ligurian Riviera, Venice and the North East, Tuscany, Emilia and Romagna, Naples and the Toe of Italy, Puglia, Sicily and Sardinia. These reflect the fact that Italy has been politically unified only since 1871 when the King of Italy entered Rome and made it his capital.

The Netherlands is a constitutional Kingdom. Queen Juliana abdicated in 1980 in favour of her daughter Queen Wilhelmina. There are two chambers; members of the first are elected for six years by the Provincial Council; members of the second are elected by popular suffrage for four years. In 1977 eleven parties had representatives in the second chamber, the Labour Party with 53 members, the Christian Democrats with 49, and the Liberals with 28 being the strongest parties in this and the first chamber. The administration of education is centralised and in all matters the claims of the religious groups, non-sectarian organisations and parents are taken into account.

Switzerland is a confederation. There is a Federal Assembly of two Chambers, and the National Council *(Nationalrat)*, with

200 members and a Council of States *(Ständrat)*. Executive power is in the hands of a small Federal Council presided over by the President of the Confederation. Education is, however, controlled by cantonal and communal authorities.

In spite of the large number of political parties in many of the nations in north-west Europe, and in spite of the fact that on some issues party political differences are considerable, educational stability has been considerable and reform has taken place rather slowly.

The same may be said about the Scandinavian countries where, except in Denmark, the number of political parties is not large. In 1980 there was a Social Democrat minority government in Denmark; a coalition government in Finland (Social Democratic Party, the Centre Party, the Finnish People's Democratic League and the Swedish People's Party of Finland); a Labour government in Norway and a Social Democratic government in Sweden. Insofar as concensus politics prevail the political emphasis in Scandinavian education tends to be left of centre. In the Kingdom of Denmark there is one chamber, the *Folketing* of 179 members. The Conservative, Progress and Socialist People's Party represent with the Social Democrats the major political parties. In Finland the highest executive power is held by the President elected for six years. There is a single Chamber of 200 members *(Eduskunta)* elected by universal suffrage. Norway has a king and two chambers: Parliament *(Storling)* elects one quarter of its members to form the upper chamber *(Lagting)* ; the rest constitute the lower chamber *(Odelsting)*. A council of Ministers *(Statsråd)* is responsible in Sweden to a Diet *(Riksdag)* of 349 members elected for three years.

In Spain and Portugal long periods of government under one leader (General Franco and Dr Salazar respectively), were followed by constitutional change and elections. In new legislative elections in Spain in 1979 the Union of Centre Democrats gained 167 seats out of 350 in the Congress of Deputies. The Socialists (PSOE) 126 and the Communists (PCE) 23. Several provisional governments followed the death of Salazar in Portugal. In 1979 a coalition of centre-rightist parties - Social Democrats, Centre Democratic and Popular Monarchist - came to power. These changes have coincided with wider debates about education and new proposals for reform.

In Eastern Europe the structure of those governments which are Communist reflects the influence of the Soviet Union. Yugoslavia is a Federal Republic. Several constitutional changes have been made since 1953. Under the 1974 Constitution a ruling Presidency was created, a Federal Assembly with two chambers (the Federal Chamber with 270 delegates and the Republican/Provincial Chamber with 8 delegates). The Federal Executive Council (i.e. the government) has to be sensitive to the needs and demands of the Republics which constitute the Federation and have their own administrative powers. In Czechoslovakia a Federal system of government was set up and consists of the Czech Socialist Republic and the Slovak Socialist government. Each has its government responsible to its National Council.

Certain aspects of policy are reserved to the Federal Government which is responsible to a Federal Assembly. Members of the Chamber of Deputies are elected on an all-country basis and the Chamber of Nations has an equal number of Czech and Slovak deputies. The Communist party has national responsibilities. The present Constitution of the German Democratic Republic dates from 1968. Power is vested in the People's Chamber *(Volkskammer)*, which can elect and dismiss the Council of State, the Council of Ministers, the Chairman of the National Defence Council, the Supreme Court and the Procurator-General. Members of the *Volkskammer* were elected in 1976. The Country is divided into fourteen administrative regions *(Bezirke)* . By 1949 the Communists had gained control of the government of Hungary. the Communist Party (the Polish United Workers' Party) came to power in 1948 and a new Constitution along Soviet lines was adopted in 1952 and modified in 1976. Elections to the National Assembly have been held at regular intervals and the Constitution provides for religious freedom, the private ownership of property and the separation of State and Church. A constitution based on the Soviet model was introduced in 1952, a new constitution adopted by National Assembly stated that the Communist Party was the leading political force. Only one candidate stands in each constituency.

In all these countries the role of the Communist Party is to formulate policy and through the presence of its members in key institutions is able to monitor the implementation of policy. Educational policy reflects Soviet views and is based on interpretation of Marxist-Leninist theory. The stability of the various regimes has varied and where political stability has been affected so has education. For the most part educational reform has been initiated by Party members.

The political and economic consequences of the most recent post 1945 division of Europe into East and West are well known. Most theorists of social change concede, however, that educational systems, committed to transmit the accumulated wisdom of previous generations to the next, change slowly and may well lag behind technological change. Political systems may change and politicians may attempt to transform education, but the process is inevitably slow. Thus Soviet leaders from Lenin on have always stressed that the creation of a 'new Soviet man' through education would take time. The Czarist system was not transformed overnight although in terms of literacy and the expansion of provision great progress has been made. The Soviet model, moreover, has certainly influenced policy in the German Democratic Republic, Poland, Hungary, Czechoslovakia, Romania and Yugoslavia but each of those systems retain features which are a product not only of long-standing European traditions but their own national histories. It is not therefore surprising that while the rhetoric and ideology associated with Eastern European systems of education may differ from those associated with Western European systems similar practices can be observed in schools on both sides of Churchill's Iron Curtain.

Certainly after World War II there developed trends which gave an international flavour to educational models. In the United Nations Declaration of Universal Rights one such model was prepared. Article 26 asserted that education was a human right and primary education should be provided free for all young children, secondary and higher education should be available to all who could benefit regardless of the ability of parents to pay for it. It is against this model that the provision of education in Europe can be judged and some of the problems of providing equality of educational opportunity and achieving equality of provision can be analysed.

In working towards the achievement of these aims national policies have varied, particularly in terms of details. General aims have been stated in somewhat different ways, emphasising either child or society centred objectives. Administrative arrangements have tended to follow those established in the nineteenth century although there have been debates about the relative advantages of centralising or devolving power. Methods of financing education have changed relatively little although changing economic conditions have influenced the amount of money made available to schools. Almost immediately after 1945 the way in which systems of education were organised in terms of the movement of children into and through the schools system and in terms of the choices open to pupils at each level became the subject of educational and political debate. The outcome of these debates is described in individual national profiles.

Somewhat after reform movements designed to re-organise systems of education had met with success in Eastern and Western Europe the problems of curriculum change began to receive attention. Over this aspect of educational policy teachers in most if not all countries have much greater control whether at the national or local levels. Protagonists in debates about content tend to be university academics, secondary and primary school teachers and inspectors. Traditions of academic freedom worked their way into school systems and even today serve to justify the view taken by many teachers that what is taught is their concern.

What is taught and how it is taught depend to a considerable extent on how teachers are trained. Historically in Europe those who taught in academic secondary schools were university graduates; a university degree being in itself a licence to teach. Elementary school teachers in the nineteenth century were trained as apprentices or in normal schools - secondary schools for teachers. Some teachers in Europe are still trained in schools in which they complete their secondary school education and receive some knowledge of teaching methods in lectures and on practice teaching. Reform movements are designed to ensure that all intending teachers receive a university or higher education course and follow professional courses designed to introduce them not only to appropriate methods of teaching but also to give them some understanding of the aims (philosophy) of education and the needs of children (psychology) in society (sociology). Some knowledge of the development of their own system (history) and that of other countries (comparative education) are also constituents of broad courses of professional training.

Against these general developments national systems of education and the changes introduced in them since 1945 can be compared. Keys to understanding trends in Europe are found in claims for quality of access, opportunity and provision and in the difficulties of reconciling in educational systems the functions of ensuring that the interests of individuals and groups of individuals are protected, the functions of maintaining a sense of national unity and finally the functions of widening the commitment of children to regional international organisations in Europe and to world organisations.

Thus minority groups everywhere seek to use the schools to maintain their cultural identity. This is usually expressed in terms of their language, religion or ethnicity. They usually want to retain overtly identifiable features of their culture such as music, dance and dress. At the same time most individuals expect education to help them to enter the mainstream of economic and political life. To find a balance in educational policy between these competing demands has been difficult, and has not always been successful. Again, to find a balance between the needs of people living in the economically and politically peripheral areas and the needs of those in the centres of wealth and power has not been easy, and finally to devise policies and practices which will serve pupils living in rural and urban areas has proved extremely difficult.

In divided Europe there are in addition pressures to harmonise policies. The European Economic Community's terms of reference make no direct attack on diversity and major efforts to unify national educational systems unlikely. They remain, within the European tradition, very nationalistic. Soviet Union models have provided reform objectives in most Eastern European nations. While the general aims of education may appear to have the support of many politicians and educationists, the use made of school systems during the era of nationalism in Europe prevents changes which are seen as antithetical to national sovereignty and national culture. The similarities of structure, content and administrative patterns revealed in these profiles disguise some of the undercurrents of debate which turn on the principles of equality and liberty as they find expression in the provision of formal schooling.

POST WORLD WAR II TRENDS

Against the Condorcet and United Nations model of education provision the position of European school systems can be judged by reference to statistics collected by Unesco. On any of the criteria regarded as important in evaluating the quality of educational systems those of Europe match that of the USA, former British English-speaking Dominions and Japan. Nations which for the most part gained independence after 1945, and even those which have benefitted economically from the exploitation of their oil resources have made great strides but still lag behind. Enrolment rates, percentages of GNP and public expenditure spent on education, teacher pupil ratios and the proportion of girls and young women attending schools and colleges make it possible to place the position of Europe in world perspective. The tables following give some indication of this position.

Table V, which gives the number of persons between birth and 24 years of age as a proportion of the whole population, makes it possible to compare the responsibilities of governments in Europe with those faced by governments in the developing world. The proportion of persons within the range of those who might still be in education is declining in Europe and has for some years been below 40%. In the developing countries governments face the prospect of having almost two-thirds of their populations in educational institutions.

Table V
Projected proportion of population
0-24 years of age (in 000)

	1970	1975	1980	1985
Europe:				
Population	459,085	473,098	486,541	499,972
0 - 24 yrs	185,699	187,092	187,881	188,777
Percentage 0 - 24 yrs	40	39.5	38.6	38
Developing countries:				
Population	2,538,079	2,847,153	3,202,901	3,593,932
0 - 24 yrs	1,506,492	1,694,444	1,891,857	2,097,254
Percentage 0 - 24 yrs	59	59	59	58

Source: Unesco Statistical Yearbook

Tables VI, VII and VIII make it possible to compare pupil teacher ratios in major regions of the world. Apart from North America the lowest ratios, and therefore class size, are found in Europe.

Table VI
Distribution according to pupil teacher ratios
First level frequency distribution 1977

	21	21-30	31-40	41-50	51-59	60
Africa	1	9	18	15	7	4
Asia	8	15	11	5	1	-
Latin America	4	21	14	5	-	-
North America	2	2	-	-	-	-
Europe	15	16	2	-	-	-
Arab States	5	4	9	-	-	-

Table VII
Distribution according to pupil teacher ratios
Second level frequency distribution 1977

	11	11-20	21-30	31-39	40
Africa	-	25	25	2	2
Asia	2	16	18	4	-
Latin America	2	28	11	3	-
North America	-	4	-	-	-
Europe	6	23	4	-	-
Arab States	2	8	8	-	-

Table VIII
Distribution according to pupil teacher ratios
Third level frequency distribution 1977

	5	6-10	11-15	16-20	21-24	25
Africa	7	18	13	6	2	1
Asia	2	9	14	6	3	1
Latin America	1	11	8	6	2	-
North America	-	-	-	2	-	-
Europe	2	14	7	4	1	1
Arab States	-	4	7	2	2	2

At the third level there is some evidence that, against very favourable European and North American student teacher ratios, African and Latin American universities are now very comparable.

Table XI shows how enrolments in pre-school institutions grew over the period 1970-77. In all parts of the world more and more children were enrolled in nursery schools and kindergartens. The percentage increases in teachers in Africa were very high and not matched by similar increases in the number of pupils. In Europe, on the other hand, the growth was modest but again pupil growth did not match teacher growth. In North and Latin America, however, large increases in pupil enrolments were matched by similar growths in the number of teachers. These figures reveal present trends but also imply the pre-school provision in Europe and North America pre-dates growth in other parts of the world.

Table IX
Education preceeding the first level
Percentage increases 1970-77

	Teachers	Pupils
Africa	27.6	15.8
Asia	8.0	8.1
Latin America	9.6	10.3
North America	9.9	10.3
Europe	6.8	3.9
Arab States	7.3	8.0

Table X makes it possible to compare on a world scale how much money is spent on education. Total expenditures are less revealing than expenditures per capita, that is per person, in the total population. The enormous gaps between expenditures per capita in Africa and in Europe and North America indicate clearly the relative positions of education as one of the public services.

Table X
Expenditure on education in US$, 1977

	Public expenditure (US $ million)	Expenditure per capita
Africa	9,759	24
Asia	61,825	44

Table X (contd.)

Latin America	17,368	51
North America	136,446	566
Europe	124,857	261
Arab States	11,604	81

In each of the national profiles data are provided which show how in most countries expenditure on education has increased. Naturally inflation accounts for a proportion of the increase in expenditure and the proportion of the GNP spent on education is a better indicator of the importance given to education as a service competing with others for economic resources.

Unesco statistics are of course collected with the intention of revealing the extent to which national governments are achieving the intentions of their own legislation and the United Declaration on education. The selected statistics provided at the end of each profile can be used to compare trends of development in Europe. While by 1945 universal primary education had been achieved efforts subsequently were designed to extend the period of compulsory attendance. It now ranges from 6 years in Greece and Portugal to 11 years in the UK. In many countries 10 years of compulsory schooling is effective. Elsewhere 9 or 8 years are stipulated. Diagrams taken from the IBE International Yearbook of Education of the structure of each school system show the length of compulsory education. Table XI summarises the position. The ages of compulsory school attendance vary. Children enter first level schools at the age of 5 (UK and Greece), 6 (Belgium, Czechoslovakia, France, the Federal Republic of Germany, Hungary, Italy, Luxembourg, Malta, Netherlands, Spain and Switzerland) and at 7 (Denmark, Finland, Norway, Poland, Sweden and Yugoslavia). No rules can be drawn from this information but the latest age of 7 is characteristic of the Scandinavian systems. The ages at which pupils may leave school vary with the starting age and the period of compulsory attendance which is often in terms of a number of years. While the age at which children must attend school has not been lowered the provision of pre-school education has become a characteristic of most systems. No generalisations are possible since nations in Western Europe like France and Belgium have high pre-school enrolments, but so have countries like Poland and Hungary in Eastern Europe.

In expanding the provision of education most governments have been anxious to ensure that more and more pupils pass on from first to second level schools and on to university or higher education. Table XII shows how participation ratios in higher education vary from lows of 1.23% in Luxembourg, 5.47% in Malta and 8.0% in Turkey to highs of 32.10% in Denmark, 28.84% in the Netherlands and 25.58% in Italy. In every case expansion has taken place, in most cases dramatically, between 1960 and 1970. Everywhere the ratio of females participating

Table XI
Compulsory Education

Country	Age Limits	Duration	Age of Admission to pre-schools
Austria	6-15	9	3
Belgium	6-14	8	3
Canada	6-15	8-10	5
Cyprus			
Czechoslovakia	6-15	9	3
Denmark	7-16	9	5
Finland	7-16	9	3
France	6-16	10	3
Fed. Rep. of Germany	6-15	9	3
Greece	6-12	6	3
Hungary	6-16	10	3
Israel	5-15	11	5
Italy	6-14	8	3
Luxembourg	6-15	9	4
Malta	5-16	8	3
Netherlands	6-16	10	4
Norway	7-16	9	5
Poland	7-15	8	3
Portugal	6-12	6	3
Spain	6-15	10	2
Sweden	7-16	9	3
Switzerland	5-16	11	3
Yugoslavia	7-15	8	3

Table XII
Enrolment Ratios:
Third level including universities

Country		1960	1970	1975	1978
Austria	MF	8.01	11.76	19.20	
	F	3.79	7.02	14.68	
Belgium	MF	9.09	17.49	22.01	23.08
	F	4.82	12.94	18.61	20.54
Czechoslovakia	MF	10.95	10.44	12.17	
	F	7.52	8.03	9.99	
Denmark	MF	10.39	18.28	29.69	32.10
	F	6.56	13.82	26.99	30.56

Table XII (contd.)

Finland	MF	7.38	13.34	18.62	
	F	6.94	13.26	19.08	
France	MF	9.83	19.50	24.29	24.42
	F			23.75	24.73
Fed. Rep.	MF	6.11	13.41	19.?8	25.14
of Germany	F	2.85	7.37	13.22	19.80
Greece	MF	6.52	10.11	11.67	
	F	4.19	8.79	11.54	
Israel	MF				
	F				
Italy	MF	6.61	16.69	25.48	25.58
	F	3.61	12.85	20.13	22.68
Luxembourg	MF	0.70	1.56	2.00	1.23
	F	0.46	1.33	1.72	1.06
Malta	MF	2.30	5.59	4.60	5.47
	F	1.54	3.61	2.53	2.73
Netherlands	MF	13.18	19.51	25.93	28.84
	F	6.88	11.12	17.34	20.47
Norway	MF	6.87	15.91	22.15	24.28
	F	4.77	9.94	17.08	21.47
Poland	MF	9.16	14.12	16.87	17.77
	F	7.34	13.55	18.60	19.93
Portugal	MF	3.46	7.97	11.65	13.75
	F	1.97	6.76	9.93	11.31
Spain	MF	3.95	8.91	20.77	21.54
	F	1.87	4.83	15.02	16.39
Sweden	MF	9.04	21.34	21.81	
	F	6.59	18.51	20.43	
Turkey	MF	2.86	6.09	6.59	8.00
	F	1.16	2.42	2.87	4.04
Yugoslavia	MF	8.61	15.93	20.00	22.52
	F	5.07	12.87	16.31	18.18

in third level education is considerably lower than for males and females. The extent to which the gap has been reduced since 1960 under conditions of expansion makes for interesting comparisons since the proportion of women attending universities tells us a good deal about changes in their aspirations and, given that these have raised questions of equality, the response of systems of higher education to accept womenon equal terms.

At the other levels of education participation ratios indicate that except in one or two European countries the participation ratios of boys and girls are roughly similar. A study of enrolments by level in the country statistics shows how selection takes place in each of the systems. No longer is it possible to observe a large drop in enrolments in second level education compared with the number enrolled in first level schools: exceptions are Poland (64.26); Greece (57.38); and Portugal (67.28). Economic and political factors account for these exceptions.

Sex differences are reflected in the number of teachers employed at each level. First level schools have traditionally employed a high proportion of women. Even in 1978, 79% of teachers in the first schools of Yugoslavia were women, in Italy 85%, Sweden 81% and in Portugal 92%. In other systems such as Cyprus (43%), Greece (48%) and the Netherlands (45%) the percentage of first level women teachers is less than 50%. In most cases the percentages range between the high 50s and the 60s.

The balance at the second level is much more even, with if anything a slightly higher proportion of men. But in the universities and higher education male teachers predominate. In some systems less than 10% of university teachers are women although the proportion is rising in most countries.

In general it may be said that equality of provision between the sexes is provided up to the end of compulsory education and in most countries the period of compulsory education is effectively in operation. A major issue debated in most countries since 1945 has been how second level schools should be organised. Traditional systems of selective academic secondary schools paralleled by vocation-technical schools, including secondary schools for teachers, have been re-organised so that all children leaving first level schools go on to the same second level school at least for some time. Differentiation by school type has been postponed. These reforms took place at different rates. Eastern European governments, and in the event the Scandinavian governments, were committed to a nine or ten year basic common school which encompassed former first level schools and the first stage of second level schooling. Vocational schools and upper second level schools provide different courses for children after the age of compulsory schooling. Another model has developed. First level schools are followed by middle schools where courses last three or four years. From these schools pupils enter a differentiated system of upper stage secondary and vocational schools.

Each national profile includes a diagram showing how the school system is organised. These diagrams indicate at what points in the system pupils take examinations which either confirm that they have successfully completed a stage of education or, for the most successful pupils, permit entry into the next stage of general education. The ways in which pupil performance is evaluated are changing. Although in continental schools oral examinations except in specialist subjects were common, the end of year essay type examination is giving way to a range of techniques designed to monitor the progress of pupils through their school career.

CURRICULA

It is not easy to describe curriculum trends in detail. Tradition tends to dominate the outlook of teachers. The emergence of comprehensive second level schools induced research and discussion about the relevance of the traditional academic secondary school course. As more pupils remained in second level schools the difficulties of teaching all of them what had previously been taught to a selected few became apparent.

In general, continental European primary school curricula emphasise mathematics and mother tongue teaching but many schools teach a foreign language, natural science and some aspects of the social sciences. Second level curricula are encyclopedic in the sense that as many established subjects (up to 14) are taught to second level pupils for as long as possible. The explosion of knowledge has made the provision of options at the upper stage necessary. Details of curriculum reforms are given in the text of the national profiles.

TEACHER EDUCATION

A feature of post-1945 education is the attempts made to improve the training of teachers by phasing out the secondary schools for teachers, which prepared teachers for the old elementary schools and first level schools, and by bringing the initial training of all teachers within the university systems. Academic secondary school teachers in continental countries have always been trained in the universities and for the most part have taken educational courses concurrently with their specialist studies. While in the past elementary and first level school teachers completed their academic secondary school course in special secondary schools for teachers. Then they followed courses in professional studies, teaching methods and undertook supervised teaching.

Now increasingly intending teachers complete their education prior to entering the profession in the university or some other comparable institution of higher learning. Fewer and fewer teachers consequently attend special secondary schools where they receive an education similar if not identical to that received in a normal general education second level school.

UNIVERSITIES

Dominating educational provision since the middle ages the universities of Europe remain the most prestigious of all educational institutions. Originally students collected round distinguished teachers and after completing courses of studies, entirely controlled by their teachers and examined by them either remained themselves within the university or took up positions of power and influence in the professions of law, the church, medicine and teaching. Early centres were Bologna and Salerno in Italy, Paris in France and Oxford and Cambridge in England. But in the fourteenth and fifteenth centuries universities were set up in most of the centres of population. To this expansion the Reformation gave impetus when many universities were established in Germany.

The nineteenth century witnessed another burst of activity. In England new universities in Durham and London were the first to be founded after Oxford and Cambridge. Towards the end of the century several technical colleges were transformed into Civic Universities. In Germany technical universities evolved alongside the traditional humanistic universities and in France following the establishment of a high level military school the *Ecole Polytechnique*, just before the end of the eighteenth century, a number of other *grandes écoles* were set up to train personnel for the armed services and the civil service in France. These institutions, admission to which is extremely competitive, remain the most prestigious educational institutions in France and undoubtedly still prepare future members of the French elite.

After the Second World War another wave of expansion took place. National legislation and heightened aspirations made it difficult to preserve pre-war elitism even in the provision of university education. This expansion has been well documented in publications of Unesco, OECD, and the Council of Europe. So vast and rapid was this growth that towards the end of the sixties commentators were suggesting that the trend from elite through mass to universal provision of higher education was inevitable. The human rights argument was re-enforced by claims made by economists that investment in university and higher education would inevitably bring economic rewards - a hope falsified by events to some extent.

During this period major concern was expressed about the under-representation of children of the working classes in the universities of Europe. Most policies of expansion were undertaken in the hope that the balance of representation in the former elitist institutions would be altered in favour of the children of non-professional parents. Again these aspirations have not been entirely realised either in Western or Eastern Europe although inevitably expansion itself allowed more young people than ever before to enter higher education as Unesco statistics clearly reveal.

The responses made to the demand for higher education varied. In England and Scotland established universities expanded and new universities were set up. In France the logical distribution of university faculties in regional centres allowed for expansion but by far the greatest expansion took place in Paris. A comparable growth in the number of students in the university in Rome took place.

Equally of concern to many governments was the extent to which expansion took place less in the science and engineering faculties and subjects than in the traditional subjects and the new social sciences. In response to this uneven expansion university institutes of technology were set up in France during the sixties To encourage applied studies polytechnics were established in England at about the same time. Somewhat similar responses were made elsewhere in Europe.

Attempts were also made to create new style universities. In the Federal Republic of Germany Bochum, Constanz and Kassel universities were experimental in several ways. One aim was to make the new universities 'comprehensive' in the sense that they were to include applied engineering subjects as well as humanistic studies. Sweden's reforms were designed to provide lifelong educational opportunities for young people and adults in the form of recurrent education. A central principle which informed this move was that adults would be able to leave and re-enter the educational system throughout their lives. Policies were made explicit in the report of a national Swedish commission U 68.

The period of very rapid expansion, namely the 1960s, was, however, one of growing student unrest which in France culminated in attempts made in France on the part of students to form a revolutionary alliance with workers. Street fighting and other forms of violence became common occurrences and there is little doubt that de Gaulle's period of supreme office was brought to an end partly as a result of student activism. Equally serious were disturbances in West Berlin and other parts of the Federal Republic of Germany.

Students made two claims. Some wished to overthrow degenerate capitalist societies. Others wished to change the internal management of universities which was for the most part dominated by senior professors. A new law on higher education was passed in France following the 1968 troubles. Elsewhere junior faculty members and students were brought into the management of universities. Students, for example, were brought onto university committees and the representation of junior faculty members was increased.

Several features of the 1970s contributed to a reduction in the demand for higher education in Europe and to an unwillingness on the part of governments to finance uncontrolled university expansion. The oil crisis, unemployment and a certain disillusionment on the part of young adults eased rates of expansion. In addition the size of age cohorts changed and the number of teachers required to staff schools in which enrolments were declining decreased, making it necessary to revise the number of teacher training places.

Hence in a declining market it is useful to compare the policies which have been adopted in various European countries. Again, as under conditions of expansion rather similar policies have been followed in a number of countries, some details are given in the national profiles which follow.

CANADA AND ISRAEL

Among the profiles presented in this volume those of Canada and Israel are exceptions in the sense that neither country is within the territorial area of Europe. Both countries, however, have educational systems which correspond in most details with those in Europe and which have their origins in European systems.

In Canada each province is responsible for most aspects of education. A clear and a statutory distinction has been drawn between the English and French systems of education. In Quebec the French speaking Canadians maintain Catholic and French schools. In the prairie provinces, Ontario and the maritime provinces on the east coast of Canada, English medium schools reflect the English and Scottish origins of these school systems. French and English are official languages throughout Canada but the language issue remains contentious.

Increasingly new immigrant groups and well established ones are demanding the same privileges in education as those enjoyed by the French speaking Catholics. For example, the Canadians of Ukrainian origin have long wished to perpetuate their language through the educational system. Hungarians came to the country in large numbers after 1956 and their wish to preserve their cultural identity is apparent. Moreover, new arrivals from Kenya and the West Indies have created issues of policy for educationists whose outlook is basically European, influenced though this has been by the near and powerful influence of American educational theory and practice.

Nevertheless it is possible to detect in the development of Canadian education since 1945 those issues and trends which have given a certain unity at least in terms of problems and developments, to European education.

The educational system of the relatively new state of Israel is basically European in origin. Apart from the remnants of the system set up under the British during the Palestinian Mandate most of the new leaders of Israel were, and are, Europeans educated in or familiar with systems of education in Europe. Inevitably trends of development have been similar to those in Europe. The system has expanded, attempts have been made to equalise opportunity and to democratise education. Traditional curricula have been under scrutiny and attempts have been made to reform them. Attempts have also been made to introduce more progressive methods of teaching and to modernise the system in the light of international recommendations.

Circumstances in Israel are, however, rather unique. A succession of wars with Arab neighbours have made education in the army a significant feature of the system. The arrival from all parts of the world of Jews who wanted to help create a national homeland helped to provide an enthusiasm for education. At the same time consensus on the type of education which should be provided and who should control it has not been reached.

Devout Jews have wished to retain schools based on the principles of Judism. Hebrew is a required language. Members of the Kibbutz movement have retained their hold on some aspects of the system and continue in the Kibbutzim to educate young people in accordance with their principles. A major problem has been associated with the integration of Jews from North Africa and the Yemen whose background of education was vastly different, and some would argue, inferior to that brought to the schools by pupils whose parents were of European origin. Thus diversity is very evident in the educational system of Israel. The problems linked with diversity among the Jewish community are very evident; they are complicated by the provision made by the Israeli authorities for Arabs who have remained in the country.

Thus similar problems to those which have given focus to this survey of European education are found in both Canada and Israel. In both countries, as in many European nations, linguistic, religious and ethnic diversity is found. Policies designed to equalise educational opportunity in terms of social class background dominated the early post World War Two period. Increasingly the problems of provision are the result of cultural diversity and the overt and often aggressive demand on the part of minority groups to ensure through education the preservation of their cultural identity. Governments, while aware of these demands have nevertheless wanted to ensure that children from all the cultural groups are socialised into accepting a sense of national unity. The need to satisfy the demands for cultural diversity, language, religion and ethnicity cannot always be reconciled with the desire to unify all peoples politically by ensuring that they feel they are members of the same nation. These national profiles reveal through descriptions of the origins of each system how problems of diversity have arisen and, in the accounts given of present reform movements and how each system operates, the ways in which governments in Europe, in Canada and in Israel are attempting to solve them.

Brian Holmes (Editor)

FURTHER READING

Andrew, N. (1965). *Government and Politics in the Nordic Countries*. Alonquist & Wiksell, Stockholm.
Berger, W. and Gruber, K. H. (1976). *Die Vergleichende Erziehungswissenschaft*. Jugend & Volk, Wien-Munchen.
Beck, R. H., et al (1970). *The Changing Structure of Europe*. University of Minnesota, Minneapolis.
Calman, John (Ed.) (1967). *Western Europe: a Handbook*. Blond, London.
Council of Europe, Council for Cultural Co-operation. *School Systems: a Guide*. Council of Europe, Council for Cultural Co-operation, Strasbourg.
(in a number of Council of Europe publications, aspects of education in European countries are surveyed)
Debiesse, M. and Mialaret, G. (1972). *Traité des Sciences pédagogiques: 3 Pédagique comparée*. Presses Universitaires de France, Paris.
Embling, Jack (1974). *A Fresh Look at Higher Education: Studies in Education*. Elsevier, Amsterdam.
Fragnière, G. (Ed.) (1976). *Education Without Frontiers: a Study of Education from the European Cultural Foundation's "Plan for Europe 2000"*. Duckworth, London.
Hall, P. (Ed.) (1977). *Europe 2000*. Duckworth, London.

Hearnden, Arthur (1974). *Education in the Two Germanies*. Blackwell, Oxford.
Holmes, Brian (Ed.) (1980). *Diversity and Unity in Education*. Allen & Unwin, London.
Kerr, Anthony (1960). *Schools of Europe*. Bowes & Bowes, London.
King, E. J. (1969). *Education and Development in Western Europe*. Addison Wesley, London.
Mallinson, Vernon (1980). *The Western European Idea in Education*. Pergamon, Oxford.
Neave, G. (1976). *Patterns of Equality: The Influence of New Structure in European Higher Education upon the Equality of Educational Opportunity*. National Foundation for Educational Research, Windsor.
Newcombe, Norman (1977). *Europe at School*. Methuen, London.
Organisation for Economic Co-operation and Development (1973). *Case Studies of Educational Innovation* (4 volumes - central, regional, local, school). OECD, Paris.
Organisation for Economic Co-operation and Development (various dates). *Reviews of National Policy for Education* (various including European countries). OECD, Paris.
Organisation for Economic Co-operation and Development (1973). *Short Cycle Higher Education: a Search for Identity*. OECD, Paris. (OECD publishes a great deal of material bearing on the economic and educational systems of member States.)
Poignant, R. (1973). *Education in the Industrialised Countries*. Nijhoff, The Hague.
Schöpflin, George (Ed.) (1970). *The Soviet Union and Eastern Europe: A Handbook*. Blond, London.
Thomas, Jean and Majault, Joseph (1963). *Education in Europe: Primary and Secondary Education*. Council of Europe, Council for Cultural Co-operation, Strasbourg.
UNESCO (1976). *World Guide to Higher Education: A Comparative Survey of Systems, Degrees and Qualifications*. Unesco, Paris.
UNESCO (various dates). *World Survey of Education* (5 volumes - Statistics & Organisation, Primary, Secondary, Higher, Policy Legislation & Administration). Unesco, Paris.
UNESCO/IBE (1979). *International Guide to Education Systems*. Unesco, Paris.
UNESCO/IBE (1980). *International Yearbook of Education, XXXII*. Unesco, Paris.
(Unesco and IBE, Geneva publications, provide worldwide information and statistics. They are invaluable sources of data about European systems of education and the basic statistics presented in these national profiles have been taken from these international sources.)
UNESCO/IBE (1981). *International Yearbook of Education, XXXIII*, (Trends in Education), Unesco, Paris.
Wilkinson, Max (1977). *Lessons from Europe*. Centre for Policy Studies, London.

Austria

CONTENTS

1 Geography 36
2 Population 38
3 Society and Culture 39
4 History and Politics 40
5 The Economy 42
6 The Education System 44
7 Educational Administration 57
8 Educational Finance 63
9 Development and Planning
　of the Education System 65

Practically everyone in Austria speaks German and the educational system has many of the characteristic features of the nineteenth and twentieth century systems in Germany. Traditionally the *Grundschule* or *Volkschule* provided an elementary or primary education lasting four years for children between the ages of 6 and 10. Some pupils stayed in upper elementary schools *(Volksschuloberstufen)* until leaving school. These pupils were, as in Germany, required to attend part time vocational schools *(Berufsschulen)* while in employment for three or more years.

Another group of pupils left the *Grundschule* for a middle school (the first stage of second level schooling) called the *Hauptschule*. After completing this school at the age of 14 or 15 pupils could go on to secondary technical schools or secondary schools for teachers. Thus after the middle school the system was and is highly differential in terms of vocational preparation.

A third group of pupils left the *Grundschule* at the age of 10 to enter academic or general secondary schools whose major aim was and is to prepare pupils for the university entrance examination taken by students around the age of 18. These schools, the *Gymnasia*, were and are, as in Germany, prestige institutions and closely connected as they are with the university, traditionally dominated the whole system of general education.

Parallel to the general school system are the vocational schools and apprenticeships. As in Germany these ways of preparing young people for industry and commerce were strongly influenced by industrialists and commercial interests. Historically movement between the two systems was very limited.

Since 1945 reform trends in Austrian education have been similar to those which have taken place in England. The period of compulsory attendance is now nine years. Second level education is in the process of reorganisation in order to prevent the selection of pupils for one kind of prestige school. University and higher education have expanded. In general, however, change has taken place relatively slowly and against the opposition of conservative teachers and politicians.

The Editor

1 GEOGRAPHY

Topography

Austria is a landlocked state, with a total area of 82,882 square kilometres (32,376 square miles) situated in south central Europe. Its length east to west is 560 km (350 miles). It consists of nine provincial states: Vorarlberg (2,570 sq km), Tyrol (12,344 sq km), Salzburg (7,070 sq km), Carinthia (9,420 sq km), Upper Austria (11,840 sq km), Lower Austria (18,949 sq km), Styria (16,189 sq km), the capital Vienna and its environs (409 sq km), and Burgenland (3,916 sq km). Seventy per cent of the land is mountainous, with the Eastern Alps extending across the whole west and central area of the country. Eastern Austria is comparatively flat. There are several rivers but only the Danube is navigable. There are no less than 88 large lakes (the largest, Neusiedlersee, on the Hungarian border, with an area of 320 sq km of which two thirds is Austrian territory) and hundreds of smaller ones. Vegetation varies considerably over the country though it is predominantly forest (covering 39% of the total area).

Climate

The Austrian climate shows wide variation, partly owing to differences in elevation and partly owing to transitional characteristics from the west to the continental east. The Alpine and highland areas have a moderate climate with little annual variation in temperature. Rainfall is heavy, with hills bordering the Alps getting as much as 200 cm (80 inches) a year. The far eastern part of the country has a continental climate with little rain. The average January and July temperatures in Burgenland are: 1.5°C and 20.1°C respectively, while in Salzburg the figures are: 1.9°C and 18.1°C. July is the hottest month and the July midday average temperature in Vienna is 24°C (75°F). Snowfall is heaviest between January and March.

Communications

One of the most important geographical features of Austria is its position as a route focus, surrounded as it is by seven countries and crossed by important European highways (including the Danube). Vienna stands at the intersection of the Danube

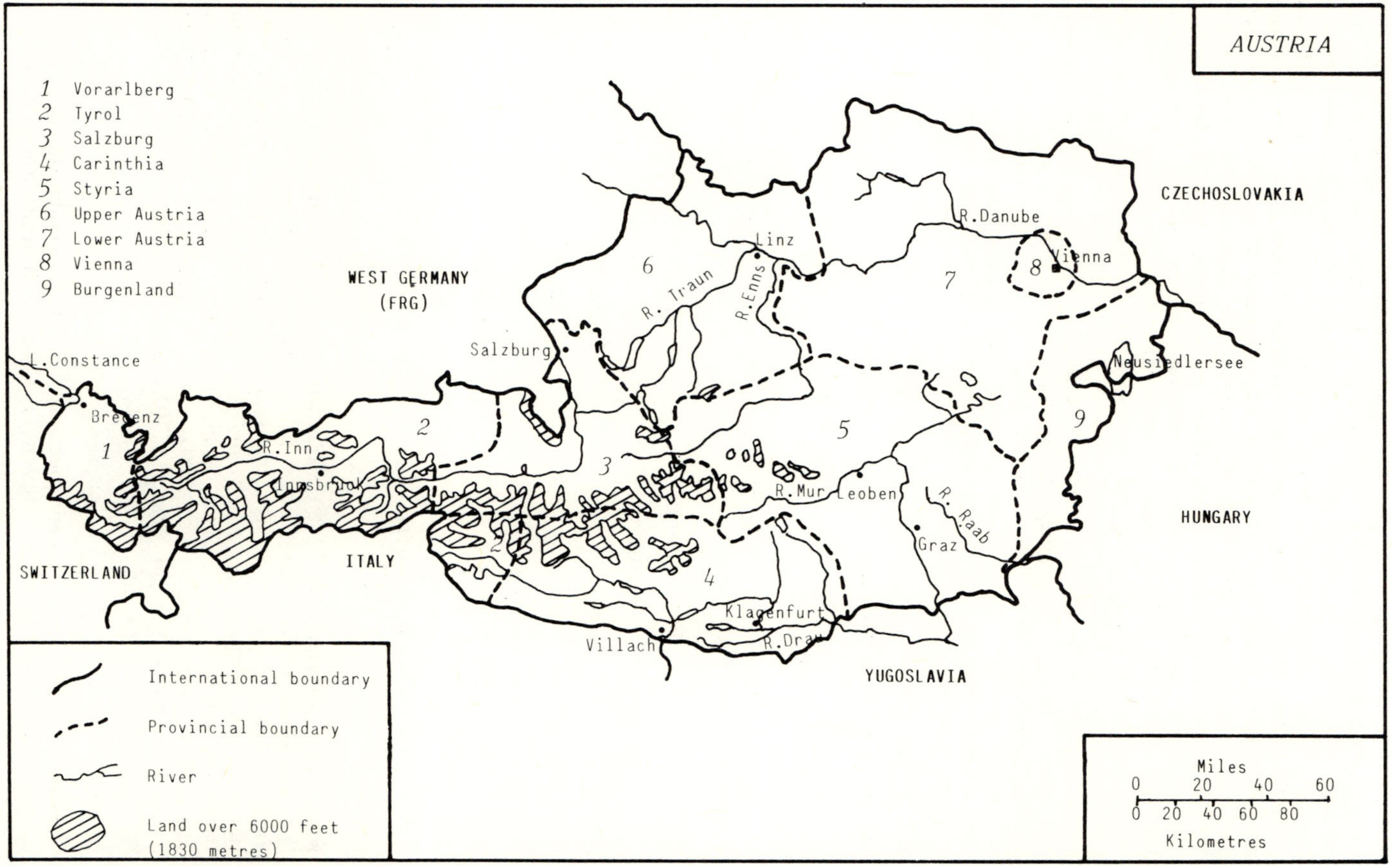
AUSTRIA
1 Vorarlberg
2 Tyrol
3 Salzburg
4 Carinthia
5 Styria
6 Upper Austria
7 Lower Austria
8 Vienna
9 Burgenland
WEST GERMANY (FRG)
CZECHOSLOVAKIA
HUNGARY
YUGOSLAVIA
ITALY
SWITZERLAND
L.Constance
Bregenz
R.Inn
Innsbruck
Salzburg
R. Traun
Linz
R.Enns
R.Danube
Vienna
Neusiedlersee
R.Mur
Leoben
R. Raab
Graz
Klagenfurt
Villach
R.Drau
International boundary
Provincial boundary
River
Land over 6000 feet (1830 metres)
Miles
0 20 40 60
0 20 40 60 80
Kilometres

and the prehistoric 'cumber road' which ran south from the Oder and Vistula rivers across the Danube and Eastern Alps to the Adriatic. The problems of transport in Austria are similar to those in Switzerland. High ranges of mountains cut off one valley from the next, snow in winter hampers communications and there is very heavy traffic in summer. The public transport system uses road, rail, air and river. The Danube carries freight traffic in coal, steel, petroleum and other raw materials. It also has a passenger service connecting the Upper Danube with Vienna and the Black Sea. There are six commercial airports. there is about 5,900 km of railway track (with all main lines electrified), 103,000 km of road and 351 km of commercial waterway. The motorway system connects Vienna with Innsbruck, (passing through Germany and thus connecting with the German system) and on over the Brenner pass into Italy. The north/south motorway system is by no means complete, however, and all north/south routes are congested, especially in summer.

2 POPULATION

Growth and Distribution

The last census in 1971 gave a population of 7,456,745 representing an increase of 380,000 over 1961. In 1978 figures produced by the Central Statistical Office put the population at 7.52 million. In 1971 the population of the nine provincial states was as follows:

Burgenland	272,119
Carinthia	525,728
Lower Austria	1,414,161
Upper Austria	1,223,444
Salzburg	401,766
Styria	1,192,100
Tyrol	540,771
Vorarlberg	271,473
Vienna	1,614,841

With a population of 1,603,900 the city of Vienna had 22% of the population, a very large proportion, which may be ascribed principally to the capital's former status but also to the mountainous nature of much of the rest of the country. Other important towns are Graz (248,500), Linz (208,000), Salzburg (137,000), Innsbruck (121,400) and Klagenfurt (84,700). The average density per sq km in 1975 was 89.7.

Groups

Austria is very mixed because of the international nature of the Hapsburg Empire. Slovenes, Croats, Hungarians, Moravians and Bohemians – even Italians and Belgians – enlisted in the imperial civil service and army. When the Empire broke up in 1918 many people of all these groups were living in Vienna and some never returned to their native countries. Since World War Two many refugees have also come to Austria from Poland, Czechoslovakia, Yugoslavia, and Hungary.

3 SOCIETY AND CULTURE

Social and Cultural Patterns

The class distinction of the Empire disappeared quickly from public life, and social classes are less segregated in Austria today than in many other European countries. Social manners are, on the other hand, more formal than elsewhere and considerable importance is attached to correct behaviour, dress and forms of address. This sense of tradition in social behaviour is matched by a conservative taste in art and culture, noticeable especially in musical life. Music is all important in Austria but theatre is well developed too, while every year exhibitions attract more and more visitors. Austria spends more public money per capita on support for the arts than any other European country.

Language

The population is 99% native German speaking, but in Carinthia and Burgenland there are two minority language groups whose rights are guaranteed by Article 7 of the Austrian State Treaty of 1955. The 1971 census showed 19,529 Slovene speakers in Carinthia and 24,526 Croat speakers in Burgenland. There is also a small Hungarian speaking minority in Burgenland (where non-German speakers represent 2% of the province's population) and small groups of Czech and Slovak speakers in Vienna.

Religion

Complete religious toleration in Austria was established in the mid-nineteenth century. After World War Two religious teaching in schools was re-established though pupils older than 14 may withdraw if they wish. The population is 89% Roman Catholic and 6% Protestant (mostly Lutheran); other groups account for a further 1% and 4% are non-denominational. There are Strong Protestant groups in south west Burgenland, central Carinthia and the eastern parts of Salzburg province and in these areas over 50% of the population is Protestant. The influence of the Protestant Church is, in fact, greater than restricted numbers would suggest. Since 1933/34 the Roman Catholic Church has been recognised as a corporate body under the law. A similar status was granted to three Protestant groups in 1961 (Lutherans, Calvinists and a group representing both where Protestants are in the minority).

4 HISTORY AND POLITICS

Historical Development

Between 955 AD, when Otto the Great regained Austria as a border province of his empire, and 1918, only two dynasties ruled in the country – the Babenbergs for 270 years and the Hapsburgs for 640. During the period of Hapsburg rule 20 emperors and kings followed in succession and at the height of its power their Empire covered large parts of Europe and the New World. The Empire was split in 1529 but the collapse of the Austro-Hungarian Empire began in 1848, the 'year of revolutions', which was also the year in which the Emperor Franz Josef succeeded to the throne. The Hungarians were agitating for independence and in 1867 a dual monarchy with separate parliaments for Austria and Hungary was set up. Liberalisation and democratisation were slow in coming and universal suffrage was only granted in 1906. By the time of Franz Josef's death in 1916 nationalism and social unrest were threatening the very existence of the Empire, and the assassination by Slav patriots of the Archduke Franz Ferdinand in Sarajevo had precipitated World War One. On 11 November 1918 the Emperor Karl abdicated and the following day a provisional national assembly was formed and Austria proclaimed a republic.

After 1918

The Treaties of Saint-Germain and Trianon established the States of Austria, Hungary and Czechoslovakia and gave land from the Empire to Serbia, Romania and Poland. But the breakdown of this major economic *bloc* created great problems, and at first the borders were closed as the country struggled to survive. With the rise of the Fascist régimes in the 1930s Austria was seriously weakened by political disagreements between the social democrats and the far right. In 1933 the lower house of parliament stripped itself of power and Chancellor Dolfuss established a dictatorship. In 1934 civil war broke out and Dolfuss was murdered in an abortive Nazi coup. The next four years saw attempts to achieve political stability in order to stave off danger from outside. Two days before a plebiscite on independence in March 1938 German troops crossed the Austrian border and imposed the *Anschluss*. Eighteen months later World War Two began.

Second Austrian Republic

On 1 May 1945 a republican constitution was declared and a provisional government confirmed in September. The four occupying powers, Britain, France, the Soviet Union and the United States, recognised the provisional government on the condition that general elections were held the same year. For ten years the four powers attempted to reach agreement on the form of a State Treaty but on 15 May 1955 the treaty was finally signed and the last of the occupying troops left Vienna. The treaty prohibits political or economic union with Germany, prohibits Nazi and Fascist organisations, guarantees the rights of minorities and protects democratic institutions. It also provides for the maintenance of the law of 1919 preventing the restoration of the royal house of Hapsburg Lorraine. In October 1955 Austria declared its permanent neutrality (though this was not mentioned in the State Treaty).

Government Organisation

The basis for the present republic is provided by the Federal Constitution, the Austrian State Treaty and the constitutional law on permanent neutrality. The Head of State is the President, elected by a compulsory vote every six years with possible re-election only once. He appoints the Chancellor, the leader of the strongest party in parliament, and also the members of the government at the Chancellor's suggestion. There is a bicameral national assembly - the National Council *(Nationalrat)* composed of 183 seats, and the upper house, the States Council *(Bundesrat)* with 53 seats. The *Nationalrat* approves new governments and all national legislation but every draft law approved by this lower house is also presented to the upper house, which may object and delay but cannot veto. For certain matters the chambers sit together *(Bundesversammlung)*.

Each of the nine provincial states has a parliament *(Landtag)* whose members elect a government *(Landesregierung)*, a provincial state governor *(Landeshauptmann)* and councillors *(Landesräte)*. Each of the provincial states may protest to the Constitutional Court if it believes that national legislation encroaches on its authority. In general, spheres of operation are clearly defined, with the national government making policy decisions on such subjects as land reform, traffic regulations, etc. and leaving administration to the provincial states. The *Landtag* then deals with all matters not expressly assigned to the national government. There are also lower level districts *(Bezirke)* under a local governor *(Bezirkhauptmann)*, who is a civil servant. There are elected local councils headed by a mayor. Eight of the nine provincial states are divided into 97 administrative districts (82 rural districts and 15 urban districts). The provincial State of Vienna is divided into 23 municipal regions.

Members of the *Nationalrat* and *Landtag* are elected by proportional representation by all citizens over 19. Candidates must be aged 25 or over. The *Nationalrat* sits for four years. The *Bundesrat* is elected by members of the *Landtag* with seats allocated in proportion to the population of the provincial states and each provincial state supplying a chairman for six months. Anyone entitled to vote may institute legislative proceedings by starting a referendum. If 200,000 or more electors provide a petition to the government it must be laid before the *Nationalrat*. Any total revision of the constitution must be submitted to the whole nation. There is an independent judiciary.

Party Politics

The two main political parties are the Socialist Party (SPO) and the People's Party (OVP). There is also the Austrian Freedom Party (FPO). The Communist Party has not been represented in government since 1959. From 1947 to 1966 government was by a coalition of the SPO and OVP with a Chancellor from the OVP. In 1966 the OVP was elected with an absolute majority and so there was one-party government till 1970. In 1970 the SPO, led by Bruno Kreisky, became the largest party in the *Nationalrat* for the first time. For 18 months there was an SPO minority government but in 1971 the party acquired an absolute majority. The elections of October 1976 left the position unchanged with Bruno Kreisky remaining Chancellor. The composition of the *Nationalrat* was in 1979: SPO - 95 seats; OVP - 77 seats; FPO - 11 seats.

International Relations

The main aim of Austrian foreign policy is to maintain and strengthen the country's independence and to relax tensions in Europe, and insofar as is possible, in the rest of the world. In this Austria's neutral status is a help, and in 1972 the Austrian ambassador to the United Nations, Dr Kurt Waldheim, became UN Secretary-General. However, relations between Italy and Austria have been strained since part of the South Tyrol was annexed by the Italians after World War One cutting off eastern Tyrol from the rest of the provincial state. Unrest in the Italian South Tyrol *(Alto Adige)* has been fiercely suppressed on occasion. The Austrians conducted long drawn out negotiations with Italy about the degree of autonomy for this region and agreement was finally reached in 1969.

Relations with Yugoslavia have also been adversely affected by the status of Austria's Slav minorities. A special census was held in November 1976 to facilitate implementation of a new law on the protection of minority rights.

5 THE ECONOMY

Economic Situation

In 1979 the percentage contribution of the various sectors of the economy to Austria's GNP may be expressed as follows:

Agriculture and forestry	6.3
Manufacturing	36.3
Construction	8.4
Electricity, gas, water	3.6
Transport	6.1
Trade	12.5
Public Administration	12.3
Other services	14.5
	100.0

The growth rate was 6.2% in 1976, 3.7% in 1977, and 1.5% in 1978. Inflation reached 9.7% in 1974 but has been reduced. The rate of unemployment did not exceed 2% during the 1970s. At the end of 1976 there were 6,830 industrial units of which only 214 employed more than 500 people. Industrial production rose in the 1970s, the percentage contribution being approximately: food and drink 24.7%; chemicals 21.3%; mechanical engineering and steel production 8.25%; iron and metal goods 12.5%; electrical engineering 12.8%; petroleum 10.2%; textiles 10%.

Investment was running at an annual rate of AS30,000 million in 1978 (an increase of 6.9% over 1977), with the emphasis shifting away from capital goods into primary materials. Within the economy in the late seventies over 60% of the population were in industry, the processing trades and services, less than 10% were in agriculture and forestry and almost a quarter of the population were pensioners.

Natural Resources

Austria is reasonably rich in natural energy resources with oil reserves of between 285 and 300 million tons, of which 35% is extractable by current methods, and 75,000 million cubic metres of natural gas, of which 60% is easily extractable. In 1975 2.3 million cubic metres were produced but the rest of the country's requirement was imported from the Soviet Union by pipeline. Two thirds of electrical power production is provided by hydro-electric power. A decision against using nuclear power was taken by referendum in 1978. Coal production provides less than a quarter of the country's requirement and the coal mining sector runs at a deficit to keep prices down and maintain employment. Iron ore supplies provide about half domestic needs. There are also deposits of magnesite, salt, brine, gypsum, copper, lead, zinc and quartz.

Agriculture and Forestry

The contribution of agriculture and forestry to GNP declined from 15.1% in 1951 to 5% in 1977; in that year the number of people employed in agriculture and forestry was 8.2% of the residential population. Mechanisation has meant that the proportion employed in these fields has declined but that high productivity has been maintained and Austrian agriculture provides 80% of domestic food requirements.

Austria has the third largest forested area in western Europe covering 39% of the total area. Two thirds of the coniferous timber felled is exported.

Tourism

Tourism is of major importance in the Austrian economy, accounting for 7.2% of Austria's GNP in 1977. Foreign currency receipts from tourism totalled AS54,906 million in 1977.

Overseas Trade

Austria imports (in value) more than she exports in the ratio of 3:2. Her main trading partners are the Federal Republic of Germany, Italy, Switzerland, France, Britain and the Soviet Union.

Economic Management

There is considerable cooperation between government and labour in the management of the economy. The Federation of Austrian Industrialists is involved in decision making. The major activity is in the control of wages and prices by the Parity Commission, a voluntarily constituted negotiating panel. The Commission is made up of representatives of the Austrian Trade Union Federation (OGB), the Chambers of Labour, Chambers of Agriculture and Chambers of the Economy (which review draft economic legislation), and appropriate ministries, under the chairmanship of the Chancellor. The Parity Commission is not in any sense an official body but it has enormous influence and any plan for wage and price rises has to be submitted to its appropriate sub-committee. Plans are considered in the light of their effect on the economy and either passed for detailed negotiation or deferred. Recommendations are presented to the government. As a result of this cooperation industrial action has been reduced to a very small scale.

6 THE EDUCATION SYSTEM

Compulsory General *(Allegemeinbildende Pflichtschulen)*

Since 1962 compulsory education has been extended from eight to nine years. It is divided into two basic cycles of four years each with a terminal ninth year, which emphasises preparation for work, for those not continuing in the school system.

Academic Year

The duration of the academic year in compulsory education is fixed by the provincial states. Usually it runs from September to June/July and is divided into two semesters with a week's holiday at Christmas, two weeks at Easter and eight weeks in the summer. There is also a week's 'energy saving' holiday in February, when everybody goes skiing. The weekly number of hours of instruction varies between 20 in the first grade of primary school and 45 in technical second level schools. In second level general schools pupils have between 31 and 36 hours of instruction per week spread over six days (with a half holiday on Saturday), except in Lower Austria. The university year is divided into two semesters (October to February and March to July).

Pre-School *(Kindergarten)*

Since 1962 pre-primary education has been the responsibility of the provincial states. Education at this level is not compulsory and caters for children between the ages of 3 and 6. Some schools operate full time and others for only half a day; some are open for the whole year and others are seasonal (for example, those provided at harvest time in rural areas). In state *Kindergarten* small fees are charged except in cases of financial need. There are also private classes mostly run by religious communities or large factories and other enterprises. The aim of pre-school education is to extend the education given by the family and to foster a community feeling among children. Emphasis is given to the promotion of the child's whole personality and to this end *Kindergarten* are organised into small classes with provision for individual activities and a wide range of materials and games. At present the number of children enrolled in pre-school education is rising steadily and so is the proportion of 3 to 6 year olds. Pre-primary schooling is rather formal and groups are large.

As well as normal *Kindergarten* there are schools for handicapped children, and children suffering from speech defects are given therapy in normal schools. Pilot projects have also been mounted in some larger cities to give special education for children of compulsory school age who are not yet ready to enter primary schools. These groups aim to give the children more individual tuition so that they may be helped to reach the appropriate standard *(Vorschulklassen)*.

First Level Schools (Volksschule or Grundschule)

First level schools are entered at the age of 6 and give a basic education common to all pupils. Subjects studied include: religious education, German, mathematics, music, physical education, arts subjects, needlework for girls, and so-called orientation subjects. In the past *Volksschulen* operated through the whole eight grades and there is still legal provision for this, but it may only happen under certain conditions, and the eight-grade *Volksschulen* tend to be found nowadays only in rural and remote areas of low population as the provision of *Hauptschulen* (secondary general schools) increases. The upper primary division of the *Volksschule* seeks to give an education specially adapted to local conditions.

Second Level General Schools (Hauptschulen)

These schools cover grades 5 to 8 (ages 11 to 14) and entry to them is dependent on successful completion of the final grade of *Volksschule*. The *Hauptschule* cycle offers a more extensive and developed general education than that offered in the *Volksschule* and subjects studied include: history and social studies, geography and economics, natural history and home economics. There is now legal provision for special forms of *Hauptschulen* with particular emphasis on fine arts or sports. The schools are organised into two streams differentiated by curricula and academic requirements. Tuition in one modern language is offered in both streams but is only compulsory in the first stream. In addition the first stream may study Latin. The first stream is intended for the selection of more gifted pupils who may subsequently transfer to top level secondary schools (AHS). This they may do without examination provided that they fulfil the language and general requirements of the particular secondary school. Other pupils may transfer to medium and top level secondary technical and vocational schools in which case an entrance examination is often required.

Pre-Vocational (Polytechnischer Lehrgang)

This grade 9 course offers a new type of terminal year, for children who will not be continuing their studies at a top level secondary or medium level school. It aims to consolidate the pupils' general education, and at the same time prepare them for practical working life (including leisure). Help is given in a choice of career by means of vocational guidance. There are compulsory courses in German, mathematics, social studies and economics, natural science (insofar as it is relevant to the modern economy), engineering drawing, hygiene and home economics and child care (for girls). On completion of the course the pupils take up employment but those who are apprentices will continue their vocational education part time.

Special (Sonderschule)

These schools cover grades 1 to 8 and the 'polytechnic' year. They give remedial teaching to physically and mentally handicapped children with a curriculum which corresponds as closely as possible to that followed in the other compulsory schools, and at the same time prepares them for a suitable job.

Second-Stage Second Level General Schools
(Allgemeinbildende Höhere Schulen)

In general, a minority of pupils (about 20% of all pupils) enter the various categories of top level secondary general school at the age of 10 after completion of the lower primary course, though as has been pointed out, pupils may also transfer from the *Hauptschule* at a later stage. Most of the top level secondary general schools offer courses divided into two cycles: a lower cycle of four years (grades 5 to 8) and an upper cycle of four years (grades 9 to 12), though some only operate at the upper level. The main aim of these schools is to provide a comprehensive academic education and prepare pupils for university entrance. The school leaving examination *(Reifeprüfung,* known as the *Matura)* gives access to higher education and consists of two parts: a written examination in German, mathematics and a third compulsory subject and an oral examination covering three subjects chosen by the candidate. It is also a qualification for certain categories of posts in the civil service, public administration, banking, and is a pre-condition for officer rank in the armed forces.

The differences between the various kinds of top level secondary general school are defined by the curricula, though there is a common core. The following subjects are studied in all *Allgemeinbildende Höhere Schulen:* religious instruction, German, history and social studies, two foreign languages (at least one being a modern language), geography and economics, mathematics, biology, physics, chemistry, introduction to philosophy (in the upper cycle), music, art, handicrafts and workshop practice and physical education. Generally speaking there is no organised sport but all pupils have one week's skiing in the winter. Promotion between grades depends on marks which are awarded both as a result of written and oral examinations and as a result of continuous assessment. It also depends on a satisfactory performance in all compulsory subjects. Though there are a few schools which emphasise fine arts and sports, the schools are broadly divided into *Gymnasia* where one modern language is studied throughout the course with compulsory Latin from grades 7 to 12, and *Realgymnasia* where one language is studied throughout with compulsory geometrical drawing in grades 5 to 8 and Latin or a second modern language in grades 9 to 12. There are also special forms of AHS offering only an upper cycle or operating part time. Of the various types and branches of AHS no more than three can be operated in a given school at one time. In larger cities all types can normally be found. In 1977/78, 176,951 pupils were enrolled in AHS.

Gymnasium

In the second cycle of the second level (grades 9 to 12) this type of school is divided into three divisions as follows:

Humanistisches Gymnasium — Latin + 1 modern language + Greek (5-6 hours Latin and Greek per week)

Neusprachliches Gymnasium — Latin + 2 modern languages

Realistisches Gymnasium — Latin + 1 modern language + extra mathematics and science.

Realgymnasium

There is a corresponding division in grades 9 to 12 in this school into:

Naturwissenschaftliches Realgymnasium — modern language + Latin + either descriptive geometry or biology, physics and chemistry (grades 11 and 12)

Mathematisches Realgymnasium — 2 modern languages + descriptive geometry.

In addition the domestic science *Realgymnasium* for girls *(Wirtschaftskundliches Realgymnasium für Mädchen)* offers in the upper cycle a second modern language or Latin + handicraft (grade 9), food science and home economics (grades 11 and 12) and education (grades 10 to 12).

Upper Cycle Schools

Since September 1976 a reorganisation of upper cycle top level secondary general schools has introduced the *Oberstufenrealgymnasium* which replaces the *Musisch-Pädagogisches Realgymnasium*. The new institutions offer three alternative specialisms: instrumental music, descriptive geometry or sciences. The *Aufbaugymnasium* and *Aufbaurealgymnasium* are primarily intended for pupils who have completed upper primary school and wish to attain the standard of secondary education. They consist of one-year transitional classes followed by a four-year course (grades 10 to 13) and are mostly found in rural areas. The curricula correspond basically to those of the *Gymnasium*, (classical or modern language branch) and the *Realgymnasium* (science branch with descriptive geometry). Other special forms of upper cycle secondary school are the *Gymnasium* and *Realgymnasium für Berufstätige* which offer part time evening courses for students over the age of 17 who are already employed. Curricula correspond to those of the *Gymnasium* (science branch) and *Realgymnasium* (mathematics branch).

Boarding Schools (Höhere Internatsschulen)

In general, State schools have no recognised facilities for boarders who may live in hostels or with families if it is impossible for them to travel from home to school and back daily. the principal boarding schools are run by religious orders (for example, the Jesuit College, Kalksburg). However, there are special top level secondary general schools with boarding facilities where academic education, character training and community life are combined. The full course lasts eight years. State boarding schools are called *Bundeserziehungsanstalten*.

Technical and Vocational

This sector is extremely complex and with an enormous variety of institutions offering technical and vocational education and training. They may be divided into three main categories:

(i) top level secondary technical and vocational schools giving access to higher education *(Berufsbildende Höhere Schulen)*

(ii) medium level secondary technical and vocational schools *(Berufsbildende Mittlere Schulen)*

(iii) compulsory technical and vocational schools for apprentices *(Berufsbildende Pflichtschulen)*.

Top Level Secondary Technical/Vocational

Courses in these schools last five years (grades 9 to 13) and in general entrants should have satisfactorily completed grades 1 to 8 and passed an entrance examination, though there are special types of institution for adult students. The schools aim to provide pupils with an advanced general and technical or vocational education to qualify them for occupations at middle management or technician level or entry to specialised higher education. The *Matura* obtained at these schools is a searching test and confers certain rights and privileges in the respective trade as well as entry to universities. Holders are regarded as fully qualified journeymen. The schools cover the industrial, agricultural and trade fields and may be subdivided into the following:

(i) *Höhere Technische und Gewerbliche Lehranstalten* - industrial and trade schools which are attended mostly by full time pupils after eight years of schooling. However, they also provide four-year part time courses for those already in employment and for graduates of other types of school who wish to be trained in a particular trade (one- and two-year courses)

(ii) *Handelsakademien* - commercial schools offering training in all branches of business including special courses for those already employed (lasting five years) and for graduates of other types of post-compulsory school (*Abiturientenkurs* - lasting one to two years). By taking a supplementary school leaving certificate *(Ergänzungsmatura)* graduates of the full course may be admitted to all forms of higher education. The *Handelsakademie Matura* qualifies holders to set up in business after one year's experience

(iii) *Höhere Lehranstalt für Wirtschaftliche Frauenberufe* - domestic and catering schools which prepare female students for jobs at executive level in domestic science and social work, including special schools for those already employed (four-year course)

(iv) *Höhere Land und Forstwirtschaftliche Lehranstalten* - schools for agriculture and forestry.

Medium Level Secondary Technical/Vocational

These schools generally offer four-year courses (grades 9 to 12), which do not give access to institutions of higher education. They are intended to provide the fundamental professional training necessary for jobs in the fields of commerce, technology, arts and crafts, women's occupations and social work. Generally candidates for admission must pass an entrance examination but here again there are schools (and more commonly special forms) for adult students. A variety of professional qualifications are awarded. The following types of school may be distinguished:

(i) *Technische, Gewerbliche und Kunstgewerbliche Fachschulen* - technical, trade and arts and crafts schools with different specialised departments each of which prepares students for one or more technical occupations through theoretical and practical instruction. Normal courses last two to four years but there are also short or long courses of up to four people who have completed primary vocational education, e.g. for master craftsman's examinations

(ii) *Handelschulen* - business schools offering three-year courses including those for people already in employment (which in this case are of the same length). There are also some private office schools at a lower level *(Buro- und Verwaltungsschulen)*

(iii) *Fachschulen für Wirtschaftliche Frauenberufe* - women's vocational schools for domestic and catering occupations which offer training at various levels, i.e. *Haushaltungsschule* (one-year housekeeping courses) *Hauswirtschaftsschule* - (two-year domestic science courses) and *Fachschule für Wirtschaftliche Frauenberufe* (three-year professional domestic and catering courses)

(iv) *Fachschulen für Sozialberufe* - vocational schools for social workers. These offer one- to two-year courses to students between 18 and 20 who have already had one year's attendance at a vocational school or one year's practical experience

(v) *Landwirtschaftliche Fachschulen* - vocational agricultural schools.

In addition there are institutions which are in level comparable to medium level technical and vocational schools such as nursing schools *(Allgemeine Krankenpflegeschulen)*, schools for medical auxiliaries *(Schulen für den Medizinisch-Technischen Fachdienst)* and midwifery schools *(Bundeshebammenlehranstalten)* which come under the auspices of the health ministry.

Compulsory Technical/Vocational

These schools are intended to start at grade 10 (after completion of the 'polytechnic year') but in fact students who have reached the age of 15 are admitted notwithstanding the grade they have previously attained. The schools provide part time education and training for one day per week or monthly on block release for apprentices in trade, industry and commerce. Courses generally last three to four years and once again the schools are subdivided into a number of different types:

(i) *Gewerbliche und Kaufmännische Berufsschulen* - compulsory industrial and commercial schools which offer day release and block release courses throughout the whole year. They cover as many grades as years of apprenticeship (two to four years) and offer subjects such as transport and tourism as well as mechanical skills

(ii) *Hauswirtschaftliche Berufsschulen* - compulsory domestic science schools. These only operate in the provincial State of Vorarlberg and offer supplementary two year part time courses for girls who are not attending any other type of school

(iii) *Land- und Forstwirtschaftliche Berufsschulen* - compulsory agricultural and forestry schools covering between one and three grades and supplementing the education of young people working in these occupations.

Teacher Training

Teachers undergo very different kinds of training (and enter training at different stages) according to the level of teaching they intend to take up. Broadly, teacher training institutions may be divided into those entered on completion of compulsory schooling *(Lehrerbildende Mittlere Schulen* - medium level secondary teacher training or normal schools) and those which require for admission completion of secondary education *(Lehrerbildende Akademien* - teacher training colleges).

'Normal Schools'

There are basically three types of institution entered after general compulsory school and the successful passing of an aptitude test. These train pre-school teachers, teachers of practical subjects and educational assistants and are as follows:

(i) *Bildungsanstalten für Arbeitslehrerinnen* - (schools for home economics teachers) which offer four-year specialised courses for women teachers of needlework and home economics in general compulsory schools. A diploma is awarded after a final proficiency examination

(ii) *Bildungsanstalten für Kindergärtnerinnen* -(schools for pre-primary teachers) which train *Kindergarten* teachers and teachers at children's day centres *(Horterzieherinnen)*. Again the courses last four years and lead to the award of a diploma. Practical training is carried out in *Kindergarten* attached to the schools

(iii) *Bildungsanstalten für Erzieher* - (schools for educational assistants) which train students for educational auxiliary work especially in residential establishments. Courses vary in length between one and five years according to the students' previous training and experience. Suitable facilities are available for practical work. Some institutions organise courses especially for work with handicapped or maladjusted chidren. Some also conduct research into boarding school education *(Institut für Heimerziehung)*

(iv) *Schulen zur Ausbildung von Leibeserziehern und Sportlehren* - (school for physical education teachers and sports instructors). Courses last between six months and four years depending on previous education; the minimum standard for admission is grade 8.

Training Colleges

These institutions train primarily teachers for compulsory schools but there are also colleges which educate specialist teachers for various kinds of vocational school. Included in this category are the institutes of education for the organisation of research as well as teaching:

(i) *Pädagogische Akademien* were established in 1965 and provide training for teachers in the *Volksschulen, Hauptschulen, Sonderschulen* and *Polytechnischer Lehrgang*. Candidates must pass an aptitude test as well as hold the school leaving certificate *(Matura)* of a top level general or technical secondary school. The courses vary in length with two year courses for *Volksschule* teachers and three-year courses for those in secondary and special schools. The syllabus for *Volksschule* teachers was revised to take into account curriculum changes at primary level. Elective major subjects include a foreign language and there is more instruction in optional subjects - music, physical education, handicraft, etc. Teaching practice is given in practice schools attached to the *Akademien.*

(ii) *Berufspädagogische Akademien* (technical teacher training colleges) and *Land- und Forstwirtschaftliche Berufspädagogische Akademien* (agricultural teacher training colleges) educate teachers of particular subjects or groups of subjects in technical schools. Conditions of admission vary - a master craftsman's certificate may be acceptable as well as the *Matura*. Courses last between one and two years

(iii) *Pädagogische Institute* (institutes of education) are designed primarily for the further training of general compulsory school teachers, for example, the upgrading of *Volksschule* teachers to work in upper primary or special schools. There are corresponding institutes for technical and agricultural teachers. All conduct research and organise conferences, seminars, etc.

Other

The training of teachers for the top level secondary general schools and certain subjects (for example, commerce) in top level and medium level technical secondary schools takes place in the universities. The students take the university degree of *Magister* in their particular field and follow this with an examination in education. They then teach for a probationary year. Teachers at the *Pädagogische Akademien* receive the same training as AHS teachers. An important development in graduate teacher training has been the foundation of the *Universität für Bildungswissenschaften* in Klagenfurt which as well as offering degree programmes is entrusted with responsibility for research into education and new education courses. Teaching practice during university studies is being pioneered by this university.

Third Level (Higher) Educational Institutions

Higher education is Austria is virtually university education when measured in terms of student enrolment (82.4% of all post-secondary students were in universities in 1977). There are 18 institutions of university standing in Austria including six schools of art and music, four general universities and nine specialist universities (formerly called *Hochschulen*). They are as follows (year of foundation in brackets):

Karl-Franzens Universität, Graz (1585)

Leopold-Franzens Universität, Innsbruck (1669)

Universität Salzburg (1623, re-established 1962)

Universität Wien (1365)

Technische Universität, Graz (1811)
    (science and technology)

Technische Universität Wien (1815)
    (science and technology)

Universität für Bodenkultur, Wien (1872)
    (agriculture and forestry)

Johannes Kepler Universität, Linz (1962, renamed 1975)
    (mainly social and economic sciences)

Wirtschaftsuniversität, Wien (1898)
    (economics)

Montanistiscne Universität, Leoben (1840)
    (mining and metallurgy)

Veterinaermedizinische Universität, Wien (1767)
    (veterinary medicine)

Akademie der Bildenden Künste, Wien (1692)
    (fine arts)

Hochschule fur Angewandte Künst, Wien (1867)

Hochscule für Künstlerische und Industrielle Gestaltung, Linz
    (industrial art and design)

Universität für Bildungswissenschaften, Klagenfurt (1970)
    (educational studies)

Hochschule für Musik und Darstellende Kunst, Wien (1817)
    (music and drama)

Hochschule für Musik und Darstellende Kunst, Graz (1963)
(music and drama)

Hochschule für Musik und Darstellende Kunst 'Mozarteum', Salzburg (1914)
(music and drama)

Admission

Access to university is open to all who have completed secondary school and obtained the *Matura*, and there is no *numerus clausus*. Graduates of the *Handelsakademien* (secondary commercial schools) are only entitled to enter the *Wirtschaftsuniversität* unless they have taken a supplementary leaving certificate which gives entrance to all faculties. tuition is free. However, the secondary school graduation group is small (about 16% of 18-year olds) and only 53% of these secondary school graduates enter university (about 8% of the appropriate age group). Applicants between the ages of 25 and 45 without secondary qualifications may enter higher education through the examination *Berufsreifeprüfung* which can be taken at any of the four general universities after preliminary application. However, in practice few students are admitted by this route. University reforms on an experimental basis in 1979/80 include the introduction of a new university qualification test for non-secondary graduates *(Hochschulreifeprüfung)* preceded by a ten-month full time preparatory course.

Degree Courses

The normal first degree course *(Ordentliches Studium)* should last between eight and ten semesters (four to five years) and is organised into two stages - the first stage being an introduction to the fundamentals of the subject and the second involving more specialisation. The first degree may be called a Diploma or a Master's Degree *(Magister)* depending on the type of college or university attended. After obtaining the first degree the student may then study for at least two more semesters to obtain the Doctorate, the highest academic qualification in Austria. Medical studies are organised differently; they are divided into three stages and conclude with the Doctoral degree for all students.

There are also special programmes *(Studium Irregulare)*, instituted in 1966, in which elements of the regular degree programmes are organised by the individual student to form a 'tailormade' course. These combinations must be approved by the academic authorities and have been used to test new programmes. In 1975 less than 1% availed themselves of this opportunity. In addition, since 1971, where a number of students (which may vary from 10 to 100) wish to follow a programme not provided by the university or college, there is legal provision for the establishment of study experiments *(Studienversuch)* for the appropriate period of time. This has led to the institution of programmes in social studies and business and economic information science. Requests to set up such experiments are considered by the National Ministry of Science and Research.

Since 1966 the structure of the regular degree courses has been rendered more flexible by the expansion of optional subjects *(Wahlfächer)* and 'free' subjects *(Freifächer)* which are additional single subjects, chosen purely at will, which may or may not relate to the student's field of study. The latter take up only a small part of study time but in the last four semesters of degree programmes optional subjects may take up as much as 65% of study time. By the General University Studies Act of 1966, students have the right to choose the courses on which they enrol and their teachers among those teaching the same subject. They may also register at the same time for courses in different universities and faculties.

Short Courses

As well as the full length degree courses, some universities also offer shorter programmes *(Kurzstudium)* though many of those leading to degree qualifications were discontinued in 1966. Such short courses include:

(i) translation at the Universities of Vienna, Graz and Innsbruck (degree course - 6 semesters)

(ii) actuarial mathematics at the Technical University, Vienna (non-degree course - 6 semesters)

(iii) computation methods at the Technical University, Vienna and Johannes Kepler University, Linz (non-degree course - 4 semesters).

Non-Degree Studies

There are also very limited opportunities for students over 18 (and exceptionally over 15) who have not obtained secondary school leaving certificates to enrol as non-degree students for a certain period of time *(Hochschulkurse* and *Hochschulvorbereitungslehrgänge)*. Some emphasis is now being given to expanding these opportunities, especially by using distance education techniques. Graduates of other higher institutes may also attend specific programmes as 'auditing' students. In addition there are State subsidised courses designed for specialists from developing countries, concentrating on medicine and veterinary medicine, prospecting and mining, tourism, customs and excise, the conservation of historic buildings, telecommunications and posts, etc. There are a small number of post-graduate non-degree courses. These include a course in international studies offered by the University of Vienna and university extension courses in business management and administration. The Institute of Advanced Studies runs two-year post-graduate courses in social sciences and business administration. But post-graduate studies as understood in Britain and the United States are not well developed.

Examinations

University examinations have the status of national examinations and the completion of degree studies gives access to the professions. Further examinations by employers do not take place unless they are intended to select candidates for promotion. Traditionally Austrian university students have had little guidance on their progress, with all examinations taken at the end of the course; only in medicine and at the technical universities were tests administered throughout the study period. In general this is changing, with a wholesale departure from major examinations before examination boards and the adoption of individual examinations on each subject with even, in some cases, part examinations on the material taught in individual sections. A cumulative 'unit' type dissertation and doctoral thesis is before an examination board.

Other Institutions

The six art schools offer a wide variety of courses but only a small proportion are academic courses of the university type which are fixed by law. These include courses in architecture, music education, instrumental music education, pictorial education, handicraft, textile work and sewing (the last five all being secondary school teaching qualifications). Mention should also be made of the *Berufsbildende Akademien* (technical academies) which, while not strictly included in higher education, do presuppose the completion of secondary school and the *Matura*. These include the academies of social work *(Akademien für Sozialarbeit)* which train students for advanced social work in courses lasting usually two years with the award of a proficiency diploma on completion. There are also medico-technical colleges *(Schulen für die Gehobenen Medizinisch-Technischen Dienste)* offering courses varying in length from 21 months to three years.

Adult

Increasing attention is being paid to this sector of the education system as one of the government's principal objectives is to ensure a higher standard of specialised training thus providing for bettern professional qualifications and easier transfer from one job to another. Except for the Vienna School of Economics, most non-degree students attend language courses. There is, of course, provision for adult students in almost all the different varieties of secondary and vocational schools operating in the evenings. But there is room for much development in the area of professional and vocational adult education.

The more general type of adult education *(Volksbildung)* is much more in evidence, and already courses are transmitted by radio and television backed up by literature, group discussions and computerised tests. The ultimate aim is the development of an Austrian Academy of the Air. However, the main sources of general adult education are the 300 *Volkshochschulen* (area centres) backed up by 1,750 local organisations. There are also

20 residential centres run by public bodies, churches, the Austrian Trade Union Federation and the Employers' Federation.

Guidance and Counselling

As befits an education system of multiple choices, guidance and counselling are highly developed at all levels of the Austrian system. Each school has on its staff educational counsellors, who are members of the teaching staff specially trained in vocational guidance and psychology. The school staff must also include a doctor. In 1975 there were 66 school psychologists engaged in educational counselling in 36 special centres. The educational counsellors are kept continually briefed on changes in the education regulations and are mainly responsible for vocational guidance, though they are also equipped to help students with learning or behavioural difficulties and may refer pupils to the counselling centres, etc. In 1975 there were also 224 consultants advising pupils, teachers and parents on the work of the vocational schools and in 1973/74 educational counselling was officially instituted in upper primary schools with three-semester courses for selected teaching staff. Counselling for primary schools is under discussion. Each of the four general universities has a student counselling service, and so has the Johannes Kepler University in Linz. As at school level these provide both vocational assessment and advice and help with academic and/or emotional problems.

Mention should also be made of the numerous vocational information publications produced by the national education ministries and by the Ministry of Social Administration which runs the national vocational guidance service for graduates of the system at all levels. The service is operated through the provincial state labour exchanges and involves the provision of information, assessment and advice.

7 EDUCATIONAL ADMINISTRATION

Federal Agencies

The administration, organisation and inspection of the school system is the responsibility of three separate authorities: the National Ministry of Education and Art *Bundesministerium für Unterricht und Kunst)*, the boards of education *(Landesschulräte)* in each of the nine provincial states, which are to some extent subordinate to the National Ministry, and the district school boards *(Bezirksschulräte)* which function at regional and local level and answer to the provincial state boards. In January 1975 in addition *Ombudsmen* were appointed by the Minister of Education and Art to aid and advise him in all matters regarding teachers and schools. Their work produced suggestions on rationalising school administration as well as inspectors, etc. Private schools are under state control to the extent that they are frequently inspected by the public authorities to ensure that standards are maintained.

ADMINISTRATION
*National Science and Technology
Policy Structures and Mechanisms*

ZONE OF PARLIAMENT

- National Council
  - Committee for Science and Research
- Federal Council

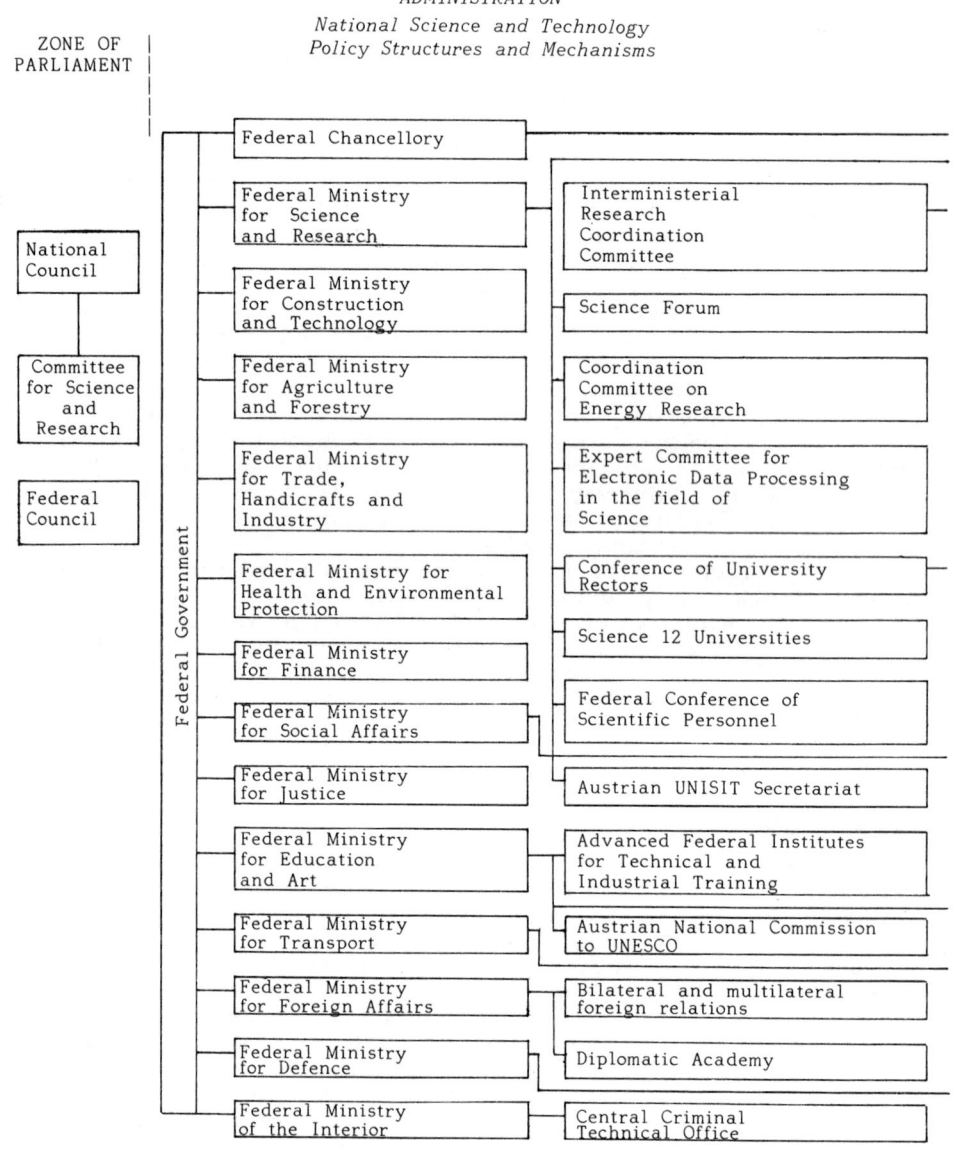

Federal Government

- Federal Chancellory
- Federal Ministry for Science and Research — Interministerial Research Coordination Committee
- Federal Ministry for Construction and Technology — Science Forum
- Federal Ministry for Agriculture and Forestry — Coordination Committee on Energy Research
- Federal Ministry for Trade, Handicrafts and Industry — Expert Committee for Electronic Data Processing in the field of Science
- Federal Ministry for Health and Environmental Protection — Conference of University Rectors
- Federal Ministry for Finance — Science 12 Universities
- Federal Ministry for Social Affairs — Federal Conference of Scientific Personnel
- Federal Ministry for Justice — Austrian UNISIT Secretariat
- Federal Ministry for Education and Art — Advanced Federal Institutes for Technical and Industrial Training
- Federal Ministry for Transport — Austrian National Commission to UNESCO
- Federal Ministry for Foreign Affairs — Bilateral and multilateral foreign relations
- Federal Ministry for Defence — Diplomatic Academy
- Federal Ministry of the Interior — Central Criminal Technical Office

/contd...

ADMINISTRATION

National Science and Technology Policy Structures and Mechanisms (contd.)

ZONE OF GOVERNMENT

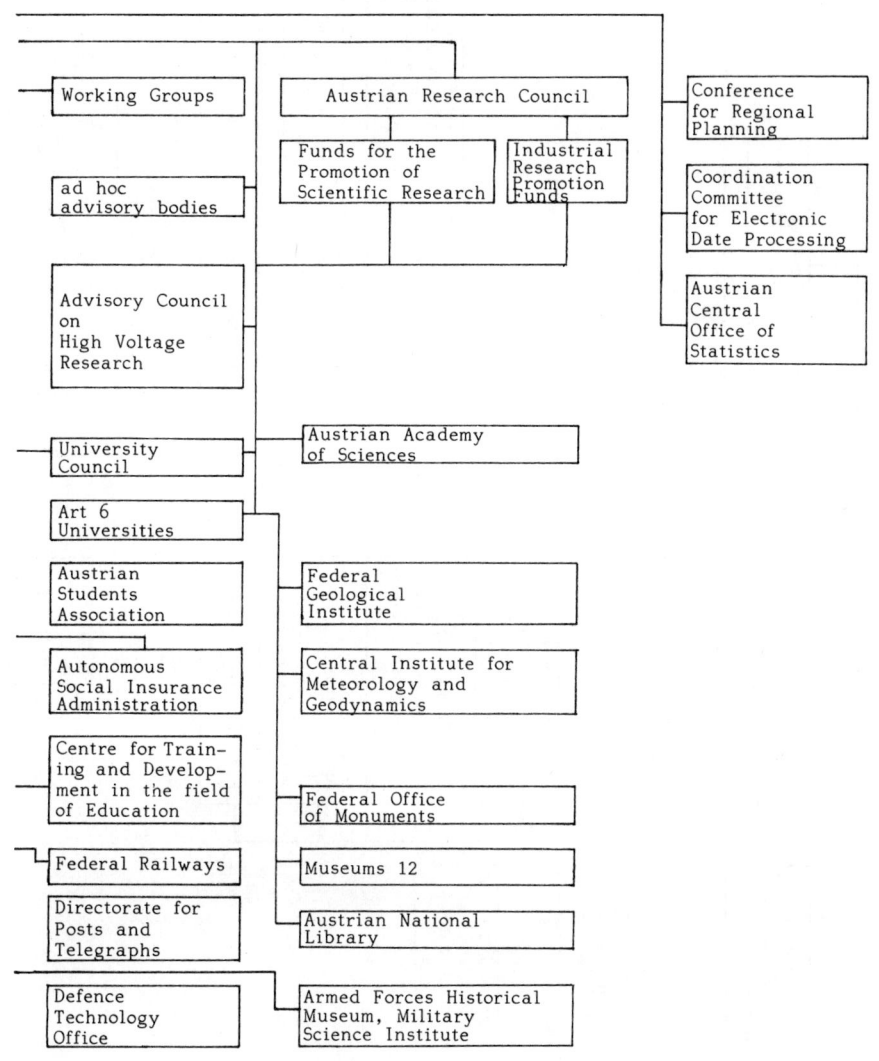

- Working Groups
- ad hoc advisory bodies
- Austrian Research Council
  - Funds for the Promotion of Scientific Research
  - Industrial Research Promotion Funds
- Conference for Regional Planning
- Coordination Committee for Electronic Date Processing
- Austrian Central Office of Statistics
- Advisory Council on High Voltage Research
- University Council
- Austrian Academy of Sciences
- Art 6 Universities
- Austrian Students Association
- Federal Geological Institute
- Autonomous Social Insurance Administration
- Central Institute for Meteorology and Geodynamics
- Centre for Training and Development in the field of Education
- Federal Office of Monuments
- Federal Railways
- Museums 12
- Directorate for Posts and Telegraphs
- Austrian National Library
- Defence Technology Office
- Armed Forces Historical Museum, Military Science Institute

/contd...

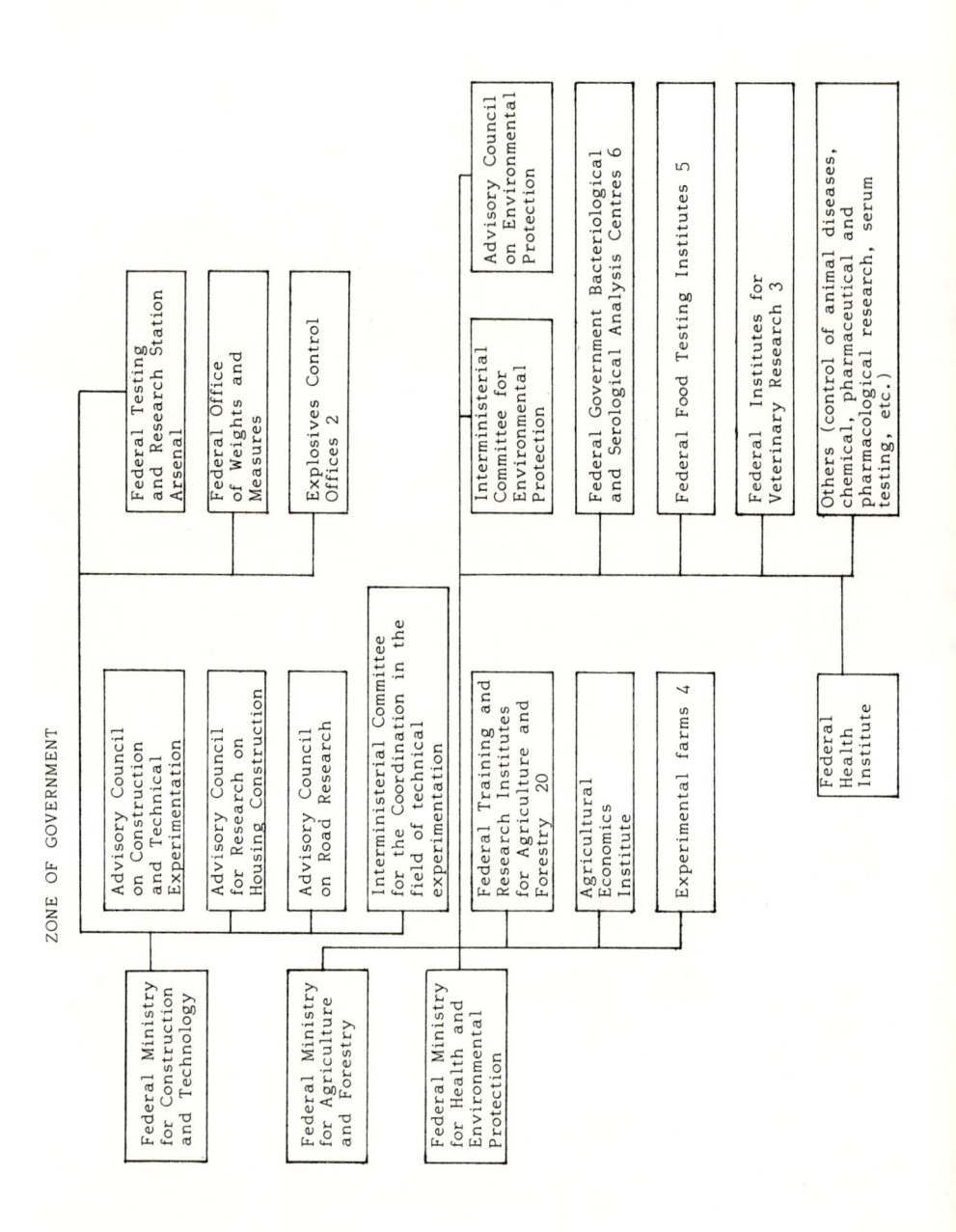

ZONE OF GOVERNMENT

- Federal Ministry for Construction and Technology
  - Advisory Council on Construction and Technical Experimentation
  - Advisory Council for Research on Housing Construction
  - Advisory Council on Road Research
  - Federal Testing and Research Station Arsenal
  - Federal Office of Weights and Measures
  - Explosives Control Offices 2

- Federal Ministry for Agriculture and Forestry
  - Interministerial Committee for the Coordination in the field of technical experimentation
  - Federal Training and Research Institutes for Agriculture and Forestry 20
  - Agricultural Economics Institute
  - Experimental farms 4

- Federal Ministry for Health and Environmental Protection
  - Interministerial Committee for Environmental Protection
  - Advisory Council on Environmental Protection
  - Federal Government Bacteriological and Serological Analysis Centres 6
  - Federal Food Testing Institutes 5
  - Federal Institutes for Veterinary Research 3
  - Others (control of animal diseases, chemical, pharmaceutical and pharmacological research, serum testing, etc.)
  - Federal Health Institute

60

ZONE OF THE CITIZEN AND SCIENTIFIC COMMUNITY

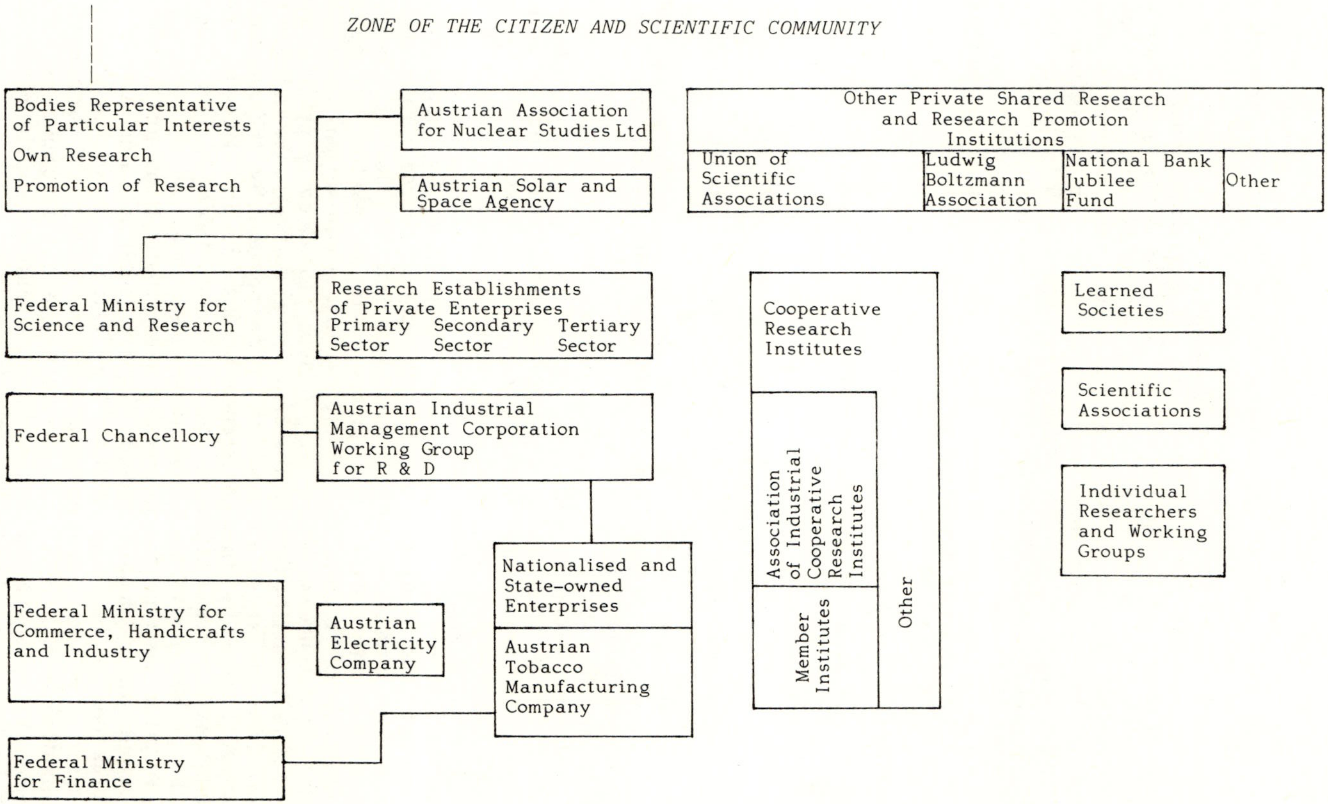

[Organizational chart showing relationships between Austrian research and government bodies]

- Bodies Representative of Particular Interests Own Research Promotion of Research
  - Austrian Association for Nuclear Studies Ltd
  - Austrian Solar and Space Agency

- Other Private Shared Research and Research Promotion Institutions
  - Union of Scientific Associations
  - Ludwig Boltzmann Association
  - National Bank Jubilee Fund
  - Other

- Federal Ministry for Science and Research
  - Research Establishments of Private Enterprises
    - Primary Sector
    - Secondary Sector
    - Tertiary Sector

- Federal Chancellory
  - Austrian Industrial Management Corporation Working Group for R & D

- Cooperative Research Institutes
  - Association of Industrial Cooperative Research Institutes
  - Member Institutes
  - Other

- Federal Ministry for Commerce, Handicrafts and Industry
  - Austrian Electricity Company
  - Nationalised and State-owned Enterprises
  - Austrian Tobacco Manufacturing Company

- Federal Ministry for Finance

- Learned Societies
- Scientific Associations
- Individual Researchers and Working Groups

The 1920 Federal Constitution did not clarify and lay down the distribution of authority between the national government and the provincial states on education and this matter was only finally resolved by the Federal Constitutional Act of 1962. This states that the national government determines the organisation of the school system (types of school etc.), fixes school district limits, class size and the establishment of new public non-compulsory schools and maintenance of existing ones. (The National Ministry of Education and Art and the Ministry of Public Works decide the volume of building for each year and then the Provincial State Ministry of Education sets priorities and decides on the location and type of schools.) The establishment and maintenance of public compulsory schools belongs to the provincial state administrations who are authorised to make the appropriate legislative enactments. Specifically local issues are dealt with at school district level with parents and teachers able to attend council meetings.

Universities

Higher education is the responsibility of a separate national ministry - the Ministry of Science and Research *(Bundesministerium für Wissenschaft und Forschung)*. The institutions of university status are national establishments and are directly responsible to the Ministry for matters in the public sphere. As the basic principles of any public measure in Austria must be enshrined in national legislation central government plays an important part in the administering of universities. By the General University Studies Act of 1966 individual study programmes are regulated on three levels: the Studies Act passed by parliament; the study regulation of the national ministry and the academic study regulations produced by the academic authority. Thus the State decrees the structure and general principles of university study, with the Ministry specifying the minimum number of hours per semester that a student has to register for individual courses in each examinable subject, while the university teachers are responsible for organising the content and methods of the individual course. This seems a cumbersome procedure but is perhaps less so than it looks, because the universities are involved at an earlier stage in the drafting of legislation. Participating organisations are the Austrian Conference of University Rectors (the legally established organ of all institutions with university status), the Academic Council (five of whose 15 members are appointed by the national government, five by the Conference of Rectors and five by the Ministry mainly from academic staff), the Austrian Student Union and the authorities of the universities concerned.

In all other matters the university level institutions are autonomous and their organs adopt legally binding administrative measures on the basis of existing legislation much as the provincial states do in administering schools. Under the University Organisation Act of 1975 the universities are autonomous in such matters as: preparation of budget estimates; appointments of chair holders and other staff; establishment of rules for university bodies; the awarding of degrees and diplomas; guarantees of courses, etc. The individual academic bodies within the universities are assigned responsibilities for these areas. Since 1969 these university bodies have included the study commissions *(Studienkommissionen)* which advise on courses and examinations and generally oversee teaching in the university.

8 EDUCATIONAL FINANCE

Education Budget

Between 1955 and 1963 education's share of the total national budget did not increase, but fluctuated between 6.9% and 7.4%. By 1967 it had risen to 9.2% but this figure did not include agricultural education, money spent by other ministries, teachers' pensions or capital expenditure on new buildings. Between 1970 and 1978 the total national expenditure increased by 193%. During the same period expenditure on higher education increased by 217%. This reflects the priority given to third level education and science. The breakdown of expenditure was as follows:

	1970	*1973*	*1977*	*1978*
Basic general	4.2	6.5	10.4	12.1
Secondary general	1.3	2.0	3.3	3.8
Vocational education	1.2	1.6	2.7	3.2
Higher education	2.3	3.0	–	7.3

Sources of Funds

The national government is responsible for the financing of public and private secondary general and technical schools, teacher training institutions and higher education. The provincial states finance vocational compulsory education and the municipalities general compulsory education and about one third of commercial education. More than three quarters of all expenditure on school education is provided by the national government, about 18% by the municipalities and 6% by the provincial states. All teachers in compulsory schools are paid by the national government but where the provision of teachers exceeds the legally fixed number the provincial states are obliged to refund the salaries of the extra teachers to the national government. The salaries of non-teaching staff in compulsory schools and all other current expenditure is provided by the municipalities. They are also responsible for capital expenditure with the help of the provincial states who contribute to special school building funds. The national government also makes substantial grants for building and has overall authority over the school building programme. The salaries of teachers in the compulsory vocational schools are paid by both the provincial states and the national government which contribute equal shares: all other expenditure (both current and capital) on these schools is met by the provincial states.

Regional Variations

There is a complex system of allocation designed to offset differences in wealth and strengthen the financial position of the weaker provincial states and municipalities. But the regional differences in school expenditure are still very marked, and range from 75% to 113% of a national average. However, it is not clear how far price levels differ between regions or whether the discrepancy is based wholly on differences in funds provided or also on differences in the supply of resources; for example, some provinces may find it difficult to recruit sufficient teachers or build schools sufficiently quickly.

Private Education

The contribution of private sources to education is likely to be much smaller than the percentage share of private education would suggest. Most private schools are 'confessional' and belong to the Roman Catholic Church. All teaching staff are now paid by the State. All other expenditure is met by the Church. But it is probably that the costs in these schools are lower than for public schools partly because non-teaching staff members are religious and therefore do not receive normal salaries. If it is assumed that the government subsidy accounts for about 50% of current expenditure the Church contribution to school education would probably amount to about 2% of public school expenditure. Non-Church private schools are on the wane and are gradually being taken over by the government. Officially they are financially independent but the major part of their finance is provided by the national government which pays the teachers and makes substantial grants for buildings and equipment.

Universities

The universities were taking approximately 0.86% of GNP and 2.7% of the national budget in 1978. By that year the universities' income had doubled in five years. The major part of the money is spent directly on the institutions, and the rest goes to improve library and other study facilities. About 38% is spent on materials, 7% on building costs, 38% on staff and 10% on research subsidies.

Grants and Fees

There are no fees in State compulsory and top level secondary schools. Since 1971 transport to and from school has been free and since 1972 so have school textbooks. After the compulsory stage financial support is available to the children of poorer parents. University fees were abolished for most students in 1972 (though some foreign students still pay nominal fees). University grants are available to students in financial need, though their continued payment depends on academic success; (students on grants must not exceed the number of semesters prescribed for a course by more than one semester). Students on grants, however, may spend two semesters of their studies abroad and still receive the grant. Student hostels and cafeterias are heavily subsidised by the government.

Allocation of Funds
Expenditure on Education: Distribution by Level
Percentage of Expenditure 1977

Pre-school	First Level	Second Level	Third Level	Other
5.3	18.8	52.8	15.3	12.8

9 DEVELOPMENT AND PLANNING OF THE EDUCATION SYSTEM

History

As in many other European countries the first educational institutions in Austria were the monastery and cathedral schools with the cathedral school at Salzburg founded as far back as the eighth century. Municipal schools developed in the mercantile towns during the thirteenth century and in the fourteenth century two universities were founded in the Empire: the University of Prague in 1348 and the University of Vienna in 1365. Both Roman Catholic and Protestant schools proliferated but after the defeat of the Hussites in 1620 and the succeeding Treaty of Westphalia all schools became Roman Catholic and most were administered by the Society of Jesus. For 100 years until their expulsion in 1773 the Jesuits exerted enormous influence over Austrian education, but except for a brief period between 1855 and 1868 education was henceforth a State responsibility. At first matters did not improve; the reintroduction of school fees in the late eighteenth century meant that few poor people could acquire an education. But in 1848 a Ministry of Education was set up and in 1849 it published an 'organisation draft' creating the eight-grade *Gymnasium* and the *Realschule* (non-classical secondary school) with six and later seven grades. In 1869 the Imperial Primary School Act established eight-year compulsory school attendance and at that time too provincial State and local Boards of Education were constituted.

Adult education also began to develop in the nineteenth century with the growth in the 1890s of workers' educational associations *(Arbeiterbildungsveriene)* offering a wide range of courses backed up by workers' libraries. The People's University in Vienna, where eminent scholars gave free lectures, worked parallel with more middle class insstitutions such as university extension departments. Vocational education had started as far back as the seventeenth and eighteenth centuries and from the very beginning there was a two-fold development of part time vocational schools for apprentices and full time vocational schools. This sector also grew rapidly in the latter half of the nineteenth century with the development of the tripartite system of today.

Educational Innovation

As early as the beginning of this century a significant movement developed in favour of a more liberal and more flexible form of education than that presided over by the Church and the imperial government. The Free School Association *(Verein Freie Schule)* was established in 1905, composed of students, teachers, and liberals and anti-clericals generally. In 1907 the association opened two private schools in Vienna to experiment with teaching methods and curricula. In due course a school programme was published, produced with the cooperation of teachers' organisations, and the association began to exert a significant influence. In 1918 it really came into its own when one of its first members, a one-time teacher called Otto Glöckel, became Secretary of Education in the national government. He immediately began to plan the reorganisation of the school system and teaching methods. The Ministry was professionalised, and in rapid succession a number of reforms were made. Compulsory religious activity was abolished, parents' associations and teachers' advisory groups were founded, women were admitted into *Gymnasia* and into all university faculties.

Glöckel's Reforms

The two major elements in Glöckel's theories were his belief in one school for all children between the ages of 10 and 14, a comprehensive school *(Gesamtschule)*, and his advocacy of education centres on the development of the individual child; beginning with the child's familiar surroundings, subjects were to be taught not as separate academic disciplines but related to each other and to the life of the child *(Arbeitsschule* method). Education was thus to be primarily aimed at developing the child's initiative so that he might learn by observation and experience, rather than from textbooks. In 1920 the Reform Division of Glöckel's ministry produced a plan for a single ladder school for all children between the ages of 6 and 14 - divided into two cycles, but in the same year Glöckel was ousted from his post before his plan could be generally accepted. Nevertheless in succeeding years as President of the Vienna Education Committee he was able to implement his policies in Vienna schools. In 1918 he had established the four-grade *Hauptschule* and this form of school was established by law in the Compulsory Secondary General School Act of 1927 which also provided for transfer from *Hauptschule* to *Gymnasium* and for special secondary schools for those already employed.

1962 Education Acts

After 1945 the education system was reconstructed on pre-war lines. But further attempts were being made to broaden the access to higher education and the process of transfer from *Hauptschulen* to secondary general schools. This trend was re-emphasised in the Education Acts of 1962 which were the product of years of public debate reflecting an increasing demand in Austria for education for everyone. The overall objectives of the School Organisation Act of 1962 are defined as follows:

> "It shall be the task of the Austrian school to foster the development of the talents and potential abilities of young persons in accordance with ethical, religious and social values and the appreciation of that which is true, good and beautiful, giving them an education corresponding to their respective stages of development and to their respective courses of study. It shall give young people the knowledge and skills required for their future lives and occupations and train them to acquire knowledge on their own initiative."

The major results of the 1962 legislation were to improve school provision generally and to increase the number of types of school available for those of different abilities and interests in the following ways:

(i) the curricula of *Hauptschulen* and *Gymnasia* were brought further into line and obstacles to easy transfer thus removed; (e.g. no Latin in science *Gymnasia* grades 1 to 4)

(ii) *Gymnasium* education was expanded for late starters

(iii) vocational secondary education was expanded

(iv) all pupils were guaranteed the opportunity to attend *Hauptschulen* (though this has not been possible in all regions).

In addition, compulsory education was increased from eight to nine years (with the creation of the 'polytechnic' courses) and teacher training for primary teachers was upgraded with the introduction of the *Pädagogische Akademie* to follow secondary education.

Planning Institutions

Since 1964 and particularly since the promulgation of the 1962 Acts, the planning capacity of the Austrian education system has been substantially increased. In 1969 a Parliamentary School Reform Commission was established to oversee the development of increased flexibility in the Austrian education system with proposals to be tested in scientifically based projects. the Centre for Educational Experimentation and Development *(Zentrum für Schulversuche und Schulentwicklung)* was set up by the Ministry to produce, check and evaluate projects. Around the same time a committee was established to advise the Ministry on university development *(Arbeitgemeinschaft für Hochschulentwicklung)*. The new university established at Klagenfurt in 1970 has a general brief to establish empirical and interdisciplinary investigations

ADMINISTRATION
ORGANISATION OF SCHOOL REFORM

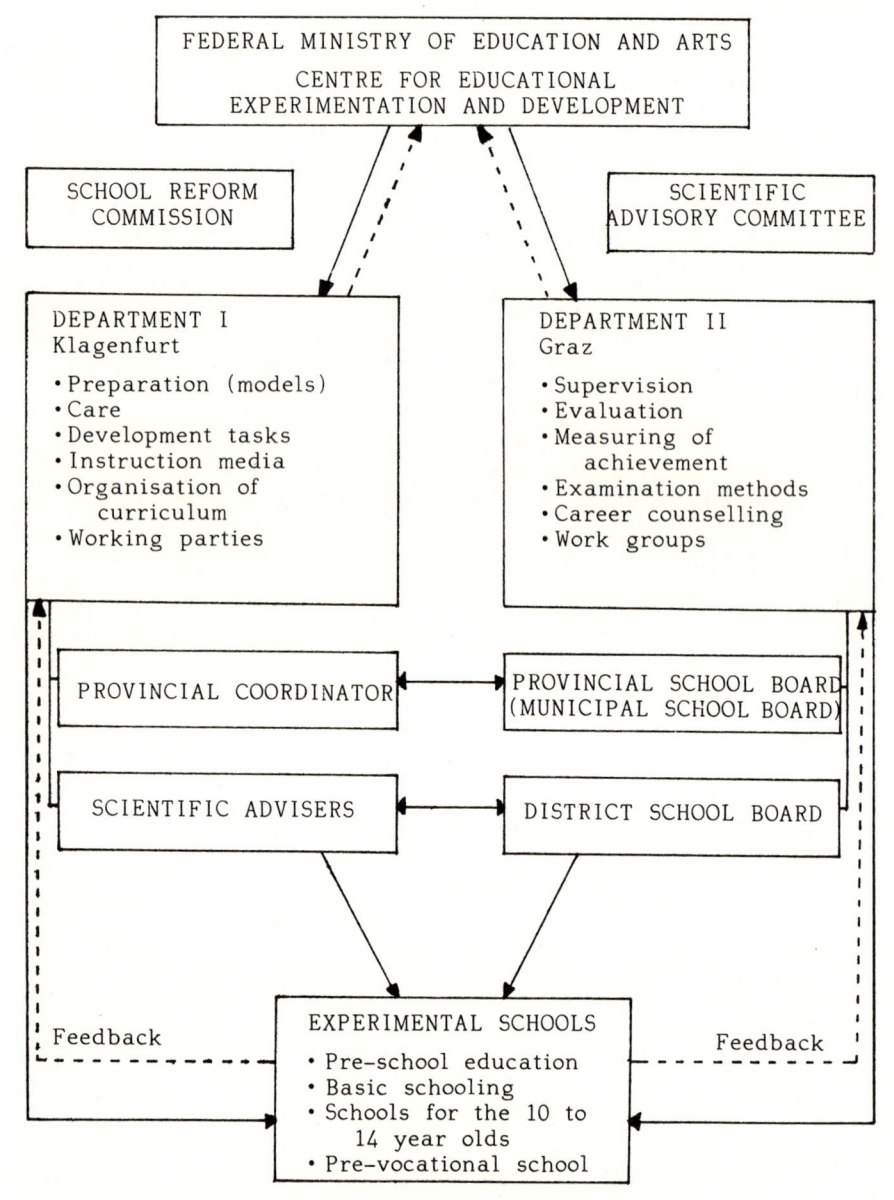

```
┌─────────────────────────────────────────┐
│   FEDERAL MINISTRY OF EDUCATION AND ARTS │
│        CENTRE FOR EDUCATIONAL            │
│      EXPERIMENTATION AND DEVELOPMENT     │
└─────────────────────────────────────────┘
```

SCHOOL REFORM COMMISSION

SCIENTIFIC ADVISORY COMMITTEE

DEPARTMENT I
Klagenfurt
- Preparation (models)
- Care
- Development tasks
- Instruction media
- Organisation of curriculum
- Working parties

DEPARTMENT II
Graz
- Supervision
- Evaluation
- Measuring of achievement
- Examination methods
- Career counselling
- Work groups

PROVINCIAL COORDINATOR ↔ PROVINCIAL SCHOOL BOARD (MUNICIPAL SCHOOL BOARD)

SCIENTIFIC ADVISERS ↔ DISTRICT SCHOOL BOARD

Feedback ← **EXPERIMENTAL SCHOOLS** → Feedback
- Pre-school education
- Basic schooling
- Schools for the 10 to 14 year olds
- Pre-vocational school

Source: Bundesministerium für Unterricht und Kunst

into the problems of education. Finally the Statistics and Planning Division of the Ministry of Education and Art has been expanded in order to prepare surveys for each of the provincial states as well as national assessments, to ensure that planning in all regions and at all levels is liked to the activities of economic agencies as well as educational research institutions. The express intention of the Ministry in the long term is to develop decentralised planning with large scale participation. A Central Planning Commission is to be set up to coordinate future planning activities.

School Reform

At present the School Reform Commission and Centre for Educational Experimentation and Development are presiding over a large number of pilot projects. These are in the following areas:

(i) development of comprehensive schools for 10 to 14 year olds *(Gesamtschulen)*

(ii) development of vocational courses in general secondary schools

(iii) changes in the curriculum and further development of adult education

(iv) ability streaming and subject setting in both general and vocational schools with the provision of intensive courses for lower streams

(v) preliminary foreign language teaching for 8 to 10 year olds

(vi) changes in the special education sector with a move towards either more integrated or more differentiated schools

(vii) *Eingangsstufe:* introduction of assessment techniques in the first weeks of *Volksschule* followed by placing in either the *Volksschule, Sonderschule* or special pre-school class *(Vorschulklasse)*

(viii) training of secondary general school teachers in political education prior to its introduction in the general secondary curriculum

(ix) provision of half and full day boarding schools for the in-school care of children after normal working hours (including *Ganztagschulen* and *Tagesheimschulen* - two kinds of full day school)

(x) various other projects concerning the curriculum at basic and higher school level.

The Medium Term School Development Programme was first set out in 1971, and updated in 1973. In 1977 a report on its implementation was presented to the *Nationalrat*. The programme aimed to improve the organisational network and the accessibility of medium level and top level secondary schools especially in rural areas by better distributing facilities while keeping schools of an economic size. An increase by one third in the provision of educational centres for the 15 to 19 year age group was envisaged with approximately equal numbers of medium level and top level secondary technical schools, and secondary general schools.

University Reform

Since the promulgation of the General University Studies Act of 1966 which criticised mass lectures and the cumbersome administrative process in universities, the Ministry of Higher Education and Research in cooperation with representatives of higher education terminated in a major reform programme, basically on two fronts: study reform and administrative reform.

Study Reform

Generally speaking, priority was first given to study reform and the continuing reorganisation of university study programmes since 1966, with the setting up of the study commissions in 1969, and with the introduction of more varied forms of teaching (seminars, tutorials etc.), and reorganised examination and course structures. The legal reform of regular degree studies is complete, but the reform is seen as a continuing process and further experiments are being conducted. The work of the study commissions in the developing of curricula and teaching methods will continue and there are a number of small scale experiments in progress on such matters as: part time training for employed persons, short and post-experience courses and distance education. The *Hochschulreifeprüfung* remained experimental until 1980. The distance education *(Fernstudium)* research involved a work group advising the Ministry of what subjects and levels might be appropriate for this method of education and conducting cost comparisons with normal studies. Preparatory courses *(Vorbereitungslehrgänge)* in English, theology and mathematics were chosen to begin with. The aim of the reforms was to develop university education in Austria towards a more flexible system highly differentiated in study aims, qualification levels and subject matter – and geared to producing a wide range of highly qualified experts in professional fields rather than simply graduates of academic courses.

Administrative Reform

This was chiefly concerned with two areas: participation and efficiency. The traditional administrative structure involved decentralisation of tasks and a high proportion of administrative work done by the teaching staff, leaving less resources for teaching and research. Just as the mass lecture gave little scope for student-staff contact, decisions were normally arrived at with little recourse to the students. The University Organisation

Act, passed in April 1975 and gradually introduced in practice provided for:

(i) freedom of academic research and teaching

(ii) strengthened autonomy of the universities with greater control over budgets

(iii) a new administrative structure based on economy and efficiency rather than tradition and involving more centralised control

(iv) more participation by students and junior staff (co-determination) in academic decision making and also in study and research (they will be represented on the study commissions for the first time)

(v) more cooperation between the universities and society.

The Act set out the new university structure involving a basic division into departments with a head elected from the professors assisted by a departmental conference (including staff and students). At the higher level the collegiate faculty may set up commissions and delegate to them the power of decision on such matters as budget, planning, staff and appointments. This considerably lightens the load of the faculty and reduces the length of its meetings. At the highest level the Academic Senate changed its composition to give a more balanced representation of all groups. This three-level structure is headed by the Rector whose term of office is now two years, preceded and succeeded by one year as Prae- and Pro-Rector, thus giving continuity. the Rectors' and Bursars' officers were to be reorganised on modern management lines with the use of computer installations, and given an increased role in central management control. The administration is headed by a *Universitätsdirektor* appointed by the Ministry. The Academic Council which links universities and society was to be reconstituted so that major social groups can be represented. New university posts of associate professor were created to improve the staffing structure.

REFERENCES AND FURTHER READING

Bushbeck, E. H. (1949). *Austria*. Oxford University Press.
Europa Year Book 1978 (1978). Vol. I. Europa Publications, London.
Federal Press Service (1973). *Austria, Facts and Figures*. Vienna.
Lloyd's Bank (1976). *Economic Report: Austria*. London.
Organisation for Economic Cooperation and Development (OECD) (1968). *Educational Policy and Planning: Austria*. Paris.
OECD (1970). *Reviews of National Policies for Education: Austria*. Paris.
OECD (1975). *Educational Policy and Planning: Higher Education and Research in Austria*. Paris.
OECD (1976). *Reviews of National Policies for Education: Austria Higher Education and Research*. Paris.

Österreichischer Bundesministerium für Unterricht und Kunst (1975). *Report*. Vienna.
Österreichischer Bundesministerium für Unterricht und Kunst (1978). *Austrian School Statistics 1977/78*. Vienna.
Österreichischer Bundesministerium für Unterricht und Kunst (1979). *Austria: Organization of Education in 1977-79* (Report presented at the 37th International Conference on Public Education, IBE/UNESCO, Geneva, 1979). Vienna.
Österreichischer Bunderministerium für Wissenschaft und Forschung (1978). *Hochschulbericht 1978*. Vienna.
Österreichscher Bundesverlag (1965). *School Organisation Act, 1962*. Vienna.
Österreichischer Landerbank (1978). *Statistical Data on Austria*. Vienna.
Papanek, Ernst (1962). *The Austrian School Reform*. Frederick Fell, New York.
UNESCO/IBE (1981). *Country Education Profile: Austria*. Geneva.
UNESCO/IBE (1980). *International Yearbook of Education* XXXII. Unesco, Paris.
Whelpton, Eric (1970). *Austrians: How they Live and Work*. David & Charles, London.

Structure of the Education System in Austria

Age	3 4 5	6 7 8 9	10 11 12 13 14 15	16 17 18	19 20 21 22 23 24
Level		I	II		III & IV
Stage		1 & 2	3 4	5	6 7
Compulsory					
School type		Volkschule	Volkschule		Universities and Akademien
			Hauptschule		
			Allgemein Höhere sch. Diff. Obs.	Gymnasium Real Gym. etc.	
				Poly. Lehr gang	
				Technical schools	

Education preceding the first level

Examinations: (a) 'Certificate of Completion', grade 4
(b) special examinations at end of second level
(c) *Reifeprüng* at end of grade 12

Special schools

Source: UNESCO/IBE International Yearbook of Education
Compulsory Education: Age Limits 6–15 duration (years) 9
Entrance age to pre-school education: 3

73

AUSTRIA BASIC STATISTICS		1960	1970	1975	1978 (approx.)
1	Total population (000)	7,047	7,446	7,538	7,508
	% female	53	53	53	
2	% population 0-14 years	36.7	32.7		28.0
	% female	49	49	49	49
3	Enrolment, all levels	898,521	1,221,966	1,354,249	1,362,405
	% female	48	48	48	48
	First level	398,772	531,934	501,843	531,934
	% female	49	49	49	49
	Second level	461,216	630,254	755,670	729,621
	% female	49	50	50	50
	Third level	38,533	59,778	96,736	100,850
	% female	23	29	38	36
4	Teachers, all levels	48,615	67,007		
	% female	46	48		
	First level	21,499	24,815	26,374	26,049
	% female	54	63	71	74
	Second level	24,145	35,212		56,927
	% female	42	45		51
	Third level	2,971	6.980		
	% female	9	12		
5	Public expenditure on education:				
	Total (000) schillings	4,645,100	17,349,500	37,409,300	43,427,650
	As % of GNP	2.9	4.6	5.7	5.5
6	% enrolment (MF) by level	100	100	100	100
	First level	44	44	37	39
	Second level	51	52	56	54
	Third level	4	5	7	7
	% enrolment (F) by level	100	100	100	100
	First level	45	44	37	39
	Second level	53	53	57	54
	Third level	2	3	6	6
7	Entrance age: Duration of				
	First level education	6:4	6:4	6:4	6:4
	Second level education	10:9	10:8	10:8	10:8
8	Enrolment ratios (MF)				
	First level	105	104	102	100
	Second level	50	72	76	72
	Third level	8.01	11.76	19.20	
	Enrolment ratios (F)				
	First level	104	103	102	99
	Second level	49	73	77	72
	Third level	3.79	7.02	14.68	

Belgium

CONTENTS

1	Geography	76
2	Population	78
3	Society and Culture	78
4	History and Politics	80
5	The Economy	82
6	The Education System	84
7	Educational Administration	92
8	Educational Finance	94
9	Development and Planning of the Education System	96
10	The System in Operation	97

The history and present position of education in Belgium are intimately linked with linguistic, religious and political differences which serve to divide the country. The Flemish speaking people in the north are for the most part practising Catholics. The French speaking Walloons in the south, rather like many French people, are Catholic but secularists, free thinkers and often anti-clerics. The language boundary runs east-west across the country and passes just south of Brussels. Educational policies have had to take these sharp differences into account so that in the Flemish speaking areas the mother tongue is the medium of instruction but either French or English is a compulsory foreign language at the lower stage of second level education. Many Flemings choose English rather than French. In Wallonia the choice of foreign language is between Dutch or English. In Brussels the first foreign language has to be the other of the two national languages. Brussels is officially bilingual.

These differences also find expression in the universities. One of the two State universities is French speaking at Liège, the other at Ghent is Dutch speaking. There are two Catholic universities, and two free universities in Brussels; in both types one is Dutch the other is French.

The political parties and the balance of elected members of parliament reflect linguistic and religious differences. Coalition governments are the rule rather than the exception. National parties are in a majority, however. Moreover the language boundary serves to divide the heavy industrial regions of the south - centres of the coal, steel and metal products are Liège, Mons, Charleroi, Namur and Hainault - and the less industrialised north where Ghent and Bruges are centres of the textile industry.

In 1971 the Belgian Parliament passed legislation to ease the tension between French speaking and Dutch speaking Belgians. One Bill established a cultural council for each linguistic group. Later a cultural council for the German speaking minority was set up. The powers of these councils were laid down in a second Bill. A third Bill in 1971 brought together municipalities around major centres - Brussels, Charleroi, Ghent and Liège. In the border areas attempts were made to reduce the influence of French in predominantly Flemish speaking areas. In 1974 regional councils for Flanders, Wallonia and Brussels were established. They reflect the main cultural and political divisions of the country.

The Editor

1 GEOGRAPHY

Topography

Belgium is a relatively small country, but one of many contrasts; in terms of language, religion or politics there are wide variations. With the exception of Luxembourg, Belgium is the smallest of the member countries of the EEC: with a total surface area of only 30,513 sq km (11,775 square miles), it is only half as large again as Wales; and a coastline of 65 kilometres. However, topographical variations are slight. The terrain changes gradually from the *polders* (reclaimed land) lying below sea level on the North Sea coast to the wooded hills of the Ardennes, which rise to over 600 metres (2,000 feet) in the south east. Between the two lies the fertile plain of central Belgium including the Brussels area.

Climate

Belgium has a variable maritime climate with regular rainfall and little variation in temperature (only 58°F between the hottest and coldest months). Brussels has about 185 mm (29 inches) of rain per year and a maximum temperature of 4°C (34°F) in January and 23°C (73°F) in July. The Ardennes region has a slightly more continental climate.

Communications

Belgium lies geographically at one of the main crossroads of Western Europe. This has undoubtedly contributed to the

---

Note: Since there are two main languages in Belgium, French and Dutch, the names of many important towns have two forms. Where a recognised anglicised form exists, as with Brussels, this is used throughout; otherwise the regional form is used, such as Mons (French) and Kortrijk (Dutch).

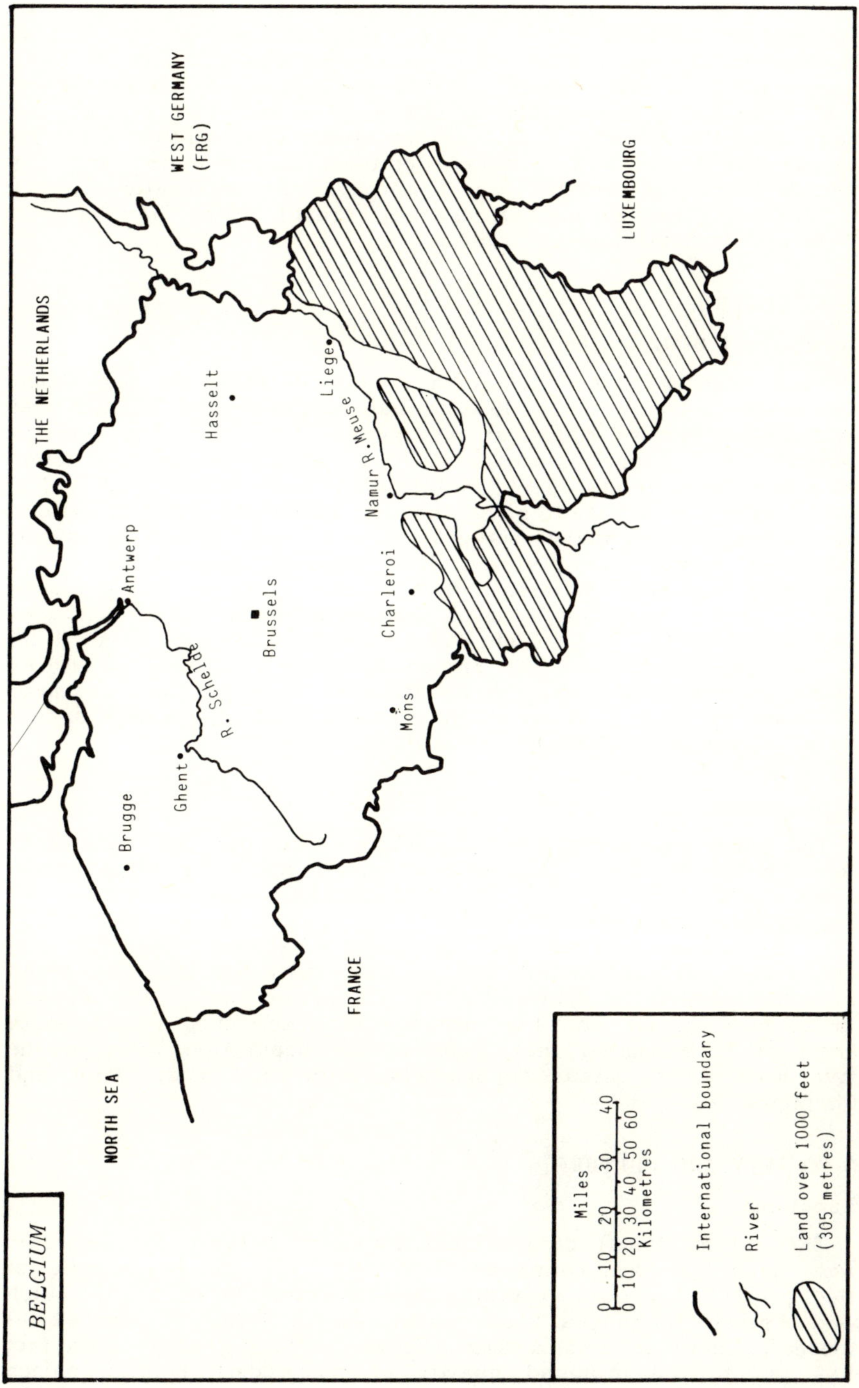
BELGIUM
WEST GERMANY
(FRG)
THE NETHERLANDS
LUXEMBOURG
NORTH SEA
FRANCE
Antwerp
Brussels
Hasselt
Liege
R. Meuse
Namur
Charleroi
Mons
R. Schelde
Ghent
Brugge
Miles
0 10 20 30 40
0 10 20 30 40 50 60
Kilometres
International boundary
River
Land over 1000 feet
(305 metres)

country's economic prosperity, and the results can be seen in the modern communications system, which is one of the densest in Western Europe. There are seven motorways, with a total length of 1,060 km, nearly 4,000 km of main line railway track and 1,700 km of navigable waterway. The two main rivers, the Meuse and the Scheldt, create natural links with Belgium's neighbours: the Meuse with France (upstream to the south) and the Scheldt with the outside world through the international port of Antwerp (the second largest in Europe) which handles 80% of Belgium's total foreign trade.

2 POPULATION

Growth and Distribution

When Belgium gained its independence in 1830, the population was under 4 million. By 1930 it had doubled to 8 million and by 1979 it was estimated at just under 10 million. The average density per square kilometre is 322, which is slightly lower than the Netherlands (329) and greater than Britain (229). But the average is misleading in that it masks the real situation: the language boundary between Flemish and French speaking provinces marks the dividing line between regions which are populated in very different ways. Leaving aside the predominantly French speaking area of Greater Brussels, which accounts for 10.8% of the population, the Flemish provinces have 56.5% of the population and the French speaking (Walloon) provinces 32.8% of the poulation. This imbalance between the two main linguistic groups (coupled with economic factors) is one of the main sources of friction in the country.

Urbanisation

The growing prosperity of Belgium during the nineteenth century led to the replacement of small towns by large urban areas separated by very short distances. Brussels today has a population of over a million; yet within 56 km (35 miles) are the cities of Antwerp (429,237), Charleroi (453,892) and Ghent (477,499) and within 105 km Liège with 616,585. This trend to urbanisation is continuing in all areas except the Kempen in the north east and the province of Luxembourg in the south east: it is estimated that 35.8% of the population lives in the five main urban areas of Brussels, Antwerp, Liège, Ghent and Charleroi.

3 SOCIETY AND CULTURE

Language

The old historical geographical boundary between the Germanic and Latin peoples runs east and west through the middle of the present kingdom, dividing the country between the Dutch and French languages, both with various forms of very local dialect. There is also a small German speaking area. This fact has led to the profound duality of the modern Belgian nation and every facet of national life has been deeply affected by it.

The earliest linguistic frontier ran in an east-west direction across the country from Maastricht in the Dutch province of Limburg to near Boulogne on the North Sea coast of France. (It has since moved north of Lille to Dunkirk and passes just to the south of Brussels.) Throughout the Middle Ages French and Dutch existed side by side; it was only in the sixteenth century that French began to gain the upper hand. This trend was reinforced during the eighteenth century and consequently the Dutch language of the Flemings suffered, especially as many of the Fleming aristocracy and bourgeoisie used French as their main social language. The successful revolution in 1830 against the rule of the Dutch led to a reaction against the Dutch language and the adoption of French as the national language. But the nineteenth century rise of nationalism led, in the case of the Flemings, to demands for parity of esteem for the French and Dutch languages. After a long struggle Dutch was finally recognised as an official language alongside French by the Law of April 1898. However, despite this apparent parity the language controversy is still very much a live issue. The language census of 1947 revealed that 51% of the population spoke Dutch, 33% French, 15% were bilingual (but predominantly French speaking) in the Brussels area and 1% spoke German in the *Cantons de l'Est* to the east of Spa and Eupen. In recent years the numerically superior Flemings have sought increasing cultural autonomy and in July 1971 a Bill was passed by Parliament establishing a cultural council for each linguistic group.

In education the medium of instruction is Dutch in Flanders (the provinces of West and East Flanders, Antwerp, Limburg and the northern part of Brabant) and French in Wallonia (the provinces of Hainaut, Namur, Liège, Luxembourg, and the southern part of Brabant). The term 'Walloon' by which the inhabitants of this region are known was first used by the French: it means 'Foreigner'. In the Brussels area the pupils attends a Dutch or French medium school according to the language of their home, and in the schools in the area east of Eupen, German is used. All schools with parallel language streams have now been abolished. As far as the teaching of foreign languages is concerned, the former ruling whereby the first foreign language taught in a Dutch speaking school had to be French and in a French speaking school Dutch, has been retained only in Brussels. Outside Brussels the first foreign language may be either of the national languages not used as the medium of instruction in the school, or English. The second foreign language may be any of the above or German, Italian, Spanish or Russian.

Religion

The religious wars in Europe left Belgium an overwhelmingly Roman Catholic country; even today the numbers of Protestants, Jews, etc. are negligible. Nevertheless throughout the nineteenth century religion divided the country almost as bitterly as the language question. Whereas the Flemings are mostly sincere practising Catholics, many of the Walloons, although nominally Catholic, have since the French Revolution been secularists and free-thinkers. During the nineteenth century this division was cemented by the political system: the majority of the Flemings suported the Roman Catholic Party (now renamed the Christian Social Party) while the Walloons favoured the Liberal Party (now the Party of Liberty and Progress). Recently, a certain indifference has developed, especially among the young, to the clerical and anti-clerical struggles of the nineteenth century.

Social Patterns

The desire for individual liberty is the key to the Belgian character. Centuries of attempted absorption by other powers led to a determination on the part of the individual to defend his language, religious beliefs and traditions. This manifests itself in the fierce independence of the municipalities. The result today is a rather traditional individualistic society. In fact, traditionalism has been a keynote of Belgian education and society since independence (particularly when the Catholics held political power) perhaps partly because it was the bourgeoisie who won the nation's independence.

4 HISTORY AND POLITICS

Origins

The language division dates from at least the third century AD when the Salian Franks began to filter into the area which is now Belgium from the east. The land to the north of the present language boundary was swampy and therefore only sparsely populated; this enabled the Franks (later known as Flemings) to retain their customs and their low Germanic language. The territory to the south of the divide was more densely populated by a people whose civilisation was more developed than that of the invaders; as a result the Franks there adopted the language of the area which was the forerunner of modern French. The two language communities were brought together politically in 843 when Charlemagne's empire was partitioned by the Treaty of Verdun: the territory of modern Belgium then became part of a buffer state between France and Germany.

Historical Development

Belgium has been aptly described as the cockpit of Europe. Its position as a strategic crossroads and its absence of natural frontiers have often made it a battlefield between the great powers of the day, and have at different times associated its peoples with Burgundy, Spain, Austria, France and the Netherlands. During the Middle Ages the country prospered and became the first great urban civilisation in medieval Europe. Political power passed to the commercial cities and the merchant bourgeoisie used this fact to obtain privileges from the nobles.

This was the origin of the provincial and municipal autonomy which is still an important feature of Belgian life. From the fourteenth century onwards Belgium was subject first to Burgundian rule and then in turn to that of the Spaniards, the Austrians and (from 1794 to 1815) the French. The period of French rule united the country and made Belgium aware of her identity and economic potential. Her subsequent incorporation in the Kingdom of the United Netherlands under William I (1815-1830) brought home to the Flemings the wide gulf (religious and cultural) which separated them from the Dutch. The hatred of William (and all things Dutch) among large sections of the population led to the revolution of 1830 and, with British support, the creation of Belgium as a nation state.

Government and Politics

According to the 1831 Constitution the form of government is a constitutional, representative and hereditary monarchy with a bi-cameral legislature, consisting of the King, the Senate and the Chamber of Representatives. Of the 175 members of the Senate, 106 are directly elected, the remainder being coopted for four years. The Chamber of Representatives consists of not more than one member per 40,000 inhabitants who is directly elected by all adult nationals (voting is compulsory). The main political parties are divided into their Dutch and French groupings: they are the Christian Social Party, the Socialist Party and the Liberal Party. There is a francophone party in Brussels (FDF) as well as other nationalist regional groupings such as the *Volksunie* and the *Rassemblement Wallon*. Most recent governments have been coalitions and rather unstable.

Egmont-Stuyvenberg Proposals

The language issue is also fundamental to the political scene and governments have fallen over questions of language. During the 1960s strong federalist and separatist movements grew up in both Wallonia and Flanders. The 'Egmont-Stuyvenberg' proposals for regionalisation in Belgium recommended important changes. These included the setting up of two completely independent community councils with their own executives. The Dutch Community Council was to comprise members of the Flemish Regional Council and Dutch speaking members of the Brussels Regional Council, whilst the French Community Council was to comprise members of the Walloon Regional Council and Francophone members of the Brussels Regional Council. The regional councils were to look to the independence and well being of the linguistic communities, and deal with 'regional matters' formerly dealt with by central government. Following local government reform to greatly reduce the number of municipalities *(communes)* sub-regions were planned, 11 in Flanders and 13 in Wallonia, which would carry out tasks delegated to them by the other national authorities. Under the proposals, the administration of Brussels presents difficult problems, lying as it does between the two communities. The city will, however, have its own regional council, but there are special arrangements for what are called 'communes with facilities' where some allowances have to be made for the rights of linguistic minorities such as francophones who have moved from the centre of Brussels to outlying suburban areas in Flanders.

Proposed changes in central government include a Senate made up of members of the Dutch and French Community Councils and representatives of Belgium's German speaking population to carry out revision of the Constitution. Decisions would be taken by double majority, i.e. a majority in each linguistic group. But the Senate would no longer have the power to block legislation: the Chamber of Representatives would have the last word. The Chamber would also retain responsibility for national affairs and elections would take place as at present, once every four years. The number of government ministers would be reduced, but parity (excluding the Prime Minister) between the two language groups would be maintained in the Cabinet. These proposals have proved controversial; they will certainly accentuate the linguistic divisions in all areas of government administration, but increased federalism may ease community problems.

International Relations

In international affairs, Belgium has been a founder member of the main international organisations including the United Nations and its agencies, OECD, the Council of Europe, the EEC, the Western European Union, and NATO. (Since France withdrew from the military organisation of NATO in 1966 the military and political headquarters of NATO have been in Brussels, which is also the seat of the EEC Commission.) Belgium is also a strong supporter of European Union. She has a substantial technical assistance programme, aimed primarily, but not exclusively, at her former African territories: Zaire, and Rwanda and Burundi (formerly UN trust territories administered by Belgium).

Belgium's membership of the EEC has had little, if any, influence yet on the country's education system although this may change when mobility of students and workers between member countries becomes commoner. Two of the 'European Schools' designed for the children of those working in Community institutions, are in Belgium – in Brussels and at Mol (in the Kempen near Antwerp). They are, of course, quite separate from the Belgian system. There is also the College of Europe in Bruges for European post-graduate studies, which receives generous financial support from the Belgian government.

5 THE ECONOMY

Natural Resources

Belgium's economic prosperity is a result of its geographical location, its once rich deposits of coal and iron ore, and the foresight of its leaders. In 1922 Belgium and Luxembourg concluded the Belgium-Luxembourg economic union, and the agreement to create Benelux (a customs union between Belgium, The

Netherlands and Luxembourg) dates from 1947. Since 1945 one of the consistent characteristics of successive governments, which have had relatively short life spans, has been their friendliness towards foreign investors. It is they, rather than local management, who are largely responsible for the consistent dynamism of Belgium's economy. However, in 1980 Belgium's economy was expanding at a lower rate than hitherto. Further problems were increasing unemployment (7.8% in 1977 and rising) and prices which are no longer as competitive in terms of exports as they were. The Belgian *franc*, however, remained firm and the country shows remarkable resilience in the face of economic crises.

Foreign Investment

The country's main exporting industries are heavily dependent on foreign investment and according to the Ministry of Economic Affairs, between 1959 and 1971 foreign investment accounted for 79% of investment in new factories in the metalworking industry, for 74% in the chemical industry, 63% in metals and 58% in textiles. The present pattern of foreign investment is quite different from the pattern between 1958 and 1968, when an average of 65% of it was American, compared with 23% from the other five EEC countries; figures for 1959-76 indicate USA 47% and EEC 36%. Membership of the European Economic Community and the choice of Brussels as its headquarters undoubtedly contributed to the country's economic prosperity. Many foreign firms have made Belgium their base for their EEC operations; although there have been some withdrawals owing to the high cost of living.

Regional Patterns

The main industrial area traditionally stretched from Mons in the west to Liège in the east, a distance of some 30 km. It owed its growth to the existence of coal, almost the only natural resource in the country. Now other industrial areas have sprung up all over the country with particular emphasis in certain parts of Flanders, such as the area between Brussels and the port of Antwerp, and the once prosperous coal mining belt of Wallonia has declined. It has been the policy of the European Coal and Steel Community to encourage governments to close uneconomic pits. The Walloon coalfields could not compete with the more easily mined (and therefore cheaper) coal from the Ruhr and the Kempen; as a result annual output which used to reach 30 million tons, had sunk to just over one million tons in 1977. The area also suffered from an inability to attract sufficient foreign investment: between 1955 and 1963 only 18% of foreign investment was in Wallonia compared with 71% in Flanders. (One explanation of this is that Flanders contains the whole of Belgium's coastline.) While Wallonia bemoans its dwindling resources and its birth rate falls, the economy of Flanders boomed.   GNP per head in 1974 averaged £4,675 in the Greater Brussels area, £3,136 in Flanders and £2,771 in Wallonia. This recent shift of economic power from the Walloons to the Flemings is one of the main causes of the present acrimony; the Fleming is enjoying what he regards as fair recompense for the inferior status he suffered in the past.

The economy of Wallonia is now being effectively diversified, however, and foreign workers (mostly from Portugal, Italy, Turkey and North Africa) are coming in diminishing numbers, mainly into the services sector of the economy. Belgium has shown foresight by providing *classes d'accueil* and *enseignement supplementaire* and the immigrants do not seem to be regarded as a problem either socially or educationally. The only other depressed area is the predominantly rural province of Luxembourg in the south east of Wallonia. Salaries and wages in industry there were, in 1979, on average 1,200 francs per day, compared with Flanders (1,315 francs per day) and the province's proportion of Belgium's total population has fallen from 4.3% in the mid-nineteenth century to only 2.19% in 1976.

6 THE EDUCATION SYSTEM

Academic Year

The school year runs from 1 September to 30 June with holidays lasting two weeks at Christmas and Easter.

At post-secondary level the academic year runs from the third week of September to 30 June, and in the universities from October to the second week of July at the latest.

Compulsory Education

Schooling is compulsory between the ages of 6 and 14 and nursery, primary and secondary education is available to all Belgian children and foreign children whose parents are resident in Belgium. Tuition is free.

There is a general trend towards co-education. But in the Catholic private sector (frequented by over 50% of the school population) there are still many single sex schools.

By an Act of 30 July 1963, it was established that the language of instruction would be French in Wallonia, Dutch in Flanders and German in the *Cantons de l'Est*. In the Brussels area parents can choose between French speaking or Dutch speaking schools.

Pre-School

Pre-primary education is divided into three stages. Crèches are provided for children from the age of two or three months (which marks the end of maternity leave for the working mother) to 18 months. From 18 months to 2½ years small children may attend a 'pre-nursery' *(pré-gardienne* or *peutertuin)*. These two stages are not free and the fees charged are dependent on parental income. The crèche and pre-nursery are either special centres or are attached to a kindergarten or primary school. They have been mainly set up in large towns. The kindergarten (*école gardienne* or *kleutertuin*) caters for 2½ to 6 year olds. Nursery education at this level is not compulsory but is available free of charge, mostly in special classes attached to primary schools.

Pre-school provision in Belgium is greater than in any other Western European country. The 1976 figures for attendance showed that 91% of children between 2½ and 4, 98% of 4 to 5 year olds and 99% of 5 to 6 year olds attended nursery schools. Normally the child will not be taught to read or write. The accent lies on language development, mathematical activity, musical education and psycho-motor functions.

Primary

Primary education caters for 6 to 12 year olds and consists of six years of study, split into three cycles of two years each. The curriculum is being reformed to cut across any subject barriers; it was felt that 'a rigid timetable' and 'compartmented' teaching cannot keep pace with the realities of modern life, and that the existing curriculum was not sufficiently child centred. Consequently there will be fewer prescribed subjects than in the past. In the French language areas modernisation began in September 1971 in the public sector. By 1 September 1974, there was some form of modernisation in 67 State schools and in 127 schools run by provinces or municipalities. In the Dutch language areas modernisation was introduced somewhat later. Specific experiments on the teaching of modern mathematics were carried out in 20 State schools. Both language sectors have introduced remedial teaching.

Compulsory subjects in the reformed system will be: mother tongue, mathematics, exploration of the environment, activities involving self-expression, second language (optional or compulsory), religion or moral instruction, physical education and road safety. A greater number of physical education classes have been planned. In the Brussels area the teaching of the second national language is compulsory.

Second Level Education

Secondary education, which is compulsory up to the age of 14, caters for 12 to 18 year olds. Figures for attendance after age 14 are as follows:

14–15 year olds	:	90%
15–16 year olds	:	80%
16–17 year olds	:	66%
17–18 year olds	:	53%
18–19 year olds	:	34%

Entrance depends on successful completion of primary education or the agreement of the 'class council', which is composed of teachers. The six-year course is divided into two cycles of three years each, and this division enables each school leaver to obtain a certificate at age 15. However, it is possible that the minimum school leaving age will be raised to 16, and the two-cycle pattern is being modified by secondary education reform.

Traditional System

This is divided into general, artistic, technical and vocational secondary education, with the different types of education offered in different schools. General or academic education is given In *athénées* (boys), *lycées* (girls), and *collèges* or *instituts* (boys or girls). In the lower cycle of the general secondary school pupils must choose either the Latin section or the modern section (which includes science and economics). Prescribed subjects are mother tongue, history, geography, mathematics, a first foreign language, biology, art, gymnastics and Latin for the Latin section. In the upper secondary school pupils can choose between the following sections: Latin-Greek, Latin-mathematics, Latin-sciences, sciences A (based on mathematics and physics), sciences B (based on natural sciences) and economics. The teaching is clearly divided into separate subjects with little or no coordination. Parallel schools offer technical secondary education (also in two cycles of three years) with a common core of secondary subjects + vocational extras. This type of education is regarded as equivalent in level to general secondary education. Vocational and artistic secondary schools are organised in a similar way, though the bias of the curriculum is more practical.

Reformed System (enseignement rénové/vernieuwd secundair onderwijs)

The introduction of the reformed system of secondary education began in 1969 in the public sector and has now been extended to all State, provincial and municipal schools. The traditional system is being phased out. However, reform began one year later in the private sector and has proceeded at a much slower pace. The traditional system is still operative in most Catholic schools though there is a general belief in Catholic education that the reform of secondary education along comprehensive lines is inevitable. The reformed system favours a multidisciplinary approach with a maximum of coordination between subjects (e.g. humanities is composed of history, political geography, economics and the social sciences). All pupils attend the same type of school. A fundamental aim of the modern system is to postpone the moment of specialisation. It is divided into three units of two years each:

(i)   observation

(ii)   orientation (pre-specialisation)

(iii)   determination (specialisation).

In unit 2 the emphasis may be put on specialisation for those pupils who would like to leave school at 16.

There are still four distinct types of second level education:

(i)   general
(ii) technical
(iii) artistic
(iv) vocational.

The four have a common first year and in the second year of the observation phase there are still a large number of common classes for pupils in all but the vocational areas. From the third year, the beginning of the orientation phase, the four distinct types of education appear, though there are common classes in religion or ethics, mother tongue, second language, humanities and physical education. Up to the fourth year it is still possible to switch from one type of education to another. During the determination phase, the number of common classes is reduced to three: religion or ethics, humanities, and physical education.

With the exception of the common classes, the structure of the reformed system is a flexible one in which the pupil can choose his own options and thus build a programme tailor made to his own interests and ability and yet which provides a properly balanced education. Pupils in the general stream may follow courses in mathematics, physics and natural science, economics and social sciences, modern languages, Latin, Greek, technical sciences, industrial chemistry and electromechanics. Options offered in the technical stream include agriculture, horticulture, mechanics, electricity and woodwork. Applied and decorative art, interior design and architectural drawing may be studied in the artistic stream and steelwork, building, construction, dressmaking and hairdressing in the vocational stream. Under the reformed system there is a minimum of 32 teaching periods and a maximum of 38 (40 in special cases) per week.

Foreign Language Learning

A first foreign language is compulsory from the first year of the lower secondary cycle. In Wallonia it can be either Dutch or English, in Flanders, French or English. In the Brussels area the first foreign language has to be the other national language: Dutch in French language schools, French in Dutch language schools. In the reformed system a second and third language can be chosen in the subsequent years. In the traditional system a second foreign language is compulsory for the modern sections from the second year and for the Latin section from the third year. A third foreign language (usually German but sometimes Spanish or Italian) is compulsory from the fourth year for the economics section only.

Assessment

Under the reformed system the traditional pattern of examinations twice a year has been replaced by a system of continuous assessment and the system of marking has been abolished. This means that the decision about whether a pupil has successfully completed a year's study is no longer reached by adding up all his marks. The Class Council decides whether or not a pupil is ready to move on to the next class.

School Leaving Qualifications

The school leaving qualification of the reformed system is the same as in the traditional system. Pupils who successfully complete secondary education are awarded the *certificat d'enseignement secondaire supérieur/certificaat van hoger middelbaar onderwijs*. The certificate has to be ratified by the *commission d'homologation* which keeps an eye on standards. A special jury, known as the *Jury d'Etat* is set up to examine pupils who have either attended unrecognised schools or studied externally.

Pupils who wish to enter a university or a university level institution have to take an additional qualification known as the *maturité* in three subjects, usually related to their chosen field of study. In the reformed system the pupils of the artistic and technical sections can also take the *maturité*. However, in view of a widespread dissatisfaction with the *maturité* it is possible that this examination will be abolished. In 1979 Ministers of Education were thinking of introducing a one-term preliminary university course which would aim at guiding the student towards an appropriate field of study and would at the same time replace the *maturité*.

Teacher Training

Since 1974 all types of teacher training have been part of higher education. For all three types (pre-school teacher training, primary teacher training, secondary teacher training) there is a two-year course at a teacher training college called an *Ecole normale/Normaalschool*.

Pre-Primary

Apart from general courses there are courses in drawing, music, child psychology, pedagogics, handicraft and professional training. The course ends with an examination which confers the title of *diplôme d'institutrice(eur) préscholair/diploma van kleuterleidster*.

Primary

The course is similar to that for pre-primary teacher training and it ends with an examination which confers the title of *diplôme d'institutrice(eur) primaire/diploma van onderwijzer(es) lager onderwijs*.

Lower Second Level

Non-graduate teachers from an *école normale* are only qualified to teach at the lower secondary level. In the general and arts stream there are the following specialised courses available:

(i) mother tongue and history

(ii) modern languages

(iii) mathematics

(iv) sciences and geography

(v) physical education and biology

(vi) arts.

In the technical stream there are specialised courses in industry, commerce, economics, decorative arts, home economics, dressmaking and cutting. The course ends with an examination which confers the title of *regent* or *agrégé de l'enseignement secondaire inférieur/geagregeerde van het lager middelbaar onderwijs.*

Upper Second Level

Teachers in the upper secondary school are university graduates. They may take their teaching qualification *(agrégation de l'enseignement secondaire supérieur/agregaat van het hoger middelbaar onderwijs)* at the same time as their degree or later. Most students take both examinations together.

In-Service

Each education authority is free to decide on how to organise in-service training for teachers. In the State system the inspectors are largely responsible for the in-service training in their own subjects. Working parties, residential training periods, and conferences are organised. Teachers are released for 'study' days. The Minister of Dutch Education has said there should be more in-service training, preferably in regional and national centres.

Third Level Education

Higher education embraces all post-secondary education including both the universities and the non-university sector.

University

University education is organised in 19 institutions. There are six full scale universities:

2 State universities: *Université de l'Etat à Liège* (French)
Rijksuniversiteit te Gent (Dutch)

2 Catholic universities: *Université catholique de Louvain*
                           (French)
                           Katholieke Universiteit te Leuven
                           (Dutch)
2 Free universities: *Université libre de Bruxelles*
                           (French)
                           Vrije Universiteit Brussel (Dutch).

The free universities were originally set up in opposition to the Catholic University of Louvain. There are also 13 university institutions, mainly created in the 1960s, where tuition is limited to a few disciplines or to the first stage of studies. These are as follows:

(i)   Université de l'Etat à Mons

(ii)   Universitaire Instelling Antwerpen

(iii)   Rijksuniversitair Centrum te Antwerpen

(iv)   Universitaire Faculteiten Saint-Ignatius te Antwerpen

(v)   Faculté polytechnique de Mons

(vi)   Faculté des sciences agronomiques de l'Etat à Gembloux

(vii)   Facultés universitaires Notre-Dame de la Paix à Namur

(viii) Facultés universitaires catholiques de Mons

(ix)   Facultés universitaires Saint-Louis à Bruxelles

(x)   Universitaire Faculteiten Saint-Aloysius te Brussel

(xi)   Faculté de théologie protestante à Bruxelles
        Protestantse Theologische Faculteit te Brussel

(xii)   Ecole royal militaire
        Koninklijke Militaire School.

The six full scale universities have faculties of philosophy and arts, law, science, applied science and medicine as well as a varying number of faculties, schools or institutes which offer courses in economics, social and political sciences, psychology, archeology, history of art, etc.

In order to gain admission to university a student must have passed the *maturité* examination, but this involves very little selection. In 1976/77, 93% to 99% of the upper secondary school leavers obtained their *maturité*. There is no *numerus clausus* except in applied sciences. There are two examination sessions per year: in June/July and in September. Students must pass the examination at the end of one year before proceeding to the next. In the event of failure they are only allowed to resit the examination once.

University study is divided into two stages: the first stage leads to the qualification of *candidat/Kandidaat* which is obtained after two or sometimes three years of study of a rather general nature. It means that the student has acquired the basic training essential to start specialisation and carries no weight outside the university. The second stage leads to the qualification of *licence/Licenciaat*. It is obtained after two or three years of further study of a more specialised nature and involves the submission of a final thesis *'mémoire de fin d'études'*. In some faculties, the second qualification is that of doctor, pharmacist or engineer. In not less than one or two years after the *licence:* the public defence of a dissertation is required. The highest qualification is that of *agrégé de l'enseignement supérieur* (the teaching qualification for higher education institutions). This qualification cannot be granted until at least two years after the doctorate has been obtained. The candidate must present an original dissertation and three subsidiary theses, defend the dissertation in public and give a lecture.

Non-University

Non-university higher education comprises colleges of technology, agriculture, economics, para-medical studies, social studies, art colleges and teacher training colleges. A distinction is made between short and long types of course. For admission to a short course a student has to have successfully completed upper secondary education., The course consists of a cycle of two or three years and leads to a sub-degree qualification. This category includes, for instance, the qualifications for nursing, midwifery, secretarial studies, commercial studies, marketing, etc. For admission to a long course a student has to have the *maturité* i.e. be qualified for entry to university. The course lasts four to five years and leads to a degree qualification. This category includes degrees in industrial engineering (construction, mechanical, electrical, chemical, etc.), interpreting, translating, administration and architecture.

Adult

Funds for this sector have been cut back recently in a government economy drive. Nevertheless several hundred organisations in this field receive state subsidies. Adults who wish to improve their qualifications can do so by part time evening study in technical subjects (provided on a fairly wide scale by the municipalities) or by taking correspondence courses. The two large union movements, the Socialist FGTB and the Social Christian CSC, have strong educational movements. The latter has 16 centres of advanced education where almost 2,000 people study social sciences, politics and economics. Belgian legislation of 10 April 1973 granted certain workers an amount of extra paid holiday leave equal to the number of hours of approved study they followed after working hours. (Half the funds are provided by the State and the other half out of a fund to which all employers contribute.) The Law *(La loi sur les crédits d'heures)* represents a significant compromise between management, government and union interests.

There is much interest in the possibility of starting an 'Open University', but it has not yet got off the ground. For financial reasons it would probably have to be bilingual, but the Flemings are considering a joint project with the Dutch as an alternative solution. One reason is probably that while the Flemings favour sub-degree courses the Walloons do not. Another is that there are already two quite separate radio and television networks for the two main linguistic communities, a fact which is likely to accentuate the tendency towards separate initiatives.

7 EDUCATIONAL ADMINISTRATION
Cultural Communities

The educational and cultural administration reflects the trend towards increasing autonomy between the linguistic regions and cultural communities. And in view of the considerable importance attached to the cultural communities - Flemish, French and German - the Constitution provides for three Cultural Councils. The Cultural Councils govern by decree and have certain powers in the field of education within the limits of national policy on educational structures, duration of compulsory schooling, diplomas, grants, etc.

Ministries of Education

National policy on education is laid down in basic legislation which is valid for the country as a whole. There are two Ministries of Education: The Ministry for National Education and French Culture (which is also responsible for administering education in the German speaking region), and the Ministry for National Education and Dutch Culture. In each Ministry there are two Ministers responsible for policy, one for national education and one for culture. Some aspects of education (e.g. adult education and physical education) are administered by the Minister of Culture. A joint Secretary-General coordinates the two branches and the administrative services common to both Education and Culture are grouped together in a special department. Adaptation by the cultural communities and the application of the decrees of the Cultural Councils means that the structure of the two Ministries differs to some extent, principally at the level of the Directorates for Education and Culture. The present Ministers of Education meet once a fortnight and their *chefs de cabinet* once a week.

Local Responsibilities

Under the Constitution several different authorities can be responsible for schools: the State, the provinces, the municipalities and private bodies (usually Catholic). The schools run by private bodies are called free schools. Most technical education is organised at provincial level and primary education at municipal level. The Catholic Church has its own schools administration although government inspectors ensure that educational standards are maintained. All schools receiving a subsidy from the State must fulfill certain conditions such as agreeing to inspections, maintaining certain minimum standards, teaching

ADMINISTRATION

MINISTRIES OF EDUCATION
Ministry for National Education and French Culture   Ministry for National Education and Dutch Culture
Minister Education   Minister Culture   Minister Education   Minister Culture
REGIONAL COUNCILS
Flanders   Wallonia   Brussels
CULTURAL COUNCILS
Dutch   French   German
REGIONAL ADMINISTRATION
Provinces   Municipalities   Private Bodies (usually Catholic)
NATIONAL INSPECTORATE
General   Subject Experts

certain subjects, length of courses, etc. An authority (State, provincial, communal) can either adopt the curriculum offered by the State or submit its own programme for approval to the Minister of Education. The curricula of the State schools are established by teams composed of inspectors, teachers, university research assistants and representatives of parents' associations. The Minister is responsible for the programmes. Each authority is free to decide its own teaching methods and the distribution of hours allotted to each subject in accordance with the minimum overall requirements laid down by the Ministry of Education.

Inspectorate

The inspectorate consists of about 60 former subject teachers recruited by examination. It wields most inclence in curricular reform where inspectors help the *conseils de perfectionnement* to decide on curricula and textbooks. Most inspectors are responsible for a specific subject. When inspecting State schools they represent the governing authority; in free (private) schools they represent the subsidising body and their powers are strictly controlled and limited by law.

8 EDUCATIONAL FINANCE

Education Budget

The combined budget for the Ministries of Education and Culture (French and Dutch speaking) rose from 10.7% of the total budget corresponding to a bare 2% of GNP in the early 1950s to 22.3% of the budget (approximately 6% of GNP) in 1976. The combined budget for 1976 amounted to 160 billion Belgian francs of which 148 billion went to the Education Ministries (81.8 to the Dutch, 64.7 to the French and 1.9 for joint expenditure). Of the 1978 budget 103 billion francs were allocated to the Dutch language educational sector of which 101.7 billion was for current expenditure and 1.3 billion for capital expenditure. The corresponding figure for the French language sector was 79.8 billion of which 78.6 was for current expenditure and 1.2 billion for capital expenditure. However, the national education budget does not record total expenditure on education since it does not record expenditure incurred by either the provinces and municipalities or, more importantly, by the Church authorities, for which no figures are available.

Approximately 25% of each Ministry's budget goes to primary education, 5% to special education for the handicapped and around 45% to the secondary sector. Expenditure on higher education, of which two thirds goes to the university sector, in 1978 came to just over 16 billion francs in each Ministry's budget, i.e. 22% of the French language budget and 16% of the Dutch. The Free and Catholic universities used to differ from their State counterparts in their administrative organisation and in the amount of funds they received from the State. Under the law of 27 July 1971, however, each university now receives the same amount per capita.

Allocation of Funds
Expenditure on Education: Distribution by Level
Percentage of Expenditure 1977

Pre-school	First Level	Second Level	Third Level	Other
-	25.7	45.2	16.1	13.0

Subsidies and Fees

Each chapter in the combined budget has three separate sets of credits covering respectively the state school system and the two subsidised school systems (provincial and municipal on the one hand, free [i.e. Catholic] on the other). The subsidies for the free school system now amount to over half of the total budget (approximately 60% in Flanders). For many years the Catholic schools were only allowed to exist if they were completely independent and financially self-sustaining. But at the end of World War One the State assumed responsibility for the salaries of all primary teachers, both in the State and 'free' secondary schools. The abolition of all fees in both public and recognised private schools has been made possible by the State becoming responsible for the payment of salaries to *all* teachers.

A law of 5 January 1976 introduced restrictions on the subsidies universities could receive for foreign students from industrial countries. It was decided that for this category of student each university could only receive subsidies for a maximum 2% of the total student population. The universities most affected by the new law were the French language universities of Brussels and Louvain which have the largest number of foreign students. The restriction resulted in a dramatic increase in tuition fees for foreign students who do not come under one of the following categories:

(i) students of Luxembourg nationality

(ii) foreign students whose parents (or legal guardian) are or have been employed in Belgium and are nationals of a member state of the European Community

(iii) foreign students who are stateless or with the status of refugee

(iv) students from developing countries which are included in the list of countries with which Belgium has a special aid agreement.

(v) foreign students who have received a Belgian Government Scholarship.

The normal tuition fee is 6,600 BF per annum. The additional fees charged vary according to the subject and level of studies from about 60,000 BF for arts, languages, economics, etc., to 180,000 BF for medicine, applied sciences, etc.

9 DEVELOPMENT AND PLANNING OF THE EDUCATION SYSTEM
Development

Before 1794 education in Belgium was a private responsibility, and managed almost exclusively by the Catholic Church. Since the French period (1794-1814) it has been under State control. In 1815 when Belgium was incorporated into the Kingdom of the United Netherlands, King William I introduced a secular school system using Dutch as the medium of instruction. This venture failed since it alienated the French speaking Walloons (and also the Catholic Flemings on religious grounds).

After Independence

Belgium's history of subjection to other powers made the people determined after 1830 to find their own identity as a nation rather than model themselves on others. This was as true in education as in other spheres. Article 17 of the 1831 Constitution established the *freedom of education:* schools could be set up by the public authorities (State, provincial or municipal) or by private persons. But during the nineteenth century disagreements developed between the Catholic and Liberal parties, and since the party in power decided educational policy, these were inevitable. While the Catholic party thought the entire education system should be controlled by the Church, the Liberals favoured a State controlled secular system. This led to the so-called 'education war'. The schism between Catholic and free thinker was also reflected in higher education: of the four original universities, two (Ghent and Liège) are State foundations, one (Louvain) is Catholic and the fourth (Brussels) was opened by the secularist Liberals to counter the influence of Louvain.

The language division was also important - then as now. In education, as in other fields, the Flemings won concessions gradually, first in the primary schools (1883) and later (1932) in the secondary schools. At university level all teaching was in French until 1930 when the Flemings finally attained their aim at Ghent which became a purely Dutch medium university.

Educational Planning

Educational Planning is by project, though a more developed structure is regarded as desirable. There is no formal coordinating body. The decision to introduce change or reform in educational methodology or programmes is made by the Minister of Education in each sector and his cabinet. A non-permanent commission is then set up composed of general inspectors who enlist the help of specialised inspectors to work on a specific reform project. However, decisions on whether to propose new legislation and the manner of introducing reforms are taken by the Ministers and their cabinets.

10 THE SYSTEM IN OPERATION

Education Pact

During the 1950s the 'education war' broke out again when the State proposed direct and equal payment to teachers in both sectors in return for exercising stricter control over 'free' schools. The government laboured to end this, and by the Education Pact, *(Pacte Scolaire)*, of 29 May 1958 a settlement was achieved. Schools were divided into two categories: State and subsidised. The Pact guaranteed complete freedom of education for all, school fees were abolished and the State agreed to pay all teachers in full, to bear the administrative expenses of all schools and to contribute towards the costs of improving equipment and facilities in the long neglected 'free' sector. Freedom of education means that the choice for parents between Catholic and non-Catholic education should always be available and is guaranteed by law. The law also prescribes that State education should be neutral. This means that parents can decide whether their children will attend a religious course or one of non-confessional moral instruction. The Law of 1958 is still the basis for the organisation of the education system in Belgium.

In recent years the strong links between the Roman Catholic Church and the Christian Social Party have been much weakened; this made it possible for Catholic schools to receive subsidies as one of the provisions of the Education Pact. (The Catholic schools cater for almost 50% of the population.)

Primary Reform

The process of rationalisation, that is abolishing and regrouping primary schools when the number of pupils falls below a certain minimum level, began in 1967 but only acquired its present form under the Law of 14 July 1975. The minimum number of pupils varies according to the population density of the municipalities concerned. However, in order to ensure the free choice of parents, education of the same level, both Catholic and non-Catholic, must be available within a reasonable distance - 4 km. A considerable number of primary schools have been either closed or regrouped as a result. The Law of July 1975 also introduced the notion of the pluralist school that would provide both confessional and non-confessional education, i.e. respect the principal of parental free choice between the two types of education within a single school. In practice, however, no pluralist schools have so far been established.

The final stage in the rationalisation of the primary school sector, which is due as from the 1982 academic year, will involve the pre-primary sector as well. It revolves round the notion of 'basic education' *(enseignement fondamental)* covering the ages from 3 to 12 when children of all social classes receive the same teaching in the same schools. The so-called basic school will include the three cycles of primary education and at least two age groups from the present pre-primary sector. The aim is to ensure the child's progressive development from the age of $2\frac{1}{2}$ to 11 or 12, avoiding the present abrupt transition from the play oriented pre-primary sector to the more intellectual disciplines of the primary school. The key innovation in this respect is the creation of vertical groups of pupils from age 5 to 7 or 8, which has already been introduced experimentally in a certain number of schools.

REFERENCES AND FURTHER READING

Blackstone, T. (1973). 'Early Childhood Education'. *Trends in Education*. HMSO, London.
Bureau de Statistique (1979). *Annuaire Statistique de l'Enseignement*. Brussels.
Council for Cultural Cooperation of the Council of Europe (1970). *School Systems - a Guide* (revised edition). Strasbourg.
Council of Europe (1970→). *Newsletter* (various articles in issues since 1970). Strasbourg.
Dupuy, R. J. and Tunkin, G. (1973). *Comparability of Degrees and Diplomas in International Law*. UNESCO, Paris.
Fondation Universitaire, Bureau de Statistiques Universitaires (1971). *Annual Reports*. Brussels.
Gerlo, A. (1973). 'Access to the University in Belgium'. *CRE - Information*, No. 22, April 1973, Geneva.
International Bureau of Education (1979). *Country Education Profile: Belgium*. IBE, Geneva.
IIEE Bulletin, (various articles). Brussels.
Kerr, A. (1960). *Schools of Europe*. Bowes & Bowes, London.
de Keyser, C. C. and Falleyn, J. A. C. (1973). *Comparative Repertory of European Qualifications*. 2: Belgium, Luxembourg and The Netherlands. Acco, Leuven.
La Cité. (Various articles in edition of 5 June 1973). Brussels.
'Les Universites en Belgique', *European University News*, No. 55, November 1971. Paris.
Mallinson, V. (1969). *Belgium*. Ernest Benn Ltd., London.
Mallinson, V. (1963). *Power and Politics in Belgian Education*. Heinemann Educational, London.
McGuinness, K. (1973). *Small Town in Belgium: Education and Life in an Area of the Province of Luxembourg*. Unpublished paper, Oxford.
Neumeister, H. (1973). *Modern Languages in School*. II: Country Reports. Council of Europe, Strasbourg.
OECD (1969). *OECD Study on Teachers*, (volume covering Germany, Belgium, United Kingdom). OECD, Paris.
OECD (1972). *Classification of Educational Systems in OECD Member Countries* (volume covering Belgium, Denmark, United States). OECD, Paris.
OECD (1973). *OECD Economic Surveys: B.L.E.U.* OECD, Paris.
Schultze, Walter (Ed.) (1968-70). *Schools in Europe*. Julius Beltz Verlag, Weinheim and Berlin.
The Times. 2 March 1972; 21 February 1973; 28 September 1973; 24 November 1973. London.
The Times Educational Supplement. 23 March 1973. London.
The Times Higher Education Supplement. 17 November 1972. London.
Tribune. (The official journal of the teachers' section of the

Centre General des Services Publics, a PSB trade union). No. 8, April 1973.
Unesco/IBE (1980). *International Yearbook of Education XXII*. UNESCO, Paris.
Unesco (1981). *UNESCO Statistical Yearbook 1980*. Unesco, Paris.
Unesco (1971). *World Survey of Education*. **V**. Unesco, Paris.
University of London Institute of Education and Teachers College, Columbia University, New York. *The World Year Book of Education* (various articles). Evans Brothers, London, and Harcourt, Brace and World, New York.
Van der Motten, J. P. (1973). 'Belgium: Some Recent Developments in Higher Education'. *International Newsletter.* Society for Research into Higher Education, April 1973, London.
Wanner, R. E. (1973). 'Expanding on Career Education'. *American Education*. United States Department of Health, Education & Welfare. **9**, No. 9, November 1973, Washington.

Structure of the Education System in Belgium

Age	3 4 5	6 7 8 9 10 11	12 13 14	15 16 17 18	19 20 21 22 23 24
Level		I		II	III
Stage		1 2 3	4	5 6	7 8 9
Compulsory					
School type		1st 2nd 3rd cycle cycle cycle *Primaire*	Observ. Orient. Déter. *Secondaire*	Technical Vocational	Non-university short and long term / University

▨ Education preceding the first level

Examinations: (a) *Certificat d'études primaires* after sixth year
(b) technical certificates at end of stages 5, 6 and 7
(c) *Maturité* gives access to third level

Source: UNESCO/IBE International Yearbook of Education

Compulsory Education: Age Limits 6–14 Duration (years) 8
Entrance age to pre-school education: 3

BELGIUM BASIC STATISTICS	1960	1970	1975	1978 (approx.)
1 Total population (000)	9,153	9,637	9,846	9,840
% female	51	51	51	51
2 % population 0-14 years	23.5	23.7		22.0
% female	49	49	49	49
3 Enrolment, all levels	1,497,553	1,870,071	1,912,692	1,880,784
% female	47	48		
First level	918,822	1,021,511	940,961	878,514
% female	48	49	49	49
Second level	526,729	723,703	812,071	832,621
% female	47	48		49
Third level	52,002	124,857	159,660	169,649
% female	26	36	41	42
4 Teachers, all levels				
% female				
First level	47,119	51,692	48,625	46,484
% female		56	57	58
Second level	51,486			
% female				
Third level				
% female				
5 Public expenditure on education				
Total (000) Francs	26,201,000		143,856,800	186,656,000
As % of GNP	4.6		6.2	6.5
As % of public expenditure				19.2
6 % enrolment (MF) by level	100	100	100	100
First level	61	55	49	46
Second level	35	39	42	44
Third level	3	7	8	9
% enrolment (F) by level	100	100	100	100
First level	63	56		47
Second level	35	39		45
Third level	2	5		8
7 Entrance age: Duration of				
First level education	6:6	6:6	6:6	6:6
Second level education	12:6	12:6	12:6	12:6
8 Enrolment ratios (MF)				
First level	109	108	106	102
Second level	69	82	84	86
Third level	9.09	17.49	22.01	23.08
Enrolment ratios (F)				
First level	108	107	105	102
Second level	66	81		87
Third level	4.82	12.94	18.61	20.54

Canada

CONTENTS

1	Geography	104
2	Population	106
3	Society and Culture	108
4	History and Politics	109
5	The Economy	111
6	The Education System	112
7	Educational Administration	117
8	Educational Finance	118
9	Development and Planning of the Educational System	120
10	The System in Operation	121

The origins of the educational systems in Canada are European. Major influences stem from Britain and France. The maritime provinces have their own characteristics which are different from the prairie provinces and British Columbia in the far west which retains, particularly on Victoria Island, many features associated with England. Quebec is French and since bilingualism was officially introduced there has been pressure on the part of some French speaking Canadians to separate Quebec from the rest of Canada.

It should be remembered, however, that the majority of the Canadian population lives in a relatively narrow strip of land running east-west across the country and bordering the USA. American influence has been strong, particularly in the urban centres of Ontario and American educational thought and practice has influenced developments particularly during the expansionist period after 1945.

The tradition of local and provincial control over education dies hard. The Federal government has little power in the sphere of education. It runs schools for Indian children, for servicemen overseas and education in prisons. Each of the ten provinces has a department of education and is responsible for its own school system. Local school boards in each of the provinces have considerable autonomy. Certain duties such as school buildings, the appointment of teachers and the local school budget are delegated to them by provincial ministers.

Thus Quebec has an education system which, while European, is French. French is the mother tongue of the majority of inhabitants and since 1974 has been the language of the provincial government. Against the pressure to Anglicise education the French speaking Canadians of Quebec have maintained schools for their children which maintains their identity.

The historical solution to French-English differences now seems attractive to groups of people who arrived in Canada more recently. A large number of immigrants from China and Hong Kong settled in the Vancouver area. Inhabitants whose origins were in the Ukraine have a strong sense of their cultural heritage. Asians now constitute more than 1.3% of the population. This diversity explains the Federal Government's concern to promote multi-cultural education and development while giving Canadians a sense of national identity.

The Editor

1 GEOGRAPHY

Topography

With an area of 3.8 million square miles (9.9 million square kilometres) Canada is the second largest country in the world, covering more than half of the North American continent. It is more than 40 times the size of Britain and its dimensions are 2,875 miles north to south and 3,223 miles east to west. Politically Canada is divided into ten provinces and two territories. British Columbia on the Pacific coast is separated from the rest of Canada by the Canadian Rockies, east of which lie the agricultural plains of Alberta, Saskatchewan and Manitoba. The two largest provinces, Ontario and Quebec, occupy most of the eastern half of the country, bordered on the Atlantic coast by New Brunswick, Nova Scotia, Prince Edward Island and Newfoundland. As one would expect with so extensive an area, the territory is extremely diverse, ranging from almost semi-tropical vegetation in the south and west to wide prairies and large areas of mountains and lakes; much of the northern part of the country is wasteland and arctic tundra, uninhabited and in some places still uncharted. There are five major regions:

(i) the arctic tundra
(ii) sub-arctic area and Canadian shield
(iii) eastern temperate forest
(iv) the prairies
(v) the Rocky mountains (Cordillera).

This last is Canada's most impressive physical feature. Many peaks are over 15,000 ft (4,500 metres) and a total of 580 miles (1,502 sq km) is over 10,000 feet. It has been estimated that an area of 292,000 square miles of Canada (756,276 km) is covered by lakes (7.6% of the total area of the country).

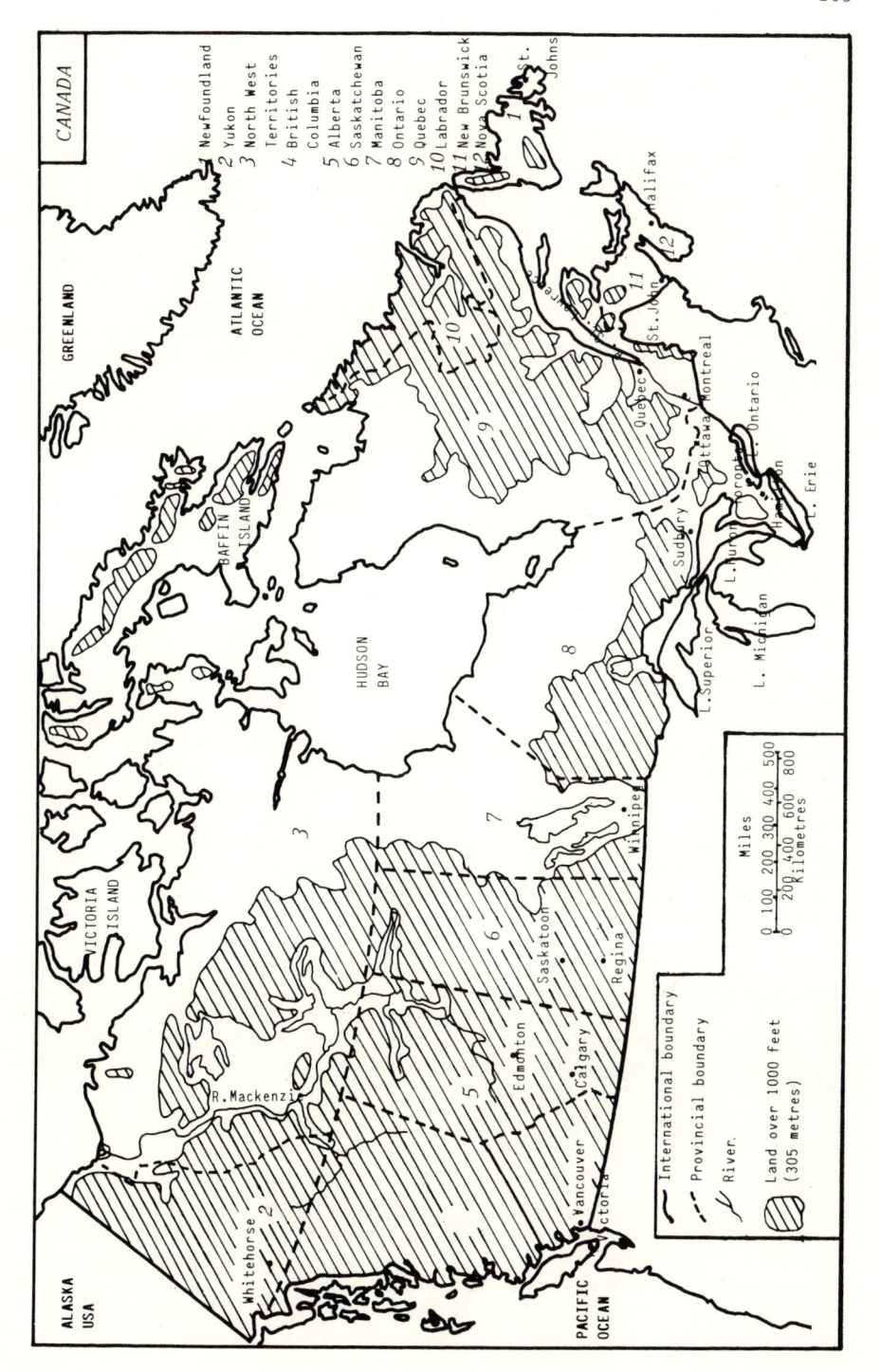

CANADA

1 Newfoundland
2 Yukon
3 North West Territories
4 British Columbia
5 Alberta
6 Saskatchewan
7 Manitoba
8 Ontario
9 Quebec
10 Labrador
11 New Brunswick
12 Nova Scotia

Climate

Canada has many regional climates. These may be described as follows:

(i) *the mountains* — varying most with altitude
(ii) *the far north* — arctic conditions with only a few months having average temperatures above freezing point
(iii) *the interior* — (from the mountains to the Great Lakes), having a continental climate with long cold winters, short warm summers and little rainfall
(iv) *the south* — (south Ontario and Quebec) having a humid climate with cold winters, hot summers and plenty of rain
(v) *the north east* — (between the arctic and southern climates) having a transitional climate similar to the interior, but with appreciable rainfall in the east
(vi) *the Atlantic coast* — having a humid continental type climate but with maritime influence
(vii) *the Pacific coast* — cool and fairly dry summers and mild, wet winters.

Communications

Canadian railways are dominated by the two great national systems, the Canadian Pacific Railway (a private company) and the Canadian National Railway (operated by the federal government). The latter covers all provinces and the North West Territories, the former eight provinces. There is a number of regional railways. In 1975 Canada had 96,633 km (60,395 miles) of track. In 1972 there were 404,512 km (251,352 miles) of roads under federal or provincial control and 446,105 km (277,198 miles) of roads under local government control. In 1974 11 million motor vehicles were registered, of which 8.5 million were private cars. There are 25 large deep water ports and about 650 smaller ports on the coasts, in the Arctic, on the Great Lakes and along the St Lawrence Seaway and inlets. Air transport is extremely important, especially in remote areas. In 1976 Canadian carriers transported an estimated 21 million passengers. The national carrier is Air Canada, and the other international airline is Canadian Pacific Air, which is private. There is a number of regional airlines.

2 POPULATION

Growth

The total population of Canada in 1976 was 22,992,604, an increase of 26% on the 1961 census figure, and 6.6% on the 1971 figure. The 1980 population estimate was 23,869,700. The provinces of Alberta and British Columbia recorded the biggest growth rates over the period, at 12.9% each. Ontario was next with 7.3%. The overall annual growth rate 1971-76 was 1.3%, which is low. Population growth has been declining since 1956, when immigration began to fall. About 30% of the population is of school age.

Distribution

In 1975 Canada had an estimated overall population density of six persons per square mile (2.5 per sq km), making it one of the most sparsely populated countries in the world. If the administered territories were omitted the figure would be ten persons per square mile (3.9 per sq km). But some urban areas are very densely populated and PE Island, Nova Scotia and New Brunswick with limited land areas have population densities well above the rest of Canada. Over 80% of Canada's total population is now concentrated in Quebec, Ontario, Alberta and British Columbia. The population is predominantly urban (i.e. living in settlements of 1,000 and over where population density is at least 1,000 per square mile or 386 per square kilometre). According to the 1971 census 76.1% of the population was urban, ranging from 38.3% in PE Island to 82.4% in Ontario. Quebec and British Columbia are also highly urbanised.

Toronto is Canada's largest city, and with a population of 2.8 million it is slightly bigger than Montreal, which is the world's second largest French-speaking city. Other major cities include Vancouver, Winnipeg, Edmonton, Quebec and Hamilton (all with over 500,000 inhabitants).

Groups

Canada's population has increased greatly through immigration, and the country contains many different ethnic groups. In 1975/76 there were 176,792 immigrants of which 31,102 were from Britain, 19,469 from the United States, 12,225 from China (including Hong Kong), and 9,589 from India (these were the single largest groups). At the same time the current trend is towards a decline in the proportion of British Isles groups, and an increase in European ethnic groups other than French. In 1971 British Isles groups represented 44.6% of the population, French 28.7% (a fairly constant proportion from the beginning of the century) and other Europeans 23%. In 1971 groups from Asia accounted for only 1.3% of the population, and others (including the indigenous peoples) 2.4%. Except for the long standing antipathy between the French and the English in Quebec there are few significant ethnic conflicts. It is the federal government's policy to encourage multi-cultural development, believing that a multi-cultural mosaic will give Canada an identity very different from that of the United States. This is of prime concern for cultural, political and educational leaders are all aware of the dangers of sharing a border with such a powerful and influential neighbour.

Indigenous Peoples

In 1975 there were 282,762 people registered as Indians under the provisions of the Indian Act of Canada. There were 574 bands in 2,284 reserves with a total area of 6.2 million acres (2,484,000 hectares). The number of people of Indian ancestry who have given up Indian status, married non-Indians, etc., is not known. In 1971 there were 18,000 Eskimos (*Inuit*) living in North West Territories, Arctic Quebec, Labrador and Northern Ontario.

3 SOCIETY AND CULTURE

Language

In the 1971 census 60.2% of the population reported English as mother tongue, and 26.9% French; however, other languages play an important part in some areas, for example Italian in Toronto and Ukranian in Winnipeg. 1971 figures showed that numbers of Italian, Greek, Chinese and Portuguese speakers had increased, while Ukranian, German, Dutch, Polish and Yiddish registered declines. Several provinces require that instruction be given in a foreign language in schools where there are considerable numbers of 'ethnics'.

Throughout its history Canada has consisted of two major linguistic groups, English and French, and since 1969 the two languages have enjoyed equal status. Canada is now officially bilingual. Citizens have the right to address, or be addressed by federal agencies in either French or English. All government documents are in both languages, bilingual districts have been created where at least 10% of the population speaks the minority language, and a Commissioner of Official Languages reporting to parliament ensures compliance with the Bilingualism Act. A massive second-language programme for federal civil servants is in operation and also a federally subsidised plan for the development of English as a second language and French as a second language in the provinces. Quebec remains the only province where French is the mother tongue of the majority (and since 1974 the language of the provincial government). Interest in French as a second language is considerable in Ontario and New Brunswick, but further west and east the expenditure of public funds on French as a second language is resented. It is too early to predict whether the Bilingualism Act will eventually lead to a bilingual population.

Religion

As well as different languages, immigrants to Canada have also brought many different religions. However, in the 1971 census three out of four people in Canada reported themselves as belonging to either the Roman Catholic Church (46%), Anglican Church (12%) or the United Church of Canada (consisting of Methodists, Presbyterians and Baptists). This last is Canada's largest Protestant denomination with 17.5% of the population enrolled and it has recently merged with the Evangelical United Brethren. The remaining 24.5% of the population are divided among more than 30 other denominations and sects including Adventists, Baptists, Pentecostalists, Presbyterians, Lutherans, Greek Orthodox, Ukrainian Catholics, as well as Jehovah's Witnesses, and followers of the Jewish faith. Recent immigrants have also introduced Islam, Hinduism, Buddhism and Sikhism.

4 HISTORY AND POLITICS
Historical Development

Though visited by John Cabot in the late fifteenth century and Jacques Cartier in the mid-sixteenth, the territory which is now Canada was first settled in the seventeenth century. At the very beginning of the century the French began to settle the area around the St Lawrence river, and founded Quebec, the capital of New France. In the 1670s, the English settled on Hudson Bay and in the eighteenth century pressed south and west in an attempt to gain the hinterland of the country from the French. British forces were numerically superior and in 1759 Quebec fell to General Wolfe; the Treaty of Paris 1763 ceded all French territories in North America to Britain. Settlement grew steadily, and was strengthened by loyalist refugees from the American War of Independence. Political development followed, with the division of the province of Quebec into Upper and Lower Canada, each with its own assembly (Nova Scotia had had a representative assembly since 1758). But the various colonies remained separate, despite economic difficulties and an increasingly hostile United States, until in 1867 the Canadas, Nova Scotia and New Brunswick were joined in confederation by the British North America Act. At this stage Prince Edward Island and Newfoundland refused to join, the prairies belonged to the Hudson Bay Company, and British Columbia was far away. But by 1894 there were nine provinces and the North West Territories had been founded; Newfoundland was the last province to join the union in 1949.

Two major wars in the twentieth century changed Canada radically. Its development from colonial status during World War One was recognised in the Statute of Westminster 1931. World War Two turned the country into a major military and industrial power and rapid economic development continued during the 1950s. During this period too, Canada moved into closer economic relations with the United States. But by the late 1950s the economy was slowing down, relations with the US were not so good, and above all, Quebec was beginning to question confederation. In 1968 Pierre Trudeau led his party to victory for the first time, a Quebecer who held strong federalist views. But the success of Parti Quebecois (PQ) in the 1976 Quebec provincial elections raised the whole question of separation once more. This year's provincial referendum was a decisive defeat for separatism, at least for the present. Meanwhile, after a short period of Conservative government, Canada had a Liberal government once more and Pierre Trudeau, at least temporarily, abandoned plans of retirement to lead it.

Government and Politics

Canada is a constitutional monarchy under the Crown. The Governor-General (who is always a Canadian) represents the Queen, and is appointed by her, on the advice of the Prime Minister. The Governor-General in turn appoints ministers, deputy ministers, and members of the Senate, judges, and lieutenant-governors of the provinces. There is a bicameral parliament consisting of a 104-seat Senate, whose members are appointed in proportionate numbers from each province, and a 264-seat House of Commons whose members are elected for single-member constituencies roughly in proportion to the population of each province. It is usual for cabinet ministers to be members of the House of Commons. In the provinces the pattern is similar except that provincial parliaments are unicameral. the Yukon and North West Territories are administered by commissioners but there are also small elected councils. All municipalities are governed by elected councils (4,500 in all). The main political parties are the Liberal Party, the Progressive Conservative Party, the New Democratic Party, and the Social Credit Party of Canada. In the general election of February 1981 the number of seats obtained by each were as follows: Liberals 147; Conservatives 102; NDP 32; 1 vacant; total 282. A new Constitution was ratified in March 1982.

International Relations

Canada's most important relationship is that with the United States, the rich and powerful neighbour with whom Canada shares a boundary of 3,986 miles. There is not always full agreement on everything, but in general relations between the two countries are excellent, and are marked by regular consultations. There is considerable trade and financial interdependence. Europe represents Canada's second most important trading partner, and Japan its third. Relations with Europe are important, and Canada, as a Pacific power, is also looking for links with Asia. Canada has long held close relations with the Commonwealth Caribbean, and recently relations with Latin America have also been strengthened.

Canada is an active member of the Commonwealth and several UN agencies, and plays a not unimportant part in NATO. It is also a member of OECD and contributes to the IMF and World Bank. It also belongs to a number of organisations of francophone countries and favours stronger links with *La Francophonie*. Canada's role in international affairs has hitherto not attracted the interest of the Canadian public though the government now appears to be striving towards an active neutralist policy, which will include greater involvement in aid to the developing countries. This is likely to lead to greater public interest in the problems of the Third World countries.

5 THE ECONOMY

Agriculture and Fisheries

Agriculture, forestry and fisheries together contributed only 3.8% of Canada's GDP in 1976, and the importance of this sector has declined since World War Two. About 80% of the wheat crop is exported and Canada provides 20% of the world's supply; 1979 saw the establishment of an important agreement to sell wheat to China. Barley, rye and rapeseed are also grown. Of late, high prices have characterised agriculture, with important effects on the consumer price index. Canada now has a 200 mile fishing limit and catches are rising.

Natural Resources

Canada is one of the richest countries in the world in terms of natural resources. At the end of 1978 oil reserves were estimated at 7.6 billion barrels. But this does not include the currently inaccessible deposits in the Athabasca Tar Sands, the Mackenzie delta, the northern islands and the Atlantic off Novia Scotia. At present Canada is a net importer of oil. Natural gas is increasing in importance as an energy source. At the end of 1978 it was estimated that reserves were 66 billion cubic feet and there is likely to be much more. Natural gas is still imported, but it is hoped that by 1990 self-sufficiency will have been achieved. Some natural gas is exported now and sales should increase by 4% annually during the next few years.

Mineral production in 1977 was to the value of C$18 billion and contributed 8.7% of GNP. Forty six per cent of mineral production is exported, accounting for 26.5% of Canada's total exports. Deposits include iron, copper, gold, silver, lead, zinc, nickel, uranium, asbestos, platinum and coal. The world's largest deposit of uranium has been discovered in Saskatchewan and exploration is continuing there. Canada is aiming to increase its processing of natural resources, thus reducing the amount of raw material exported to other industrial countries.

Industry

Since World War Two Canada's industrialisation has proceeded rapidly, and industry now employs about 30% of the labour force. In 1976 it accounted for about 19% of GDP. Important industries include motor vehicle manufacture, paper and pulp production and meat packing. The automobile industry has expanded particularly during the last 15 years and 100,000 workers are now employed in it. A new Ford plant is to be constructed in southern Ontario. The steel manufacturing industry has also expanded in response to this. Canada is the world's second largest producer of pulp and provides 15% of world supplies of newsprint.

Economic Situation

The economy is broadly based, but heavily tied to the United States. Since 1976 the growth in output has slowed (GNP rose by 3.4% in 1978). Inflation remains a problem, and stood at 9% in 1978, high food prices being cited as the prime factor. In previous years the strategy to fight inflation had been handled by the Anti-Inflation Board which monitored wages, prices and profits. But the unemployment rate (8.5% in 1978) seems likely to keep wage settlements low. Unemployment is highest in the Atlantic provinces (12.5% in 1978) and lowest in Alberta. The main group of unemployed is in the 15-24 age group. About 70% of trade is with the US and the forecast for 1979 showed a healthy trade surplus of C$4 billion but a current account deficit of C$4.7 billion, largely as a result of high debt servicing costs. Canada's small domestic market, its geography and its dependence on the US economy are seen to be limiting factors, but its immense natural resources should augur well for the future. There remains a shortage of technical personnel and of technological know-how, leaving exploitation of some of its natural resources open to foreign companies, especially from the United States. Development of training facilities for technologists and of first class research establishments is therefore of paramount importance.

6 THE EDUCATION SYSTEM

Academic Year

The school year consists of 180 to 200 teaching days and is divided into two semesters - from September to December and from January to June. There is a ten-day holiday at Christmas and a week's holiday at Easter. The university year runs from early September to late April or early May with breaks at Christmas and in the spring. Some universities have instituted half courses or one-semester courses and a few have a three-term system. Throughout Canada universities offer summer sessions. These sessions do not, however, provide a full range of courses.

Private Schools

Only about 3.4% of Canada's elementary and secondary school enrolment is in private schools. Four provinces - Alberta, British Columbia, Saskatchewan and Quebec - provide some financial assistance to private education. In most cases private schools follow the curricula laid down for public education and are required to meet standards set by the provinces in which they are situated.

Pre-School

Pre-primary education consists of day-care centres, nursery schools and kindergartens. Most day-care centres are privately run, though licensed with the Department of Education or Social Services, but some school boards provide public education for three and four year olds. Kindergartens which provide one year of pre-primary education for five year olds are provided by all provinces except Prince Edward Island, Nova Scotia, New Brunswick and Alberta. In Nova Scotia children are admitted to primary school at 5, and in Alberta children of $4\frac{1}{2}$ to $5\frac{1}{2}$ participate in the 'early childhood services programme'. In 1977/78 pre-primary enrolment was estimated at 363,910.

Kindergarten curricula provide opportunities for singing, playing games, dancing and drawing, to aid coordination, social skills, and the development of independence. Formal classes should develop oral and written language skills. Open education methods and the 'integrated day' approach are commonly used. Most classes contain no more than 25 children.

First Level (Elementary)

At one time the pattern of eight years of primary education followed by four years of secondary was universal throughout Canada, except for Roman Catholic schools in Quebec Province. However, nowadays, though elementary schools usually take pupils from grade 1 to grade 6 or 8 (age 6 to 11 or 13) the point of transition varies between provinces and even between school boards. In some places there are six grades of elementary school, followed by three 'middle' grades (junior high) and three grades of secondary education (senior high). In other places the pattern is 6-3-4. Some authorities divide the elementary course into two cycles of three years each. Elementary education is compulsory in all provinces, though the starting age is six in Alberta, Nova Scotia, Ontario and Quebec, and seven elsewhere.

The elementary curriculum represents an interdisciplinary approach to basic studies in the three Rs, plus science, social studies, music, art and physical education. Some vocational studies begin in the second three years and instruction in the second official language at this level is growing. Most of the provinces have introduced some sort of continuous assessment system for grading, and repetition of a year is now less common. Open-plan schools have been introduced widely at this level. The present system makes provision for remedial and enrichment programmes and generally speaking, the old year-by-year promotion policy has been discarded.

Second Level (Secondary)

Secondary schools vary from single classrooms in remote rural areas, to enormous schools with up to 3,000 pupils. Some cover grades 9 to 11, others 9 to 12, others again 10 to 12, and some secondary courses begin at grade 7 or 8. At one time secondary education was predominantly academic, though there were specialised vocational schools to be found in large cities. Now most secondary schools (except in the remote areas) offer a wide range of academic, commercial and technical courses. Some part of secondary education is compulsory everywhere in Canada except in the North West Territories where compulsory schooling ends at age 12. Pupils must stay at school up to age 15 in British Columbia, Newfoundland, New Brunswick, Prince Edward Island, Quebec and the Yukon, and to age 16 in Alberta, Manitoba, Nova Scotia, Ontario and Saskatchewan. In Quebec five years of secondary education (grades 7 to 11) are followed by two or three years at a *collège d'enseignement général et professionel* (CEGEP).

The comprehensive programme includes academic and vocational subjects, physical education, music, drama, fine arts and special interest activities. Through these broad experiences it is expected that students will be prepared for further education, whether in full or part time study, and be able to enter directly into the labour force or continue their studies, as they may choose. The first two years of secondary education are transitional and exploratory, so that students may test their skills and interests before choosing the more specialised courses of the later years. Most secondary schools now operate a system whereby pupils take certain compulsory 'core' subjects laid down by the province, but then select options as they wish. This has produced very individualised timetables and means that credit promotion is by subject rather than by grades over the year. Transfer from one course to another is very straightforward. Ontario's core of compulsory subjects in the first two years of secondary education is English, mathematics, science and either history or geography. Pupils who are aiming for university entrance would be likely to opt for other 'academic' subjects such as languages, economics, art, music, etc.

High school graduation is at grade 12 in all provinces except Newfoundland and Quebec where secondary education ends at grade 11. In Ontario there is an (optional) grade 13. Traditionally graduation diplomas were based on compulsory examinations set by the provinces. Now such examinations are only required in Newfoundland, Quebec and Saskatchewan (this last only under certain circumstances). Where examinations are compulsory they constitute 50% of the final grade, the other 50% being provided by the teachers' marking. Elsewhere the grading is based on the secondary school record, performance in school examinations, and teachers' assessment.

Special

Children with disabilities are educated in special schools, in separate classes, or are integrated into the normal school system. The two latter methods are the ones favoured. At present there are about 20 schools for the deaf and five for the blind directly administered by the provinces. There are also special schools for those with mental disabilities. The four Atlantic provinces have agreed to make joint provision of education for the blind and deaf, and eventually hope to combine in providing services for all those with disabilities.

Indigenous Groups

The education of Indians and *Inuit* (Eskimos) is a federal responsibility and schooling takes place either in federal schools in communities or in provincial schools. Indian education is being integrated into the general system and the Indians are being encouraged to join in the planning of curricula and the teaching of native languages. In some provinces special teacher training programmes for indigenous people have been started and there are some curriculum projects in the native languages.

Third Level (Higher) Education

Tertiary education in Canada is composed of degree-granting institutions (universities) and non-degree-granting institutions which award diplomas instead.

Universities

In 1980 there were 68 public universities, 16 of which are affiliated to others. In 1977/78, 390,050 full time students were enrolled. In 1976 ten universities had enrolments of over 14,000 students, and of these the five largest were the Universities of Toronto, British Columbia, Alberta, Montreal, and McGill University. The largest group of universities provides instruction in English; in addition to these and the French language institutions, there are some bilingual universities, notably the University of Ottawa and Laurentian University, Sudbury.

Admission to university requires high school graduation except in Quebec where students must have completed a two-year course at a CEGEP after grade 11. Many universities now also require applicants to complete aptitude tests operated by the Service for Admission to Canadian Universities, though mature students are admissible without formal qualifications. A degree in arts or science is normally an entrance requirement to courses in architecture, law, medicine, business administration and theology. Engineering and education are sometimes first degrees, sometimes second. Courses for a pass bachelor's degree last three or four years with an extra year of more intensive or higher quality work for an honours degree; requirements for professional degrees mentioned above can lengthen the period of study considerably. A master's degree takes one or more years after the bachelor's; a doctorate requires at least two additional years of research after a master's. Part time students are also admitted to university and there is a provision for off-campus courses. Most universities are organised into faculties, each headed by a dean. There are major central faculties of arts and science. Faculties are subdivided into departments which are headed by members of the teaching staff in rotation on the American model.

Community Colleges

The term 'community colleges' describes non-university post-secondary institutions. They are called by various names - colleges of applied arts and technology (CAAT) in Ontario, *collèges d'enseignement général et professionnel* in Quebec, regional or community colleges elsewhere. In Alberta, British Columbia and Quebec the colleges offer the first two years of university level study after which students may transfer to a university. They also run vocational programmes and a variety of general courses. In other parts of Canada community colleges provide general, technical and vocational courses as an alternative to univerfsity. All community colleges have flexible admission policies; some courses require high school graduation, but mature student status may be used to waive this and in general there are no such requirements. Tuition fees are below those of universities. The normal duration of professional courses is three years (two years for pre-university studies) but specialised one-year courses are also offered often in response to local needs. This local aspect of community colleges is extremely important. There are some privately operated colleges, but the provinces are responsible for coordinating and financing community colleges. Most specialised trade and vocational schools and schools of nursing have now been incorporated into the college system. In 1978 there were 173 community colleges in Canada, with an enrolment of 247,000.

Technical and Vocational

In the seventies there was a rapid development of technical and vocational education in Canada. The pattern varies between provinces and even within provinces but in general instruction is offered in trade and occupational training schools, post-secondary institutes of technology and community colleges. This is apart from the technical education offered in secondary schools. Trade and occupational schools (both public and private) are open to those over school leaving age. They do not normally require school graduation, completion of grade 8 to grade 12 being sufficient. The schools offer specialised courses training for a trade or other occupation. Vocational education is also provided under the apprenticeship system whereby on-the-job training is combined with evening or day release classes in trade schools. Post-secondary institutes of technology require high school graduation for admission, and offer technician level courses up to four years in duration. Similar courses are offered in technical departments of community colleges. A wide variety of subjects is offered, reflecting the manpower requirements of the particular region, and including engineering, architecture, health sciences, applied arts and business administration.

Teacher Training

At one time only teachers at secondary level were required to have university degrees, and elementary school teachers were trained in normal schools or teacher training colleges. Now almost all teachers must have university degrees and the teacher training colleges have been largely phased out, or absorbed into the university system.

Non-Formal and Adult

Continuing or adult education has now become an important part of the Canadian education system. Most school boards, trade schools, institutes of technology, community colleges, universities and adult vocational centres offer part time day and evening courses. The provincial departments of education provide correspondence study courses and ETV programmes, while extension services are provided by several government agencies. Non-profit-making organisations also run general interest courses and many employers and professional associations provide training.

In 1973/74 registration in school board classes reached 1,280,228. In the same year 107,883 people were taking provincial department of education correspondence courses. Schools now play an important part in adult education, offering evening classes for elementary and secondary school credit courses plus special interest activities. Several provinces provide secondary legal diploma programmes (reduced syllabus) or have a special adult diploma course. All provinces except Ontario and Quebec have a system of tests and examinations by which adults can receive an equivalent of the final high school diploma. Community colleges are and always have been extremely important in adult education, running part time courses and general interest classes, sometimes in partnership with local school boards. Universities are also included in non-credit courses and community development programmes as well as extra-mural courses. At present part time enrolment is increasing rapidly and in 1975/76 there were 213,669 part time students on non-credit courses.

7 EDUCATIONAL ADMINISTRATION

Federal Government

The federal government does not have direct responsibility for the administration of education, except for specific subjects. It runs schools for Indian children through the Department of Indian Affairs and Northern Development, schools for servicemen overseas, and education in prisons. It collects statistics and information on education and disseminates it throughout Canada. Elsewhere its involvement is limited to financial support.

Provincial Governments

Each of the ten provinces runs its own education system, and has its own department of education, though since 1970 there has been a trend towards the foundation of two separate provincial departments, one for post secondary education. Universities, however, are administratively independent. Each of the provincial departments is administered by a deputy minister, who is a civil servant. There are also a chief inspector, local inspectors and directors responsible for specialised aspects of education. A provincial department of education might have sections covering supervision, curriculum, primary education, secondary education, guidance and counselling, educational technology, textbooks and libraries, correspondence and adult education. Provincial responsibilities include inspection, certification of teachers, curricula and selection of textbooks, regulations for teachers. Schools are requested to make regular reports to the provincial department. However, recent changes have seen a lessening in the supervisory work of provincial departments with more autonomy given to school boards. Most provinces operate regional offices of the department in order to localise administration and consultative services.

Local Level

For the purposes of administration all provinces are divided into school districts, each governed by a school board (in Quebec *commission scolaire*) of elected or appointed trustees. The province's education (or school) Act gives it power to determine the number of school boards, number of trustees, and whether they are elected or appointed. In larger school districts there may be a superintendent and even assistant superintendents appointed to assist the board, and in some districts there are specialised boards for different levels of education. The provincial minister delegates certain duties to the trustees. These normally include school building and maintenance, the employment of teachers, and the local school budget. In some provinces there are still denominational school boards.

The Two Territories

The North West Territories Department of Education has, since 1970, administered its own education system. There are two school districts in Yellowknife, the Territories' capital. The Yukon Territory education system is administered by the Yukon Department of Education through a superintendent and staff at Whitehorse. There are no school boards.

8 EDUCATIONAL FINANCE

Education Budget

Canada ranks among the top countries for the amount of national wealth spent on education. In 1977/78 approximately C$16.4 billion was spent on education. The figure for 1978/79 was C$18,660 million and for 1979/80 C$20,170 million.

Sources of Funds

Elementary and secondary schools are financed by municipal property taxes and by provincial funds. Local taxes, which used to contribute the largest share of the revenue, now provide less than a quarter of the total. Provincial governments have steadily increased their grants and are now overall the largest contributors. The revenue from fees and other private sources is now a minor factor in the total budget. Meanwhile the federal government has increased its share from about 5% in 1950/51 to over 20% in 1970. The federal contribution has traditionally taken the form of programmes sponsored by individual departments. However, in an effort to reduce disparities between different provinces the federal government in the 1960s began a system of equalisation payments and also, through the Department of Regional Economic Expansion, offered suppot for special projects, a number of which were in the field of education. The operation of these programmes is still the subject of some controversy and their exact effect on disparities is not easy to determine. Nevertheless there appears to be a growing reliance on the federal government to correct the imbalances which are bound to arise in a federal state, although the machinery for achieving this has not yet been fully developed. Budget procedures have also been adopted within most provinces to assure a minimum standard of service and equalise local taxes. Foundation programmes and guidelines for approved expenditures are used to provide local school boards with essential revenue.

Post Second Level Financing

This is governed by the Federal-Provincial Fiscal Arrangements and Established Programs Financing Act 1977. Previously provinces received 50% of post-secondary operating costs from the federal government; the new system gives the provinces greater freedom in the use of these funds, and provides for a more even distribution among provinces. One part of the federal payment is in the form of a fiscal transfer, and the other part is in the form of a cash payment to each province. In 1977/78 total expenditure on post-secondary education amounted to C$4.6 billion. Universities and colleges receive about 70% of operating costs from federal and provincial governments, 20% from fees, 1.4% from endowments and 8.6% from other sources.

Allocation of Funds
Expenditure on Education: Distribution by Level
Percentage of Expenditure 1977

Pre-school	First Level	Second Level	Third Level	Other
-	-	60.4	26.3	13.3

Grants and Loans

Since 1964 the federal government has guaranteed loans to graduates and undergraduates. Up to C$1,800 per academic year may be borrowed to a total of C$9,800, interest free while the student is enrolled. The student after graduation is expected to repay it within five to ten years. In 1976/77 C$175.1 million was loaned. All provinces administer the federal plan except for Quebec which has its own scheme. There are various bursaries, student assistance schemes etc. at provincial level.

9 DEVELOPMENT AND PLANNING OF THE EDUCATIONAL SYSTEM
Development

The education systems of the provinces of Canada may be said to be based on the systems brought by the immigrants of the nineteenth century - French in Quebec and British in the rest of Canada. From the sixteenth century French literature and philosphy have influenced Canadian educational practice, perhaps especially in the adherence to the classical tradition in the humanities. The Scottish and English contributions came in the sending of well qualified teachers and educators in the early days. The religious orders were the first to establish schools in Canada of which the earliest were founded in Quebec in the early seventeenth century. Protestant missionaries and teachers also founded schools at this time, and itinerant teachers were common. The churches continued to play a significant role in the development of education in Canada. The proliferation of small universities in the Maritimes can be put down to religious rivalry in the early twentieth century. The state school system developed in the eighteenth and nineteenth centuries with individual initiatives from the various provinces. Since confederation in 1867, the ten provinces have been empowered 'exclusively to make laws in relation to education' without federal intervention. The systems have therefore developed independently.

Objectives

Since traditionally education in Canada was influenced by ideas from France and Britain, there was a strong emphasis placed on academic learning with only a few passing through the system to the higher education level. Since World War Two, however, and strongly influenced by ideas from the United States, a more democratic spirit has pervaded Canadian educationtion. The introduction of comprehensive schooling has been symptomatic of this and the social development of children - and adults - is now considered to be equally as important as academic success. With growing unemployment in certain areas of the country concern is now being expressed for education that is 'relevant' or more directly related to employment opportunities than has hitherto been the case. As with many education systems in the western world the Canadian one is undergoing great changes and much rethinking.

10 THE SYSTEM IN OPERATION

In the past decade Canada's administrators in the field of education have become increasingly aware of the need for young people to receive the type of education that will prepare them for their future careers; for professional, technological and cultural education to be diversified and of a high standard and for the provision of equal educational opportunity for each individual regardless of socio-economic status, sex, ethnicity or location. The necessity of assuring equality of opportunity and of providing diversified programmes has led education planners to offer a wide choice of courses at all levels of education. At the post-secondary non-university level, a proliferation of new structures has evolved. The most innovative type of institution that has emerged recently is undoubtedly the 'community college'. Further changes in Canadian education have been brought about by the interest and ability of students in different subjects. This has resulted in a drastic revision of policies to include non-graded systems, subject promotion, changes in methods of examination and the extension of guidance facilities.

During the 1960s, Canadians showed a deep commitment to education. They attended schools and universities in greater numbers and they more than quadrupled their spending on educational budgets. Moreover there were indications that they had begun to realise that education is not a brief experience concentrated in childhood and youth but a lifelong process, and that, in modern times, it cannot be reserved for a privileged elite but must be made accessible to everyone. These two principles are now widely recognised and educational policies, structures and administration are being adapted accordingly. To meet the growing demand for lifelong education, new emphasis is being placed on early childhood and adult education, both of which have usually been considered marginal activities in the educational systems.

Throughout the world, the priority given to education is very different now from what it was after World War Two, or even in 1960. What is even more significant, however, is that the scope and spirit of education have also changed. The depth of this revolution is well described in the report of Unesco's International Commission on the Development of Education, which recommended that the essential elements of reform on which concrete work should begin in the 1970s were:

(i) the concept of education limited in time (to school age) and confined in space (to school buildings) must be superseded
(ii) closed educational systems must be made open
(iii) special attention should be paid to fostering education for pre-school children by selecting and cultivating the most positive forms of family and community associations in this work

(iv)   general education and technical training should be reconciled
(v)   there should be more diversified higher education institutions
(vi)   education should be individualised and personalised to the utmost and constitute a preparation for self-learning
(vii) educational management should be democratised.

Educational leaders in Canada appear to be in sympathy with these objectives and concepts and are moving slowly toward their attainment; and, in education, it is less important to move swiftly than it is to move in the right direction.

Provincial Education Systems

Newfoundland

Until recently education in Newfoundland was denominational; some denominations still operate their own schools, e.g. Roman Catholic, Pentecostal, Seventh Day Adventist.

Pre-primary education is not compulsory, but most five-year olds attend kindergarten.

There are two basic patterns:

(i)   elementary school (kindergarten and grades 1-6) and central high school (grades 7-11)
(ii) elementary school (kindergarten and grades 1-8) and regional high school (grades 9-11)

There are some junior high schools (grades 7-9) and district vocational schools.

Prince Edward Island

Kindergarten classes are not provided though there is some private provision.

The educational pattern consists of: elementary school (grades 1-6), junior high school (grades 7-9) and senior high school (grades 9-12).

About 30% of elementary and secondary pupils are taught in French.

Nova Scotia

Nearly all five-year olds are accommodated in publicly operated kindergarten classes.

The basic pattern is: elementary school (pre-primary and grades 1-6), junior high school (grades 7-9) and senior high school (grades 10-12). There are also some high schools offering grades 7-12, and some primary schools to grade 9 with high school grades 10-12. High school graduation is either at grade 11 (junior matriculation) or grade 12 (senior matriculation).

New Brunswick

There are no publicly operated pre-primary classes.
There are two basic patterns:

(i) elementary school (grades 1-6), junior high school (grades 7-9) and senior high school (grades 10-12)
(ii) elementary school (grades 1-6) and high school (grades 7-12).

About 35% of pupils in primary and secondary schools are taught in French.

Quebec

Kindergarten for five-year olds is now part of the education system.
The rest of the pattern consists of: elementary school (six-year course from age 6), secondary school (five-year course - grades 7-11). Two years' attendance at CEGEP (grades 12-13) is necessary for university entrance. Four CEGEPs are English medium.

Ontario

Ontario has a 13-grade education system with pre-school provision. There are two main educational patterns:

(i) elementary school (pre-primary and grades 1-8) and secondary school (grades 9-13)
(ii) elementary school (pre-primary and grades 1-6), junior high school (grades 7-9) and senior high school (grades 10-13).

Manitoba

Public kindergarten classes are included in most elementary schools.
There are two main patterns of organisation:

(i) elementary school (pre-primary and grades 1-8), and high school (grades 9-12)
(ii) elementary (pre-primary and grades 1-6), junior high school (grades 7-9) and senior high school (grades 10-12).

Saskatchewan

Kindergarten is not compulsory and public classes tend to be found only in large centres.
The traditional 12 grades of schooling have been replaced by four divisions each consisting of three years.

Alberta

Kindergarten classes are not compulsory though some local authorities do provide them. There are also privately operated pre-primary institutions.

The two main educational patterns are as follows:

(i) elementary school (grades 1-6), junior high school (grades 7-9) and senior high school (grades 10-12)
(ii) elementary school (grades 1-8) and high school grades 9-12).

British Columbia

The predominant educational pattern consists of: elementary school (grades 1-6), junior school (grades 7-9) and senior high school (grades 10-12).

FURTHER READING

Belanger, Pierre (1970). *Ecole et sociéte au Québec.* HMH.
Burton, A. P. (1972). *The Horn and the Beanstalk: problems and possibilities in Canadian Education.* Holt, Rinehart and Winston.
Gayfer, M. (1978). *An Overview of Canadian Education.* Canadian Education Association.
Katz, Joseph (1974). *Education in Canada.* David & Charles.
McGill University (1969). *The University and Society.* McGill-Queen's Press.
Lloyds Bank Economic Review (1979). *Canada.* June, 1979.
Mathews, Robin (1969). *The Struggle for Canadian Universities.* New Press.
Munroe, D. (1974). *The Organisation and Administration of Education in Canada.* Information Canada.
Ostry, Sylvia (1972). *Canadian Higher Education in the Seventies.* Information Canada.
Pke, R. M. (1971). *Who doesn't get to University and Why.* AUCC.
Statistics Canada (1977). *Canada Handbook.* September, 1977.
Statistics Canada (annual). *Canada Year Book.* Contains a good chapter on education in Canada.
Statistics Canada (annual). *Education in Canada.* Contains full educational statistics.
Walmsley, N. E. (1970). *Canadian Universities and International Development.* AUCC.
Wilson, T. D. (1970). *Canadian Education: a history.* Prentice-Hall.

Newfoundland

Rowe, F. W. (1964). *The Development of Education in Newfoundland.* The Ryerson Press, Toronto.

Report of the Royal Commission on Education and Youth. (Warren, 1967-68), Government of Newfoundland, St John's.
Legislation passed 1968 and 1969 Relating to the Reorganisation of Education and Statement by Hon. F. W. Rowe, Ministry of Education. Queen's Printer, St John's.

Prince Edward Island

Report of the Commission on Educational Finance and Related Problems in Administration. (Lazerte, 1960). Queen's Printer, Charlottetown.
Report of the Commission on Higher Education. (Bonnell, 1965). Queen's Printer, Charlottetown.
Report of the Commission on Post-Secondary Education. (Sheffield, 1969). Queen's Printer, Charlottetown.
Department of Education. *Annual Reports.* Queen's Printer, Charlottetown.

Nova Scotia

Royal Commission on Public School Finance. (Pottier, 1954). Queen's Printer, Halifax.
University Grants Committee (1964). *Survey Report.* Queen's Printer, Halifax.
Tribunal on Bilingual Higher Education (1969). *All Eyes Toward the Future.* Queen's Printer, Halifax.
University Grants Committee. *Annual Reports.* Queen's Printer, Halifax.
Department of Education (1972-73). *Programme of Studies in the Schools of Nova Scotia.* Queen's Printer, Halifax.
Department of Education (1970). *Amalgamation of School Boards.* Queen's Printer, Halifax.
Department of Education. *Atlantic Institute of Education.* Queen's Printer, Halifax.

New Brunswick

Report of the Royal Commission on Higher Education. (Deutsch, 1962). Queen's Printer, Fredericton.
Report of the Royal Commission on Finance and Municipal Taxation. (Byrne, 1963). Queen's Printer, Fredericton.
Higher Education Commission (1969). *Investing in the Future, a programme for government assistance to universities, technical schools and their students.* Queen's Printer, Fredericton.
Department of Education (1969). *The Organisation of Instruction for New Brunswick Schools* (revised 1972). Three volumes. Contents: Vol.1 - Elementary Education; Vol. 2 - Junior High School Programmes; Vol. 3 - Senior High School Programmes. Queen's Printer, Fredericton.
Department of Education. *Annual Reports.* Queen's Printer, Fredericton.

Quebec

Report of the Royal Commission of Enquiry on Education in the Province of Quebec. (1963-66). 5 volumes, Commission Parent, Queen's Printer, Quebec.
Department of Education (1966). Bulletin, Document 1: *Associated and Private Institutions*.
Department of Education (1966). Bulletin, Document 2: *The Cooperative School*.
Department of Education (1968). Bulletin, Document 3: *College Educations and the General and Vocational Colleges*.
CEGEP (1973). *Programmes and List of Colleges*. Quebec.
Department of Education (1971). *Education in Quebec*. Queen's Printer, Quebec.
Superior Council of Education (1964-65). *Participation in Educational Planning*. Queen's Printer, Quebec.
Superior Council of Education (1965-66, 1966-67). *The Teacher Faces Social and Educational Change*. Queen's Printer, Quebec.
Superior Council of Education (1972). *3rd Annual Report*. Queen's Printer, Quebec.
Department of Education, Information Services. *Education Quebec*. (French only).

Ontario

Harris, Robin S. (1967). *Quiet Evolution. A Study of the Educational System of Ontario*. University of Toronto Press, Toronto.
Committee of Presidents of Universities in Ontario (1971). *Towards 2000, the Future of Post-secondary Education in Ontario: Brief to the Commission on Post-secondary Education in Ontario*. McClelland & Stewart, Toronto.
Fleming, William G. (1972). *Education: Ontario's Preoccupation*. University of Toronto Press, Toronto.
Report of the Royal Commission on Education (Hope, 1950). King's Printer, Toronto.
Department of Education (1968). *Living and Learning: Report of the Provincial Committee on Aims and Objectives of Education in Ontario*. Newton Publishing Company, Toronto.
Commission on Post-secondary Education in Ontario (1972). *The Learning Society*. Ministry of Government Services, Toronto.
Ministry of Education. *Annual Reports*. Queen's Printer, Toronto.
Ministry of Colleges and Universities. *Annual Reports*. Queen's Printer, Toronto.
Ministry of Education. *New Dimensions*. Ten issues per year. Toronto.
Ministry of Education. *Ontario Department of Education News*. Internal Quarterly, Toronto.

Manitoba

Report of the Manitoba Royal Commission on Education (Macfarlane, 1959). Queen's Printer, Winnipeg.

Department of Youth and Education (1970-71). *Annual Report*. Queen's Printer, Winnipeg.

Saskatchewan

Report No. 6, Royal Commission on Agriculture and Rural Life. (1956). Queen's Printer, Regina.
Department of Education. *Annual Report*. Queen's Printer, Regina.

Alberta

Commission on Educational Planning (1972). *A Future of Choices: A Choice of Futures*. Queen's Printer, Edmonton.
Department of Education (1971). *Annual Report*. Queen's Printer, Edmonton.

British Columbia

Johnson, F. Henry (1964). *A History of Public Education in British Columbia*. University of British Columbia Publications Centre, Vancouver.
Report of the Commission of Enquiry on Education. (Chant, 1960). Queen's Printer, Victoria.
Department of Education (1972). *100 Years of Public Education in British Columbia*. Queen's Printer, Victoria.

Structure of the Education System in Canada

Age	3	4	5	6	7	8	9	10	11	12	13	14	15	16	17	18	19	20	21	22	23	24
Level				I									II									
Stage				1									2				3					
Compulsory																						
School Type	(a) Playschools / (b) Nurseries / (c) Kindergartens			Elementary									Comprehensive schools				Universities / Colleges / Technical institutes / Trade schools / Community colleges / Open learning centres					

Education preceding the first level

Source: UNESCO/IBE International Yearbook of Education

CHART 1
*NEWFOUNDLAND
DEPARTMENT OF EDUCATION*

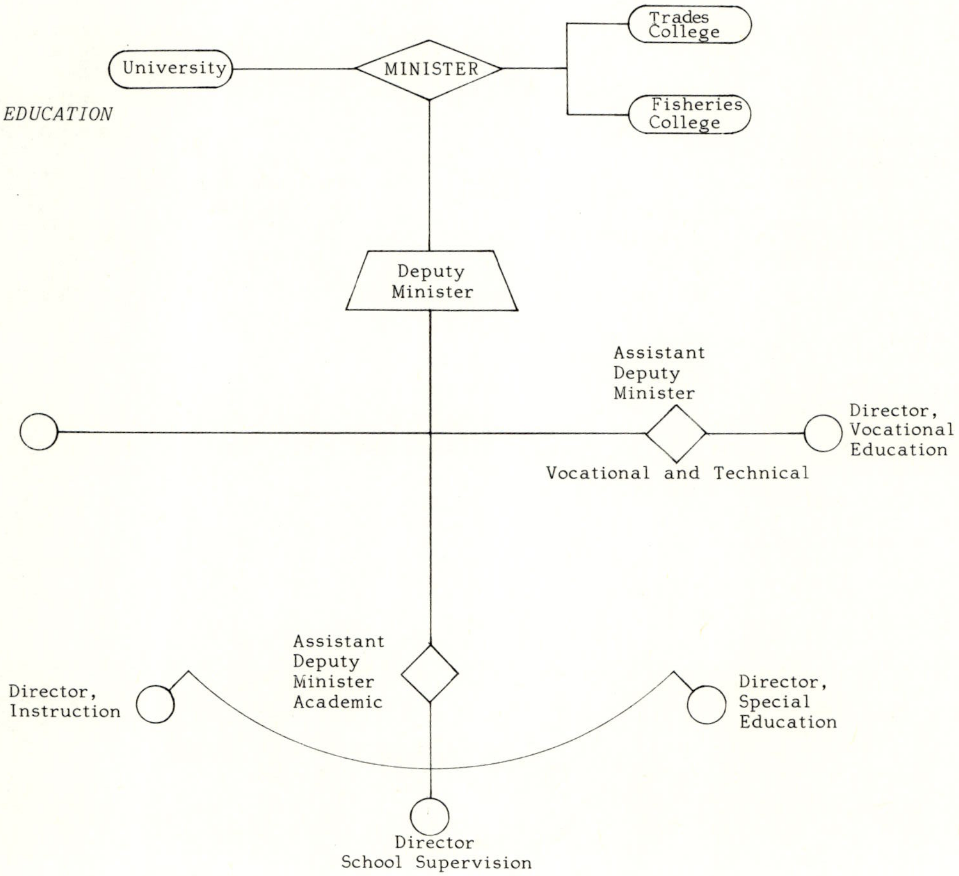

CHART 2
PRINCE EDWARD ISLAND
DEPARTMENT OF EDUCATION

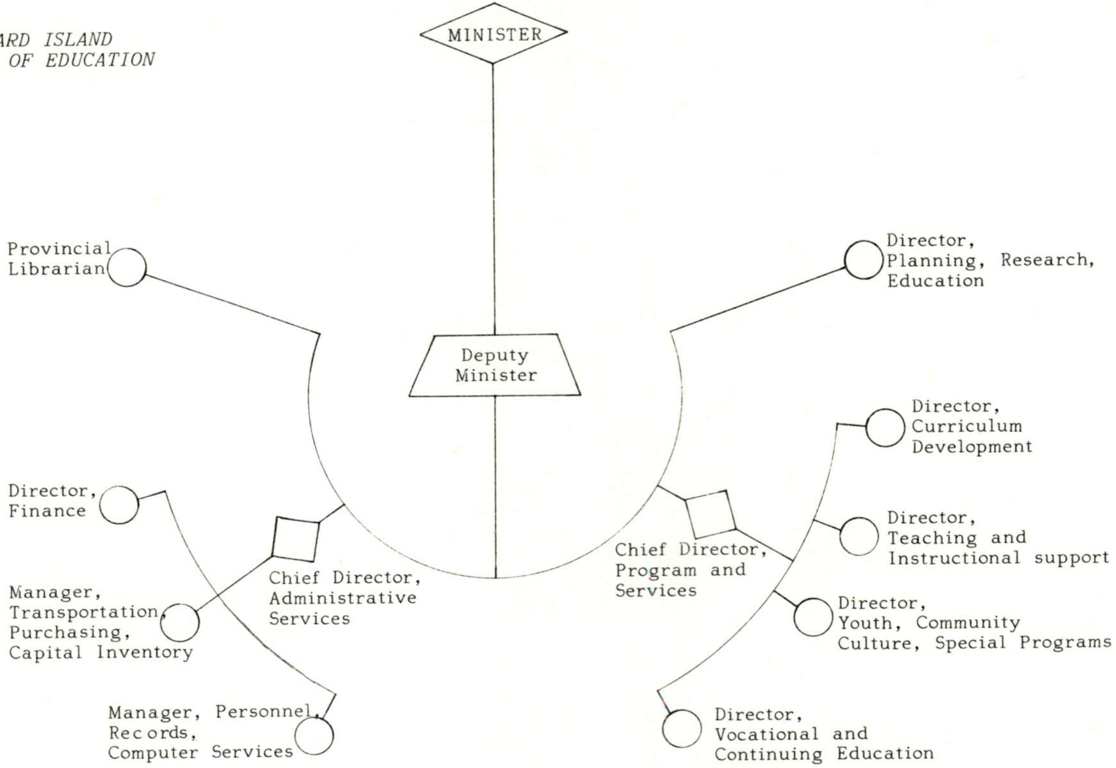

MINISTER

Deputy Minister

Chief Director, Program and Services
- Director, Planning, Research, Education
- Director, Curriculum Development
- Director, Teaching and Instructional support
- Director, Youth, Community Culture, Special Programs
- Director, Vocational and Continuing Education

Chief Director, Administrative Services
- Provincial Librarian
- Director, Finance
- Manager, Transportation, Purchasing, Capital Inventory
- Manager, Personnel Records, Computer Services

CHART 3
NOVA SCOTIA
DEPARTMENT OF EDUCATION

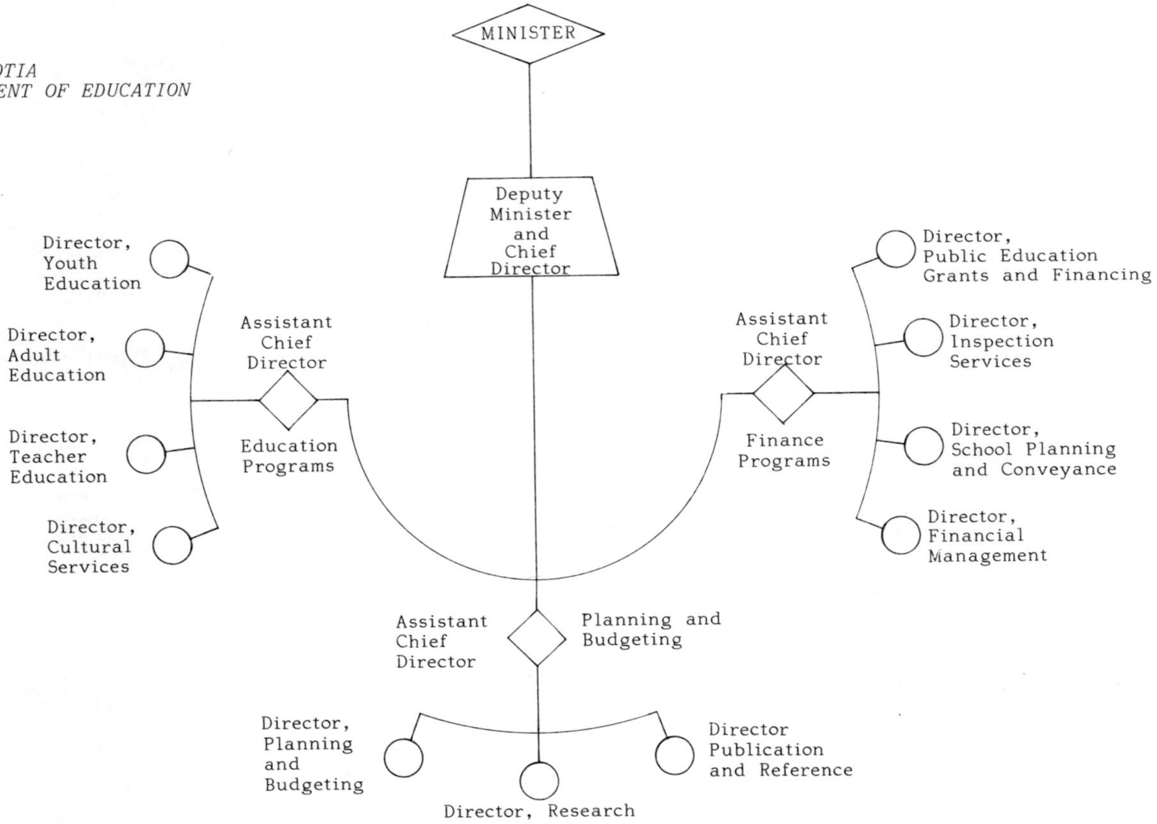

MINISTER

Deputy Minister and Chief Director

Assistant Chief Director — Finance Programs
- Director, Public Education Grants and Financing
- Director, Inspection Services
- Director, School Planning and Conveyance
- Director, Financial Management

Assistant Chief Director — Education Programs
- Director, Youth Education
- Director, Adult Education
- Director, Teacher Education
- Director, Cultural Services

Assistant Chief Director — Planning and Budgeting
- Director Publication and Reference
- Director, Research
- Director, Planning and Budgeting

CHART 4
NEW BRUNSWICK DEPARTMENT OF EDUCATION

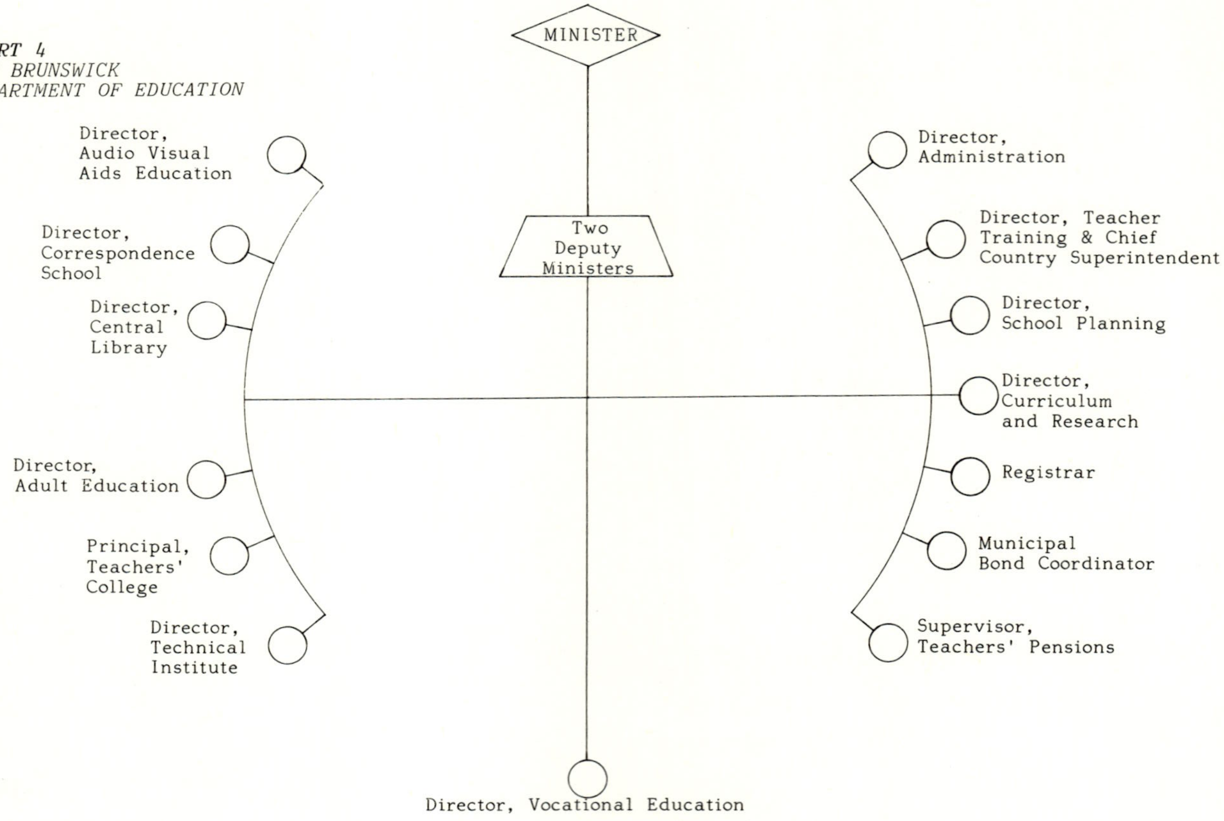

MINISTER

Two Deputy Ministers

- Director, Administration
- Director, Teacher Training & Chief Country Superintendent
- Director, School Planning
- Director, Curriculum and Research
- Registrar
- Municipal Bond Coordinator
- Supervisor, Teachers' Pensions

- Director, Audio Visual Aids Education
- Director, Correspondence School
- Director, Central Library
- Director, Adult Education
- Principal, Teachers' College
- Director, Technical Institute

Director, Vocational Education

133

MINISTER —— (Superior Council of Education)

Deputy Minister

Associate Deputy Minister (Protestant)

Associate Deputy Minister (Catholic)

Planning
Finance
Building and Equipment
Regional Bureaus

Assistant Deputy Minister
Assistant Deputy Minister
Assistant Deputy Minister
Assistant Deputy Minister

Elementary Secondary Education
College Education
Higher Education
Continuing Education
Private Institutions

CHART 5
QUEBEC DEPARTMENT OF EDUCATION

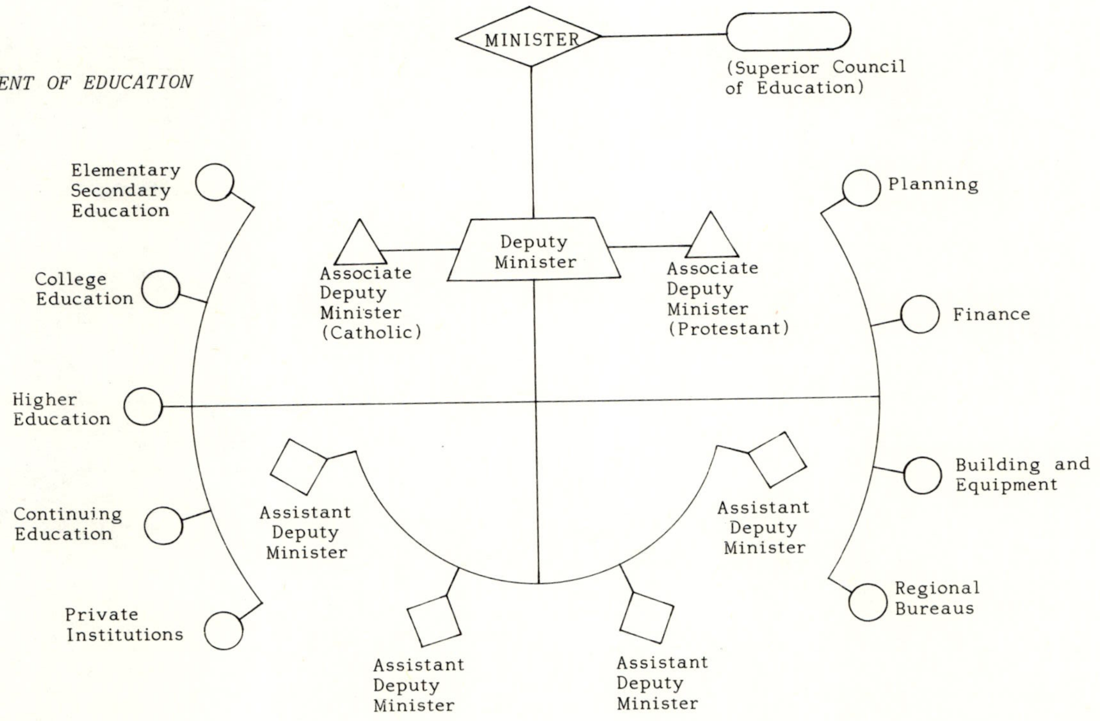

CHART 6
QUEBEC
DIVISION OF RESPONSIBILITIES
FOR EDUCATION

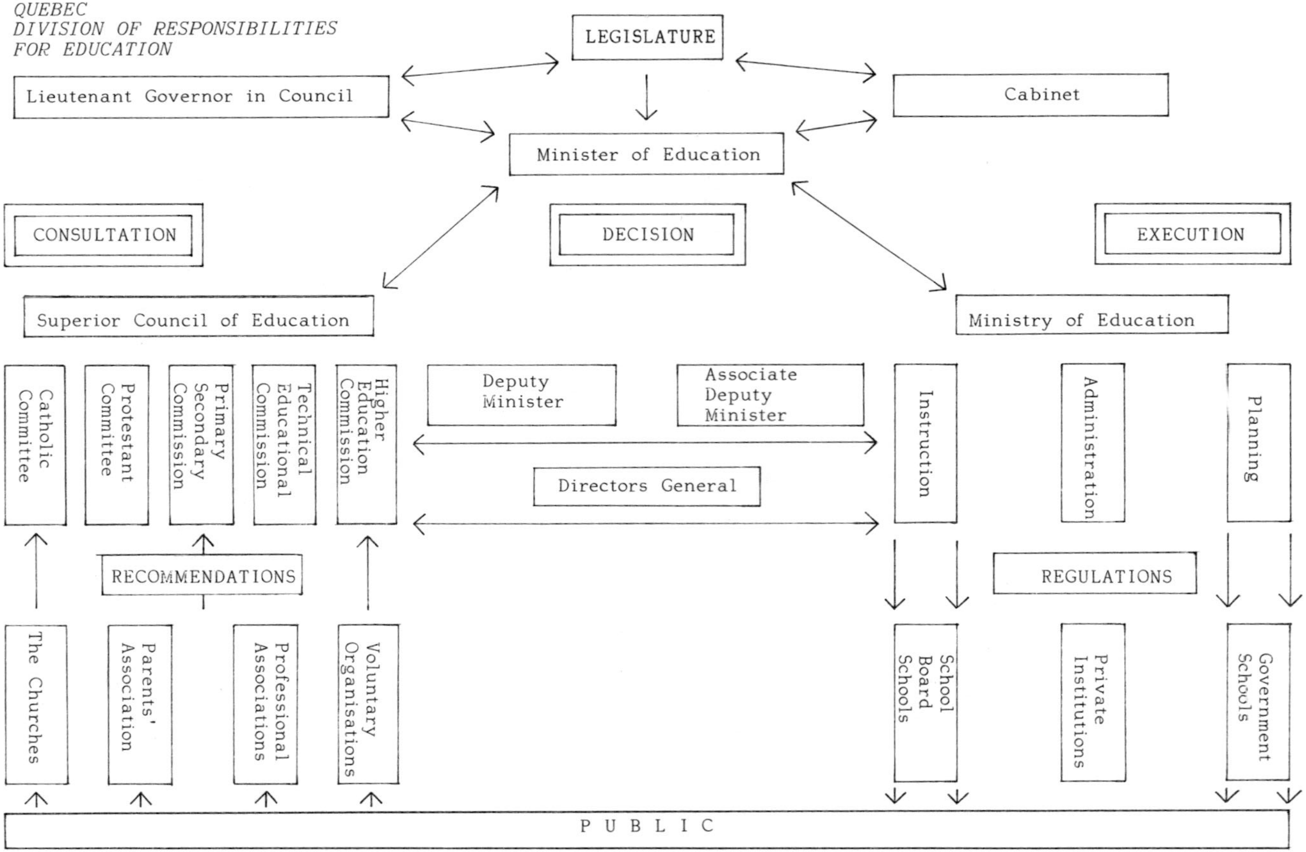

CHART 7
ONTARIO
MINISTRY OF EDUCATION

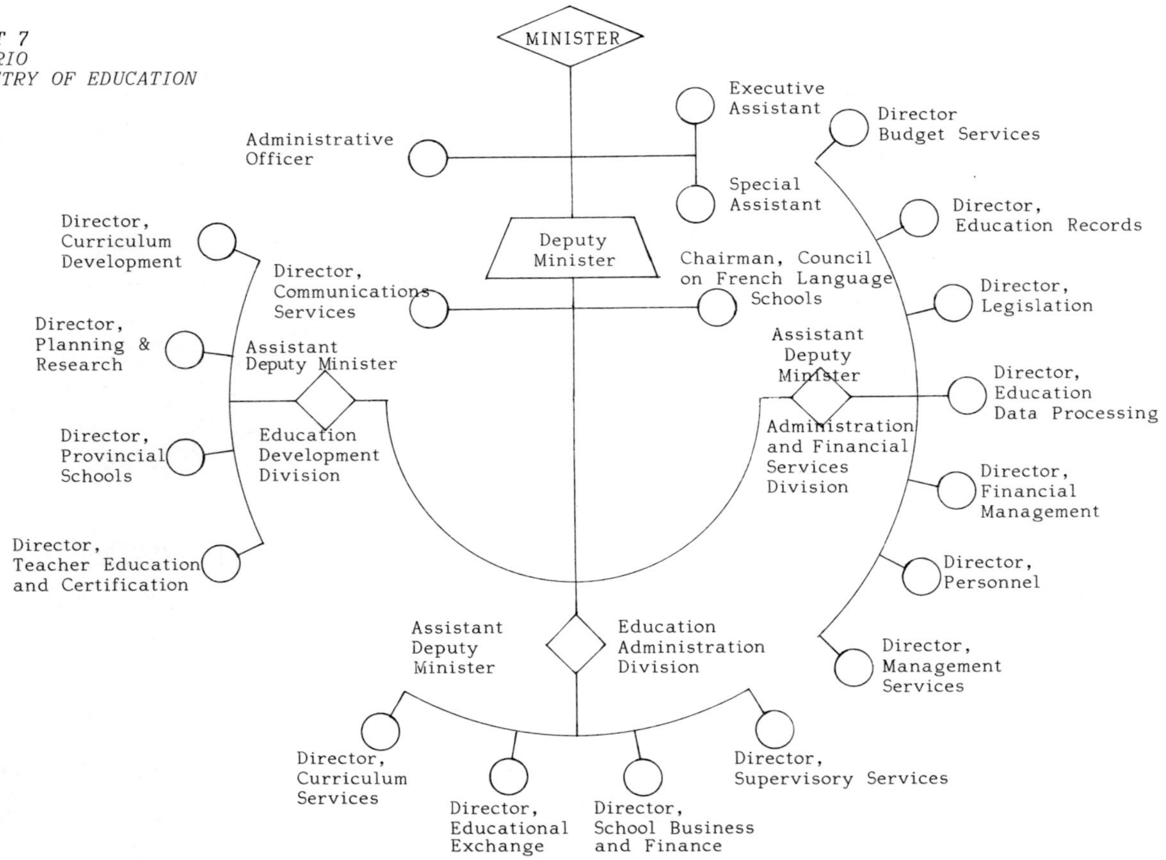

MINISTER

Executive Assistant
Special Assistant
Administrative Officer

Deputy Minister

Director, Budget Services
Director, Education Records
Director, Legislation
Director, Education Data Processing
Director, Financial Management
Director, Personnel
Director, Management Services

Chairman, Council on French Language Schools
Assistant Deputy Minister
Administration and Financial Services Division

Director, Supervisory Services
Director, School Business and Finance
Director, Educational Exchange
Director, Curriculum Services

Assistant Deputy Minister
Education Administration Division

Director, Communications Services
Assistant Deputy Minister
Education Development Division

Director, Curriculum Development
Director, Planning & Research
Director, Provincial Schools
Director, Teacher Education and Certification

135

CHART 8
ONTARIO
MINISTRY OF COLLEGES AND UNIVERSITIES

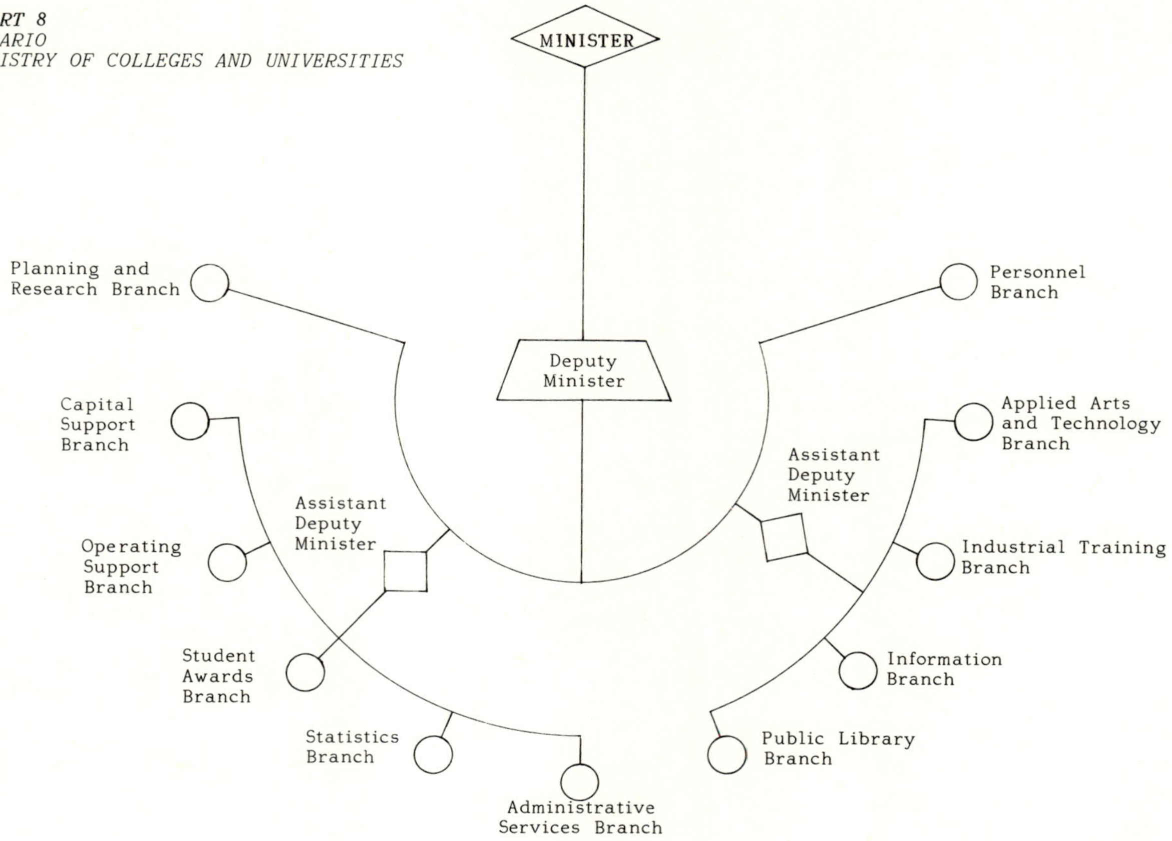

MINISTER

Deputy Minister

Assistant Deputy Minister
- Personnel Branch
- Applied Arts and Technology Branch
- Industrial Training Branch
- Information Branch
- Public Library Branch

Assistant Deputy Minister
- Planning and Research Branch
- Capital Support Branch
- Operating Support Branch
- Student Awards Branch
- Statistics Branch
- Administrative Services Branch

137

CHART 9
MANITOBA
DEPARTMENT OF EDUCATION

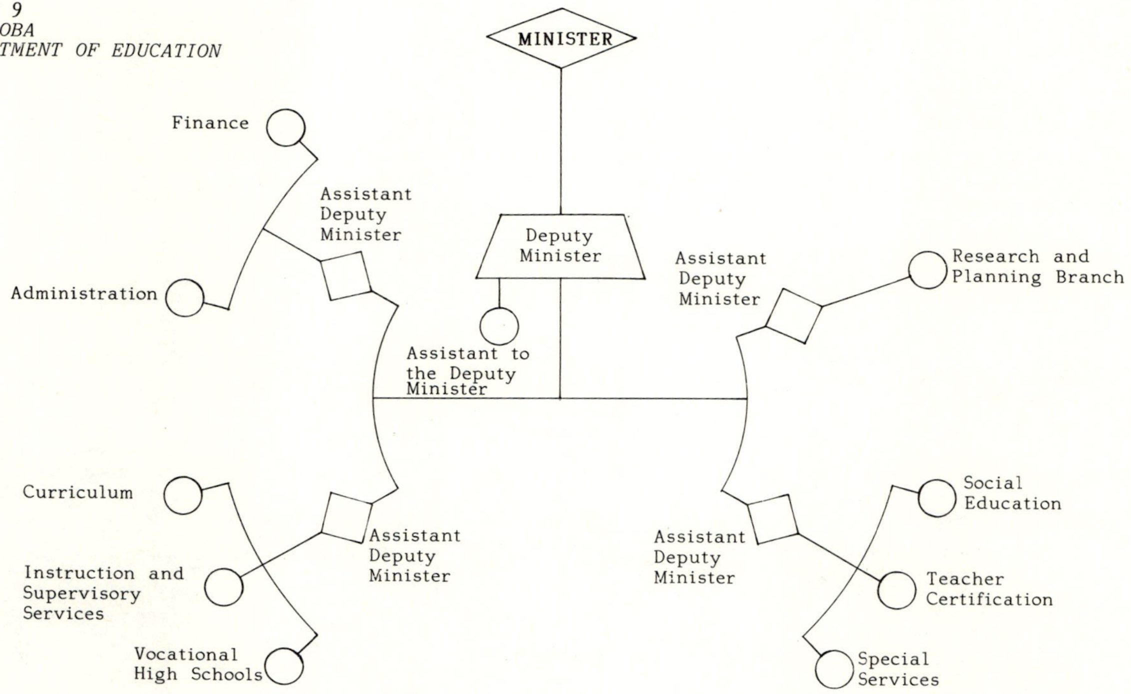

MINISTER

Deputy Minister

Assistant to the Deputy Minister

Assistant Deputy Minister
- Research and Planning Branch

Assistant Deputy Minister
- Social Education
- Teacher Certification
- Special Services

Assistant Deputy Minister
- Finance
- Administration

Assistant Deputy Minister
- Curriculum
- Instruction and Supervisory Services
- Vocational High Schools

138

CHART 10
MANITOBA
DEPARTMENT OF COLLEGES
AND UNIVERSITIES AFFAIRS

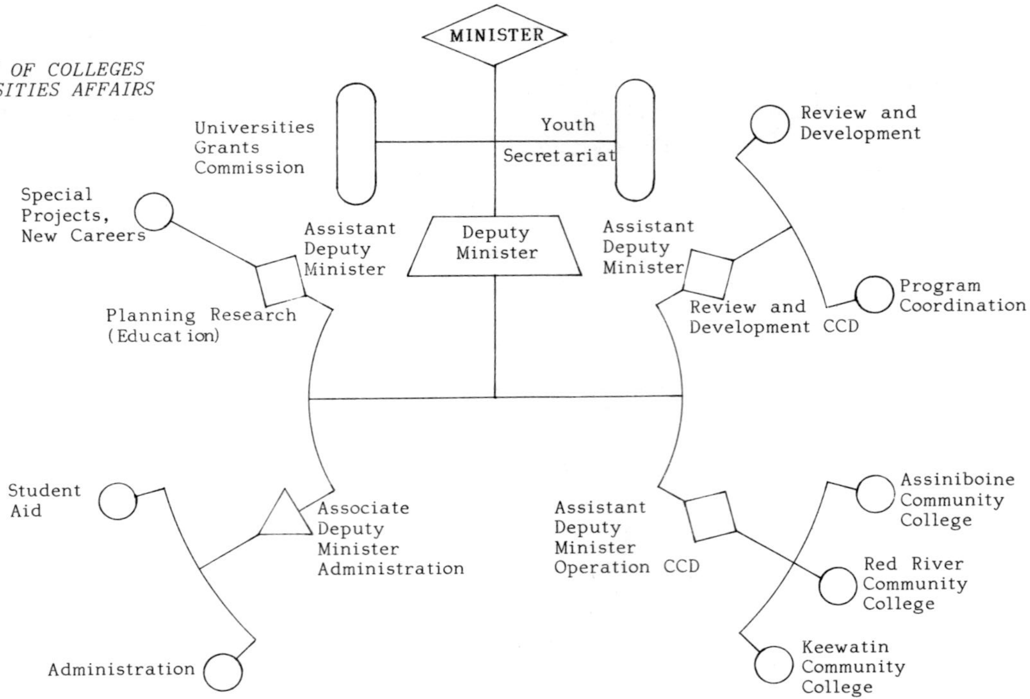

- Review and Development
- Program Coordination
- Assiniboine Community College
- Red River Community College
- Keewatin Community College
- Review and Development CCD
- Assistant Deputy Minister
- Assistant Deputy Minister Operation CCD
- MINISTER
- Youth Secretariat
- Deputy Minister
- Universities Grants Commission
- Assistant Deputy Minister
- Associate Deputy Minister Administration
- Special Projects, New Careers
- Planning Research (Education)
- Student Aid
- Administration

CHART 11
SASKATCHEWAN
DEPARTMENT OF EDUCATION

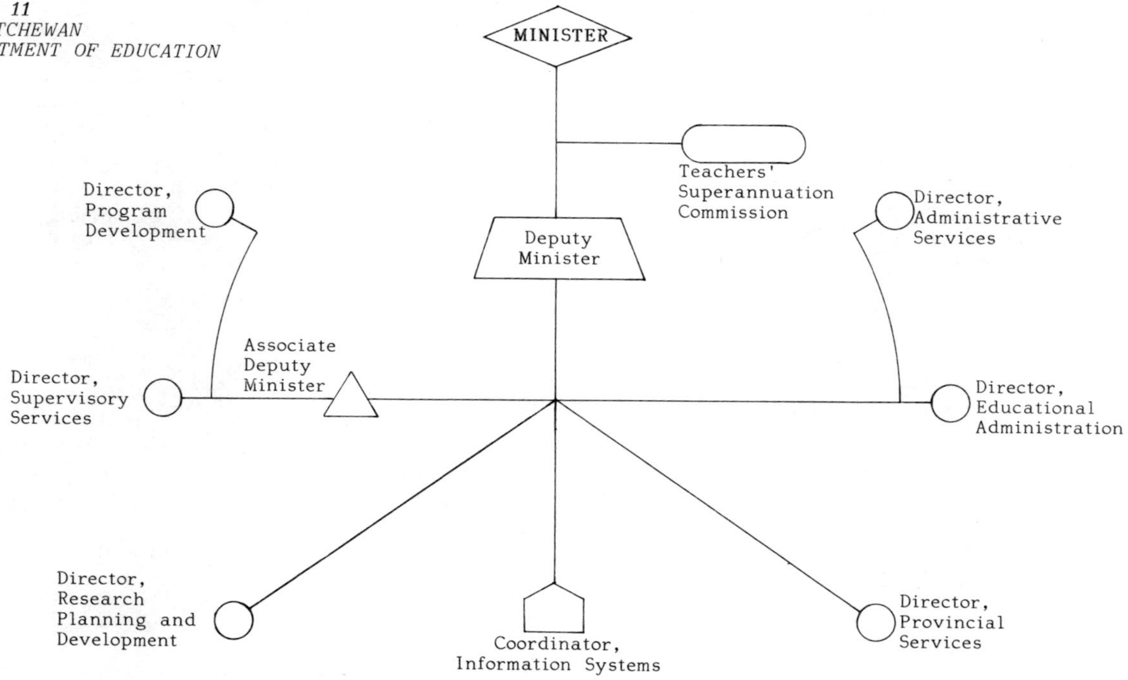

MINISTER

Teachers' Superannuation Commission

Deputy Minister

Director, Administrative Services

Director, Educational Administration

Director, Provincial Services

Coordinator, Information Systems

Associate Deputy Minister

Director, Program Development

Director, Supervisory Services

Director, Research Planning and Development

139

140

CHART 12
SASKATCHEWAN
DEPARTMENT OF CONTINUING EDUCATION

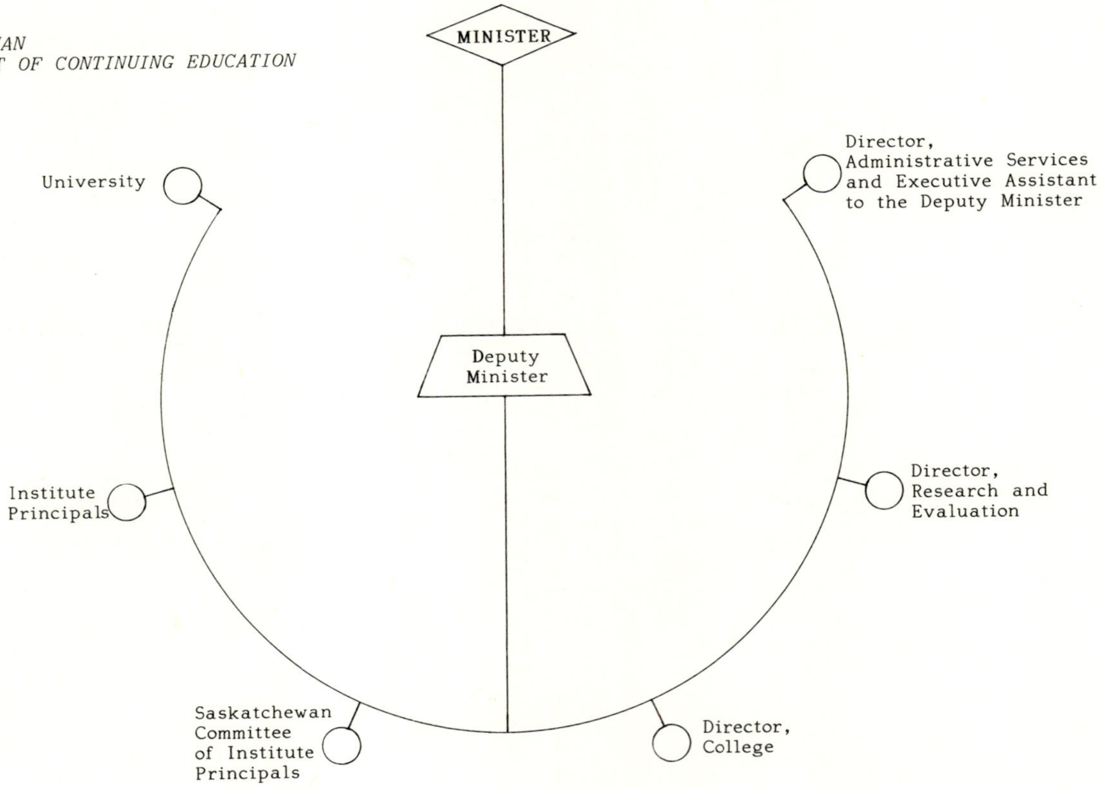

MINISTER

Deputy Minister

Director, Administrative Services and Executive Assistant to the Deputy Minister

Director, Research and Evaluation

Director, College

Saskatchewan Committee of Institute Principals

Institute Principals

University

141

CHART 13
ALBERTA
DEPARTMENT OF EDUCATION

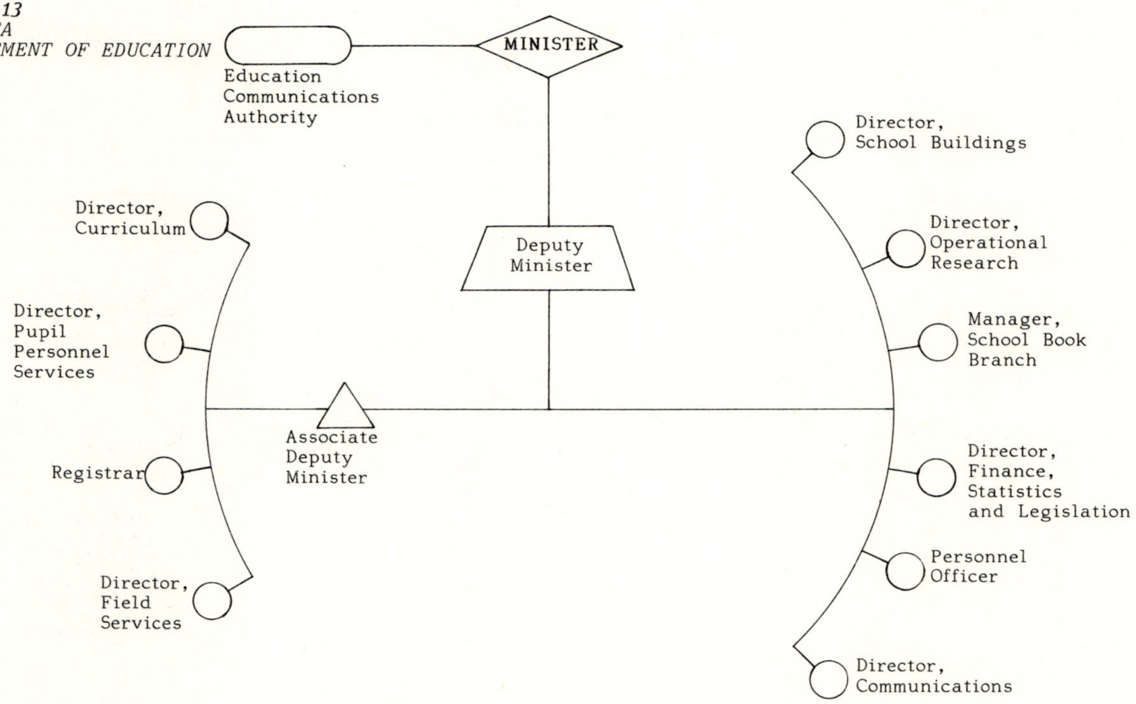

MINISTER

Education Communications Authority

Deputy Minister

Director, School Buildings
Director, Operational Research
Manager, School Book Branch
Director, Finance, Statistics and Legislation
Personnel Officer
Director, Communications

Associate Deputy Minister

Director, Curriculum
Director, Pupil Personnel Services
Registrar
Director, Field Services

CHART 14
ALBERTA
DEPARTMENT OF
ADVANCED EDUCATION

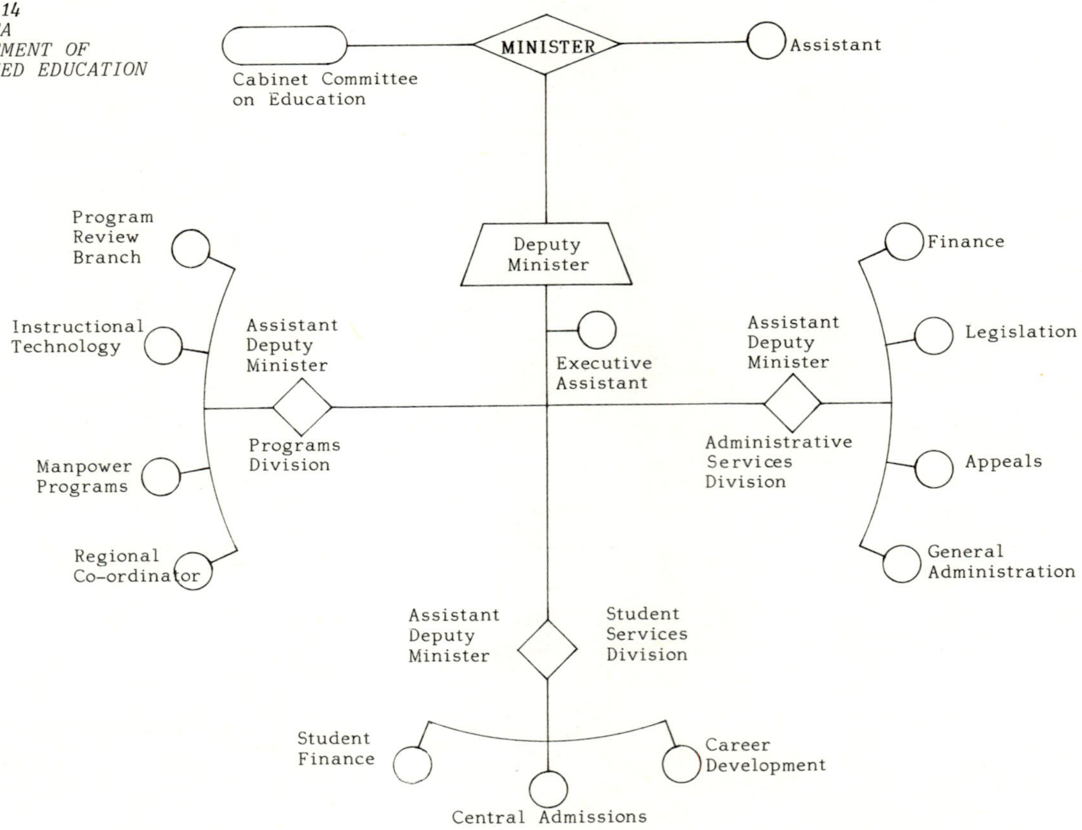

MINISTER
— Assistant
— Cabinet Committee on Education

Deputy Minister
— Executive Assistant

Administrative Services Division — Assistant Deputy Minister
- Finance
- Legislation
- Appeals
- General Administration

Programs Division — Assistant Deputy Minister
- Program Review Branch
- Instructional Technology
- Manpower Programs
- Regional Co-ordinator

Student Services Division — Assistant Deputy Minister
- Career Development
- Central Admissions
- Student Finance

CHART 15
BRITISH COLUMBIA
DEPARTMENT OF EDUCATION

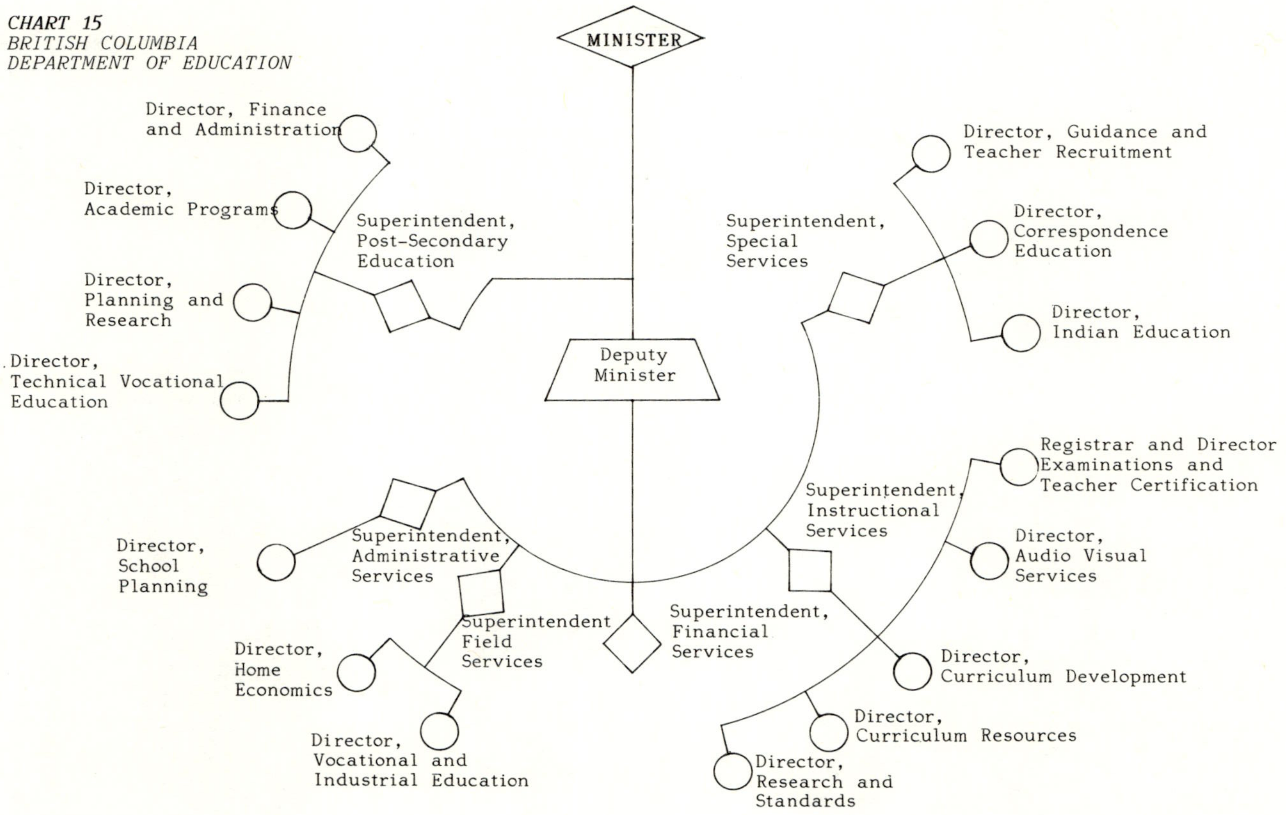

MINISTER

Deputy Minister

Superintendent, Special Services
- Director, Guidance and Teacher Recruitment
- Director, Correspondence Education
- Director, Indian Education

Superintendent, Instructional Services
- Registrar and Director Examinations and Teacher Certification
- Director, Audio Visual Services
- Director, Curriculum Development
- Director, Curriculum Resources
- Director, Research and Standards

Superintendent, Financial Services

Superintendent, Field Services

Superintendent, Administrative Services
- Director, Home Economics
- Director, Vocational and Industrial Education
- Director, School Planning

Superintendent, Post-Secondary Education
- Director, Finance and Administration
- Director, Academic Programs
- Director, Planning and Research
- Director, Technical Vocational Education

143

Cyprus

CONTENTS

1 Geography 146
2 Population 148
3 Society and Culture 149
4 History and Politics 150
5 The Economy 152
6 The Education System 153
7 Educational Administration 158
8 Educational Finance 161
9 Development and Planning of the Educational System 162
10 The System in Operation 164

Since 1945 the history of education in Cyprus has been dominated first by the struggle for independence from the British and secondly by the Turkish invasion and virtual partition of the island in 1974.

The Greek Cypriots' claim for independence was associated with a call for 'union with Greece'. The campaign involved school children and teachers. Proposals to Hellenise the content of education and to weaken the position of English and UK approaches to the curricula, organisation and examinations were legitimised by this political slogan. After independence working agreements between the two communities and the constitution placed education in the hands of two Offices of Education. The assumption by the Greek Office of the title Ministry of Education left the position of the Turkish office unclear. After the invasion of 1974 a Turkish Federated State of Cyprus was declared in 1976 and the separation of the two communities became a reality and cooperation between the two Offices of Education has been extremely limited. Official reports, such as that submitted to the International Bureau of Education in Geneva virtually describe the Greek Cypriot system. The Turkish system is, however, similar in many respects.

The mandate of the UN Peace Keeping Force in Cyprus (UNFICYP) was renamed on 13 June 1980. Since 1974 attempts to reach a settlement have been made through intercommunal talks. Education was one of the issues discussed but until such time as an overall settlement is reached it is likely that the two systems of education will remain in the hands of the two communities.

In the Greek Cypriot system there is evidence to suggest that the re-introduction of some elements in the British inspired pre-independence system are favoured in some quarters. Parents are anxious that their children should learn an international language, English. Although the creation of a university has been discussed most Greek Cypriots must travel abroad for degree courses either to Greece, Britain or the USA. A sound knowledge of English is consequently useful to them both academically and economically in view of the tourism and the growth of manufacturing industry.

The Editor

1 GEOGRAPHY

Topography

Cyprus is the third largest island in the Mediterranean and lies at the easternmost end, 70 km (40 miles) south of Turkey, 100 km (60 miles) west of Syria and not much further north west from Lebanon and Israel. It is 224 km long (of which 80 km is the narrow eastern Karpass peninsula) and 96 km wide at its broadest. The area is 9,144 square kilometres (3,572 square miles) and there is 777 km of indented and rocky coastline which includes many sheltered bays and sandy beaches. There are only seasonal rivers.

The island can be divided into five natural regions:

(i) the Northern Range (forest and scrub), rising to 3,000 feet
(ii) the Troodos Massif (also forested), rising to 6,000 feet
(iii) the fertile central plain - usually called the *Mesaoria* - which extends right across the island between the mountain ranges a few hundred feet above sea level
(iv) the southern slopes
(v) the coastal plains.

Climate

The climate (mountains excepted) consists of a mild winter, a short spring accompanied by rain, and a dry hot summer and autumn during which temperatures over 38°C are frequently maintained. As a result of the low rainfall, water supply is a chronic problem. For eight months of the year the countryside is brown and barren; during July and August the intense heat of the plains slows down human activity. Snow falls on the south western mountains between January and March.

Communications

Communications throughout the country are excellent. There are no railways but there is a comprehensive network of tarred

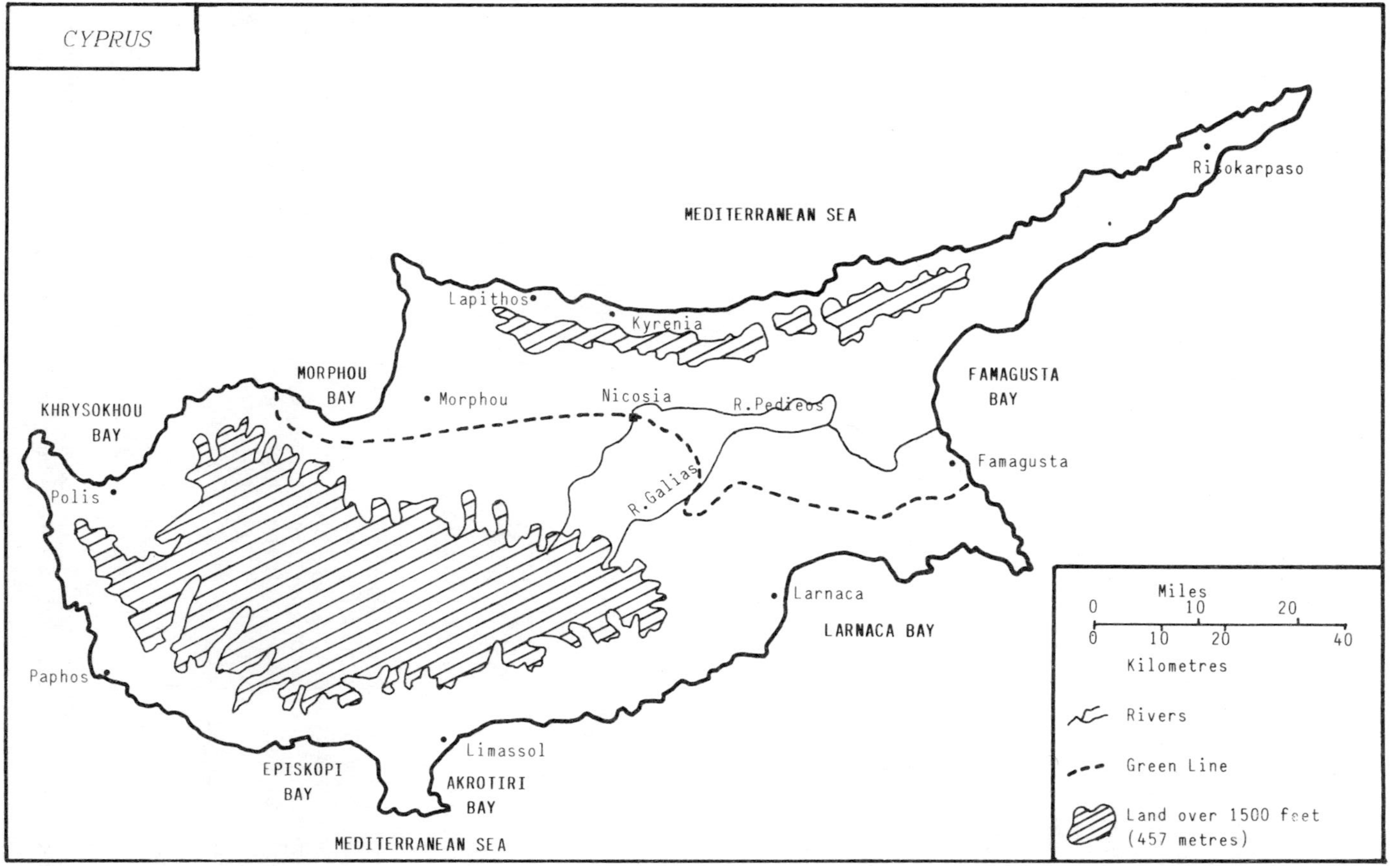
CYPRUS
MEDITERRANEAN SEA
Risokarpaso
Lapithos
Kyrenia
MORPHOU BAY
Morphou
Nicosia
R.Pedieos
FAMAGUSTA BAY
Famagusta
KHRYSOKHOU BAY
Polis
R.Galias
Larnaca
LARNACA BAY
Paphos
Limassol
EPISKOPI BAY
AKROTIRI BAY
MEDITERRANEAN SEA
Miles
0 10 20
0 10 20 40
Kilometres
Rivers
Green Line
Land over 1500 feet (457 metres)

roads which reach to all but a handful of small villages. Main roads between the towns are good, though not all are usable because of the presence of the Turkish military. Roads in the Troodos Massif are blocked by snow at times during the winter but clearance is regular. Outside communication is easy physically but difficult politically: those needing access to the government controlled part of the island may not use any of the illegal ports of entry, including the hydrofoil service between Kyrenia and Turkey and the air service between Ercan (Tymbou) and Istanbul. Ships may not use both Turkish occupied and Greek Cypriot sea ports. Nicosia airport has been closed since 1974, but numerous international flights are available from Larnaca.

2 POPULATION
Growth

The first census in Cyprus was taken in 1881 when the population was 186,000. The most recent census was 1960 when the figure was 578,000. The estimated population in 1978 was 618,300. The average annual growth rate between 1946 and 1960 was 1.7%; between 1960 and 1972 it was 1.0%. The drop in the rate is due to exceptionally high emigration during 1960 and 1961 and a declining birth rate.

Reliable figures for the Turkish Cypriot population are not available.

Distribution

The overall population density is 174 per square mile. Until August 1974 one third of the population lived in the six main towns of Nicosia, Limassol, Famagusta, Larnaca, Paphos and Kyrenia, and almost one fifth (118,000) in Nicosia alone. the rural population lived in some 630 villages. A substantial proportion of the village population could still be described as peasant, but large numbers travelled daily to the towns for work. And there was indeed a marked shift to urban settlement. Since 1974 the situation has changed dramatically with the postwar population movements. Some 180,000 Greek Cypriot refugees have moved south from the area now controlled by the Turkish army to be replaced by only 20,000 Turkish Cypriots. Famagusta (formerly the main port) with a population of 40,000, is partly uninhabited. The northern area generally is underpopulated, with a corresponding increase in the population density in the south.

Groups

The population is basically divided into Greek Cypriots (78%) and Turkish Cypriots (18%), an approximate ratio of 4:1. Armenians, Maronites, Britons and others make up the remainder. The division of Cyprus between Greek Cypriot and Turkish

Cypriot is sharp. It is the all-consuming factor which has dominated Cypriot politics since Independence in 1960, and to a lesser extent previously. 'The Cyprus Question' has always been a question of whether the Greek and Turkish population can agree to live together in peace. As a result of the events since 1960 tension between the two populations has grown and in 1974 physical separation became complete.

External Migration

Very large concentrations of Cypriots live in Britain, America and Australia. Efforts have been made to entice back emigrés with their skills and capital, but these have not been entirely successful.

3 SOCIETY AND CULTURE
Social Patterns

Cypriot society is either Greek Cypriot or Turkish Cypriot. Both societies manifest gradations of wealth from the rich entrepreneur to the (in money terms) poor peasant. Until 1974 there was no real poverty. But wealth was rare among the Turks whereas it was common among the Greeks. The Greek Cypriot is a good businessman, the Turkish an indifferent one. The pursuit of wealth and social standing is general. But there is no hereditary class structure or the class consciousness it brings. Families are much intermixed, village connections carefully retained by those who have become urbanised and there exists a social unity throughout the country. The family unit is a strong one and a relation by birth or marriage may command preferential attention. As no point in the island is farther than 192km from the capital by road, no areas can be called remote. But many of the villages are still little changed by the modern world, except for the absence of young men.

Role of English

In the present situation where some sort of dialogue between the two sides must be revived and where a common language for international and commercial relations is essential, the role of English can hardly be exaggerated. Before 1960 Turkish was taught in Greek Cypriot schools and Greek in Turkish Cypriot schools. Since then a generation has grown up knowing nothing of each other's language. English, however, is taught in all schools, starting at the first level. While Greek and Turkish are prized as the national language of each side there is every encouragement for the learning of English, and a good command of it is an essential qualification for government employment and indeed for most jobs in the professions or commerce, and also for prospective emigrants.

Religion

Cyprus was one of the first places to be converted to Christianity. Barnabas was himself a Jew of Cyprus and in AD 46 with John Mark and St Paul they converted the Roman proconsul. (Cyprus thus was the first country to be ruled by a Christian governor.) Christianity rapidly spread throughout the island. The autocephalous Church of Cyprus is one of the oldest of the Eastern Orthodox churches. For the Greek Cypriot population the Church is equated with Hellenism. The efforts of the Lusignans and later the Venetians to submit the Orthodox Church to the Pope's authority may or may not have been successful (authorities differ), but at least to the people their priests and bishops were their ever present visible leaders. Certainly, under Turkish rule the Church was allowed to re-establish its power, which it did to such effect that its leaders were martyred en masse in 1821 by an administration grown suddenly frightened. Throughout the struggles for *Enosis* (union with Greece) during British rule, and indeed since Independence, the Church has been to the fore. The perfect realisation of its power was the election as the first President of the Republic of the Head of the Church. Greek Cypriot education is closely tied to a loyalty to the Church, for the Church as a leader has always had as its aim to keep alive the national feeling for Greece and Hellenism. The power of the Church is further enhanced by its very great wealth.

Islam among the Turkish Cypriot population is no longer a strong force. Taking their lead from the reforms of Atatürk, younger Turks are seldom in the mosques, though the invading army brought some religious customs back into fashion.

4 HISTORY AND POLITICS

Origins

Earliest settlements in Cyprus were late Neolithic Age (c.3000 BC) and the interest of the history of the island since then is primarily due to its geographical position. It was during the Late Bronze Age (2000-1000 BC) that Greek settlers from the Aegean introduced the culture of the Mycenaean period. They mixed with a presumably indigenous race probably incorporating Phoenician traders and settlers. They were a rich and cultured people, knew the Greek alphabet and probably spoke some sort of Greek. This is of vital importance in the subsequent history of the island; and after centuries of various foreign influences and occupations - Egyptian, Phoenician, Assyrian - Cyprus was finally 'liberated' by a local Greek prince in 410 BC. The predominance of Greek culture was established from that time.

Later, Cyprus fell to the Ptolemies for 200 years and then to the Romans from 58 BC to AD 395. The administration of Rome became that of Byzantium and the island enjoyed 200 years of prosperity, followed by two centuries of Moslem attacks and finally the usurpation of Byzantine rule by the brutal Isaac Comnenos who was in turn defeated by Richard Coeur de Lion on the Third Crusade. Richard found the Crusade demanded all his men and money, sold the island to the Knights Templar who in turn passed it to Guy de Lusignan, King of Jerusalem, whose family ruled Cyprus for 300 years. The island was ravaged by the Genoese in 1464, misfortunes occurred in the royal house, and the Venetians took possession of Cyprus in 1489. They regarded it as a military post, fortified it, drew an extortionate revenue and misgoverned and oppressed it for 100 years until the Turkish conquest in 1571, which led to Ottoman rule for three centuries. This rule, at first comparatively enlightened, became neglectful and oppressive; there were serious risings and the Church developed so great an influence that the Turks became alarmed and in 1821 executed the Archbishop and bishops on a charge of conspiracy with Greece, then fighting Turkey for its independence. Thereafter governmental reforms threatened the politico-economic supremacy of the Orthodox Church. In 1878 as a result of an Anglo-Turkish convention arising from the rivalry of Britain and Russia the island was handed over for administration by Britain. In 1914 with the entry of Turkey into World War One Cyprus was annexed and became a Crown Colony.

Independence

In 1931 serious disturbances arose out of a demand by sections of the Greek population for *Enosis*. After World War Two agitation for *Enosis* was renewed and became violent in 1955. British, Greek and Turkish foreign ministers failed to agree on a solution and a five year period of terrorism began led by George Grivas. His organisation, the National Organisation of Cypriot Combatants (EOKA) enjoyed wide support from the Greek community. Attempts to suppress it failed, and efforts to produce a settlement came to nothing in the face of the Greek community's desire for union of the island with Greece and the Turkish desire for partition. But in 1959 agreement between the Greek, Turkish and British governments was reached for an independent state whose security they would guarantee. British sovereignty was to be retained over two military bases. Executive power was to be vested in a Greek Cypriot President (the Ethnarch, Archbishop Makarios) and a Turkish Cypriot Vice President. There would be a Council of Ministers consisting of seven Greek Cypriots and three Turkish Cypriots, and a House of Representatives in proportion. The Republic came into being in 1960 with a complicated and unalterable dual constitution which never really worked.

International Relations

Cyprus belongs to the 'non-aligned' group of countries and votes with the 'Third World' in the United Nations. It is a member of the Council of Europe and has associate membership of the EEC. Links with Britain which result from the economy, the military bases, the large Cypriot population there, and historical association, remain strong.

5 THE ECONOMY

Natural Resources

The economy is a capitalist one which expanded vigorously in the 1960s. It was mainly rural, with agriculture providing about 50% of exports; but by 1974 it included secondary industries and a considerable tourist trade (250,000 visitors per annum). The chief visible exports are fruit and vegetables, wine and minerals. Chief visible imports are machinery, manufactured goods, food and fuel. The main natural resource of Cyprus is its soil, which is dependent on a low and erratic rainfall. Developments in irrigation stimulated a large citrus and early vegetable export industry. The most valuable mineral resources are iron pyrites and copper concentrates; there are also deposits of asbestos, chrome and gypsum. Cyprus has no fuel resources of its own and relies for power on imported oil.

The war of 1974 greatly dislocated the country's economy with the destruction of agriculture and factories and the loss of lucrative tourist revenue. The Greek and Turkish zones function as separate economic units. Partition cut off factories from raw materials and owners from hotels. Citrus groves (now in the Turkish zone) and vineyards (in the Greek zone) are in the hands of those without experience of cultivating them, and Turkish Cypriots also now hold most of the potato and cereal fields.

Economic Situation

The Greek Cypriot economy has showed amazing resilience, due on the one side to sound financial policy, strict economic planning and the natural business acumen and entrepreneurial vigour of the people, and on the other to the highest per capita aid figure in the world, good export crops of potatoes while Europe suffered two years of drought, and massive inflows of foreign exchange during the Lebanese civil war. Agriculture remains the backbone but manufacturing industry (now including the booming construction industry in Arab countries) and tourism are well on their way to establishing themselves at pre-war levels. There is some structural unemployment in certain key skills and employment prospects for graduates are poor; many of them emigrate.

The Turkish Cypriot economy is less buyoant; the lack of international recognition is a potent adverse factor and the more relaxed style of the Turkish Cypriot does not give him the commercialist instinct of his counterpart across the Green Line. The foreign exchange position is acute; prices continue to rise and the Lira has been effectively devalued by the free market; industrial disputes have been numerous and sometimes protracted. Capital accumulation is low and shortage of all kinds of skills and expertise as pronounced as ever; the labour shortage can only be alleviated by contentious settlement of mainland Turks. There was a substantial trading deficit in 1977 of about C£30 million with the value of imports estimated to be about treble that of exports. Britain is thought to have taken 46% of exports and provided 25% of imports, though reliable figures are rarely available from the Turkish-controlled area. Turkey is not only the largest supplier, with 40% of the market and an outlet for 28% of exports, but an important prop to the economy by way of financial aid and technical assistance.

6 THE EDUCATION SYSTEM

As a result of the division of Cyprus into two separate communities there are two autonomous education systems both run independently from separate 'ministries'; one identifying itself with Greece and Hellenism and the other with Turkey. There is no official contact whatever between the two, nor have they ever answered to a common government. While certain aspects are common to both systems, it is necessary when discussing the education system of Cyprus to refer separately to the Greek Cypriot and the Turkish Cypriot systems. This Education Profile is primarily a description of the Greek Cypriot system, partly because it is the majority system, partly because the Turkish Cypriot is not dissimilar, and partly because reliable statistics from the minority administration are not available.

Academic Year

The academic year extends from mid-September to late June and at school level pupils attend on average five hours a day six days a week. There are about 17 holidays, with two-week breaks at Christmas and Easter and a long holiday of over two months in the summer.

Pre-School

Pre-school education in Cyprus is still in its early stages, with most kindergartens in private hands. The government is showing an increasing interest in this level, and is starting to look for overseas training and support for it. The purpose of nearly all kindergartens is to provide pre-school education and care for children in the age range $2\frac{1}{2}$ to 5, and they fall into one of the following categories:

(i) public or communal: these are almost all financed and supervised by the Department of Primary Education
(ii) private approved: these have to meet the Ministry's requirements for qualified teaching personnel and suitable accommodation
(iii) private day nurseries: these do not meet the Ministry's requirements. They are under the control of the Department of Welfare
(iv) private foreign language: these are mostly non-profit-making, run by foreign religious organisations or Armenians.

First Level Schools

Primary education has always been free and coeducational and since 1962 it has been compulsory. Children begin school at the age of five (since 1975/76) and leave when they have completed the prescribed six-year course, or have reached the age of 13, whichever comes first. Most schools cover the full six-year course, though some are divided into separate upper and lower sections. There is only one eight-grade school offering an additional two-year terminal course to 34 boys and girls. Private primary schools function independently, though they are liable to inspection and supervision by the Ministry. There are three Armenian primary schools (150 pupils) and seven foreign language schools (715 pupils), run mainly by religious groups on a non-profit-making basis.

The curriculum consists of: Greek, English, religious knowledge, mathematics, natural sciences, history, geography, hygiene, physical education, handwork and art, music, agricultural subjects, domestic science. The eight-year school offers in addition woodwork and metalwork for boys and domestic science for girls in the last two years. Divided primary schools have a wider and freer curriculum in the first three years than the equivalent classes in the six-year schools, with emphasis on art, music, drama and physical education. The amount of time devoted to each subject depends mainly upon the size of school and the number of teachers. The number of minutes allocated to each subject each week is laid down by the Ministry of Education and it is left to the headmaster to draw up the timetable.

General Second Level Schools

Secondary education in the *gymnasium* or academic school, consists of two cycles of three years each. It is not yet compulsory, but it is free up to the age of 15 except for a small fee to meet extra-curricular expenses. At upper secondary level the cost ranges from nothing to a maximum, according to a means test. Entrance to secondary education is by examination. This consists of written and oral tests in mother tongue, arithmetic and general knowledge. Each school conducts its own examination. Greek-English schools, which are private, cover the full six-year course and prepare pupils for General Certificate of Education examinations. They boomed with the economy in 1969-74, suffered a sharp setback thereafter, but are now well set on an upward path again.

Lower Second Level

The lower secondary school is a period of general education. Its self-contained general study course aims to provide an adequate amount of knowledge and skill for a useful intelligent life for the 30% who proceed no further. The curriculum is heavy and includes Ancient and Modern Greek, English, religious instruction, mathematics, natural sciences, history, civics, geography, music, art and physical education. Some schools also include two or three periods a week of woodwork, metalwork and technology.

Upper Second Level

The senior secondary school provides a more specialised education and is divided into streams, each concentrating on one particular branch of learning - classical, commercial and scientific. The classical stream emphasises humanities, the scientific stream mathematics, physics and chemistry. Pupils in the commercial stream concentrate on foreign languages as well as commerce and economics. A fourth experimental stream of students in the main streams was: commercial 39%; scientific 29%; classical 24%. Any two of the streams in the same building can constitute a school under a headmaster. To this extent the system is comprehensive and some pupils do transfer during the first year of the three-year course, though after this it becomes more difficult.

Technical and Vocational

Secondary

The technical schools, which used to be separate from the vocational schools, aim mainly at providing local industry with technicians and craftsmen. The curriculum for the first three years is the same as in the *gymnasia*; specialisation begins in the fourth year with the introduction of technical and vocational subjects, as the same time as *gymnasia* students are choosing their streams. In 1978, 19% of the secondary school population was in technical schools, most of this number being made up of boys. They studied either electricity and electronics (37%), fitting, welding, mechanics, auto-mechanics and foundry technology (29%) or building, carpentry and plumbing (28%).

Post-Second Level Institutions

There are a variety of separate institutions operating at post-secondary level. The Higher Technical Institute (a joint ILO/government project) offers three-year technological courses to secondary graduates who are selected on the results of a highly competitive examination. Its object is to supply qualified technicians for industry, and teachers for the technical schools. Courses are conducted for the most part in English and all students are given minimal training for teaching. There is a Hotel and Catering Institute which provides one- or two-year courses at middle level in cooking, waiting, housekeeping and reception work. The Forestry College, situated at Prodromos in the Troodos Mountains, offers a two-year course. For many years it had a British principal. New entrants must be secondary school leavers, though 25% of the places are reserved for overseas students (from Rhodesia, Jamaica, Libya, Ghana, Lesotho) who are scholars of the Cyprus government, under the Commonwealth Scholarship Scheme. There is also a School of Nursing and Midwifery attached to the Nicosia Hospital and offering four separate courses:

(i) a three-year course for the Certificate of General Registered Nurse

(ii) a two-year course for assistant nurses

(iii) a two-year course in midwifery

(iv) a three-and-a-half year course in community health visiting.

Nearly all entrants are secondary graduates and this is likely to become an official requirement. Since 1964 the school has been recognised by the General Nursing and Midwifery Council of England and Wales as equivalent to similar institutions in Britain. A School of Psychiatric Nursing attached to the Psychiatric Hospital provides courses lasting two years.

Third Level Institutions

At tertiary level there is the Higher College of Technology which is a private institution offering more advanced courses in the subjects covered at the Higher Technical Institute. There is also a Mediterranean institute of Management (MIM) which is part of the Productivity Centre jointly funded by ILO and UNDP. This American-style institute offers a ten-month postgraduate course in management to 30 students (only ten of whom are Cypriot).

University

There is no university in Cyprus, though there are proposals to establish one. All those wishing to take degree courses must travel abroad to do so - usually to Greece, Turkey, Britain, the Soviet Union, or Western Europe.

Teacher Training

Kindergarten

Kindergarten teachers are trained at the Pedagogical Academy (in 1977/78 there were roughly 20 girls in each of the three years) and there are signs that they may be able to find employment in the lower classes of the primary school, as well as in the private pre-primary sector. Their course differs little in length or content from the primary teacher training course, and the level of student ability is at least as high. A kindergarten specialist was appointed inspector for pre-primary teaching in 1977.

Primary

Students who have completed Greek-Cypriot upper secondary education may sit for the fiercely competitive entrance examination to enter the Pedagogical Academy for three years' training as primary school teachers. As the number of primary school children is expected to fall, the number of students admitted is being reduced (12 in 1977 - a drop of six on the previous year and eight in 1978). But even this may be too many. The course covers a wide range of subjects and there are opportunities for teaching practice in all types of primary schools. Turkish Cypriot students attend the Turkish Teacher Training College at Kyrenia. This is at present housed in a building within a military complex, without free access and lacking many of the facilities associated with teacher training. There is a normal entry of 30 students per year but there was no new intake in 1978 because of pressure of space and teacher unemployment.

Secondary

Those who have attended university or other institutions of higher education are automatically entitled to apply to join the secondary teaching force, though there is a long waiting list. Primary school teachers who wish to move to the better paid secondary ladder can only do so by obtaining a degree: since the demise of the University of London external BA, the only practicable way for them to do this is to obtain a UK scholarship leading to a Master's degree (a Diploma does not count for such promotion).

In-Service

The Pedagogical Institute runs courses for serving teachers at all levels (primary, secondary, probationary, etc.). It is staffed by a small number of full time and part time lecturers and course designers, which includes several who have been on scholarship to Britain. Courses are mandatory for probationer teachers to be made permanent and for teachers with seven years' service to pass the 'promotion bar'. Teachers also receive support in their schools. Increasingly effective educational broadcasts are made regularly, supported by back-up visits and materials. Teaching aids and activity methods are widely in evidence. Inspectors inspect and advise.

Non-Formal and Adult

The role of adult education is not highly developed in Cyprus but during the 1960s and early 1970s a system of further education centres was set up to enable young people, especially in the rural areas, to acquire additional skills and pass their leisure time. Work is informal but studies usually include English, arithmetic, general knowledge, agriculture, first aid, domestic science, etc. There are discussions on the life of the community, film shows, and organised games.

Apprenticeship/Technical Evening Classes

The curricula of both of these schemes aim towards the same end, which is the technical training of young working people in various trades who did not have the opportunity or the means to enjoy a full technical education. The ultimate aim of both schemes is to offer better craftsmen and technicians to the country's infant industries. The courses offered are wide ranging and cover nearly all trades (furniture making, dress making, building, plumbing, goldsmithing, electronics, etc.). Tuition is provided by staff of the technical schools, where the classes take place.

Foreign Language Institutes

These also use regular school buildings in the evenings. Before 1974 there were nine with 15,000 students enrolled. In 1978 there were six with 6,000 students, providing courses in foreign languages and commercial subjects. Most of the clientele is made up of school children seeking to improve their English for which the secondary schools allow only four periods per week. French, German and Greek are also taught. Classes meet for 90 minutes twice a week, and courses last three to five years. Apart from these institutions which are run by the Ministry there are language classes run by the German and Soviet Cultural Centres. These attract students who have been, or who are hoping to be, awarded scholarships for under-graduate study in the respective countries.

Part Time Institutes

Subjects taught at these private institutions cover all possible requirements. Teaching takes place mainly during the afternoons and evenings, and the schools are attended by secondary school pupils and adults who are trying to supplement other teaching and their own efforts to pass various examinations.

7 EDUCATIONAL ADMINISTRATION

Under the constitution there were two Offices of Education, but with the passing of time the Greek Office of Education appropriated for itself the title of Ministry. Outsiders did not officially deal with the Turkish Cypriot 'Minister', but only with his 'Under Secretary' in his capacity as Director General of the Turkish Office of Education.

Ministry of Education

The Director General of the Ministry of Education is the chief administrative officer who assists the Minister and Deputy Minister of Education in coordinating and supervising the various sections of the Ministry. These sections include, apart from the educational services, a cultural relations service, technical

ADMINISTRATION
ORGANISATION OF THE MINISTRY OF EDUCATION

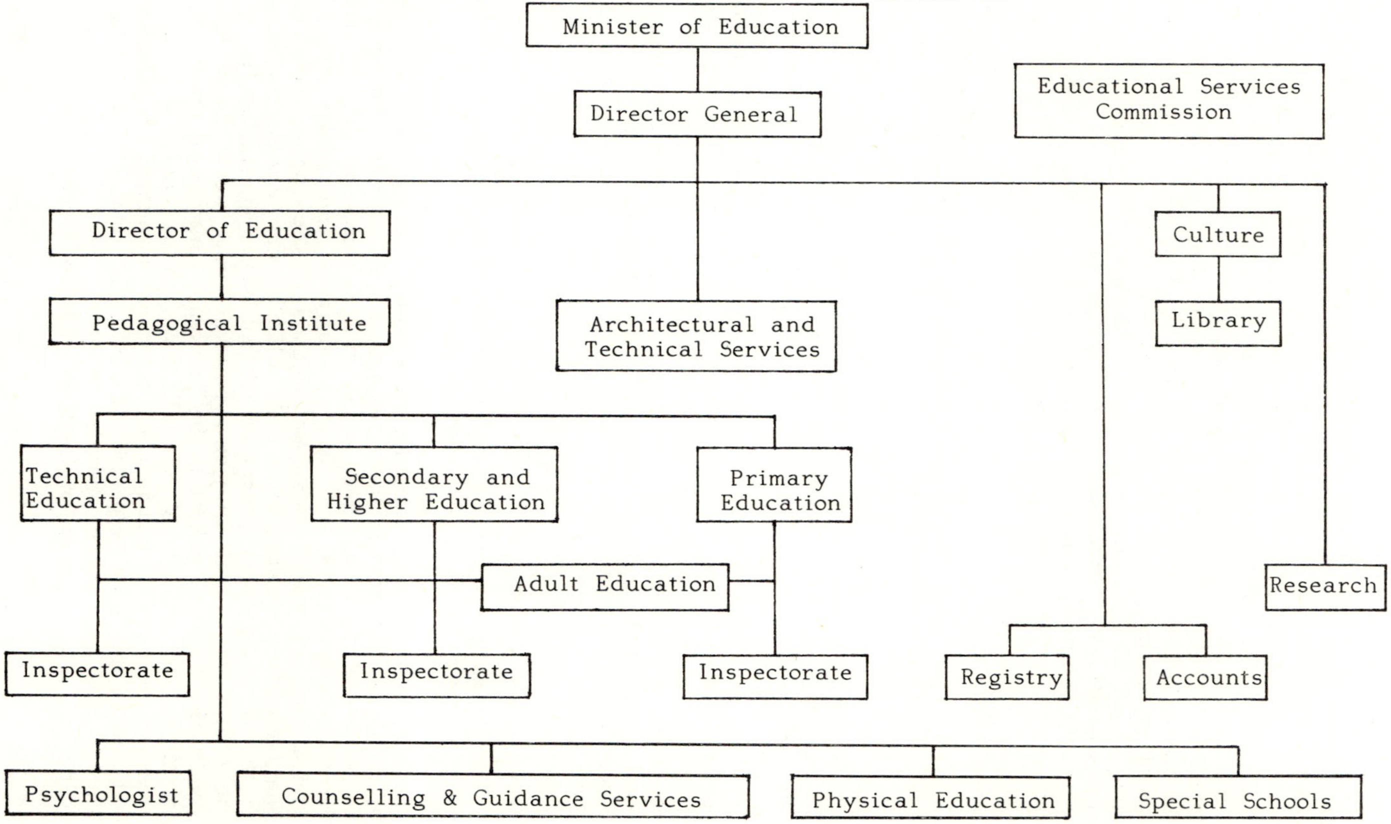

- Minister of Education
  - Educational Services Commission
  - Director General
    - Architectural and Technical Services
    - Culture
      - Library
    - Research
    - Registry
    - Accounts
    - Director of Education
      - Pedagogical Institute
      - Secondary and Higher Education
        - Inspectorate
      - Primary Education
        - Inspectorate
      - Adult Education
      - Technical Education
        - Inspectorate
      - Counselling & Guidance Services
        - Psychologist
      - Physical Education
      - Special Schools

services, and a centre for scientific research with its own director. The Director General is in charge of the educational services of the Ministry and works closely with the heads of departments. There are at present three departments for the school system, dealing respectively with secondary and higher education, technical and vocational education, and primary education. Functioning as adjuncts to these departments because they concern more than one level of education and type of school are the educational services for in-service teacher training, vocational guidance, special education, physical education, radio and television, adult education, foreign language institutes and educational psychology. The system is a highly centralised one with syllabi, curricula and books to a large extent prescribed by the Ministry.

Other Agencies

Apart from the Ministry of Education, four other ministries have certain educational responsibilities: the Ministries of Labour and Social Insurance, Agriculture and Natural Resources, Justice, and Health are responsible for vocational education which is pertinent to their functions. The Educational Service Commission is the employing authority for teachers and inspectors responsible for appointments, transfers and promotion. It is an entirely independent committee of five members appointed directly by the President of the Republic for a three-year period. The chairman of this committee is a lawyer of high standing while the members are ex-teachers conversant with the problems of schools and teachers. Each departmental head of the educational services sits on the Commission when matters concerning personnel within his jurisdiction are under consideration.

Inspectorate

The primary, secondary and technical departments of the Ministry each have their own bodies of inspectors. A Chief Inspector in each of the primary and secondary departments establishes guidelines and coordinates activity. There are two types of primary inspector: those assigned to districts for general subjects and those assigned to special subjects or subject areas. Secondary inspectors are all specialists, and come under the jurisdiction of the Director of Secondary and Higher Education. The secondary inspectorate is unified, not divided according to the three types of secondary school. Some specialists in technical and vocational subjects, however, may work almost exclusively in technical schools. The principle function of the nspectorate is to report to the Ministry on schools, whether for example they have reached a maximum standard of efficiency, but they are also expected to help the teachers by comment and suggestion. Other equally important responsibilities of the inspectors are to give professional advice to the Ministry, conduct courses for serving teachers, prepare advisory pamphlets and advise on the prescription of books. Because the system is centralised, the inspectors are also required to assess the work of individual teachers and advise the Educational Service Committee on their promotion and transfer.

School Committees

School committees, of which there is one in every town and in every rural centre where there is a secondary school, are appointed by the government for a two-year period. Their main function is the building, maintenance and equipment of schools and the provision of school medical inspection and treatment. They also assist the headmasters in the internal organisation and administration of the schools. School committees exercise a large part of the authority associated with the day to day running of schools, but the jurisdiction of the school committees as regards school building and equipment does not extend over the technical schools, which are the direct responsibility of the Ministry.

8 EDUCATIONAL FINANCE

Sources of Funds

Public education is financed by government grants, some foreign aid and local funds. Local authorities are responsible for the running of primary education in rural areas; for this purpose they levy local school taxes. In urban areas the financial management of primary education belongs to the school committees who also manage secondary schools. However, the main financial burden is borne by the government which pays teachers' salaries and offers specific grants to the managing authorities. Rural grants are twice the urban grants per capita. Capital expenditure (i.e. school buildings and equipment) for public primary education is borne by the local authorities which raise funds by means of an educational tax imposed on all residents of the rural areas; its basis is the fiscal capacity of each tax payer, i.e. both income and wealth. In poor rural communities the government may pay up to 50% of the total cost of school buildings. Funds are allotted to the Ministry of Education by the House of Representatives in the annual budget. The Ministry of Finance must approve any further allotments needed. The annual budgets of school committees must be approved by both the Ministries of Education and Finance. Private schools (at all levels, including evening institutes) are mainly financed from tuition fees paid by pupils. Full time private secondary schools receive a per capita grant from the Ministry.

Education Budget

Public and private expenditure on education as a percentage of GNP has risen. Between 1968 and 1972, there was a very much greater proportional increase in central government expenditure (78% increase) than in local government expenditure (19% increase in the same period). This reflects steeply rising recurrent costs especially salaries, and comparatively static capital costs with falling enrolment. It also reflects a steady centripetal tendency, with centralised finance, bureaucracy, curricula and teaching service all combining to erode the traditional hegemony of village and town school committees. The latter used to provide 25% of funds and had much say over book supplies, but now provide 10% and simply use the Ministry's approved list of textbooks as a shopping list.

Allocation of Funds
Expenditure on Education: Distribution by Level
Percentage of Expenditure 1977

Pre-School	First Level	Second Level	Third Level	Other
-	39.1	50.6	3.8	6.5

Overseas Aid

Foreign aid for education in Cyprus before the war was mainly for books supplied free of charge by the Greek government. Since the war, foreign aid in various forms has increased greatly. Scholarships for higher education abroad are provided by both the Cyprus government and some foreign governments, notably Greece, Turkey, Britain and the USA.

9 DEVELOPMENT AND PLANNING OF THE EDUCATIONAL SYSTEM
Origins

Greek education in Cyprus was in the Church, for the Church and by the Church. Turkish education in Cyprus was endowed by the faithful for religious purposes. In the Ottoman period grants were made to Moslem schools but Greeks received no aid. The head of the Orthodox Church was their supreme authority and schools were maintained voluntarily. The British recognised the division of education, appointed a Director of Education in 1880 and appointed two Boards of Education, one for each community. The British colonial power only very gradually, and for political reasons, attempted to secure control of the education systems - particularly the Greek - increasingly abrogating to itself powers over pay, discipline, transfer and eventually appointment of teachers, and over curricula, textbooks and languages to be taught. Fierce and sometimes violent resistance met colonial attempts to ban the import of Enosist activists and textbooks from Greece and to impose to some extent the English language.

Post-Independence

Independence in 1960 brought a triumphant return to communal autonomy in educational matters, triumphant abolition of the English medium in a communal teacher training college, and the resumption of the wholesale import from Greece of textbooks, teachers and ideas whose effects are clear today. The 'Zurich' Constitution had virtually only one provision that was universally popular and indubitably workable; separate educational systems. Under articles 86 and 87 of the Cyprus Constitution, the Greek and Turkish Communal Chambers were responsible for the education of their respective communities. On 31 March 1965 the Greek Chamber was dissolved, and replaced by the Council of Ministers. Its Ministry of Education was made responsible for the provision and control of education subject to the approval of the Council, notwithstanding some educational activities which are under the jurisdiction of other ministries. The Turkish Cypriot education system is on the whole similar, and is administered by the Turkish Communal Chamber through its Office of Education. The latter now claims the title of ministry. Apart from that claim, it is the only feature of the 1960 Constitution surviving in a form acceptable to the Greek Cypriot central government. In fact, it is questionable whether the (Greek Cypriot) post of Minister of Education is legally constituted and whether, if it is, the Turkish Cypriot post is so too. The former claim is normally respected, however, and the latter not.

Planning

Because constitutionally education is a separate communal responsibility, there can be no such thing as a national education plan. The Turkish Four-Year Plan 1963-67 was wrecked by civil strife and grossly abnormal conditions. Over 100 elementary schools were abandoned when Turkish Cypriots withdrew to their own enclaves. Planning since then has inevitably been short term. Within the Greek Cypriot Ministry of Education the post of Director of Education is responsible for educational planning backed up by the Planning Bureau and the Department of Statistics and Research of the Ministry of Finance which produce the finance, buildings and manpower figures. However, except for a brief period, this post was vacant for many years.

10 THE SYSTEM IN OPERATION*
Effects of the War

Greek schools suffered heavily in 1974. As a result of the Turkish invasion, 171 of the 548 Greek primary schools (31%) now fall within the Turkish occupied zone. A similar percentage of Greek secondary schools are now in Turkish held territory (19 out of 49) with three out of the eight technical schools and about half of the special education institutions lost. Almost £250,000 worth of elementary school furniture, books and equipment was destroyed or lost and twice as much in secondary schools. The Ministry's central store of books, stationery and aids was totally destroyed by bombing and £500,000 worth lost.

Enrolments decreased overall but not in proportion to the drastic cut in school provision. Of the present enrolment at primary level no less than 35% are refugees of which 55% have been placed in rural schools and the remaining 45% in urban schools.

District	1973-74	1974-75	Increase (+) Decrease (-)	Refugee & displaced pupils
Nicosia	21,637	19,497	- 2,140	7,086
Kyrenia	3,297	-	- 3,297	-
Famagusta	13,680	3,227	-10,453	1,168
Larnaca	6,152	10,670	+ 4,518	5,526
Limassol	12,469	16,656	+ 4,187	4,880
Paphos	4,985	5,390	+ 405	720
TOTAL	62,220	55,440	- 6,780	19,380

*Note: This Education Profile tries to give as complete a picture of the system's structure as is commensurate with brevity. However, certain imbalances must be acknowledged in that this section concentrates on problems rather than what is done well. Concern for the problems educationists in Cyprus face is inevitable given the political circumstances which have prevailed since 1975.

At secondary level about 32% of all pupils and teachers are refugees, but the overall enrolment figure fell by 3,033 (or 6.1%) in 1974/75. This decrease was unprecedented. The total secondary school enrolments were expected to reach the figure of 51,000, but the total number of pupils enrolled plus the enclaved and those transferred to schools overseas only reached the figure of 48,435. Thus the expected roll fell short by 2,565 pupils and it is believed that most of these pupils emigrated. Private secondary schools lost over 40% of their pupils. About 25% of the private schools were occupied by the Turks and this, together with special concessions being made for the transfers of pupils from private to public schools, has accelerated the already downward trend of their enrolments.

Turkish Cypriot elementary and secondary schools in the south are not operating. Many were destroyed with their contents. No statistics are available. The English medium Turk Maarif Koleji school in Nicosia has been swollen to 800 pupils.

Planning

Within the present Greek Cypriot Ministry of Education the post of Director of Education, whose brief was educational planning, was vacated in 1973 with the promotion to Minister of the then incumbent. He made an indifferent Minister and alone among the June 1974 ministers displaced by the Junta coup, did not return to his ministry. There is thus at present rich evidence of ignorance of basic educational planning concepts within the professional elite of the Ministry of Education. Indeed, the absence of clearly formulated educational standards apart from the label Christian Hellenism, has resulted in lowered standards of teaching, much ossification of the curriculum, and massive emigration.

Provision

Two years after independence primary education was made compulsory and even before compulsory schooling 98% of the age group was enrolled at primary level. Parental demand for education is very great. Most villages have their own elementary school. there is a discernible trend to urbanisation though not as steep as might be expected. In 1962/63, 29% of all school pupils were in town schools and in 1972/73, 37%. School buildings are generally good, though furniture and equipment tend to be old fashioned. Drop-out rates are minute (primary: 0.3%; secondary: 1.6%) and show no difference between urban and rural areas, though rather more girls than boys fail to complete elementary school. Very few children repeat (2.3%), and failure rates are around 2%. There was a fall in enrolment from 73,000 in 1965 to 63,000 in 1973. This resulted from unstable conditions and massive emigration after independence; it was expected to pick up in the late 1970s, but did not.

Teachers

Teachers are respected and enjoy high status especially in villages. They are also the most politically active profession in Cyprus and have been so since World War One. Nowadays male primary teachers (80%) predominate in rural areas, and female teachers (60%) in urban areas. All are fully qualified and the general quality is exceptionally high. Since Cyprus has no university, the Pedagogical Academy attracts students of considerable ability, many of whom in other countries would walk into degree courses. In 1973 there were ten candidates for every place available. However, professional training is only nominally a component of Greek university degrees. The latter, however, must receive automatic recognition as qualifying anybody to do anything, so secondary schools are now flooded with virtually untrained teachers.

Teachers are well paid and their Teachers' Union acquired considerable financial advantages during the later years of the recent boom. Cost of living allowance based on the retail price index, a 'thirteenth month salary', reduced working hours and no holiday or afternoon training courses were benefits demanded and won by the militant secondary school teachers' union in 1972/73. Now all teachers offer 20% of their salaries to the government's fund for refugees, COLA is frozen, and the thirteenth month salary halved. But not a single teacher has been dismissed. Teacher overemployment was threatening even pre-war, and no intake was planned for September 1974. The staffing ratio has improved from 34.6 pupils per teacher in 1960 at primary level, to around 27 pupils per teacher in 1974. But this ratio conceals the fact that 14% of the elementary school population were in one-teacher and two-teacher schools.

In the foreign language institutes only the Principal is full time. British CEC teachers taught full time in six FLIs, pre-war, but most other teachers are inexperienced, untrained, and awaiting employment. Standards have dropped low and private language tuition is in greater demand than ever.

Study Abroad

The system works by exporting virtually all third level students. Greeks go to Greece or Britain or Europe or the United States. Turks go to Turkey or Britain or, a very few, elsewhere. Demand for English medium education and British examinations at every level and in all fields of study had risen enormously by 1974 and has in fact dropped very little since the war. The reasons for the urge to study English are not far to seek. To get on in Cyprus, you need English; and to get out of Cyprus, you need even more English. Legalised ambivalence operates here; State schools are Greek medium and teach only four periods of English per week but State foreign language institutes provide what the schools do not. State schools work to Cyprus *Gynmasium* examinations valid for entry to Greek universities but not elsewhere, whereas many students of these very same schools sit for GCE as private candidates through private tutors or tutorial institutions. Lip service is paid to the ideas of Christian Hellenism, but the demand is for English and American degrees, cars, clothes and standards. As employment prospects fall in Britain, America and Australia, they rise in Libya and the Gulf.

Relevance

The tourist boom has proved more ephemeral than the early vegetable and vine produce boom which may outlast it. The skills needed to participate in these aspects of economic development are indeed being catered for. The educators concerned were aware in 1974 of the need to trim the sails of technical education to the winds of the labour market. But although the last five years show an encouraging swing away from hellenistic 'classics' the vocational gain is not as solid as it should be. The farming villages of Cyprus are still emptying, and the business studies courses in London still filling.

Since 1974, the number of registered unemployed has risen from 1.4% to 9.2% and many more do not think it worth registering since they do not expect to find a new job. Emigration and exchange control regulations narrow the natural outlet, and potential receiving countries abroad have their own unemployment problem. There is a glut on the market of Greek graduates in arts and science subjects, agriculture, commerce. Education has always been seen as a most desirable thing, respected and sought, and parents spare no pains to pay for extra tuition or fee-paying schools for their children or to send them abroad to study. But they are sure to demand more and more fiercely that State education should be relevant to employment opportunities; but what these may be in the foreseeable future is impossible to say.

FURTHER READING

Commonwealth Youth Seminar, Nicosia (1972). *Youth and Development in Cyprus: Report.* Commonwealth Secretariat, London.
Cyprus Planning Bureau (1972). *Five Year Plan 3rd 1972-1976.* Government Printing Office, Nicosia.
Koullos, L. K. (1964). *Greek Education in Cyprus.* Education Office Greek Commercial Chamber, Nicosia.
Weir, W. W. (1952). *Education in Cyprus: Some Theories and Practices in Education in the Island of Cyprus Since 1978.* Cyprus.

Structure of the Education System in Cyprus

Age	3 4 5 6 7 8 9 10 11 12 13 14 15 16 17 18 19 20 21 22 23 24
Level	I • II • III • IV
Stage	1 • 2 • 3
Compulsory	
School type	Primary • Gymnasium • Classical/Commercial/Scientific Lyceum of optional subjects • Technical and vocational courses • First Teacher Training • Other Higher Education

⬚ Education preceding the first level

Examinations: compulsory at end of stage 2 onwards

Source: UNESCO/IBE International Yearbook of Education

Compulsory Education: Age Limits 6-12 Duration (years) 6
Entrance age to pre-school education: 3

	CYPRUS BASIC STATISTICS	1960	1970	1976	1978 (approx.)
1	Total population (000)	573	633	681	
	% female	51	51	51	
2	% population 0-14 years	36.7	32.7		28.0
	% female	46	45	46	46
3	Enrolment, all levels	116,371	112,163	106,781	
	% female	46	48	48	
	First level	83,617	69,160	55,366	
	% female	48	48	49	
	Second level	32,337	42,305	50,633	
	% female	41	46	47	
	Third level	417	698	782	
	% female	26	44	43	
4	Teachers, all levels	3,898	4,355	4,874	
	% female	36	39	43	
	First level	2,487	2,280	2,163	
	% female	37	40	45	
	Second level	1,376	2,011	2,621	
	% female	34	38	41	
	Third level	35	64	90	
	% female	20	22	23	
5	Public expenditure on education:				
	Total (000) pounds	2,640	7,060	11,421	
	As % of GNP	2.3	3.0	4.4	
6	% enrolment (MF) by level	100	100	100	
	First level	72	62	52	
	Second level	28	38	47	
	Third level		1	1	
	% enrolment (F) by level	100	100	100	
	First level	75	63	53	
	Second level	25	37	47	
	Third level		1	1	
7	Entrance age : Duration of				
	First level education	6:6	5:6	5:6	
	Second level education	12:6	11:6	11:6	
8	Enrolment ratios (MF)				
	First level	102	82	69	
	Second level	47	52	61	
	Third level	0.89	1.21	1.26	
	Enrolment ratios (F)				
	First level	100	81	70	
	Second level	39	49	60	
	Third level	0.45	1.07	1.10	

Czechoslovakia

CONTENTS

1 Geography 172
2 Population 174
3 History and Politics 174
4 Society and Culture 178
5 The Economy 178
6 The Education System 180
7 Educational Administration 186
8 Educational Finance 187
9 Development and Planning
   of the Education System 187
10 The System in Operation 190

The new republic of Czechoslovakia was created in 1918 after the collapse of the Austro-Hungarian monarchy. Its relatively recent creation as a sovereign state, the linguistic diversity which exists within its borders, the concession of parts of Bohemia and Moravia, which had a majority of German speaking people, to Germany in 1938 and the later occupation in 1939 of the whole country provide a context of political instability within which changes in educational policy can be examined. After 1945 for a brief period a coalition government gave hope to the Western allies of stability within a liberal democratic framework. The *coup d'état* of 1948 placed the communists in control of the government. Proposed reforms under Alexander Dubček in 1958 provoked intervention by Warsaw Pact Forces. Among the reforms were some which were intended to hold up educational changes in the direction of Soviet practices.

Similarities between the two systems and those in other Eastern European countries can be discerned. Pre-school education, for example, has been expanded – a threefold increase having taken place since 1945. A basic school for children between the ages of six and fifteen reflects the Soviet model. Russian language as a subject in the curriculum indicates the ties between the two countries. The child's mother tongue, Czech or Slovak, is the medium of instruction: the introduction of all day or extended day schools reflects Soviet moves to keep schools open in the afternoon.

At the age of 15 pupils can go straight into employment, enter apprenticeships, training centres and schools or go into the four year *gymnasium* which leads to university entrance. Competition for this kind of school is keen and only a small proportion of pupils who apply for the *gymnasium* are admitted. Secondary schools for workers and People's Universities and Academies provide opportunities for those who have not attended the *gymnasium* to improve their qualifications.

The aims of education - to educate the youth and working people in the spirit of a scientific world outlook and to be enthusiastic builders of communism - are those which would be accepted by educationists in most Communist countries. Strong academic traditions which have their origins in Charles (Karlova) University, founded in Prague in 1348, run deep and will not be changed easily. Tensions between academics who accept the ideals of Western and Eastern Europe are bound to arise. Religious diversity exists, 70% of the population is nominaly Roman Catholic, only a small number of Jews remain, and there is an important Protestant minority. However, there are now no Church schools or monasteries, although freedom of worship is allowed. Hungarians, Poles and Germans now constitute small minority groups. The Czech speaking population is more than double the Slovak speaking population.

As in other countries influenced by Soviet educational policies and practices, cultural diversity in terms of language, religion and ethnicity creates problems of policy found in many politically created nation states which are culturally very heterogenous.

The Editor

1 GEOGRAPHY

Topography

The Czechoslovak Socialist Republic covers a land-locked area of less than 129,000 square kilometres (50,310 square miles). The length of its frontiers is about 3,472 km (2,170 miles). In the east, the country borders on the USSR; in the north, on Poland and the German Democratic Republic; in the west, on the Federal German Republic; and in the south, on Austria and Hungary. The country is divided into three main areas - Czechoslovak speaking Bohemia in the west, Moravia-Silesia in the centre, and Slovak speaking Slovakia in the east. The scenery is varied with several mountain ranges; some peaks in the High Tatras reach an altitude of 2,655 metres above sea level. There are several karst regions in Bohemia and Moravia with large subterranean caverns which have remarkable stalactites. Although land-locked, many rivers and waterways cross the country, and the navigable rivers Labe (Elbe), Danube, and Odra provide access to the sea. Natural and artificial lakes also abound.

Climate

Situated in the centre of Europe, the country is a temperate zone with marked differences of weather according to the time

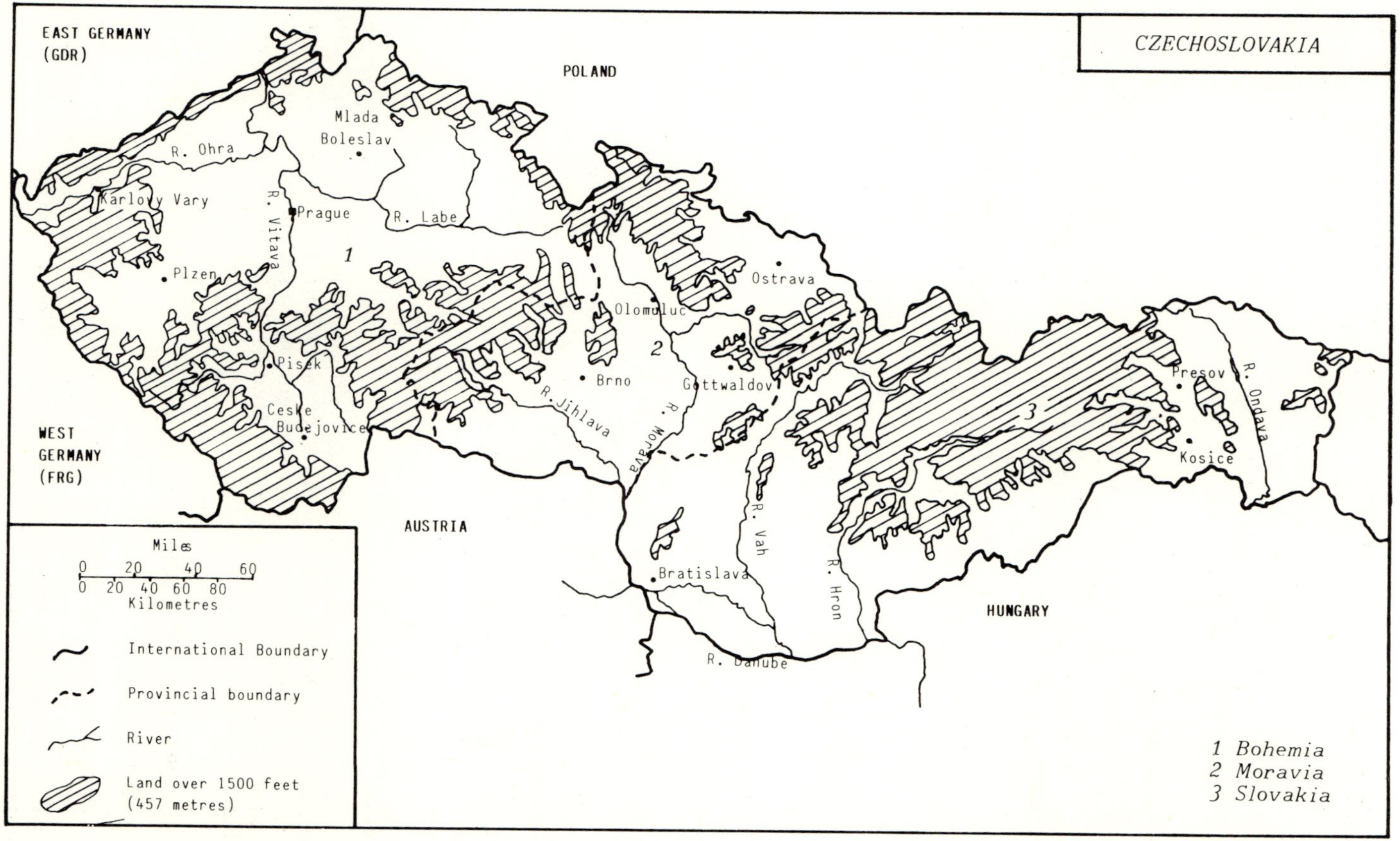
CZECHOSLOVAKIA
EAST GERMANY (GDR)
POLAND
WEST GERMANY (FRG)
AUSTRIA
HUNGARY
Mlada Boleslav
R. Ohra
Karlovy Vary
R. Vitava
Prague
R. Labe
Plzen
1
Pisek
Ceske Budejovice
Ostrava
Olomouc
2
Brno
R. Jihlava
R. Morava
Gottwaldov
R. Vah
Bratislava
R. Hron
R. Danube
3
Presov
R. Ondava
Kosice
Miles
0 20 40 60
0 20 40 60 80
Kilometres
International Boundary
Provincial boundary
River
Land over 1500 feet (457 metres)
1 Bohemia
2 Moravia
3 Slovakia

of year. The average annual temperature is 8°C to 10°C (46°F to 50°F). December, January and February are the coldest months and June, July and August the warmest. In winter the temperature can fall to -20°C (-68°F) and in summer can sometimes reach over 30°C (86°F). The weather in spring and autumn is usually very pleasant. Rain falls throughout the year and there are frequent thunderstorms in the summer.

Communications

The country is covered by a railway network of 13,241 km (8,276 miles) and there are 73,538 km (45,961 miles) of major roads. Internal air routes between the major cities total 4,700 km (2,938 miles) and there are several hundred kilometres of navigable waterways. There are over 4,500 regular bus and coach lines and very few places without a regular bus service. Czechoslovakia's overseas bulk freight traffic passes along her two main rivers, the Elbe (and its tributary the Vltava), which flows north through the German Democratic Republic to Hamburg and the North Sea, and the Danube, which flows east through Austria and Hungary into the Black Sea. Civil aviation is important and there are about 60 regular internal services. All transport facilities are nationalised.

2 POPULATION

Growth and Distribution

The total population in 1978 was 15.14 million, with twice as many people in the Czech lands (Bohemia/Moravia) as in Slovakia. More than a million people live in Prague. The density of population is 115 per square kilometre. After World War Two an intense effort was made (especially in Slovakia) to replace a dispersed rural population with a concentrated urban economy, and by the late 1960s over 70 new towns had been established. One of these, Havirov, had 74,510 people in 1966 and ranked eighth among the cities of Czechoslovakia. Over 80% of the population is now urban.

Groups

Over 94% of the population is Czech or Slovak, with Hungarians, Poles and Germans forming minority groups. Before World War Two minorities represented one third of the population, chiefly Germans (23.4% in 1921) living in Bohemia and Moravia-Silesia.

3 HISTORY AND POLITICS

Before Independence

Czechoslovakia is one of the successor states to the Austro-Hungarian monarchy, which collapsed in 1918, and now incorporates Bohemia, Moravia, parts of Silesia (called the Czech lands), and Slovakia.

Bohemia was renowned in the Middle Ages as a centre of learning and Charles University in Prague is the oldest in Central Europe. After the Thirty Years' War and the Counter-Reformation, Bohemia was subjected to a process of Germanisation. The Czech language was discouraged, and large numbers of Germans moved into an area surrounding Bohemia on three sides, the Sudetenland, with disastrous consequences for the later Czechoslovak republic. However, the Bohemians retained a strong national awareness, increasingly manifest in the nineteenth century, and evident in the fact that the Hapsburg Emperor was not only entitled King of Hungary and Archduke of Austria, but also King of Bohemia. By a language decree of 1880 the Czech language was placed on the same footing as German in the Bohemian administration and courts of the land. Slovakia, on the other hand, was simply administered as part of the kingdom of Hungary and, particularly from 1867, suffered from an extremely oppressive policy of Magyarisation under the Hungarians. Before World War One, large numbers of Slovaks were driven to emigrate, particularly to America.

When World War One broke out in 1914 Czech and Slovak sympathies tended to be on the side of Russia and the Serbs, and their western allies, while the Germans of Bohemia supported the Austro-Hungarian and German war effort. Under pressure from Czechs and Slovaks outside Austro-Hungary, notably Tomaš Garrigue Masaryk and Edvard Beneš, in 1917 the Allies included in a declaration of their war aims the liberation of the 'Czech-Slovaks'. In 1918 the Czechoslovak State was formally recognised. Masaryk was the first President.

The First Republic (1918-1938)

From the very beginning the new republic was dogged by racial problems. The Czech majority (about 6.5 million in Bohemia and Moravia) was in command, with about 3.1 million Bohemian and Moravian Germans (in the Sudetenland) who were unwilling to accept their place in the new state. As the economic situation worsened Hitlerism and Nazism grew amongst the Sudeten Germans. In elections in 1935 Konrad Henlein's pro-Nazi *Heimatfront* party became the biggest single party in the republic and his pro-Nazi and anti-Czech activities rapidly increased. On 12 March 1938 the Germans annexed Austria and Czechoslovakia's situation became extremely precarious. The Munich agreement of 1938 between Germany (with Henlein and his followers) and Italy, Great Britain, and France, forced Czechoslovakia to cede to Germany all those districts of Bohemia and Moravia which had a 50% or more German speaking population. Other parts were ceded to Poland and Hungary, in all depriving Czechoslovakia of about one third of its population. Shortly afterwards, on 15 March 1939, Czechoslovakia was occupied by the German army.

Post-1945

In May 1945 the republic was restored with a coalition government which included communists. Most Germans and Magyars were expelled. The most easterly part of the country, sub-Carpathian Ukraine, was ceded to the USSR. In the elections of 1946 the Communist Party emerged as the largest single party (38% of the votes cast) and a coalition was formed under the communist leader Klement Gottwald. In February 1948 the communists launched a *coup d'état* and gained control of the government. Many non-communists were expelled from the party and party purges soon followed. The reversal of Stalinist policies was slow. The First Secretaryship of the Communist Party was held by Antonin Novotný from September 1953.

1968 and After

In January 1968 Novotný was relieved of his post following a Central Committee Plenum to discuss the position and role of the party. He was succeeded by Alexander Dubček, a member of the Czechoslovak Party Praesidium and First Secretary of the Slovak Communist Party. A new government was formed with General Ludvik Svoboda as President. Far-reaching reforms were discussed, aiming at 'socialism with a human face', but in August 1968 the country was invaded by the Warsaw Pact forces, excluding those of Romania. There followed a gradual reversal of the reforms. Party membership was reduced by over 300,000 to 1.2 million. Mr Dubček was expelled from the party in June 1970, having been succeeded as First Secretary in April 1969 by Gustav Husák, previously leader of the Slovak Communist Party. In 1973 attempts were made to normalise the political situation resulting from the events of 1968. In 1975 Dr Husák was appointed President of the Republic while still holding the position of Chairman of the National Front and Secretary of the Communist Party. He was re-elected party leader in May 1980.

Central Government

In 1960 Czechoslovakia was given the official title 'Czechoslovak Socialist Republic' (CSSR). The constitution defines the country as a 'socialist state based on the firm alliance of workers, peasants, and intelligentsia headed by the working class' and (since January 1969) as a 'single state of two fraternal nations possessing equal rights: the Czechs and the Slovaks'. Political franchise is accorded to all citizens over 18 years, and the right to be elected to all citizens over 21 years.

Czechoslovakia now, since 1968, consists of the Czech Socialist Republic and the Slovak Socialist Republic. The federal government has the right to suspend or annul the execution of a measure of either of the two republican governments if it does not comply with federal government policy. The Federal Assembly consists of two chambers of equal rights: the Chamber of the People which has 200 deputies elected from the whole federation (but proportional to the population of the republic - 138 Czechs and 62 Slovaks); and the Chamber of Nations, with 150 deputies of whom 75 are Czech and 75 Slovak elected by their respective National Councils. The two chambers have equal powers; the government may submit Bills to either of them but the consent of both chambers is needed for the passing of the Law. The Head of State is the President of the Republic who is elected by the Federal Assembly for a term of five years and is accountable to the Assembly. The President appoints and dismisses members of the federal government including the Prime Minister, and also the highest State officials.

Regional Government

The separate Czech and Slovak governments each consist of a prime minister, three deputy prime ministers, and 15 other ministers. Each republic has its own parliament: the Czech National Council in Prague, and the Slovak National Council in Bratislava. The members are elected for five year terms. Both Councils delegate to the Federal Assembly responsibility for State constitutional affairs, foreign relations, defence, civil and penal law, education and certain economic matters.

Both republics are divided into regions, districts, and municipalities, where the organs of popular self-government are the national committees. These rely on the active participation of the working people of the area and they cooperate with other organisations of the people. They direct local and economic cultural development, ensure the protection of socialist ownership, the maintenance of socialist order in society, and the implementation and observance of laws, etc. The committees take part in drafting and implementing State plans for the development of the national economy and draw up their own budgets which form a part of the State budget. The committees appoint commissions (which may include a large number of citizens who need not be national committee elected members) to deal with various aspects of public work.

Communist Party

The centralised Communist Party of Czechoslovakia (CPCZ) dominates the National Front which includes four other minor parties. The Party's highest authority is the Party Congress, which elects the Central Committee (121 members were elected in April 1976) to supervise party work, and takes important decisions on the problems, the present situation, and the future development of the whole society. The Committee elects a Præsidium (11 full members and 2 alternate members) to direct policy.

International Relations

Czechoslovakia is a member of the Eastern European Mutual Assistance Treaty (the Warsaw Pact). For trade purposes Czechoslovakia is a member of the East European Council for Mutual Economic Assistance (COMECON). In 1973 some attempts were made to improve relations with Austria, Romania, and Yugoslavia. In 1974 a treaty with the Federal Republic of Germany established normal relations between the two countries for the first time.

4 SOCIETY AND CULTURE

Culture

Czechoslovakia has given the world several outstanding writers and musicians, such as Karel Capek, Jaroslav Hašek, Franz Kafka (who wrote in German), Bedrich Smetana, Antonin Dvořák and Leos Janaček. In May 1949 legislation was passed making the publication, printing, illustration, and distribution of all books and music the prerogative of the State. Churches and religious bodies are permitted to publish if the State will accept their work for printing. Czech and Slovak writers and other intellectuals were prominent in the struggle to oust president Novotný in the 1968 reform movement. Subsequently they and other people in the arts world have been subjected to tighter State control.

Czechoslovakia has a rich heritage of castles and other historical buildings which are all in the care of the Ministry of Culture. In recent years more effort and finance has been expended on the preservation of these historical monuments which had been very neglected. Many of the buildings are used to house exhibitions for the general public to visit or to store books and records. Some are used as homes for children or pensioners.

Language

The official languages, which are mutually understandable, are Czech and Slovak, members of the west Slavonic group. there is a Hungarian speaking minority in Slovakia.

Religion

About 70% of the population is nominally Roman Catholic. There is an important Protestant minority (about 15%) belonging to different denominations, and including the spiritual descendants of the reformer Jan Hus. There were about 15,000 Jews in Czechoslovakia in 1966 but an anti-Zionist campaign has forced many Jews to leave the country on one-way passports; an estimated 4,000 remain. Since 1949 all Church administration has been under the State and the churches are dependent on it. There are no church schools, nor monastaries. The constitution guarantees religious freedom so long as there is no contravention of the law.

5 THE ECONOMY

Economic Planning

Before 1939 the Czech lands were well advanced industrially, while Slovakia was still largely agricultural. After 1949 economic development was implemented in a series of five-year plans on the Soviet model, with socialisation of the means of production and detailed planning of the national economy. There was a vigorous growth of investment and industry in Slovakia; between

1948 and 1960 the increase of people industrially employed in Slovakia was 60%. The First Five-Year Plan (1949) effected changes from a liberal to a Soviet type 'command economy'. Investment was channelled towards heavy industry, agriculture was nationalised, and low priority given to consumer needs.

The Third Five-Year Plan (1961-65) switched the emphasis from heavy industry and engineering to light industry, and in January 1965 a plenary meeting of the CPCZ Central Committee approved more flexible economic and management reforms, to include a relaxation in the influence of the central authorities and the reintroduction of a price mechanism. The new system was to provide a financial interest in profitability, quality, and marketing, and an incentive to workers in the wage element. However, inflationary trends soon appeared: inefficient industries benefited and many greatly increased their profits without a comparable rise in the quantity and quality of goods produced for the market.

When Mr Hušak came to power in April 1969, a policy of stabilisation was introduced. Increased industrial production made it possible to fulfil the export plan and restore a favourable trade balance. The targets of the Fifth Five-Year Plan (1970-75) were exceeded.

The Sixth Five-Year Plan (1976-80) stressed the need for increased productivity and the more efficient use of resources. Priority was given to chemicals, engineering, power, and long established industries such as textiles, and those which use indigenous raw materials, like paper manufacture. In 1978 a measure of responsibility was given to 150 enterprises and in 1980 a plan to introduce some devolution of production and profits control was introduced to encourage production.

Agriculture

Although traditionally the manufacturing industry has been the greatest strength of the Czechoslovak economy, agriculture is now quite highly mechanised and further improvements in productivity are planned. Between 1971-75 production increased by 15.5%, but for certain domestic requirements Czechoslovakia is still dependent on imports of agricultural products. Agriculture has been collectivised, and about 93% of the land is under agricultural cooperatives, State farms, or communal enterprises. The main crops are wheat, barley, potatoes and sugar beet.

Industry

Although Czechoslovakia has few natural resources, and depends on the USSR for many raw materials, it is now a highly industrialised country. In 1971 the industrial sector employed 38% of the working population. Engineering is of prime importance, with a considerable output of cars and cycles, together with construction of new chemical plant, new and modernised iron and steel plans, paper mills, and mining. The most rapid development has taken place in the chemical and petrochemical industry. In recent years there has been substantial development of hydroelectric resources, particularly in Slovakia. Other important industries are traditional, such as textiles, glass and ceramics, and beer.

Trade

Czechoslovakia's internal trade network is State managed. As a member of COMECON a large proportion of her trade is with the countries of Eastern Europe, particularly the USSR. However, there is also considerable trade with west European countries, notably the Federal Republic of Germany, Austria, and Britain. Principal exports include machinery and equipment, chemicals and fuels, glass and other manufactured goods.

Living Standards

Living standards compare with those in Western Europe. The traditional diet has, however, a high carbohydrate content and for much of the year there is a shortage of fresh fruit and vegetables. There are shortages of labour and materials. In some parts, especially in Prague, there is a housing shortage. The statutory living space allowance is 12 square metres (14.40 square yards) for each member of a family plus 6 square metres (7.20 square yards).

Average salaries are rising. Most wives have to work but an improved system of family allowances allows mothers to take longer maternity leave than in the 1960s. All prices are fixed by the State but since 1972 there have been increases in hotel and restaurant prices as well as rents. Public transport and most basic foodstuffs are cheap but clothes and materials and most consumer goods are expensive. The range and quality of consumer goods is limited but enough Skoda cars are now available for everyone who can afford to buy and run one. It is possible now to obtain credit facilities for the purchase of some cars and household goods.

6 THE EDUCATION SYSTEM

Academic Year

The school year runs from 1 September to 30 June. It is divided into two semesters (September to January and February to June) with a two-month break in the summer.

Pre-School

Pre-school education is provided free by the Ministry of Health for children up to 6 years of age. From infancy to three years the children of working mothers may attend nurseries *(jesle)* and from 3 to 6 years they go to nursery schools *(mateřska škola)*. In 1975/76 there were 475,004 pupils in these schools; the number has more than trebled since before the war and it is now possible, though not compulsory, for all five-year olds to enter nursery school. Day nurseries are usually open from 6.00 a.m. to 6.00 p.m. to fit in with the mothers' working hours and it is also possible to attend for half days as well as whole days. They are staffed by personnel trained in secondary vocational schools and doctors visit the nurseries regularly. Children are divided into age groups for games and other activities; no group has more than 25 children and they follow a careful timetable of work and play with exercise in the fresh air, regular meals and rest periods, based on the principle of Comenius that "Children should learn by tiny steps, without being aware of it, as if playing". Activities are picked for their educational value and children are also encouraged to join in 'socially useful' work - tidying their toy cupboards, laying tables, etc.

First Level (Primary)

Education is free, compulsory and coeducational between the ages of 6 and 15, during which children attend the basic school *(základni devítiletá škola)*. In 1979 there were more than 9,000 basic schools with 1.88 million pupils. Proposals have been made to reduce the length of compulsory basic schooling from nine to eight years. The curriculum is set by the three regional education ministries and all children receive a unified education based on the 1960 Education Act. In the lower forms a general curriculum is provided, followed from the sixth class onwards by more specialisation. Subjects taught are mother tongue, literature, Russian language, social relations, history, geography, mathematics, civics, general science, physical education, art and music. Roughly 37.9% of the timetable is devoted to languages, 11.3% to social studies, and 27.5% to mathematics and sciences; the rest of the time is spent on physical education, arts subjects, and work training. Children are taught either Czech or Slovak, according to their location, but since the languages are mutually comprehensible, this causes no problems. Special efforts are made to popularise certain subjects - for instance Mathematics Olympiads are held in which up to 25,000 secondary school children and pupils of the upper forms of the basic school participate. Pupils are promoted from one year to the next on the basis of their assessment on the five-point scale. Physical education, civics, art and music are not included and a pupil may still be approved for promotion with one or two subjects in the 'unsatisfactory' grade, provided one is not the mother tongue or mathematics. The pupil does, however, have to take extra classes to improve his performance.

Children must attend school for five days a week, usually from 8.00 a.m. to 1.00 p.m. The State pays 40% of the cost of school meals. In the afternoon children of working mothers can attend centres and clubs where under the guidance of trained supervisors they take part in a variety of activities such as singing, dancing, sports, film shows, visits to theatres and museums, etc. An all day school system was tested in 1974 in a selected 67 schools, with the aim of creating a new type of school to provide conditions for all pupils to prepare their lessons and engage in special interest activities after school lessons. At these schools pupils in the first cycle prepare 'homework' at school clubs, and older pupils work in school study rooms under the supervision of a teacher. Special interest activity includes educational work, sports, defence education, working, technical and aesthetic education.

Second Level Schools

At the age of 15 children can leave school and go straight into employment or they can follow a free course of secondary education, in apprentice training schools, vocational schools, or for the most . academically inclined, four-year courses in *gymnasia* leading to university entrance.

Gymnasia (středni všeobecné vzdělávací škola)

There is keen competition for places at this type of school and only about 20% of those who apply are selected. Selection is made by an admission board of the secondary school, headed by the school director, on the basis of the applicant's school record and an interview. The pupils enter the school at 15 for a three- to four-year course leading to a school leaving examination *(Matura)*. Pupils who succesfully complete their examinations can apply for entry to university. The children study a wide range of subjects with emphasis on arts or natural sciences according to their varying interests. In order to avoid excessive specialisation there is a large common core to the curriculum. All students must learn Russian as their first foreign language but can choose a second foreign language of which English is most popular.

Vocational and Secondary Vocational Schools (středni odborná škola)

The latter provide four-year courses of vocational training combined with general education for pupils from the basic schools who are destined for less skilled employment. The courses lead to a professional qualification and the *matura*. There are also two-year courses, without general subjects, for students who already have the *matura*. Vocational schools provide two- or three-year courses for pupils from the basic schools but with less general education, and they award only a professional qualification without the *matura*. Some professions are taught in four-year secondary vocational schools only, but in many there are both types of course. Most of the students are released from their places of work to attend these schools part time or in the evening. The trade and industry courses offered in the schools include carpentry, tailoring, and dressmaking, dry cleaning, office work, the preparation and distribution of food, etc. There are also specialised conservatories which train artists and musicians, and these are highly selective, requiring demonstration of special talents as well as general educational competence.

Apprentice Training Centres and Schools
(odborne uciliste and učeňovská škola)

About 60% of basic school leavers enter apprenticeship. The centres are run by major industrial concerns; the apprentice schools are run by national committees and give training in trades where the numbers are so small that factory centres are uneconomical. General education is continued in these schools (about 20% of curricular time), concurrently with specialist trade subjects. Students follow a course in one of 15 categories: mining, foundry work, chemical industries, engineering and metalwork, electrotechnology, building, ceramics and glass-making, woodwork and musical instrument making, film, photography and polygraphy, textiles, leatherwork and shoemaking, food industries, agriculture and forestry, transport and communication, commerce, catering and non-productive services. The system covers 288 apprentice trades with some courses taking two years and others three to four years. Students intended for the printing industry take a four-year course. For the first half of the course chosen, the students are paid at apprenticeship rates, and later they earn between 60% and 100% of the normal wage. Concessions (e.g. free board and lodging) are given to apprentices in 'preferential trades' in order to tempt trainees into the most essential sectors of the economy. Courses lead to an examination in theory and practice and the award of the Certificate of Apprenticeship, the skilled worker's qualification. A student who completes his course satisfactorily may apply for admission to a technical university.

Special

Over 40,000 children are in special schools for the handicapped, grouped according to the pupil's disabilities. There are also a few experimental projects to provide schooling for highly gifted pupils. Special basic and even secondary schools exist for children of national minority groups. The curriculum at these schools is taught in Polish, Hungarian or Ukrainian, but is otherwise identical to the Czech and Slovak schools. Textbooks are published in the minority languages.

Third Level (Higher) Institutions

In 1978/79 there were 183,632 students in 36 degree-granting institutions of higher education *(vyoské školy)* comprising universities, technical universities and colleges, schools of fine arts, and teacher training colleges. Each institution is headed by a Rector, assisted by a Prorector, and each faculty is run by a Dean and sub-Deans. Nearly a quarter of the students are part time.

Universities

There are six universities; the oldest is Charles (Karlova) founded in Prague by the Emperor Charles IV in 1348. In 1970/71 the university had 13 faculties, the most recent being the Faculty of Mathematics and Physics and the Faculty of Social Sciences and Journalism. In 1974 the university absorbed the University of 17th November, which had been established mainly to accommodate overseas students (mainly from Afro-Asian and Latin-American countries) as part of Czechoslovakia's international aid programme). The most important Slovak university is Comenius University in Bratislava, founded in 1919, with faculties providing tuition in almost all fields of university study. Other important universities are the Palacky in Olomouc, founded in 1573, and the J E Purkyne in Brno, founded in 1919.

The universities deal principally with the humanities, pure sciences, economics, and older professions such as medicine and law. There is a good deal of competition for entry to the arts faculties. Study is free; all students are granted scholarships to provide for costs connected with studies and student life, and as far as possible are required to live in student hostels and eat in student cafeterias, where the food is cheap. the courses last for some four to six years and successful candidates who pass the final State examination become graduates with a diploma in their particular field of study. Selected students can continue with post-graduate courses of a more specialised nature. University graduates (with the exception of graduates in medicine) who have passed a doctoral examination are awarded the degree of Doctor of Law (JUDr) or Doctor of Science (RNDr) or Doctor of Philosophy (PhDr). Graduates in medicine receive the degree of Doctor of Medicine (MDRr), and graduates of veterinary science receive the degree of Doctor of Veterinary Science (MVDr). Graduates in science, economics and agriculture receive the degree of Graduate Engineer.

Technical Universities and Colleges

There are 14 of these, including the Czech Technical University of Prague, the Technical University of Brno, and the Slovak Technical University in Bratislava. Some offer courses in several branches of technology, while others are more specialised. Most courses last five years, though engineering, electrical engineering and building take five and a half, and six years' study are required for architecture. At most technical faculties the students receive thorough theoretical training in the first two to four years with some general subjects, and in the final years they take up their specialisation. The last term of all is devoted to work on a particular project and the final State examination.

Schools of Fine Art

There are six: the Academy of Fine Arts in Prague and the college of Fine Arts in Bratislava; colleges of music and dramatic arts in Prague, Bratislava, and Brno; a faculty of film and television and a college of applied arts in Prague. Graduates in painting, sculpture and architecture are awarded the titles Academic Painter, Academic Sculptor, and Academic Architect.

Czechoslovak Academy of Sciences

The Czechoslovak Academy of Sciences is concerned with the training of new scientific workers. The students are either full time post-graduates or part time post-graduates and follow planned research projects. Their courses last from three to five years and, as well as their own research topic, they must study Marxism/Leninism and languages. On completion and successful defence of the candidates' degree theses, degrees are awarded in two grades: either Candidate of Science (CSc) or Doctor of Science (DrSc) in the respective field of study. All matters concerning the awarding of these degrees are the responsibility of the State Council for Academic Awards.

Teacher Training

Pre-school teacher training at pedagogic schools is open to students with the *matura;* courses last two years. For students with the *matura* intending to teach in first and second level schools there are pedagogical faculties in universities (where teacher training forms part of the normal course), or seven colleges providing degree and diploma courses normally lasting four years. After passing the State examination, students teach under supervision for a further year, at the end of which they take a proficiency examination to confirm their qualification. Graduates at all types of universities are entitled to use the professional title of 'secondary school professor' when they take up teaching at second level schools. Teachers of vocational subjects follow one-year training courses after the completion of technical college studies.

In-service training is important. Every major city has an institute for the organisation of refresher courses and courses leading to higher qualifications, and every district has a pedagogical centre for the exchange of information, dissemination of literature, etc.

Adult

Second level schools for workers *(střední škola pro pracující)* give courses leading to the *matura*. The length of course varies to accommodate workers of varying ages and educational standards, but the maximum is three years. Most schools are run by large industrial concerns for their own employees, and others are run by national committees. There are three types of course specialising in physics, chemistry, or biology, and a fourth of a more general nature. The curriculum is narrower, and the time more limited, than in the general secondary school.

Further part time education is also provided for employed people in the form of People's Universities and Academies, administered by the Society for the Dissemination of Political and Scientific Knowledge, and other mass organisations. The People's University of Science, Technology and Arts aims to supplement knowledge obtained in the basic school and keep students abreast of the latest trends, by means of courses, lectures, and seminar cycles. There is also the specialist Agricultural People's University. Youth universities are set up in all regional cities and are being established in district towns for students from the age of 17 to enable them to acquire knowledge in the fields of social, natural, technical, and agricultural sciences. The People's Academy of Science, Technology and Arts differs from the People's University in being broader in scope, including for instance courses on the correct upbringing of children, etc.

7 EDUCATIONAL ADMINISTRATION
Central Administration

There has been no private education in Czechoslovakia since 1948. The present system is based on a 1960 Education Act and other laws and governmental decrees. The government alone administers education, through the two education ministries in Prague and Bratislava. The ministries decide on curricula and textbooks to be used throughout the school system. They appoint teachers, readers in higher education, and administrative personnel; though the President of the Republic appoints professors. Salary scales, other conditions of employment, and in-service training are also arranged by the ministries, and they administer directly institutions of higher education, research institutes (pedagogical and vocational), the State pedagogical publishing houses, teaching aids centres, etc.

Regional Administration

Both the Czech and the Slovak republics are divided into regions and statutory cities for administrative purposes: seven regions and four statutory cities in the Czech Socialist Republic and three regions and the city of Bratislava in the Slovak Socialist Republic. The executive organs of the national education administration in the individual regions are the education departments of regional national committees; regions are further divided into districts with district national committees which have departments of education and culture. Districts are further subdivided into municipalities with local or town national committees. The statutory cities are divided into wards. The regional national committees (or national committees in the statutory cities) administer secondary schools (vocational and general, secondary schools for adults, apprentice training centres and schools) and the basic nine-year schools, in accordance with the principles and directives approved by the Ministry of Education.

Attached to all regional national committees and national committees of both capital cities are the regional pedagogical institutes. Their main task is the further education of school teachers and improvement of teaching techniques in general.

Inspectorate

There is a network of school inspectors: the district school inspector looks after the secondary schools, and the work of institutions of higher education is controlled by different commissions of the State Committee for Higher Education. The central school inspectorate of the Ministry of Education evaluates the work of the primary and secondary schools in the various regions of the country, carries on general methodological activities, accumulates experience in educational work and, in particular, directs regional and district school inspectors in specific inspection and methodological tasks.

8 EDUCATIONAL FINANCE

Education Budget

In 1974 6.5% of all public expenditure was allocated to education (or 4.5% of the net material product). Total expenditure on education was 17,598 million koruñas, of which 90.8% went on recurrent expenditure. All expenses for the construction, equipment, and operation of schools are covered by the State, through the budgets of the statutory cities.

Allocation of Funds

The distribution between the various educational levels is approximately as follows (1977 figures):

Allocation of Funds
Expenditure on Education: Distribution by Level
Percentage of Expenditure 1977

Pre-school	First Level	Second Level	Third Level	Other
11.4	42.2	14.4	16.5	15.5

In technical education the operation of school farms or forests is guided by the same financial principles as that of State farms or forests: part of the profit goes to the teachers and pupils, part is used by the school for the improvement of its equipment and facilities, while the third part goes to the national budget.

9 DEVELOPMENT AND PLANNING OF THE EDUCATION SYSTEM

Pre-1960

The pre-war system of education was organised in three tiers: the elementary schools (ages 6 to 11), the 'civic' school (an advanced primary or lower secondary school for ages 11 to 15), and the secondary schools. From 1922 schooling was compulsory until the age of 14. This, together with comparatively greater industrialisation and minimal illiteracy, meant that Czechoslovakia was later spared many of the post-war problems of educational backwardness and low living standards. In 1948 all schools were brought under State management and a law passed 'to make culture, training, and education democratic'. The system was organised in three tiers: the basic school (from 6 to 11), middle schools (11 to 15), and four-year *gymnasia* and vocational secondary schools (15 to 19). Later developments brought into being the basic comprehensive schools followed by different types of secondary school on the present patterns.

Present System

The most important reforms of the 1960 Education Act were the lengthening of the basic school course to nine years, the further expansion of vocational and technical education, the increased emphasis on polytechnical and technical studies in the schools, and the introduction of new types of schools for adults.

The present education system was developed in accord with the humanitarian principles of Jan Amos Comenius, pedagogical reformer of the seventeenth century (1592-1670), and the revolutionary social elements and ideas in the teaching of Jan Hus (1371-1415), together with the teaching of Marx, Engels, and Lenin. The general aims and objectives of the system are expressed in the preamble to the 1960 Education Act:

> "It is the function of schools in the Czechoslovak Socialist Republic to educate the youth and the working people, in the spirit of the scientific world outlook, to be educated citizens who are able to acquire the results of modern science and technology, who are well prepared for socially useful work; to be citizens who are physically well prepared, who find pleasure and satisfaction in the community and in work for society, who are imbued with the ideas of socialist patriotism and internationalism; to be conscious citizens of the Czechoslovak Socialist Republic – to be enthusiastic builders of communism."

The management and organisation of the universities is laid down by the Universities Acts of 16 March and 17 December 1969. The Czechoslovaks define the task of the universities as follows:

(i) to train highly educated and qualified professional workers who, on the basis of Marxism/Leninism, are morally and politically prepared for all fields of life in a socialist society

(ii) to develop scientific or artistic activities and to educate new scientific workers or workers in the field of art

(iii) to deepen and widen professional knowledge of the workers with university education

(iv) to be the centres participating in the development of culture and people's education.

The number of pupils in secondary education and under-graduates in each branch of study is carefully planned to suit the requirements of the national economy, science and culture. As in the case of vocational school leavers there is strict adherence to the principle that the graduate should find employment in the field for which he or she was trained.

Planning Institutions

Research on education and curriculum development is conducted by the pedagogical research institute in each area. They also advise on textbooks which are produced by the pedagogical publishing houses in Prague and Bratislava. The institutes in the two main cities are concerned with improving the content and methods of work in pre-school institutions, in primary schools, in special schools, in general secondary schools, and adult secondary schools. They are concerned too with school hygiene, and the work of teachers. The Research Institute of Vocational Schools exercises a similar function for vocational schools and apprentice training institutions. General pedagogical problems are considered by the J A Comenius Pedagogical Institute of the Czechoslovak Academy of Sciences: chiefly basic problems of the all round development of man, the effectiveness of the educational process and the theory of adult education.

In the light of research and new developments, fundamental education policy is decided by a Council for Education which coordinates the activities of the two ministries. The Communist Party Central Committee exercises control of the education system through its Department of Schools, Science and Art, which reviews policy and reinforces political influence on the running of the system.

Current Plans

In 1974 experiments were made in some schools with a view to shortening compulsory and advanced education. Elementary school attendance was to be gradually reduced from five to four years, based on a new view of the basic school as a stepping stone to individual branches of secondary education rather than a closed cycle, and based too on the view of Czechoslovak educationists that children are developing both physically and mentally at a faster rate than in the past. Reducing the first level to four years will automatically reduce school attendance at the basic nine-year school to eight years. In the 1974/75 school year eighth grade pupils entered *gymnasia*, and in the next stage of the reform will enter secondary vocational schools. There are plans to shorten courses at universities and technical colleges from five to four years, with a corresponding extension of the system of post-graduate studies so that every graduate could then take post-graduate courses after intervals of five and ten years of work.

10 THE SYSTEM IN OPERATION
Provision

The majority of schools (about two-thirds) do not at present have the full number of classes to accommodate the whole nine-year basic course, and indeed a proportion of them are one-class schools. While it is considered unrealistic to introduce full scale schools in small villages (many of them cater for less than 20 children) there are plans to introduce schools of at least two classes where no alternative solution is possible. After the reduction of the five-year first cycle of the basic school to four years conditions for teaching in the lower grades of the basic school should be improved. The main trend, however, is on providing more central nine-year schools, with a transport system for children in the surrounding areas.

Apprentice Education

There is a continuing stress on improving the standard of apprentice education. A concerted effort is also being made to give the largest possible number of young people a complete secondary education to ensure that future qualified workers not only master their own subject, but are also capable of adapting quickly to changing situations. Continued further expansion of four-year training centres aimed at workers' qualifications and the *matura* examination is one method being used to achieve this.

Education and Ideology

In the nine-year basic school, history emphasises the motherland against a background of world events. In the sixth year ancient history is taught; in the seventh Czechoslovakian history in its world context up to the rise of capitalism and the transition to imperialism. In the ninth form the teaching matter deals with 'the period beginning with the victory of socialism in the Soviet Union right up to the present day'. The geography programme also deals primarily with the geography of Czechoslovakia and other countries, in particular the socialist countries, beginning with the Soviet Union. Stress is laid on economic and political aspects. Civics is more directly political in content, with the purpose of 'providing instruction about the most important aspects of political and economic institutions in Czechoslovakia, making the pupils familiar with all the essentials of the scientific world outlook of Marxism-Leninism, and to bring home to them the principles of Communist morality'. Unlike most other subjects, no marks are awarded in the subject of civics.

Almost all children belong to one of the country's official youth organisations - *Jiskry* (Sparks) for 6 to 9 year olds, the Pioneer Organisation of the Czechoslovak Youth League for 9 to 15 year olds, and the Czechoslovak Youth League for 15 year olds and above. These organisations play a strong political role which is closely integrated with all sorts of spare time activities, cultural circles, sports clubs, holiday camps, etc., reflecting communist aims to make not only school but society as a whole an educational environment for future citizens.

FURTHER READING

Czechoslovakia Ustav Skolských Informacć (1976). *Project of the further development of the Czechoslovak educational system.* Prague Institute of Educational Information.
Feser, Jeri (1978). "New programme of teacher education in Czechoslovakia", *Universita Karlova,* European Information Centre Newsletter, 2, nos. 1-2, November 1978.
Groombridge, Brian (Ed.) (1966). *Adult education and television: a comparative study in Canada, Czechoslovakia, Japan.* National Institute of Adult Education with Unesco, London.
Richmond, W. Kenneth (1966). *Educational Planning: old and new perspectives.* Michael Joseph, London.
Turosienski, Severin K. (   ). *Education in Czechoslovakia.* Bulletin 1935, No. 11. US Office of Education, Washington DC.
Shalka, Jarolim (1977). *Adult education in the Czechoslovak Socialist Republic (CSSR).* European Centre for Leisure Education, Prague.
UNESCO (1978). *Economic aspects of special education: Czechoslovakia, New Zealand, United States of America.* Unesco, Paris.
UNESCO/IBE (1980). *International Yearbook of Education.* XXXII. Unesco, Paris.

Structure of the Education System in Czechoslovakia

Age	3	4	5	6	7	8	9	10	11	12	13	14	15	16	17	18	19	20	21	22	23	24
Level						I								II			III			IV		
Stage					1				2					3			4					
Compulsory																						
School type	(a) Creches (b) Nurseries and children's centres			Eight-year basic school									General academic secondary / Apprentice schools and centres / Vocational/technical / Nursery teacher training				Teacher training					Universities

☒ Special schools: for handicapped

Examinations: compulsory at the end of stage I onwards

Education preceding the first level

Source: UNESCO/IBE International Yearbook of Education

Compulsory education: Age Limits 6-15   Duration (years) 9
Entrance age to pre-school education: 3

CZECHOSLOVAKIA BASIC STATISTICS	1960	1970	1975	1978 (approx.)
1 Total population (000)	13,654	14,339	14,793	15,138
% female	51	51	51	51
2 % population 0-14 years	27.4	23.1		23
% female	49	49	49	49
3 Enrolment, all levels	2,460,314	2,418,176	2,357,004	2,417,098
% female	49	50	50	50
First level	2,152,834	1,966,448	1,881,414	1,877,773
% female	49	49	49	49
Second level	213,440	320,629	320,531	355,314
% female	55	61	61	62
Third level	94,040	131,099	155,059	184,011
% female	34	38	40	41
4 Teachers, all levels	113,640	136,618	141,812	139,952
% female		61	64	64
First level	87,465	97,712	95,634	91,876
% female		73	77	78
Second level	15,671	22,504	24,880	25,481
% female		43	49	50
Third level	10,504	16,402	21,298	22,595
% female	*17	20	25	25
5 Public expenditure on education				
Total (000) Korunas	6,085,821	13,625,000	19,104,801	
As % of GNP	3.7	4.4	4.7	
6 % enrolment (MF) by level	100	100	100	100
First level	88	81	80	77
Second level	9	13	14	15
Third level	4	5	7	8
% enrolment (F) by level	100	100	100	100
First level	88	80	78	76
Second level	10	16	17	18
Third level	3	4	5	6
7 Entrance age: Duration of				
First level education	6:9	6:9	6:9	6:9
Second level education	15:4	15:4	15:4	15:4
8 Enrolment ratios (MF)				
First level	93	98	96	94
Second level	25	31	36	40
Third level	10.95	10.44	12.17	15.25
Enrolment ratios (F)				
First level	93	98	97	95
Second level	28	39	45	50
Third level	7.52	8.03	9.99	12.64

*

Denmark

CONTENTS

1 Geography	196
2 Population	198
3 Society and Culture	199
4 History and Politics	200
5 The Economy	204
6 The Education System	205
7 Educational Administration	213
8 Educational Finance	215
9 Development and Planning of the Educational System	216
10 The System in Operation	218

The Danish Folk High Schools are world renowned. Based on the idea of Bishop Grundtvig, whose methods of teaching emphasised the 'living word' and put into practice by Kristen Kold the Folk High Schools were designed to protect Danish culture against German imperialism in the nineteenth century. Many of them were established near the Schleswig Holstein/Denmark border. Danish literature, music, folk lore and traditional crafts provided the core of studies and activities designed to keep alive in the young people of Denmark a sense of their national identity. Religion gave these activities an overall ethos in some cases closely associated with the Inner Mission.

The Folk High Schools served other functions. They provided for the children of farmers residential colleges during the long winter months. In the informal atmosphere provided young adults learned how to cooperate in running their affairs. Denmark's economic growth, based on dairy produce cooperatives, owed much in the nineteenth century to the development of a farming industry. The high quality of products – milk, bacon and butter – was carefully monitored and cooperatives made it possible for the Danish farmers to win an international market for them. Some Folk High Schools offer vocational training while others specialise in, for example, gymnastics. Others are run by trade unions and Askov in effect provides courses for those who have already attended Folk High Schools.

The spirit of the Folk High School movement, while it does not dominate the national system of education, has certainly influenced it. The family and small community remain important educative agencies and while, as in most continental European countries, the Central Ministry of Education has considerable powers, municipal councils are very much involved in the planning and running of first level schools.

Trade with Britain no doubt stimulated cross fertilisation and while the structure and content of the Danish school system are rather similar to the German model there is less rigidity in the Danish approach to the provision of education.

As in most countries the reform of secondary schools has occupied the attention of educationists since 1945. After the Act of 1975 a comprehensive nine year compulsory and a tenth form non-compulsory school was created. This kind of common basic school lasting nine years is rather typical of new schools in the Scandinavian Countries, Eastern Europe and of course the USSR.

A spate of legislation in the late seventies reflects the changes in emphasis on the provision of education. The comprehensive common school leads to new sixth form colleges and vocational training (*folkskole* Law, 1975). The examination system has been simplified. The broadly based core curriculum has been unified and options to meet individual needs introduced (Act No. 370, June 28, 1977). Teacher training is being raised to the third level of education. A resolution in 1980 on Youth Education referred to all education and training following the end of compulsory education and included proposals designed to provide young people with a genuine choice of courses in the context of a single, overall system of education.

The Editor

1 GEOGRAPHY

Topography

In setting, Denmark is essentially a Scandinavian country. Excluding Greenland and the Faroe Islands, which still form part of the Kingdom of Denmark, the country is the smallest of the Nordic nations, covering 16,571 square miles (one eighth the size of Norway) with a population of over five million. Half of the surface area is taken up by the Jutland peninsula; the rest being scattered over some 500 islands, the largest of which are Zeeland on which Copenhagen is built, and Funen.

Of the total surface area, 10% is forest and 75% agricultural land. In spite, however, of Denmark's fame as an agricultural producer the soil is naturally poor and infertile. In appearance the landscape is almost universally flat and undulating, packed with small farms and marked periodically by the white gables towers of its churches. The country's highest hill rises to 586 feet - a source of amusement, it is said, to visiting Norwegians.

Climate

As the country lies between 54° and 57° North, the climate is generally hard with summers which are wet and winters which are cold in spite of the influence of the Gulf Stream.

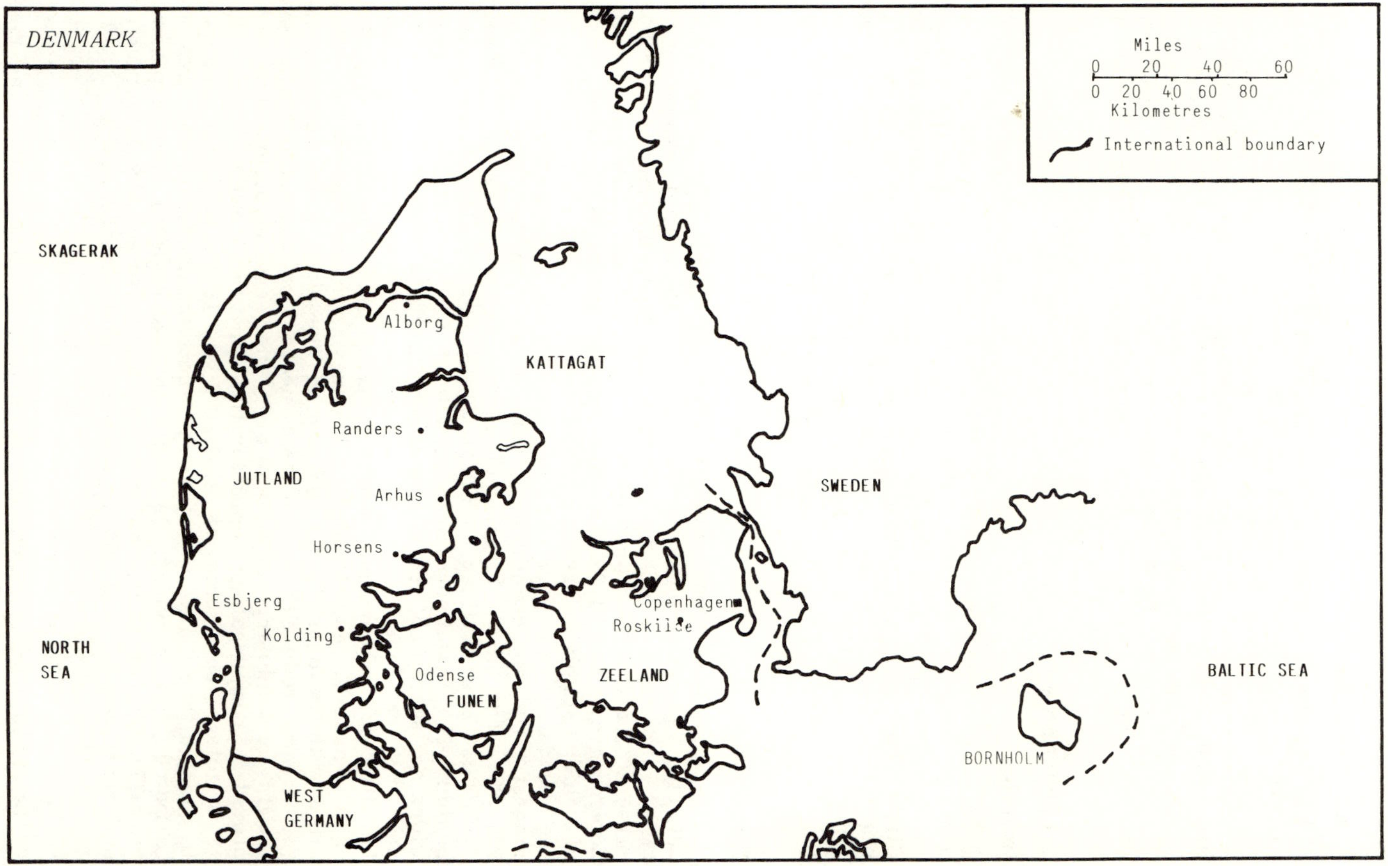
DENMARK
Miles
0 20 40 60
0 20 40 60 80
Kilometres
International boundary
SKAGERAK
KATTAGAT
Alborg
Randers
JUTLAND
Arhus
Horsens
Esbjerg
Kolding
Odense
FUNEN
SWEDEN
Copenhagen
ZEELAND
NORTH
SEA
WEST
GERMANY
BALTIC SEA
BORNHOLM

Communications

For a small country, the population (outside the capital) is widely and fairly evenly scattered and internal traffic plays an important part in securing national and economic cohesion. With few physical problems apart from the sea, communications are good; towns and settlements inland are linked by an efficient road network and the islands are well served by bridges or ferry routes from the numerous harbours which stud the eastern coast, while frequent domestic flights link Copenhagen with 11 provincial airports.

2 POPULATION

Growth

In 1979 the population of Denmark was 5,111,534 with an average density of 325 to the square mile - by far the highest in Scandinavia. As elsewhere in the region, the percentage of births has declined steadily in recent years as a result of smaller urban families and the availability of birth control methods; the growth in population is due more to the decline in the death rate. In 1979 there were 59,582 live births and 54,721 deaths.

Distribution

The distribution of population between rural and urban zones reflects, as elsewhere in the region, the rapid expansion of cities and towns and the drift away from the countryside. At present 2.4 million are in the rural areas, 2.4m in greater Copenhagen, and 1.0m in the smaller provincial towns, most of which supply marketing facilities or industrial support for the needs of the surrounding countryside. Copenhagen is the largest city in Scandinavia with a metropolitan population of 905,000. The next largest cities of Aarhus (121,000), Odense (110,000) and Ålborg (86,000) fall numerically a long way behind. The disproportionate growth of the capital and the ever-widening scatter of rural population are the source of numerous problems not the least of which are those providing equal facilities for school and, particularly, higher education.

In Denmark, as elsewhere, urban expansion has been associated with changes in the pattern of the work force as mechanisation has reduced the numbers needed on the land while the growth of industry and, notably, the service occupations has provided compensatory opportunities in the towns. Thus, out of a total work force of 2,071,000 in 1965, 16% were engaged in agriculture, 42% in industry and construction, and 42% in commerce and services; by 1980 the work force had expanded to 2,250,000, of which 8% were in agriculture, 42% in industry and construction, and 50% in commerce and services.

Groups

The population of Denmark is ethnically homogenous and has the same language and religion. Danish is the language of all; it is close enough to Norwegian (the written languages are very close) and Swedish to be widely understood in Scandinavia. The country is officially 90% Lutheran and although most take their religion lightly many of Denmark's educational and social traditions can be traced to this source. This fundamental unity of origin and view, tempered by centuries of evolution without internal discord of revolution is the basis for much of the tolerance, community activity, egalitarianism and the strong sense of 'Danishness' which is such a feature of the country.

3 SOCIETY AND CULTURE
Social Patterns

As in most of Scandinavia, the most striking feature of Danish society is the apparent lack of class distinctions and discrimination. The small size of the country, the homogeneity in ethnic origins and religion and the historical experience no doubt account for the cohesiveness, if not conformity, of the people. Allied to this is the political liberation, the community consciousness and the egalitarian principles inherited from the rural and Lutheran past; and the tradition of State involvement in industry, employment and social welfare, manifested in deliberate policies aimed at spreading the wealth of the country and eliminating both ends of the social spectrum. Whatever the basic reasons, Denmark is a very democratic country.

Certainly the overall impression is that in Denmark there is one way of life for all. Leisure pursuits are shared and enjoyed without regard to social origin. Flats and houses may vary in size but the decor and furnishings are uniformly elegant - the Danes having managed to combine mass production with quality. Education too is seen in terms of training and certificates gained rather than in the prestige of the institution attended. All this is not to say that Danes are not differentiated. On the contrary, Danes value their individual freedom and are as interested in 'getting on' as anyone else; educational certificates are highly prized and social etiquette demands that full recognition of qualifications or profession must be given, for example, in modes of address. But Danes refuse to attach prestige rating to these distinctions. The general attitude is that everyone should be free and should have the opportunity to make the most of himself. For this reason none of the various branches of the education system is a dead end; all can lead equally to the top.

With harmonious industrial relations, social harmony, a comprehensive welfare state and one of the world's highest standards of living and consumption rates the Danes, through sheer hard work and ingenuity, seem to have solved many of the problems of modern living. But such an impression is an oversimplification. Urbanisation has begun to undermine many of the traditions of life and there is less involvement in the old communal activities. One third of mothers now go out to work and with the economy demanding more in the way of schooling, the family is no longer in a position to exercise the responsibilities which the Lutheran tradition bestows. People are tending more to see themselves as individuals rather than parts of greater social-family entities. Alcoholism is on the increase; abortions are a problem; the permissive society and the 'generation gap' a worry; and the divorce rate is higher even than in the United States. Prosperity, leisure and modern living bring their problems but with the advantage of a stable community and a tradition of democratic sharing and cautious practicality the Danes are well placed to find the answers.

Religion

The majority of the population are Lutherans. A strongly religious flavour informed the development of education in the nineteenth century. Education was supervised by the clergy until 1933. Secularism and non-sectarianism rather than anti-clericalism characterises present day relationships.

Language

The Danish language is rather similar to Swedish and Norwegian. Familiar nineteenth century authors include Hans Christian Anderson (1857-1875) and Sören Kierkegaard (1813-1855). Henrik Pintoppidan (1857-1943) and Karl Gjellerup (1857-1919) shared the Nobel Prize for literature in 1917 and Johannes V Jensen (1873-1950) received the same aware in 1944). Folk traditions, finding expression in language, are strong but the Danish people are generally speaking anxious to learn English for economic and other reasons.

4 HISTORY AND POLITICS

Origins

Far back in history the Danes were the scourge of the western world. Viking freebooters harried the seas and raided the whole of northern Europe, England and Ireland. Their longships penetrated as far as the Mediterranean and Greenland and they settled or established their authority over a wide area bordering the North Sea. Danish power in France and England was beaten off in the eleventh century, but their dominance persisted over the whole of the Scandinavian area and was confirmed in 1397 by the Treaty of Kalmar. In 1523 Sweden broke away; but until 1814 the authority of the King of Denmark still extended over Norway, Greenland and Iceland. The half century which followed was a time of depression and disillusionment; the Napoleonic wars left Denmark bankrupt and deprived of Norway and in 1864 Southern Jutland (Schleswig Holstein) was lost to the German powers.

It was out of this period of poverty, national trauma and economic stagnation that modern Denmark was born. After a lengthy liberal agitation the absolute power of the monarchy was surrendered and a constitutional parliamentary system introduced in 1849. Deprived of so much of their old territory the Danes began to make the most of their limited assets, expanding their trade and developing their commercial and banking facilities. Transport improved; towns grew; and industrialisation began. Internally, land reform went apace and, after 1864, the Danes, as if to compensate for the loss of Southern Jutland, threw themselves with determination into the cultivation of the inhospitable heathland which remained. Cooperatives were formed and the area of cultivated land steadily increased until what had been an infertile waste supporting a poverty stricken and subsistence level population had become rich and intensely worked farmland. Agriculture was diversified towards the production of dairy produce and away from the supply of grain - a move which did much to save the country when North American wheat flooded the world market in the 1870s.

Parallel developments took place in education whose role in national regeneration was readily appreciated. For many reasons Denmark was one of the earliest nations to take popular education seriously and it was no exaggeration when one European traveller remarked in the nineteenth century that "in Germany the large buildings are barracks, in England they are factories and in Denmark they are schools". In 1814 education was made compulsory from seven years and by the middle of the century a network of elementary schools had been established all over the country. In the second half of the century attention was concentrated on the creation of a secondary system and on the reform of the old Latin schools. In 1850, 1871 and 1899 their organisation was steadily overhauled and their curricula reformed to include modern languages and science. In 1903 the various ingredients were combined to form one formal education system composed of three successive tiers - elementary, middle school and *Gymnasium* - an arrangement which remained substantially unaltered until 1958.

The development of the formal system was, however, accompanied by far reaching developments in the non-formal sector partly in response to a German threat to the country's cultural independence. N F S Grundtvig (1789-1878) was strongly opposed to the traditional methods of academic education which he regarded as uninspired cramming and advocated a system outside the control of the State where spiritual nourishment and personality development were as important as basic skills and where oral methods would predominate over the literary. In 1852 Kristen Kold (1810-1870) established the first *Friskole* of this type and inspired by his example parents in other parts of the country established similar institutions. The number of these schools was never great but their educational influence was considerable. In the field of post-school education Gruntvig's theories were even more potent and played a great part in arousing the people to a new endeavour and a new national consciousness. He was convinced that in order to enable him to participate fully in national life a new style of non-classical education was needed for the rural common man - one which concentrated on 'awakening' rather than knowledge and on national cultural language, and the truths of real life. The result of his efforts was the Folk High School movement. The first school was opened in Funen in 1851 and by 1870 the number had increased to over 50 with 2,000 students. With the support of the Liberal party and the rural cooperatives the movement grew from strength to strength until by the middle of the twentieth century it represented one of the most notable and well known features of Danish education.

Government and Politics

Denmark is a constitutional monarchy – the oldest monarchy in Europe – with legislative and judicial authority lying with the Queen and, respectively, the parliament or *Folketing* and the courts. Power lies in the *Folketing*, the Upper House having been abolished in 1953; this consists of 179 members elected by universal suffrage. The Danish political tradition is one of stability and moderation, the rural background of the country in particular exerting a conservative influence. Elections are by proportional representation, resulting frequently in coalitions, and the largest of the six or so parties which have been active in recent years is the Social Democratic Party. The governmental system resembles that of Britain except that there is less in the form of Cabinet responsibility and more individual ministerial accountability. The constitution permits the use of referenda on questions of national importance – such as Common Market entry. The role of the *Ombudsman* is well known.

At local level there was total reorganisation throughout the country with effect from 1970, reducing the number of country authorities from 25 to 14, further subdivided into 277 municipalities, of which Copenhagen and its adjacent Frederiksberg have special status. The governing boards of all the entities are democratically elected.

Although the absolute power of the monarchy was removed in 1849, full parliamentary government only dates from 1901, and until 1919 the mayors of cities were appointed by the State. Democratic government therefore developed comparatively late and fell heir to a strongly centralised system of administration and a tradition of State involvement in many aspects of life. In the early days many social and economic reforms were enacted from above rather than being the result of agitation from below, and the use of State power to achieve practical results for the national (rather than the narrow class) interest meant that its exercise never became a bone of contention. Now the State's role in all aspects of economic and social life is accepted and widespread: in economic terms it has resulted in a happy compromise between State socialism and unbridled private enterprise; in social terms it has produced a comprehensive 'welfare state' covering all aspects of social life from maternity care, unmarried mothers, children from broken homes and the handicapped to old age pensions, unemployment insurance and health provision.

Parallel with the tradition of State involvement, however, is the tradition of local government and communal activity. Rooted in a rural past where scattered communities of small craftsmen and farmers were left to solve their own problems or devise methods of complying with instructions from the King, the habit of local involvement and cooperation remains strong both in political life and in industry. The prevalence of small establishments and the craft traditions of Denmark are basic to the comparative harmony and stability of industrial relations. Trade unions are extremely important and still have many of the characteristics of the old Craft Associations; the State's role in regulating such things as minimum working hours, paid holidays and factory safety has long been recognised; and the employers tend to be representatives of small human entities rather than great faceless corporations. In large organisations joint worker-management councils help establish common views. The result of all this is an effective and sensible tri-partite involvement of State, employees and workers in industrial affairs.

International Relations

The international position of Denmark can therefore be said to be rooted in a combination of history, cultural affinity, geographical position and trading links. As observers have indicated there are many reasons why Denmark, Norway and Sweden can be regarded as a single expression of a way of life. Historically they have been closely linked and for long periods were under one crown: they are homogeneous in the Nordic race and the Lutheran religion; their languages are closely related - with a Scandinavian Language Committee to restrain any divergent tendencies; and their traditions of State control and social welfare are similar. In 1954 this community view was marked by the founding of The Nordic Council, established to provide a forum for discussions of mutual interest and a stimulant to the introduction of common welfare legislation, legal codes and economic activity in numerous sectors.

From the point of view of economic and political involvements, however, the Nordic nations are not complementary. Only one eighth of their trade is with each other and Denmark is in competition with its neighbours in its shipping, trade and commercial interests. Similarly political outlooks are different; whereas Sweden is a Baltic state and Norway looks to the Atlantic, Denmark is a geographical extension of the North German plain and has strong European connections. Throughout history, from the Reformation onwards, Denmark has been a gateway for the passage of European influences into Scandinavia and in recent history while Sweden was able to remain neutral in the Second World War, Denmark was under German occupation (in varying degrees) the whole time.

With its European connections and its worldwide trading interest it is not surprising that Denmark is a supporter of both regional and international groupings. It is an active member of UNO, NATO, the Council of Europe, OECD and, most recently, of the European Communities.

5 THE ECONOMY

Agriculture

Denmark is pre-eminently an agricultural country, its dairy products in particular - eggs, bacon, butter, etc. - being widely known and distributed. Produce of this nature accounts for 23% of Denmark's exports; 7% are made up of tinned meat and milk; while the remaining 70% consists of industrial goods and a small percentage of fish products.

The general picture of Danish agriculture is one of small farms run by owner-occupiers and their families. Of a total of some 200,000 holdings almost half are under 25 acres in size, and half of this figure are of 12 acres or less. A Central Land Board backed by a central fund controls the sale and amalgamation of land into economic units as this becomes necessary. Perhaps naturally, most agricultural activity is carried out through farmers' cooperatives which cover all aspects of the industry and back the individual producer with a highly developed and modern system of purchasing, food processing and marketing.

Natural Resources

Denmark lacks natural resources. There are no such sources of power as coal, oil or water; in the past Danish industrialisation was fuelled by Tyneside colliers; in the future it is hoped that Norwegian or Swedish hydro-electricity can be utilised. The advantage of this universal lack of natural wealth is that, outside the capital, development has taken place evenly and without any one locality enjoying and attracting more investment than any other. On the other hand, the difficulties of maintaining a high standard of living and a generous system of social services on such an unfavourable economic basis are obvious and maximum use of all its resources is a condition of survival. Here again it should be stressed that Denmark's prosperity depends upon its trading skill, which in turn depends on the hard work, technical knowledge and ingenuity of the population and on an effective and responsive education system able to provide the level of skills and attitudes required.

Industry

As elsewhere in Europe and Scandinavia, the growth of industry in this century has resulted in a rapid change in both the economic structure of Denmark and the distribution of the labour force. Now industry offers more employment than does the land (though less than the service occupations) and contributes 65% of all exports. The largest single activity is iron and metal working which employs 35% of all industrial workers and produces one third in terms of value. Next in importance are food and drink, paper, textiles, clothing and footwear, wood and furniture, chemicals, cement and glass. In total there are some 6,000 industrial establishments and over half the labour force is employed in concerns with less than 100 workers.

Danish crafts have a high reputation for skill and good design and small craft workshops account for 90% of all manufacturing establishments. The tradition of small scale craft activity still persists and accounts - amongst other things - for the emphasis on long and thorough apprenticeship training which is only now being reviewed. It was indeed the existence of a large class of independent craftsmen and farmers which helped to soften the harsher effects of industrialisation in the second half of the nineteenth century by preventing the domination of the economy by large scale enterprises.

Economic Situation

The prosperity of the Danish economy depends to an overwhelming extent upon its foreign trade - a fact which is reflected in a highly developed business sector covering banking, insurance, exporting and general commerce. The importance of international trade and the effect of the country's maritime tradition are reflected in the extent of Denmark's overseas commercial interests. Danes have always been great engineers and navigators, and today their businessmen, scientists and technicians range the world. Seafaring has always been a natural Scandinavian occupation; ships flying the white and red ensign of Denmark can be found in every corner of the globe and over 70% of its merchant marine are involved in trading between foreign ports. Fishing too provides an important subsidiary activity and annually the Danes land some 750,000 tons from the rich fishing grounds which fringe the Scandinavian coast. In the industrial sector the sea has its impact and the Danish shipbuilding firm of Burmeister and Wain is world famous. In per capita terms the level of exports and the size of the Danish merchant fleet is among the greatest in the world.

Denmark's principal imports are petroleum and its products, machinery, vehicles and textiles. It exports agricultural and dairy products and machinery. In 1979 the country had a balance of payments deficit on current account.

6 THE EDUCATION SYSTEM
General

Nine years of compulsory, comprehensive first level schooling is based on the aim of ensuring equal educational opportunity for all young people.

Academic Year

The school year starts in August. Schooling is for five days a week and traditionally there are ten weeks annual holiday. Lessons last fifty minutes and the number of lessons per year increases from 720 to 1,200 after the fourth year.

Structure and Organisation

The structure of the school system in Denmark was reformed in 1958, the previous arrangement consisting of seven years primary schooling followed by a selective secondary system which was regarded as inegalitarian and of dubious value for the majority with no academic bent. The present structure is based on the ten year *Folkeskole* with its two major divisions, the elementary *Hovedskole* and the lower secondary *Realafdeling*, (*real* department).

The New School Act, of June 1975, decreed that the *Folkeskole* should become a comprehensive school in which pupils will in principle be together with the same group throughout their entire school life – from the one year nursery class through the nine year compulsory basic school and the non-compulsory tenth class. This new organisation was fully implemented in the year 1978-79.

Pre-School

Nursery and pre-school classes are voluntary from the age of 1 to 6 and can be provided by either municipal or private entities. They are under the general supervision of the Ministry of Social Security.

First and Lower Second Level Schools *(Folkeskolen)*

Prior to the 1975 Act the *Folkeskole* was a divided school. After the seventh form pupils were placed either in a three year *real* department or in three forms leading to State controlled examinations or technical examinations. The Act created a comprehensive school which pupils attend from the nursery class, the nine year compulsory school and the tenth non-compulsory form.

During the first seven years Danish, arithmetic/mathematics, athletics, Christian studies, creative art, music and free class discussion constitute a common curriculum. History, geography and biology are offered in the third and subsequent forms. English is commenced in the fifth form. Handicrafts, woodwork and domestic science can be made compulsory according to local decisions. Indeed, regulations for curricula issued by the Ministry of Education are to be considered merely as suggestions; the municipal authorities having the power to issue curriculum regulations.

Pupils progress through the first seven forms without taking annual examinations although parents receive regular reports on their children's progress. The majority of schools do not create homogeneous teaching groups. New school leaving examinations were introduced in the eighth form (1977), ninth form (1978) and the tenth form (1979). The new examinations are called 'The Leaving Examination of the *Folkeskole'* and 'The Advanced Leaving Examination of the *Folkeskole'*. The Leaving Examination may be taken in accordance with pupil choice, in up to 11 subjects and at the Advanced Examination in up to five subjects. There is no overall examination but individual subjects are examined. Handicrafts, woodwork, domestic science and typing may be taken as Leaving Examinations in the eighth, ninth and tenth forms. Danish, mathematics, English physics, chemistry and German are ninth and tenth form Leaving or Advanced Leaving subjects. Latin may be taken in the ninth and French in the tenth form.

The Upper Second Level School *(Gymnasium)*

The *Gymnasium* is a three year school ending in a final examination (written and oral) set by the Ministry of Education. An Act of 1977 amended admission regulations laid down in the 1970 Act. Admission to the first form of the *gymnasium* is conditional on completion of nine years of compulsory education, on having taken German in forms 7 to 9, having passed written examinations in Danish and mathematics, having passed the oral part of the leaving examination in English and German for the language side of the *gymnasium* or in physics/chemistry for the mathematics side. The pupil's former school must judge that he/she is capable of following the *gymnasium* course satisfactorily. Admission after the beginning of the tenth year is on the basis of an admission examination. There are two main branches of subjects (mathematics and languages) in the first year. In the second and third years there are two main and seven side branches from which to choose. On the language side there are the following branches: modern languages; music; social science and classics. On the mathematics and science side there are: mathematics; physics, social science and biological branches.

A core of subjects – religion, Danish, English, German, Classical culture, history and civics, French (or Russian) and mathematics are common to both sides, along with physical training, music and art. The number of weekly lessons in each of these subjects varies depending on the side. Special subjects appropriate to broadly based language or science courses make up a very broadly based curricula.

Comprehensive Upper Second Level Schools *(Enhedsskole)*

According to the 1975 Act the Ministry of Education may approve proposals made by the Teachers' Council, the School Board and the School Commission in any municipality or district to abolish the division between language and science in the eighth and ninth forms. In such districts it is therefore possible to find a unified school system in which experiments to individualise teaching in foreign languages, mathematics and physics/chemistry may be decisive in the creation of a totally unified comprehensive school system. The Act does not allow the two sides to be brought together in the tenth form but such a prospect is not wholly out of the question.

Special Education

Within the school system children whose development requires special consideration and special teaching participate, wherever possible, in ordinary classes on the clear understanding that special educational assistance will be given to them. The Upper Secondary Schools and Upper Secondary Courses Act of 1977 makes provision for handicapped pupils to receive "special teaching or other pedagogical aid".

Training in Firms and Institutions

Continuation schools for pupils aged 14-18 emphasise practical subjects. The 1975 Act makes it possible to send pupils in the eighth to tenth forms out to firms and institutions for practical work training. Such schemes acquaint pupils with conditions in the labour market and in society outside the school. Training service may be part of the teaching on an optional subject or in the shape of a period of training for the whole class for a short period. The first possibility implies that 'work knowledge' is on a par with other optional subjects and that visits to firms will not interfere with the school based programme. The second scheme implies that pupils will spend up to 20 days in the eighth and 30 days in the ninth and tenth forms out of school in places of trainee service. Teaching in schools is suspended during these periods.

Leisure Time Education

Out of school hours teaching is available on a voluntary basis primarily in music and athletics. These activities should not be confused with the optional subjects which are offered within the fixed class hours and are part of the work of a certain form.

Non-compulsory teaching out of school hours is coordinated under the School Commission, individual School Boards and municipal Leisure Time Commissions. Parents may be required to pay for the participation of their children, particularly in music classes.

Completion of Compulsory Education

It is possible to complete compulsory education after the seventh form by full time education in a municipal youth school or by occupational employment. Such exemption is granted if the pupil himself wants to start occupational training, that he will not benefit from ordinary schooling and that on the contrary, the training or employment will really offer the pupil possibilities of developing in accordance with his abilities and qualifications. Finally some pupils may be excused from the optional subjects and may complete compulsory education by attending a maximum of 22 weekly lessons in the eighth and ninth forms and taking only the compulsory subjects. For school leavers there are several possibilities for vocational training.

Unskilled Workers who have completed minimum compulsory schooling and are under 18 years of age can follow vocational courses in the *Ungdomskoler* (Youth Schools). Courses and re-training courses are also available for workers over 18 in special State institutions.

Apprenticeships (Laerlingeuddannelse) provide the main road to the skilled labour force. Apprentices must be over 14 years of age having completed the ninth year of education.

Commercial Apprentices follow a 2-4 year programme which in addition to practical work in an office or shop includes attendance at a special training school working towards the theoretical part of the apprentices examination. A certificate is issued to confirm the completion of the apprenticeship.

Industrial/Handicraft Apprentices follow 3-4 year programmes of practical work and theoretical training in special training institutions. The certificate signifying the completion of the apprenticeship also gives access to further technical training.

The general educational element in the apprenticeship system has increased.

Commercial Schools

Handelsskoler (Commercial Schools) offer 2-year day or evening classes leading to the *Handelseksamen* in general subjects, languages, accounting or the retail trade. Applicants must have passed the ninth/tenth form or commercial apprentices examination.

Handelsgymnasier (Higher Commercial Schools) offer full time courses leading to the higher commercial examination. For holders of the *Handelseksamen* the course lasts two years; for those with the former *Studentereksamen*, one year.

Further Technical Training Access to the numerous basic technical courses available depends on the previous basic training of the applicant. Entrants are normally expected to have passed the leaving examination or its equivalent or have completed their apprenticeship. Training for technicians is both theoretical and practical (the latter omitted in lieu of experience) and lasts from 1-2 years.

Engineers (Teknikum) Studies leading to the *Teknikum* qualification take four years and are divided into five branches – civil engineering, electrical engineering, mechanical engineering, production engineering and shipbuilding. Applicants must have completed class ten, or completed their apprenticeship training.

Agricultural Schools (Landbrugsskoler) There are no apprenticeships in agriculture. Possibilities for training do, however, exist in the residential *Landbrugsskoler* – offshoots of the Folk High School movement – without examinations but with State support.

Third Level Education

Danish higher education, although beginning to feel the winds of change, is still on the continental European tradition, comprising on the one hand separate institutions preparing for the higher professions and, on the other, universities organised into traditional faculties offering courses basically orientated towards research. Many features of the older Danish universities reflect the early nineteenth century German tradition that universities were concerned with the unhampered pursuit of pure knowledge and that teaching and research should be closely coordinated.

There are universities at Copenhagen (founded 1478), Aarhus (1933), Odense (1966), Roskilde (1972) and Aalberg (1974). In 1981 further universities were being planned. Higher professional schools cover such specialisms as veterinary science and agriculture, dentistry, fine arts, architecture and business administration. The official status of institutions of higher education varies; most of them are autonomous though in receipt of State subventions and under the general control of the Ministry of Education, whose regulations ensure uniformity in respect of examinations, degrees, enrolment and staffing.

The older universities of Copenhagen with 23,000 students and Aarhus with 11,000, are organised in the five traditional faculties of Theology, Arts, Economics and Law, Science, and Medicine. Odense has fewer faculties. In both specialist institutions and universities the traditional link between higher education and the preparation for the higher professions lives on and by law (for example) senior officials in government departments must have degrees in law or economics. Roskilde has been a very experimental institution based on student participation and incorporating a two year junior college.

Entry to higher education is open to all who possess the Advanced Leaving examination, formerly the *Studentereksamen* or, in relevant subjects, the *Højere Forberedelseseksamen*. Access to universities is unrestricted for those with these qualifications and the suitability for a course is left to the candidate's judgement. The professional institutions of higher education are, however, able to control their numbers by instituting entrance tests of specific requirements as to standards attained.

Courses in universities last from 5-8 years and in theology, law and medicine are crowned by the award of a *candidate* degree specifying the speciality, e.g. *cand theol,* or *cand jur* etc. Arts and science faculties award the degree of *magister.* Courses tend to be a mixture of honours degree, post-graduate research and professional training and examinations, held when the student feels ready, are a mixture of written and oral. The traditional concept of 'academic freedom' combined with the research orientation of the university means that the student is left free to decide what, how, and how long to study. Lectures (open to all) are available but there are no structured courses, regular assessment or advice on progress. Drop-out rates are accordingly high. Post-graduate doctorates are a rare and esteemed accolade taking up to 15 years to achieve through the public defence of a thesis.

Courses in professional institutions are completed in 3-4 years and drop-out rates are accordingly lower. Like universities, these institutes have strong research orientations. Traditional power in the universities lay with the professors, who held established Chairs. They were selected by the existing professorial staff on the basis of their research abilities - who dominated the administrative and faculty boards and from whose number the Rector and Deans were elected. Protests by junior staff and students during the 1960s have resulted in recent years in the breaking of this monopoly. All university committees must now be made up of between one third and one half of student delegates, the remainder representing the teaching staff regardless of rank. The amount of student representation on a university board is, within these limits, generally in inverse proportion to its importance: the adjustment therefore neither satisfies conservative academic opinion nor radical student organisations.

In addition to the universities and the higher institutes, there are a number of post-secondary institutions offering 3-4 year professional courses at a lower level though in similar fields. They cover, for example, teaching, library science, journalism, nursing, etc., and unlike the higher institutes are concerned solely with providing training.

Teacher Education

First level school teachers are trained for three years (two years for holders of the Advanced Leaving Examination, formerly the *studentereksamen)* or for four years in teacher training colleges *(Laererseminarium)* which may be publicly or privately owned. Special training courses are available for nursery teachers. Basic training is supplemented by frequent in-service courses.

The courses offered include practical training together with educational psychology, educational theory, teaching methods, basic academic (teaching) subjects and folk lore, two specialisms, creative activities, contemporary orientation and civics. First level teachers are appointed as public servants and are placed on an appropriate salary scale and pension scheme.

Teachers in the *Gymnasium* are university graduates who complete a short period of post-graduate professional training. They are employed as *adjunkts* or more highly paid *lektors*. They are either public servants or employed on the basis of a negotiated contract. A high proportion of *Gymnasium* teachers are men.

Non-formal and Voluntary Education

Adult (i.e. post-school) education occupies a central position in Danish life and has been a feature of the national scene for over a hundred years. Extra-mural courses, whether of a cultural or vocational nature, and whether aimed at educational qualifications or personal enrichment are a widespread leisure activity throughout the country and are enjoyed by approximately 15% of the adult population. Some institutions are run by the municipal authorities but the field is generally characterised by private initiative in the form of cultural associations, religious groups or the labour movement.

Folk High Schools (Folkhøjskoler) - the Folk High School movement is undoubtedly Denmark's most original contribution to international education and has been widely copied throughout Scandinavia and elsewhere. Based on the ideas of N F S Grundtvig and translated into practicality by Kristen Kold, the movement was designed to provide non-formal and non-classical education relevant to the needs of the common man living at that time in rural areas. The creation of the movement was the Folk High School - a full time residential college for young adults offering spiritual awakening rather than knowledge, with no examinations or fixed syllabi but with an almost romantic concentration on Scandinavian culture carried out in a religious and almost Spartan atmosphere. In recent years, urbanisation and other factors have caused changes in the original patterns (the curricula, for example, now reflect a more realistic and less romantic view of life and problems) but many features remain - their independence, their emphasis on awakening and broadening the minds of youth, and their lack of examinations and entrance requirements. Annual enrolments at the present time are around 15,000.

Outside the Folk High Schools are a variety of institutions of a general and vocational kind for the post-school education of youth and adults. Some of these grew originally from a desire to found a Grundtvigian non-boarding institution more suitable for the urban worker; others have since arisen as a response to particular vocational needs. All, however, take a broad view of their responsibilities, e.g. the all round social development of young adults.

7 EDUCATIONAL ADMINISTRATION

Responsibility for education in Denmark is shared between the central and local entities. Central authority is vested in the Ministry of Education; the local authorities comprise municipal councils *(byråd)* and rural district councils *(sogneråd)*.

The Ministry of Education has overall responsibility and control. It has three divisions (legal, personnel and planning). As departmental authority for the Minister it prepares bills, issues regulations and circulars, prepares the educational budget and administers funds allocated for educational purposes. The administration has five directorates responsible for aspects of general, technical, commercial, agricultural, post-second level, third level and teacher training. The Ministry is assisted by advisory committees.

The powers of the central government over the national system of education are considerable and the tradition of central control is strong (although beginning to weaken as more authority is given to local councils and parents). The Ministry (planning) advises on curricula, teaching methods, public examinations, teacher selection and promotions; it establishes minimum building standards, appoints senior staff in schools and in the administration, and most *Gymnasier*.

Municipal councils appoint Education Committees *(skolekommission)* to carry out their responsibilities as regards educational supervision, administration, the appointment of staff and the drawing up of building plans. To a large degree within the framework established by the Ministry, local authorities (both municipal and county) have administrative and financial control of the *folkeskole* and some responsibility for *Gymnasier*. One of their main functions is the preparation of the school plan – giving the distribution of schools, their catchment areas, size, organisation, staff details, health and welfare facilities, etc. – and the teaching plan – providing details on subjects, timetables, syllabi and progress. Municipal councils report direct to the Ministry.

Rural District Councils also appoint *skolekommission*, but their powers are more restricted by the existence of an additional county level education authority between the RDC and the Ministry. This comprises the School Council *(skoleråd)* made up of elected members from the county and RDCs who administer all educational funds; and the School Directorate *(skoledirektion)*. The School Directorate consists of the County Governor and four members and its function is to supervise the lower tier authorities, confirm their school and teaching plans before despatch to the Ministry, appoint staff and approve building plans.

Copenhagen has an independent status zealously maintained since 1658. The City Council is the authority responsible for the maintenance of schools and discharges its administrative responsibilities through a small School Directorate. It reports directly to the Minister.

THE ADMINISTRATION OF EDUCATION IN DENMARK

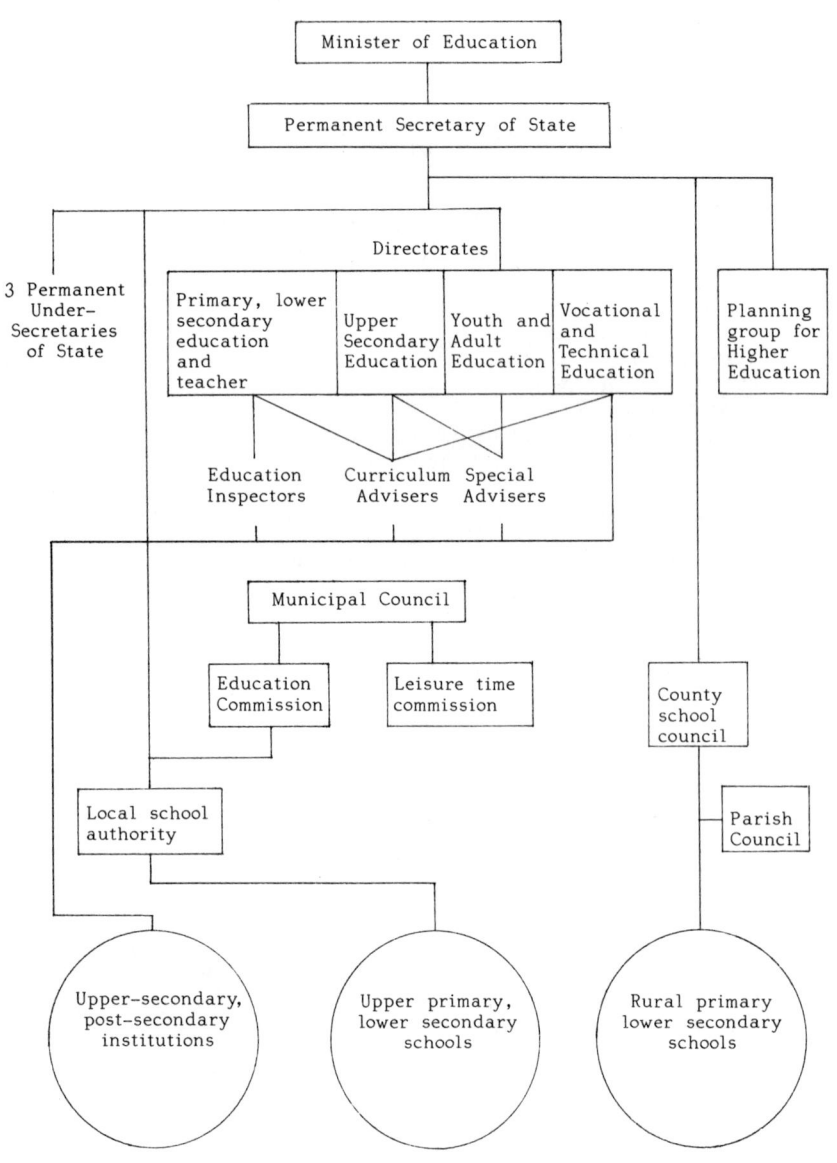

```
                    ┌─────────────────────────┐
                    │   Minister of Education │
                    └────────────┬────────────┘
                                 │
                    ┌────────────┴────────────┐
                    │ Permanent Secretary of State │
                    └────────────┬────────────┘
```

- 3 Permanent Under-Secretaries of State

Directorates
- Primary, lower secondary education and teacher
- Upper Secondary Education
- Youth and Adult Education
- Vocational and Technical Education

- Planning group for Higher Education

- Education Inspectors
- Curriculum Advisers
- Special Advisers

- Municipal Council
  - Education Commission
  - Leisure time commission

- County school council
  - Parish Council

- Local school authority

- Upper-secondary, post-secondary institutions
- Upper primary, lower secondary schools
- Rural primary lower secondary schools

Danish anxiety to harness the interest of parents and others outside the political/administrative framework can be seen in the existence below the local authority tier of a system of school boards, one for each school. Membership consists of one councillor with two, three or four representatives of the parents; two members of the local authority *skolekommission* must be elected by the school boards. The Danish tradition of community/consumer involvement is thus respected. Teacher-parent contact is also strongly encouraged. Careful attention has been paid to giving teachers a part in the administration. In all but the smallest schools teachers' councils exist and Joint Teachers' Councils are elected covering the wider local authority area: these are strongly represented on school boards and attend without voting rights meetings of the *skolekommission*.

8 EDUCATIONAL FINANCE

Public education in Denmark is free and largely financed by public funds, the only exceptions being vocational instruction, where facilities for practical and theoretical apprenticeship training are provided or financed by industry, and private schools which receive only partial public support. Higher education is funded directly from the central government; but the financing of other sectors is divided between the Ministry of Education and the local authorities. A complicated system of expenditure and reimbursement exists, but in general terms central government aid is given for teachers' salaries and pensions, to redress regional inequalities and in the form of grants-in-aid related to specific purposes such as school buildings. In 1961, 747.8 million kroner were spent on education by the local authorities compared with 707.3 million (half of which was disbursed to local authorities) from the central government. As elsewhere there has been a tendency for the central contribution to increase in recent years. Comparisons are, however, difficult for in 1970, in line with official policy, greater financial authority was granted to the local authorities. Now they will receive a per capita sum per pupil and in return must defray for example 40% of the cost of *folkeskole* teachers' salaries compared with the previous figure of 15%. As elsewhere teachers' salaries absorb over two-thirds of recurrent costs.

Quantitative expansion, qualitative change and rising costs and salaries have led to increasingly larger sums being allocated to education during the seventies. As a percentage of the GNP, expenditure rose steadily from 3% in 1956 to 6.5% in 1970, in the latter year comprising 6.8 million kroner - or 17.7% of all public expenditure.

Allocation of Funds
Expenditure on Education: Distribution by Level
Percentage of Expenditure 1977

Pre-school	First level	Second level	Third level	Other
-	52.0	15.9	17.5	14.6

9 DEVELOPMENT AND PLANNING OF THE EDUCATIONAL SYSTEM
Origins

Like so many countries in the European tradition, Denmark has enshrined the aims of its education system in legislation, in ministerial guides and in its constitution. Section 76 of the latter, for example, lays down that education shall be compulsory (whether provided by school or family) and free in public institutions. Ministerial guides amplify this basic statement, declaring that education should be seen in terms of developing the pupil's personality, aptitudes and needs: and in terms of social behaviour, spiritual values and community consciousness as well as academic achievement and the acquisition of skills. The dangers of excessive examination emphasis, and overloaded curricula, and the need for up to date education programmes are both stressed. Unlike those of some other countries, however, the declared aims of Danish education are reflected to a large extent by what goes on in the schools: largely because they are not abstract ideals plucked from philosophy, but have their roots deep in the concepts and traditions which have been inherited from the past. Present educational objectives result from the fusion of this inheritance with the idiosyncracies of national character and the demands of modern social, economic and political circumstances.

Without doubt the greatest historical influence on the formation of Danish and Scandinavian education was that of the Lutheran church. Institutionally its influence is now weak, but its traditions can still be seen in many aspects of national life and particularly in educational thought. The Reformation Statutes of the 1530s laid down the foundation of an education system which survived until the end of the nineteenth century. State supremacy was accepted by the Lutherans with the result that Church and State were never in conflict: it was accepted that the old Latin or Grammar Schools should teach Latin and the Liturgy and that education should be supervised by the clergy - an arrangement which remained in force until 1933. Religious teaching is still a compulsory subject at the primary level of education and the fact that the local Deacon was often Pastor, parish clerk and schoolmaster is one of the main reasons why teaching in Denmark is an unusually prestigious occupation, enjoying good salaries and attracting a high proportion of men. The Lutherans' belief in individual salvation and the resulting necessity for all to be able to read the Bible led them also to advocate compulsory schooling and - when such a thing was physically impossible - the supremacy of the family and its obligation to educate its children in basic skills and religion.

The State, for its part, responded to the obligation to see that schools were provided, and limited attempts were made to do this from the sixteenth century onwards. In the Lutheran tradition again, however, the objects of such schooling were conceived in narrow instructional and religious terms - designed at the upper levels to train officials and priests and at the lower to provide a Christian supplement to the 'training for life' given in the family. Thus infant schools in Denmark are very recent phenomena, and the bookish and formal tradition in Danish education is strong.

The Lutheran emphasis on individual salvation and equality in the face of God resulted not only in the need for universal compulsory education but also in a conviction that this should equally be available to boys and girls. There was no discrimination by sex. During the eighteenth century the Pietist movement gave an extra dimension to the Lutheran ideal: confirmation was made compulsory and in 1739 universal elementary education from the age of 7 until the age of confirmation was enacted but never achieved.

The Enlightenment, the impact of the French Revolution, and the rise of the merchant classes who needed a more mathematical and commercial style of schooling all combined to cause widespread dissatisfaction with the Church's grip on the education system. The need to promote a national consciousness and to educate and 'awaken' the brutalised peasantry who made up so much of the Danish nation combined with this dissatisfaction to produce a secondary powerful tributary which began to flow into the mainstream of education - the philosophies of Grundtvig. Grundtvig endorsed the supremacy of the family and the importance of community action (so much so that he opposed State monopoly and even compulsory education) and his influence on the Folk High School movement has already been noted. But his contribution was much broader than this: his emphasis on spiritual values and the development of personality introduced a new element into the old formal concepts of education; he gave dignity and real value to rural life; and, significantly, he cut the link which bound education to a concept of class culture and made it relevant and available to all.

The education system which existed in Denmark from 1903 to 1958 resembled very closely the selective 'grammar/secondary modern' structure which could be found, for example, in Britain: plus at the upper levels a Germanic style university education, and at the non-formal level the uniquely Scandinavian Folk High School. It was in some cases a fusion and in others a coexistence of different Danish educational traditions modified to some extent by national character - for example, the bookish strain has always been relieved by the very practical outlook of the Danes; similarly the democratic outlook of the people made 'parity of esteem' more of a reality than elsewhere.

Since the Second World War Denmark, like other countries in Europe, has felt the effects of increasing democratic opportunity, rising expectations, changing occupational patterns and the new requirements of science and technology. Educational change has, and is, taking place. Scandinavian countries are frequently regarded as exemplars of progressive methods and thought: it should be understood, however, that Denmark is essentially a conservative country and that education change has occurred slowly if continually. Both the agrarian and Nordic backgrounds may help to account for this; but so too must the range and often contradictory nature of the educational traditions which have been inherited. Readjustment of patterns of thought rather than revolution is the keynote.

Planning

The conservatism of the Danes, the tradition of community action and the comparatively small size of the country have all combined to delay the advent of comprehensive planning in Denmark. The obvious increase in demand, the considerable acceleration in educational expenditure, and the need for curricular and structural change have, however, made the Ministry of Education extend its activities into the field of planning and the determination of long term goals and trends through the appointment of specialist committees covering the appropriate level or the particular area of enquiry. A major report on educational trends and programmes published in 1962, for example, gave vital basic statistics for educational expansion 1961 to 1980; and permanent planning committees in the Ministry cover higher, engineering and *Gymnasium* education. The emphasis in government documentation remains, however, on the 'coordination' of local/central activities and efforts and the provision of information on trends and long term goals rather than executive action. The tradition of the central government giving the ground rules while the local authorities apply them remains.

10 THE SYSTEM IN OPERATION

Trends, Problems and Possibilities

Danish commentators detect the following problems confronting their system:

The Internal Efficiency of the System

(a) Problems of school provision resulting from a scattered rural population; but more serious imbalances in higher education resulting from the disproportionate size of Copenhagen

(b) The impact of rising demand on admissions policies, organisation and teaching traditions in higher education

(c) Drop-out rates in higher education

(d) The need for the recruitment of more teachers to meet the increased length of schooling

(e) Need for curriculum revision in teacher training colleges to meet the requirements of the increasingly unselective school system

(f) The serious financial implications of educational expansion.

The impact of changes in occupational patterns, in the increasing complexity of technical operations and automation, in increases in democratic opportunity and in social expectation have had an educational impact in Denmark similar to that in the rest of Europe. The trends are broadly the same: the lengthening of basic schooling for all: the postponement of vocational specialisation; the steady removal of selection and discrimination in the school system; the widening choice of subjects; and the adaptation of the institutions of higher education to rising demand and the entry of students with different ambitions, needs and interests. But due to Danish conservatism - rooted in an agrarian past and the mixture of traditions which form its educational inheritance - change since 1958 has been slow and cautious: advancing on a broad front rather than rushing ahead in isolated sectors.

FURTHER READING

Begtrup, H., et al (1949). *The Folk High School of Denmark and the Development of a Farming Community* 4th ed.. Oxford University Press, London.
Blegvad, M. and Jeppesen, S. L. (1975). 'Danish Universities in Transition', in P. Seabury (Ed.) *Universities in the Western World*. Free Press, New York.
de Danske Selskab. *Schools and Education in Denmark*, Det Danske Selskab, Copenhagen.
Denmark, Ministry of Foreign Affairs (Annual). *Denmark: An Official Handbook*. The Ministry, Copenhagen.
Dixon, W. (1959). *Education in Denmark*. Harrap, London.
Mannicke, P. (1952). *Living Democracy in Denmark*. Gad, Copenhagen.
Rordam, T. (1965). *The Danish Folk High Schools*. Det Danske Selskab, Copenhagen.
Thomson, O. B. (1967). *Some Aspects of Education in Denmark*. University of Toronto Press, Toronto.
UNESCO/IBE (1980). *International Yearbook of Education XXII*. Unesco, Paris.

Statistics

UNESCO (1981). *Statistical Yearbook 1980*. Unesco, Paris.

Regulations

Ministry of Education:
(1979). *Curriculum Regulations for the Gymnasium (Upper Secondary School) in Denmark*. Ministry of Education, Denmark.
(1977). *The Danish Upper Secondary School System*. International Relations Division, Copenhagen.
(1980). *Parliamentary Resolution on Youth Education*. Ministry, Copenhagen.

Structure of the Education System in Denmark

Age	3 4 5 6 7 8 9 10 11 12 13 14 15 16 17 18 19 20 21 22 23 24
Level	I / II / III / IV
Stage	1 / 2 3 4 5
Compulsory	
School type	Comprehensive / Sixth form college / Vocational training / Teacher training / University

▨ Education preceding the first level

Examinations: compulsory at the end of stages 2 to 5

Source: UNESCO/IBE International Yearbook of Education

Compulsory Education: Age Limits 7-16 Duration (years) 9
Entrance age to pre-school education: 5

221

DENMARK BASIC STATISTICS	1960	1970	1975	1978 (approx.)
1 Total population (000)	4,581	4,928	5,025	5,111
% female	50	50	50	50
2 % population 0-14 years	25.2	23.3		21
% female	49	48	49	49
3 Enrolment, all levels	868,314	916,968	969,205	872,804
% female	45			
First level	559,292	513,458	567,793	461,838
% female	49	49		
Second level	277,540	327,486	291,141	293,310
% female	39			
Third level	31,482	76,024	110,271	117,656
% female	31	37	44	46
4 Teachers, all levels				
% female				
First level	17,888	47,314	58,012	58,957
% female	51	51		52
Second level				
% female				
Third level				
% female				
5 Public expenditure on education:				
Total (000) Kroner	1,286,429	8,137,000	16,801,000	18,441,000
As % of GNP	3.1	6.4	8.2	6.7
6 % enrolment (MF) by level	100	100	100	100
First level	64	56	59	53
Second level	32	36	30	34
Third level	4	8	11	13
% enrolment (F) by level	100	100		
First level	70			
Second level	28			
Third level	3			
7 Entrance age : Duration of				
First level education	6:7	6:7	6:7	6:6
Second level education	13:5	13:5	13:5	12:6
8 Enrolment ratios (MF)				
First level	103	96	104	100
Second level	65	94	77	83
Third level	10.39	18.28	29.69	32.10
Enrolment ratios (F)				
First level	103	97		
Second level	52			82
Third level	6.56	13.82	26.99	30.56

Federal Republic of Germany

CONTENTS

1	Geography	226
2	Population	227
3	Society and Culture	229
4	History and Politics	231
5	The Economy	233
6	The Education System	235
7	Educational Administration	246
8	Educational Finance	248
9	Development and Planning of the Education System	249
10	The System in Operation	255

Among the great educators Germans loom large; John Sturm was born near Cologne; Martin Luther gave to education a radically different character from that offered by the Catholic orders; Ratechus studied in Hamburg; Comenius studied in several German towns; John Bernard Basedow was born in Hamburg; Froebel and Herbart are names associated with new educational ideas in the nineteenth century. Moreover, Prussia was the first state to introduce legislation about compulsory education and to set up institutions in which elementary school teachers were trained. Wilhelm von Humbolt's notions about teaching and research and the freedom to learn inspired reforms in German universities and elsewhere. This history and the commitment of German scholars to it help to explain the relatively slow rate of change in German education and its importance as a model which has been widely copied.

A feature of nineteenth century German education was the isolation of education from politics while expecting that it should contribute to the spirit of a nation state. A feature of Nazi policies in the thirties was the extent to which education was used to legitimise Nazi slogans and policies.

After the Second World War a new school system had to be created out of the devastation. In the Federal Republic of Germany the Americans, the British and the French had some influence on the kinds of developments which took place. Traces of these influences remain, particularly in those *Länder* which formed part of the separate zones. Nevertheless, strong German traditions continue to inform educational provision in each of the 11 *Länder* which are autonomous in educational matters. Policies cannot always be reconciled in spite of an overall Federal Education Plan. While the general trends of reform are similar – and the introduction of a reorganised system of second level comprehensive schooling has been one of these trends – each *Land* has moved at its own rate and on the basis of its own interpretation. Reforms have taken place more rapidly in the city state of progressive Hamburg than in more conservative Bavaria. These distinctions are reflected in the relative strengths of the major political parties.

As in most continental European countries the traditional education system was one in which a large proportion of children entered an elementary school (at 6) and completed their education in the same school. Over a period of time the period of compulsory education was increased. A highly structured system of vocational and technical schools took care of pupils leaving the elementary schools and trained them for specific jobs in an industrial society.

A favoured minority of pupils used to be selected at the age of 10 for admission to the academic secondary school which trained them for the university entrance examination, the *Abitur* (possession of which confers a legal right to enter a university or institution of higher learning). In the course of time middle schools were set up to accommodate the majority of pupils leaving *Volksschulen* at the age of 10. Upper second level schools retain the name *Gymnasium* and prepare young adults for higher education. Previously there were several distinguishable branches. Reforms created basic and main course options so that the traditional examination load has been reduced. The reorganisation of the upper secondary school along comprehensive lines has a long history during which many issues have been hotly debated.

Parallel to the academic schools there has traditionally existed a well developed and differentiated system of vocational and technical schools. At the third level of education technical universities emerged in the nineteenth century to compete with the humanistic universities. Since 1970 colleges of advanced technology *(Fachhochschulen)* have provided specialised training in a number of fields, especially in engineering and commerce.

Characteristic of the Federal Republic of Germany are the many and detailed laws and regulations which govern the provision of education at all levels. Increasing party political influences, which differ from *Land* to *Land*, dominate the formulation of policy in spite of the determination after World War Two on the part of many German educationists to prevent politics from entering again into the running of schools.

The Editor

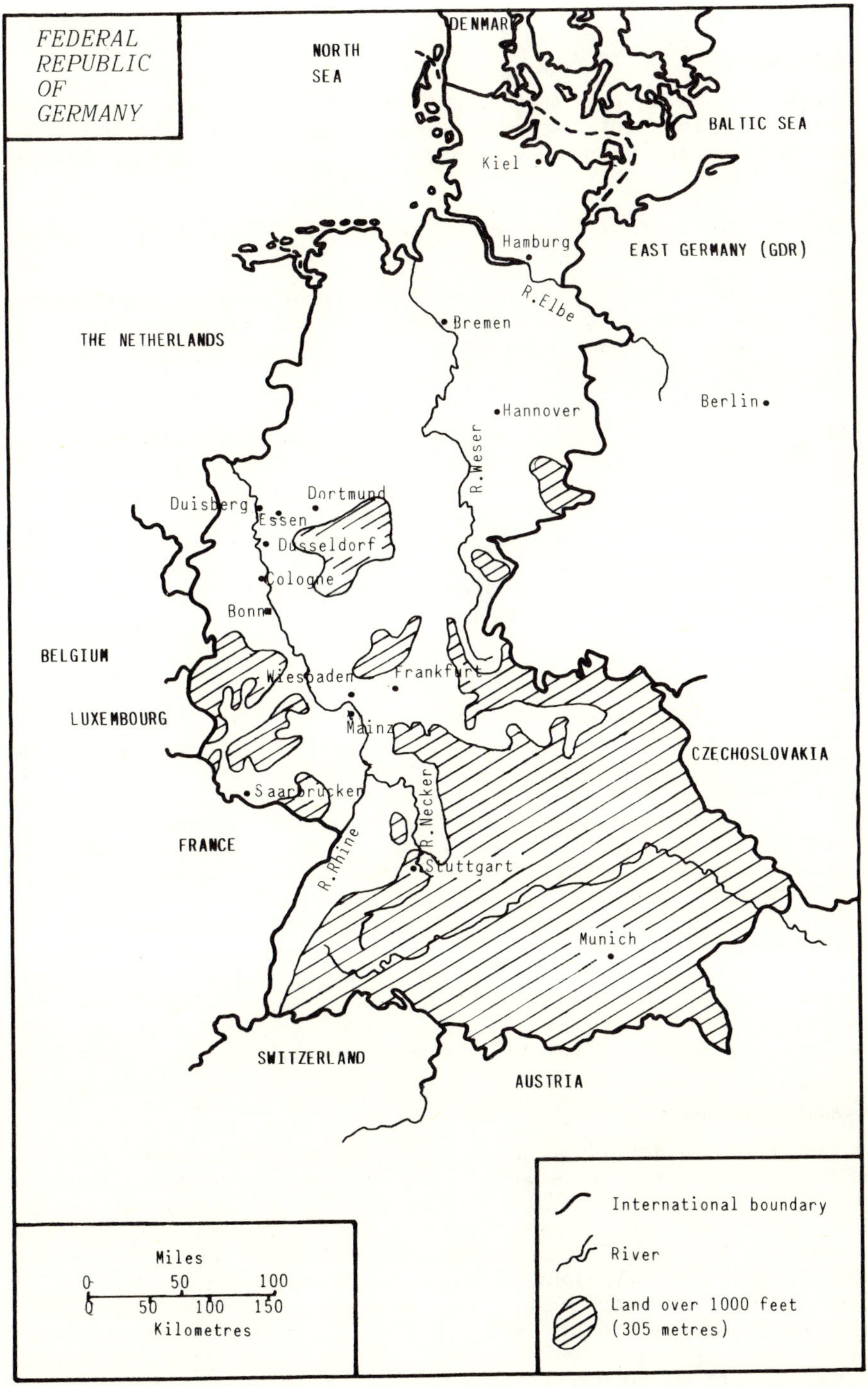
FEDERAL REPUBLIC OF GERMANY
NORTH SEA
DENMAR
BALTIC SEA
Kiel
Hamburg
EAST GERMANY (GDR)
R.Elbe
Bremen
THE NETHERLANDS
Berlin
Hannover
R.Weser
Dortmund
Duisberg
Essen
Düsseldorf
Cologne
Bonn
BELGIUM
Wiesbaden
Frankfurt
LUXEMBOURG
Mainz
CZECHOSLOVAKIA
R.Necker
Saarbrücken
FRANCE
R.Rhine
Stuttgart
Munich
SWITZERLAND
AUSTRIA
International boundary
River
Land over 1000 feet (305 metres)
Miles
0 50 100
0 50 100 150
Kilometres

1 GEOGRAPHY

Topography

With an area of 248,606 sq km (95,978 square miles) the Federal Republic of Germany contains within its boundaries all the three main physical regions that make up central Europe. These are:

(i)   the North German plain or lowland, extending eastwards into Poland and Russia

(ii) the central uplands (the largest region), presenting a varied landscape with scattered areas of highland, e.g. the Harz Mountains

(iii) the Alpine foothills (south of the Danube) and the Alps.

There are no definite geographical frontiers between these regions. Three major rivers cross the country from north to south - the Rhine, the Weser and the Elbe. Topography has little direct influence on German education except for some of the mountainous and isolated areas of southern Bavaria. Provision of education here is difficult and children have to be 'bussed' for long distances, or boarded, particularly those who wish to attend intermediate or grammar schools.

Climate

Germany lies within the temperate zone and hence rainfall occurs throughout the year. In the north west the climate is influenced by the ocean, with moderately warm summers and mild winters - similar to the climate of Britain. As one moves towards the east and south east the climate becomes more continental in character, with warm to hot summers and cold winters. In the central uplands the climate varies according to topography and altitude; in the Alpine foothills and the Alps heavy falls of snow occur in winter. Average mean temperatures in January, the coldest month, range between 1.5°C in lowland areas and below -6°C in the mountains. In July, the warmest month, average mean temperatures range between 17°C and 18°C in the lowland areas; in the Rhineland area the mean can rise to 20°C; in Munich (Bavaria) the mean is 17.2°C.

Communications

The Federal Republic has a highly developed network of railways, roads and waterways. The Federal Railways *(Deutsche Bundesbahn)* had in 1979 a rail network of 28,576 km (10,349 km electrified). The road system grew to 470,000 km in 1979, of which 6,500 km were motorways. Germany has the densest and, after the USA, longest network of motorways in the world. The number of registered motor vehicles rose from 2.4 million in 1950 to 24 million in 1980, of which 22 million were passenger cars. The inland water transport system is highly developed, consisting of 4,400 km of waterway. The Rhine accounts for two thirds of all goods traffic carried by inland waterways. Canals link the Rhine, Main and Danube rivers and these are being widened and deepened to form a waterway which will link the North Sea to the Black Sea. Among seafaring nations, Germany ranks in eleventh place, with a merchant fleet of some 9 million gross registered tonnes, 2.5% of the world's merchant tonnage. There is an efficient internal and external air service run by the national airline, Lufthansa. The major airports are Frankfurt, Munich, Hamburg, Cologne-Bonn, Stuttgart and Hannover. There are road and rail connections through the DDR.

2 POPULATION

Growth

The population in December 1979 was 61,439,300. The growth rate is declining and the ratio of live births to population in 1978 was only 9.4 per 1,000 inhabitants, compared with 16.1 per 1,000 in 1968 and 19.5 per 1,000 for the same area in 1938. Germany has the lowest birth rate in the world and if the decline continues at the same rate the population is expected to fall by 3 million by 1990. The reasons for the decrease are: a drop in the number of women of child bearing age, an increase in the number of working women and a shortage of large, reasonably priced accommodation. The decline in the birth rate is now the most important factor affecting future educational policy and planning. At present the upper levels of the system are still under pressure for places.

Distribution

The breakdown of population among the Federal States *(Länder)* is as follows: *(Source: Whitaker's Almanack 1981)*.

State	Capital	Population
Schleswig-Holstein	Kiel	2,599,000
Hamburg		1,653,000
Lower Saxony (Niedersachsen)	Hanover (Hannover)	7,234,200
Bremen		695,000
North Rhine Westphalia (Nordrhein-Westfalen)	Düsseldorf	17,017,100
Hesse *(Hessen)*	Wiesbaden	5,576,100
Rhineland Palatinate (Rheinland-Pfalz)	Mainz	3,633,200
Baden-Württemberg	Stuttgart	9,190,100
Bavaria *(Bayern)*	Munich *(München)*	10,871,000
Saarland	Saarbrücken	1,058,600
Berlin (West)		1,902,300

The pattern of population distribution is very uneven. The average population density is 247 per square kilometre, one of the highest in the world. Nine percent of the population is found in the Ruhr district, with a density in places of 5,500 per sq km. Every third person in Germany lives in a large city or town of more than 100,000 population. The largest cities are West Berlin (1,909,700), Hamburg (1,664,800), Munich (1,297,000) and Cologne (976,500). Other cities with populations between 50,000 and 700,000 are Essen, Frankfurt, Dortmund, Düsseldorf, Stuttgart, Duisberg, Bremen and Hannover. Yet some 25 million people (41%) still live in small towns or villages with less than 20,000 inhabitants and of these 5 million live in villages with fewer than 2,000 people. In addition, there are vast areas of unspoilt open countryside, heathland, forests and mountains with thinly distributed populations.

Movements

Since World War Two Germany has experienced one of the greatest displacements of population known to European history. During this time at least 12 million people of German origin have been resettled. The Federal Republic makes a distinction between expellees and refugees. Expellees are those who lived formerly in areas other than the present German Democratic Republic, e.g. East Prussia, Poland and Czechoslovakia; by 1950 there were about 8.5 million expellees from these areas. Refugees are those who have lived previously in the German Democratic Republic; by 1961 3.5 million of them had settled in the Federal Republic. Both these groups are completely integrated within the Federal Republic and no longer form a separate section of society. A further group, the 'later resettlers', are Germans who have only recently come in from Eastern Europe - a process that is still continuing. They give rise to special problems, e.g. lack of proficiency in the German language and often the need for job retraining.

Immigrants

In 1973 Germany had over 2.5 million immigrants workers *(Gastarbeiter)* living in the country. Since then the recruitment of foreign workers has been cut, except those from EC member countries. In 1977 there were 1,877,100 foreign workers in Germany, the largest group being Turks (514,700), followed by Yugoslavs, Italians, Greeks, Spaniards and Portuguese. Most of these undertake unskilled and menial jobs, although a number have contributed significantly to the variety of restaurants and small food shops in most German towns. Many foreign workers have their families with them and they tend to live in ghettos in the less desirable areas of towns and cities. Many of the women do not speak German and for practical purposes it is often the children who act as interpreters. Although non-EC foreign workers are only allowed to stay for fixed renewable periods, in practice many have already been in Germany for more than five years. The children therefore consider themselves to be German and attempts to effect a major reduction in numbers would cause serious resettlement problems. The total number of foreigners living in Germany is 3.9 million. One child in every five born is non-German, which has far reaching implications for the education system, particularly in zones of industrial concentration. Since many of these children are disadvantaged to begin with, apart from the language problem, the risk of under-achievement is great. Their prospects for performing well at school, for job training and an integrated future in society are not great. It is a problem to which the German authorities are paying more and more attention.

3 SOCIETY AND CULTURE
Language

German is the mother tongue of more than 100 million people. As well as being spoken in the two German States, it is the official language in Austria and Liechtenstein and one of the official languages in Switzerland. There are also some $4\frac{1}{2}$ million German speakers in the United States. Dialects of German are spoken in most parts of the Federal Republic: there are considerable differences, for example, between Bavarian German and that spoken in the north or the Rhineland. Education, however, enables dialect speakers to write Standard German and to speak it, although always with the accent of their region. English is the first foreign language in West Germany. It is accepted as an international language of manifold utility and as a major language in the EC. About 98% of secondary school pupils learn it as their first modern language. A recent survey of young people indicated that 45% of them can read a newspaper in English. In the top educational group 90% speak English and in a survey of language needs in business 92% of those interviewed stated that English was the language needed most. The desire to learn English shows every sign of growing, a factor that is causing some concern in educational circles as they see the popularity of other languages declining.

Social Patterns

The general picture of post-war Germany is one of general prosperity. Apart from those of the business elite, about 2% of the population, the outward style of living and appearance of all social groups have become very much alike. A noticeable trend is that this constant levelling process has increasingly narrowed the difference between industrial workers and other classes in society. In Germany, employees are placed in three categories: officials or civil servants *(Beamten)*, office workers or white collar workers *(Angestellten)* and workers *(Arbeiter)*. The *Beamten* previously formed the core of the leading class in society but their influence and prestige has declined. The growth of *Angestellten* could be said to represent a new middle class but they have not coalesced to form a homogeneous group, and represent varied political and social outlooks. The main dissenting voices from the materialisation of present-day Germany have until recently come from students and extreme left wing or nihilist groups; but there are signs that this dissent is now on the wane. The new and growing form of protest comes from environmental groups and the relative success of the Green Party *(Grüne Partei)* in elections is an indication of this. There are almost 3 million more women than men in Germany; over the age of 45 the surplus of women is as much as 4 million, most of them war widows. Almost every second woman between 15 and 50 is in employment and women as a whole make up about a third of the total workforce.

Culture

From the point of view of both quality and quantity, German cultural life is probably as developed as any in the world. Because there has never been a real cultural metropolis comparable to Paris or London, cultural life is diffused throughout the length and breadth of the land. For example, the central library of the Federal Republic is situated in Frankfurt, which is also the centre of the book trade; the press is largely concentrated in Hamburg; Munich has the most theatres; the central State archives are in Koblenz; there are scientific academies in Düsseldorf, Gottingen, Heidelberg, Mainz and Munich; the major museums are in Berlin; even medium sized towns often have fine art galleries, symphony orchestras and theatres. Decentralisation is one of the major characteristics of German culture. Musical life has always been extremely active in Germany, and there are over 60 theatre/opera houses, almost 80 symphony orchestras and a large number of independent chamber orchestras as well as others composed of members of the great symphony orchestras. Most of the opera houses are heavily subsidised by the city or *Land* (state), and are freed from the financial worries of institutions in other countries. Out of a total of 188 theatres in the Federal Republic, 30 are subsidised by *Land* governments and 100 by municipal administrations, while 58 are privately run. Since the mid-1960s the German film industry, centred on Munich, has undergone something of a renaissance. After a long period of silence German literature experienced a revival in 1945. The first writers expressed a feeling of despair as a result of war-time and post-war experiences - a 'literature of ruin'. In the 1950s and early 1960s, the mood was one of disquiet over the negative aspects of materialism and economic prosperity, as articulated in the novels of Heinrich Boll. In the late 1960s literature became politically aware again as a result of the student movement of 1967/68. 'Expatriate' writers and poets from the DDR are now a significant part of the literary scene. Apart from Boll, the best known German writer is probably Gunter Grass, an author of inexhaustible imagination who populates his novels with weird and fanciful characters. The Federal Republic's book production is the third largest in the world, after the USA and the Soviet Union. There are more than 2,000 publishers. In 1976 5,499 titles were translated into German, of which just under two thirds were from English. In 1973, 3,400 German titles were translated into foreign languages, of which 18.9% were into English. The International Frankfurt Book Fair, held every autumn, is the largest in the world; in 1978, 5,089 publishers exhibited there.

Religion

Approximately 90% of the population belong to either the Roman Catholic Church or the Evangelical Church (an alliance of Lutheran, Reformed and *Land* churches). In the Federal Republic as a whole the ratio between the two denominations is more or less equal. The Protestants preponderate in the north and the Catholics in the south. In the Rhineland Palatinate, Saarland and Bavaria the Catholics are in the majority. In the other *Länder* the Protestants predominate with the exception of North Rhine Westphalia and Baden-Württemburg, where there are equal percentages. It is estimated that about one third of the Catholics are regular churchgoers, compared to less than 10% among Protestants. In spite of this, Church taxes are still levied on their members, unless they make a legal declaration that they have left the Church.

4 HISTORY AND POLITICS

Historical Development

Germany did not become a single nation until 1871. The death of Charlemagne in 814 precipitated the division of his Empire between his sons and further division followed. For the next 1,000 years, Germany was part of what later became known as the Holy Roman Empire, while at the same time becoming divided into ever smaller units of government. In the mid-seventeenth century there were 360 of these. The activities of Napoleon and the congress of Vienna reduced the number to 39. But one of them, Prussia, had grown steadily in importance during the eighteenth century and it was the brilliant Prussian minister, Bismarck, who finally united Germany under the Prussian King. World War One led to the fall of the monarchy but the country preserved its unity. In 1933 the appointment of Hitler as Chancellor ended Germany's period as a democratic republic; the Nazi government established a one-party state and embarked on an expansionist policy which took as its first objective the revision of the Treaty of Versailles. World War Two ended in complete defeat for Germany, which was partitioned among the Allied Powers. The country was in chaos: most of its large towns and cities lay in ruins and the problems were exacerbated by the millions of refugees who had fled or been expelled from the east.

Post-War Period

After the failure of negotiations to establish a unified administration, the three western zones were integrated economically The Basic Law *(Grundgesetz)* of 23 May 1949 declared the three zones a federal republic. In October of the same year the Soviet Union announced the establishment of a separate republic in its zone of occupation. After three elections Dr Konrad Adenauer formed a government which began the highly successful period of reconstruction. Gradually the three Western occupation powers relinquished their authority during this period and on 5 May 1955 full sovereignty was restored to the Federal Republic. From this time on Germany became a partner of the Western powers. At the same time the German Democratic Republic became more and more integrated with the Eastern bloc, politically, economically and militarily. The attainment of German unity, which the Federal Republic had fought hard to achieve, became less and less likely as time went on. In the late 1960s Chancellor Willy Brandt set out to put the relations between the two German states on a new footing and on 21 December 1972 a treaty was signed whereby the two states agreed to develop normal interstate relations. However, the Berlin wall and the border barrier running the whole length of the boundary between the two states constitute one of the world's most impenetrable buffer zones. The GDR holds the view that the two German states are completely separate nations; the Federal Government continues to maintain that they form one nation.

Government and Political Organisation

According to the Basic Law, government is shared between the 11 component states *(Länder)* and the federal government *(Bundesregierung)*. The Law defines the areas of national and provincial authority and guarantees the rights of the *Länder*. Each *Land* has its own parliament elected by suffrage. The Federal Parliament and major legislative organ is the *Bundestag*, whose 496 members are elected by universal suffrage. Federal elections are held every four years, while those in the *Länder* are staggered. West Berlin is not technically part of the Federal Republic but its links are extremely close and it sends deputies to the Federal Parliament in Bonn. In addition to the *Bundestag* there is also a Federal Assembly *(Bundesrat)*. This body is not elected but consists of members of the *Länder* governments or their delegates. Laws require the express approval of the *Bundesrat* if they concern *Länder* interests, as more than half of them do. In other cases, the *Bundesrat* has the right of objection: the Federal Assembly, therefore, provides useful checks and balances in the running of a democratic system.

There are at present four main political parties. They are: the Social Democratic Party of Germany (SPD); the Christian Democratic Union (CDU); the Christian Social Union (CSU); and the Free Democratic Party (FDP). The CSU - a party corresponding to the CDU - operates only in Bavaria, but at national level they operate as one joint parliamentary CDU/CSU block. Until 1966 the country was governed by the CDU in coalition with the FDP; from 1966 to 1969 there was a 'grand coalition' between the CDU and SPD; since 1969 the SPD has been in power in alliance with the FDP, although in the 1976 elections it had a considerably reduced minority. The President of the Republic was elected for five years in 1979.

International Relations

The Federal Republic has very close relations with the Western allies whose support was initially felt necessary for the survival of the State. It is an active and cooperative member of the EC, the Council of Europe, NATO, OECD, and other international organisations. At the same time it must be remembered that Germany is a country on the dividing line of Europe: East and West confront each other in a divided Germany. For Germany the policy of detente is a cornerstone of its relations with its eastern neighbours. Chancellor Willy Brandt (1967-1974) paved the way towards this end by his policy of *Ostpolitik*. Treaties were concluded with Poland and the Soviet Union in 1970, the GDR in 1972 and Czechoslovakia in 1973. The Federal Republic's recognition of the GDR led to the admission of both German States to the UN in 1973. This policy of detente has been patiently continued by Helmut Schmidt since 1974. A third, and increasingly important, object of German foreign policy lies in its relations with the Third World and the leading role it plays in the North-South dialogue. Responsibility for foreign cultural policy lies with the Federal Government. Its implementation, however, is mainly carried out by intermediary organisations. The Goethe Institute plays a major part in cultural work abroad, especially through teaching the German language and disseminating information about Germany. The German Academic Exchange Service *(Deutscher Akademischer Austauschdienst, DAAD)* is responsible for the exchange of academics, researchers, and students. *Inter Nationes* is chiefly concerned with looking after foreign visitors as well as the production and distribution of information and cultural material. The Institute of Foreign Relations *(Institut für Auslandsbeziehungen, IFA)* specialises in organising exhibitions in foreign countries. The Federal Republic also actively supports a number of schools abroad *(Auslandsschulen)* as follows: Europe 37, Americas 40 (39 in Central and South America), Africa 14 and Asia 17.

5 THE ECONOMY

Agriculture

Agriculture with forestry and fishing now contributes only 2.7% of GNP and employs 7% of the labour force. Its share of both has decreased considerably over the last 20 years. Farms are small because the traditional system of inheritance led to land being divided, and in some areas where there is also industry many small farmers have an industrial job. The government has attempted to increase the size of holdings with some success, but smallholdings are still in the majority. Nevertheless, the Federal Republic produces 70% of its own foodstuffs. About a quarter of the land in the Federal Republic still consists of forest yet, even so, much timber is imported.

Natural Resources

Germany is not particularly rich in natural resources and depends largely on imports for its raw material and energy needs. Coal and lignite (the latter obtained by opencast mining) are the largest sources of fuel; small reserves of oil supply 5% and natural gas 40% of the country's needs. Natural gas is also imported from the Netherlands and the USSR. The government's policy is to reduce dependency on imported oil and to turn to nuclear power. There are 14 nuclear power stations in operation (three experimental) but there is growing population resistance to the extension of this form of energy production.

Industry

In 1977 manufacturing and construction contributed 48.5% of GNP and employed 40% of the labour force. The country is heavily industrialised, with the major emphasis on heavy industry, including iron and steel production, electrical engineering, vehicle production, and shipbuilding; the chemical industry is the largest sector.

Economic Situation

The German economy is basically a free market economy with the government pursuing a policy of maximum competition and limiting its intervention to maintaining or increasing competition rather than reducing it. Since the currency reform in 1948, Germany has made rapid strides in expanding the economy and is now the major industrial power in Western Europe, with a GNP approximately twice that of Britain. The growth of the Federal Republic's economy is one of the success stories of the post-war era - for between 1950 and 1970 GNP increased by over 250%. Part of the success in rebuilding the economy is attributed to Marshall Aid and the plentiful supply of labour, first from the east and subsequently from Mediterranean countries. But it is also attributable to the willingness of German manufacturers to invest in new plant machinery, a hard-working and disciplined labour force and a non-militant trade union movement. Since the late 1950s Germany has been the second largest trading nation in the world and is now contributing 11% of the combined exports of the West (exports represented 20% of GNP in 1979). The 1974 oil crisis, precipitating a decrease in world trade, brought problems to the German economy, so dependent on exports. But since then the economy has revived and is likely to continue to do so. Industrial production for August 1979 was running at a level 5.2% above the previous year, compared to 3.3% in the USA and a nil growth position in the UK. The per capita GNP is still among the highest in the EC and the rate of inflation the lowest (only 4.5% in 1979). The balance of payments has until recently shown a healthy surplus, but in 1979/80 this situation changed because of a large increase in the country's oil bill. Unemployment since 1975 has, on average, been over the one million mark, but by December 1979 was down to 866,783 (3.8%). The average level of negotiated tariff round wage and salary increases in 1979 was a comparatively modest 4.5%, but total improvements to incomes (i.e. including increased family benefits, profit sharing schemes, tax reductions, etc.) averaged out at 7.5%. In common with other industrialised nations Germany views the immediate future with grave concern and sees the continuing world recession, increasing energy costs and the unstable international situation as factors likely to lead to higher inflation and increased unemployment. But the position from which Germany faces these problems is much stronger than that of most other industrialised countries.

6 THE EDUCATION SYSTEM
General

Since the states *(Länder)* are autonomous in educational matters, there are 11 distinct and separate systems and 11 major administrative authorities. There is a broad uniformity between these systems, the instruction offered and the qualifications gained, but sometimes nomenclature varies and qualifications are not always valued uniformly. Most parts of the system have been undergoing a thorough overhaul since the 1960s. There is an overall Federal Education Plan but the *Länder* are moving at different speeds, often with differing interpretations, towards the objectives outlined in the Plan. The basic pattern is a four-year primary school *(Grundschule)*, commencing at age 6, followed by selection into one of the types of secondary school. Between *Grundschule* and final selection is an orientation/observation/promotional stage (years 5 and 6). This can be in the form of:

- a separate school - notably Lower Saxony
- continued attachment to a *Grundschule* - Bremen, Berlin
- attachment to one of the three types of secondary school *(Gymnasium, Realschule* or *Hauptschule)* - most states
- a cooperative or additive comprehensive school (multi-lateral school); here there is a common orientation stage prior to streaming into a *Gymnasium, Realschule* or *Hauptschule* branch.

Only a few states have made significant progress with fully integrated comprehensive schools; in Hesse roughly 25% of the age group, in Berlin roughly 30%.

The Academic Year

The school year is considered a single unit (sometimes, at upper secondary level, the term 'school half-year' is used). The year is punctuated by short holidays: in autumn (two weeks), at Christmas (two weeks), Easter (three weeks), and a longer six-week holiday in the summer. Summer holidays are on a staggered rotation system, each state (Bavaria excepted) advancing each year by one week up to the earliest possible starting date (June). Thus the opening day of the school year varies accordingly. Most schools work a six-day week, mornings only, plus occasional extra-curricular afternoon activities but there is an increasing number of full-day schools which work a five-day week.

Pre-School

Schools or classes which precede the first grade of *Grundschule* are of three types. First, the *Kindergarten* which caters for children aged 3, 4 and 5. *Kindergarten* fall broadly within the competence of the Ministries of Health, Family, Youth and Social Affairs although education ministries *(Kultusministerien)* are expected to advise on curricula and are collaborating in pilot projects. Most schools (80%) are financed by local municipal and district social welfare authorities, the Churches, youth organisations and other charitable organisations. The teachers are trained child care and social workers, whose salaries are not borne by the *Kultusministerien*. Provision of places in *Kindergarten* has noticeably increased in recent years as part of a deliberate policy of positive discrimination in favour of less privileged school groups. The federal average of 32.7% in 1965 rose to 65.5% in 1975. Provision in Baden-Württemburg and Saarland in 1978 was well over 90%. Actual attendance figures, as far as they are available, suggest that supply exceeds demand. Provision for five year olds including *Vorklassen* (see below) reached 100% in most *Länder* in 1979, thus earily fulfilling the target of the Federal General Education Plan. The second type of pre-schooling is known as the *Vorklasse* which, as distinct from the *Kindergarten*, is attached to a *Grundschule* and caters for the age group 5-6 (children who are below compulsory school age or are considered not yet mature enough). Staff are trained child care/social workers as in the *Kindergarten* (i.e. they are not graduates and not the responsibility of the *Kultusministerien*). The *Kultusministerien* have, however, been collaborating closely with social affairs ministries over pilot projects to determine whether five year olds should spend this pre-school year in a primary school, *Vorklasse* or in a *Kindergarten*. Results and decisions have varied. In Berlin, where in 1975/76 over 55% of five year olds were already in *Vorklassen* it is intended that the *Vorklasse* should become general. In Baden-Württemberg, where provision in places in *Kindergarten* is high, five year olds will remain in the *Kindergarten*. There is no conclusive evidence whether *Vorklasse* or *Kindergarten* five year olds get a better start. There is evidence that children who start at 3 or 4 do better in the first year of *Grundschule*. The third type is the *Schulkindergarten*, which is also attached to the *Grundschule* but is specifically a preparatory class for children of 6+ who are not deemed mature enough to begin school.

Activities in the pre-school system *(Elementarbereich)* are play oriented: attempts to pre-empt teaching of basic reading, writing and arithmetic are frowned upon. Children are educated in the use of materials, construtive work, basic implements for painting, drawing, etc. There are in some quarters complaints that the two to three year training of pre-school teachers is not enough and there are pressures for more highly specialised, pedagogically trained graduates. Nominal fees are payable in the *Elementarbereich:* in practice only those who can afford to contribute do so.

First Level Schools *(Grundschule)*

Primary school is universal and free. At the beginning of the school year (August), children who have reached the age of 6 by 30 June, and who are considered mature enough, begin a four-year *Grundschule*. There is a further discriminatory entry period *(Karenzzeit)* up to 31 December for those who can convince the school authorities that their children are mentally and physically capable of coping. Berlin and Bremen have a six-year primary school system, Hamburg has reverted to the four-year system. The atmosphere nowadays in these schools is becoming less authoritarian and more informal; work is in groups and teaching is child centred. The introduction of reading, writing and basic mathematics is the most important element of the teaching, but the longer term objective is to provide pupils with knowledge and experience of the modern world and help them to come to terms with their environment. The teaching programme includes German, religious knowledge, local studies, arithmetic, music, art, craftwork and physical education. The schools are open in the mornings only. In the first two years there are usually 20-26 periods a week, while there are 24-30 periods in the third and fourth years. New Maths, in particular set theory, was introduced in 1972 in a published form which is being updated regularly every five years or so by trained working parties of teachers, inspectors and researchers. Most schools are involved in some form of curriculum reform. There is still heated controversy over the appropriateness of New Maths to children's needs. The *Kinderhort*, sometimes confused with the *Kindergarten*, is essentially a child-minding establishment for the benefit of families where both parents are working. Here school children can be left in the afternoons in the care of qualified child-minders; there is some loosely organised activity, play facilities, and children can be helped with homework, language difficulties, etc.

Second Level Schools

There are basically four types of secondary school:

(i) *Hauptschule* (main school) covering grades (school years) 5 to 9

(ii) *Realschule* (intermediate school) covering grades 5 to 10

(iii) *Gymnasium* (grammar school) covering grades 5 to 13

(iv) *Gesamtschule* (comprehensive school) covering grades 5 to 9/10 or 13.

Secondary education is conceived as consisting of two levels, *Sekundarstufe I and II*, which is based on the conviction that divisions in the educational system should be horizontal rather than vertical. To *Sekundarstufe I* belong all schools/classes covering the school years 5 to 10 (in Berlin and Bremen there is a six-year primary school system, school years 7 to 10. This corresponds to ages 10+ to 16 and includes the four types of school listed above as well as the various types of special schools for children with disabilities *(Sonderschule)*. The minimum school leaving age is 15, usually corresponding to the final year, grade 9, at the *Hauptschule*. To *Sekundarstufe II* belong all schools in the post-compulsory school sector from school year 11 (age 16+) and onwards, i.e. the upper classes of the *Gymnasium* (years 11 to 13) and the various types of vocational school *(Berufsbildende Schule)* described later. The first two years at secondary school are known as the orientation stage *(Orientierungsstufe)*. This takes various forms, as outlined at the beginning of this section. The aim is to palliate, in a tripartite system, the worst effects of selection at 10+. Children are normally recommended by their primary school, in consultation with their parents, for one of the main types of secondary school. This recommendation, however, is not final until the end of the orientation stage, thus leaving open the possibility of transfer between different types of school. Parents can challenge the final decision; if they do, the child goes first to the type of school chosen by the parents, but must pass a test after a probationary period or be transferred.

Hauptschule

The *Hauptschule* is, as the name implies, the main type of secondary school. Until comparatively recently, the *Grundschule* and *Hauptschule* were one unit, embracing ages 6 to 14 and known as the *Volksschule*. This type of school is now comparatively rare although the name still persists in the vernacular. The *Hauptschule* is characterised by high intake from lower social group workers, one-parent families and foreign workers' children. It mainly caters for the less academically gifted children and aims largely at providing them with an introduction to the working world. The typical timetable consists of the following (figures relate to the number of periods): religion (2), German (4), one foreign language (3), mathematics (4), physics/chemistry (2), biology (1), history (2), geography (1), social studies (1), world of work (2), sport (1), art, music, handicraft (4), optionals (2). The weekly number of lessons varies between 30 and 33. At the end of grade 9 pupils take a qualifying school leaving certificate *(Hauptschulabschlusszeugnis)*, which qualifies them for entry into apprenticeship and day release at a vocational school, the possibility of continuing for an optional tenth year, transfer to a *Realschule* course or entry to full-time vocational education. Those who leave school without an *Abschluss* (about one in five) are awarded a non-qualifying certificate *(Hauptschulabgangszeugnis)* and largely join the ranks of the 'unskilled'.

Realschule

The *Realschule* comprises grades 5-10 or 7-10 concluding at age 16+ with the Intermediate Certificate *(Realschulabschlusszeugnis)* - often referred to as 'middle maturity' *(Mittlere Reife)*. There is a parallel continuation *(Aufbau)* type of school for those who transfer from the *Hauptschule* in that it offers a more demanding curriculum in the basic subjects; an additional foreign language and a second science subject are also offered and a business administration/legally oriented option is usually included. There are between 30 and 34 hours of instruction per week. The *Realschule* is a very popular choice among lower middle class, craft workers, and industrial workers. It offers a safe passage to white collar jobs in middle management or technical status: an alternative to those who do not aspire to the more abstract intellectual rigours of *Gymnasium* courses and lengthy university study. At the same time it still leaves open the possibility of transfer to a course leading to various types of vocational training (part time or full time), general university entry via a continuation *(Aufbau)* type of *Gymnasium* or restricted university entry via a specialist *Gymnasium*. The importance of the *Realschule* has grown considerably in the last few years.

Gymnasium

The *Gymnasium* spans both second levels I and II. There are many different types, but its charateristic feature is that it offers courses beyond the compulsory school leaving age up to a thirteenth year of school. On completion, pupils sit for their higher school certificate examination *(Abitur or Reifeprufung)*, which qualifies them for university entry. Traditionally the *Gymnasium* is the most academic and prestigious branch of the secondary school system. The three main traditional categories are: classical *(altsprachliches Gymnasium)*, modern languages *(neusprachliches Gymnasium)* and scientific *(mathematisch-naturwissenschaftliches Gymnasium)*. These still persist although the subject bias is not so marked nowadays. Depending on the duration of primary school, the *Gymnasium* includes classes 5-13 or 7-13. In addition to the previously mentioned continuation forms of *Gymnasium* for promising transfer pupils from the *Hauptschule* (years 7 or 8) or from the *Realschule* (year 11), there are also specialised vocational *Gymnasium* with a social studies, musical/artistic, economic, textiles, agricultural or domestic science bias. These offer important vocationally oriented training courses with direct outlets into jobs or entry to specific university faculties.

In the standard type of *Gymnasium* the timetable in classes 5 to 10 includes German, mathematics, biology, geography, music, art, physical education, at least two foreign languages, history, social studies, physics and chemistry. The number of lessons varies from 30 to 36 a week. Streaming is the general rule with some setting for modern languages and mathematics. Repeating a year is also very common as promotion from one class to the next depends on a rigorous system of marks for tests and classwork. Pupils can if they wish leave the *Gymnasium* at the end of class 10 and if their performance is satisfactory are awarded the *Mittlere Reife* certificate, equivalent to that obtained in the *Realschule*.

At the upper secondary level (classes 11-13) reorganisation has taken place following an agreement reached in 1972. The subject distinctions - classical/modern languages/science - merge to form the new reformed upper level *(reformierte gymnasiale Oberstufe)*. The traditional *Abitur* used to be taken in all subjects in a mammoth examination at the end of the final year. Now, in the reformed upper level, a system of options has been introduced. Pupils select two main courses *(Leistungskurse)*, each comprising five to six lessons a week, and basic courses *(Grundkurse)*, two to three lessons a week, which are compulsory in three broad subject fields: language/literature/art, social sciences, and mathematics/natural sciences/technology. Further options now offered in addition to more traditional subjects are pedagogy, psychology, sociology, law, geology, astronomy, statistics and data processing. In the final *Abitur* which is internally set and marked by each school, candidates sit a written examination in two main subjects and one optional subject (from a different subject field). In addition they are examined orally in a further option subject. These subjects must include at least one living foreign language, mathematics or natural sciences and German. The final grade is on a scale of 1-6 (1 = high), but prior to the final grading candidates are awarded points for each course or examination completed. Main courses are weighted in the ratio of 3:1 to basic courses.

Gesamtschule

The comprehensive school is still a hotly debated issue, although some headway has been made in introducing the system, especially in Hesse and Berlin, as well as North Rhine Westphalia and Hamburg. In most *Länder*, however, this type of school is still being treated as experimental. Two basic types of comprehensive predominate: the 'integrated' school *(integrierte Gesamtschule)* and the 'additive' or 'cooperative' type *(additive* or *kooperative Gesamtschule)*. The integrated comprehensive provides a uniform teaching and organisational pattern for all pupils, although there is streaming in the basic subjects: in Hesse, for example, pupils are divided into three levels (A, B, C) tending to correspond to the three main types of secondary school. the cooperative or additive comprehensive incorporates the *Hauptschule, Realschule* and *Gymnasium* on the same site, sometimes under one head teacher, but the three types of school nevertheless remain distinct. On completion of classes 9 or 10 pupils sit for the corresponding examinations taken in other types of secondary school. Those comprehensives which include classes 11 to 13 are modelled along the lines of the *Gymnasium*.

Vocational

Vocational schools *(Berufsbildende Schulen)* correspond roughly to what is known as the Further Education Sector in Britain but exclude advanced work at degree or diploma level. In Germany they are classified as upper secondary. Three basic points need to be grasped in order to understand the complexity of vocational school types. First, all vocational schools are entirely within the jurisdiction of the 11 *Land* education ministries: second, there is a statutory obligation (following minimum school leaving age) of three years' part time attendance at a vocational school. This applies to all school leavers between 15 and 18, irrespective of whether they are in training apprenticeships or under contract (only a tiny percentage are not). It does not apply to those staying on at school on a full time basis to obtain a qualification. Third, by far the vast majority of school leavers follow the part time day or block release system (1.7 million in 1978). For students following this training the *Länder* continue to be in charge of the school element while the federal government is responsible for on-the-job training and other forms of training outside schools. This is called the dual system.

While there are variations in types of vocational schools in individual states the following are the most important:

- *Berufsschule* (part time vocational school). This type is the cornerstone of the vocational school system, catering for the majority of those leaving school at 15 or 16, who then proceed to a vocational training in industry or who are employed but receive no on-the-job training. Courses consist of practical and theoretical training (about 60%), plus a timetable devoted to general subjects such as German, social studies, economics, English, religion and sport (about 40%). At the end of training, trainees take a final examination administered by local Chambers of Commerce.

- *Berufsfachschule* (full time specialised vocational school). The entry requirements are a successful completion of *Hauptschule* or *Realschule*. This type prepares pupils for a future field of employment or provides vocational training, while at the same time improving their general education. There are various types of *Berufsfachschule*, such as those specialising in commerce, child care or technical assistant careers. Length of attendance varies, but in most cases lasts one year. All courses end with final examinations.

- *Berufaufbauschule* (continuation part time vocational). This type caters for young people who are currently doing vocational training or who have completed it. The teaching of both the vocational and general courses is at a higher level than that of the *Berufsschule*, leading to the equivalent of the *Realschule* intermediate certificate. The minimum course length is 1,300 hours and there are five areas of specialisation, all of which incorporate economics and business management. These are: general commercial/industrial, industrial/technical, home economics/nursing, social work and agriculture.

- *Fachoberschule* (senior full time technical school). These full time schools comprise grades 11 and 12 for those who have completed *Realschule* or equivalent. The teaching programme offers specialised theoretical and practical knowledge and skills, as well as general subjects. The specialisations include engineering, economics and administration, domestic science, design, navigation, etc. The final examination, the *Fachhochschulreife*, is the entry qualification for colleges of technology *(Fachhochschule)*.

In addition to these four main types of vocational school there are others: the *Hohere Berufsfachschule* (higher full time specialised vocational school), of which the most common sort is commercial, and which prepares students for lower to middle management positions or for entry to the *Fachhochschule;* the *Berufliches Gymnasium* (vocational grammar school) which takes *Realschule* leavers and prepares them for entry to higher education; and the *Fachschule* (advanced technical school), which trains middle level personnel in management. The vocational education sector, as will have been seen, is highly complex and is still undergoing change.

Third Level (Higher) Institutions

At present there are 64 institutions of higher education listed as being of university status; these include specialised institutions such as the Medical University in Hannover, the Army Universities in Hamburg and Munich, and the Sports University in Cologne. The bulk of the higher education institutions, however, fall into three groups, the traditional type of university *(Universität)*, of which there are 37, with the usual faculties (arts, sciences, social sciences, law, etc.); the seven technical universities *(Technische Universität/Hochschule)*; and a new type, the comprehensive university *(Gesamthochschule)*, combining in one entity and sometimes on one campus existing institutions of higher education, such as a college of education and a technical college. They are the result of recommendations made in 1970 and are intended to promote greater flexibility and opportunities for transfer in higher education. Including a few religious foundations, 11 of these new institutions are listed as *Gesamthochschulen*. The best known are in Duisburg, Essen, Paderborn, Siegen, Wuppertal, Kassel and Bamberg. There is also the new multimedia Open University *(Fernuniversität)* in Hagen, which opened in 1976 and now has nearly 12,000 students. Its teaching programme is mainly by correspondence operating through 26 regional study centres. There are, in addition, higher institutions which do not have full university status, for example the 17 colleges of education, 9 theological colleges and 26 fine arts and music institutions *(Kunsthochschule* and *Musikhochschule)*. The best known music schools are in Berlin, Cologne, Detmold, Essen, Hamburg and Munich. The normal requirement for entry is the *Abitur*, but in both art and music schools students of outstanding ability are accepted without formal academic qualifications.

Entrance

The normal route to the university is via the Gymnasium and the possession of an *Abitur*. However, in recent years attempts have been made to make university education available to wider sections of society by what is termed 'the second route to education' *(der zweite Bildungsweg)*. The two most common means are through night schools *(Abendgymnasium)*, which offer the *Abitur*, or through a *Studienkolleg*, which is an institution, usually attached to a university, designed to enable mainly foreign students to prepare for university entrance. The third way, the hard way, is by progression through the educational institutions described in the section on vocational education, as well as the college of technology *(Fachhochschule)*. Universities are under severe pressure for places. Although not strictly constitutional, restricted entry *(numerus clausus)*, based on *Abitur* grade, has been introduced into the hardest hit faculties, e.g. medical, dental and pharmacy studies. A Central Office for the Allocation of Study Places has been set up, by agreement between the *Länder*, and controls entry into seven disciplines in which *numerus clausus* has been universally imposed. About 60% of the places are awarded on the basis of school performance; the allocation of the remainder depends largely on the length of time students have been waiting for admission, as well as other factors such as 'hardship cases' and the special public need for certain occupational skills.

Courses

A course of study is usually divided into semesters, which as a rule run from October until March and from April until September. There are, however, no classes during 5 months of the year. The pattern of study and qualification in Germany is quite different from Britain. Students present themselves for an examination when they feel ready for it. The first of these is usually the preliminary examination (e.g. *Vordiplom* or *Zwischenprufung)* on completion of four or six semesters, (two or three years) of foundation studies. After a minimum of eight semesters, but usually between ten and 12 semesters, students take either a qualifying diploma examination, e.g. *Diplomingenieur*, *Diplomkaufmann*, etc. or the first *Staatsexamen*, depending on faculty and future profession. The normal conclusion of studies in science and engineering is the *Diplom;* the *Staatsexamen* is an examination controlled by the *Land* and necessary for the exercise of certain professions (for example, law and teaching). After a probationary *(Referendar)* period there is a second State examination. In the arts and humanities there is no equivalent to the British BA and until recently all humanities students had to proceed to the doctorate. A new degree of *Magister Artium* was introduced in the 1960s. This is a shorter course equivalent to the *Diplom*, and caters mainly for students of the humanities who do not want to teach, and it is also recognised as a qualifying examination for those who wish to proceed to a doctorate. A doctorate is more commonly awarded in those disciplines in which the normal termination of studies is a *Diplom*. It is a research degree, consisting of a dissertation and a stiff oral examination, and usually requires two to four years' further study after a *Diplom*. Attainment of the doctor's degree is known as *Promotion*. For those who wish to take up university teaching as a career one further academic hurdle needs to be overcome: the *Habilitation*, a scholarly thesis which confers eligibility for a professorship.

Other Institutions

The *Fachhochschule* (college of advanced technology) is a recent addition to higher education, having been established in 1970/71. It provides specialised training in a number of fields, especially in engineering or commerce. It offers a six semester course, which includes periods of practical training, and the final qualification confers the title of *graduiert*. This is lower than a *Diplom*, but grants exemption from at least one year of a *Diplom* course for those who wish to proceed to a university course of study; in most cases, however, the title of *graduiert* leads directly into employment. (Some *Fachhochschulen* are now awarding a *Diplom* which, especially in the case of engineering, can lead to confusion with the *Diplom* awarded after the longer university course.) In 1978 there were 172,800 students in 106 of these institutions; numbers are likely to expand in future.

Teacher Training

Training takes place at either colleges of education *(Pädagogische Hochschulen)* or in the universities. In general training of teachers for the *Grundschule* and the *Hauptschule* is separate from that of teachers for the *Realschule* and the *Gymnasium*. However, some states now train teachers for a specific level of education, i.e. for primary level (grades 1 to 4) and the lower secondary level *(Hauptschule, Realschule,* and grades 5 to 10 of the *Gymnasium*. The training for all teachers is divided into two periods; academic training and preparatory training. Teachers of vocational subjects also have practical training in firms and factories.

Colleges of Education

The *Pädagogische Hochschulen* (PH) are becoming much more closely associated with the universities. In Bavaria they have been incorporated as departments of education into the universities; in Bremen, Hamburg, Hesse and Lower Saxony the universities carry out the functions of the PH; in Berlin and North Rhine Westphalia the process of merging is now under way. The 17 colleges of education (31 including branch institutions) specialise mainly in training *Grundschule* and *Hauptschule* teachers and sometimes *Realschule* and *Gesamtschule* teachers for grades 5 to 10. The course lasts a minimum of six semesters and subjects studied include theory of education, psychology and sociology as well as two subjects to be taught in the schools (this applies also to future primary school teachers). This course of study leads to the First State Examination *Erste Staatsprüfung für das Lehramt)*, which is roughly equivalent to the BEd. After this examination the preparatory training period begins (see below).

Universities

The universities train teachers for the *Gymnasium* and *Realschule* and for the upper secondary level in general, including full time vocational schools and special schools. The course lasts a minimum of eight semesters and leads to the First State Examination. In practice, few *Gymnasium* teachers take the examination in under ten semesters. The normal pattern of study is two specialist subjects taught at the school (all secondary school teachers teach at least two subjects) plus theory of education, psychology and sociology. The course may include a practical introduction to teaching. As with *Pädagogische Hochschule* students, the preparatory training period begins after the First State Examination.

Preparatory Training Period

The second stage *(Referendarzeit)* consists of a further 18 months (two years in some states) of theory and practical teaching leading to the Second State Examination *Zweite Staatsprüfung für das Lehramt)*. This part of the training is completely separated from previous training at a *Pädagogische Hochschule* or university. Students are based on small institutes usually called a *Studienseminar* and are attached to a particular type of school or level of school. Administratively they are now under the ministries for Schools *(Kultusministerium)* or regional departments *(Bezirksregierung)*. Students spend approximately 12 hours a week on teaching practice, starting with observation and going on to supervised teaching with the specialist subject teacher. Seminar work varies from state to state but a fairly typical pattern is as follows: a weekly seminar attended by the whole training group, at which general lectures on pedagogics, psychology, comparative education, etc. are given; a weekly seminar for a small subject specialist group of 5-15 trainees, under a tutor *(Fachleiter)*, devoted to methodology, peer group teaching and evaluation of experience during teaching practice; private study and independent work for seminar papers; and finally a short, pedagogical dissertation of 80 pages or so for the final examination. Grades (1-6) in the Second State Examination are based on: the tutor's final assessment, two observed teaching periods (one in each subject area), an oral examination and the dissertation already mentioned. Once qualified, teachers normally obtain full civil servant status *(Beamter)* after a further probationary period of two to four years depending on examination grade and subsequent performance.

Adult

Outside the formal education system the *Volkshochschulen* (Adult Education Centres) are a flourishing part of public life. Traditionally these have offered general courses covering everything from languages and science to leisure preparation. Nowadays there is increasing emphasis in the VHS on courses for catching up on school leaving qualifications and various certificates of professional competence (e.g. language). Some regret this tendency because it detracts from the ideal of education for leisure and pleasure. Many towns now boast their own modern VHS building, but the essence of the VHS movement, as in Britain, lies in the courses conducted in the evenings in school buildings in both towns and outlying districts. In 1978 there were 904 adult education centres with approximately 4,500 subsidiary local centres; 235,000 courses were run with 4.14 million participants. Each state has its own VHS association *(Verband)*, with the federal headquarters in Frankfurt. *Volkshochschulen* are either run by local authorities themselves or sponsored by independent organisations with considerable local authority financial support. Private sponsors include churches, political parties, trade unions, chambers of commerce, etc. Apart from the *Volkshochschulen* few other bodies have any interest or tradition in offering continuing education; the universities, for example, show little interest. Since 1969 the federal government has taken on extensive responsibilities for organising and financing adult vocational and further training, and this area is expanding. Some states have introduced statutory periods of study leave for workers. The armed forces run their own adult education institutions for service personnel. These provide a variety of courses, including ones leading to secondary and vocational certificates. The pattern of VHS certificates in various foreign languages and some sciences has now been adopted in a number of neighbouring European countries.

7 EDUCATIONAL ADMINISTRATION

Background

During the Nazi period education was highly centralised, its policy and aims dictated by the government. The Basic Law of 1949 restored to the *Länder* their traditional independence. Education is the only area of public life in which they are fully autonomous. The *Länder* were given the right to develop their own school and university systems with only academic research and extra-mural vocational education left to the central authority. However, the *Länder* were obliged to remain 'loyal to the federation *(Bund)*', i.e. they were obliged to observe federal law and to respect developments in the remaining federal area of authority in education. In 1969 the constitution was altered to provide for a greater degree of federal involvement in education affairs. Under paragraphs 91 (a) and (b) of the Basic Law the federal government gave itself the right to participate with the *Länder* in 'common projects', of which the most important was the building of new universities. For the first

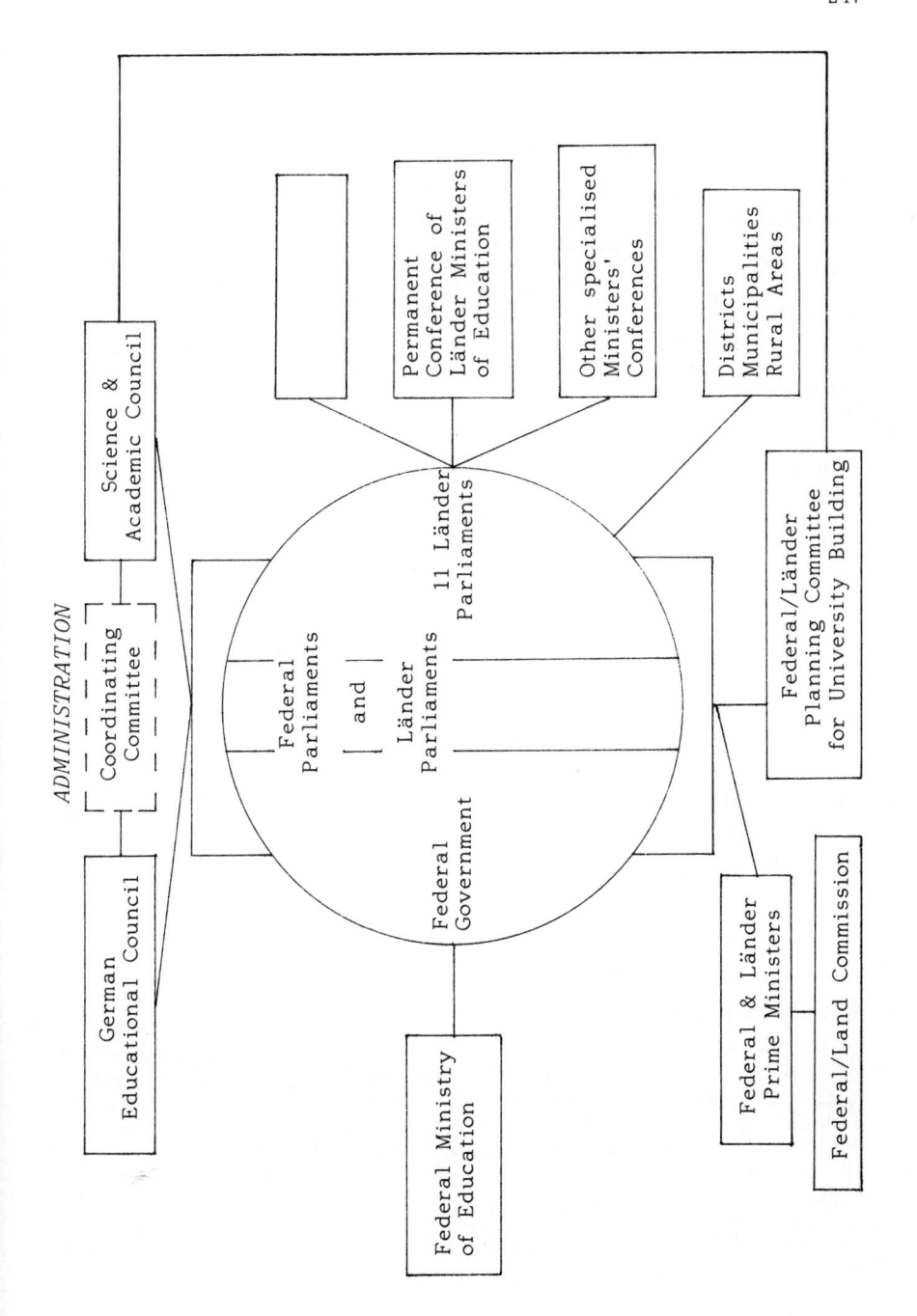

247

ADMINISTRATION

- German Educational Council
- Science & Academic Council
- Coordinating Committee
- Permanent Conference of Länder Ministers of Education
- Other specialised Ministers' Conferences
- Districts Municipalities Rural Areas
- Federal Parliaments and Länder Parliaments
- 11 Länder Parliaments
- Federal Government
- Federal Ministry of Education
- Federal & Länder Prime Ministers
- Federal/Land Commission
- Federal/Länder Planning Committee for University Building

time a Federal Ministry of Education and Science *Bundesministerium für Bildung und Wissenschaft)* was set up. The BMBW's responsibilities and influence are, however, strictly limited.

Responsibility of the *Länder*

The administration of the system basically belongs to the *Länder*, and there is no system of federal inspection. Each *Land* has its own Minister of Education *(Kultusminister)*, (called *Senator für Schulwesen* in Berlin, Bremen and Hamburg), and has the right to draw up its own syllabi, recommend textbooks and organise its schools and teaching. All examinations, including the *Abitur* are local and are set and marked by the teachers under the supervision of the *Land* education staff. The *Länder* also train, appoint, promote and recruit teachers. Because the Basic Law guarantees freedom of movement, the freedom to choose one's place of work as well as one's place of education, some coordination among the *Länder* was found necessary. The chief organ for cooperation is the Standing Conference of State Education Ministers, usually known as the *Kultusministerkonferenz* or KMK, which was first set up in 1948, with a permanent secretariat in Bonn. Over a thousand voluntary agreements have been reached through this body, which have ensured that the structures, institutions, curricula and leaving certificates are broadly comparable in all the *Länder;* uniformity has also been attained in such spheres as the length of the school year and the recognition of academic and professional training. Success in these areas is partly due to the tight central control which exists within each *Land*.

District Responsibility

Below the level of the *Land*, educational administration is the responsibility of smaller regions, called *Regierungsbezirke*. These are further sub-divided into *Kreise;* a *Kreis* may be a town or a more widely scattered rural area.

8 EDUCATIONAL FINANCE

Education Budget

In the 1970s public expenditure on education reached a high of 16% of the total domestic budget and 5.5% of the GNP compared with 11% and 3.4% respectively for the previous decade. Both federal and *Länder* governments are committed to further substantial increases in the next decade and the current rate of growth of this sector is among the highest of any head of government expenditure. About 70% of educational expenditure is provided by the *Land* government, 23% by local district authorities and 7% by the federal government. A large proportion of the *Land* budget goes towards teachers' salaries.

Administration of Finance

As far as schools are concerned, the normal rule is that the *Land* employs the teachers and pays their salaries while the local authorities pay the administrative costs (including salaries of office and domestic staff) and pay for the upkeep of buildings and equipment. In four *Länder* responsibility for the *Realschulen* and *Gymnasien* is shared with local authorities, according to the status of the schools; the *Land* meets the entire costs of some of the schools, the local authorities pay for the remaining schools and employ the teachers for them. At school level the contribution of the federal government is minimal, but at university level it is significant, constituting about one third of the total. The federal government contributes 50% of the capital costs of new universities, in accordance with the 1969 amendment to the Constitution, although with a few exceptions they are all *Land* institutions.

Fees and Grants

Since 1971 all student grants (known as *Bafög*) have been coordinated throughout the country. The federal government provides 65% of the money and the *Länder* the rest. Grants are awarded on the basis of a means test and cover both fees and living expenses for full and part time students past the compulsory stage. Part of the grant is in the form of a loan. As the awards are tied to fixed periods of the study, the grants system should help to reduce the length of courses. There are also grants available to assist students undergoing vocational training.

Allocation of Funds
Expenditure on Education: Distribution by Level
Percentage of Expenditure 1976

Pre-school	First Level	Second Level	Third Level	Other
-	19.2	51.7	13.6	14

9 DEVELOPMENT AND PLANNING OF THE EDUCATION SYSTEM

Origins

As in other European countries the foundations of the higher school system were laid down by the Church, though the first secular schools were started as early as the thirteenth century, to meet a need in the cities for trained merchants and craftsmen. At the time of the Reformation the secular rulers assumed joint responsibility with the Church for providing schools in the reformed states. Those were for only a very narrow upper stratum of society, grammar schools with strict academic curricula but influenced by the ideals of the Humanists. In states which remained Roman Catholic the Jesuit order founded new grammar schools with even stricter curricula. The task of both sets of schools was to prepare students for the university; by the end of the eighteenth century Germany had 42 (mostly very small) universities, more than any other country in Europe. It was not until the seventeenth and eighteenth centuries that there was any serious move towards providing schooling for a broader section of society. In the last third of the eighteenth century the secular authorities gradually took over the school system, led notably by Prussia, then one of the most progressive states with influential proponents of educational reform. Nevertheless the churches, both Catholic and Evangelical, remained closely connected with education; until 1919 they shared responsibility for the *Volkshochschule* with the secular authorities.

Traditional Objectives

The education system is closely allied to power structures and has traditionally been an area of fierce controversy between religious, political and class groups. For many years the traditional educational pattern in Germany was the *Gymnasium* (grammar school) for the middle and upper classes and the *Volksschule* (elementary school) for the working class. The traditional function of the *Gymnasium* was most cogently defined by von Humboldt (Director of Education in Prussia 1809-10). Himself a product of the Enlightenment and an admirer of the liberal ideas of Schiller and Fichte, Humboldt saw education as a means of stimulating individuals to their full intellectual capacity. This was to be achieved through a dedication to *Wissenschaft* - the pursuit of knowledge as a creative activity. The core of the curriculum in Humboldt's *Gymnasium* was the classical languages and culture - especially the culture of ancient Greece - with mathematics and German. The *Gymnasium's* decline began with the replacement of Greek by Latin, and the ideals of Greek democracy by the authoritarian attitudes of Rome (echoed by the growing authoritarianism of Prussia). *Wissenschaft* degenerated into a sterile amassing of facts and a rigidity of mind. Curricula became increasingly academic, there were frequent examinations to weed out the intellectually unworthy and mechanistic methods of teaching. (Later during the period of Nazi rule there was a determined effort to reduce the cultural dominance of the *Gymnasium* with its remnants of the classical tradition by replacing it with the *Oberschule*, with an emphasis on German culture.) The idea which inspired Humboldt and his fellow founders of the University of Berlin, created in 1810 (now the Humboldt University in East Berlin), was similarly a dedication to *Wissenschaft* - not as an end in itself, but as a means to an end; a creative activity from which would arise the close interaction of teaching and research. Both teacher and student were to be seekers after truth; it was therefore essential that both should have complete freedom - *Lehrfreiheit und Lernfreiheit*. These concepts have dominated German university life until the present day (and influenced university development elsewhere, notably in the USA).

The *Volksschule*, because the goals set for it were less ambitious, suffered less of a fall from grace than the *Gymnasium* in the nineteenth century. The reformers who at the beginning of the century determined its future in Prussia, and whose ideas were more or less closely followed throughout Germany, saw it as a place where the broad mass of children would receive a sound general education, based on the three Rs, religious instruction, singing and gymnastics. The liberal teaching methods of Pestalozzi and Herbart were generally adopted, and managed to survive for a long time, even when reactionary pressures were turning the grammar schools into training grounds for pedants.

Planning Institutions

In 1957, following the first phase of university redevelopment, the federation and *Länder* began to cooperate more closely in scientific and university policy. The result was the establishment of the *Wissenschaftsrat*, (Science or Academic Council), a joint advisory committee consisting of representatives of scientific and academic life. In 1965 a further federal government/*Land* agreement resulted in the founding of the *Deutscher Bildungsrat* (German Education Council). Its responsibility was to advise on the entire educational system with the exception of the university sector. It was disbanded in 1975. An important development was the creation in 1970 of the *Bund-Länder Kommission für Bildungsplanung und Forschungsforderung* (Commission for Educational Planning and Advancement of Research), which has subsumed the functions of the former *Deutscher Bildungsrat*. The BLK is given the task of preparing long term overall plans for education and monitoring pilot projects. The federal government and the 11 *Länder* are together represented in the Planning Commission with an equal number of votes (the federal government has 11, each *Land* one). Decisions can be approved with a three quarters majority. Any decision requires the approval of at least nine heads of the 12 governments and is binding only on those who have given their approval.

Educational Plans

Wide ranging recommendations for federal reforms were made by the Education Council (1965-1975). In 1970 the newly formed Ministry of Education published its own blueprint for reform *(Bildungsbericht '70)*. This had little effect among the *Länder* some of which disregarded it completely. In 1973 the BLK produced its own long term plan entitled 'General Plan for Education'. This contained an overall framework for the whole of the education system up to the year 1985 and also included estimated financial requirements. The Plan was well received by both the federal government and the *Länder* and it has largely determined the development of the education system since then, although there are still considerable variations among the *Länder*. Its main recommendations were as follows:

(i)   expansion of kindergarten places from 27% for 3 and 4 year olds to 70% by 1980; places for 5 year olds to be increased from 54% to 100% by 1985

(ii) improvement of teacher/pupil ratio in primary education to 1:19–23 (mostly through reduction in primary enrolment)

(iii) increased financial provision of the first stage of secondary education (though number of pupils expected to decline)

(iv) increased provision in the second stage of education (numbers of full time pupils expected to double between 1970 and 1985)

(v) increased provision at tertiary level (numbers expected to rise from 16% of age group in 1970 to 22–24% by 1985).

These will be discussed in the next section.

Educational Reform

Educational reform – in particular the question of opportunity – has been a subject of continuous heated public controversy since the mid-1960s. All political parties are committed to the reform ideal, but with different solutions as to its realisation. Reform has been taking place at all levels of education from the Kindergarten to the university, and presents a picture that is often hard to disentangle and analyse.

Pre-Primary

The policy of positive discrimination in favour of less privileged groups of children has borne fruit. Provision of places for children at this level has virtually reached 100% in most *Länder* thus achieving the target of the 1973 Plan at an early date.

Primary

Although the target teacher/pupil ratio set out in the 1973 Plan has not yet been reached, the rapid decline in the number of pupils at this stage (from a 1972 peak of 4.17 million) should ensure that the size of classes reaches a more desirable educational level in the not too distant future (it is already down to approximately 27:1). Reforms in the primary school curriculum are under way in many schools, but there is still considerable controversy over a number of aspects, particularly the introduction of New Maths. In general, education at this level is still rather traditional.

Secondary

With the vastly increased number of pupils at both the lower and upper second level schools, expenditure on education in this sector doubled between 1970 and 1980. Two dominant themes have emerged: equality of opportunity for pupils and equality of status for different types of schools. Concern has been expressed at the rigid labelling of children at the age of 10+ and their subsequent separation into various kinds of secondary schools. Attempts have been made to obviate the worse effects of this vertical system in a number of ways: by the introduction in grades 5 and 6 of the 'orientation' stage, described at the beginning of section 6; by attempts to make the system more 'permeable', i.e. a trend towards the coordination of courses in grades 7 and 10 of all types of secondary schools so as to ease the process of transfer from one type of school to another; by the gradual reorganisation of secondary education into two horizontal stages, notably the upper level of the *Gymnasium* and the various types of vocational school; and finally by the introduction in certain states of the comprehensive school. Full recognition of the integrated comprehensive school is, however, a long way off and the result is that most of them continue with the practice of early streaming. Some *Länder* have emphasised parity of esteem and the expansion of the *Gymnasium* and the *Realschule* rather than adopting a policy of comprehensivisation. The result is that *Hauptschule* pupils now constitute only 40% of the age group whereas previously they represented 70%.

Vocational

The separation of the general educational system from the vocational education system has been a serious problem in the past. This resulted in divisions of status, finance and curriculum. Reform has taken place by the creation of more full time vocational educational institutions such as the *Berufsfachschule*, *Fachoberschule* and *Berufliches Gymnasium*. Public attention and larger injections of State (as against industrial) finance have helped to produce a greater equality of esteem in this sector of education. The curriculum reforms of the upper secondary level also take account of this problem of status enhancement. In recent years, beginning in 1974, the concept of the Vocational Foundation Year *(Berufsgrundbildungsjahr)* has gained importance. It has the function of providing a broader based theoretical and general education combined with practical training and can be completed either as a full time training year or in 'cooperative' form, i.e. half in the factory, half in the school. The main idea is to give greater flexibility to the apprentice training system and enable workers to change job direction or retrain more easily. The foundation year counts as the first full year of apprenticeship. Courses are grouped into 13 broad vocational areas (electrical engineering, business administration, metallurgy, nutrition, etc.) instead of being too closely tied to a specific job operation or firm. There has, however, been much opposition from the employer's side, particularly from those industries or occupations with shorter two-year apprenticeships. It is still an open question how far or how soon the vocational foundation year will become the general norm throughout the country.

Third Level Institutions

The main changes in the late seventies were in the area of study reform, democratisation of university government and the creation of alternative systems of higher education. In 1977 a Standing Commission on Study Reform was set up, whose objectives were as follows:

(i) to ensure that courses open up a broad spectrum of possible vocational developments in view of a changing professional world

(ii) to adapt the different forms of study to new methods of teaching

(iii) to equip the students to handle material scientifically and independently and be aware how it is applied in practice

(iv) to guarantee the equality of corresponding university certificates and to make it possible for students to change universities.

The involvement of junior university staff and students in faculty government has been a continuing process: the all-powerful figure of the German university professor is fast disappearing from the scene. Some universities are moving away from organisation into faculties towards the concept of a larger number of relatively small 'areas of knowledge' *(Fachbereiche)*, corresponding to the British term 'school'. The very great increase in student numbers (about every fourth young person born in a given year is seeking a university place) has meant the State has been under pressure. New universities have been built or are under construction; teaching staff has doubled over the last few years; funds for universities multiplied four-fold between 1970 and 1980; and between 1970 and 1975 fully 200,000 new places for students were created. Attempts to bridge the former distinctions among various types of higher education institutions have led to the creation of the comprehensive university *(Gesamthochschule)*, while the creation of the *Fachhochschulen*, with their emphasis on more practical and shorter courses, is an important new development. As in the case of other levels of education, the higher education sector is in a constant state of flux.

Teacher Training

There have been two developments which have already been touched upon: first, some *Länder* now train teachers for specific school levels rather than for different types of school; and second, there is a strong and growing tendency for the *Pädagogische Hochschulen* to be merged with universities.

Research

Educational research has greatly expanded since 1965. Hitherto there had been more interest in institutional and structural issues, but subsequently interest is shifting towards such topics as child development, the educational impact of the parent, social worker and teacher, and the possible forms of cooperation between home and school. Greater emphasis is being given to the teaching and learning processes, particularly in such areas as fear of school, and stress which affect the child's performance at school. Model experiments are also being carried out, particularly with regard to the transfer from one level of education to another, e.g. from primary to secondary school, from general secondary education to vocational training at 15 or 16, or from school to university.

10 THE SYSTEM IN OPERATION

Future Trends

Demographic developments will play a large part in educational planning for the 1980s. Since the peak year of 1964 (nearly 1.1 million births) the annual birth rate had nearly halved by 1978 (576,000 births), although a slight increase is anticipated in the next few years. These demographic factors will have the following consequences for education: a diminishing primary school population up to the mid-1980s; a considerable decline in numbers at the lower secondary level; a marked rise at upper secondary level until the early 1980s, followed by a marked decline 1987/88, followed by a drop, first slowly then more rapidly, until the 1990s. A considerable problem in the future will be to provide all members of the peak birth rate year groups with suitable training courses and employment opportunities. As one means of alleviating this problem, pressure for a tenth year of compulsory, full time schooling is growing and some *Länder* have already legislated to this effect.

Apart from the continuation of the educational developments mentioned in previous paragraphs other trends are discernible. It is expected that the lower number of pupils in the schools will provide the opportunity for qualitative developments in the system, e.g. smaller classes, more child centred teaching and greater provision of in-service courses for teachers. At present the vast majority of pupils attend school in the mornings only; there is evidence that the demand for all-day schools, based on the five-day week, is growing. This is linked with two other trends: greater participation by teachers, pupils and parents in the management of schools and demands for the 'human school', i.e. one that is not simply a teaching institution but a focal point for the needs of the pupils and the community as a whole. The problem of the integration of foreign pupils into the education system is also one that is likely to receive more urgent attention in the future, if severe social problems are to be avoided. Finally, the universities and other institutions of higher education will be under considerable strain in the next decade, as they attempt to cope simultaneously with the large, but temporary increase in student numbers and the demands made on them to adapt to the changing needs of society. At all levels of education, then, reform and change are in the air, a process that will continue well into the foreseeable future.

REFERENCES AND FURTHER READING

Bundesminister für Bildung und Wissenschaft, (1979). *Grund- und Strukturdaten*. Bonn.
Bund-Länder Commission for Educational Planning (1973). *General Plan for Education* (abridged version). Bonn.
Council for Cultural Cooperation (1970). *School Systems: a Guide*. Council of Europe, Strasbourg.
Federal Government Press and Information Office (1979). *Facts about Germany*. Bertelsman Lexikon-Verlag.
Federal Republic of Germany (c.1980). *Framework Art for Higher Education (Hochschulrahmengesetz)*, Federal Ministry for Education and Service, Bonn.
Federal Republic of Germany (1980). *Information on the Bund-Länder-Commission for Educational Planning and Research Promotion*, (BLK). Federal Ministry for Research and Technology, Bonn.
Further Education Staff College (1979). *The German Vocational Educational System*. (Comparative Papers in Further Education, no. 4). Coombe Lodge, Blagdon, Bristol.
Goldschmidt, D. (1972). 'West Germany', in M. S. Archer (Ed.) *Students, University and Society*. Heinemann.
Hearnden, Arthur (1976). *Education, Culture and Politics in West Germany*. Pergamon Press.
Inter Nationes: Bildung und Wissenschaft. *Education and Science in the Federal Republic of Germany*. Published at frequent intervals by Inter Nationes, Bonn.
Inter Nationes (1979). *The School System in the Federal Republic of Germany*. (Bildung und Wissenschaft, Special Topic 12/79.) Bonn.
Littman, Ulrich (1977). *An Introduction to the Confusion of German Education*. DAAD, Bonn.
OECD (1970). *Innovations in Higher Education: Three German Universities*. OECD, Paris.
OECD (1972). *Reviews of National Policies for Education: Germany*. OECD, Paris.
Secretariat of the Standing Conference of Ministers of Education (1979). *Federal Republic of Germany: Educational Developments 1976-1978*. Bonn.
Secretariat of the Standing Conference of Ministers of Education, et al (1979). *The Education System in the Federal Republic of Germany*. College Entrance Examination Boards, 888 Seventh Avenue, New York 10019.

Structure of the Education System in the Federal Republic of Germany

Age	3	4	5	6	7	8	9	10	11	12	13	14	15	16	17	18	19	20	21	22	23	24
Level					I					II								III				IV
Stage					1					2			3		4			5				
Compulsory																						

School type:
- Kindergarten
- Grundschule
- Orientierungsstufe
- Hauptschule
- Realschule
- Gesamtschule
- Gymnasium
- Fach oberschule
- Fach hochschule
- Vocational schools
- non-graduate teacher training
- University
- Higher education institutes

Legend:
- ▨ Education preceding the first level

Examinations: professional certificates at the end of stage 4

Source: UNESCO/IBE International Yearboook of Education
Compulsory Education: Age Limits 6-15
Duration (years) 9
Entrance age to pre-school education: 3

257

FEDERAL REPUBLIC OF GERMANY BASIC STATISTICS	1960	1970	1974	1978 (approx.)
1 Total population (000)	55,433	60,700	61,259	61,310
% female	53	52	52	52
2 % population 0-14 years	21.3	23.1		21
% female	49	49	49	49
3 Enrolment, all levels	6,862,320	9,553,389	10,910,915	11,059,237
% female	48	48	48	48
First level	5,081,014	6,344,774	6,481,775	6,019,128
% female	49	49	48	48
Second level	1,490,080	2,704,796	3,642,429	3,966,376
% female	46	48	51	52
Third level	291,226	503,819	786,711	1,073,733
% female	23	27	33	39
4 Teachers, all levels	307,757		623,743	668,643
% female	36			
First level	172,178	248,499	275,830	274,576
% female	43	55	59	62
Second level	111,916	219,112	248,528	240,835
% female	31	34	37	40
Third level	23,663		99,385	153,232
% female	7			
5 Public expenditure on education				
Total (000) Deutschmarks	8,345,402	27,038,700	44,965,000	46,691,000
As % of GNP	2.8	1.0	4.5	4.2
As % of public expenditure				8.8
6 % Enrolment (MF) by level	100	100	100	100
First level	74	66	59	54
Second level	22	28	33	36
Third level	4	5	7	10
% enrolment (F) by level	100	100	100	100
First level	77	68	60	54
Second level	21	29	35	38
Third level	2	3	5	8
7 Entrange age: Duration of				
First level education	6:4	6:4	6:4	6:4
Second level education	10:9	10:9	10:9	10:9
8 Enrolment ratios (MF)				
First level				
Second level	67	78	82	
Third level	6.11	13.41	19.28	25.14
Enrolment ratios (F)				
First level				
Second level	67	79	82	
Third level	2.85	7.37	13.22	19.80

Finland

CONTENTS

1 Geography	260
2 Population	262
3 Society and Culture	263
4 History and Politics	265
5 The Economy	267
6 The Education System	270
7 Educational Administration	283
8 Educational Finance	288
9 Development and Planning of the Educational System	290
10 The System in Operation	294

Finland's educational system has many features shared by other countries in Scandinavia; a basic school for children between the ages of 7 and 16 is followed by a diversified system of academic and vocational schools, the former leading to admission to universities. The curriculum of the basic schools follows the usual continental European pattern. Emphasis is given to mother tongue, the second national language or first foreign language, religion, mathematics, the natural sciences, geography, history, social studies and civics, music, art, handicraft and physical education. Frequently English is introduced in the third grade when pupils reach the age of 10.

Since there are two official languages - Finnish spoken by some 94% of the population and Swedish spoken by the rest - both languages are compulsory in both the Finnish and Swedish medium schools. This is one way of ensuring loyalty to the nation but allows the Swedish Finns to retain their own identity. The nomadic Lapps, being small in number, speak their own language.

Reform in education has taken place slowly although provision has expanded. Pre-school enrolments trebled between 1965 and 1977, although annual population growth has been in the region of 0.3%. During the same period university enrolments doubled and teacher training numbers in third level institutions more than trebled. Finland, for such a small population, has a large number of universities (17), ten of which have been founded since 1945, and three have been upgraded from technical institutions. Expenditure on education as a percentage of the GNP has remained fairly high but at about the same level, namely 6%. Not until 1977 were proposals to reduce selection by creating a nine year basic school implemented although discussions have been going on for more than fifty years.

Poor natural resources, poor soils and, for agriculturalists, a brief growing season may help to explain why since 1945 many Finns have emigrated to the USA and increasingly to Australia. They participated in the economic boom and have suffered from the world recession since 1974. Traditional interests in the arts and education have probably helped to constrain major and rapid changes in a school system which until the middle of the nineteenth century was in the hands of the clergy and powerfully influenced academically by the University of Helsinki which was established in 1640.

The Editor

1 GEOGRAPHY

Topography

Finland, with an area of 337,032 sq km (130,100 square miles) is the sixth largest country in Europe. Its maximum length is 1,160 km (721 miles) and maximum width 540 km (336 miles). About one third of the country's area is north of the Arctic Circle. Finland is bordered in the north by Norway and Sweden and shares a long eastern frontier (1,269 km) with the Soviet Union. There is 1,100 km of coastline and 30,000 offshort islands mainly in the south and south west. Inland water (either lakes, canals or rivers) accounts for 9% of the total area (31,577 sq km) and in the Lake District proper as much as 50% of the area is water. There are more than 60,000 lakes (17 with areas of more than 200 sq km) and the largest lake, Iso Saimaa, occupies 14% of the lake area and is the fifth largest lake in Europe. Apart from the lakes the major physical feature is the forests, with 73% of the land area forested. The soil is mainly morainic deposits left by glaciers and is so thin that the shape of the landscape follows the contours of the bed rock. The hills are low and gently rounded ridges and it is only in Lapland that high fells are found – rising to 4,350 feet in the north west near the Norwegian frontier.

The country may be divided into 4 main regions:

(i)   the southern and western coastal area (including the vast archipelago of the Åland Islands)
(ii) the lake plateau – with fertile and cultivated land in the west changing to stony and poor soil in the east
(iii) the north eastern forest area

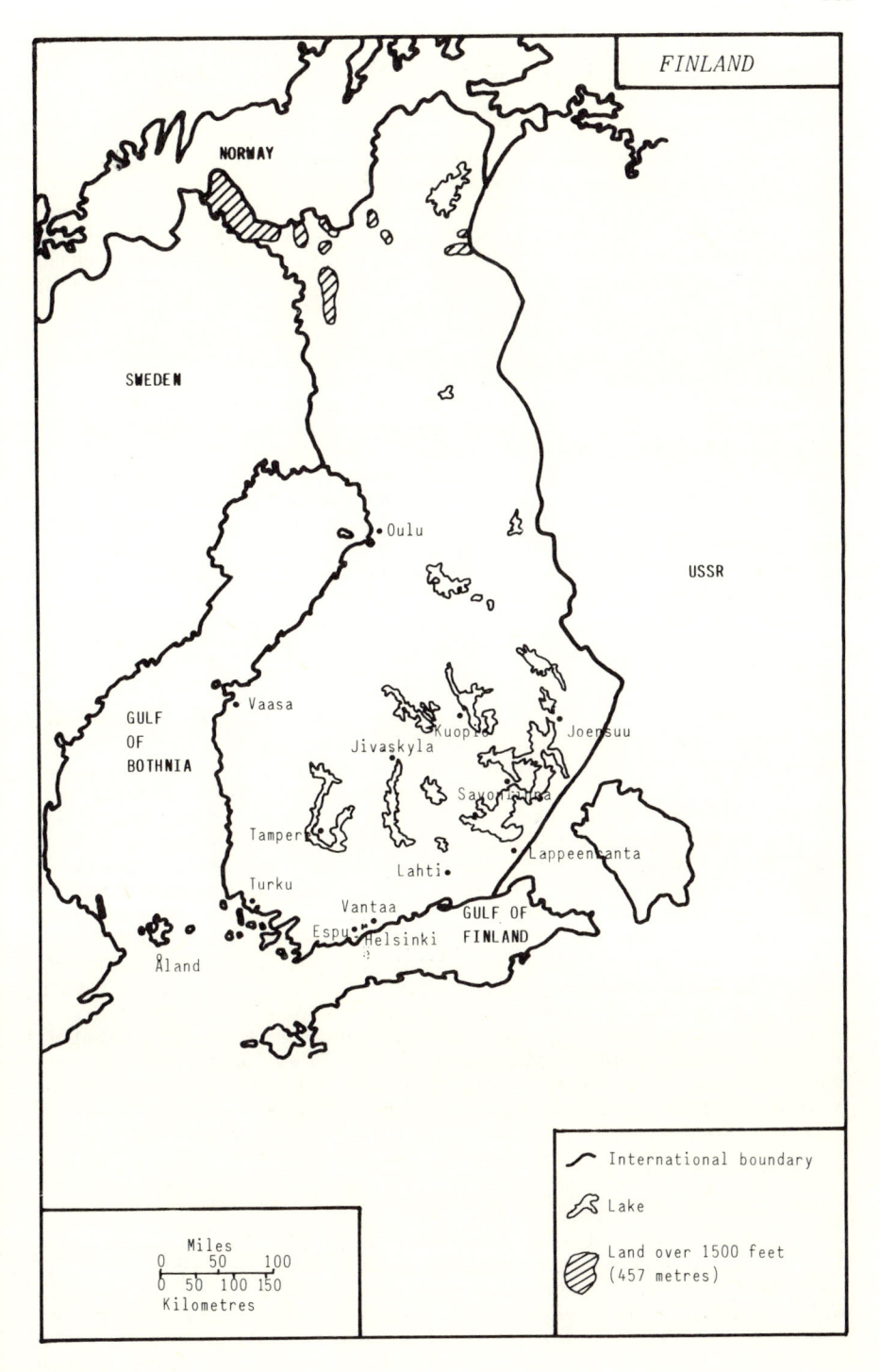

FINLAND

NORWAY

SWEDEN

USSR

- Oulu
- Vaasa
- Jivaskyla
- Kuopio
- Joensuu
- Savonlinna
- Tampere
- Lahti
- Lappeenranta
- Turku
- Vantaa
- Espoo
- Helsinki

GULF OF BOTHNIA

GULF OF FINLAND

Åland

International boundary
Lake
Land over 1500 feet (457 metres)

Miles
0 50 100
0 50 100 150
Kilometres

(iv)   the fell area of Lapland - with marshes, slow growing forests and, in the far north, treeless wilds.

Climate

For its latitude Finland enjoys a temperature climate (for its most southerly point, the island of Bogskär, is at a latitude of 59.8°N. This relative mildness may be ascribed to the moderating maritime influence of the North Atlantic Drift. The mean annual temperature in Helsinki is 5°C (41°F) and in the summer the average temperature is 16°C (61°F) though it can rise to as much as 36°C. The mean annual temperature in the far north is -4°C. Summer in Finland is reckoned as those days when the average temperature is over 10°C (110-122 days in the south, 50 days in Lapland). In southern Finland there are 19 hours of daylight at midsummer and in the north there are 73 days of perpetual daylight in the summer months, balanced by 51 days of perpetual twilight around Christmas. Precipitation is light - only 620 mm (25 inches) in south and central Finland and less than 225 mm in the Arctic Circle. About 30% of this falls as snow. Winter begins in Helsinki in November and lasts until March or April with lowest temperatures in January and February. Snow falls from mid-December for 100 days, but in the central region there are 150 to 180 days of snow and in Lapland 200 days.

Communications

There are over 6,000 km of railway track (395 km electrified) and there are railway links with Sweden and the Soviet Union. The railway service is cheap and efficient, though hampered by natural barriers in the shape of the lakes; (routes are rarely direct). There are 73,552 km of roads (over 27,000 km paved) and these are very good, though traffic is light; (about one million private cars were registered in 1976). However, minor roads suffer considerably from frost damage in winter and the road network as a whole requires more maintenance than any other in Europe. Bus services connect most main towns and, in the north, buses are a principal form of transport. Much use has always been made of inland waterways, with canals connecting the lakes, and there are now 6,600 km of navigable waterway. Water buses are a popular form of transport in the summer months. There is a well developed internal air network with 40 airfields, half of which are served by scheduled traffic operated by the national airline, Finnair.

2 POPULATION

Growth and Emigration

The 1970 census gave a population of 4,598,336; the 1980 estimate was 4,787,751 and the projection for the year 2000 is 4,904,000. the average annual rate of increase 1970-75 was 0.4% and in 1975/76 the population increased by 0.3%. There has been fairly large scale emigration from Finland since World War Two. There are 59,200 Finns in Canada (of whom 29,000 were born in Finland) and about 45,500 of the Finns in the USA are first generation immigrants. In the last 25 years as many as 300,000 Finns have emigrated to Sweden and a small but growing number has moved to Australia (15,000).

Distribution

Of the population 59% now live in urban settlements as against 51% in 1970 and 32% in 1950. There are about 63 cities and towns, of which the largest is the capital Helsinki (population 492,000) which with the neighbouring townships of Espoo (125,000) and Vantaa (123,000) forms a conurbation whose total population is 740,000. The only other settlements with populations of over 100,000 are Tampere (166,000) and Turku (164,000). All these towns are situated in the south west. This region (which represents only one tenth of the total area of the country) now holds over half of the population and migration is increasing as the vitality of remote areas has declined in the wake of socio-economic problems. The overall population density is 15.5 per sq km (37.4 per square mile) but the density increases southwards with 4 per sq km in the north, 13.3 in the eastern and central regions and 46.1 in the south. In some parts of the south west the density is as high (for Finland) as 100 per square kilometre.

Groups

The Finnish people developed from two tribes; the Tavasts, who settled in central Finland, and the Karelians who settled in eastern Finland. These people were distinctive in appearance and character; the Tavasts being short, stocky and fair in colouring, the Karelians taller, with dark colouring and slim build. Over the centuries these two groups mingled together and were joined by numerous Swedish immigrants from the west. Now only one recognisable group remains - the Lapps of the far north, an Arctic people who are related to the Finns linguistically. But there are only 1,500 Lapps in Finland (a very small group compared with the 20,000 in Norway), and very few of the Finnish Lapps are true nomads.

3 SOCIETY AND CULTURE

Social Patterns

Finnish society is in the Nordic tradition of democracy, with an absence of hierarchies and social strata. It is characterised by a high degree of social mobility and could be described as meritocratic. Certain professional groups, for example those successful in academic life and the arts, enjoy wide respect, whatever their origins, and as a class the nobility no longer exerts any influence. In farming communities the basic social and working unit is still the family, generally a large one, though this pattern is now breaking down as elsewhere in Europe. But despite the decreasing proportion of the population directly involved in agriculture, many urban Finns retain close ties with their rural origins. There is a tradition of female emancipation, and Finland was the first country in Europe and second in the world (after New Zealand) to give votes to women - in 1906. Legally women have equality and enjoy equal pay and pensions. About 50% of married women work and half the university population is female.

Language

There are two official languages in Finland; 93.4% of the population speak Finnish as the first language and the remaining 6.6% speak Swedish. The Swedish speakers are mainly concentrated in the south west and along the west coast. If 10% or 5,000 of the population of a unit of local government speak a minority language then both languages must be used. There are 26 of the 464 units in which Swedish is the official language and 39 units in which both languages are used (22 with Swedish speaking majorities). Both are compulsory in education, and both language groups have their own schools with Finnish and Swedish institutions at all levels following identical curricula. There is no language problem; at one time there was some rancour between the two language groups but this has largely disappeared and the division is no longer so rigid as it was. Nevertheless, while giving their wholehearted loyalty to Finland, the Swedish Finns wish to retain their own identity. The Lapp population speaks Lappish but the numbers involved are very small.

Finnish is one of the small groups of Finno-Ugrian languages which includes Estonian and Hungarian: this group is quite separate and different from other European languages. Since neither Finnish nor Swedish is widely spoken the Finns must learn to speak a foreign language. The first language in schools is now English; up to World War Two it was German. The interest in English is widespread and many of the Finnish-British societies based in the major towns appoint teachers of English.

Culture

There is a very active interest in the arts and in literature; the Finns are great readers and buyers of books. Many write themselves, especially poetry, and since the publication of the great national epic poem, the *Kalevala*, in 1835, literature has been closely allied to nationalism. Drama is also very popular with 85 theatres and no less than 5,000 amateur groups (for in this art as well participation is important). Despite its small size there are two symphony orchestras in Helsinki, as well as the opera house orchestra, and many of the provincial towns have their own orchestras. Sibelius was an enormous source of pride to the whole population and his memory is greatly revered. As singers the Finns are internationally distinguished, for example, the world famous bass Martti Talvela, and choral singing is popular. There is also considerable activity in fine art, but this has attracted less interest outside Finland, though twentieth century Finnish architecture and design have proved influential and are widely respected. As one would expect in a country that was for so long predominantly rural, folk culture is popular and serves as an important source of inspiration to more sophisticated work.

Religion

There are two State churches, both of which have the right to tax their members. The larger of the two is the Evangelical Lutheran Church of Finland to which 92% of the population belong; the other is the Orthodox Church of Finland with around 60,000 members (1.3%). There are also small groups of Roman Catholics, Methodists and Jews. The Church took a dominant role in society until the middle of the last century, with local government and education in the hands of the clergy. Nowadays, though the 92% are sufficiently loyal to the Lutheran Church to register as members and pay Church taxes, only about 5% or 10% actually attend services.

4 HISTORY AND POLITICS

Origins

Finland's first official contacts with Sweden were made in the twelfth and thirteenth centuries, partly as a result of missionary (and political) expeditions. (Eastern Finland had received the Orthodox faith somewhat earlier.) Gradual assimilation followed and from the fourteenth century the Finns participated in the elections of the Swedish kings. In 1523 Finland became a Duchy of Sweden ruled by the Crown Prince. She also became, and remained, a battlefield between Sweden and Russia. Independence movements did not succeed and by a Russo-Swedish treaty of 1809 Finland passed into the hands of Russia, becoming a Grand Duchy. But despite this change the use of Swedish law and the Swedish ecclesiastical and administrative tradition continued. Tsar Alexander I gave Finland a legislative assembly but it was never convened and the Finns had to wait until 1863 before it became operative under Tsar Alexander II. He also gave the Finnish language equal status with Swedish and Russian and for these acts is the Tsar most honoured in Finnish history. Under Nicholas II harsh and restrictive measures were introduced and a policy of Russification pursued. The revolution in 1917 gave Finland the opportunity to free herself from Russia and on December 6 an independent republic was declared. A civil war then followed between Red and White Guards, as on the newly emerging Russian stage. In Finland, the Whites won.

World War Two

At the beginning of World War Two, war broke out between Finland and the Soviet Union after failure to reach agreement over exchanges of territory. Finland fought a gallant but inevitably doomed defensive campaign which became known as the 'Winter War' of 1939-40. An uneasy peace followed the Finnish surrender. As the enemy of Russia, Finland unfortunately became also the enemy of the Allies and so turned for help to Germany, a friend from the past. In June 1941, when Germany attacked the Soviet Union, war broke out anew and the 'Continuation War' lasted until 1944. By the 1944 truce Finland ceded 12% of her territory to the Soviet Union and paid the equivalent of US$300 million (1938 values) in reparations, mainly in the form of industrial equipment. One of the conditions of the truce was that German troops should be expelled from Finnish territory, but in the event they did not go quietly and adopted a 'scorched earth' policy, destroying all that lay in their way. Finland's losses from the war were 86,000 dead, 60,000 disabled, a refugee population of 400,000 and the whole northern half of the country laid waste. On top of this the Finns had to pay relatively the severest war reparations ever. But they had escaped occupation and had retained their political independence.

Political Organisation

The constitution now in operation was promulgated in 1919. It provides for a parliamentary system and a strong presidency. There is a unicameral legislature, with 200 members elected by universal adult suffrage every four years (subject to dissolution by the President). Elections are by a form of proportional representation. The President holds supreme executive power and is elected for six years by a college of 300 electors, who are themsleves chosen by popular vote. The President then appoints the Council of State (or cabinet), headed by the Prime Minister.

There are numerous political parties (nine represented in parliament), with four major groups - the Social Democrats, People's Democrats (Communist), Centre Party and National Coalition (Conservative). These four represent four fifths of the electorate. The multitude of parties and electoral system have meant that since 1944 no single party has gained more than 56 seats. There were 59 cabinets in the first 59 years of independence, including 20 minority coalitions. Inevitably there has been a lack of strong government programmes and this situation places great pressure on the office of the President as a source of political stability. President Urho Kekkonen has been in office since 1956 and is supported by all the major parties. In January 1978 he was elected for a further six-year term at the age of 77. It is customary for the non-socialist and socialist parties to form groupings in Parliament and when elected in 1979 a coalition government was formed.

Regional Government

The Åland Islands, whose inhabitants are Swedish-speaking, have a special status and are self-governing. They return one member to the Finnish parliament. Elsewhere there is a lesser but still considerable degree of regional autonomy. The country is divided into 12 provinces *(lääni)* each administered by a governor *(maahera)* and a regional government. Each province is divided into one or two electoral areas for general and presidential elections. The smallest administrative unit is the municipality *(kunta)*, which is governed by a municipal council. There are 464 municipalities in all, of two types: cities or towns and rural districts. There are 380 rural municipalities and 84 urban and they are remarkably independent. Municipal councils are elected by proportional representation every four years and the municipal boards appointed by the councils have executive authority.

International Relations

In the light of the experiences of World War Two it was decided that alliance with anti-Soviet power groups was not the answer to Finland's security problem. Post-war Finnish foreign policy is based on the maintenance of friendly relations with the Soviet Union and with the West - a difficult position that has so far been maintained with success. In 1948 the Finno-Soviet Pact of Friendship was signed; it was extended for 20 years from 1955 and for a further 20 years from 1970. Finland has trade agreements with both COMECON and the EEC; there are other international agreements, for example with the Soviet Union on tourism and transport (including the lease of the Soviet sector of the Saimaa Canal). Finland attempts to adopt a position of strict neutrality (though this is not officially recognised by the Soviet Union), and often hosts international conferences such as the Conference on Security Cooperation in Europe in 1973. In the last two decades Finland has participated in international cooperation with the aim of strengthening peace and security. She has taken part in United Nations peacekeeping efforts and has a permanent standby force for UN service. Finland joined the UN in 1955 and the Nordic Council in the same year. The Council makes recommendations on integration to the five member states and has been instrumental in the introduction of a common labour market, free movement between countries and a number of joint institutions. Finland became an associate member of the European Free Trade Association in 1961 and is also a member of the Organisation for Economic Cooperation and Development.

5 THE ECONOMY

Natural Resources

Finland is characterised by a high degree of energy consumption and poor natural resources. There is a fairly good supply of minerals including iron ore (50% of the country's needs), zinc, copper (the largest deposits in Europe), lead and cobalt (5% of the world's supply); Finland is also the world's largest producer of vanadium. But the country's largest and most important natural resource is still wood. Hydroelectric power resources are being exploited already in the north, but peat bogs cover 35% of the total area of the country and peat is now being utilised as much as possible. However, no oil has been discovered (though this is the largest single source of energy used) and as there is no coal or natural gas the Finns have turned to nuclear power with equipment purchased largely from the Soviet Union for four plants.

Agriculture

Finland is the most northerly agricultural country in the world, with generally poor soils and a brief growing season. It represents the northern limit for the cultivation of wheat, rye, barley, oats, potatoes and vegetables. Yields are low and most of the sugar, fruit and vegetables consumed are imported, (agricultural imports representing 6.5% of the total in 1976). But Finland is self-sufficient in dairy products and even exports butter, eggs and cheese, for animal husbandry has always been more profitable than cereal growing, and milk yields are now high. In 1976 2.6 million hectares were cultivated (less than 10% of the total land area) and there were 258,000 holdings of which only 172,400 consisted of more than 5 hectares. There was never a tradition of large manorial estates and most cultivated land is owned by independent farmers in small plots. There are undoubtedly too many small holdings producing too much dairy produce, heavily subsidised by the government. Fishing is important for food. Agriculture, hunting and fishing provided 6.4% of GDP in 1976, their contribution having been halved over the previous 15 years. Farmers obtain 45% of their income from milk, 34% from meat and 11% from grain. In 1970 98.1% of arable land was in private hands and 0.6% in State hands.

Forestry

Finland has the third largest forest area in Europe (after the Soviet Union and Sweden). There are 22 million hectares (approximately five hectares per inhabitant). Each farm has at least four times as much forest as field which provides a solid livelihood and work in winter. As much as 60% of the forest is privately owned. Wood is the cash crop, the backbone of Finland's economy and can provide three quarters of the income of a small farmer. Forestry and forest products constituted 43.9% of exports in 1976 and 4.5% of GDP. Most of the forest is pine (44%) and spruce (38%). The Forestry Plan (a large scale improvement programme) is designed to achieve a position in which 50 million cubic metres can be cut each year without jeopardising supplies, rising to 80 to 100 million cubic metres in a further 70 to 80 years. In 1975, 40 million cubic metres were cut as against an annual growth of 57.5 million cubic metres and an overall resource of 1,513 million cubic metres. The long term plan is to alter the balance between forestry and agriculture so that the profitability of forestry is increased. In 1975 15% of the labour force was engaged in agriculture and forestry (only 3% in forestry full time because of mechanisation).

Industry

Until 1939 Finland had only one large scale industry - wood working. But World War Two and the reparations paid to the Soviet Union completely changed the Finnish economy and led to the development of a large metal and engineering industry. In the 1950s and 1960s total production increased by an average of 5% a year but industrial production by 6%. In 1976 manufacturing and mining accounted for 31.2% of GDP and 28.1% of exports. Finland has long term contracts with the Soviet Union for metal and engineering products which followed directly from the reparations. So now Finnish industry depends on two resources - wood and metals. In engineering the Finns specialise in the production of heavy equipment and shipping most closely related to their own needs and experience, for example icebreakers and paper making machines. Textiles and chemicals have shown rapid growth and the manufacture of consumer durables is now important (especially glass, ceramics, furniture and footwear). Electrical and electronic equipment are increasingly home produced. Industry and construction now employ the major proportion of the workforce with metals and engineering the biggest employer (35% of the working population). The extent of State ownership in industry is high. The government is involved in industry through government departments of State, industrial enterprises, and joint stock companies in which the State owns most of the capital.

Trade

The Finnish economy is heavily dependent on exports and is the world's largest exporter of pulp and paper and the second largest exporter of newsprint. No less than 25% of GNP and the same proportion of industrial output is exported, which leaves Finland very exposed to the vagaries of the international economic climate. The collapse of the paper market in late 1974 was a particularly serious blow. In 1975 the Soviet Union replaced Britain as the major trading partner (by far the largest single import being Soviet oil) and to compensate for this reliance on oil and the payment for Soviet nuclear reactors the trade balance has swung towards COMECON. In 1975 exports to COMECON rose by 37.5% and to the EEC fell by 19.5%. One fifth of Finland's trade is now with Eastern Europe. In 1976 the USSR provided 18.5% of Finnish imports and took 20.2% of exports. Britain is now in fourth place behind Sweden and the Federal Republic of Germany, providing 7.9% of imports and taking 14.2% of exports. By agreement with the EEC tariffs have been reduced and were abolished in 1977 on most industrial goods.

Economic Situation

Since 1960 industry has replaced agriculture in economic importance, and Finland was becoming increasingly prosperous until hitting the economic recession of 1974. The annual growth rate was 5%. Since then the world recession has had a disastrous effect on the Finnish economy which is now facing its worst crisis since World War Two. The inflation rate was up to 18% in 1975 but at the end of 1977 it was running at 13%. Greater progress has been made with the reduction of the balance of payments deficit which reached a record 8 billion Fmk in 1975 but was cut to 4 billion Fmk in 1976 and to 0.75 billion in 1977. However, unemployment rose (7.5% at the end of 1977). For a time left wing influences kept public spending up but subsequently expenditure was cut and taxes raised. The government which took office in May 1977 announced plans to stimulate the economy which included the provision of funds for industrial investment and regional development and the alleviation of unemployment. Wages were to be restrained, with official guidelines suggesting wage rises of 4.2% in 1977, and 5.5% in 1978. The plan was for an annual growth rate of 4%.

6 THE EDUCATION SYSTEM
General

All levels of the Finnish education system are undergoing major changes. Reform began in the sector of basic education and this was completed by the beginning of 1977/78. Reform of university degrees and upper secondary and vocational education is currently taking place. Pre-primary education is to be developed.

Academic Year

The school year runs from mid-August to 31 May with 190 days attendance over the five-day week and with a five to seven hour working day. The year is divided into two terms with a one-week holiday at Christmas and ten weeks in the summer. There is also a few days holiday at Easter and one week in February/March for skiing. But there are some variations from this pattern in vocational education. The university year runs from September 1 to May 31 and is also divided into two terms.

Pre-School

Pre-primary education is administratively not part of the education system and comes under the Ministry of Social Affairs. There are various kinds of crèches and day nurseries providing primarily social day care for the under-threes. Kindergartens (*päiväkoti*) which cater for three to six year olds, are mostly concentrated in the cities and are financed by municipalities, industrial enterprises, even individuals and organisations - though some receive State subsidies. A number of private kindergartens employ English teachers. Nursery schools operate both full and part time and about one third of the children attend full time (usually for special educational or social reasons). the system provides for about 30% of six year olds. There is no fixed curriculum but activities are generally creative, or designed to increase vocabulary and promote social skills. It is very likely that the official school beginning age will be lowered by one year but it has not yet been decided whether this year should be made compulsory or left optional. There are also plans to develop pre-primary education and day care and incorporate them into the system.

Basic (First and Second Levels)

Under the Constitution compulsory education is available for every child between the ages of 7 and 16 in his own language in bilingual municipalities and in unilingual municipalities in the language spoken there. The new basic school *(peruskoulu)* for this age group came into operation over the whole country at the beginning of the academic year 1977/78 though 89% of children were already in such schools in 1976/77 (581,127 out of an age group of 661,508). The basic school replaces the old combination of primary and civic school (6 years + 2 or 3 years) or primary and junior secondary school (4 years + 5 years). The curriculum was being phased in for operating overall in 1981. Some pupils still follow the old junior secondary curriculum.

The course is divided into two cycles - a lower cycle of six years (grades I to VI) and an upper cycle of three years (grades VII to IX). In the lower cycle teaching is by class teacher, in the upper cycle it is by subject teacher. There is a maximum number of 32 pupils per class laid down at national level but some schools have more than this with special permission. A grade X class has been introduced in two provinces in the north of the countrry and in some other provinces. This measure was largely a response to the problem of youth unemployment. Pupils in grade X have the opportunity to consolidate their previous studies and prepare for their working lives by means of work practice. This small scale programme may or may not increase in size.

Curriculum

The basic school curriculum lays down the subjects studied and the number of teaching periods allocated to each. In the lower cycle pupils study: mother tongue, second national or first foreign language, religion (according to their own faiths, Lutheran or Orthodox, unless the numbers involved are too small), environmental studies (grades I to IV), mathematics, natural history and geography (grades III to VI), history, social studies and civics (grades V and VI), music, art and handicraft, and physical education. The first foreign language/second national language course begins in grade III and in most schools this is English (with Swedish studied in the minority). In Swedish language schools Finnish is generally the first language with English introduced two years later in grade V. Normally the second language course begins in grade VII. There is one hour per week of counselling in grades V and VI.

At upper level two courses of differing difficulty are offered in mathematics in grade VII and three in grades VIII and IX. There are also three courses in the first language and two in the second language. The choice is made by the pupils with their parents, and it is an important choice as 'intermediate' courses in mathematics and the first language and the 'long' course in the second language are required for entry to senior secondary school *(lukio)*. However, there are opportunities for subsequent change. Other subjects studied in the upper cycle include: mother tongue, religion, history, social studies and civics, physics and chemistry, natural history and geography, physical education, home economics, music, art and handicraft. There are also optional courses (in grades VIII and IX) in technical subjects, home economics, commercial subjects, agriculture, forestry and a third language. A maximum of four hours per week is allocated to optional subjects, with about 26 hours spent on compulsory subjects. The curriculum has been modified and simplified since it was first introduced and may well change further. It has been suggested, for example, that streaming in mathematics and foreign languages should be abolished. Counselling is provided in all grades.

Assessment

Pupils receive marks during the school year for every subject taught together with conduct and application, though in grades I to III marks are not recorded for every term's work. Marks are awarded on a scale from 4 to 10 (with 10 representing 'excellent'). Those with marks of 5 or more in all subjects may proceed to the next grade, and if only two marks of 4 are received they can proceed on passing a supplementary examination. Pupils who receive marks of 4 in three or more subjects (except singing, arts or physical education) must repeat the year.

Second Level General

The senior secondary school *(lukio)* continues to provide a three-year course. If the number of pupils wishing to attend senior secondary schools exceeds the places available there is selection based on all round performance at basic level (though in some cases outstanding ability in a particular subject is acceptable). At present about 46% of the age group continue their education in these schools. There are also evening schools which give the older generation the opportunity of completing a senior secondary course. Assessment is similar to that operating in the basic schools with repetition of the year if the pupil gains marks of 4 in three subjects.

Curriculum

The curriculum at this level includes religion, mother tongue, second national and first foreign language, second foreign language (German, French or Russian), mathematics ('short' or 'long' course), geography (for those following the 'short' course in mathematics), biology, history and social studies, physical and health education, art or music. Optional subjects are physics, chemistry ('short' or 'long' course), philosophy and psychology, geography (for those following the 'long' course in mathematics), a third foreign language (generally French, Russian or Latin) and art or music. The course is divided into three main branches specialising in mathematics, languages, or science and humanities but the curriculum is now more flexible than it was and offers more options. The maximum size of any one group is 36 pupils, the minimum 16 or 20 depending on the subject.

Matriculation

The course culminates in the Matriculation examination *(ylioppilastutkinto)*, which consists of four compulsory and two optional written tests. There are also oral tests examined by the teachers and for which the pupils arrange the timetable themselves. The written examinations are set by the Matriculation Examination Board but marked by the teachers who pass on their assessment to the pupils before returning the papers to the Board for second marking. The compulsory papers are in mother tongue composition, second national language and first foreign language, and either mathematics or a general paper *(reaalikoe)*. The two optional papers are chosen from *reaalikoe*, mathematics and two foreign languages. Pass marks are graded either *approbatur, lubenter approbatur, cum laude approbatur, magna cum laude approbatur* or *laudatur*, and a fail in mother tongue composition ensures a fail overall. In fact, the failure rate is low. If students do fail or wish to improve their grades or gain extra passes they have two chances of resitting the examination within two years of the original attempt. At present successful matriculands receive two certificates - the Matriculation Board Certificate and the Secondary School Leaving Certificate. Since 1972 the right to take the Matriculation examination has been extended to graduates of vocational and technical institutes.

Foreign Language Schools

Outside the general school system there are four foreign language schools in the capital offering schooling from kindergarten level. The English and French schools introduce more teaching in Finnish as the course proceeds, while the German and Russian schools begin in Finnish and work towards more instruction in the foreign languages. The German and French schools offer classes up to Matriculation and in the German school it is also possible to take the German *Abitur* examination.

Technical and Vocational

In 1976 there were 130,000 students in vocational education. Of these 71,753 were new students (up 5.4% on 1975) and 23.6% of new students were entering the vocational sector after completing secondary education. There were about 600 institutions of which 30% were State owned, 48% municipal and 22% private. This abundance of institutions offers a wide variety of different kinds and levels of courses in commerce, technology, health and welfare, agriculture and forestry, nautical studies, etc. As well as the institutions offering vocational training to school leavers there are vocational course centres providing manpower training for those who have not had the opportunity to acquire vocational skills or who require new skills to gain employment.

The government is now committed to the development of vocational education as an alternative route to higher education. At present courses tend to be specialised, and vocational students do not prepare for the Matriculation examination though some students may take it after two or three years of study and the completion of certain supplementary courses in foreign languages. However, in the context of the reform, and over the next ten years, new curricula will be introduced in the vocational institutions which will rationalise the number of courses offered, orient the study programmes towards specific goals and introduce a greater general education component into those courses which may lead on to higher education. All courses within the same field will have the same general first year and it will be possible to choose subsequently the level of course to be followed. In some cases different fields may be able to share a common first year.

Vocational

These institutions include municipal vocational schools *(yleinen ammattikoulu)* and vocational institutes. The vocational schools take pupils straight from basic education. In the first year about 50% of the instruction is practical, in the second year 60% and in the third year 75% to 80%. Regulations state that these schools must offer training in metalwork, machine **repairs, electrical work,** building and construction, carpentry and joinery, clothing and catering. To improve training opportunities many municipalities have joined **together into** federations to set up and run vocational schools. There are also central State owned vocational schools *(keskusammattikoulu)* which teach courses not generally available in municipal vocational schools. Factory training schools usually provide one to two years' instruction based on vocational school training. There are also special vocational schools for the handicapped. Vocational institutes provide training for basic school leavers and also advanced training for skilled workers. These tend to be specialised institutions and include the School for Dental Technicians, Institute for Opticians, Institute of the Meat Industry and Institute of Advanced trade (a general training school). Vocational institutes now also provide classes for matriculands who follow the same curricula but complete the courses in one year less than those students entering from basic education. There is an apprenticeship scheme which entails attendance on short block release courses run by the vocational schools, but the numbers involved are very small (only 2,300 to 3,000 apprentices) as there is no tradition of apprenticeship in Finland.

Technical

In 1977 there was a total of 30 technical education institutions in Finland. Technical schools *(teknillinen koulu)* admit basic school leavers with some work experience and graduates of vocational schools. The three-year course is for prospective technicians such as draftsmen, planners and master mechanics. Technical institutes *(teknillinen opisto)* admit graduates of basic or technical/secondary schools who have obtained satisfactory grades in general subjects and mathematics. Applicants must also have 16 months work experience (12 months for secondary school graduates) and must pass an entrance examination in mother tongue and mathematics. Courses generally last four years but only three for technical and secondary school graduates. Applicants from secondary schools are required to have taken the 'long' course in mathematics. The curriculum in both types of institution includes general subjects - mathematics and science, mother tongue and a foreign language (together occupying from 25% to 35% of teaching time). From 4% to 9% of teaching time is devoted to other non-technical subjects including economics and management and there is vocational training in the form of exercises and laboratory work. Technical school graduates receive a lower diploma, technical institute graduates a higher diploma (which is close to the level of the former 'lower' first degree at university).

Commercial

This type of education is also provided at two levels in commercial schools *(kauppakoulu)* and commercial institutes *(kauppaopisto)*. Commercial schools provide two-year courses for basic school graduates with specialisation in the second year in either general, commercial (wholesale/retail), accountancy or office work branches. The certificate awarded is the *merkantti*. Commercial institutes offer three-year courses leading to the *merkonomi* certificate. Applicants must have completed basic education or junior secondary education or have obtained the *merkantti* certificate with two foreign languages. The first year provides a general commercial course and in subsequent years students opt to specialise in either marketing, accountancy, secretarial studies, or social studies. Commercial institutes offer similar courses to secondary school graduates but in their case only two years' study is required to obtain the certificate (one year's specialisation). There are also special schools for business training which provide professional education and retraining for those already employed.

Agricultural and Forestry

These branches of vocational education are particularly complex with both basic and supplementary training offered at a wide variety of institutions. Applicants to the various kinds of agricultural vocational school *(maatilatekninen koulu)* must have completed basic or junior secondary education and have attained the age of 17. There are general schools and ones offering specialised training, for example in dairy farming, pig breeding, poultry and fisheries. Some offer two-year courses though most tend to be shorter than this. An important part of the work of the agricultural vocational schools is the arrangement of short courses for working farmers in cooperation with local extension advisers. The agricultural vocational institutes *(matalousopisto)* traditionally train specialised consultants for organisations promoting agriculture. Qualified entrants must be graduates of agricultural schools, and some institutions also require work experience. Courses last two and a half years and include commercial subjects, mother tongue and English, as well as agriculture. Other farm institutes provide courses of approximately two years in length.

Over 1,000 students follow some kind of forestry course, ranging from 8 to 16 month courses in the various kinds of forest workers' schools *(metsäkoulu)* to two and a half year courses in forestry institutes *(metsäopisto)*. Both these types of institution require entrants to be over 18 and to have obtained 12 months' work experience. There are also schools for forest owners which provide courses lasting about five months. Special courses have been mounted for students from developing countries and a forestry industry training centre is to be built to cater especially for their needs.

Horticultural education is given in horticultural and advanced horticultural schools which offer one-year courses, and in horticultural institutes which accept graduates of the horticultural schools who have obtained 18 months' work experience to follow two-year advanced courses.

Other

Other subjects studied in the vocational sector include home industries and industrial arts, public health (including nursing) and home economics, hotel and catering, and nautical studies. Home industry schools *(kotiteollisuuskoulu)* offer two-year courses in woodwork, metalwork, weaving, etc. to basic school graduates over the age of 16. Two thirds of study time consists of practical training, though mathematics and in some cases science and design are included in the curriculum. Rural housekeeping schools *(emäntäkoulu)* run one-year courses for 16 year olds who have completed basic school. Two courses are offered – one general and one geared specifically to home economics. Housekeeping schools *(talouskoulu)* run courses lasting one term in basic housecraft while home economics institutes *(kotitalousopisto)* take graduates of rural housekeeping schools for one-year courses leading to qualifications as home economics specialists. In the field of health education, institutes of health personnel *(sairaanhoito-opisto)* offer two and a half year courses to basic and junior secondary school graduates between the ages of 18 and 30. They prepare students for first level examinations in nursing, physiotherapy, radiography, medical laboratory work and occupational therapy. After this students proceed to one year's specialised training in separate centres. Lower level courses are also offered in this field and in some places these also take place in the institutes. In addition there are courses at various levels offered in specialised institutions in hotel and catering, tourism and food technology lasting usually one or two years. The Institute of Tourism in Provoo offers a two-year course for secondary school graduates.

Third Level (Higher) Institutions

Finland had 22 universities and equivalent institutions of higher education in 1979. All, with the exception of the University of Helsinki, were established in the twentieth century and many after 1945.

	Founded	Number of Students 1977
University of Helsinki (originally at Turku)	1640	20,593
Abo Akademi, The Swedish University of Turku (Abo)	1918	3,294
University of Turku	1920	8,776
University of Oulu	1959	7,200
University of Joensuu	1966	2,390
University of Jyväskylä	1966	6,103
University of Kuopio	1966	1,046
University of Tampere	1966	9,246
Helsinki University of Technology	1908	6,922
Lappeenranta University of Technology	1966	639
Tampere University of Technology	1972	2,500

	Founded	Number of Students 1977
Helsinki School of Economics	1911	4,336
Helsinki Swedish School of Economics	1927	1,567
Swedish University of Turku School of Economics (Åbo Akademi)	1927	640
Turku School of Economics	1950	1,326
Vaasa School of Economics	1968	988
College of Veterinary Medicine	1945	241

Other institutions of higher education include: the College of Industrial Design (982), the Sibelius Academy (713), the Swedish School of Social Science and Local Administration (341), and the *Ateneum* (School of Fine Arts). All these offer four to five year programmes. There are also four language institutes, training interpreters in two to three year courses at Kouvola, Savonlinna, Tampere and Turku. In 1976/77 there were approximately 73,700 students receiving higher education. Of these 55% were studying humanities, social sciences, education, economics, law and theology, 19% were studying mathematics and science, 16% technology and 7% medicine.

Admission

At present there are first year university places for less than half the matriculands and so a *numerus clausus* operates. Entrance examinations are held in June and July and marks are considered together with those from previous examinations. There are about 12,000 places available annually to new students (about 16% of the age group). The Ministry of Education has recommended that 5% to 10% of first year places be reserved for students from vocational education (usually non-matriculands). In 1976 only 3% of new students came from vocational education but their presence is forcing a change in admission criteria with more emphasis on factors such as special interests and experience.

Courses

The traditional pattern of university courses in Finland includes two levels of first degree and two levels of higher degree – all obtained by passing examinations covering specific syllabi in major and minor fields and presenting dissertations. The Schools of Economics also award diplomas. In a degree course each subject may be studied at one of three levels: *approbatur, cum laude approbatur,* and *laudatur,* and a certain number of passes at each level is required to gain the appropriate certificate. For the 'upper' or 'basic' first degree *(kandidaatti)* students take a major subject and two or three minor subjects. For the *licensiaatti* (lower postgraduate degree) two subjects are studied and the major subject may be different from the one taken at *kandidaatti* level; the degree also involves the presentation of a thesis *pro gradu*. Each student keeps his own study book *(opintokirja)* in which attendance and/or marks are recorded. Holders of the degree *kandidaatti* may apply for the title *maisteri* which confers on them certain voting rights in the university. In medical faculties (those training doctors and dentists) the licentiate is the first degree. The doctorate is a title bestowed on a licentiate who has successfully defended a full dissertation. At present each of the degrees is necessary to proceed to the next and there are no limits fixed on the time taken to acquire them.

Changes are being made. The 'lower' first degree was never available at all institutions and is being phased out. In future students will also be able to proceed to the doctorate without first taking the licentiate. The new degree course will be organised as study programmes directed towards the attainment of certain goals. They will be divided into general studies (25% of study time), subject-oriented studies (50% of study time) and advanced specialised studies (the remaining 25%). General studies will be designed to introduce the student to the theoretical foundations of his major subject, the development and practical applications of the general field, and give him some training in study skills. Subject-oriented studies will give the basic knowledge of the subject (the core of the course), and advanced specialised studies will explore the subject's research applications through group and project work. These programmes have started in certain disciplines in individual universities and higher institutions. By 1980 all new students should be admitted to the new degree programmes. The programmes will be designed by the faculties on the basis of the 'credit' system. Students will collect credits, some of which will be compulsory, some optional. The basic unit for calculating the length of studies will be the 'study week' (not necessarily coinciding with the calendar week). The length of most first degree programmes will be 160 study weeks, with some variations, but the medical faculties have decided that their programmes will continue to be reckoned as taking six years.

Though the university is divided into two terms there are opportunities to continue studies during the three months summer holiday. Certain parts of degree courses can be taken in the so-called 'summer universities', basically institutions of adult education, some of which are located in university towns. In future there may be some tendency for students to move more towards continuing their studies in their own institutions and hence to an optional 'third term'.

Staff

University students in Finland are taught by a wide variety of staff. As well as 'full' professors (appointed by the President of the Republic) there are also associate professors and docents *(dosentti)*. The title of docent is an honorary one, and docents are paid for the lectures they give (which may be a regular allocation of two hours per week or a few lectures in a given term). They often hold positions in other institutions. Lower down the scale are lektors *(lehtori)* and assistants *(assistentti)*, most of whom are studying for their doctorates. There are also part time specialist teachers. The present percentage distribution of staff in the various categories is: full professors - 14%; associate professors - 11%; lektors - 23%; assistants - 34%; and part time staff - 18%.

Teacher Training

The old system of teacher education was extremely complex, with a variety of institutions training teachers at different levels and in different fields and in some cases with more than one type of institution training teachers in the same field or at the same level. The educational reform provided an opportunity to raise standards in teacher education and rationalise the training system. To this end seven teacher education units have been established in university faculties of education to provide tertiary level education for all basic and senior secondary teachers. Each of these units has a practice school attached to it. The reform of teacher education included the abolition of the old institutions and the reform of study programmes along the lines of the degree reform. During the transition period the old pattern is being followed with certain modifications to the curricula.

Pre-Primary

At present teachers for pre-primary education are still trained in special institutions *(lastentarhanopettajaopisto)*, but also now in teacher education units. In both the training takes two years and leads to the Pre-primary Teacher's Certificate. The curriculum includes childcare, psychology, educational theory, teaching methods and teaching practice. The entrance requirement is either the Matriculation certificate or completion of basic/junior secondary education supplemented in various ways. There is an aptitude test and stiff competition for entry. At least 10% of places are reserved for men and 10% for non-matriculands.

Class Teaching

The education of basic school class teachers (grades I to VI), lasts three years and candidates for admission must have completed senior secondary school. Again competition for places is fierce and there is a quota of places reserved for men. The curriculum involves study of all the academic subjects taught in the lower cycle with educational subjects constituting the single most important element in the course (the 'major' subject). The current Class Teacher's Certificate is approximately equivalent to the former 'lower' first degree, but under the reform the course will be lengthened to four years and will then be comparable to the 'upper' or basic first degree and the subject teachers' qualification.

Subject Teaching

Senior secondary school teachers and teachers in the upper cycle of the basic school undergo very similar education and training, with slightly higher subject qualifications required of the senior secondary teachers. At present the training consists of a one-year post-graduate teachers' course leading to the Subject Teachers' Diploma which is open to holders of the *kandidaatti* or *licensiaatti* degrees. The curriculum consists of educational theory and teaching practice. At this level there is little competition to enter training. Trainees include some teachers of practical subjects who have followed their subject studies in the teacher education unit. The reform of subject teachers' training will be thorough - abolishing the present two-stage training and replacing it with study programmes in which study of the subject to be taught, educational theory and teaching practice will be integrated and take place more or less simultaneously.

Vocational

Teachers for vocational education are still trained in separate institutions and most receive anything up to two years training in addition to their vocational qualifications. In some cases the period of training is shorter than this and in a few cases no training is required. Most courses consist of educational theory and teaching practice but in the shorter courses there may be only teaching practice. However, training is offered at two different levels: the upper level requiring completed professional or vocational education, a university degree or practical experience and the second requiring only completed basic education. This type of training entails combined vocational education and educational studies and may take four to six years; teachers of home economics, for example, are trained in this way. There is a move towards strengthening the educational element in vocational teachers' courses, but the wholesale reform of vocational teacher education is still at the planning stage.

Other

Special education and counselling training now also takes place in the university teacher education units. In order to enter this type of training, applicants must have already qualified as class teachers or subject teachers. In the autumn term of 1977 there were 89 trainee counsellors and 150 teachers being trained for special education and remedial work.

In-Service

Further training is now regarded as equally important as initial training and a Centre for In-Service and Retraining has been established. The educational reform has necessitated considerable training for teachers, for example in comprehensive school teaching methods, the use of language laboratories, audio-visual aids and educational broadcasting. In every province between one and four supervisors have been appointed from the teaching cadre to be involved in in-service training. Teachers at basic and senior secondary level attend three compulsory study days in each academic year. These take the form of one-day weekend schools at which lectures and seminars are given by supervisors, central inspectors, teacher trainers and educationists. Teachers' organisations are now involved in the planning of the study days. Many teachers also participate in the courses offered by the summer universities and in courses for teachers overseas. Supervisors must attend annual courses run by the central inspectorate and are regularly briefed. Teacher trainers also have a compulsory in-service element in their work. Every seven years it is their 'right and duty' to take six months' sabbatical leave for further study.

Non-Formal and Adult

The variety of adult education courses and the number of different kinds of institution offering them reflects the respect and enthusiasm for education in Finland. Though this sector of education is subsidised by the State most is the result of private and municipal initiative. Adult education is offered in both Finnish and Swedish. In 1970 an Institute of Adult Education was founded at the University of Tampere to organise courses both on its own initiative and on request and to set up examinations based on these courses. It also mounts courses for workers in adult education and researches into adult education. The major sources of adult education are the folk high schools and civic and workers' institutes. Each has a coordinating institution - the *Suomen Kansanopistoyhdistys* (Finnish Folk High School Association) and the *Työväenopistojen Litto* (Union of Civic and Workers' Institutes). There is also a Finnish Association of Adult Education Institutions which arranges meetings and courses for members of affiliated organisations. It is involved in international cooperation in adult education and is participating in a Joint Nordic Programme for research into adult education.

Folk High Schools

The high schools *(kansanopisto)* offer a wide variety of courses. In general they are boarding schools whose main work is in improving general knowledge among the rural population aged 16 to 30, as a preliminary to more advanced studies. A full course for basic school graduates can take between one and three years. Subjects studied include the national languages and literature, history, sociology, geography, natural sciences, education, religion, ethics, music, health education and physical education. In the first year (basic course) instruction is also offered in home economics, handicraft, mechanics, shorthand and typing. The second and third years are often spent in a folk academy *(kansankorkeakoulu)* which prepares students for admission to the higher vocational institutions. The folk high schools also offer 6-9 month courses and special one-month programmes. Music education is now available to the under 16s. About 6,000 students follow full time courses in these institutions. Students in remote areas have their transport costs subsidised.

Civic/Workers' Institutes

The civic institutes *(kansalaisopisto)* and workers' institutes *(työväenopisto)* are situated in every city, town and municipality and offer part time and evening courses in a wide variety of subjects. However, the majority of students take languages, with social, artistic and economic studies. At present there are about 500,000 students following evening courses.

Other

This varies between institutions as disparate as residential Sports Institutes offering ten month courses for physical education instructors and evening Study Circles organised in Study Centres under the National Board of General Education. Series of lectures are also organised at the Study Centres. There are English teachers running classes in most of the main towns under the auspices of the Finnish-British Societies. Correspondence education in Finland is non-profit-making and provides about 500,000 students a year with instruction, mostly in school subjects. For formal extra-mural studies, evening classes are provided in secondary and vocational and technical schools leading to the appropriate examinations. There are also some university classes provided in regional centres for external degree students. These are described as 'open university' classes. Trade and industrial organisations and private firms have set up their own residential education centres and also provide on-the-job training. The summer universities are open to anyone. Apart from the degree studies for university students there are also courses for teachers, vocational courses, and studies in liberal arts, languages and subjects of general interest.

7 EDUCATIONAL ADMINISTRATION

Ministry of Education

The supreme authority in educational administration in Finland is the Ministry of Education. Two ministers are responsible for education and culture assisted by the Permanent Under Secretary (the highest permanent official). The Ministry is divided into six departments: General Department, Department of International Relations, School Department, Department of Higher Education

ADMINISTRATION

THE ORGANISATION OF THE SCHOOL SYSTEM

STATE

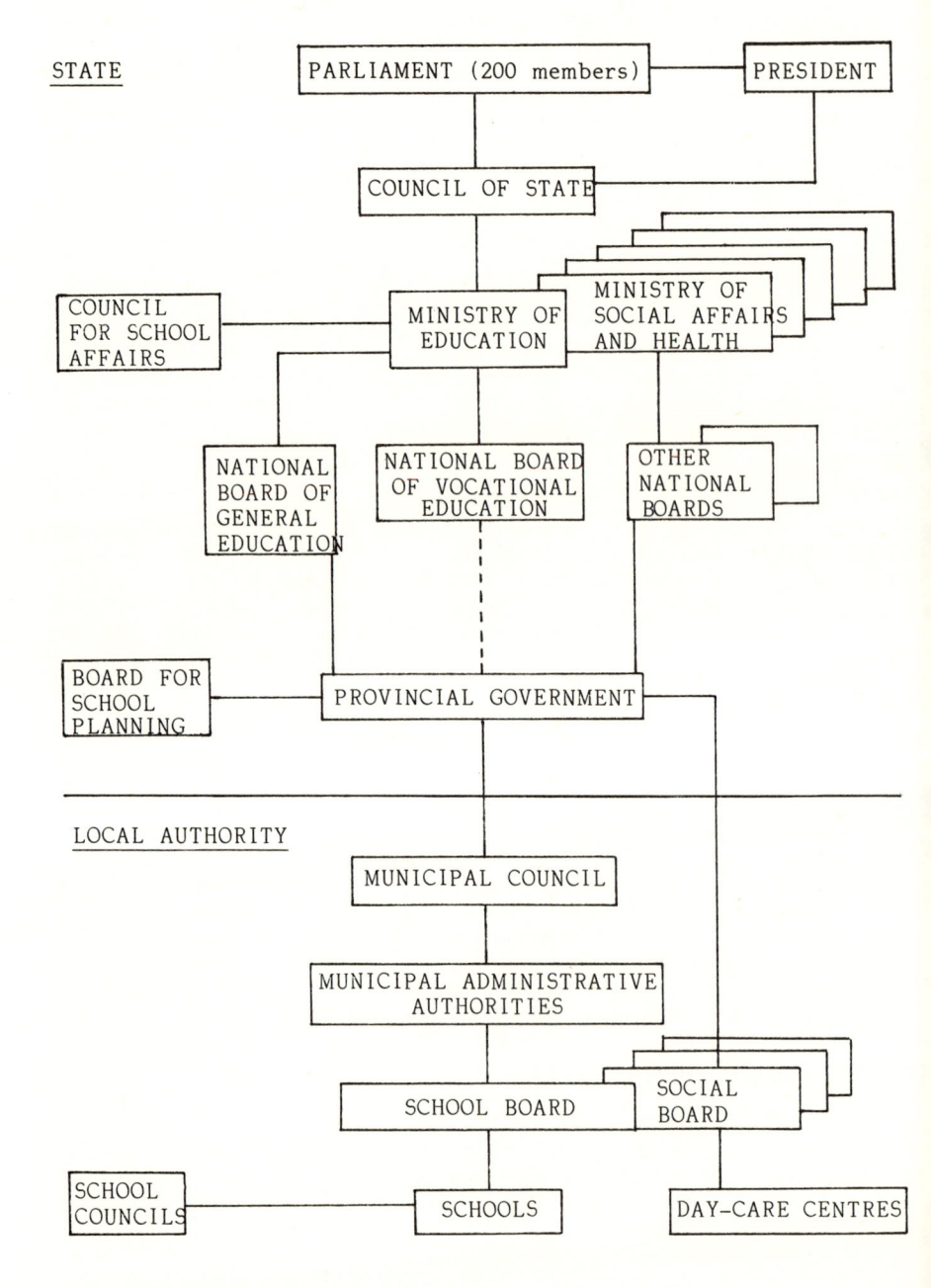

```
PARLIAMENT (200 members) — PRESIDENT
            |
     COUNCIL OF STATE
```

- COUNCIL FOR SCHOOL AFFAIRS
- MINISTRY OF EDUCATION
- MINISTRY OF SOCIAL AFFAIRS AND HEALTH
- NATIONAL BOARD OF GENERAL EDUCATION
- NATIONAL BOARD OF VOCATIONAL EDUCATION
- OTHER NATIONAL BOARDS
- BOARD FOR SCHOOL PLANNING
- PROVINCIAL GOVERNMENT

LOCAL AUTHORITY

- MUNICIPAL COUNCIL
- MUNICIPAL ADMINISTRATIVE AUTHORITIES
- SCHOOL BOARD
- SOCIAL BOARD
- SCHOOL COUNCILS
- SCHOOLS
- DAY-CARE CENTRES

and Research (including a Teacher Training Bureau), Department of Arts, and Department of Youth and Sports. Subordinate to the Ministry are two central offices – the National Board of General Education *(kouluhallitus)* and the National Board of Vocational Education *(ammattikasvatushallitus)*.

The National Board of General Education manages and supervises basic and secondary education (public and private), some teacher training, adult education and libraries. The National Board of Vocational Education controls all aspects of vocational education directly. All important development projects are drawn up by the Boards and then submitted to the Ministry for approval. The Department of Higher Education and Research is responsible for the general administration of all institutions of higher education and is not dependent on an additional administrative organisation between the Ministry and the institutions. The administration of teacher education is complex, with pre-primary teacher training institutions and in-service training under the National Board of General Education and other institutions of teacher education (i.e. university faculties of education) under the Teacher Training Bureau of the Department of Higher Education and Research. The Ministry drafts the legislation for the implementation of decisions taken by the Council of State or cabinet. There are advisory bodies attached to the Ministry – the Council for School Affairs, the National Council for Higher Education, and the National Council for Teacher Training. Some specialised educational institutions are administered by other ministries.

Regional Responsibilities

Each of the 11 provincial governments has a school department responsible for the monitoring and guidance of general and adult education and libraries. Some of the State's administrative responsibilities for schools are delegated to the provincial authorities. Each provincial school department has its own inspection staff and in bilingual provinces there is also a Swedish school department with a full complement of staff. At municipal level there is an educational board assisted by a municipal Director or Secretary for School Affairs and each school may have its own separate board (though its tasks vary according to the school). The National Board of Vocational Education is now strengthening its contacts with the provincial governments with the creation of one post in each provincial administration responsible for the planning of vocational education, with a particular brief to develop systems of selection and make plans for the reform.

Administration of General and Vocational Education

In schools the subjects to be studied and the number of periods allotted to them are laid down by the National Board of General Education. Within this framework the school board and teaching staff draw up the curriculum, subject to the National Board's approval. In practice variations in the curriculum are quite small. The guidelines provided by the Board basically lay down the objectives of the curriculum but they do specify something of its content and the teaching methods to be used, though each teacher has the right to choose the method which best suits the situation. The National Board also offers advice on evaluation. The choice of textbooks is made by the school board, but all textbooks are approved by the National Board before acceptance for use in schools, and are written in cooperation with the Board's Teaching Materials Office. When deciding whether a textbook is acceptable the Board consults separately individual teaching staff, teacher training institutions, provincial education staff and the national inspectorate. Extra book materials need not be approved at national level, but general guidance on selection is provided by the Board. For vocational education the institutions draw up the curricula, subject to the approval of the National Board of Vocational Education. However, under the reform the rationalisation of vocational courses will mean that there are standardised curricula laid down by the Board with possible local modifications.

All basic and senior secondary schools have a School Council. In basic schools the Council consists of representatives of parents, teachers and upper cycle pupils. Its tasks are mainly concerned with parent-teacher cooperation. The School Council at senior secondary level has six to ten members representing equally teachers and students; it has the right of decision on discipline and working conditions and also makes suggestions on the development of the curriculum. Senior secondary schools also have a Parents' Council whose members are chosen by the local municipal council.

Administration of Higher Education

The Council of State or cabinet and the Ministry of Education are responsible for general administration of higher institutions except in those areas designated to the institutions themselves. Some institutions are more independent than others - for example the University of Helsinki is traditionally more autonomous. However, the new system of degrees is regulated at national level with guidelines laid down centrally for each field of study. These do not specify the contents of the curricula in detail, but declare the objectives and basic structure of the programmes.

Since the late 1960s the reform of the internal administration of higher institutions has been one of the major issues of educational policy in Finland. More efficiency and more democracy was called for. The traditional administrative system placed authority in the hands of the full professors who met in the Faculty Councils and in the University Senate. Seven university level institutions still operate the old system, but gradually a new reformed system is being introduced into each institution separately by government decree. This allows for a two-tier administration - a central administration elected on a tripartite

THE ADMINISTRATION OF HIGHER EDUCATION AND RESEARCH

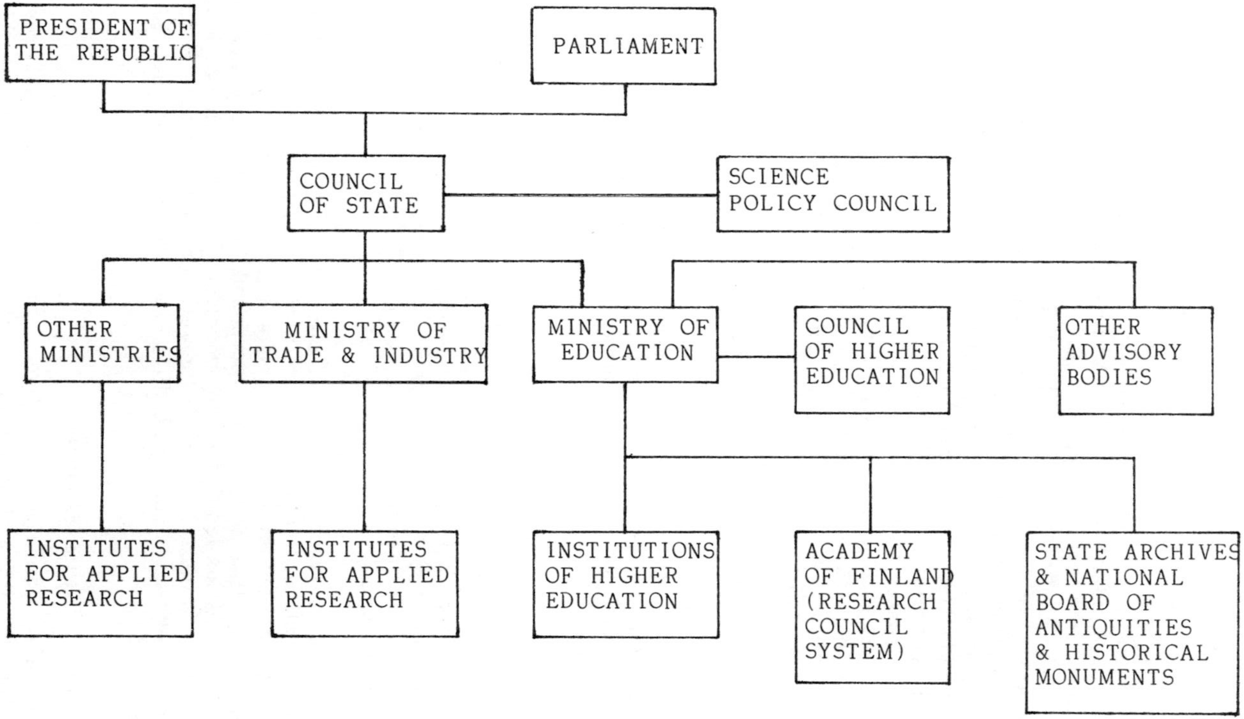

Source: Ministry of Education

quota system (one third each of professors, teachers and students with each group electing its representatives), and a departmental administration. The central administration consists of the University Council, Board of Administration, the Rector and the Office of Administration. The University Council sits for two years; it can have any number between 18 and 60 members. It drafts regulations and comments on government directives, makes budget proposals and financial plans, elects the Rector, the Vice-Rector and members of the Board of Administration. The Board, which has 6 to 12 members, appoints staff and deals with major issues of general administration. The Rector, who is appointed for two years, undertakes general management and supervision assisted by the Director of Administration, who is head of the Office of Administration). In the University of Helsinki and some other universities the Chancellor *(kansilieri)* is the highest administrative authority - and the Chancellor is appointed by the President from three candidates nominated by the university. The departmental administration is in the form of a Council consisting of between 6 and 16 members, half of which are staff and half students. The Council considers teaching and research in the department, the syllabus and the use of funds. In larger institutions there are also Faculty Councils which consist of heads of departments and two representatives of each Departmental Council elected by members. This body suggests candidates for appointments, considers theses and awards degrees, though these matters are confined to Council members of appropriate standing. Where there is no Faculty Council, the Departmental Council, Board of Administration or a special body is made responsible.

8 EDUCATIONAL FINANCE

Educational Budget

Though most school level institutions are municipal and the State runs only 30% of vocational institutions and senior secondary schools it provides on average 75% of recurrent costs to non-State institutions in the vocational and adult sectors, 85% of recurrent costs to senior secondary schools and 80% to basic schools. All university level recurrent and capital costs are met by the State budget, though higher institutions may acquire additional sources of finance. The amounts allocated to vocational and higher education have increased considerably in recent years. In 1975 expenditure on vocational education was up 28% on 1972. The annual growth of government expenditure on higher education between 1968 and 1973 was running at between 12% and 13%.

School and Institute Finance

Since basic education is almost entirely a municipal responsibility the municipalities receive either directly or in the form of a redeemable loan a sum amounting to between 60% and 95%

of the construction costs of each school building. The State also refunds two thirds of the amount spent on furniture, equipment, libraries and social benefits and guarantees 90% of teachers' salaries. The amount of expenditure actually covered has varied between urban and rural municipalities and subsidies now take the financial position of individual municipalities more into account. In technical institutions over 80% of teachers' salaries and 50% of other expenses are covered by State subsidies. Schools may not deviate from the purposes for which the money is given. Individual institutions may order equipment and books, and arrange modernisation and building repairs within the limits of their budgets but their expenditure is scrutinised by the National Board and inspectors supervise the way in which they treat their equipment. Permission of the government is necessary for school construction in most areas and plans are approved at central administrative level.

University Finance

The budgets of higher education institutions are decided annually as part of the State budget. Individual institutions submit proposals for recurrent and non-recurrent expenditure to the Ministry. The Ministry's proposals go first to the Finance Ministry and then to the Council of State which in its turn makes a proposal for submission to Parliament (for inclusion in the State budget). The funds approved by Parliament are finally confirmed by the President.

Fees and Grants

At basic school level everything is provided free. At senior secondary schools all pupils pay a small fee though this is reduced if the pupil has a brother or sister already in the school and abolished in cases of severe financial difficulty. Textbooks are purchased by the pupils but can be borrowed by the less well off. There are also scholarships available for poorer pupils. At higher levels there are no fees but students must meet most of the cost of course materials and living expenses. There are subsidised refectories, housing assistance schemes and health services - mostly provided by student organisations - but these simply lessen financial problems rather than solve them. Through the State Centre for Aid to Education and its local representatives, grants and low interest loans are paid to students, and since 1970 grants and loans have also been offered to pupils at senior secondary level.

Allocation of Funds
Expenditure on Education: Distribution by Level
Percentage of Expenditure 1977

Pre-school	First Level	Second Level	Third Level	Other
-	49.8	27.5	12.7	10.0

9 DEVELOPMENT AND PLANNING OF THE EDUCATIONAL SYSTEM
Origins

As in most countries the early history of education in Finland is closely connected with the Church. The first schools, begun in the thirteenth and fourteenth centuries, were attached to cathedrals and the Reformation interrupted and delayed educational development. Major moves were made in the seventeenth century; the first university was founded at Turku in 1640, the first secondary school in 1649 and the first proposals for the organisation of general education were made by Bishop Gezelius in 1683. The Religious law of that year declared that it was the duty of all citizens to learn to read and that those who could not were barred from communion and marriage. Until the mid-nineteenth century all post-primary education was in Swedish hands and the first Finnish language secondary school, opened in 1858, was the result of private initiative. It was followed by the setting up of associations all over the country to promote Finnish secondary education - and even today many secondary schools are private foundations. By 1880 half the students at the University of Helsinki were Finnish speaking and by 1900 the enrolment of Finnish speaking pupils in secondary schools was twice that of Swedish speakers.

The first efforts to introduce compulsory education were resisted by the Russians but in 1893 the Compulsory School Founding Act was passed by which each district was required to set up a primary school wherever as many as 30 pupils could be enrolled. The systematic development of adult and popular education had begun in 1866 with the setting up of folk schools by law, followed in 1874 by the foundation of the Society for Popular Culture. In 1921 came the law on Compulsory School Attendance which laid down an eight-year compulsory period of schooling consisting of six years at primary school and two years additional education for those not progressing further. This basic pattern survived until 1962 when an optional extra year was introduced.

Educational Planning

The State lays down the principles of educational policy through the Ministry of Education and the National Boards. Innovative and reformative projects have traditionally been the work of special committees appointed by the Council of State. The reports of the committees then form the basis for decision making. In 1966 a coordinating body, the Bureau of Educational Planning, was set up within the National Board of General Education. Five-year medium term plans are prepared and updated annually and the extent of implementation is decided when the budget is considered. However, planning cannot be entirely centralised because of the degree of regional devolution. Other bodies such as the Finnish Population and Family Welfare League and the Union of Rural Municipalities may be involved. At the higher level the National Council for Higher Education was established in 1966 and at the request of the Ministry considers problems of planning and development.

Educational Reform

During the period since World War Two education expanded dramatically. Between 1950 and 1960 the number of children in primary education rose on average by 3% annually. Secondary, vocational and higher education saw an annual increase in numbers of 7% and in the 1960s universities were taking 11% more students each year. It was recognised that this sort of expansion could not continue in an *ad hoc* fashion and that the education system should be examined in the light of Finland's economic and social development and future needs. In addition, the primary school had failed to meet educational aspirations and an increasing number of pupils was leaving after four years. This, combined with migration to the cities, closed over 1,000 primary schools. The introduction of municipal junior secondary schools allowed poorer pupils to succeed at this level, so that more and more children were seeking secondary and higher education. In 1963 43% of 11-year olds were in junior secondary schools; by 1971 the proportion had risen to 64%. In the same period the proportion of the age group in senior secondary schools had risen from 20% to 30%. In 1963 there were 10,000 graduates, in 1971 over 20,000 and the number of university students doubled between 1962 and 1972. A broader based and more flexible system was needed. In 1963 the Finnish Parliament accepted the government's proposal to remodel compulsory education on a comprehensive basis. The reform of basic education proved to be a starting point for the reform and reorganisation of the whole education system. Throughout, a leading principle of reform has been the promotion of educational equality.

Pre-Primary

Since 1968 pre-school classes and kindergartens have been allowed to be included in the municipal school system. Because of limited resources it is widely felt that the extension of compulsory education can only be achieved by lowering the age of school attendance. Successive reports have attempted to define the objectives of pre-primary education and draw up general plans for development. The compulsory attendance of all 6-year olds has been recommended to eliminate educational inequality, promoting the social development of children and fostering the equality of the sexes by freeing women to enter the labour market.

Basic

The introduction of a comprehensive school system has been discussed since the 1920s. After the draft bill was introduced in 1965 experimentation continued through the rest of the sixties and the curriculum was issued in 1970. Modifications were made to this subsequently before the new system was introduced overall in 1977/78. The comprehensive system is seen as a means to the cultivation of the whole personality as opposed to the purely intellectual development fostered by the junior secondary school. It should teach all pupils to learn for themselves, remove blind alleys and alleviate any anxiety caused by classification at 11 and give everyone the opportunity to progress further if they wish. Further major priorities in the context of basic school reform are seen as:

(i) integration of subject divided curricula
(ii) development of educational content in relation to the demands of scientific, technical and social development
(iii) development of teaching material
(iv) reform of pupil grading
(v) development of special education.

Secondary and Vocational

At post-comprehensive level the major aim has been to find the appropriate balance between secondary and vocational education, recognising both the aspirations of individuals and the demands of society. Both types of education must expand but in the past secondary education has expanded two or three times more rapidly. Without changes half the age group would have attended secondary schools by 1980. Vocational education was not growing sufficiently to meet the demand for skilled labour. In 1960 less than one sixth of the population had received vocational training. The curricula of both systems were regarded as inadequate - the secondary curriculum being too old-fashioned and the vocational curriculum lacking a sound basis in general studies. Consequently the decision was taken to:

(i) reform the curriculum of secondary education in relation to current developments and demands
(ii) reform vocational training to work through a system of successive choice
(iii) broaden the possibilities for further training by increasing the provision of general subjects in the vocational sector.

The law on Secondary Education describes the general framework of secondary education (both general and vocational). During the planning stage a number of proposals were made by the various committees working on secondary education. Among them was the remodelling of the Matriculation examination to cater for the needs of vocational as well as senior secondary students. There was also a recommendation of a general first year for senior secondary schools and certain vocational institutions so that pupils could opt for academic or vocational education after one year of secondary level studies. This would have entailed a reduction in specialisation in these secondary schools. In the event none of the proposals was accepted for immediate implementation but vocational curricula are being extensively reformed and vocational students following certain courses will be given easier access to higher education. Post-compulsory education will be more unified than hitherto, the senior secondary curriculum will be more flexible and the proportion of pupils entering senior secondary and vocational education will be adjusted.

Another ground for concern was the very unequal provision of vocational education over the whole country (with more places than applicants in Helsinki but only 25% to 30% of applicants gaining vocational places in remote areas). Vocational education is being expanded especially in remote areas though this must be a temporary measure as the birth rate is falling and the demand will decrease. It is designed primarily to enable adults who have not had the opportunity to acquire a vocational education to rectify this omission. Free accommodation and transport are provided for students. In 1979 between 12,000 and 12,500 students were in temporary vocational education (10% of all students in the vocational sector).

Higher and Teacher Training

As early as 1935 a committee was formed to consider the problems of the 'excessive' number of applicants to universities - lately the concern has extended to the disproportionate numbers in humanities and social sciences, the need for reform in degree programmes, admission, length of courses and so on. In 1950 there were 15,000 university students, in 1970 55,000, with a forecast of 75,000 in 1986. In 1966 the Act on the Development of Higher Education stipulated the number of places for students in 1981 and the proportion in each discipline. These targets have since been deferred to 1986 but the 1975 figures showed that the movement was in the right direction, i.e. towards science, technology, agriculture and medicine and away from humanities and social science. A centralised and standardised admission system for each field of study was also a long term aim and the trend is towards this with certain faculties joining together to set joint entrance examinations backed by ministerial financial support. The Ministry has recommended that 5% to 10% of first year places should be held for students from vocational education.

At present priority is being given to the reform of degree programmes, the coordination of the reforms at secondary and higher levels and the regional development of the higher education system. The changes in the degree structure which involve the phasing out of 'lower' first degrees (now complete), the rationalisation of the 'basic' first degree, and the restructuring of post-graduate courses (not yet clearly defined) are based on several years research. The aim is to develop degrees so that:

(i) all first degree programmes have vocational relevance
(ii) education offers a better basis for the broad development of vocational skills
(iii) education equips students with the capacity to play a fuller social role.

Working groups - which include students - have been appointed by the Ministry for each field of study. These have drafted lists of study programmes for each discipline and made proposals on the part to be played by the universities in planning and implementing these programmes. Some new programmes have been operating for some time. Others, for humanities, natural sciences and education, are planned. When the appropriate decree is passed teacher education programmes will be reorganised along similar lines to the degree programmes and there are proposals for extending the length of pre-primary teacher training.

The Committee on the Regional Extension of Higher Education reported in 1976. The Committee divided the country into six planning areas (with Swedish language education separate) and recommended that:

(i)   efforts be made to relate the number of student places in each area to the number in the relevant age group
(ii) regional development be coordinated with secondary education development
(iii) the disciplines available be relevant to the area's economic structure, production and labour requirements
(iv) in each area priority be given to regions with the poorest educational opportunities when an increase in student places is planned.

The Committee also suggested that the planning and administration of educational development be delegated to new cooperative bodies set up to encourage coordination of plans between institutions and to relate educational plans to needs. At present three new institutions are proposed. It is also proposed that forestry and veterinary science be moved from Helsinki to the University of Joensuu and the University of Kuopio respectively.

10 THE SYSTEM IN OPERATION
Future Trends

The reform is now well under way, with the transition to basic school over the whole country, the introduction of the law on secondary reform and the reorganisation of degree programmes. A committee set up by the Ministry of Education considered the question of further integration of post-compulsory education (1979-83). In future research may assume a greater role in planning. In 1976 an unofficial joint consultative group representing teachers' organisations and education authorities was set up under the National Board of General Education. This group provides advice and assistance to research workers in the field of general education. The Department of Higher Education and Research in the Ministry is also providing financial support for a number of research projects. The Institute of Educational Research at the University of Jyväskylä is the key institution here, carrying out basic and applied research and also providing an information service on Finnish education both within the country and overseas.

FURTHER READING

Bacon, Walter (1970). *Finland*. Robert Hale & Co., London.
Europa Year Book Vol. I (1977). Europa Publications, London.
Hall, Wendy (1967). *The Finns and Their Country.* Max Parrish, London.
Mead, W. R. (1968). *Finland*. Ernest Benn, London.
Ministry for Foreign Affairs (1967). *Education in Finland by Matti Gustaffson*. Reference Publication No.2, Helsinki.
Ministry of Education (1970). *Educational Reform in Finland in the 1970s*. Reference Publication No.4, Helsinki.
Ministry of Education (1973). *Higher Education and Research in Finland*. Reference Publication No.6, Helsinki.
Ministry of Education (1975). *Educational Development in Finland 1973-75*. Reference Publication No.7, Helsinki.
Ministry of Education (1977). *Educational Development in Finland 1974-76*. Reference Publication No.8, Helsinki.
National Board of Vocational Education (1973). *Vocational Education in Finland*. Helsinki.
Nickels, Sylvie, Kallas, Hillar and Friedman, Philippa (Eds.) (1973). *Finland - an introduction*. Allen & Unwin, London.
Otava Publishing Company (1976). *Facts about Finland*. Helsinki.
Unesco/IBE (1979). *International Guide to Educative Systems*. Geneva.
Unesco/IBE (1980). *International Yearbook of Education XXXII*. Unesco, Paris.
Unesco/IBE (1981). *International Yearbook of Education XXXIII*. Unesco, Paris.

Structure of the Education System in Finland

Age	3	4	5	6	7	8	9	10	11	12	13	14	15	16	17	18	19	20	21	22	23	24
Level					I					II					III				IV			
Stage					1			2			3			4								
Compulsory																						
School Type				Comprehensive							Lukio / Vocational College				Universities / Institutions of higher education / Teacher Training

Education preceding the first level

Examinations: matriculation *(ylioppilastutkinto)* at the end of stage 4 gives access to university
Source: UNESCO/IBE International Yearbook of Education
Compulsory Education: Age Limits 7-16   Duration (years) 9
Entrance age to pre-school education: 3

FINLAND BASIC STATISTICS	1960	1970	1975	1978 (approx.)
1 Total population (000)	4,430	4,606	4,651	4,752
% female	52	52	52	52
2 % population 0-14 years	30.4	24.6		21
% female	49	49	49	49
3 Enrolment, all levels	925,152	955,690	950,751	936,127
% female	49	49	50	50
First level	544,652	386,230	453,737	406,921
% female	48	47	48	49
Second level	356,948	509,691	419,808	446,041
% female	52	51	52	52
Third level	23,552	59,769	77,206	83,165
% female	46	48	50	50
4 Teachers, all levels	37,665	55,874		63,757
% female		51		
First level	20,727	17,360	24,494	25,096
% female	66	60	61	
Second level	14,442	32,247		32,651
% female		53		
Third level	2,496	6,267	5,429	6,010
% female	12	19		21
5 Public expenditure on education:				
Total (000) markkas	760,220	2,678,872	6,497,103	8,765,000
As % of GNP	4.8	6.2	6.7	7.0
As % of public expenditure				12.9
6 % enrolment (MF) by level	100	100	100	100
First level	59	40	48	43
Second level	39	53	44	48
Third level	3	6	8	9
% enrolment (F) by level	100	100	100	100
First level	57	39	46	41
Second level	40	55	46	50
Third level	2	6	8	9
7 Entrance age : Duration of				
First level education	7:6	7:4	7:6	7:6
Second level education	13:6	11:8	13:6	13:6
8 Enrolment ratios (MF)				
First level	97	82	89	85
Second level	74	102	81	89
Third level	7.38	13.34	18.62	
Enrolment ratios (F)				
First level	95	79	88	85
Second level	78	106	86	96
Third level	6.94	13.26	19.08	

France

CONTENTS

1 Geography 302
2 Population 302
3 Society and Culture 304
4 History and Politics 307
5 The Economy 310
6 The Education System 312
7 Educational Administration 326
8 Educational Finance 330
9 Development and Planning of the Educational System 331
10 The System in Operation 335

The French system of education has provided a model for most of Europe. The principles upon which it is based were outlined by a succession of thinkers including Condorcet during the late eighteenth century and many of them were put into practice under Napoleon's leadership. His military successes in Europe influenced the development of school systems so that in Western Europe including the USSR important features of this French model remain. The model was characterised by universal primary or elementary schools, where children should learn about their civic rights and duties, followed by selective secondary schools where an aristocracy of talent should be educated for the university and for the service of France.

Napoleon introduced an administrative system consisting of a powerful central authority, regional academies, departments and local communes run by a corps of bureaucrats who would be protected from political interference. State *lycées* for the most able were created; and following an earlier precedent *grandes écoles* were established to train engineers, military personnel and teachers. In the secondary schools a broadly based encyclopedic curriculum was to be provided with emphasis on mathematics and modern (rather than classical) languages.

The training of elementary school teachers took place in local *écoles normales primaire*. University trained teachers for the *lycées* were selected on the basis of rigorous competitive examinations *(concours)* called the *agrégation*.

The history of nineteenth century educational development is one during which Church-State conflict over the control of education was particularly bitter and when competition between the classical languages and modern subjects for a place in the secondary school curriculum dominated debates. Throughout the nineteenth century, however, every attempt was made to keep the French language 'pure' and to unify the country by insisting on a mastery of it.

After 1945 the reform recommendations symbolised in the Committee chaired jointly by Paul Langevin and Henri Wallon were debated without being accepted for some 15 years. Objections to the reorganisation of secondary education along comprehensive lines (a policy which had its roots in the *écoles uniques* of the 1920s) came from the defenders of the *lycées* the *société des agregés* and as a consequence of political and religious differences in the French National Assembly. Under de Gaulle progress was possible and a comprehensive set of decrees delayed selection at the point of entry to second level education, introduced guidance and counselling procedures and moved towards the creation of a new type of general secondary school.

In spite of these debates the system, partly in response to the immediate post-war baby boom, has expanded very considerably. During the sixties university enrolments trebled to more than 600,000 students. Serious student unrest in 1968 contributed to the downfall of de Gaulle and led to major legislative changes designed to create new universities out of the old faculties, to ensure autonomy and student and junior faculty participation in the running of the universities.

Recent changes in the system have included attempts to lengthen the period of general secondary education and to diversify its content. Greek and Latin are now options, the position of a second modern language is debated but may be chosen from a wide range including Arabic, Hebrew, Chinese or Polish. In 1979 against long traditions one of five regional languages (Basque, Breton, Catalan, Corsican or Occitan) may be taken. Pupils leaving the four year *collèges uniques* go on to a *lycée* or into vocational education.

The Haby reforms were introduced by law in July 1975 and are being introduced progressively; not, however, without continuing debate and on some aspects, resistance. As stated, university reform stems from the *Loi d'Orientation* of November 1968 but the university institutes of technology had been set up in 1966 to meet the need for scientifically and technically trained personnel. In 1980 government regulations reduced the autonomy won in the sixties by placing restrictions on the number of 'education' courses which could be offered in the universities.

Although there have been changes, represented in the number of national Directorates in the system of administration with the intention of devolving authority, and in 1974 a new Secretary of State for the universities was established and in 1978 became a separate Ministry, the administrative system retains many features introduced by Napoleon.

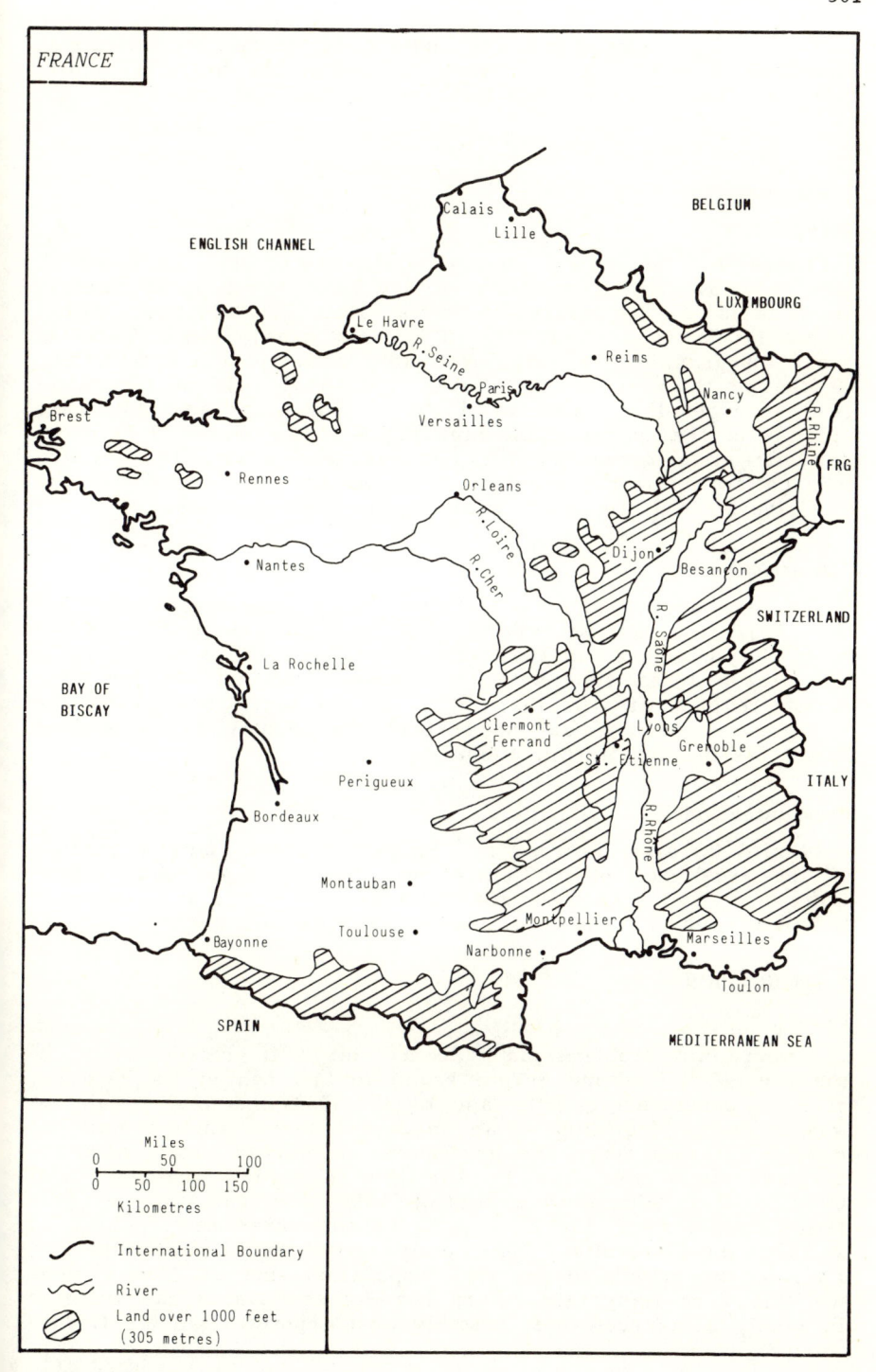

FRANCE

De Gaulle's reforms in 1959 helped to defuse the historical Church-State conflict which made it impossible to make public funds available to the large number of Catholic schools.

The Editor

1 GEOGRAPHY

Topography

France is the second largest state in Europe, exceeded in size only by that part of the Soviet Union which is in Europe. Its area is 547,000 square kilometres (about 211,200 square miles) including Corsica. About 30% of this is arable land. There is great topographical variety, from the fertile plains and valleys of the north west and the drab industrial belt of the north east through the vine-clad hills of Burgundy and the bare uplands of the centre to the high peaks of the Alps and Pyrenees and the olive groves of the Mediterranean coast. The country is rich in natural resources of all kinds: fertile soil, forests and rivers, iron ore, coal, bauxite and other minerals.

Climate

The size of the country and its varied topography mean that the climate is equally varied. For most of France the climate could be described as temperate, though in the south it is of the Mediterranean type with hot summers and mild winters. The driest regions are in the centre of the Paris basin and the Mediterranean coast, but no part of the country has less than 500mm (20 inches) of rain annually.

Communications

Despite its size, France is a compact country, largely because of the excellence of communications; the railway, road, inland waterways and external air networks are extensive. Most of the motorways, for instance, radiate from Paris.

2 POPULATION

Growth

Demographic problems have loomed large in recent times. In the nineteenth century France began to fall behind its European rivalsin population growth, and by the 1930s the total population was actually declining – an important factor in the national *malaise* of that time. The government introduced family allowances and other measures to stimulate a higher birthrate, and by 1939 their efforts were meeting with some success. The pro-family policies of the Pétain government helped to sustain these results. Immediately after World War Two, in 1945/46, the growth in the total population shot up. The reasons for this were many: the return home of combatants, an increase in family allowances and, possibly most important, the confidence and optimism arising from the resurgence of what has been called 'the collective national conscience'. The birth rate remained at a high level until the mid-1960s, after which it declined again. In 1946 the population was 41 million; by 1969 it had reached 50 million. In 1972 about one third of the total were under 20. By 1978, however, the birth rate of 1.8 child per woman was lower than it had been in 1941.

The official policy of stimulating population growth was defined in 1920 in a strict anti-contraception law which was repealed, under growing pressure of educated public opinion, only in 1967. Birth control and, even more, abortion are still controversial issues. The family planning movement had to develop without official support and with much opposition from the bulk of the medical profession and from the powerful Communist Party. Sex education was formerly banned in schools. Since 1973, however, the school curriculum has provided for a progressive provision of information about the human body and its functions.

Numbers and Distribution

By western European standards, France is still underpopulated, with an average population density of about 97 per square kilometre. In 1980 the total population was 53,589,000, over 4 million of whom were foreigners. As much as 80% of the population live in urban areas. Paris and its suburbs have the largest and densest population, some 8.5 million in 1979; 21 other conurbations have populations of around 200,000 and a further 28 over 100,000.

School Population

The post-war sudden increase caused an *'explosion scolaire'* In the mid-40s the school population was about 6.5 million; in 1979 it was over 13 million. Other reasons for this increase have been a voluntary tendency to stay at school longer and the raising of the school leaving age. In the 1980s, however, the total will drop.

Groups

The people of metropolitan France are of mixed ancestry: short, stocky men from the mountains of central Europe, taller men of Nordic type (who came from the east centuries before the invasion of the Norsemen who founded Normandy in the ninth century), sea-borne settlers from the eastern Mediterranean. Though most of the original differences are now obscured, there still remain on the periphery substantial groups distinguished in language or culture from the majority: the Bretons, of Celtic descent, the Basques and Catalans in the south, the Alsatians and some Dutch speakers in the east, the speakers of Occitanian in the Languedoc, and off the mainland, the people of Corsica. The nationalist movements of Brittany and Corsica resort to violent expressions of their demands for more regional power or for complete autonomy. The Occitan language movement in the south, though less violent, is also making its presence increasingly felt.

Immigration

There was a large influx of foreign workers into France after World War Two, but further immigration was stopped in 1974 because of the economic situation. At 1 January 1978 the number of foreigners (including families) was officially estimated to be 4,097,295, of whom over 1.5 million were actively at work. They represent 7.5% of the total active population of the country and 98% of them do manual work. The largest groups (1978) are from Portugal (nearly 882,000), Algeria (804,000), Spain (486,000) and Morocco (376,000). The housing of many of these workers, especially those from North Africa, poses a serious social problem. Thousands live in near-slum conditions in shanty towns, especially in the Paris region and on the south coast. In Marseille and elsewhere outbreaks of violence have been associated with a white backlash against coloured immigrants.

3 SOCIETY AND CULTURE

Social Patterns

A society as complex, as ancient, and as deeply rooted as that of France cannot be described even superficially in a few short paragraphs. Moreover, it is undergoing a profound change under the impact of the technological revolution and the country's own economic renascence. It is a society of contrasts and conflict: between traditional conservative Catholic values and fiercely secular iconoclasm; between the authoritarian centre and what Ardagh calls "the honeycomb of little sectional interests"; between a widespread feeling that France is unique and the enforced awareness that no country, least of all in Europe, can stand alone; and between the strength of closely-knit family ties and the disruptive effect on the young of the present discontents and the contemporary media-fed culture. Despite great technologycal advances, the foundations of French society are changing only slowly: these still reside in the small individual unit, whether it be the small local *commune*, the family firm, or the peasant smallholding. It is a fiercely competitive society at all levels; outstanding achievement of any kind, especially intellectual and cultural, is rated very highly. This leads to an elitism of an intellectual rather than a social kind; but, paradoxically, intended reforms in education and other fields can be frustrated by an intense egalitarianism inherited from the Revolution.

Status of Paris

One significant change is the decline in the comparative status of Paris. The dominance of the capital in the past was such that one could fairly refer to the provinces as '*le désert français*'; it was the centre of gravity of learning, culture, government, and industry, and its pull drained the provinces of their finest talent. This applied to cultural life particularly: until about 1945 the gulf between Paris and the provinces was nowhere so obvious as in the arts and intellectual activity. Recent governments, however, have been making efforts at decentralisation and at reducing the power and influence of central bureaucracy. The importance of the regions is slowly growing, often under the influence of powerful mayors and chairmen of regional councils who are also politicians of national and even international repute. The first significant effort at cultural decentralisation was made by André Malraux, then Minister of Culture, in the 1960s, when he inaugurated a network of regional arts centres, the *Maisons de la Culture*. Many of these were in splendid new buildings, superbly designed and equipped. The problem was to turn them into living centres of the arts. On the whole the Maisons have not attracted the ordinary man in the street and his family, as they were meant to do, and some provide depressing evidence of the difficulty of trying to impose 'culture' from above where there is no real demand for it. But less ambitious arts centres, which have grown naturally from small beginnings, flourish in many places. The authorities have also recently signed a series of 'cultural charters' with cities, to coordinate local and national action.

Nevertheless, Paris retains its predominant place as the source of important decisions. It is significant that more than 60% of all scientific and medical research workers still live and work around Paris. In the arts, too, an important development of recent years has been the foundation in Paris in 1977 of the huge and very expensive *Centre National d'Art et de Culture Georges Pompidou* which, despite gloomy prognostications and much criticism, has been a distinct success. It has attracted worldwide attention.

French Culture

France's contribution to the world's culture, in the narrower sense of the term, is immense and hardly needs description. In the past many countries turned to France for cultural inspiration and the French themselves were keenly aware of their *mission civilisatrice*, which has left a deep imprint on their former colonies and elsewhere. The French language, the major instrument in this mission, was for long the principal medium of diplomatic interchange, and many Frenchmen resent the growing use of English as a world *lingua franca*. There is a close identity for them between *la langue* and *la patrie*. The *Academie Française* continually strives to protect the language from the encroachment of alien terms and there has recently been legislation to check the use in the public services of *Franglais* which is a current fashion in the entertainment media and commerce.

Mass Media

The mass media are contributing to the 'democratisation' of culture in its narrower sense, though their impact has been slow. In 1963 there were only 3 million television sets, compared with 12 million in Britain, but the gap has closed considerably since then. There are three television networks, the last started in 1973. Until 1974 these, like sound radio, were controlled by the State through the ORTF *(Office de la Radio et Télévision Française)*. The subservience of the ORTF to the government was widely criticised, and its dismantling was one of President Giscard d'Estaing's first reforms after his election in May 1974. The three TV channels, sound radio and ancillary services operate independently of each other. The success of this reform is debatable though there is less political interference in the running of the networks.

Leisure

The Frenchman's leisure interests are changing under the impact of the mass media and cheap travel facilities. In the past he tended to stay at home and spend much of his income on food — the largest single item in the average Frenchman's budget, a reason for the excellence of French cuisine. Holidays are, however, beginning to supplant the traditional pleasures. Over half the population takes holidays away from home, twice as many as before the 1939-45 war. The French have the longest statutory holiday allowance in Europe: 24 working days is the legal minimum and a five-week holiday is common. There is a 'back to nature' movement, in a society becoming more urbanised; the popularity of *colonies de vacances*, by the sea or in the mountains, with meals taken communally, is steadily growing. (Schoolchildren have for many years been sent to such colonies during the summer.) In 1979 two thirds of all households had a private car. Even the farming community is beginning to shake off the engrained habit of never leaving home: 10% in 1970, 21% in 1978, went away on holiday. Recent governments have been making strenuous efforts to stagger holidays, but with little success so far: the weekend after 14 July still finds millions en route for the sea or the country. France's own immense potential as a holiday centre is being intensively developed, with an emphasis on regions other than those which have traditionally attracted tourists.

Religion

The French State has been formally secular since 1905, when the separation of Church and State was confirmed. The present constitution lays down that "France is a republic, indivisible, secular, democratic and social . . . It ensures equality before the law for all citizens, without distinction of origin, race, or religion." Nominally, about 80% of the population is Roman Catholic. Over the last century, the numbers of those who actually practice their religion have greatly declined; about one adult in five attends Mass regularly on Sundays. In most of France the parish priest is no longer an influential local leader; only in the most Catholic areas, such as Brittany and Alsace, is the Church, in its traditional form, still a potent force. There are some 800,000 Protestants, divided among six churches which are federated, and an active Jewish community of about 500,000, mainly in Paris, Marseille and Alsace. Among the immigrant workers there are many Moslems.

Since World War Two, however, there has been a significant Catholic revival of a new kind, distinguished not in number but in effectiveness from the pre-war Church. This neo-Catholic movement is militant, reformist, and led for the most part by laymen, allied with the younger clergy. The movement started during the last war with the creation of the *Mission de France* - an organisation created to bring back Christianity to the 'pagan' working classes. This culminated in the remarkable worker-priest experiment, which was so effective in making contact between the Church and factory workers that the Vatican, worried about the Marxist influence on some of the priests, ordered its virtual suspension in 1954. The neo-Catholic movement continues, however, and is widely involved in all fields of French life: in business, industry, agriculture, among students and even in the pressure for family planning.

4 HISTORY AND POLITICS

Political Developments

France's political record in the past was normally one of instability. Betwen the French Revolution in 1789 and 1870, government alternated between republican and monarchical systems. In 1870, the present period of republican rule began. The Third Republic survived, often precariously, until 1940, and the Fourth, after the German occupation and the wartime Pétain régime, from 1946 to 1958, a period in which there were 26 cabinets with an average life span of $5\frac{1}{2}$ months. In 1958 the long crisis in Algeria, insurrection in Corsica, a threatened revolt by the armed forces and the possibility of civil war led to a request to General Charles de Gaulle, the outstanding wartime leader, to form a government. After a referendum the present constitution, that of the Fifth Republic, came into force and de Gaulle assumed wide personal powers as President, a position to which he was elected for a seven-year term; he was re-elected in 1965.

For ten years, until 1968, France enjoyed a period of comparative political peace which enabled the country to maintain a remarkable rate of economic growth and rebuilding. But in May 1968 there occurred the 'events' which rudely shattered the calm. Growing discontent among students about the archaic structure of the university system and its impossible overcrowding, was fanned by left wing extremists, mainly in Paris, and the new University of Nanterre, and culminated in large scale fighting and the 'night of the barricades' in Paris. The protest spread outside the universities. Not only industrial workers at the Renault factories and elsewhere, but also white collar and professional workers joined in; at one time there were eight million on strike. The government was forced to resign, but the strength of de Gaulle's personal authority prevailed; in the ensuing elections the party which owed allegiance to him won a huge majority. These events, particularly those of 1968, had an impact on the education system and above all on the organisation of universities.

President de Gaulle resigned in 1969, after defeat in a referendum on which he had staked his future, and was succeeded by Georges Pompidou who, though less idiosyncratic and authoritarian than his predecessor, continued many of his policies. When M Pompidou died in 1974 he was succeeded by his former Minister of Finance, Valéry Giscard d'Estaing, who had a very narrow majority over his Socialist opponent. He instituted a programme of gradual and cautious reform, stressing the need for changes in French society. Presidential elections took place in 1981 and François Mitterand was elected.

Parties and Trade Unions

The French party political system is complicated. After the parliamentary elections of 1978 a coalition government was formed of the majority centre parties supporting the President, led by M Raymond Barre, a former professor of economics. The largest single party in the Assembly was the neo-Gaullist *Rassemblement pour la République* (RPR), led by M Jacques Chirac, which had ministers in the government but nevertheless had strained relations with the President. In opposition were the two large left wing groups, the Socialists and the powerful Communist party. An electoral alliance between these two in 1973 and 1974 came near to unseating the government, but their alliance in 1978 was less successful than expected.

The trade unions are divided on lines of politics or ideology, not according to craft or industry; this reduces their effective power. the majority of French workers are not union members. The largest union is the Communist-led *Confédération Générale de Travail* (CGT); Two others, respectively Catholic and Socialist, are each of about a third of its size. The teachers' unions are active political pressure groups, mainly left wing. The overarching organisation is the *Fédération de l'Education Nationale* (FEN), which has 40 constituent unions. The *Societé des Aggregés* includes among its members *lycée* teachers and the leading figures in academic and professional life.

Government

France is a parliamentary democracy. Under the present constitution, the Head of State, the President of the Republic, is elected by direct universal suffrage for a term of seven years which is renewable. He appoints the Prime Minister and also the cabinet on the former's recommendation, and has considerable reserve powers: for example, to dissolve the National Assembly or to submit disputed legislation to national referenda. The execu-

tive (the Prime Minister and other ministers) is constitutionally separate from Parliament, which has two houses, the National Assembly and the Senate.
The governmental structure is tightly centralised though in the seventies some 'deconcentration' of powers took place. The present structure derives from the organising genius of Napoleon. He divided the country into departments, each governed by a prefect responsible to him, whose first task was to maintain law and order. There are now 95 departments in metropolitan France. (The colonies of Guyane, Martinique, Guadeloupe and La Réunion are also departments, having in practice rather more local independence that those within France.) The prefects, men of the highest calibre, are appointed by the Minister of the Interior as personal representatives of the central government. Since reforms in 1964 they, and their staff of administrators and specialists, have more local autonomy than previously when even minor matters had to be referred to the appropriate ministry in Paris. Paradoxically, government at the local level is fragmented; the unit of local government is the commune, a term which embraces both large cities and small hamlets. In 1975 there were over 38,000 communes, over 90% of which had fewer than 2,000 inhabitants and 22,500 even fewer than 500. Each commune has its *mairie* and its jealously guarded local rights. The government has attempted to rationalise this structure, first by the creation of economic regions and secondly by the merging of small communes.

International Relations

France is an active member of the principal international and European organisations - the United Nations and its agencies, SEATO, OECD, the Council of Europe, the European Communities and Western European Union. Three of these bodies, UNESCO, OECD and the Council of Europe, are based in France, and the European Parliament (of the European Communities) though housed in Luxembourg, meets in Strasbourg. A notable exception is NATO; in 1966 France withdrew from the military organisation of this body, of which it was a founder member, and its military and political headquarters were subsequently moved from Paris to Brussels.
The European Economic Community is probably the most significant organisation in French thinking. It was two Frenchmen, Robert Schumann and Jean Monnet, who presented in May 1950 the Declaration which, supported by a small group of imaginative Duropean statesmen, laid the basis for the eventual unification of western Europe. Their aims were twofold: reconciliation between France and Germany, and the setting up of a European federation. The first step was the creation of the European Coal and Steel Community, of which M Monnet became the first president. France in international relations shows the same propensity for independence of attitude which is to be found in its citizens and has the same reluctance to engage in any form of association or alliance which would limit freedom of action, while at the

same time recognising the importance and need for such associations. It thus remains a vigorous proponent of the EEC while insisting on the importance of conserving the identity of the nations within it.

Less at variance with other western countries than some years ago, France still preserves this independence of policy in its relations with eastern Europe, the Arab world and in Africa. Aid *(coopération)* is an important element in French policies and in the developing world. It is largely concentrated on francophone countries which were previously within the French colonial empire or spheres of influence. France thus gives a great deal of educational aid to North Africa and such countries as Senegal and Chad. With the international decline in the use of the French language, France is particularly concerned to maintain cultural influence in those areas where French is still well rooted. Language policy has great significance for France as a factor in diplomacy. The notion of cultural relations was a French invention in the nineteenth century and it remains a living diplomatic instrument.

5 THE ECONOMY

Mixed Economy

France has a mixed economy, in which State enterprises co-exist with private enterprise but the State plays an unusually important role in the control of the economy. Not only does it run public services such as the railways, but it also controls large sectors of banking and insurance, car and aircraft manufacture and armaments. Private industry has traditionally accepted a high measure of State finance, and is consequently responsible to State involvement in policy and planning. The central direction of the economy is made up of a multiplicity of small firms, with few really large ones. It is concentrated in the north east and the Paris region; other important centres are Lyon, Marseille, Bordeaux, St Nazaire and Grenoble. Agriculture (including wine production) is also of considerable importance.

Current Performance

Until the current world economic crises began with the steep rise in oil prices in 1973, the French economy was expanding at a rate of 5-6% p.a. In 1979 France, like the other industrialised countries of the west, was trying to cope with the energy crisis, inflation (about 10% p.a.), a high rate of unemployment (about 1.3 million, of whom about 10% are immigrants), the running down of traditional industries (especially steel, mining and textiles), competition from Asia, and an aging population. An egalitarian austerity programme introduced by the President and Prime Minister was fiercely contested by the unions and partly frustrated by the innate determination of many Frenchmen to use any means to avoid paying taxes. Nevertheless, the economy remained reasonably strong. One of M Barre's achievements was to close the trade gap. After 1981 with Mitterand as President policies were designed to reflate the economy.

Within the country there are particular regional problems. In the north and east steel mills and mines closed. On the other hand, new industries are needed in rural areas, especially in the west and south west, where agricultural mechanisation has led to a surplus of labour. The number of agricultural workers was almost halved from 1954 to 1968; in 1971 they constituted 14% of the total work force, in 1976 11.6%.

Economic Planning

Where so much of industry is owned or guided by the State, the idea of a national plan is more readily accepted than it would be in Britain or the USA. The idea is indeed not new in France; Colbert attempted it under Louis XIV. The need for reconstruction after World War Two coincided with the emergence of a remarkably far-seeing and imaginative man, Jean Monnet, who had spent the war in the USA and come to admire American efficiency. His advocacy of national planning won the support of General de Gaulle and the government, and in 1946 the first five-year plan was approved. M Monnet gathered round him a group of outstandingly able, mostly young, men in the *Commissariat-Général du Plan*, whose basic task was to set targets for growth, in all the different sectors of the economy, over five-year periods. The planners, whose office now comes directly under the Prime Minister, have no executive function or formal authority; neither the govrnment nor private firms are under any obligation to accept their advice. The Plan has, however, worked, partly because of its psychological effect on industry, particularly on the larger and medium sized firms; it helped to create a new spirit of competition as well as a readiness to cooperate and to consider mergers for the sake of efficiency. By 1980 there had been seven Plans of which two, in 1958-61 and 1962-65, were those most concerned with the development of education.

To assist in the development of the Plan, France has been divided into 22 economic regions, including Paris and Corsica. To some extent these coincide with the old traditional regions of France (Brittany, Aquitaine, etc.); they therefore have a meaning for the ordinary Frenchman which Napoleon's departments, with artbitrarily fixed boundaries, did not have. Each region has a *préfet de région* at its head - normally the prefect of whichever department contains the chief city of the region. Regional planning was a major preoccupation of M Monnet and his team, and in some cases the Plan has achieved a notable regeneration of declining areas, particularly in the south east (Grenoble's development has been astonishing) and parts of the north west (Rennes, for example, is now a flourishing city).

6 THE EDUCATION SYSTEM
General

Education is compulsory from 6 to 16. The school leaving age has been progressively raised from 14 (since 1936) to 16 (1967). Pre-primary schooling normally begins at 3, sometimes 2 or 4. Students may finish a course at university in their late twenties, so that it is possible to spend an uninterrupted period of 25 years in education. The whole school system is being progressively revised under the law of 11 July 1975 (the 'Haby reform'), initiated by M Haby and continued by his successor M Beullac. One of the major principles of this reform is that the system should be planned as a continuous whole, the objectives of each stage being coordinated.

Academic Year and Hours

The school year runs from mid-September to the end of June. In 1979/80 the *rentrée* (the term generally applied to the beginning of a new academic year, at all levels) is on 12-13 September; there are short holidays at the end of October and early November, at Christmas, one week in February according to zone, and two weeks in spring, again starting according to zone. The summer holidays last 11 weeks. (The division of the country into zones is part of the attempt to stagger departures on holiday.)

The school day is long: typically 8.30 - 16.30 in a primary school and 8.15 - 17.15 in a secondary school, followed in the latter case by homework. Most schools are closed on Wednesdays and open on Saturday mornings; local authorities now have power to alter this system. The working pattern of schools *(le rhythme scolaire)* is a controversial issue; many parents and psychologists think it too exhausting for their children.

Pre-School *(Ecoles Maternelles)*

These schools were started during the Third Republic, in the 1880s. Teaching is in separate nursery schools or in infants' departments attached to primary schools. Attendance is voluntary. The proportion of the age group undergoing such education is higher in France than in any other European country except Belgium: in 1975 80.3% of the 3-4 year olds were enrolled at school, and almost all 4-5 year olds. Communes with more than 2,000 inhabitants are required by law to provide such schooling. It was planned to provide enough places for all 2-5 year olds by 1978. The children receive the care needed for their physical, intellectual and moral development; the methods used are partly based on Montessori and Decroly theories. The older children (5-6) are prepared in the Three Rs, for entry into the primary school, and also, in many schools, in a foreign language (there is a number of *écoles bilingues*, in which the second language is English or German).

Primary *(Ecoles Elémentaires)*

The normal age of entry to the primary school from the *école maternelle* is 6. Individual children who are advanced for their years may, however, start at 5, as do children in communes where there is no nursery provision for 5 year olds. The course is divided into three stages of two years each:

(i) cycle *préparatoire*
(ii) cycle *élémentaire*
(iii) cycle *moyen*.

The structure is flexible. A bright newcomer may after a few weeks of observation be promoted into the second year of the preparation cycle; in exceptional cases such a child might subsequently skip the first year of the following cycle, being given instead a special 'revision' course. The below average child could also benefit from this revision course; in his case the reinforcement of what he had learned in the previous year is meant to replace the former need for him to repeat a whole year. (The abolition of the old system of repetition was one of the cardinal features of the Haby reform.)

The primary curriculum, which is common to all children, is based on the Three Rs, the fundamental tools which every individual must master. The ability to reason, powers of observation, imagination, taste and physical control must also be developed as soon as possible.

The school week of $4\frac{1}{2}$ days (27 hours) is made up as follows in all three cycles:

(i) 15 hours of basic studies: French (9 hours) and mathematics (6 hours)
(ii) 7 hours of *'activités d'éveil'* history, geography, moral education, observation projects, handwork, modelling, music
(iii) 5 hours of physical education and sport (including the popular 'classes in the snow' or by the sea during the term).

Special

The general policy concerning children suffering from physical or mental handicaps is so far as possible to integrate them into ordinary schools. There are special schools of various kinds for children too severely afflicted to attend ordinary schools.

Second Level Schools – First Cycle (the *collèges*)

Transition from primary to secondary education *(l'enseignement du second degré)* is now automatic, unless the primary school can show in a particular case that the child must repeat some of the primary work. Instruction in the first cycle (11 to 15) is mainly given in the *collèges uniques* (the name given since

1977/78 to the former *(collèges d'enseignement secondaire)*. These comprehensive schools have almost completely replaced the *collèges d'enseignement général* (dating from 1959), which recently existed only in rural areas, and the lower forms of the *lycées* (grammar schools), only a few of which have retained classes for this age group.

Streaming has been abolished in the first two years (the observation stage) of this cycle, the 6th and 5th classes. There is a common core curriculum of 21 hours a week for all pupils, designed to consolidate the knowledge and skills gained in primary school. This consists of the traditional subjects: French - 5 hours; mathematics - 3 hours; one foreign language - 3 hours; history/geography (including elementary economics and civics) - 3 hours; and (new subjects introduced under the Haby reform) experimental science - 3 hours; artistic activities (including music and drawing) - 2 hours; and manual and technical education - 2 hours, designed to familiarise the pupils with tools and equipment in everyday use. For every subject there is a precise national programme, defining the aims and content. All children have 3 hours a week of physical education and sport; schools may, according to their resources, offer a further 2 hours a week for optional sporting and/or artistic activities. In addition, 3 hours are set aside each week for extra classes of 1 hour each in French, mathematics and the modern language: either remedial classes *(enseignement de soutien)* for the slower learners or fuller studies in depth *(activités d'approfondissement)*, including individual project work, for the more gifted children. In the academic subjects (i.e. all except sport, art, music and manual education) each class lasts 50 minutes, leaving 10 minutes for relaxation and informal contacts between teachers and pupils. The normal size of class is 24; the maximum is 30.

At the end of the observation stage, after the 5th class, the orientation stage begins. The pupil may then either continue general education in the 4th and 3rd classes, or start classes with a vocational bias. If he stays in the general stream he has a $24\frac{1}{2}$ hour weekly timetable, made up of the common core stubjects studied in the 6th and 5th, plus one additional obligatory subject for 3 hours a week, except where indicated, to be chosen from the following list: an additional foreign language (the possibility of withdrawing this option is being studied by the Ministry), reinforced study of the first foreign language (2 hours a week), Latin, Greek or one of three technical subjects. A second 'voluntary' subject may also be chosen from this list. The second language may be chosen from a wide range, limited or course by the school's resources and location: the list can include, for example, Arabic, Hebrew, Chinese or Polish and, from 1979, one of the five regional languages: Basque, Breton, Catalan, Corsican or Occitan.

At the end of the four years of the collège, a pupil may apply for a *brevet d'études du premier cycle*. This is awarded by a jury without further examination to a pupil who has been advised to go on to a *lycée* or to do advanced studies in an LEP (see below); in other cases the pupil must pass an examination. Pupils who have opted for vocational education on leaving the 5th class may start on a three-year course leading to a *Certificat d'Aptitude Professionnelle* (CAP) in one of over 300 different subjects (technical, commercial, catering, etc.) or begin their pre-apprenticeship or agricultural training, as appropriate. They do this in a *Lycée d'Enseignement Professionnel* (LEP), formerly called *Collège d'Enseignement Technique* (CET) - an institution which provides various vocational and craft courses, at different levels.

Second Level Schools - Second Cycle (15+)

In the second cycle a distinction is made between long and short types of course, *enseignements longs* (3 years of study) and *enseignements courts* (2 years). Pupils are guided towards the appropriate type by counselling, according to their aptitudes, interests and achievement.

Enseignements longs: the lycées

The three-year courses are provided in the *lycées*; some cover only the non-technical subjects, others are specifically designated *lycées d'enseignement technique*. These schools fall into 3 groups, according to whether they are maintained wholly by the State, wholly by a municipality, or jointly. The oldest *lycées*, such as the distinguished schools Louis-le-Grand and Henri IV in Paris, fall into the first group.

These courses are in a form decreed in 1965, but since modified. Their aim is to provide a sound academic grounding in *culture générale* combined with preparation for a future career. The 2nd class has 4 streams: literary (A), literary and economic (AB), scientific (C) and technical (T), with certain basic subjects (French, history, geography, civics, one modern language, mathematics, physical sciences and physical training) common to all four, plus optional extras including both scientific and literary subjects. In the 1st (penultimate) and Terminal classes, there is greater specialisation, in preparation for the chosen *baccalauréat*. In the Terminal class philosophy is at present a compulsory subject for the *baccalauréat* A (except A6), B, C, D and G; the possible diminution of the place accorded to this time-honoured subject aroused fierce opposition in 1979. The number of hours spent on each subject varies according to the stream. The workload is heavy; in addition to the long school day, much homework is required. The C stream is generally reckoned to be the most demanding.

The *baccalauréat* is an examination which, because of its long history and its academic and social significance deserves a longer description than can be given here. It is both a school leaving examination and an automatic passport to higher education. Success in it ensures acceptance by a French university, though not – as previously – for study in any department. There were in 1978/79 five general *baccalauréats* (A-E), with 11 different options, and three *baccalauréats de technicien* (F-H), with 16 options, as follows:

A1-7   Literary, linguistic and philosophical studies
AB   Economics and social sciences, including pure and applied mathematics
C   Mathematics and physical sciences
D   Sciences of nature and applied mathematics; specialisation in agricultural sciences is possible (D1)
E   Mathematics and technology
F1-10 Industrial subjects and applied sciences
F11   Music
G1-3   Business and commercial studies
H   Information science.

Since 1965 the examination has undergone various modifications, with the dual aims of modernising the syllabus and of lightening the load which it imposes on both students and examiners. For the majority, however, it is still a gruelling ordeal, with a high failure rate: in 1979, of the 235,558 candidates, only 155,013 (65.8%) succeeded. The pass requirement is 10 out of 20 in every subject. French (a compulsory subject) is taken at the end of the 1st class, the other subjects in the last year. Candidates with an 8-9 overall mark may take an extra oral examination and still pass; if they do not succeed at this second attempt they are awarded a consolation prize, the *Certificat de Fin d'Etudes Secondaires* (CFES).

Other streams of the three-year second cycle, with a greater industrial or technical bias, lead to a different qualification, the *brevet de technicien*. Many specialisations are possible: for example, agriculture, applied chemistry, hotel management, leather technology, musical instrument manufacture, radiology. The courses are provided either in technical *lycées*, in technical departments of the big general *lycées* or, in the case of agriculture, in one of the specialised agricultural *lycées*.

Enseignements courts

The short second cycle lasts two years or in some cases only one year, depending on the pupil's age, ability, academic record and interests. A pupil with fairly decided ideas about his future vocation may, if he has already started on a CAP course in the first cycle, complete it in an LEP. Alternatively, if he has not yet started on his vocational training, he can take a complete two-year craft course in an LEP leading to a *Brevet d'Etudes Professionnelles* (BEP). Both the CAP and the less narrowly-specialised BEP are recognised for entry to jobs in industry and commerce.

There are various options open to the pupil who wishes to give up full time schooling after the end of the first cycle.

If he is 16 or over, he can simply start looking for a job. If he wishes to acquire a skill or qualification, he can either sign a two-year contract or apprenticeship, preparing for a CAP with a course in an apprentice training centre interspersed with work in industry, etc. (for which he receives a basic salary), or sign a contract of *emploi-formation* (for which the normal minimum age is 17) of at least six months. In this case he is employed and paid by a firm and is guaranteed certain training, either within the firm or at an outside training centre.

Technical and Vocational

As shown above, this all comes within the school system, but at all levels there is contact between the school and the outside industrial and commercial world. In brief:

(i) *Basic level* (semi-skilled jobs):
The first secondary cycle followed by apprenticeship or a contract of *emploi-formation*
(ii) *Middle level* (skilled):
The first secondary cycle followed by completion of the CAP course or a two-year BEP course
(iii) *Higher levels:*
The first secondary cycle followed by a long second cycle course leading to a *baccalauréat* or *brevet de technicien*. This may be followed by a two-year more specialised course in a technical *lycée* leading to a *Brevet de Technicien Supérieur* (BTS), or by an appropriate course of higher education.

Guidance and Counselling

In every school there are advisory councils, including the *conseil d'établissement* (school council) and the *conseil de classe* (class council), both of which include elected representatives of parents and pupils. (There are several rival national organisations of parents of children in State schools, the two most influential being respectively secular left wing and Roman Catholic.) At the end of the 3rd class the school, together with the pupil and the parents and aided by a trained guidance counsellor, decides on the future 'orientation' of the pupil. The actual decision is taken by the appropriate *conseil de classe* but the parents can if they wish contest the decision. An elaborate record system, computerised, is maintained for each pupil throughout his or her school career; the amount of personal information which this record should contain has recently been a controversial issue.

Private Schools

The system described in detail above is that provided by the State. About 15% of pupils, a high proportion by European standards are, however, educated in private schools, 95% of whom are Roman Catholics. The essential difference between Church and State schools is, of course, that the former are confessional, the latter secular; as all examinations are State controlled, the curriculum in the Church schools, given the religious bias in some subjects, resembles that in comparable State schools.

Third Level (Higher) Institutions

The French higher education system, already unusually complex by normal European standards, has during the last decade undergone radical reforms. The universities have suffered a complete overhaul of their structure, and alongside them new types of institution have been created; only the *Grandes Ecoles* have remained more or less untouched. Certain features are common to the whole system:

(i) The State has a monopoly of the right to confer degrees (under the law of 1880, confirmed in the *Loi d'Orientation* of 1968)

(ii) Higher education in State institutions, though not free, is provided at a low cost to students: the fees for enrolment, examinations, use of libraries and laboratories, and presentation of a thesis are of nominal amounts. Students must also pay medical, insurance and social security contributions. The fees for private institutions are higher

(iii) Students who can prove financial need may receive grants or scholarships from the rector of the relevant academy, from private donors or foundations, from the State or from the municipal council of a university city. The proportion of students receiving direct grants is low. At some *Grandes Ecoles* and other establishments, students are paid a salary. Subsidised restaurants and lodgings are generally provided.

Universities

The *Loi d'Orientation* of 12 November 1968 transformed the university system. Plans for reform had been under consideration for some years, and a new degree structure was implemented in 1966, but the need for more thorough revision was dramatically shown by the unrest in the universities culminating in the 'events' of May 1968. The law substituted for the Napoleonic *Université* and the small number of traditional universities created in the 1890s, with their constituent faculties, a much larger number of 'public scientific and cultural establishments having legal status and financial autonomy'. Each of these universities comprises several *Unités d'Enseignement et de Recherche* (UERs), partly based on the old faculties, which have academic and administrative but not financial independence. There are some 80 institutions of university status comprising over 700 UERs. There are 13 separate universities in the Paris area alone, and three each in some other cities, such as Grenoble, Lyon, Montpellier, and Lille. The university at Compiègne, opened in 1973, stands apart from the others in being a technological institution. The universities vary in size from the huge establishments in Paris (several with over 25,000 students) to Valenciennes with about 1,600 students.

A holder of the *baccalauréat* is at present entitled to claim admission to a university, to a discipline relevant to the branch of studies in which the *baccalauréat* was taken. There is no *numerus clausus* for admission to the first year, except at the university at Compiègne (though, unofficially, some universities in great demand such as Paris also limit entry). From 1974, however, entry to the 2nd year of medical studies has been restricted, because of the serious overcrowding in medical schools. The examination at the end of the first year is competitive, not merely qualifying, in order to relate the number admitted to the number of posts available in the hospitals for students. Similar restrictions have been applied since 1975 to studies in pharmacy.

The degree structure in the arts, law, economics and sciences, reformed by a law of June 1966, was left unaltered by the *Loi d'Orientation* but the first cycle was altered in 1973. Briefly, there are three cycles, followed by higher degrees:

First Cycle:
Two years of studies leading to the *Diplôme d'Etudes Universitaires Générales* (DEUG). This multidisciplinary diploma replaced the former *Diplôme Universitaire d'Etudes Littéraires* (DUEL) and *Diplôme d'Etudes Scientifiques* (DUES) in the academic year 1973/74.

Second Cycle:
There are two degrees, the *licence*, taken one year after the DEUG, and the *maîtrise* (two years). Students can go straight to the *maîtrise*, which often entails specific training for a profession, including a compulsory practical period outside the university. Both degrees are normally made up of a number of different *unités de valeur* (credits).

Third Cycle:
Research in preparation for the *doctorat de 3ème cycle*, taken at least two years after the *maîtrise* and for other degrees and diplomas including the *Diplôme d'Etudes Supérieures Spécialisées* (DESS), which follows a one-year course of training directly related to a profession. At the end of the first year of research for a doctorate, students who have made satisfactory progress are awarded the *Diplôme d'Etudes Approfondies* (DEA).

Above the third cycle doctorate there is a higher degree, the *doctorat d'état ès lettres et sciences humaines*, awarded to candidates who have defended a thesis (or a principal and a subsidiary thesis), or who have presented a corpus of original work of high quality. A period of five years must normally elapse between registration and presentation; many university teachers take longer to finish their theses. In other disciplines the degree structure varies: in medicine, the system for which is under review, the second cycle lasts four years followed by one year of internship and leads to the *doctorat de médicine*. In dentistry and pharmacy there is a five-year course leading to a State diploma. In all disciplines the *doctorat d'état* may be awarded.

The keynotes of the 1968 law are 'autonomy, participation, multidisciplinarity'.

(i) The autonomy of the universities is greater than it used to be. Article 19 enables universities to determine their teaching activities, research programmes, teaching methods, and within limits, their procedures for evaluating students' knowledge and aptitudes. The apparent conflict between this and the fact that the State awards all degrees has been countered by a compromise system, first tried out in the academic year 1972/73. Under this degrees are still national but the common regulations are limited to such matters as entrance requirements, length of course, minimum content of course, teachers' qualifications and, where relevant, the balance between theory and practice. Each individual establishment is free, within these limits, to determine how a course should be taught and the students examined, and what optional subjects should be added. In financial matters also universities have more freedom than hitherto; a global sum is allocated to each establishment by the Ministry, based on the university's own estimate of its needs and on advice given by the *Conseil National de l'Enseignement Supérieur et de la Recherche*. The university then allocates the necessary sums to its constituent UERs. Its accounts, which must be published, are subject to audit by government financial bodies.

(ii) Participation means in effect the sharing of responsibility within universities between teachers, of all ranks, administrative and research staff and students. In the aftermath of May 1968 students were promised parity with staff in university councils, and Article 13 of the Law provides for this; but in practice the rules governing the election of student representatives have resulted in a much lower proportion of students. The politically active minority of students have refused to vote; an apathetic majority have not bothered to do so.

(iii) Multidisciplinarity has been achieved only to a limited extent: some of the UERs are organised on traditional faculty lines and narrow specialisation still widely exists. The growth of new disciplines and the breaking down of the barriers between some of the older subjects, especially in the sciences have, however, resulted (as in other countries) in the creation of departments on new lines and new degree courses, particularly for the *maîtrise*.

Grandes Ecoles

These institutions are probably unique; in no other higher educational system are there institutions which as a group enjoy their peculiar prestige. The term has never been officially defined, so that one cannot state precisely how many there are. Broadly speaking, there are some 150, of which about 30, mainly in or near Paris, have the highest prestige. This select group includes the *Ecole Polytechnique* founded in 1794, which has an unusual blend of military and engineering education, the *Ecoles Normales Supérieures* and the *Ecole Nationale d'Administration:* all of them training grounds for the highest posts in public life. Some, such as the *Ecole Nationale Supérieure des Ponts et Chaussées*, date from the eighteenth century; many were founded during the scientific and technological revolution of the nineteenth century; others are post-war foundations, including the *Ecole Nationale d'Administration* (ENA), created in 1945 to train administrators and 'technocrats'. Their graduates occupy most of the seats of power in French life, especially in government and industry. All of the *Grandes Ecoles* are specialist institutions preparing students for senior posts in particular professions: for example, the *Ecoles Normales Supérieures* (teaching in *lycées* and research), *Ecole Nationale Supérieure des Mines, ENS des Télécommunications*. Most have a scientific or technological specialism. Many of them are controlled and financed by other ministries, for example, those for defence, agriculture, finance, transport. Plans to bring them into closer contact with the rest of the higher education system have so far failed, largely because of the influence which they can bring to bear.

Entrance, particularly to the select group mentioned above, is highly competitive. For the majority a candidate must normally follow a two- or three-year course after the *baccalauréat*, in special classes *(cours préparatoires)* run by *lycées* and then take a competitive entrance examination. These courses are of a high intellectual level and demand much stamina and application. The *Ecole Normale Supérieure* for men in Paris usually accepts only one in eight of those who compete. A few, such as the ENA, are post-graduate institutions. At the engineering *Grandes Ecoles* the course of study lasts three years, with a strong theoretical bias, and leads to the *diplôme d'ingénieur* (engineering diploma). No higher academic qualification is available; a graduate who wished to continue in research would transfer to a university to prepare for a *doctorat de 3ème cycle* and is exempt from the first year of study for this. Courses at other *Grandes Ecoles* vary in length from one year to three, and lead to diplomas or certificates.

Instituts Universitaires de Technologie (IUTs)

These institutions, of which the first were founded in 1966, have precisely defined aims: to provide scientific and technical training adapted to contemporary needs. Their functions imply a narrower specialisation than that of the professional engineer but a wider education than that of the technician; they demand an adequate mastery of the means of expression and communication and the capacity to adapt oneself to an environment in a constant state of evolution. The courses last two years and lead to a national qualification, the *Diplôme Universitaire de Technologie* (DUT). The IUTs, of which there are over 60, cover between them the following range of disciplines: applied sciences, engineering, (civil, electrical, mechanical, etc.), information science, social work, public and business administration, commerce and public relations. Each IUT constitutes a UER of the university with which it is linked.

Other Higher Institutions

There are many other institutions recognised by the State, some privately owned, such as the Catholic Institute of Paris, where students prepare for State degrees and diplomas and also for degrees recognised by the Holy See. The following should be particularly mentioned:

(i) *Instituts Nationaux Polytechniques,* of which there are three, in Grenoble, Nancy and Toulouse. Founded in 1970 under the 1968 law, their admission requirements and courses are similar to those of the engineering *Grandes Ecoles.*

(ii) *Instituts Nationaux de Sciences Appliquées* (INSA). The INSA, of which there are also three, in Lyon, Rennes and Toulouse, were set up by the government to train engineers and to carry out research. They provide a five-year ncourse and are selective to the extent that entrants coming straight from school must have one of the science or technical *baccalauréats* and are interviewed before selection. (there is provision for later entry, after the 1st cycle of two years.) The *diplôme d'ingénieur INSA* to which the course leads, ranks with the *diplôme* of the *Grandes Ecoles* in similar disciplines.

(iii) *Ecoles Nationales Supérieures d'Ingénieurs* Higher engineering schools forming specialist UERs of universities but ranking with the *Grandes Ecoles* and having similar entry conditions.

(iv) Business Schools with varying titles, such as the *Ecole des Hautes Etudes Commerciales* in Paris and the *Ecoles Supérieures de Commerce et d'administration des Entreprises* (ESCAE) in several large cities, which rank as *Grandes Ecoles*. There are also many other schools of lower ranking, public and private.

(v) *Education in the Arts*. Various establishments under the control of the Ministry of Culture, providing courses in the fine arts, dancing, music, etc.

There is also a group of eminent *grands établissements* performing special functions: for example the *Collège de France*, founded in 1530, the *Ecole Pratique des Hautes Etudes* and the *Fondation Nationale des Sciences Politiques*, centres of post-graduate education and research at the highest level.

Coordinating Bodies

The *Conseil National de l'Enseignement Supérieur et de la Recherche* was created in 1971, as one of the last stages of the implementation of the 1968 Law. It has 90 members serving a three-year term, 60 representing the universities and other higher establishments, including students, and 30 persons nominated by the Secretary of State, representing major national interests, including members of parliament, trade unionists and administrators. It has sub-commissions, one of which is responsible for examining research programmes of universities etc. and teaching and examining in the 3rd cycle. The council advises the minister on the allocation of funds to universities but has no real power: it was recently stated in a university journal that in the eight years 1971-79 the minister accepted its advice in less than 20% of cases.

There are various other university coordinating bodies, notably the *Conférence des Présidents d'Universités*. This body was not provided for in the 1968 Act but proved in practice, with the new conditions, to be necessary. The president of a university is elected for a term (not immediately renewable) of five years by the university council, which includes representatives of teaching staff, administrators and students. He must normally be a titular professor, holding a Chair in the university. The *Office National des Universités et Ecoles Françaises* is concerned *inter alia* with the recruitment of *lecteurs* and *assistants* to work abroad. It also publishes information about courses for foreign students in French Universities. The *Comité Consultatif des Universités*, concerned with staff matters, was replaced by a *Conseil Supérieur des Corps Universitaires*.

Teacher Training and Qualification

The training system for school teachers is complex and widely regarded as unsatisfactory. The system of initial training varies with the type of school being prepared for, and in France the distinctions between the various programmes are clear and strong and are reflected in the social status and pay of the teachers. The *professeurs* at *lycées*, especially those in the top ranks who are *agrégés* enjoy a high status in society; the standing of primary school teachers (known as *instituteurs*), who in the nineteenth century were regarded as important local functionaries, has declined, but attempts are being made to improve it. There is therefore a continual pressure among teachers to improve their (paper) qualifications and hence their pay and status. For this complex hierarchy of teaching staffs in schools is reflected in an equally complicated salary structure, in which the aristocrats of the profession, the *agrégés*, receive much the highest rates on national civil service scales.

Pre-School and First Level Teachers

The system of training pre-primary and primary school teachers in the *Ecoles Normales* is being revised. Since 1972 students have been recruited by competitive examination after they have taken the *baccalauréat*. Until 1978, students had taken a two-year course of professional training at the end of which they were awarded a *Certificat de Fin d'Etudes Normales* (CFEN), which also qualified them for the *Certificat d'Aptitude Pédagogique* (CAP) necessary for teaching in a State school. From the entry *(rentrée)* of 1979 the training course will last three years after the *baccalauréat*, culminating in a *diplôme d'enseignement supérieur* as well as the CAP. There have until now been two *Ecoles Normales* in each department, for men and women respectively; henceforth there will be one only.

Second Level Teachers

Teachers for the first cycle of secondary education hold one of a variety of qualifications, according to the type of subject which they teach. The staff of a former *collège d'enseignement secondaire* were required to have either a *Certificat d'Aptitude au Professorat de l'Enseignement Public du Second Degré* (CAPES), or a *Cert. d'A. au Professorat de Collège d'Enseignement Général* (CAPEGC), which was also the qualification for teaching in a college of that designation. With the abolition of streaming in the *collège unique* a CAPES became the general qualification. Those who acquire it are entitled to be called *professeurs*. Candidates for this certificate must hold a *licence d'enseignement* in the appropriate discipline. This licence may be acquired either at a university or in one of the specialist *Instituts Préparatoires aux Enseignements de Second Degré* (IPES). The CAPES examination is in two parts, theory and practice; the latter is taken after professional training lasting one year. The number of successful candidates is restricted by the Ministry, in accordance with the number of posts available; in 1978 only 1,576 out of 27,229 candidates were accepted.

Teachers in the *lycées* i.e. the long second cycle of secondary education, are also called *professeurs*. The majority are holders of the CAPES; a minority (less than a quarter) hold the higher qualification of *agrégation*. Candidates for this must have either the appropriate *licence d'enseignement* and the pre-1966 diploma of higher studies (DES) or (since 1966) the appropriate *maîtrise*. The one-year course of preparation for this stiff competitive examination, passed in 1978 by only about 8% of the candidates (674 out of 8,350), is provided in one of the seven *Ecoles Normales Supérieures*, an IPES, or can be taken by correspondence. Holders of the CAPES may enter for the examination, without further training. An *agrégé* has a lighter teaching load than a *professeur certifié*, as well as a higher salary. (Many *agrégés* do not teach in schools; in 1963, for example, 400 of the 1,000 new *agrégés* took up university posts or CNRS research assignments.)

There are specialist courses of training and certificates for teachers of technical subjects, physical education, etc. There are also various categories of assistant teachers – *maîtres auxiliaires* – a source of much discontent. Teachers for the short second cycle are trained in a variety of ways according to the subjects which they teach.

Higher Education Teachers

Teachers in higher education receive no formal professional training, but there are minimum qualifications laid down for each grade, varying according to discipline. In universities the principal grades are at present, in descending order:

Professors and *maîtres de conférences*, who teach, supervise research and often have administrative responsibilities (from 1979 the latter grade is to be abolished; the holders will become professors)

Maîtres-assistants who teach, supervise students and carry on their personal research

Assistants who supervise students in their studies and practical work while working for their own doctorates.

To become a professor, in the arts or sciences, a candidate must be at least 30, hold a *doctorat d'état* and have taught for at least two years in a university or comparable institution. *Maîtres-assistants* are recruited from among the holders of *doctorats de 3ème cycle* or the *agrégation*. In law, medicine and pharmacy there are equally, or in some cases more, stringent requirements. The new *Conseil Supérieur des Corps Universitaires* will have wide responsibilities in the recruitment and promotion of university staff.

Adult and 'Recurrent'

Until the late 1960s, the adult education provision was mainly limited to vocational training or retraining schemes, organised by the Ministry of Labour or of Education. Training courses were run under the auspices of the Ministry of Labour, by the *Association Nationale pour la Formation Professionelle des Adultes* (AFPA). The Ministry of Education's responsibility was exercised primarily through the *Conservatoire National des Arts et Métiers*

(CNAM) founded in 1819. This institution, which has over 36 outposts, runs lecture courses and practical training in science, technology, economics, and human sciences, mostly in evening classes. Various diplomas are available. There are many voluntary organisations with official support, such as *Peuple et Culture*, which also promote courses for adults.

In the past the universities played a minor role in adult education. There were a few exceptions: Grenoble, Nancy and Vincennes led the way in opening courses to adults without the normal paper qualifications. The 1968 *Loi d'Orientation*, however, specified that permanent education was one of the fundamental concerns of the universities. Many universities now provide classes in languages, in communication and in economics and social sciences, making use of radio and, to a lesser extent, television. To cut the costs, some universities have formed regional groups, to make joint television and radio programmes. Toulouse I pioneered a new type of course in France, the *Université du Troisième Age*, aimed particularly at raising the standard of living of the retired and those preparing for retirement. It offers socio-cultural activities for the elderly. Other universities, notably Grenoble II and Nanterre, have followed its example.

The law of 16 July 1971, on continuous vocational training in the framework of permanent education, required every firm with more than ten employees to devote at least 0.8% of its salary bill to the training of its employees. Although the trade unions would like this training to include general, non-vocational education, it is almost entirely professional in type. The *Agence Nationale pour le Développement de l'Education Permanente* (ADEP) was set up in 1973 to advise industry and the Ministry of Education on the planning of courses. In 1973 1.5 million workers throughout the country received training leave for courses varying from a few days to several months. The great majority of these were white-collar and skilled workers; the aim since then has been to do much more for unskilled and unemployed workers.

7 EDUCATIONAL ADMINISTRATION

Centralised Control

In 1969 the then Minister of Education, M Guichard, described the Ministry to the OECD examiners who conducted a review of French education as "the largest administration in the world except for the Red Army". It is also the country's largest single employer: 834,000 in 1979, plus another 160,000 paid by the Ministry (over 100,000 of whom are teachers in private schools). Though the educational system, like government as a whole, is no longer so tightly controlled from the centre as it once was, the Ministries of Education and the Universities administer the whole State system, with the exception of certain institutions of higher and vocational education which come under the control of other Ministries, such as Agriculture and Defence.

Education Ministries

The Ministry of Education was reorganised in 1973 and again with the change in government in 1974 by M Rene Haby, who remained in office for four years. the major changes in 1974 were the dropping of the word *'Nationale'* from the title of the Ministry and the creation of a new *Secrétariat d'Etat aux Universités.* After the 1978 elections the latter department became a separate ministry. The central administration of the Ministry of Education now consists of nine directorates, responsible respectively for planning and coordination: pre-school and first level schools; the first cycle and the second cycle of secondary education; teaching staff in the *lycées;* administrative staff; general administration; equipment and building; and finance. There are also separate departments concerned with statistics and information (which works also for the Ministry for the Universities) and with international relations. The general inspectorate and the information service work directly to the minister, one of whose priorities is to keep the education service and the general public well informed about his policies.

The Minister for the Universities is responsible for higher education (the universities and certain *Grandes Ecoles*), the national libraries and research. Two organisations with international responsibilities come under this Ministry, the *Centre National des Oeuvres Universitaires et Scolaires.* which has regional branches and is concerned with student welfare, and the *Office National des Universités et Ecoles Françaises* which deals with the interchange of students and teachers.

Advisory Services

The two ministries are assisted by numerous advisory services. The principal advisory councils are:

(i) Le *Conseil Supérieur de l'Education Nationale* created in 1965. This comprises representatives of educational administrators, teachers, parents' and students' associations, and of private education, and individuals selected because of their special qualifications. This council is consulted and gives advice on all questions of national interest relating to education and teaching, including draft legislation.

(ii) Le *Conseil National de l'Enseignement Supérieur et de la Recherche.* set up in 1971, under the *Loi d'Orientation.*

(iii) Le *Conseil de l'Enseignement Général et Technique.* created in 1965.

CENTRAL, REGIONAL AND DEPARTMENTAL ADMINISTRATION OF EDUCATION

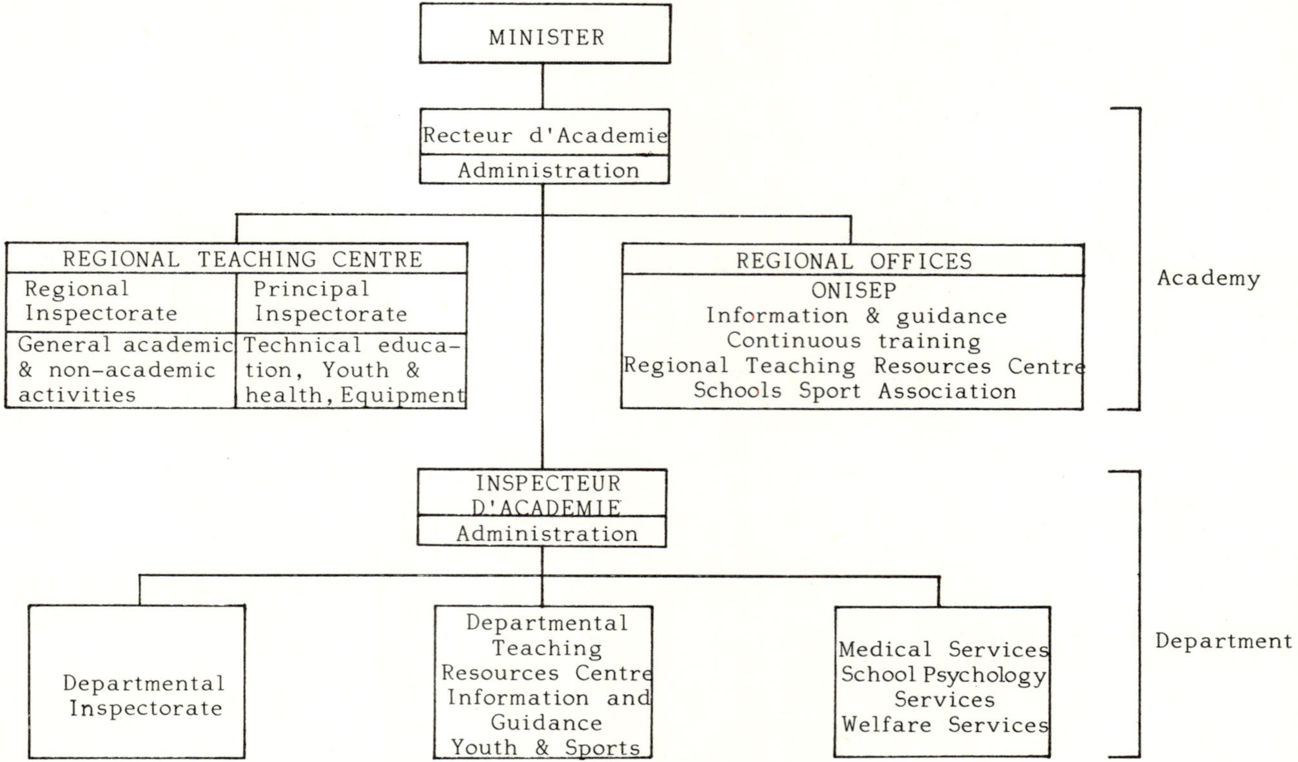

```
                              ┌──────── Academy ────────┐  ┌──── Department ────┐

              ┌──────────┐
              │ MINISTER │
              └────┬─────┘
                   │
         ┌─────────┴──────────┐                              ┌─────────────────┐
         │ Recteur d'Académie │                              │                 │
         │ Administration     │                              │   INSPECTEUR    │
         └─────────┬──────────┘                              │   D'ACADEMIE    │
                   │                                         │ Administration  │
         ┌─────────┴────────────┐                            └────────┬────────┘
         │                      │                                     │
┌────────┴──────────────┐  ┌────┴──────────────────────┐   ┌──────────┼──────────────┬─────────────────┐
│ REGIONAL TEACHING     │  │ REGIONAL OFFICES          │   │                         │                 │
│ CENTRE                │  │                           │   │ Departmental            │ Departmental    │  Medical Services
│ Regional  │ Principal │  │ ONISEP                    │   │ Inspectorate            │ Teaching        │  School Psychology
│ Inspect.  │ Inspect.  │  │ Information & guidance    │   │                         │ Resources Centre│  Services
│ General   │ Technical │  │ Continuous training       │   │                         │ Information and │  Welfare Services
│ academic  │ education,│  │ Regional Teaching         │   │                         │ Guidance        │
│ & non-    │ Youth &   │  │ Resources Centre          │   │                         │ Youth & Sports  │
│ academic  │ health,   │  │ Schools Sport Association │   │                         │                 │
│ activities│ Equipment │  │                           │   │                         │                 │
└───────────┴───────────┘  └───────────────────────────┘   └─────────────────────────┴─────────────────┘
```

Source of information: French Embassy Publication 1976

Local Administration

The external services of the two ministries are administered through 26 academies, including Paris, which has its own special organisation, and one in the Caribbean colonies. At the head of each is a rector, nominated by the President of the Republic, who, under the authority of the ministers, controls all the educational services of his academy and is a man of high academic and administrative standing. He is assisted by a permanent administration, an inspectorate and various regional advisory councils. The rectorate is increasingly becoming a decision making body, less an interpreter of orders from the centre, particularly in the organisation of education and the administration of the teaching force. At the departmental level the prefect is the head of all civil administrative services and the *inspecteur d'académie* directs the educational services, under the authority of the rector.

Inspectorate

The inspectorate works at three levels. The general inspectorate, within the ministry, has professional oversight of the whole system, and is concerned not only with pedagogical matters but also with organisation and methods. It is divided into over 15 specialist groups, each concerned with specific matters. Within each academy there is a second corps of inspectors (one for each department), who work at two levels, reporting both to the rector of the academy and to the prefect of the department on other defined matters. An *inspecteur d'académie* is an important regional functionary, the personal representative of the rector at departmental level, with delegated powers of financial control, and wide duties of inspection covering all matters except teaching staffs of *lycées* and specialist teachers in technical schools, who are inspected from Paris. He is assisted in each department by local inspectors.

Documentation and Research

The major institution is the *Centre National de la Recherche Scientifique* (CNRS), founded in 1939, which covers a very wide field, from nuclear physics to anthropology. It is funded by the government, under the Minister for the Universities, and commissions and sponsors fundamental and applied research in universities, etc., and in its own institutes and laboratories. It has close links with the universities; no important university laboratory could subsist without its financial support in the form of the provision of expensive equipment and the payment of research workers' salaries, and 70% of the research workers whom it sponsors work in university laboratories. A project for its reform (concerning particularly its relationship with the Ministry for the Universities) was being studied in July 1979.

Four other important national agencies should be mentioned. The *Agence Nationale pour le Développement de l'Education Permanente* (ADEP) was set up in 1973 to advise the government and industry on the development of continuous and recurrent vocational training. The *Centre National de Documentation Pédagogique* (CNDP) is concerned with the development of educational technology (audio-visual aids, etc., in relation to both hardware and software) and documentation for both teachers and pupils. The *Institut National de Recherche Pédagogique* (INRP) is responsible for research on the curriculum, teaching methods (except educational technology), and teacher training. The *Office National sur les Enseignements et les Professions* (ONISEP) is responsible, in conjunction with the universities, the administration and the professions, for providing information about educational facilities and professional activities; and for advising on the training of teachers responsible for educational professional guidance.

8 EDUCATIONAL FINANCE

Education Budget

The State system of education is mainly financed by the central government. Between 1948 and 1973 education's share of the national budget was doubled. In 1975, the total allocation for education, including that for the universities, which are now on a separate vote, was 18.03% of the national budget; in the budget for 1978, the total figure was 20.3%. In 1979 the budget of the Ministry of Education alone represented 15.8% of the total State budget. Salaries, of teachers and administrative staff, take up 87% of the budget.

Sources of Funds

In discussions with the OECD examiners in 1969 the French representatives pointed out "that the breakdown of the cost of educational financing between the State, the local authorities, the private sector and households was still very imperfectly known owing to the absence of adequate statistics". In particular it was difficult to assess the expenditure of communes, since the statistics available related only to the very small number with populations of over 5,000. With many reservations, the educational expenditure for 1968 was roughly estimated to be shared as follows: over 80% borne by the State; less than 10% by local authorities (e.g. in the apprenticeship tax - see below) and private households.

Apprenticeship Tax

The vocational part of the second cycle of secondary education and other forms of technical and vocational education (including studies in the *instituts universitaires de technologie*) are partly financed by the *taxe d'apprentissage*. The tax, first introduced in the Third Republic, is levied on all establishments, societies and associations carrying on industrial, commercial or artisan activities. The amount of the tax is based on a percentage of the total wages bill of the establishment etc. concerned.

Allocation of Funds

*Allocation of Funds
Expenditure on Education:
Distribution by Level*

Pre-school	First Level	Second Level	Third Level	Other
6.7	17.5	51.9	13.6	10.3

Aid to Private Schools

About 10% of the budget of the Ministry of Education goes on aid to private schools, under the Barangé and Debré Laws. The Barangé Law of 1951 permitted subsidies to be paid to private as well as State primary schools; the Debré Law of 1959 offered State aid in one of three optional forms to Church schools involving more or less assimilation into the State system. This law was renewed in 1971 and 1977; the latter modification is known as the *Loi Guermeur*. By far the largest proportion of this aid is spent on teachers' salaries and the conditions of service of teachers in private schools (pensions, tenure, etc.) are gradually being brought into line with those of State teachers. There are now two principal forms of contract with the State: the *contrat simple*, under which teachers are paid by the State while parents and others pay for the running of the school; and the *contrat d'association*, which brings the school much closer to the State system, involving financial, administrative and in many cases pedagogic control as a result of greater subsidisation. It is claimed that the effect of this State aid has been to raise overall standards in private education.

9 DEVELOPMENT AND PLANNING OF THE EDUCATIONAL SYSTEM

Origins

The roots of French education may be traced in ancient Gaul where, according to tradition, the sons of the aristocracy were educated by the Druids, and then in the Roman system, influenced by Hellenist ideals. By the Middle Ages the Church, as elsewhere, had a near monopoly which survived for several centuries, though after the religious wars of the sixteenth century the Protestants were allowed to found schools. For about 200 years, the Jesuits, with their authoritarian ideas and subservience to Rome, were predominant. Their position was, however, challenged and finally destroyed by the liberalising influence of the great French philosophers: first the Humanists (Montaigne, Descartes and Pascal) and later Voltaire and the other men of the eighteenth century Enlightenment. These men brought into French education those characteristics which are at once its finest glory and a source of weakness: the concept of *culture générale*, a schooling, traditionally based on literature and the humanities, which will enable the recipient to attain that wisdom which is an essential of civilised life; and an emphasis on training in the art of rational, objective thinking - *l'art de bien penser*. Such an education can only be for the elect, the children of the aristocracy (whether of position or of achievement). By the end of the eighteenth century, schools and universities providing this type of education were well established; but the great mass of children were receiving only the most elementary instruction, in the rudiments of the Three Rs and religion, in schools provided locally by parishes and charitable institutions.

The Revolution to Napoleon

The French Revolution brought utterly new ideas. The reformer Condorcet, inspired by the philosophy of Jean-Jacques Rousseau, laid down the principles which have continued to guide later reformers. Education was a right to which all were entitled: it would be free, provided by the State, lay-controlled, and available equally to boys and girls. Primary schools providing compulsory four-year courses were to be set up, and the higher schools were to offer a much wider choice of studies, according to natural aptitudes. Some progress was made in implementing these principles, but there was too little time before the advent of Napoleon Bonaparte, who rejected all except one of them: that education should be provided by the State. Napoleon's aim was the negation of those of the Revolution: to train select cadres to carry out his ambitious designs. For this purpose he founded *lycées* in the principal towns and new institutions of higher education. The structure which he created, being rational and soundly based, survived until the present time. He combined the whole of the education system in *l'Université Imperiale*, a secular corporation under the control of one sole authority, assisted by an advisory council. To aid administration the country was divided into a number of academies, each controlled by a rector nominated by and responsible to the central authority. These academies and the rectorates still exist, although the *Université* was dissolved in the reforms of the 1960s.

Nineteenth Century

Between the end of Napoleon's Empire and the birth of the Third Republic, the educational system varied with the political fluctuations of the day: the pendulum swung between the elitist and the egalitarian concepts. Some progress was achieved in the period between 1830 and 1848, followed by reaction, typified by the Falloux Law of 1850, which restored the dominance of the church. The Third Republic built on the ideals of Condorcet and laid the foundations of the present system: a basis of free primary education, obligatory from 6 to 13 and neutral in religion; normal schools for the training of teachers; nursery schools for the 3-6 year olds; and, from 1880 onwards, a system of technical education. At the end of the century a law to reconcile the conflict in education between the classical ideal and modern needs was passed: in the secondary schools two different courses were given equal status, both leading in two cycles to a single *baccalauréat* with different options. Thus for the first time the concept of a change of course during the school career was introduced. The 17 universities which came under *l'Université* were reorganised in the 1890s into faculties of letters, sciences and law. Private universities (i.e. Catholic institutions) were also given liberty to teach, but in 1880 a law giving the State the sole right to grant degrees was passed.

Twentieth Century

In the period from 1914 to 1939 various attempts were made to rationalise and reform the primary, secondary and higher education systems, which had developed independently, but they were hampered by doctrinal conflicts, political weakness and financial stringency. World War Two brought new problems to be solved at the end of hostilities. Many school buildings had been destroyed, there was a shortage of teachers and equipment, and there was the astonishing rise in the birth rate. The Langevin-Wallon commission, set up in 1944 to advise on the planning of post-war education, made far-reaching proposals for reform. Not much, however, was achieved in practice, though 1946 saw the beginning of the *classes nouvelles:* experimental, child-centred teching methods, initiated by a group of teachers with official support. One of General de Gaulle's first measures when he became President was to initiate actual measures for reform based on the following principles, still declared to be valid:

(i) democratisation of education
(ii) adaptation of education to individual aptitudes
(iii) adaptation of education to the modern world
(iv) pedagogic renewal.

The following year, 1959, was a landmark in the development of French education; many changes were then implemented or started. Their outcome is seen in the description of the present system.

Church and State

Nowhere else in western Europe was there such a long and bitter struggle between Church and State for the control of education. French Catholicism, like so much of French thinking, is informed by rational intellectual principles; it is therefore a particularly tenacious opponent, unwilling to compromise. The conflict started even before the French Revolution, and a truce has been achieved only since World War Two.

Napoleon's creation of the Imperial University gave the State a monopoly of education, except for seminaries for priests. The Guizot Law (1833) and the Falloux Law (1850) restored freedom to private education, which in practice meant the right of the Catholics to run their own schools. During the Third Republic there was a struggle between the Church and the republican parties; in the 1880s, for example, laws were passed, against fierce opposition, confirming the secular nature of State schools and forbidding members of religious orders to teach in State schools. The Dreyfus affair exacerbated anti-clerical feelings, and by 1903 there was a widespread demand for the separation of Church and State. In 1905, 13,000 Catholic schools wre closed, on the abrogation of a Concordat with the Vatican; many were later privately reopened by parents' associations. Between the two World Wars, the issue was not so burning, though it was briefly revived during the Vichy régime. Since World War Two, the point at issue has been mainly financial, turning on the amount of aid which private schools should receive from the State. The Barangé Law was passed in 1951, but the Catholic schools continued to find it difficult to meet their costs. After much heated political debate, the then Prime Minister, M Debré, forced through a Bill in 1959, with the active help of President de Gaulle, which (though since modified in 1971 and 1977) governs the present relationship. The private schools are still strong, but their position is again under challenge from the left. The Socialist Party campaigned in 1978 for the withdrawal of State aid from confessional schools and some Socialist local councils are threatening to put this policy into practice, so far as the law permits.

Educational Planning

The *Commissariat Général du Plan* initiated by M Monnet has a subsidiary commission which has been responsible since 1951 for planning the development of education within the context of the National Plan. Until recently this has been limited to quantitative matters, including forecasting the investment to be made, even where educational reform has been involved. For the VIth Plan (1971-75) wider terms were drawn up. Efforts were to concentrate on completing a number of pedagogical policies already decided on, and secondly on preparing for future reforms, covering *inter alia* the provision of schooling for almost all 4 year olds and all 5 year olds; the reform of French and mathematics teaching in elementary education; an estimated increase of numbers in the first cycle of secondary education; various improvements in the second cycle of secondary education; higher engineering education; agricultural education; and teacher training. The education provisions of the VIIth Plan were concerned mainly with the contribution that the education system would make towards reducing social inequalities and improving the employment situation.

An outstanding feature of the planning to date has been the *carte scolaire*. This term is used in two senses: the descriptive sense of a geographical inventory of existing educational establishments, and the forecasting sense of the planned distribution of new establishments according to the estimated demand for places. It is promulgated by the Ministry of Education, on the basis of plans drawn up at departmental, regional and national level.

The Ministry of Education has remained in full control of general educational policy, in cooperation with the planning commissariat, and implements the plans.

10 THE SYSTEM IN OPERATION

Educational Objectives

The traditional major objectives of the French system have been touched on above. On the one hand, there is the aim of providing the pupil with the essential *culture générale*. Though the pressures of modern life have perforce modified this traditional concept of the curriculum, it still pervades the French system. For example, an official French statement in 1973 on objectives in upper secondary education said that: "the concept of culture remains the foundation of the educational system to be established. Any modern definition of culture implies. . . a good grounding in science. . . opportunities for methodical development of the means of expression and of the capacities for intellectual and artistic perception (and) an insight into the realities of the contemporary world."* The other major objective of French education, as first defined by the leaders of the Revolution, is enshrined in the Constitution. Under the 1946 Constitution, confirmed in 1958, "the nation guarantees the equal access of children and adults to instruction, vocational training and culture. The organisation of state education, which is free and non-denominational, is a duty of the state". The system has sought to guarantee equality through its emphasis on uniform standards, centralised administration, and national examinations. The 'freedom' of education makes it possible for the State system to coexist with private establishments which can receive aid from the State. There is thus a dichotomy in the objectives of the French system. On the one hand there is the traditional curriculum, inevitably suitable only for the academic minority; on the other there is the egalitarian principle. The clash between these two contradictory concepts has been one cause of the periodic stresses and strains which have affected French education.

In the twentieth century, and particularly since World War Two, succeeding governments with the support of the French nation, have declared the democratisation of education to be one of their main objectives. It is realised that the traditional

---

* Paper on 'Problems and Pressures in Education Policy' for the Standing Conference of European Ministers of Education, 1973.

system can no longer serve the needs of a modern industrial democracy. The aim is now to achieve a system of *éducation permanente* – one designed to meet the educational and cultural needs of every person in accordance with his abilities throughout his life.

FURTHER READING

Ardagh, J. (1977). *The New France: A Society in Transition, 1945-1977*. 3rd edition, Penguin Books, London.
Aron, R. (1969). *The Elusive Revolution: Anatomy of a Student Revolt*. Pall Mall, London.
CNOUS (annual). *Je vais en France* (a guide for foreign students). Paris.
Coveney, J. and Kempa, S. (1978). *Guide to French Institutions*. Harrap, London.
Cros, L. (1961). *L'Explosion Scolaire*. Paris Comité Universitaire d'Information Pédagogique. (English translation: *Explosion in the Schools*. Sevpen, Paris.)
Doucet, L. (1973). *The Engineers' Training in France*. French Embassy, London.
Fraser, W. R. (1971). *Reforms and Restraints in Modern French Education*. Routledge & Kegan Paul, London.
Halls, W. D. (1976). *Education, Culture and Politics in Modern France*. Pergamon Press, Oxford.
King, E. J. (1973). *Other Schools and Ours*. 4th edition. Holt, Rinehart & Winston, London.
Majault, J. (1973). *L'Enseignement en France*. McGraw-Hill, London.
Ministere de l'Education (1977). *La réforme du système éducatif français*. Paris.
OECD (1971). *Reviews of National Policies for Education: France*. OECD, Paris.
OECD (1973). *Economic Surveys: France*. OECD, Paris.
Prost, A. (1968). *Histoire de l'Enseignement en France, 1800-1927*. Colin, Paris.
UNESCO/IBE (1980). *International Yearbook of Education XXXII*. Unesco, Paris.

Laws: Decrees

Institut Pédagogique National (1961). *La Réforme de L'enseignement*. Imprimerie Nationale, Paris.
'University Reform in France' (1969). *Minerva*, 7, No. 4, Summer 1969, pp.706-727.

Structure of the Education System in France

Age	3	4	5	6	7	8	9	10	11	12	13	14	15	16	17	18	19	20	21	22	23	24
Level					I						II					III					IV	
Stage				1	2	3	4	5	6	7												
Compulsory																						
School Type			*Ecole Elémentaire*					General Secondary / Obs. / Guid.			Short / *Lycée*		University / Higher Institutions								

▨ Education preceding the first level

Examinations: the *baccalauréat* is taken after stage 7

Source: UNESCO/IBE International Yearbook of Education

Compulsory Education: Age Limits 6–16 Duration (years) 10
Entrance age to pre-school education: 3

337

FRANCE BASIC STATISTICS		1960	1970	1975	1978 (approx.)
1	Total population (000)	45,684	50,669	52,913	53,371
	% female	51	51	51	51
2	% population 0-14 years	26.4	24.8		24.0
	% female	49	49	49	49
3	Enrolment, all levels	8,384,734	10,022,295	10,514,278	10,710,979
	% female				
	First level	5,821,500	4,939,683	4,601,550	4,647,552
	% female	49	49		48
	Second level	2,279,900	4,281,446	4,874,152	4,976,489
	% female	52	51		51
	Third level	283,334	801,156	1,038,576	1,086,938
	% female			48	49
4	Teachers, all levels				
	% female				
	First level	170,555	184,326	256,781	230,634
	% female	65		65	67
	Second level	87,603	270,949	306,718	358,916
	% female		40		54
	Third level	8,078			
	% female				
5	Public expenditure on education:				
	Total (000) francs	7,194,167	38,386,800	80,475,045	108,150,500
	As % of GNP	2.4	4.7	5.6	5.8
6	% enrolment (MF) by level	100	100	100	100
	First level	69	49	44	43
	Second level	27	43	46	46
	Third level	3	8	10	11
	% enrolment (F) by level	100	100	100	100
	First level				42
	Second level				48
	Third level				10
7	Entrance age : Duration of				
	First level education	6:5	6:5	6:5	6:5
	Second level education	11:7	11:7	11:7	11:7
8	Enrolment ratios (MF)				
	First level	144	117	109	112
	Second level	46	75	85	83
	Third level	9.83	19.50	24.29	24.42
	Enrolment ratios (F)				
	First level	143	117		111
	Second level	48	77		87
	Third level			23.75	24.73

GUIDE TO FRENCH ABBREVIATIONS IN COMMON USE

ADEP	Agence nationale pour le développement de l'éducation permanente
AFPA	Association nationale pour la formation professionelle des adultes
BEP	Brevet d'études professionelles
BEPC	Brevet d'études du premier cycle
BTS	Brevet de technicien supérieur
CAP (1)	Certificat d'aptitude professionelle
CAP (2)	Certificat d'aptitude pédagogique
CAPES	Certificat d'aptitude au professorat de l'enseignement public du second degré
CAPET	Certificat d'aptitude au professorat de l'enseignement technique
CAPEGC	Certificat d'aptitude au professorat d'enseignement de collège général
CEG	Collège d'enseignement général
CEP	Certificat d'études professionelles
CES	Collège d'enseignement secondaire
CET	Collège d'enseignement technique
CFEN	Certificat de fin d'études normales
CFES	Certificat de fin d'études secondaires
CNAM	Conservatoire national des arts et métiers
CNDP	Centre national de documentation pédagogique
CNESR	Conseil national de l'enseignement supérieur et de la recherche
CNOUS	Centre national des oeuvres universitaires et scolaires
CNRS	Centre national de la recherche scientifique
DEA	Diplôme d'études approfondies
DES	Diplôme d'études supérieures
DESS	Diplôme d'études supérieures specialisées
DEUG	Diplôme d'études universitaires générales
DUEL	Diplôme universitaire d'études littéraires
DUES	Diplôme universitaire d'études scientifiques
DUT	Diplôme universitaire de technologie
ENA	Ecole nationale d'administration
ENS (1)	Ecole nationale supérieure
ENS (2)	Ecole normale supérieure
FEN	Féderation de l'éducation nationale
INSA	Institut national de sciences appliquées
INRP	Institut national de recherche pédagogique
IPES	Institut préparatoire aux enseignements de second degré
IPN	Institut pédagogique national
IUT	Institut universitaire de technologie
LEP	Lycée d'enseignement professionel
ONISEP	Office national sur les enseignements et les professions
ONUEF	Office national des universités et écoles françaises
SFA	Service de la formation administrative
SNE	Syndicat national des enseignants de second degré
SNESup	Syndicat national de l'enseignement supérieur
SNI	Syndicat national des instituteurs
UER	Unité d'enseignement et de recherche

Greece

CONTENTS

1 Geography 342
2 Population 344
3 Society and Culture 345
4 History and Politics 346
5 The Economy 349
6 The Education System 351
7 Educational Administration 358
8 Educational Finance 361
9 Development and Planning of the Educational
   System 362
10 The System in Operation 363

The achievements of classical Greece still inform debates about the content of education in modern Greece. In most of these debates appeals are made to preserve Greek culture through the study of classical literature and the retention of the classical Greek language. The medium of instruction in first level schools is the language of common speech *(demotiki)*, but its position has been contentious, and the formal literary dialect *(katharevousa)* is the language of instruction in second level schools. The importance of classical Greek is reflected in the number of lessons per week devoted to it in the lower and upper stages of second level education in the general and technical schools.

The extent to which these classical traditions have inhibited reform may account for the dissatisfaction expressed by parents and students who would like to see the content of education modified. The demand for technological and technical training and the growing interest in modern languages, especially English, represent some of the pressures to reform education to meet the requirements of modern life.

Post Second World War politics, a succession of weak governments after the death in 1964 of King Paul, the Cyprus conflicts, (the call for independence by the Greek Cypriots was associated with 'Union with Greece' and the Hellenisation of the Cypriot schools' curriculum) and periods of non-parliamentary government all contributed to the relatively slow pace of educational reform.

The Constitution of 1975 clearly stated that the aims of education were: the ethical, intellectual, vocational and physical training of the population; the development of national and religious identity; and the creation of self-sufficient and responsible citizens. The spoken language of the people - demotic Greek - was made the official language of instruction in 1976.

The Editor

1 GEOGRAPHY

Topography

After substantial adjustments of her territorial boundaries during the present century, mainland Greece now covers an area of 107,194 sq km (41,883 square miles) of continental Europe, bounded to the east by Turkey, to the north by Bulgaria and Yugoslavia, and to the north west by Albania. An additional 24,804 sq km (9,688 square miles) is accounted for by her myriad islands in the Ionian Sea to the west, the Sea of Crete to the south, and the Aegean Sea to the east. The largest island is Crete. Many of the Dodecanese (ceded to Greece by Italy in 1947) and other Greek islands of the eastern Aegean are only a few miles from the Turkish mainland of Asia Minor. Mountains, rising in places to over 2,695 metres (9,000 feet) cover most of the mainland both north and south of the Gulf of Corinth, which cuts the country almost in two. The islands too are mountainous, although Crete and the larger islands of the Ionian Sea have considerable areas of fertile land unlike the barren and rocky Cyclades of the Aegean Sea. There are no navigable rivers in Greece. Although a few rivers flow all the year round, most streams dry up from June to September.

Climate

The climate is generally Mediterranean, with mild winters (usually from November to the end of February) and hot summers. In islands like Rhodes, Corfu and Crete there is very little distinction between winter and summer; the daily average temperature throughout the year is about 22°C (71°F), with a rainy season from November to March. The great plains of Macedonia, Thessaly, Boetia, Attica, and Sparta have a more continental climate, hot and dry in summer, and cold in winter. In July, August and early September, shade temperatures in Athens sometimes rise to 38°C (100°F) or more but the heat is usually a dry heat, attenuated, especially in August, by strong winds. In winter, temperatures of around freezing point occur in Athens.

Communications

The mountains divide; the seas unite. Maritime traffic has always been of the greatest importance; Greece has a large mercantile marine of over 25.5 million tonnes. The 5 km Corinth Canal links the Corinthian and Sardonic Gulfs, shortening the

343

GREECE

sea journey from the Adriatic to the port of Athens (Piraeus) by 325 km. On land the picture is very different. Until the end of World War Two most villages in the interior of the country were approached only by mule tracks. Town and village were physically isolated. Since the war an expanding road network (by 1979 over 36,000 km in length) has drawn villages into closer contact with the provincial towns and with the capital, but many of the roads are unclassified, and in spite of continuing substantial government investment in construction, road communications are generally poor by western European standards. Rail communications are not much better. Greece's railway system was almost completely destroyed during World War Two; the length of track was in 1980 2,577 km. An extensive system of air transport facilitates travel between the capital and the major provincial towns and islands.

2 POPULATION

Growth and Distribution

The last census in Greece was taken in 1971. The population then was 8.8 million, an increase of 4.5% on the 1961 figures. Just over 2.8 million are under 19 years of age. Of the population 53% are urban dwellers, 12% semi-urban and 35% rural. About one million of the population are islanders. More than half the population lives in the plains of Macedonia and Thessaly, Boetia, Attica and Sparta, and along the coastal stretches of the north Peloponnese. Athens has 2.54 million people, accounting for 28% of the total population, and Salonika 557,000 (6%). In the country, people generally live in compact villages or hamlets and not on their farms. A great number of these settlements are very small. The 1961 census identified 11,516 settlements or urban 'agglomerations'. Of these 5,677 had fewer than 200 inhabitants, 5,500 were between 200 and 2,000, and together these two categories accounted for 43% of the total population. There is a wide dispersal of population throughout the countryside but the population density of 67 per sq km is considerable in relation to the country's resources.

Groups

No serious problems have been found among ethnic and religious groups since the exchange of populations between Greece and Turkey imposed by the Treaty of Lausanne in 1923, whereby Turkey received 355,000 Moslems hitherto living on Greek territory while over-populated Greece was called on to absorb some 1.3 million Greeks from Turkish territories, most of whom arrived completely destitute. At the time of the 1928 census there were only 126,000 Moslems in Greece, of whom 86,000 were Turks, 18,000 Albanians and 17,000 Pomaks, or Bulgarian Moslems. The Turks and the Pomaks live mainly in the north. The Albanians are scattered throughout the country and most are descended from the Albanians who were encouraged by the Turks for political reasons to settle in Greece during the eighteenth century.

The number of Greeks of Albanian descent is accordingly much higher than the 18,000 mentioned above. The most important of the racial minorities are the Macedo-Slavs, of mixed Greek and Slav descent. The Greek census of 1928 put the number of Macedonian speaking Greek subjects at about 82,000, although the Bulgarians consider that they number about 300,000. Although no comparable figures are available from the 1971 census, there is little doubt that the number of Moslems in Greece has diminished over the past 50 years, although their concentration in Thrace, near the Turkish border, is a continuing source of unease to the Greek authorities.

Emigration

Emigration has always been a major factor in Greek national life. So poor and destitute was the country that close on 500,000 Greeks emigrated, mostly to Russia, Egypt and America, in the first century after Greece achieved independence. By 1950 the annual exodus was at the rate of about 20,000 still mostly to destinations outside Europe. The sudden change came in 1960, first in numbers which rose in that year to 50,000, and second in the geographical pattern, since fewer than 40% left Europe. The principal destination since 1960 has been Germany, whence the steady flow of remittances from the substantial Greek labour force has contributed significantly both to the maintenance of their families in Greece and to Greece's invisible export earnings. In the three years before the 1971 census, emigration was at the rate of 82,000 per annum, but changes in the West German labour laws helped to bring about a reversal of this trend, and in 1974 the total was 24,448 per annum. Nearly half the emigrants are from 20 to 30 years of age, mostly from the provinces on Greece's northern borders.

3 SOCIETY AND CULTURE

Social and Cultural Traditions

The Greek is heir to two stupendous traditions, those of Byzantium and of ancient Hellas. For 1,000 years Constantinople was the heart and centre of the Greek people; the Turkish occupation of Greece was an interlude, but when it passed it was not a revived Roman Empire of the east, centred on Constantinople, which emerged, but a revived Hellas with its capital eventually in Athens. Both traditions have been irrevocably breached, and the modern educated Greek feels himself rootless in consequence. The strongest social and cultural forces are those which have survived the vicissitudes of centuries - the family, kinship and the church, and a vague but powerful sense of Greek identity. The physical configuration of the country, the pervasive influence of the church, and the centuries as a subject people have combined to give the Greek a strong code of personal and family behaviour. This involves both rights and obligations and confers sensitivity and self-reliance which together with individual energy and enterprise can contend with and sometimes beat, the official system. "They feel compelled", one writer has said, "to take time by the forelock, exploit favourable currents and wrest fortune from unpromising circumstances"; and the values of personal and family advancement exist side by side with conservative loyalties to the values of the Orthodox religion and of family ties. Education is naturally regarded as a means of advancement, and educational qualifications are highly desired, and competed for by all possible means. The severance of cultural roots has led the educated Greek to look abroad, and especially to western Europe, for intellectual and cultural nourishment.

Language

Basic to some understanding of modern Greece, and especially of its educational and cultural life, is the language problem. The spoken language is descended by a process of natural development from the 'common Greek' of Alexander's empire, and its contemporary form, *demotiki*, is the language of common speech, creative writing, elementary education and, with varying degrees of admixture, the press. But the revival of Hellenism and the re-emphasis of the classical Greek heritage - an emotional consequence of the severance from Turkish domination - encouraged a linguistic separation which crystallised in *katharevousa*, a conservative literary dialect created out of Attic, Byzantine and demotic Greek in the nineteenth century which became the official language of modern Greece. Partisanship for the two idioms has led to rioting in the streets of Athens, to bloodshed and even death. Children are taught in *demotiki* at the first level and in *katharevousa* at second and post-second levels. The use of *katharevousa* for official communications effectively excludes from public life and public employment all those who have not received a second level education; many villagers are unable to understand the mixed *demotiki/katharevousa* of the Greek newspapers, much less a political speech.

Religion

The Orthodox Church, perhaps more than any other force, enabled the Greeks to retain a sense of national identity throughout the period of Turkish rule, and to be Greek is to be Orthodox even for those who seldom enter a church. The Patriarchate remains at Constantinople; the distinction between national Hellenism and ecclesiastical Hellenism accentuates the tension of Greek life.

4 HISTORY AND POLITICS

Greek Independence

Despite her evocative and tangled ancestry, Greece is a new state. Between 1820 and 1826 independence from centuries of Turkish domination was finally achieved, and in 1829 formally recognised by the Treaty of Adrianople. Greece owed her independent existence, and the choice of the Bavarian prince Otho as her first sovereign from 1832, largely to the decisions and interventions of the major European powers, whose main interest lay elsewhere. The original State covered about half its present area and consisted of the mainland, extending as far north as Thessaly with the Sporades and Cyclades Islands in the Aegean Sea. Athens was chosen as the capital in 1834.

Formation of Modern Greece

The past 150 years of independence have been marked by chronic instability in Greece's internal politics (producing about 150 governments in as many years), recurrent struggles with Balkan neighbours, and territorial adjustments shaped largely by outside influences. In 1864 the Ionian Islands were ceded to Greece by Britain. After the Balkan war of 1912-13 the northern frontier was extended to include Epirus and Southern Macedonia and the Aegean Islands near the Turkish coast. In 1912 Greece annexed Crete. She remained neutral in World War One until the enforced departure of King Constantine on 12 June 1917 and the succession of his second son Alexander. The postwar treaty of Sèvres gave Greece certain parts of Turkish and Bulgarian Thrace which were used partly for the settlement of Greeks from Asia Minor. Constantine returned to the throne on 20 December 1920 after a plebiscite following Alexander's death, but shortly afterwards (27 September 1922) abdicated in favour of his son George, in the revolution following the Turkish victory over the Greeks in Asia Minor. From 1924 to 1935 King George was exiled and Greece was a republic. Germany invaded Greece in World War Two (April 1941) after Greek opposition to Italian aggression. The liberation of Greece was followed by a civil war which lasted until 1949. With the help of the USA, the Communist forces were defeated, and constitutional monarchy re-established. King George II died in 1947 and was succeeded by his brother King Paul. The Dodecanese Islands, which had been Italian since the Italian-Turkish war of 1911/12 became part of Greece in 1947.

After 1960

In 1964 King Paul died and was succeeded by his son King Constantine II. A succession of weak governments and conflicts between the King and his ministers, and an alleged conspiracy involving Centre Union Officers, resulted in a coup led by right-wing army officers in April 1967, who suspended parliamentary government. Following an unsuccessful royal counter-coup in December 1967, the King went into voluntary exile and was subsequently deposed. Greece was ruled by cabinet decree and martial law. George Papadopoulos emerged as the dominant personality in the new régime, becoming Prime Minister in December 1967, Regent in March 1972 and President of the Republic in July 1973, when martial law was ended and a civilian cabinet appointed in abortive preparation for elections. A second military coup took place in November 1973 but the ensuing military régime of President Phaidon Ghizikis, Adamantios Androutsopoulos and Brigadier-General Demetrios Ioannides collapsed in July 1974 as a result of the failure of the régime's attempt to overthrow President Makarios of Cyprus and its inability to prevent the Turkish invasion of the island. Civilian government was restored and elections held in November 1974 gave the party of Constantine Karamanlis an overwhelming majority in parliament. A referendum in December 1974 rejected proposals for a return to constitutional monarchy and in June 1975 a new republican constitution providing for a parliamentary democracy, was promulgated. In the same month Constantine Tsatsos was elected President. In elections in 1977 the New Democratic Party gained a reduced majority. Karamanlis was elected President of the Republic in 1980 and a New Democratic Party government was formed under George Rallis.

Government Organisation

Under the constitution of June 1975 the President is Head of State and is elected by parliament for a five-year term. He appoints the Prime Minister, and upon his recommendation, the other members of the government. The government must enjoy the confidence of the unicameral parliament of 200 and 300 deputies who are directly elected by universal adult suffrage for four years.

International Relations

The aspirations and realities of Greece's recurrent struggles with her Balkan neighbours in the present century are never far from the threshold of contemporary Greek national consciousness, and these, together with memories of the civil war of the late 1940s and the continuing problems of Cyprus, have created a deep-seated sensitivity in relations with the communist countries on the northern borders and with Turkey in the east, which any single current issue is liable to jar into violent reaction. Relations between Greece and Turkey deteriorated markedly during 1976 with a dispute of offshore rights in the Aegean. Combined with the continuing failure to reach a settlement in Cyprus, this brought the two countries close to war in July 1976. Talks followed. Hopes that Turkey would acquire a strong one-party government ready to negotiate effectively were dashed by inconclusive results in elections in June 1977.

Greece remains a member of NATO. She is a member of the Council of Europe and became a full member of the EEC on 1 January 1981.

5 THE ECONOMY

Natural Resources

Natural resources are limited. Timber is abundant, but access and transport are difficult. The seas are rapidly being depleted of fish. There are no known large deposits of minerals although oil has been found in the north Aegean and bauxite and, in smaller quantities, other minerals such as iron ore and manganese are mined. Major developments have been the processing of an expanding proportion of the ores in Greece, rather than the export of raw materials. The development of the country's electric power resources, irrigation and land reclamation schemes, and the exploitation of Greece's lignite resources for fuel and industrial purposes are being undertaken. Electricity output nearly doubled between 1966 and 1971. But perhaps the country's greatest potential lies in its Mediterranean climate, long coastline, and thousands of islands, for the development of tourism, which already makes a substantial contribution to Greece's invisible earnings.

Agriculture

Although there has in recent years been a substantial measure of industrialisation, Greece is still predominantly an agricultural country, with about 25% of the working population engaged in farming. Inheritance laws and customs mean that the average peasant holding is small (3 hectares) and fragmented, but since World War Two the adoption of cooperative organisation and the increasing amount of capital made available to agrarian enterprise have gone some way to making agricultural production more efficient. Although less than one third of the surface area of the country is suitable for cultivation, the range of climate and therefore of agricultural produce is wide. The most important product is tobacco, but since the war the production of wheat, cotton and rice has been substantially increased, partly in an attempt to make the country's economy less dependent upon tobacco. The most important of the fruit trees are the olive, vine, orange, lemon, fig and almond, and considerable efforts have lately been made to develop exports of fresh fruit and vegetables as well as the more traditional currants and other dried fruits.

Industry

From small beginnings, manufacturing industry grew steadily between the two world wars, but its orientation was to the small domestic market, protected by high tariffs. Its scale of production was small, it could afford to be inefficient and since domestic costs were high it was little concerned with production for export. Manufactured goods (chiefly textiles, chemicals, cement, glass, metallurgy and shipbuilding) contributed only 3.4% in 1963 and 11.6% in 1966 to the total value of the country's exports. Since then there has been a great drive for rapid industrialisation, and in 1970, for the first time, manufactured products contributed more to GDP than agricultural goods. By 1974 industrial products represented 63.72% of all exports. However, the country is not self-sufficient industrially and against the rapidly growing contribution of manufacturing industry to exports must be set the import of a wide range of manufactured consumer and capital goods. In 1979 total imports were more than three times the value of exports.

Economic Situation

Greece continues to suffer a serious and chronic deficit on her visible trade balance. The extent to which in any year this can be offset depends on invisible earnings from tourism, shipping, and emigrants and on the inflow of foreign investment. The problem of the balance of payments has been a recurrent theme in many of the crises in Greece's modern history, and its contribution to her dependence on other powers has been significant. Recent external trade figures (excluding the free trade areas of Piraeus and Thessaloniki) are as follows (in million drachmae):

	1971	1974	1979
Imports	62,943	132,181	434,730
Exports	19,276	60,891	168,990

Greater Athens dominates the economy of the country in wealth and present productive capacity, accounting for over 25% of its total population and over 50% of its manufacturing industries. Two thirds of the labour force in firms employing more than 100 workers live there. Although the growth of the national product in recent years has averaged 6% per annum, the average income per head is low, inflation is rising steeply and the disparities of wealth and living standards between Athens and the rest of the country are notable.

The Future

The achievement of development objectives requires the continued modernisation of agriculture and transport, the expansion of the industrial sector and the further exploitation of the country's natural resources, including the oil bearing deposits recently found in the north Aegean, which in turn require substantial capital investment, changes in the economic structure and skilled managerial, technological and technical personnel; but the present role of national education is rather to promote stability than to produce qualified manpower.

6 THE EDUCATION SYSTEM

Compulsory Education

Education is free and compulsory from the age of 6 to 15.

Academic Year

The academic year extends from September to June at school level and October to June for universities.

Pre-School *(Nepiagogeion)*

Schooling is optional at this level and, in the State sector, free. Both State and private schools cater for infants between the ages of 3½ and 5½; classes are limited to a maximum of 30. Of the total population of 300,000 within this age range, about 87,000 infants attended nursery schools in 1975; 72,000 in the 2,180 State schools and 15,000 in private schools. These schools have morning sessions only of up to four hours, and extensive use is made of play and child activity approaches. A start is made on an introduction to the correct usage of the mother tongue and the first principles of numeracy.

First Level *(Demotikon Scholion)*

Primary education is provided both in private and in State schools, and in the latter it is free. Attendance is compulsory for all children. Primary education is available throughout the country, even in the smallest and most remote village, subject only to the legal requirement that there is a minimum enrolment of 15 pupils. Schools are officially categorised on the basis of their staff complement, for example single post schools, two post schools, etc. up to the largest which is the 15 post school. There is a legal provision which states that the number of pupils per teacher may not exceed 40.

The curriculum and syllabus are uniform throughout State schools and in practice most private establishments follow suit. Textbooks are prescribed by a committee set up by the Ministry of Education. Subjects taught are religion, Greek language *(demotiki)*, environmental studies, history, arithmetic, elements of science, geography, handicrafts, music and physical education. The aggregate allocation of class hours by subject for all classes over one working week is as follows:

Greek language	56	Music	11
Arithmetic	24	Physical Education	11
Handicraft	21	Geography	10
Religion	14	Environmental Studies	10
Elementary Science	14	History & Social Studies	9

The medium of instruction is *demotiki* (the language of common speech) and all textbooks for this level are written in this idiom, with a very few specialised exceptions, e.g. gospel texts. End of year promotion depends on the pupil passing the end of year examination. After successfully completing the first cycle a pupil will gain a primary leaving certificate, the *Apolyterion*, which qualifies him to register for the entrance examination for one of various types of second level school.

Second Level Schools

Secondary education is optional and covers the age range 12 to 18 years. Admission is determined on the results of a combination of the primary leaving certificate and specific second level entrance examinations held in July and September. Those who fail the first examination can take the second. There are three main subdivisions of schools:

(i) general secondary *gymnasia* (including pilot/experimental schools)
(ii) commercial and naval *gymnasia*
(iii) *gymnasia* of technical education.

Most pupils attend general secondary schools. There are several experimental schools including demonstration schools *(peirainatikon)* attached to the Universities of Athens and Salonika, practical/demonstration schools used for in-service teacher training, and the Anavryta National School near Athens, a full boarding school in the public sector and a prestige establishment with the highest admission requirements. Commercial and naval *gymnasia* exist in certain areas to supply the specialised needs of specific sections of the community. The *gymnasia* of technical education were established following proposals made in 1959 and emphasise technical and vocational studies. State and private schools exist in both general and specialised categories. In the State sector tuition and textbooks are free. The language of instruction throughout was formerly the formal literary dialect *katharevousa*. In 1976 demotic Greek was established as the official language of instruction.

The second level course is divided into two cycles, a lower and an upper, each lasting three years. The lower cycle is concerned with rounding off the general education begun in primary school, while the upper cycle is intended to promote studies leading eventually to specialised careers. All types of *gymnasia* follow a common curriculum in the lower cycle. In remote villages second level schools may function with only the lower cycle to provide at least some *gymnasium* education for those who find it impossible to travel to the towns. In general *gymnasia* the upper cycle is divided, whenever enrolled numbers permit, into science and humanities streams (called 'practical' and 'theoretical'). There is a marked preference for humanities (76% as against 24% sciences). However, this streaming is not rigidly exclusive since the curriculum allows for students following one branch of studies to maintain contact, at reduced level, with subjects in the other.

The distribution of *aggregate* hours study among subjects for one working week in a general *gymnasium* is as follows:

	Lower Cycle (3 years)	Upper Cycle (3 years)
Classical Greek	17	22
Modern Greek	12	12
Mathematics	12	12
History	9	9
Physical Education	9	9
Science	12	9
Modern Languages	9	6
Religion	6	7
Geography	5	2
Domestic Science	4	2
Handicrafts	3	1
Music	3	1
Biology	1	1
Anthropology	1	1
Hygiene	1	1
Latin	–	8
Philosophy	–	4

In a *gymnasium* of technical education the distribution of *aggregate* hours study among subjects for one working week (both cycles) is (6 years):

Mathematics	38	History	9
Classical Greek	30	Geography	
Laboratory Work	30	Cosmography	6
Physics/Chemistry	28	Industrial Arts	6
Modern Greek	23	Gymnastics	6
Mechanics or	20/21	Religion	6
		Civics/Philosophy	2
Electricity	18	Hygiene	2
English	19	Economics	1
Drawing	10/11	Organisation of Work	1

During the School year a check on pupils' progress is maintained by regular oral tests, often on a lesson by lesson basis. Major written examinations covering all subjects studied are held twice a year, once in February and again at the end of the year in June. Promotion is decided on the results of the end of year examination, *(endeiktikon)*, in conjunction with grades given for work throughout the year. At the end of the final year of secondary studies, pupils sit for the leaving certificate, *(Apolytirion)*. Those who gain fewer than 10 points at the end of year examination are required to re-sit in September those subjects in which they have failed; if they fail again, they are required to repeat the full year.

Vocational

The main source of vocational education in Greece are those schools which train pupils for employment in technical and skilled trades essential to the economic development of the country. Running parallel to the *gymnasia* system are lower and intermediate technical vocational schools and recently higher technical institutes have also been introduced. In the State sector such education is free. Those attending private schools are eligible for grants from public funds, and the best 5% of pupils enrolled at vocational schools are awarded annual bursaries by the Greek State Scholarships Foundation. In addition, there are a number of highly specialised vocational institutions, for example music schools, tourism schools, and schools for librarians, which provide courses of various lengths at appropriate levels.

Technical Vocational

Lower Schools *(katotera)* are open to holders of the primary leaving certificate after an entrance examination. Day schools follow a three-year programme; evening schools four years. All students must complete 200 to 500 hours of practical training and pass an examination set by the Ministry of National Education and Religion if they wish to receive a diploma. Admission to intermediate schools *(mesi)* is open both to holders of a *gymnasium* third year promotion certificate and to pupils who have successfully completed a lower vocational school course. Programmes of study also last three and four years respectively. In addition one- or two-year specialist courses are offered to pupils who hold either the *gymnasium* leaving certificate, or a certificate of promotion from the fifth form of the *gymnasium*. In 1973/75 higher technical schools *(kentra anoteras technikis ekpethenseos* - KATES *)* were established with World Bank capital grants. They offer programmes in engineering, food technology, business management and health services and provide vocational education for potential technicians and middle level management from 18 years upwards.

Specialised Vocational

These include the privately run aircraft mechanics school (offering a three-year course for pupils with three years of *gymnasium* education), music academies (called literally voice schools - *odeia*) offering four year courses, correspondence schools *(alilografias)* offering courses of up to three years to *gymnasium* graduates and librarianship and tourism schools (both offering one-year courses to graduates of the *gymnasia*).

Special

Special schools are maintained by State authorities for the education of children who cannot be absorbed into the normal school system because of physical or mental handicaps or social maladjustments. There are 52 such schools, of which 26 are for the mentally retarded. Some have boarding facilities.

Ecclesiastical

The purpose of ecclestical schools is to instruct those who are to be ordained as Orthodox priests and to help them to understand their responsibilities towards the Church and modern society. Within the framework of secondary schooling there are six establishments known as middle ecclesiastical schools. Admission is open to boys below the age of 16 who hold the primary leaving certificate and have passed an entrance examination. The course of study covers seven years, the first six years' programme corresponding broadly to the general *gymnasium* curriculum, while the final year is devoted to religious studies. There is a further school, the Athonias Ecclesiastical School, which prepares monks for the communities of Mount Athos by a six-year course concentrating on theological studies.

Military

Military academies come under the direction of the Ministry of National Defence, and are for training maritime officers, gendarmerie officers, police officers, army cadets, aviation cadets, navy cadets and military doctors, dentists and pharmacists. Graduates of secondary *gymnasia* are admitted to these schools to pursue a three-year course of study and after successfully passing their examinations they become commissioned officers.

Third Level Institutions

Higher education is provided by the following institutions:

(i) the University of Athens, founded in 1837, which has six schools: Theology, Philosophy and Literature, Law and Economics, Medicine, Pharmacology, Dentistry. The Faculty of Philosophy includes the departments of Archaeology, History and Foreign Languages

(ii) the Metsovian National Technical University (Polytechnic) of Athens, founded in 1836, which has five schools: Civil Engineering, Mechanical and Electrical Engineering, Architecture, Chemical Engineering, Topography-Agronomy

(iii) the University of Salonika, founded in 1925, which has nine schools: Theology, Philosophy and Literature (including History, Archaeology and a separate Institute of Foreign Languages), Law and Economics, Medicine, Dentistry, Agriculture and Forestry, Veterinary Science, Polytechnic, Pharmacology

(iv) the University of Patras, founded 1964, with two faculties: Physics-Mathematics (Mathematics, Physics, Chemistry, Biology) and Polytechnic (Electrical-Mechanical Engineering and Civil Engineering)

(v) the University of Ioannina, founded in 1966 and given independent status in 1971, which has two faculties of Mathematics and Philosophy

(vi) the University of Thrace, established at Komotini in 1975, with faculties of Law (at Komotini) and Engineering (at Xanthi)

(vii) the Athens Graduate School of Economics and Business Sciences, founded in 1920

(viii) Panteios School of Political Sciences, Athens, founded in 1930

(ix) Piraeus Graduate School of Industrial Studies, founded in 1938

(x) Salonika Graduate School of Industrial Studies, founded in 1958

(xi) Athens Graduate School of Agriculture, founded in 1920

(xii) Athens Graduate School of Fine Arts, founded in 1836.

There are special university areas (university cities) in Athens, Salonika, and Patras. All higher education is free. Since 1968 textbooks have been issued free to university students, and grants are made towards the cost of medical attention, meals and accommodation.

Admission

Admission is based on competitive entrance examinations which are open to all who have successfully completed secondary general education. The entrance examinations take place in the autumn and the results are valid for the following academic year only. Scholarships are awarded by the Greek State Scholarships Foundation to those who secure a high mark in the entrance examination.

Courses

The faculties of the universities and of the institutions with para-university status are grouped in 12 cycles. A candidate may state a preference for more than one faculty provided that his choice remains within the same cycle. Courses in higher education (excluding teacher training) last a minimum of four years up to the first degree. Degree courses in technical and medical subjects take five to six years. Of the total student enrolment about 20% study law, 15% business studies, 15% pure science, 12% medicine, 10.5% humanities, 8% applied science. Law studies have maintained their traditional prestige and importance. Post-graduate courses exist in the Faculties of Law, Physics-Mathematics and Agriculture-Forestry at the University of Salonika; in the Faculty of Physics and Mathematics at the University of Athens; and at the Graduate School of Economics and Business Sciences in Athens. These courses are free and normally last two years. Candidates for post-graduate diplomas must be graduates and must submit a thesis in Greek.

Examinations

Examinations are held twice a year, in June and in October. They may be written, oral, or both. A student may repeat the year if he fails in one or two subjects only; re-examination is restricted to those subjects. Alternatively a student may proceed to the following year, transferring his failed subjects for re-examination at the end of the following year. Failure in a transferred subject requires a repetition of the earlier year. Final examinations are held in June, October and February; students are examined on only the final year's work.

Teacher Training

Teachers receive full pre-service training for pre-school, primary and vocational schools. Secondary teachers must be university graduates in the subject they intend to teach. The provision of in-service training for secondary teachers is expanding.

Pre-School

Teachers for this level are trained in specialised schools at Thessaloniki, Florina, and Yannena, offering a one-year course to holders of the secondary school leaving certificate *(Apolytirion)*. Pierce College in Athens admits women who have the primary leaving certificate to a four-year course of study.

First Level

First level teachers are trained in one of 15 State pedagogical academies, of which 12 are coeducational and three are for women. Candidates for admission must hold the secondary school leaving certificate and must take an entrance examination in ancient Greek, composition, modern Greek, modern Greek history, science and mathematics. After a two-year course (soon to be extended to three years) and the passing of written and oral examinations, a diploma is awarded. The Ministry of National Education and Religion certifies and appoints primary teachers to specific districts. It is mandatory for all State school teachers to teach for two years in rural areas. After three years of service in rural areas teachers are entitled to receive two years of additional training at the University of Athens on full salary.

Second Level

Newly appointed teachers at secondary level are given three-month courses in teaching methods and attend demonstration/practice classes. Candidates usually have a university degree, the normal qualification for a secondary teaching post. Specialisation by subject is officially the basis of appointment to a post, although teachers are often required to teach more than one subject. After a period of three years, each teacher is entitled to a two-year refresher course at the Didaskaleion College in Athens, opened in 1971. The College offers long courses of two years to about 70 secondary teachers (mostly of mathematics and science). They receive instruction in their own subjects as well as in educational theory, psychology and methodology, and some time is set aside for pratical teaching in the model school attached to the College. Some short courses of six months are also provided. In-service training for teachers in all branches and specialities is also provided by the College for the In-Service Training of Secondary Teachers.

Vocational

Teaching staff in vocational schools are recruited from graduates of vocational schools, technical universities or other university faculties, and their pre-service training takes place at the UNESCO-assisted technical teacher training school, SELETE *(Scholi Ekpeudeutikon Litoyrgon Epagelmatikis Technikis Ekpedeyseos)*, near Athens, which also offers in-service courses. The course lasts from one to two years depending on the area of specialisation. Three years of practical training must be completed before the diploma *(ptychion)* is awarded.

Non-Formal and Adult

The official aim of adult education is to supplement and improve the education of adults on the basis of Hellenic-Christian moral values, and to enable them to meet their everyday needs more effectively. Adult education also aims to combat illiteracy and near-illiteracy; the illiteracy rate was reduced from 72% to less than 10% in the last 30 years. There are nearly 1,000 education centres in the country, ranging from centres in their own premises to a single individual using a village school. A limited number of evening secondary schools exist in towns for people in daytime employment. There, because of the shorter daily schedule, the usual six forms of secondary education are expanded to seven forms. As a means of overcoming the teacher shortage in schools regular radio and television schools programmes are provided.

7 EDUCATIONAL ADMINISTRATION

Centralised Control

The administration of the Greek education system is highly centralised, reflecting the focus of political power in modern

ADMINISTRATION

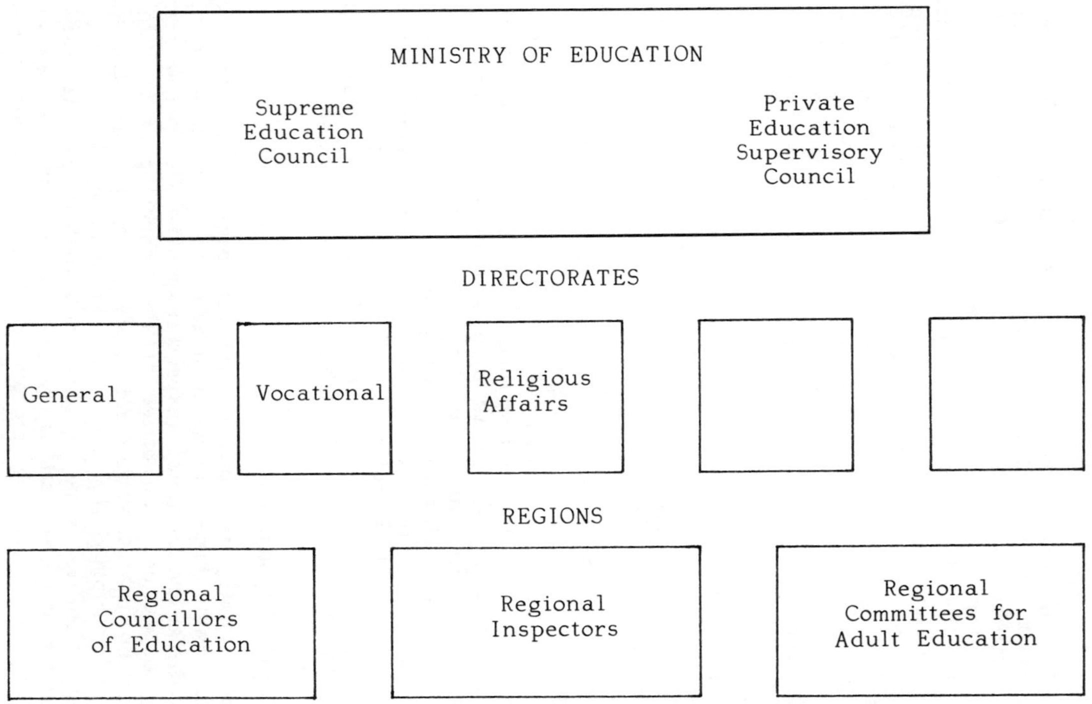

MINISTRY OF EDUCATION

Supreme Education Council

Private Education Supervisory Council

DIRECTORATES

| General | Vocational | Religious Affairs | | |

REGIONS

| Regional Councillors of Education | Regional Inspectors | Regional Committees for Adult Education |

Greece. Though the country is divided into regions for administrative purposes no independent departures from the countrywide uniformity of the education system are permitted. The private sector is as strictly regulated by the Ministry as the State sector. There is a Private Education Supervisory Council but it performs only a consulting role. Under Decree Law No. 651 (1970) a Supreme Education Council was formed to assist the minister in top level administration and supervision, and in determining general directions in the planning of school curricula and syllabi, together with the form of language to be used in the writing of school texts. Its directions are promulgated as law in the Government Gazette. The Supreme Education Council is composed of the councillors of education (the top regional administrators), and the directors-general (heads of the directorates of general education, vocational education, and religious affairs in the Ministry). At the end of each academic year the SEC reports to the minister on the state of education in each region and makes recommendations for improvements in the education system.

The directorate of vocational education supervises all State vocational schools and was established when the Ministry took over the administration of certain independent foundations hitherto supervised by the Ministry of Industry. The General Directorate of Ecclesiastical Education supervises the seven ecclesiastical schools administered by the Church of Greece. Although in the field of adult education other government departments (for example, the Ministries of Labour and Agriculture), and private bodies (such as the YMCA and YWCA) run their own programmes, main responsibility rests with the Directorate of Adult Education. There is also a General Directorate of Teacher Training. Greek institutions of higher education are independent and self-governing with an elected governing body of full professors but they are supervised and financed by the State through the Ministry's General Directorate of Higher Education. Until 1974 a government State Representative was appointed to each university; this office has now been abolished.

Regional Responsibilities

The country is divided into ten regions for educational purposes. Each of the regions is headed by a Councillor of Education, and there are regional inspectors-general for primary and secondary education. The office of the Inspector General for Primary Education is responsible for implementing policies and administering and supervising all staff at primary level. The Inspector General shares some of his responsibilities with an associate inspector general, and they are assisted in detailed administration by a descending hierarchy of nomarchy inspectors, district inspectors and primary head teachers. The administration and supervision of *gymnasia* are the responsibility of the regional office of the Inspector General of Secondary Education, who may share his duties with an associate. Supervisory staff in each region consist of district administrative inspectors, subject specialist inspectors and *gymnasiarchs* (principals of *gymnasia*).

Private *gymnasia* have independent boards of control and are largely self-financing, but they must conform to ministry established curricula and criteria for staffing, accommodation, etc. and are subject to ministry inspection. Directors of teacher training establishments are under the authority of the respective Councillor of Education. Adult education is administered through regional committees which operate the 952 adult education centres under the supervision of the directorate of adult education.

8 EDUCATIONAL FINANCE

Education Budget

The cost of public sector education is met entirely from the national exchequer; there are no local authority contributions. In the private sector, expenditure is met from fees with assistance in a few cases from foreign trusts. For the five years 1967-71 the average percentage of the GNP allocated to education was 2.8, indicative of the comparatively low status of education among the government's priorities. A tight rein is kept on educational spending; for example, decisions on the establishment or enlargement of pre-primary or primary schools require the approval of the Minister of Finance as well as the Minister of Education.

Allocation of Funds

The distribution of available funds between the different levels of the education system is a matter for government decision. In recent years there has been a notable increase in the allocation of funds for higher education; for example, the University of Athens received three times the grant for the five-year period 1967-71, compared with the grant for 1962-66. Unesco figures for 1974 give the following percentage breakdown:

Allocation of Funds
Expenditure on Education: Distribution by Level
Percentage of Expenditure 1974

Pre-School	First Level	Second Level	Third Level	Other
3.5	40.6	29.9	22.0	4.0

Foreign Aid

The World Bank has made substantial grants for capital expenditure in the development of higher education, and concluded a loan agreement with the Greek government to finance feasibility studies for educational development and research, especially at secondary level. Unesco provides a few advisory/teaching staff for technical education.

9 DEVELOPMENT AND PLANNING OF THE EDUCATIONAL SYSTEM
Origins

The core of Greek education is national, secular, and Hellenistic, with particular emphasis on the teaching of classical and modern greek, history, philosophy and logic. In 1830, after the War of Independence, the total school population of Greece was about 9,000, of whom some 6,500 were in 71 primary schools and 2,500 in the 39 'Hellenic' schools which provided some post-primary education in *katharevousa*. Nearly a century later they were finally absorbed, fundamentally unchanged, into the secondary school system. Only higher education has been affected to any noticeable extent by outside influences (for example the University of Athens was heavily influenced by foreign models), irrespective of whether the resulting hybrid was likely to become a satisfactory part of Greek life.

Educational Aims

The Hellenic schools aimed to lay the foundations of national pride and of religious and moral education, and to equip their pupils for a proper and useful role in society. Despite the enormous expansion in education subsequently, these social and national aims have remained, broadly speaking, paramount. The development of the individual is seen as generally desirable within the framework of approved values of the national society, and Government Decree No. 651 of 1970 sets out the objectives of general education in Greece on this basis. The declared objectives of primary education are:

(i) to lay the foundations of national pride and of religious and moral education
(ii) to equip pupils for a proper and useful role in society
(iii) to develop their capacity to learn
(iv) to train them in correct habits of self-expression and communication
(v) to impart a groundwork of knowledge essential both for everyday living and for the furtherance of study;

and of secondary education:

(i) to achieve a balanced harmonious development of moral and intellectual faculties within the framework of values of Greek society
(ii) to consolidate and extend the rudiments of knowledge gained in primary education
(iii) to prepare pupils for the pursuit of higher specialised studies relevant to the careers they may envisage.

Planning

Until the seventies there was nobody with particular responsibilities for planning but a Directorate of Educational Planning was set up in the ministry, responsible directly to the minister, for formulating plans for educational development at all levels. Its recommendations are not made public, but may be assumed to influence the minister in his periodic announcements of educational reorganisation.

10 THE SYSTEM IN OPERATION
Provision

Only at the first level is there a close correspondence between the total age group and pupil enrolment since education is compulsory. Below six years of age the nursery enrolment is about 25% of the age group, while at second level it is approximately 55%. The figures for school attendances in the seventies show an increase at all levels other than primary, where numbers remained fairly constant; the increase at kindergarten level was about 8%, mostly in the public sector, and at secondary level about 3%, again mostly in the State schools. Unfortunately the expansion in enrolments has not been matched by increased provision of schools. Only about 84% of schools enjoy sole occupancy of premises; elsewhere buildings are shared by two, three or more schools. Even when a school is the sole occupant, its size may be such that shift working is necessary, usually with the lower cycle attending in the morning, and the upper cycle in the afternoon. There seems to be little regional variation in provision for the required deployment of teachers corresponds broadly with the distribution of population, 36% of posts being in greater Athens and Salonika.

Schools are distributed between the State and private sectors in proportions heavily weighted in favour of the former. This is most marked in the area of compulsory education where the division is 93% State and 7% private, although above this level where private enterprise is more active, the imbalance is somewhat reduced and private establishments account for about 25% of the total number of secondary schools. Pre-first level education expanded in the seventies. Private enterprise finds it a profitable investment – about 20% of schools are in the private sector – while the State planned 500 new nursery schools in 1972 alone. The percentage of schools by category is as follows.

	State day	State (evening)	Private (day)	Private (evening)
Pre-primary	87.0		13.0	
Primary	90.0	3.0	6.5	0.5
Secondary *(gymnasia)*	71.0	2.5	22.0	4.5
Vocational	49.0		51.0	

Buildings and Equipment

School buildings constructed during the last 30 years have had to conform to standards laid down by the Ministry of Education and are therefore adequate, although generally utilitarian and stark rather than stimulating. Many schools, however, especially in rural districts, occupy buildings of earlier date, and these vary from good to dilapidated. Nonetheless, classrooms generally provide reasonable basic working facilities, with an adequate supply of serviceable furniture. Textbooks are supplied free in primary and secondary State schools, and while they are not in short supply, many are locally produced and their content may leave much to be desired. Following Decree Law 749, passed in 1970, an effort has been instantly made to appreciably improve the quality of textbooks at all levels of education, both in content and general design. School libraries may or may not exist, depending on the initiative of the headmaster, but are seldom integrated into the teaching programme. Physics equipment is possessed by 90% of primary schools and 50% have chemistry equipment adequate for the experimental work prescribed in the syllabus, but class numbers are such that generally pupils remain passive observers of practical demonstrations and have little opportunity to experiment themselves. Audio-visual teaching aids, maps, etc. are available in all schools and much of this material, together with some laboratory equipment, is manufactured in workshops run by the Ministry of Education, Tape recorders exist in some schools, although they may be securely guarded in the headmaster's office.

Wastage and Repetition

The drop-out rate at secondary level has been estimated at 36%. The causes are mainly economic: the need to supplement family income, expenses incurred in travelling long distances to school or having to board away from home. At primary level, where such considerations are less applicable and school attendance is in any case compulsory, the drop-out figure is only 3%. Repeaters at primary level form about 5% of the total enrolment. Of the secondary schools enrolment about 9% are repeaters in the ratio of roughly two boys to one girl, a ratio that remains constant over forms 1 to 5. Thereafter it alters to 6:1.

Curricula and Examinations

The mandatory countrywide curricula determined by the Supreme Education Council tend to be academic and traditional, and throughout the system no departure from them is permitted for public schools. Philology is the central feature of the Greek curriculum comprising classical and modern Greek, history, philosophy, logic and Latin, and occupies 44% of all teaching staff, far outweighing all other subjects. By contrast it is noteworthy that appointments in the natural sciences account for only 10%. Private sector gymnasia have been allowed to set up supplementary courses for specific outside examinations, for example GCE, AEB, if they have the staff. This has meant in a few schools the provision of courses additional to those officially prescribed, in certain subjects such as English and other modern languages and mathematics, and these courses are tolerated, if not explicitly welcomed, by the Ministry. The distribution of subject teachers at secondary level generally is about the same in the public and private schools, but it is interesting to note a marked disparity in the number of modern languages staff, where there are proportionately twice as many posts in the private schools.

The traditional type of examination plays a prominent role and as well as annual promotion examinations pupils are subjected to written tests at regular monthly or even weekly intervals. Generally speaking, at both primary and secondary level examinations perform a selective function, as a basis for interclass promotion. The same selection purpose governs entrance examinations to the various types of secondary education. Leaving examinations, after both primary and secondary courses are essentially attainment tests. The basic timetable and rigorous testing is extremely demanding of the pupil, if not overwhelming, and when to this is added the prevalent practice of attendance at teaching institutes outside school hours, either to remedy inadequacies in school teaching or to prepare for university entrance, it is unusual to find secondary pupils with time for any further work. An additional burden is the fact that children are taught in *demotiki* at elementary level and in *katharevousa* at secondary or post-secondary level which in itself forms a continuing and very real impediment to educational development.

Teachers

Although some teaching qualification is required of teachers for appointment at kindergarten and primary level, teacher training shares the weaknesses of all the higher education institutions. Too many students are admitted without meeting the basic entrance requirements; classes contain 50 to 60 students and occasionally more. There is a wide range of subjects in the curriculum with few options and the manner of learning and teaching is almost wholly verbal. There is no continuous supervised teaching practice; students may watch demonstration lessons in the experimental schools associated with the universities but may not actually conduct a lesson. Buildings are generally poor and educational technology seriously lacking. Teachers appointed in secondary schools are graduates but suffer from the lack of full pre-service teacher training. In general teaching methods remain formal and conservative. In-service training has expanded. In the Universities of Athens and Salonika the Faculty of Philosophy includes courses in methodology, child psychology and pedagogics, but such study is inevitably theoretical. The setting up of Didaskaleion College in 1971 was an important step forward.

All teachers in State supervised schools and universities have public servant status and are recruited in civil service grades for the purposes of salary and promotion. Government salary scales are comparatively low and therefore unattractive. Promotion is determined by a combination of academic qualifications, years of service, and, most important, end of year inspectors' reports. Theoretically inspections take place annually, but in practice and in some subjects more than others, this is not always so. It is officially claimed that promotion is quicker for teachers than for other civil servants, but the only clearly established advantage for teachers is that of special bonuses.

All kindergarten teachers are women and 85% are in public sector schools. At primary level women hold rather fewer than half of the total number of teaching posts, again predominantly in State schools. At secondary schools women also hold just under half the teaching posts, 88% of which, on the national figures, are in public schools, although rather less in greater Athens.

Higher Education

In higher education as in schools, the tradition is mainly verbal and academic, and the advantages of practical experimentation largely neglected. University faculties can cater only for general instruction because of the problem of overcrowding. Little attempt is made to gear enrolments to a standard staff-student ratio since tuition is almost entirely through mass lectures and once a significant number of students are engaged in regular employment outside the university they seldom attend lectures. In these circumstances a faculty can accept large numbers of students, confident that many will not actually occupy space in a lecture hall. University attendances are also affected by political events.

There is little personal contact and no social means of bridging the gap. Lack of specialisation is a feature of courses in both the sciences and the humanities; specialised training or research must be done abroad. Most teaching is dominated by examinations at which cheating is common. It carries no social stigma and is often a competitive venture. It is a practice which belongs to an attitude born in the secondary schools, and is encouraged by the emphasis placed on the accurate repetition of professorial lectures and publications.

The Future

The Greek education system, which follows closely the classically framed traditional model, does not, in many respects, satisfy the desire of parents and students for an education geared to meet the needs and pressures of modern living. The increasing demand for technological and technical training and the growing interest in modern languages, especially English, are only two of the developments which the present form of education does not easily accommodate and which would require considerable modifications of the system to satisfy. The traditional objective of formal education is national stability, not development. The retention of a generally conservative curriculum with its heavy emphasis on classical and traditional studies, is seen as promoting the Hellenic homogeneity of the nation, and is in conformity with entrenched academic opinion, and the entrenched conservatism of bureaucracy. The instability of Greek internal politics has not helped the cause of long term educational policies and radical reform. However, under pressure from domestic public opinion, the stipulations of innovation and experiment in educational planning, to meet the development needs of the country are evident.

FURTHER READING AND REFERENCES
Main Sources (Education)

Ekpaideftikos Odigos (annual). *Greek Educational Handbook.* Hellenic Printers, Athens.
Education in Greece (1973). Publication No.10 of the General Directorate of General Education. National Printing Office, Athens. (Editions in English and French.)
UNESCO (1971). *World Survey of Education,* 5, 527-534, Unesco, Paris.
UNESCO/IBE (1980). *International Yearbook of Education XXXII.* Unesco, Paris.
OECD (1965). *Mediterranean Regional Project: Greece.* Educational Report, OECD, Paris.
OECD (1973). *Classification of Educational Systems: Canada, Greece, Yugoslavia.* OECD, Paris.
OECD (1970). *Training and Functions of Technicians, Greece.* OECD, Paris.
OECD (1968). *Study on Teachers/Elude sur les Enseignants, Austria, Greece, Sweden, Mediterranean Regional Project, Greece 1965.* OECD, Paris.
OECD (1971). *Quantitative Trends on Teaching Staff in Higher Education,* OECD, Paris.
Schultze, Walter. *Schools in Europe III.* Verlag J Beltz, Germany.

Laws, Decrees (Education)

Decree Law No. 651/1970 (1971). *Organisation and administration of general education and staff.* National Printing Office, Athens
Decree Law No. 748/1970 (1971). *Further training of secondary teachers and reorganisation of college for in-service training.* National Printing Office, Athens.
Decree Law No. 749/1970 (1971). *Textbooks.* National Printing Office, Athens.
Decree Law No. 842/1970 (1971). *Reorganisation of the Pedagogical Academies.* National Printing Office, Athens.
Ephimeris Tis Kyberniseos (Government Gazette) No. 225. Contains secondary education timetables and syllabi. 10 November 1969.

Ephimeris Tis Kyberniseos No. 218. Contains primary school timetables and syllabi. 31 October 1969, Athens.

Statistiki Tis Ekpaidefseos (1968-70) (1971). Secondary Education. National Statistics Service, Athens.

Pinax Dimosion Gymnasion Kata Nomarchias (1973). Official list of secondary schools. Ministry of Education, Athens.

Statistiki Tis Ekpaidefseos (1969-70) (1971). Tertiary Education, National Statistics Service, Athens.

Statistics

National Statistics Service (annual. *Statistical Yearbook of Greece.* National Statistical Service, Athens.

OECD (1970). *Development of Higher Education - Statistical Survey.* OECD, Paris.

OECD (1971). *OECD Economic Report on Greece for 1971.* (English text), OECD, Paris.

UNESCO (annual). *Statistical Yearbook.* Unesco, Paris.

Structure of the Education System in Greece

Age	3	4	5	6	7	8	9	10	11	12	13	14	15	16	17	18	19	20	21	22	23	24
Level				I							II				III							IV
Stage				1							2				3	4	5	6	7	8		
Compulsory																						
School Type				Primary							Ghymnasion			Tech. voc. / Lyceum a. general b. technical and vocational			Higher Education Courses / Teacher Training / Graduate Training						Post-Graduate

▨ Education preceding the first level

Examinations: compulsory from the end of stage I onwards

Source: UNESCO/IBE International Yearbook of Education

Compulsory Education: Age Limits 6-12 Duration (years) 6
Entrance age to pre-school education: 3

369

GREECE BASIC STATISTICS	1960	1970	1974	1978 (approx.)
1 Total population (000)	8,327	8,793	8,890	9,360
% female	51	51	51	51
2 % population 0-14 years	26.7	24.9		23
% female	49	48	49	49
3 Enrolment, all levels	1,224,795	1,513,545	1,660,747	1,750,705
% female	45	45	45	45
First level	895,887	907,446	927,848	938,597
% female	48	48	48	48
Second level	300,606	529,901	635,140	694,216
% female	39	43	43	43
Third level	28,302	76,198	97,759	117,892
% female	25	32	37	37
4 Teachers, all levels				
% female				
First level	23,251	29,336	30,458	32,665
% female	47	47	47	48
Second level	12,280			
% female	32			
Third level	926	3,483	5,744	
% female	7	30	36	
5 Public expenditure on education:				
Total (ooo) drachmas	1,599,919	6,239,900	10,291,047	
As % of GNP	1.5	2.1	1.7	
As % of public expenditure				8.0
6 % enrolment (MF) by level	100	100	100	100
First level	73	60	56	54
Second level	25	35	38	40
Third level	2	5	6	6
% enrolment (F) by level	100	100	100	100
First level	78	63	59	57
Second level	21	33	36	38
Third level	1	4	5	5
7 Entrance age : Duration of				
First level education	6:6	6:6	5:6	
Second level education	12:6	12:6	11:6	
8 Enrolment ratios (MF)				
First level	102	108	105	104
Second level	38	64	81	79
Third level	3.84	12.01	15.53	18.99
Enrolment ratios (F)				
First level	100	106	102	103
Second level	2.9	56	72	67
Third level	1.91	7.93	11.52	14.98

Hungary

CONTENTS

1 Geography 372
2 Population 374
3 Society and Culture 375
4 History and Politics 376
5 The Economy 378
6 The Education System 381
7 Educational Administration 386
8 Educational Finance 389
9 Development and Planning of
   the Education System 389
10 The System in Operation 391

The post-World War Two history of Hungary undoubtedly turns on the 1956 uprising and, in education, the efforts of educational reformers to introduce changes into a traditional selective European educational system along the lines of practices advocated in the Soviet Union.

Within the Austro-Hungarian Empire, which lasted for over 50 years, until the end of World War One, Hungarian schools were selective, and geared to preparing and selecting out students for admission to universities. Between the wars reform movements were sporadic and for the most part unsuccessful. After World War Two, when in 1949 the Communists gained effective control of the government, reforms have been designed to guarantee the right of all citizens to culture by making schooling compulsory for pupils from 6 to 16 years of age, by strengthening the links between school and the industrial life of society, by preparing pupils for productive work and by developing them into honest citizens with a sense of patriotism. These aims have informed proposals to create a nine-year compulsory basic school followed by a differentiated upper second level and third level institutions. At the upper stage of second level schools there are four-year academic secondary schools *(gymnazium)* and specialised technical schools *(technikum)* which prepare pupils for the universities and technical institutions. Specialised secondary schools educate able musicians, fine artists and applied artists.

Three-year apprenticeship schools and two-year continuation schools do not lead to university entrance awards except through adult education courses.

Graduates from the general and specialised technical schools can go on to one of several types of teacher training institutions, for kindergarten, lower primary and upper primary schools and for handicapped children.

Changes in the organisation of the school system have taken place along Soviet lines in spite of the evidence that before and after the 1956 uprising contacts between Hungarians and their colleagues in Western Europe were maintained.

Demographic trends are reflected in the rise in pre-school enrolments between 1965 and 1975, the decline in the number of pupils enrolled in primary schools and general secondary schools which is not matched by increases in enrolments in other types of secondary school.

Since 1945 industry has replaced agriculture as the largest sector of the economy. Most of the raw materials have to be imported, many of them from the USSR, and the latter country is Hungary's most important trading partner. The need for vocational and technical schools is obvious.

As in most countries with a sizeable Catholic population, the authorities in Hungary have regarded the Church as a potential source of political unrest. In Hungary, while more than half the population is Roman Catholic, there are sizeable minority groups, the largest of them being the Calvinists. While atheism is actively encouraged, religious instruction in the schools is not specifically forbidden. To this cultural diversity must be added that associated with the presence of Germans, Slovaks, Serbs, Croats and Slovenes, and Romanians, reflecting the ethnic and linguistic origins of groups in neighbouring states.

The Editor

1 GEOGRAPHY

Topography

Hungary *(Magyarország)* is a landlocked country of approximately 93,031 square kilometres (35,920 square miles, about three quarters the size of England), situated in the Carpathian basin of central eastern Europe, and bounded by Czechoslovakia to the north, Romania to the south east, Austria to the west, Yugoslavia to the south, and the USSR to the north east. The country is composed of three major geographic areas: the Great Hungarian Plain *(Alföld)* in the east, covering about two thirds of the country; the hilly region of Transdanubia *(Dunántul)* west of the Danube, and the Northern Uplands *(Eszak-Magyarország)*, which includes the Matra Mountains and most of the country's forests. The main rivers are the Danube, entering from Austria in the west and crossing through the capital, Budapest, to flow south to Yugoslavia, and the Tisza, flowing across the Great Plain from north east to south west. Budapest has one of the most beautiful sites in Europe, with the Danube dividing Buda from Pest. The capital was badly damaged during World War Two and the 1956 Uprising, but much money has been spent,

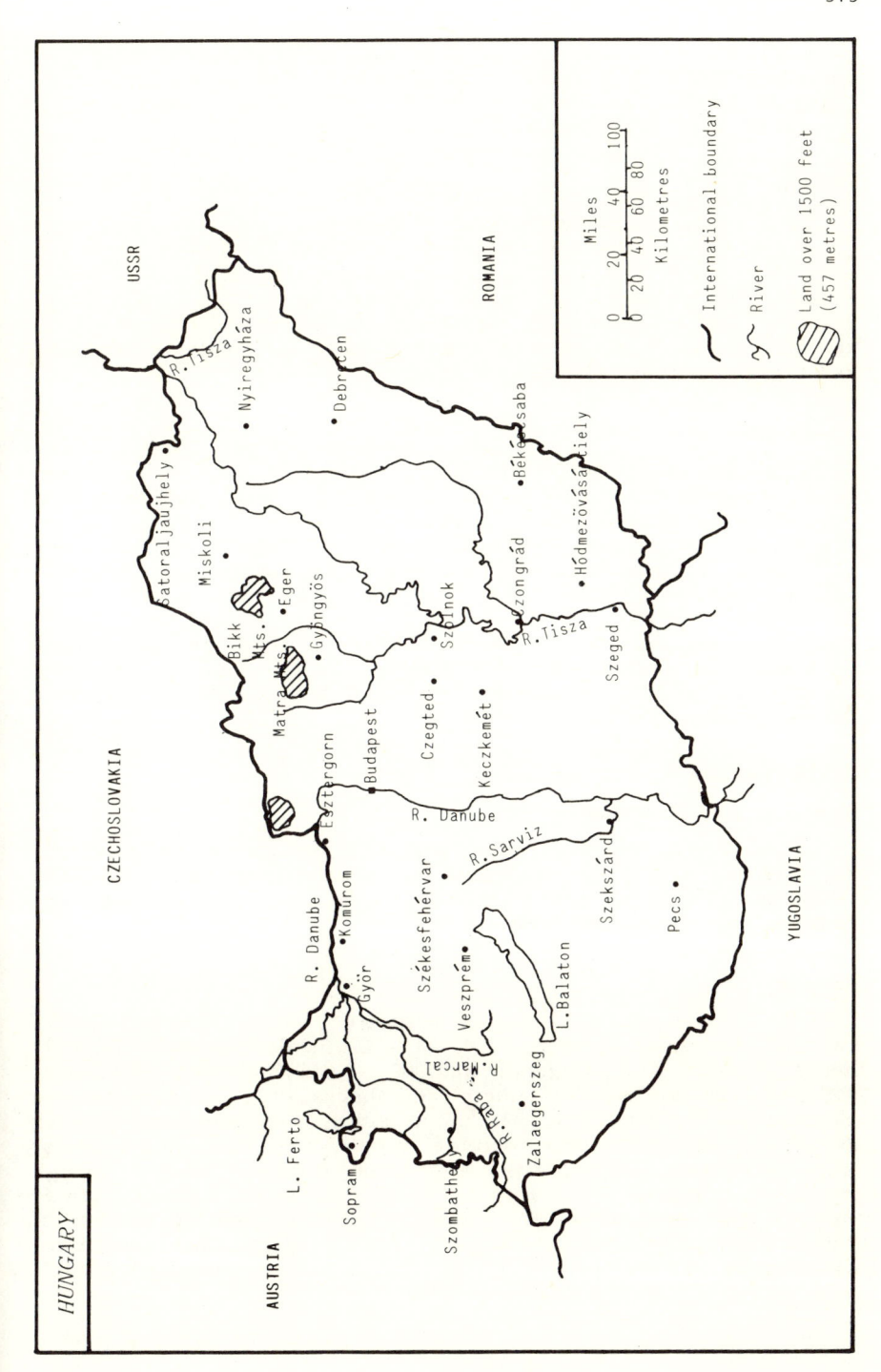

HUNGARY

particularly in Buda, on the restoration of historic buidings, including the Royal Palace and the Buda Castle district. Pest, with its wide boulevards, squares and baroque churches, is a smaller version of Vienna.

Climate

The climate is predominantly continental, with severe winters (average temperature in Budapest −3°C [25°F] in January) and long dry summers (21°C [70°F] in July). In the lowlands, annual precipitation reaches 20 to 24 inches, while 24 to 31 inches fall on the uplands. The central part of the sheltered *Alföld* is the driest part of the country with the hilly south west receiving most rainfall.

Communications

There are about 30,000 km (18,750 miles) of main or secondary roads (representing about 27% of the total road network). The Hungarian State Railway operates 8,393 km (5,246 miles) of track, connecting all main towns with Budapest and the rest of Europe. Of this 1,303 km (814 miles) are electrified. Navigable inland waterways total some 1,688 km (1,055 miles), and there is a small merchant fleet (average tonnage 1,100 tons) which operates from the Danube to Mediterranean ports and the United Kingdom. The Hungarian State Airline (Malév) has an extensive network of flights to Europe and the Middle East, but there are no public internal air services.

2 POPULATION

Numbers and Distribution

In July 1980 the population was estimated to be 10.7 million. the largest towns are Budapest (2 million), Miskolc (185,000), Debrecen (166,000), Pécs (152,000), and Szeged (125,000). The country has one of the lowest birth rates in the world.

Groups

Some 450,000 people belong to minority groups. The most important of these are: Germans (200,000 − 220,000); Slovaks (110,000); Serbs, Croats and Slovenes (80,000 − 100,000) and Romanians (25,000). Unlike most of their neighbours, the Hungarians are not Slavs; the Magyars, who have since been intermingled with peoples of Germanic stock, originally came from east of the Urals, and their language is unlike any other European tongue, though distantly related to Finnish and Estonian. Many ethnic Hungarians, equivalent to about a third of the population of the country, live outside Hungary. Almost every other inhabitant of Hungary has a relative living outside eastern Europe.

3 SOCIETY AND CULTURE

Cultural Pattern

Cultural life is intended to assist 'the construction of the socialist state'. In practice, however, in Hungary more than elsewhere in the Soviet bloc, the strength of western cultural influence is very visible.

The Media

Newspapers are the organs of the Communist Party, trade unions, and social organisations. Religious denominations produce their own. There are 2.5 million radio licence holders. Western broadcasts are widely listened to, both in English and Hungarian. There have been regular television programmes since 1958 and there are now about 2 million set owners; 70% of households have a set. In many parts of Hungary TV programmes from neighbouring countries can be received, and there is particular interest in Austrian programmes.

Religion

Party members are forbidden to practise any religion. Of the rest of the population, approximately 50-60% are nominally Roman Catholic, 30% Calvinist, 4% Lutheran, and the remainder belong to the Union of Free Churches (Baptists, Presbyterians, Nazarenes, Free Christians, Seventh Day Adventists, etc.) or to one of the five separate branches of the Greek Orthodox Church. There are also estimated to be 100,000 Jews, and Jewish observance is greater in Hungary than elsewhere in Eastern Europe. There are 30 synagogues open in the capital and the only rabbinical seminary in a Communist country is there too. Religious instruction in schools is not forbidden, but parents must obtain special permission for it to be taught. Attendance at religious classes has declined sharply, especially in the towns. Atheism is actively promoted in the schools and universities, and official encouragement is given to civil weddings, funerals, and 'christenings'.

The relationship between Church and State over the past two decades has been particularly stormy. The Hungarian Constitution of 1949 declared the separation of Church and State, but in practice the churches have remained subjugated to government control through the State Office for Religious Affairs. The land reforms of 1948 deprived all the churches of their financial independence. The National Protestant Churches signed individual agreements with the government, but the Roman Catholic Church, which was the most powerful, and from the government's point of view, the most dangerous on account of its international character, conducted a spirited resistance under the leadership of Cardinal Mindszenty. The government reacted by trying Mindszenty and he was imprisoned for life. He was released in 1956 only to take up asylum in the US diplomatic mission for 15 years. Archbishop Grosz was tried and imprisoned and the remaining Bishops developed the concept of 'dual allegiance' by which they claim to be able to remain loyal both to the Pope and to the State. The current Vatican *'ostpolitik'* has produced a dialogue between Hungary and Rome but the government will probably continue to vet all ecclesiastical appointments.

4 HISTORY AND POLITICS
Early History

In the course of their history, beginning in or about AD 896, with the foundation of the Hungarian kingdom, the people have enjoyed little real independence. The Mongol invasion in the thirteenth century left the country in ruins. In 1301 the succession of national kings ended. After the reign of the outstanding Renaissance prince, Matthias Corvinus (1458-90), who did much to advance the country's intellectual life, a decline followed with a major peasant rebellion in 1514. The Turks overran the country at the battle of Mohacs in 1526 and, at the end of the seventeenth century, Hungary was conquered by the Hapsburgs. For the next two centuries Hungary was under Hapsburg rule, until 1848 when the Hungarians, led by Lajos Kossuth, formally denounced the Hapsburg dynasty and declared Hungary a republic with Kossuth as president. The Hungarian forces put up a stiff fight, but were finally beaten in August 1849, after the new Emperor, Francis Joseph, called in Russian aid. After a period of repression, a compromise was worked out in 1867 establishing the dual Austro-Hungarian Monarchy which lasted for over 50 years until the Empire fell at the end of World War One.

1918 to 1956

Under the Treaty of Trianon, Hungary lost 71.4% of her territory, and 10.6 million (60%) of her population. Her foreign policy between the wars was dominated by a desire to regain the lost territories and since the other Slav powers were protecting their own interests, Hungary turned to the Axis powers for redress. Hungary declared war on the Soviet Union in June 1941, and on the United States in December 1941. Hungary, however, proved so unsatisfactory an ally to Nazi Germany that in March, 1944, German troops occupied the country. Szálasi and his fellow members of the Hungarian Nazi Party (Arrow Cross) took over in November but in the same month Soviet troops arrived. Budapest fell after three months' siege in February 1945 and two months later Hungary was free of German troops. Behind the Soviet troops came Soviet political experts, accompanied by Hungarian Communists (including Rákosi, Gerö, and Imre Nagy) who had been living in exile in the USSR. By 1949 Communist control was complete and in the following four years the Communist Party, under Mátyás Rákosi, endeavoured to turn the country into a replica of the Soviet Union. After Stalin's death in 1953 more moderate counsels prevailed for a time but the party leadership remained divided between Stalinist and more moderate elements.

Uprising and After

Public discontent was growing and strong criticism of the régime was openly expressed by leading writers and journalists. Nevertheless the 1956 uprising was entirely unpremeditated. It began on 23 October 1956 when unarmed students demonstrated, and might have ended peacefully, but for a provocative speech, the shooting down by the State security police of unarmed demonstrators and the arrival of Soviet tanks. Street fighting lasted a week, the Soviet Army then withdrew and it seemed as if the Hungarians had won the day. By 1 November, under great public pressure, Nagy declared Hungary to be a neutral State, withdrew from the Warsaw Pact and appealed to the United Nations to support this policy. However, on 4 November Soviet troops again moved into Budapest in force and by 10 November the armed uprising was crushed. According to an official Hungarian estimate 2,700 people were killed and 20,000 wounded during the uprising. Considerable material damage was done to Budapest. Over 190,000 Hungarians fled the country; a small proportion returned, but the majority settled in western countries.

Once all traces of the uprising had been removed, Kádár, backed by massive Soviet credits, set about improving living conditions and bringing about a more relaxed atmosphere. Hungary appears to have succeeded better than any of the Warsaw Pact countries in reconciling the population to life under a Communist régime. Freer contacts with the West have increased Western influence despite party warnings of imperialist loosening-up tactics.

Government

According to the constitution of 1949, amended in 1976, the highest organ of State power is the National Assembly. It consists of one chamber elected every four years by all citizens over 18 years. In the general elections of April 1971, 98.2% of the electorate of over 7 million voted. The National Assembly elects the Presidential Council, consisting of the President, two Vice-Presidents, a Secretary and 17 members. The Council acts as a collective Head of State, fixes the dates of the elections, convenes parliament, and frames legislation, mostly in the form of decrees. Legislation is then discussed by committees of the National Assembly before being presented to the National Assembly at its next session. There are normally only about four sessions a year, lasting two or three days at a time. The members of the Council of Ministers who need not be members of the National Assembly, are appointed and dismissed by the National Assembly on the advice of the Presidential Council. The Council of Ministers, whose Chairman is *de facto* prime minister, directs the work of the ministries, supervises the execution of legislation and issues decrees and resolutions. All but four government ministries are headed by a member of the policy making, party central committee and the ministries' function is mainly executive.

The system of local government was reformed by a Law of 1971 designed to make the local councils largely self-financing and to widen their sphere of initiative. Local councils are elected (partly indirectly) at county and municipal level. At the intermediate district *(járás)* level, councils have been replaced since 1971 by non-elected district officers. Councils work under the political guidance of the party and general supervision of the Council of Ministers, which may annul any of their decisions that run counter to the law or threaten the national interest.

Communist Party

The Party hierarchy consists of the *Politburo* with 13 members, the Central Committee with about 105 members, which meets at least every three months, and the Central Committee Secretariat, headed by the First Secretary with six other members. There are also eight Central Committee departments. Before the 1956 Uprising, the party numbered about 900,000 members. Immediately afterwards membership fell to about 100,000. It has increased rapidly during recent years (by 9.3% between the summer of 1970 and the summer of 1972), and in 1980 stood at around 720,000. The Central Committee announced in March 1974 that membership was to be reviewed and the proportion of worker-members increased. The party coordinates and directs the Patriotic People's Front, a mass organisation including representatives of all walks of life. The Communist Youth organisation (KISZ) with 800,000 members, also runs the Pioneer Movement for children of between 7 and 14.

International Relations

Hungary's major foreign policy has been to express consistent support to the Soviet Union, formalised in the Soviet-Hungarian Treaty of Friendship, Co-operation and Mutual Assistance signed in 1967 (in succession to the original treaty concluded in 1948). After the invasion of Czechoslovakia a new Hungarian-Czechoslovak friendship treaty was signed in April 1969, and relations are now formally good, though less than warm. Despite traditional hostility towards Romania, because of her treatment of the 1.5 million Hungarians in Transylvania and western Romania, the Hungarians have worked at improving relations. Relations between Hungary and Yugoslavia are now good.

Relations with the west have improved greatly during the past decade. Those with the United States have become almost fully normal, after the signing of the Hungarian/US Property Rights Agreement settling pre-war and post-war claims on both sides. Diplomatic relations with the German Federal Republic were established in December 1973. Relations with Britain have also improved.

5 THE ECONOMY

Natural Resources

Hungary has few natural resources. Her only significant natural resource is bauxite, and uranium deposits near Pécs.

Although it has now been decided to maintain coal production at a maximum level the output consists mainly of low grades inadequate to meet all domestic needs. High grade iron ore and coking coal are available only in insignificant quantities, and Hungary has to import 80% of her rapidly growing oil requirements as well. Domestic gas supplies, although relatively high, do not permit self-sufficiency.

Agriculture

Agriculture now plays a greatly reduced, though nonetheless important part in the economy and 54% of the land area is given over to arable farming. Agriculture now employs about a quarter of the labour force and provides about 20% of the national income. Hungary is still a large exporter of meat, fruit and vegetables and half its exports to western European countries consist of agricultural products. As a result of the land collectivisation begun in 1948 about 94% of arable land is State or cooperatively owned. There are 2,315 cooperatives averaging about 2,000 hectares and employing about 80% of the agricultural population. There are also 175 State farms run on a basis similar to an industrial enterprise and averaging 5,500 hectares. Collective farms have about a million members, but only 578,000 are working members. Collective farmers are entitled to their own household plots, where they can earn more than on the collective, and although these plots accounted for only 7.8% of total agricultural land in 1971, they play a vital part in the nation's food supply and export trade. In 1971 they were responsible for 23% of the total value of agricultural production. To sustain the pace of advance the government is now investing heavily in so-called 'closed systems' of intensive cultivation based partly on Western technology.

Industry

Since World War Two industry has replaced agriculture as the largest sector of the economy. In 1975 it employed 37% of the labour force and produced 47% of the net material product. After 1948 the government embarked on a policy of building up heavy industry, despite the lack of natural resources. Major sectors are engineering, chemicals and petrochemicals including plastics, pharmaceuticals and fertilisers, computers, energy generation, building, aluminium, bus manufacture and telecommunications. Seventy percent of raw materials have to be imported, including crude oil, iron ore, copper and copper products, raw materials for the plastics industry, and chemical fibres. A substantial proportion comes from the Soviet Union, and increased costs have affected the planned growth rate of the Hungarian GNP since 1975, when the cost of petroleum imports nearly doubled.

Trade

Under the fourth Five Year Plan (1971-75) foreign trade went up by 60%, representing an unprecedentedly rapid growth. One important development has been the drive to increase the proportion of exported engineering and industrial goods and reduce Hungary's traditional dependence on agricultural product. the Soviet Union is Hungary's main trading partner, accounting for about 34% of total turnover, by providing a substantial part of imported raw materials and a large market for many classes of Hungarian consumer goods and foodstuffs as well as engineering products. At present almost 70% of Hungary's foreign trade is conducted with the Council for Mutual Economic Assistance (CMEA). Trade with the West accounts for about one third of turnover. Although still only a small proportion of Hungary's total, trade with developing countries has attracted growing attention. There is evidence of Hungary's taking increasingly seriously the opportunities for diversification of her raw material supplies offered by some Middle Eastern, South American and African countries. Hungary also maintains an open door for economic relations with China.

Economic Situation

The most outstanding economic change has been the rapid industrialisation under the Communist régime of a predominantly agrarian country which lost more than 40% of its national assets during World War Two. With Soviet aid, industrial output had increased four-fold and national income trebled by 1964, but only at the cost of pressure on the workers, and by 1964 it was clear that the system (based on the standard Soviet central control planning system) was not economically efficient. Party commissions set up to investigate the problems reported in late 1965 that 'fundamental and essential changes' were needed, and on 25 May 1966, the Central Committee passed a resolution outlining the New Economic Mechanism (NEM) to come into operation on 1 January 1968. The aim was to evolve a socialist market economy in which business enterprises produce what they want, engage in competition on the domestic and foreign markets, and share profits among the workers. Central planning was retained to a certain extent, in plans for the long term - expressed in five- and fifteen-year plans - and for general short term trends (expressed annually in the National Economic Plan and the Budget). The major targets of the fourth Five-Year Plan (1971-75) were exceeded. National income rose by 35%, and industrial production increased by 38% over the previous five-year period and agricultural output by 18%. The fifth Five-Year Plan (1976-80) aimed at increased productivity and efficiency, and stressed the modernisation of industry, with a rise in industrial production of 33-35%. Particular emphasis was placed on the expansion of the engineering and chemical industries and on the increased mechanisation of agriculture.

6 THE EDUCATION SYSTEM

Academic Year

The school year begins on 1 September and ends on 31 August; it is divided into two semesters: September to January and January to June, except for students in the last year of secondary studies whose year ends on 8 May. There are also two short holidays in the academic year, one at the end of December and one in April.

Pre-School

Pre-primary education is not compulsory, but children under the age of 3 may attend crèches *(bölcsödék)* and those between the ages of 3 and 6 may attend kindergartens *(óvodák)*. State schools are free, although a charge may be made for maintenance, depending on parental income. However, demand often exceeds supply, and in cases where the number of applications exceeds the capacity of the kindergartens, committees decide who will be admitted, after investigating the children's family situation. In 1973 40,000 children were refused admittance to kindergartens because capacity was already exceeded by 41,000. Crèches may be either day or boarding, run by local authorities or factories and other enterprises and supervised by the Ministry of Health. Kindergartens may be full-day, seasonal, half-day, weekly or permanent boarding and are supervised by the Ministry of Cultural Affairs. Experiments are being carried out to combine crèches and kindergartens so that parents can leave all their young children at the same place. Administration facilities would be shared although classrooms and play areas would be separate. At present work specifically designed to prepare children for primary school is only carried out in about 45% of the existing kindergartens because of lack of facilities, but Hungarian television broadcasts programmes for this age group.

First level (Basic) Schools
(altalanos iskola)

School attendance is free and compulsory between the ages of 6 and 16. School preparatory courses are run during the summer months which about 25% of school beginners attend. This means that, including those who attend kindergartens, 91% of children in the first grade of primary school have received some sort of school preparation.

Primary schools (also known as basic schools) have two cycles, each of four years. In the lower cycle a class teacher takes all the subjects, while in the upper cycle instruction is carried out by specialists. The curriculum follows the general pattern of similar schools in other East European countries, starting with an emphasis on Hungarian language and mathematics, together with art, handwork, music, and physical education. Other subjects such as history, geography, languages, and the sciences, are introduced about halfway through the course. Over the past few years a system of special classes in music and foreign languages (Russian, English, French, and German) has been developed to provide more scope for special talents. In 1966/67 over 12% of general schools ran these special classes, and more were planned. There is a system of assessment, and promotion from class to class. Children who fail more than two subjects have to repeat the year; if they fail only two they have a second chance at a supplementary examination after the summer holidays.

Upper Stage Second Level (Secondary) Schools

At 14 pupils graduate to a grammar school *(gymnazium)*, a technical school *(technikum)* or other specialised secondary school, or continue their studies in an apprentice training school. Selection for secondary schools is made by the schools themselves based on basic school reports. Just over 80% of primary school graduates continue their studies. Under a Law of August 1973, children of 14 are no longer obliged to attend school daily, and may finish their schooling in continuation schools *(továbbképző iskolák)*.

Gymnazium

These provide a four-year course of mainly academic studies, although there is some vocational training in the curriculum. The proportion of time allocated to the latter varies from two hours to a whole day. There is a common core of humanities and sciences but pupils are also able to specialise in particular areas that interest them. A new feature of secondary education was the introduction of the subject in September 1973 'The Fundamentals of our World Outlook', a course in civics and political theory, considered necessary to counteract what some term 'an alarming eclecticism' which the present young generation seems to exhibit in its thinking. The principal themes dealt with are laid down by the Ministry of Education. Another new subject was introduced in 1974, a course in preparation for family life. Further facilities are provided by extra curricular study groups which are attended by 40% of *gymnazium* pupils. Each year 300 to 800 secondary school pupils participate in national school competitions in certain subjects. The winners of the first ten places of the competitions are exempted from the university entrance examination in that particular subject. The *gymnazium* course culminates in a leaving certificate *(érettségeri)*.

Technical Secondary Schools (Technikum)

These provide practical training (together with some general education) for a group of connected professions and each school is associated with an industrial or agricultural concern where the pupils gain practical experience. Because of the demand for skilled labour the schools are very important, and their superior facilities for teaching a trade often make them more popular than grammar schools, although a shortage of places may necessitate pupils accepting grammar school places as second best. In 1972/73, 55.8% of secondary school age children entered *technikums*. Pupils may apply for admission on completion of their basic schooling, provided they are not more than 17 years old. Studies last four years; the academic year is one month longer than in the *gymnasium*, to take account of summer training in production work. Of the total course time, 35% is devoted to general education, 35% to vocational theory, and 30% to vocational practice. In all *technikums* the same syllabus and textbooks are followed for subjects unrelated to the particular craft, but the number of lessons and the emphasis placed on each subject varies according to the special requirements of the pupils. The final matriculation certificate qualifies students either to apply for university or to enter appropriate employment. University candidates are expected to do a year's industrial or agricultural work between school and university. Students who enter employment may, after one or two years' practical work, continue their studies at an industrial college or university.

Specialised Secondary Schools

Admission to specialised music schools is by entrance examination for children who have completed the music syllabus of the primary school or for children who have acquired the same level privately. Instruction is given in most instruments and in addition pupils learn the basics of music theory. A matriculation certificate from a music secondary school enables the pupil to obtain employment in choirs and orchestras or to apply to the Music Academy. Art schools train students for entry to the various branches of art industry and instruction offered includes furniture restoration, glass pattern designing, textile pattern industry, etc. Outstanding pupils may apply for higher education to the fine arts or applied arts high schools, to the fine arts departments of universities, or to the Faculty of Architecture of the Technical University.

Apprentice Training Schools
(ipari tanulók gyakorló iskolái)

These are attached to factories, agricultural cooperatives, etc. and lead to full trade qualifications. General education is not so important in the curriculum in this type of school. The courses lead to skilled workers' qualifications but not the secondary school leaving certificate. Most courses last for three years, although in some trades they may be shorter, and can be reduced to one year for students who have completed secondary schooling. At the end of the course the newly qualified workers normally go straight into employment. Some may, however, qualify for higher general or technical education by following adult education courses leading to secondary qualifications, equivalent to the grammar school certificate.

Continuation Schools
(továbbképző iskolák)

Children who leave the basic school at age 14 and do not continue with their studies in secondary or apprentice schools are required to attend continuation schools until the age of 16. They must attend two days or the equivalent (10 hours) a week.

Teacher Training

Teachers are trained in separate institutions according to the level of class taught. All intending teachers must complete secondary education before embarking on professional training.

Kindergarten

Kindergarten teachers are trained in two-year colleges *(ovónöképző iskolák)*, where they study psychology, educational theory, history of art and literature, singing, physical training and school management. They also learn teaching methods and receive basic training in educational methods for handicapped children. In the fourth term they do six weeks' teaching practice and at the end of the second year sit for a State examination to obtain their teaching certificate. There are training colleges for kindergarten teachers in Kecskemét, Sopron, Esztergom and Szarvas.

Lower Basic

These trainee teachers follow a three-year course in colleges called *tanár továbbképző kollégiumok*, where they study a broad curriculum and learn to use modern teaching aids. They spend one term on teaching practice. There are ten of these teacher training colleges in Hungary.

Upper Basic

Upper basic teachers take four-year courses in the pedagogical institutes *(pedagógiai intézetek)*, and are trained as subject specialists. In addition to specialist subjects the courses include educational theory, psychology, teaching methods, and teaching practice. This consists of one or two days a week from the sixth half-year and a continuous period of practice in the fourth year in the school attached to the institute.

Secondary

Secondary school subject specialist teachers are trained for five years at a university although some teachers of technical subjects are trained in technical colleges. Post-graduate refresher courses are organised by the Ministry of Education and by a new body, the National Institute of Pedagogy *(Országor Pedagógiai Intézet)*. The university course in humanities and the pure sciences includes educational theory, methods, psychology, philosophy, logic, and additional courses in political subjects and one or two foreign languages. In the second to fourth years the students visit schools to observe lessons, and in the final year teaching practice is carried out in 'pilot schools', under the supervision of the school staff.

Special

Teachers of handicapped children are trained in four-year courses in a special institute. Apart from the usual subjects, they have special courses in the care of backward or handicapped children.

Third Level (Higher) Institutions

The term 'higher education' in Hungary applies not only to uiniversities and colleges of equivalent standard, but also to other institutions giving shorter courses of professional training to students who have completed secondary schooling. In addition to the general universities at Budapest, Dbrecen, Szeged and Pécs, there are 46 polytechnical colleges including three arts universities, three technical universities, two for agricultural sciences, one for the chemical industry, four medical and one for economics. The Academies of Fine and Applied Arts, the Budapest Academy of Music and the College of Fine and Dramatic Art also have university status and so do pedagogical institutes. Most university students come from the *gymnazia*.

Both the number of higher educational institutes and the number of students have increased considerably since before World War Two. There are now about 107,500 students in 56 higher education institutes, but there are more applicants than places. Over half attend full time, and the rest study in the evenings or by correspondence. Before the war nearly 40% of all students were in the law faculties, compared with 10% studying engineering, whereas students of technology now outnumber law students by 7 to 1. Over half the students live in hostels, and all are entitled to scholarships, assessed according to family income, provided that their marks are satisfactory.

Admission

In addition to a school leaving certificate a prospective student must pass an entrance examination, except for a few in specially exempt categories. To help students prepare for the admission examinations many institutions organise special evening preparatory courses. An applicant who has been rejected may appeal to the head of the institution, and if again rejected, to the minister exercising immediate jurisdiction over the institution. Some institutions use a system of 'conditional admission' for applicants who cannot be admitted for lack of space but are thereby entitled to be admitted the following year.

Courses

These generally last five years though some are four-year courses, and medical courses last six years. From the first year of the course students concentrate on their special field, but they are also obliged to continue with Russian, physical education, and political economy and Marxist-Leninist theory. On the strength of a government decree of 1969 universities determine their own curricula in accordance with the training objectives laid down by the ministry. The academic year is usually divided into two terms and the average number of study hours per week is 25. Students are tested periodically and also sit a final examination before obtaining their qualification. A two-tier training system has been introduced in some technical institutions where first year students and technical college students are taught together and go on to their respective institutions after two or three years. In this way they are able to train certified engineers capable of research development and management in five years and production engineers with a thorough practical knowledge in only three years.

Non-Formal and Adult

The general educational level of all individuals has risen considerably since the introduction of compulsory schooling. However, many people now in employment have not received much education, and education in rural districts is also often below standard. Self-education is increasing and courses are being organised all over the country, especially in towns, where young people form clubs for all sorts of scientific and technical subjects (local history, astronomy, and mathematics are particularly popular) and there are more than 200,000 people who take part in amateur art movements, the majority of whom are students.

General schools for adults provide evening or correspondence courses on the same lines as the basic eight-year school, the length of course depending on the standard already reached. Secondary schools also provide part time courses to enable adults with only basic schooling to reach the leaving certificate standard or improve their vocational qualifications. Other institutions give courses for vocational improvement or general culture, for instance the peasant academies, youth academies, parents' academies, and free universities, which are organised in all major towns. The latter provide courses of between one and four years in length, but for interest only, not for any formal qualification.

7 EDUCATIONAL ADMINISTRATION

Administrative Agencies

The educational institutions of Hungary are organised and administered by central and local organs with the cooperation of various cultural, scientific, and social organisations. Ultimate decision making power lies with the central executive organs of the Communist Party, i.e. the Scientific and Public Education

387

ADMINISTRATION

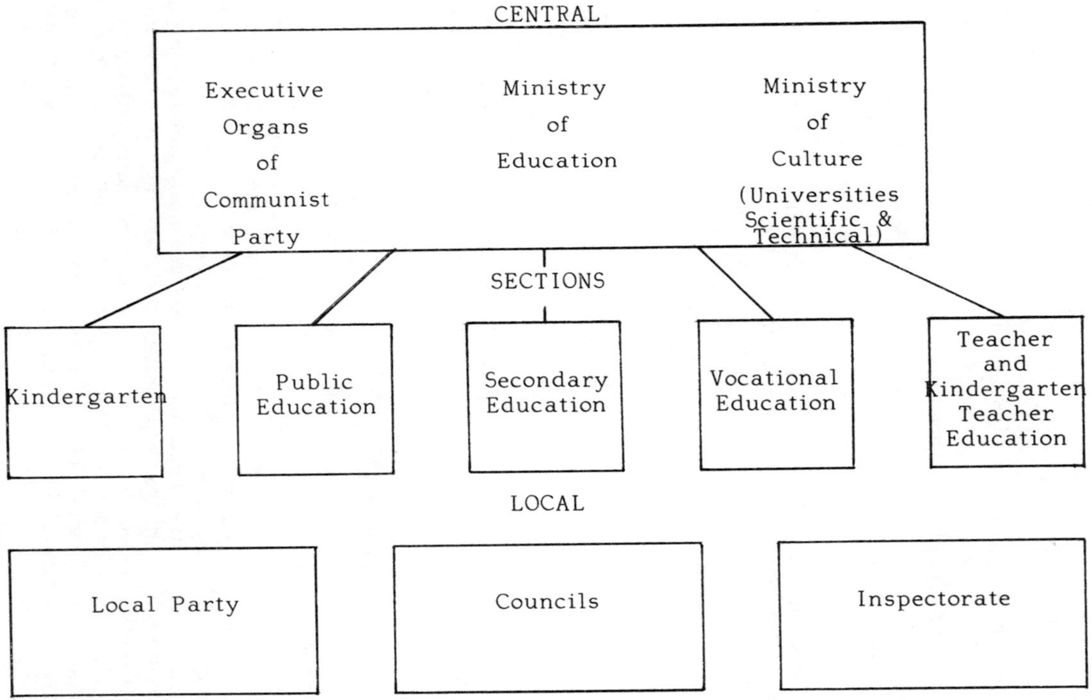

CENTRAL

| Executive Organs of Communist Party | Ministry of Education | Ministry of Culture (Universities Scientific & Technical) |

SECTIONS

| Kindergarten | Public Education | Secondary Education | Vocational Education | Teacher and Kindergarten Teacher Education |

LOCAL

| Local Party | Councils | Inspectorate |

section of the Party Central Committee. Party educational directives are issued in the form of decrees or decisions by the government, the Ministry of Culture, or other appropriate ministries. The syllabus followed in general or primary schools is discussed by the local Party branch and the Administrative Council, and each educational institution is obliged to give an account of its work. If necessary the local Party makes decisions to encourage work in certain areas and will sometimes back these decisions with financial aid. The overall result is that teachers are quite closely supervised.

Central and Local Government

Although policy formulation rests almost exclusively with the Party, the central and local governmental and school administrative organs have considerable latitude in implementing educational policy. The Ministry of Education draws up curricula, sets examinations, and legislates on qualifications. Divisions of the Ministry include the Kindergarten Section, the Department of Public Education, the Department of Secondary Education, Department of Vocational Education, and Department of Teacher and Kindergarten-Teacher Training. Much of the administrative work is carried out by local councils whose task it is to establish and maintain educational institutions. The 1973 Schools Statue requested each school to submit a work programme to the local education authority for approval by 10 September of each year. Institutes of higher education are organised with a Rector, Prorectors, and a council of senior staff at the head, all working under the general supervision of the Universities and Scientific and Technical Departments of the Ministry of Cultural Affairs (who also supervise university textbooks and curricula).

Inspection and Research

An educational inspectorate of general and special inspectors reviews the organisation and execution of the system. The former belong to the local council education departments and the latter are practising teachers who, besides their inspectorate work, also teach ten hours a week. Their work is coordinated on a national scale by the National Pedagogical Institute whose main task is to prepare syllabi, to advise on organisation, to carry out research and to authorise the writing of new textbooks. Educational research work is organised and directed by the Scientific Coordination Council which reports to the Ministry of Education. Special research is carried out by the Pedagogical Research Institute of the Hungarian Academy of Sciences and the Institute of Public Education, both of which also report to the Ministry of Education. Surveys are carried out frequently to test the professional capabilities of teachers and the testing procedure is also constantly under review as new methods and requirements are developed. The National Centre for Educational Methods was established in 1973 to further the spread of modern teaching methods and to provide refresher courses for teachers.

The National Pedagogical Library and Museum and the publication of several educational periodicals also help teachers to keep up to date.

8 EDUCATIONAL FINANCE
Education Budget

The educational budget is worked out by the National Planning Office whose estimates are submitted to the National Assembly. In 1975 4.8% of the gross national product was spent on education. The following data for 1977 gives an idea of the distribution of funds between the different levels of the educational system.

Allocation of Funds
Expenditure on Education: Distribution by Level
Percentage of Expenditure 1977

Pre-school	First Level	Second Level	Third Level	Other
13.0	38.3	13.7	21.6	13.4

The money allocated is distributed to the educational departments of local councils based on estimates received. Development depends on demographic factors. Money is allocated with a view to accommodating the variations in population estimated from census statistics.

Fees, Scholarships and Allowances

Education is free in primary/basic schools, schools for the handicapped, secondry schools, apprentice training schools, and adult education schools. Other schools charge tuition fees, which vary according to the student's grades and general educational achievement, and parental income. Fees are often offset by scholarships and family allowances. Scholarships are awarded on the basis of educational performance, and may be granted by the State as well as social organisations. They are normally awarded on contractual terms under which the recipient undertakes to work after graduation for a specified time at a location defined in the contract.

9 DEVELOPMENT AND PLANNING OF THE EDUCATION SYSTEM
Origins

Between 1920 and 1945 10% of the school age children did not register for school, and more than 10% of the population was illiterate. In 45% of general elementary schools there was only one teacher and 25% operated with two teachers. Higher elementary schools whose school leaving certificate qualified children for the so-called lower grade clerk professions were mostly attended by the children of the lower middle class who could not afford to send their children to grammar schools. It was the task of grammar schools to educate the brighter pupils destined for high office in public life. The tuition fees were so high in these schools, however, that between the wars the proportion of young people of peasant and/or working class origin did not exceed 4-5% in secondary education.

Between 1% and 2% of the children joined the universities. The Church gave scholarships to poor students but they mostly joined the clergy. Between the wars there were only 38 higher education institutions, four of which were universities of arts and natural sciences. Half the students at that time were theologians and jurists, while only 11% were medical students and 7.2% students of engineering. In 1974 over 50% of the population aged 15 and over had not completed an eight-year general school course.

Before 1945 Hungary's education system was similar to that in other Central European countries. Plans were made to raise the level of general public education and in 1940 a new Educational Law was enacted establishing eight-form compulsory general schools. It did not come into force, however, because of World War Two. The modernisation of public education really only began in 1945 when the provisional government made school attendance compulsory in eight-form general schools for all children between 6 and 14 years of age. The basis of the present school system was formed between 1945 and 1948. The 1949 Constitution laid the ground for later developments by writing in the right to free and compulsory basic education. Because of the rise in the number of students and the increased requirements of public life following social, political, economic, technical and cultural development further modernisation became necessary by the end of the 1950s. A reform of curricula and polytechnical education was effected by an Education Act in 1968. Technical secondary schools were established, new curricula were drawn up, textbooks and/or lecture notes were written. By virtue of Act VI of 1969 vocational schools were established as a sector of secondary education.

Planning Institutions

Like other socialist countries Hungary has a National Planning System. Within each Five-Year Plan annual plans are worked out by the National Planning Office which coordinates every department from the financial point of view. Although responsibility for educational affairs lies with the Ministry of Education and Culture the local councils have education departments who consult with the local Party branch educational expert. The plans are looked at by various research institutions and are coordinated by the National Planning Office and must subsequently be accepted by the National Assembly and the Presidential Council. Once accepted, the execution of these plans is frequently hindered by unexpected factors (shortage in building materials, change in the rate of foreign exchange, etc.). A report must be made to the National Assembly in any case when the Plan is not fulfilled. Plans for the 1970s included the reorganisation of the educational system.

10 THE SYSTEM IN OPERATION
Current Developments

The present school system was laid down in the Education Law of 1961. The system aims to increase the general level of education, to produce a forward thinking socialist generation and to provide sufficient manpower for the requirements of the national economy. Social, political and economic pressures have necessitated several changes in the system. For example, economic pressures have made it necessary to distribute manpower as follows: 35% skilled workers: 40% semi-skilled workers; which means that *gymnazium* education will be required for only 15% and university education for only 10%. From time to time the objectives of the education system are redefined. In June 1972 a memorandum from the Party formulated the policy subsequently implemented by the Ministry of Education.

Research into the shortcomings of the present structure of education, among which the most significant are felt to be the lack of proper mechanism for observation and orientation of pupils in their most formative years, inadequate educational guidance, difficulties in transfer between the different sectors of upper secondary education and the difficulties in transition to higher education, is designed to recommend improvements to the system. It is clear that it will be some time before investigations are put to the test in selected experimental schools and finally, after the necessary readjustments, plans for reform are approved by the ministry and introduced into practice all over the country. Though centrally coordinated, financed and administered, the programmes of educational research leave, nevertheless, scope for original experimentation, individual initiative and team-work, which has become an important feature of the system. As a result of the investigations into alternative forms of an improved structure of the system, the content of education and educational methods, far-reaching changes are likely to be introduced, although many aspects of schooling and studying have still to be investigated and many problems to be solved.

However, the Hungarian system of education also develops and changes under the impact of more universal trends and tendencies such as the explosion of knowledge, the explosion of aspirations, progressive industrialisation and mechanisation of the economy as well as the national features such as the low birth rate, limited geographical and social mobility, and characteristic linguistic uniqueness. The concentration of talent providing the motive force for modernisation and improvement is to be found in the research institutes and the universities. It seems that, increasingly, educational changes abroad are becoming recognised by Hungarian scholars as being relevant to the solution of problems experienced in their own country.

Trends

The old model of 8 + 4 is likely to be replaced by 6 + 4 + 2, where the middle four years would be characterised by observation and orientation, a mixed combination of 'core-subjects' and electives. This is an interesting possibility, which would bring the Hungarian system nearer to the French and West German ideas on curricular reform and restructuring the system. There is also a possibility of lowering the age of compulsory education to five years of age, as in England. The persistently low birth rate in Hungary may make this reform more feasible than it would otherwise be. It appears that another area subject to change is that of evaluation. In particular the final maturity examination at the end of secondary education, should become simplified with Hungarian and mathematics taken only as a written examination. At present it is a lengthy procedure in its oral and written form, in Hungarian, history, mathematics and one of the following subjects: physics, chemistry, biology or a foreign language. In addition, some schools apparently are introducing new forms of homework assignments: instead of more frequent short exercises they set much longer written kinds of work requiring considerable intellectual effort, inventiveness and even small scale research on an individual basis.

Kindergartens

Although the government has made a real effort in recent years to increase the number of kindergartens, only an average of 60 out of every 100 children can be given places in them. Moreover, the figure is somewhat distorted, since there is less kindergarten space in the countryside than in Budapest and other major cities. Despite the fact that an additional 55,000 children were accepted for kindergartens between 1970 and 1974, instead of the 39,000 called for in the 1971-75 Plan, the shortage of space increased, indicated by the fact that in the same period some 50,000 children had to be refused admission. The shortage of personnel remains a problem; groups of 30 or 35 children under one teacher are not uncommon. In 1974 25% of kindergarten teachers were untrained. The shortage of nursery maids for the kindergartens is another problem, remedied to some extend by the practice of employing housewives for four to six hours a day. To make up for the shortage of State kindergartens, private institutions have been proliferating in the country, although they are not generally favoured by the authorities.

Provision and Wastage

School children registered in primary schools represent 98-99% of the age group and 90-91% of them will continue until they are 16. The drop-out rate is also very small in respect of children receiving education in the higher classes of specialised (technical) school where the percentage of the final certificates issues to school leavers is 94%. The small percentage of wastage is partly due to the fact that not only has the number of the teaching staff increased considerably but the number of classrooms, and new schools, has also risen. The establishment of new schools was for a long time affected by resettlement - (organisation of large scale agricultural farms, building up new industrial areas, etc.) and demographic factors. Approximately 70% of each generation receives secondary education (and in 1938 the figure was only 16.6%). The ratio of students in higher education is 11% (in 1938 only 2%). Fifty percent of children in secondary and higher education are from worker or peasant families.

Teachers

Although the number of teachers has increased considerably in recent years the numbers are still inadequate and, given the government's policy of increasing the country's birth rate, there will probably be an even greater demand for teachers in a few years' time. In 1974, of 6,247 posts advertised only 3,570 were filled, some by non-qualified teaching personnel, a measure much criticised in some quarters. There is a shortage of primary school teachers of specialised subjects, instructors in technical subjects, kindergarten teachers, and unspecialised teachers in the first four grades. In 1974 special arrangements were made to encourage recently retired qualified teachers back into the profession, and it was stipulated that non-qualified teachers might only be employed if there were no retired teachers available to fill the vacancies. The number of people who leave the profession is particularly high among educationists, nearly 7.5% of qualified kindergarten teachers, and about 15% of specialised primary school teachers are working outside education. Many teachers attributed the shortage of teachers to the negligence of the education authorities who did not properly plan the number of teachers to be trained, and also to the fact that qualified teachers do not want to teach as their salaries are lower than other people's with similar qualifications in other professions.

Conclusion

While there have been considerable advances made in education, problems still remain. One of the most serious shortcomings is the once-and-for-all nature of the decision taken at 14 as to the type of secondary school one chooses. English teaching is weak in pronunciation and intonation as teachers seldom have an opportunity to converse with English visitors. Polytechnical education is receiving less attention because of the heavy burden of academic work although teachers recognise the possibilities in this area. There is real interest in forthcoming changes in the field of secondary education to improve the quality of learning and make greater flexibility possible. It seems that there are two needs to be met first: the evening-out of the individual differences among children at the beginning of their schooling, due to the environmental differences in early childhood, through compensatory activities; and the introduction of an extended period of orientation, covering the 12-16 years age range, where interests, aptitudes, and special talents were likely to reveal themselves fully and to take final form.

Although requirements are defined in the National Plan its execution cannot be rigidly maintained. According to a survey in 1972, 55.5% of students wished to follow an intellectual occupation, 29.8% wanted to become skilled workers and 8.8% professional workers. Since these percentages cannot be maintained from the point of view of the national economy (every year Hungarian industry, agriculture, transport services and other trades require 90,000-95,000 new skilled workers - 40% of them in Budapest), and also because of the lack of places in higher education there is great competition and many students are unable to obtain the kind of education they would like. Students in general are not inclined to strive for excellence but are content with mediocre results - possibly because of the dismal employment prospects awaiting them. Generally speaking neither parents nor students are satisfied with the education system after primary school, and there is considerable conflict between the desires of the population at large and the policy followed by the government.

FURTHER READING

Berend, Ivan T. (1980). 'Educational reforms in East-Central Europe: the Hungarian example', *Prospects*, **10**, No. 2.
Fukasz, Gyorgy (1978). *Adult Education in the Hungarian People's Republic (HPR)*. Prague European Centre for Leisure and Education.
Géndos, Miktos (Ed. in chief) (1970). *Hungary 1978*. Pannonea P., Budapest.
Hungarian Embassy Great Britain (1979). *Minorities in Hungary*. London Embassy of the Hungarian People's Republic.
International Review of Education (1980). **26**, No. 3.
Norman, J. B. (1980). 'The processes of implementing educational policy in Hungary: policy and practice', *Comparative Education*, **16**, No. 2, June.
Sándor, Frigyes (Ed.) (1969). *Musical Education in Hungary* (trans.). Boosey & Hawkes, London.
Tamás, Pal (1979). 'Features of Hungarian higher education', *European Journal of Education*, **14**, No. 4, December.
UNESCO (1974). *Cultural Policy in Hungary*. (Hungarian National Commission for Unesco), Unesco, Paris.
UNESCO/IBE (1980). *International Yearbook of Education*, XXII. Unesco, Paris.

Structure of the education system in Hungary

Age	3	4	5	6	7	8	9	10	11	12	13	14	15	16	17	18	19	20	21	22	23	24
Level				I								II				III				IV		
Stage				1								2		3		4				4		

Compulsory

School type: Divided / Partly-divided / District / Associate

Academic / Vocational / Skilled workers

University / 1st & 2nd teacher training

Adult education

▨ Education preceding the first level

Examinations: secondary school leaving examination is held at the end of stages 2 and 3

Source: UNESCO/IBE International Yearbook of Education

Compulsory Education: Age Limits 6–16   Duration (years) 10
Entrance age to pre-school education: 3

395

HUNGARY BASIC STATISTICS		1960	1970	1975	1978 (approx.)
1	Total population (000)	9,984	10,337	10,533	10,685
	% female	52	52	51	51
2	% population 0–14 years				
	% female	49	48	48	48
3	Enrolment, all levels	1,717,715	1,661,853	1,530,548	1,566,350
	% female	46	46	48	48
	First level	1,392,260	1,115,993	1,051,095	1,106,744
	% female	48	48	49	49
	Second level	44,585	80,536	107,555	108,649
	% female	38	43	45	46
	Third level	44,585	80,536	107,555	108,649
	% female	33	43	48	50
4	Teachers, all levels	76,658	95,358	101,777	
	% female				
	First level	57,290	63,125	66,861	76,750
	% female	63	73		80
	Second level	13,733	22,442	22,781	24,235
	% female	24			48
	Third level	5,635	9,791	12,135	12,579
	% female		22	27	29
5	Public expenditure on education				
	Total (000) Forints	6,214,641	12,208,066	19,325,492	
	As % of GNP	4.4	4.4	4.8	
6	% enrolment (MF) by level	100	100	100	100
	First level	81	67	69	70
	Second level	16	28	24	23
	Third level	3	5	7	7
	% enrolment (F) by level	100	100	100	100
	First level	85	70	70	72
	Second level	13	26	23	21
	Third level	2	4	7	7
7	Entrance age: Duration of				
	First level education	6:8	6:8	6:8	6:8
	Second level education	14:4	14:4	14:4	14:4
8	Enrolment ratios (MF)				
	First level	101	98	99	97
	Second level	46	63	63	69
	Third level	6.52	10.11	11.67	
	Enrolment ratios (F)				
	First level	100	97	99	97
	Second level	35	55	58	65
	Third level	4.19	8.79	11.54	

Israel

CONTENTS

1 Geography	. . . . . .	398
2 Population	. . . . . .	400
3 Society and Culture .	. . . . .	401
4 History and Politics .	. . . . .	402
5 The Economy .	. . . . . .	405
6 The Education System	. . . .	406
7 Educational Administration	. . . .	414
8 Educational Finance .	. . . .	416
9 Development and Planning of the Education System	. . . .	417

The creation of Israel was designed to fulfil the desire for a Jewish homeland. The Declaration of Independence of 14 May 1948 laid down that "the State of Israel will be open to the immigration of Jews from all countries of their dispersion". In 1950 a law was passed giving every Jew who wished to settle there the right to enter Israel. Over a period of 30 years more than 1,250,000 immigrants from over 100 different countries came to Israel. The unifying purpose which lay behind the creation of Israel had its repercussions. A large number of Arabs left the country in 1948-49 as refugees. For the Arabs who remained, education is provided for their children in what should be regarded as a separate part of the system. The language used in these schools is Arabic rather than Hebrew and the curriculum is different, in that it does not include Biblical studies or Hebrew literature.

Cultural diversity among the Jewish population reflects the status and country of origin of immigrants. The majority of the early arrivals were Europeans. Jews from North Africa and the Yemen were not easily assimilated into a formal education system which was basically European. Again among the Jewish population some are very orthodox and expect the schools to retain a religious purpose and ethos. The *kibbutz* movements represent a strong educational commitment, and because of the frequent wars with Arab countries the army has played an important educational role.

Thus, in spite of the strong national commitment to an independent state, Israel is an example of a country in which education is regarded as important in creating national unity, but serves to promote considerable cultural diversity.

The Editor

Note: *All figures given in this Profile refer to Israel within the pre-1967 borders and do not include the areas administered by Israel since June 1967.*

1 GEOGRAPHY

Topography

Considering the extent to which the State of Israel figures on the world stage it comes as something of a shock to realise how small it is. Its total area is 20,700 square kilometres (7,992 square miles). From Eilat in the south to Metulla in the north is only 512 km, while at no point is the country more than 208 km wide. The traveller may drive comfortably from north to south in little more than a day and from east to west in two hours. While much of the country has what may loosely be called 'Mediterranean' appearance, in the south lies a desert area of forbidding aspect, the Negev. The heart of the country is the coastal plain, bordering on the Mediterranean. Except for Haifa Bay, the coast is unindented and for the most part lined with sand dunes. Inland runs a chain of hills, from the Galilee in the north to the Negev in the south. The 'mountains' or rather high hills, of Samaria upon which Jerusalem stands are part of this chain, much of which is over 610 metres (2,000 feet). To the east of these hills is the Rift Valley along which runs the Jordan, and in which lies the Sea of Galilee, and the Dead Sea, the lowest spot on earth, 400 metres (1,308 feet) below sea level.

Looked at from the point of view of the geography of the Middle East as a whole, Israel lies at the centre of the area. In ancient times the fertile crescent in the north east and the valley of the Nile in the south west provided the centres of social and political power in the region while communication between them was through Palestine. Biblical history is in no small measure the story of the wars fought between Egypt on the one hand and Babylon and Assyria on the other, across the land of Palestine. Today Israel occupies a no less central position within the Middle East.

Climate

Israel has the sunny and warm summers and relatively mild winters typical of the Mediterranean. No rain falls between May and October. There are, however, variations in climate. For example, the rainfall in the Galilee is about 39.4 inches per year (compared with 23.6 inches in London), while in Eilat it is only 0.98 inches. In Jerusalem the rainfall is 21.65 inches while only 19 miles away at the Dead Sea it is well below 4 inches.

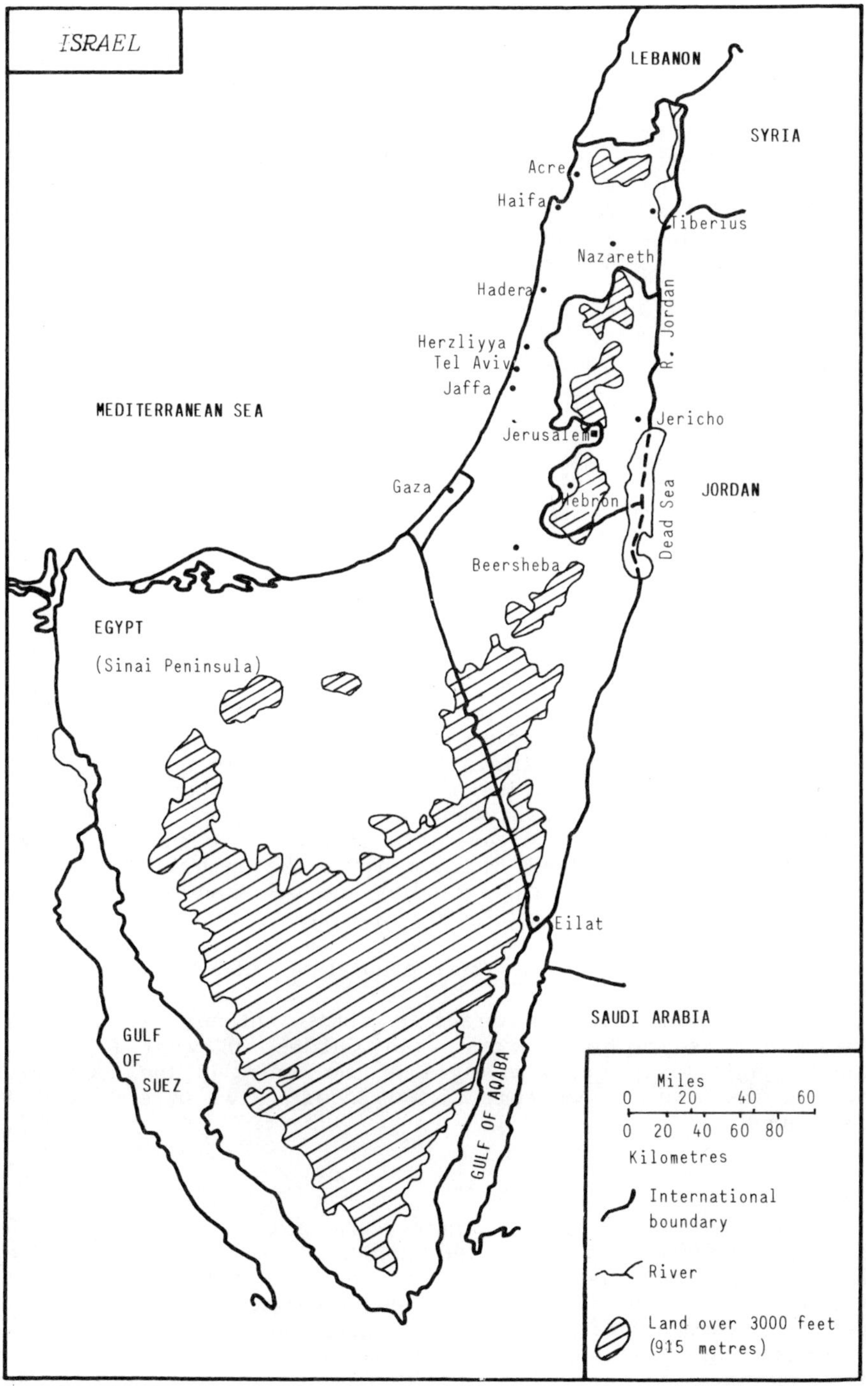

ISRAEL
LEBANON
SYRIA
Acre
Haifa
Tiberius
Nazareth
Hadera
R. Jordan
Herzliyya
Tel Aviv
Jaffa
MEDITERRANEAN SEA
Jericho
Jerusalem
Gaza
Hebron
JORDAN
Dead Sea
Beersheba
EGYPT
(Sinai Peninsula)
Eilat
SAUDI ARABIA
GULF
OF
SUEZ
GULF OF AQABA
Miles
0 20 40 60
0 20 40 60 80
Kilometres
International boundary
River
Land over 3000 feet (915 metres)

Communications

Israel has developed an extensive system of roads totalling 10,600 km (6,625 miles). Bus services connect all the cities and towns and shared taxi services the cities. The Israeli Railway Administration operates 800 km (500 miles) of railway track and when development is complete Eilat, the port on the Gulf of Aqaba, will be served by rail. El Al (Israel Airlines) operates international services and Arkia (Israel Inland Airlines) a domestic service. Israel has a merchant fleet with a gross tonnage of 4,475,000. The largest port is Haifa.

2 POPULATION

Growth

The estimated population at 31 March 1979 was 3,836,000. Since the founding of the State of Israel in 1948, about 1.5 million immigrants (about half from Europe) have settled in the country. Up to 1972, the rate of growth of population was probably the most rapid in the world (44% between 1961 and 1972 - one third by immigration). Since the 1973 War, however, immigration has slowed down. In 1975 the rate of growth dropped to 2.1% and this trend has continued.

Distribution

The people of Israel are not uniformly distributed over its area. The great bulk of the population lives in the coastal plain. Over a million people live in the Greater Tel Aviv area and half a million in Haifa, the country's principal port, and surrounding district. Jerusalem and its surrounding district have a population of about 400,000. Over 80% of the population live in towns or urban areas; these include a number of 'new' towns scattered throughout the country. The remainder live in small settlements or villages including the well known *kibbutzim* which, great as their contribution has been to the development of Israel and important as they are as a social experiment, house only about 3% of the total population (about 85,000 people in all).

The Arab population of Israel is almost entirely concentrated in certain geographical areas - in Galilee, in what is called the Triangle (a group of villages in the centre of the country), and in the south where some 35,000 Bedouin live in semi-settled conditions.

Groups

At the beginning of 1977 there were 3,031,800 Jews, 429,000 Moslems, 82,000 Christians and 44,000 Druzes in Israel. The Jewish population is made up of representatives of a great variety of communities. It includes descendants of the Jewish religious communities who lived in the holy cities of Safad, Tiberias and Jerusalem throughout Mameluke and Turkish times; the descendants of pioneering groups from Russia and East Europe who entered the country in the late nineteenth and early twentieth centuries, and of the German Jews who fled from Hitler. After 1947 the greater part of the Jewish communities from the Arab world, from Iraq, Morocco, Libya and Egypt, came to Israel where they mingled with the remnants of European Jewry who had escaped the Holocaust, and with smaller numbers of Jews from Western Europe, Latin America, the United States, South Africa and a number of other countries. As time passes an increasing percentage (it is now over 50%) of the population are 'sabras' (the popular term for Israelis born in Israel) but these young people still retain certain of the characteristics of the Jewish communities of the countries from which their parents came. This diversity of background, which is in some ways a source of strength, helping as it does to give the country a sense of vitality, is in others a source of difficulty, particularly perhaps in education, since the educational standards of the various groups vary very much.

Nor is the Arab population of Israel homogeneous. There are still considerable differences in outlook between the Moslem and Christian communities (though of late these have been less in evidence), while the 35,000 Bedouin in the south of the country still live quite different lives from the rest of the Arab population.

3 SOCIETY AND CULTURE

Social Patterns

It is extremely difficult to generalise about social patterns in Israel since the population is made up of people from so many different parts of the world. There is one feature of society, however, that is of concern to all in Israel and that is the considerable tendency for non-western Jews to find themselves in the situations classified as disadvantaged. Their employment is often of a menial kind and their living conditions are also frequently lower than that of western Jews. A combination of government policy and natural integration is gradually reducing the size of the problem.

Religion

Palestine was for centuries the object of pilgrimages by Christians, Moslems and Jews. The 24 or more separate Christian churches which have establishments in Israel today reflect the extent of Christian interest in Palestine. Jerusalem is also a Moslem Holy City. The Mosque of Omar is one of the great buildings of Islamic religious architecture and Moslems are the majority among the Arabs of Palestine. And the importance of Jerusalem to the Jews cannot be exaggerated.

Today neither the Christians nor the Moslems have much direct political influence in Israel. Political power is to be found rather in Jewish religious quarters. The Orthodox Jews have their own political parties, one of which, the National Religious Party, is of considerable importance. The NRP has used its bargaining position to prevent the introduction of civil marriage, to stop the functioning of public transport on the Sabbath over most of the country, and to maintain the religious schools within the State education system. However, there is no likelihood at the moment of Israel becoming a theocratic Jewish State; the majority of the people go to the synagogue only on high holidays and a significant minority are resolute secularists.

4 HISTORY AND POLITICS
Origins

It is hard to understand any aspect of life in Israel without reference to its history. In the traditional religious life of diaspora Jews continual reference was made to the time when the Jewish people would return to Zion. Up to about 1850 these references had for the most part an 'other-worldly' or Messianic character (although a few enthusiasts travelled to Palestine on pilgrimage or to live a life of prayer), but in the nineteenth century the orthodox tradition was fused with nationalist ideas. Jews who were not themselves orthodox, some of whom were indeed far to the left in social terms, began to think of establishing a Jewish national home in Palestine, a state where the Jewish people would be free from persecution and able to live as they pleased. The early peasant settlements of the 1880s supported by Baron Rothschild were followed by the settlements of Russian Socialist Zionists (the *kibbutzim*) which were founded from 1880-1914. The International Zionist Movement found its first popular leader in the person of Theodore Herzl.

British Mandate

The growth of the Jewish community was slow while Palestine was part of the Turkish empire but received great impetus when the British were given the Mandate after World War One. The British government had already in 1917 adopted the Balfour Declaration with its commitment to the creation of a Jewish national home. Under the British Mandate, Jewish settlement in Palestine proceeded rapidly and a thriving community was established. The success of the Zionist enterprise, organised by the Jewish Agency for Palestine and guided by Dr Weizmann, was indeed so considerable that it awoke fears in the minds of the Arab population of Palestine that they would find themselves 'taken over' by the Zionists. There had been some trouble in 1921 but the first serious riots between Arabs and Jews broke out in 1929. From this time onwards the British government for the first time had seriously to consider the difficulty of creating a national home in an area where Arab nationalism was just beginning to take root. The period between 1929 and 1940 was largely occupied in political terms by the efforts of the British to find a 'modus vivendi'. Throughout that period Palestine offered a haven to Jews fleeing from Germany and elsewhere. The adoption of a policy of partition by the Peel Commission in 1937 recognised that a state in which Jews and Arabs could live together was not a practical possibility.

Independence

During World War Two the feud between Jews and Arabs lay dormant but immediately after its close the trouble began again. This time the plight of the Jewish refugees in Europe, many of whom wished to come to Palestine, lent added vigour to the Zionist cause. The British, weary with fighting, were in no condition to maintain public order effectively and in 1947 they gave up the Mandate. The United Nations declared in favour of partition and the Jews in Palestine accepted it. It was, however, rejected by the Arabs both of Palestine and the neighbouring countries. There followed a civil war which the Jews won. In November 1947, the United Nations recognised Israel as an independent state and David Ben Gurion became its first Prime Minister. Almost immediately afterwards the Arab armies from Egypt, Syria and Jordan invaded the country but were defeated. As they withdrew they were followed by almost half a million of the Arab population.

The creation of the State of Israel was followed almost immediately by a mass immigration of refugees from Europe and shortly afterwards by an influx of Jews from Arabic speaking countries. The Jewish population of Palestine in 1947 was about 600,000. By 1957 the population had reached 1,976,000: in 1953 alone 239,000 immigrants arrived. The absorption of these large numbers caused the new state great difficulty. Accommodation was hard to find and full employment a thing of the future. The difficulties were compounded by the fact that many of the new immigrants were from socially and educationally backward communities. There could be no thought of turning them away since the 'Law of Return' passed immediately on establishment of the state stipulated that any Jew wishing to settle in Israel should be free to do so. The energies of society were heavily committed to the task of making a unified whole from these disparate elements. Gradually work was found, accommodation provided and educational facilities created.

Later Conflicts

The internal social and economic problems posed by the rapid expansion of the population were made the more difficult to solve by the continued hostility of Israel's neighbours. The continuous incursions of armed Arab bands from Gaza and elsewhere led to a build up of tension in the period 1954/56. Israel was therefore very willing to assist Britain and France in their invasion of Egypt in 1956. Israeli troops rapidly occupied the Sinai Desert and reached the Suez Canal but withdrew under pressure from the American government. In 1967 war broke out once more after the Egyptians had blockaded the Straits of Tiran leading to Eilat, Israel's only port in the south. Fighting against Egypt, Jordan and Syria, the Israelis secured victory within six days and remain in possession of part of the Sinai Desert and the Gaza strip, the Jordanian part of what was formerly Palestine, and the Golan Heights. In these areas there is a military administration backed by civilian personnel working in education, agriculture and the social services.

Neither the war of 1956 nor that of 1967 solved the deep-rooted political problems which lay at the heart of the feud between the Arabs and Jews in the Middle East. On the contrary, each conflict hardened the resolve of the Arabs to recover what they conceive to be their lost rights, and of the Israelis to strengthen themselves against an enemy who appeared determined to destroy them. Terrorist activities of Palestinian groups further increased the tension. In October 1973, armed by the Russians, the Arabs made yet another attempt to achieve their objective by force and were beaten back only after a desperate struggle in the course of which it became clear how great was the extent to which Israel relied upon her friendship with the United States. A peace conference begun at Geneva in November 1973 led to disengagement agreements, but little further progress was made towards peace until November 1977 when President Sadat of Egypt visited Israel to begin his peace initiative which, after considerable difficulties and setbacks, led to the Camp David accords of September 1978 between Israel and Egypt, backed by the United States of America, and subsequently to the Peace Treaty between Israel and Egypt signed in March 1979.

Political Organisation

The Israeli Parliament *(Knesset)* is a unicameral legislature, elected under a system of proportional representation every four years. Until 1977 the country was dominated politically by the Israel Labour Party (MAPAI) which has existed from the 1920s onwards and to which most of the country's best known politicians belong. The MAPAI party in its turn owed much of its power to the *Histadrut*, the Trade Union Congress, which had been established in Mandatory times to protect the interests of Jewish workers and settlers. It had, by providing medical services, establishing corporate enterprises, and education, assumed an important role within Mandatory Palestine which it in some measure retains in Israel today. However, in the elections of May 1977 the Likud Party won 43 of the 120 seats in the Knesset and became the single largest party. with the support of the National Religious Party and two smaller parties Mr Menachem Begin, the Likud Party leader, formed a government the following month. The structure of the political system is perhaps of less significance than the fact that the Israelis themselves feel free to express themselves on all political topics without reserve. Israel is a western democracy in the full sense of the term and individuals who feel themselves wronged can and do call upon the press, public opinion and the courts (which are modelled on British lines) to protect their rights.

International Relations

Israeli foreign relations are dominated by the requirements of survival in a generally hostile environment. Though once committed to neutrality Israel has experienced hostility from the Soviet Union and other countries of the Eastern bloc (with the exception of Romania) and has depended on Western countries for political and economic support and arms. Israel joined the United Nations in 1949 but has incurred condemnation from the UN for refusal to reabsorb Arab refugees (1948-49), refusal to accept the internationalisation of Jerusalem and reprisals against Arab terrorists.

5 THE ECONOMY

Agriculture

Traditionally Palestine was a land of 'milk and honey', the richness of which was a temptation to the marauding Bedouin from the harsh and arid lands round about. The rich soil of the coastal plain and some of the inland valleys coupled with intensive irrigation and the use of fertilisers have given Israel a very advanced agriculture. Production is increasing by about 7% - 9% annually. So far as basic foodstuffs are concerned Israel is very largely self-sufficient though some grain and meat are imported. Agriculture provides her with her major source of export revenue. The US$380 million earned by agricultural exports in 1976/77 came not only from citrus (US$191 million) but also from the export of cotton, groundnuts and seeds (US$62 million), vegetables (US$38 million), flowers (US$32 million) and fruit (US$27 million).

Natural Resources

Apart, however, from the natural fertility of the soil, Israel is not particularly well blessed in natural resources. Geological surveys have not revealed any substantial quantity of oil (the Israeli fields produce only about 5% of local consumption). There are extensive deposits of valuable minerals including magnesium, phosphates, bromine and potash in the Dead Sea area and the Negev, but little else. Water resources are limited and every effort is being made to develop them further.

Industry

In spite of the absence of raw materials, Israel has developed a thriving industry based largely on imported materials. Amongst the most important manufacturing industries are metalworking, aircraft, electronics, textiles, chemicals, building materials and food. The relative importance of industry to GNP is steadily increasing and at 35% in 1977 is higher than for any other country in the Middle East. Between 1968 and 1972 industrial output increased by 80% while industrial exports increased by 124%. Though there is an unfavourable balance of trade, the gap between imports and exports was slowly closing before the war in October 1973. Since 1975 it has been government policy to direct manpower into industry and particularly into export orientated industries. Among the main products (other than agricultural) sold abroad are diamonds (re-exported after polishing), textiles, chemicals, fertilisers, tyres, electrical equipment, cement and pharmaceuticals. Over 50% of Israeli exports go to Europe.

Economic Situation

During recent years the high cost of imports, particularly defence imports, has put the economy under strain. A high trade deficit, a fall in investment and growth, a high rate of inflation (34.6% in 1977) represent some of the problems. Measures taken to correct the situation included drastic devaluation of the Israeli pound, import controls and tax increases. The Begin government allowed the pound to float and introduced a programme intended to foster a freer economy and encourage further foreign investment.

Every effort is being made to utilise existing resources and this effort has been greatly helped by the availability of capital for investment, most of which has been supplied by Jewish communities in America and Europe or by the American government. The cost of defence places a great burden on the economy and the isolation of the country from its natural markets in neighbouring Arab states and its difficult relations with the Common Market makes the expansion of its exports difficult. Moreover, the wish to develop the resources of the country to the utmost, coupled with the fact that Israel is so relatively small has ". . . created serious problems with regard to the rational use of natural resources and environmental pollution. The rapid expansion of industry and the constant intensification of agriculture (industrial output was IL 1,950 million in 1955 and by 1971 had risen to IL 16,925 million) . . . in one respect so necessary, was damaging as far as the environment is concerned." (Report of the Israel National Committee on Biosphere and Environment, 1972.) There is general recognition that in the absence of great natural wealth the future prosperity of the country will depend on the ingenuity, and on the technical and educational skills of its people. This lends added importance to education.

6 THE EDUCATION SYSTEM

Academic Year

The academic year runs from 1 September to 30 June in the case of schools and teacher training institutions and from November to July in the case of universities. There are approximately 200 school days in an academic year with pupils working a six-day week for four hours a day at primary level, and seven hours a day at secondary level. There are about 15 weeks holiday a year. There are three terms. At higher level most institutions operate a three-term year but some have adopted the two-semester system.

Pre-School

One-year's pre-primary education is compulsory for children at the age of 5. Almost the whole age group attend, the only exceptions being children in some Arab communities. The percentage of children aged 3 and 4 attending nursery schools and kindergartens is also high. This is because a great number of Israeli women have full time jobs. Kindergartens are run by the State, by religious and voluntary organisations, as well as privately, and vary from simple crèches to fully equipped educational institutions.

First Level (Elementary)

In spite of the introduction of junior high schools (see below) the majority of Israeli children still attend primary schools from the age of 6 to 15. The curriculum includes reading, writing, arithmetic, etc. in the first two classes, joined by geography, history, science, handicrafts, art, music, foreign languages, physical education, agriculture, home economics and civics in the following years. Foreign language study usually begins in the fifth year and the language is normally English, though some students are starting Arabic in the fourth or fifth grade. Judaic studies are compulsory in all schools and occupy three to five hours per week in State general schools with additional hours in State religious schools; (about 30% of the school population attend religious schools). The allocation of periods in selected classes at this level is shown as follows:

Subject	State Schools	
	Fourth year	Fifth year
Old Testament / Oral Law	5	5
Hebrew Language and Literature	5	5
Heimatkunde and geography / Nature study	3	2 / 2
Arithmetic	4	4
Physical education	2	2
Art and music	2	3
Handicrafts	2	2-4
Agriculture	2	
Social education	1	1
Total	26	26-28

| | State Schools | |
Subject	Seventh year	Eighth year
Old Testament	4	5
Oral law	1	7
Hebrew Language and Literature	3	3
Arithmetic and geometry	4	4
History	3	
Geography	2	4
Natural science	2	
Foreign language	4	4
Physical education	2	2
Art and music	2	1
Agriculture and handicrafts	2-4	2
Social education	1	6
Total	30-32	32

In grade 7 some children transfer to junior high schools *(hativat benaim)* where they follow a three-year course. This is the new system which thus far is fully implemented only in development towns and in Haifa, though working partially in Tel Aviv and Jerusalem.

Special

At elementary level there are separate schools for handicapped children and slow learners. In some areas separate classes operate in ordinary schools. There are also special courses for immigrant children, as well as schools for young people between the ages of 14 and 17 who have not attended primary schools. These reflect the country's concern to absorb immigrants and bridge the gap between Western and non-Western Jews.

Secondary

There are four kinds of secondary school in Israel:

(i) academic
(ii) vocational
(iii) agricultural
(iv) comprehensive.

Academic

The academic high schools have been strongly influenced by the central European tradition and are, as their name suggests, devoted to the pursuit of success in the *Bagrut* – the Israeli matriculation examination. The *Bagrut* is taken by pupils of 17 and 18 and in 1975 a new system was introduced. Prior to this, all pupils had to take a set number of given subjects at the same level. Under the new system, there are three levels of examination. Each level carries a different number of points so that a pupil can elect to take a subject, e.g. history, at the 2, 4 or 5 point level. There is also a 6 point level for very gifted children. In order to get a matriculation certificate, a pupil must accumulate a total of 20 points with six subjects, which must include Jewish studies, general studies, science and a modern language. Both the former and the revised systems are in operation. Whereas 20 points is enough for the matriculation certificate, a student wishing to enter university must have considerably more than 20 points.

A pupil can choose his own timetable provided, of course, that the school can provide teachers of the required subjects. This gives well endowed schools in areas which attract teachers an advantage over many schools in 'underprivileged' areas. Failure rates in some subjects are high, particularly mathematics. English also used to come out badly but the 1976 results showed a marked improvement with 86% receiving a pass mark. In assessing the examination, school assessments (based on a mock *bagrut*) are taken into account. In 1976, the average examination mark in English was 70.6 - in the mock it was 69.9.

Vocational

There is a wide variety of vocational schools in Israel, most of them provided by voluntary agencies, such as the Organisation of Rehabilitation through Training (ORT). The highest level of technical course runs parallel to the academic secondary course and leads to technical *Bagrut* examinations and a matriculation certificate which is accepted for entry to higher technical education. However, these courses are in the minority. The majority of vocational schools offer courses preparing students for work in trades and business. In addition to the full time vocational schools there are a number of schools offering evening classes to children who left school at the age of 15. The most usual vocational curriculum consists of 20 hours per week of practical training and 24 hours of general and technical subjects. These include Hebrew, Bible, English, history and civics. Mathematics is also studied as appropriate but is usually stronger in the agricultural schools, which also provided courses in chemistry and biology.

Agricultural

Most of the agricultural schools are boarding schools and their purpose is to prepare young people for work in agriculture. A few of them submit candidates for the *Bagrut* examination.

Comprehensive

Following a conference on comprehensive education held in Israel in 1970, in which three British experts participated, a decision was taken to establish comprehensive schools in various centres of population. There are now 61 such schools, an example being Yehud Comprehensive School, a few miles outside Tel Aviv, which has over 1,000 pupils in the 14-18 age range.

Educational Broadcasting

The educational television service was established in the early 1960s. It offers programmes in English, Hebrew Language and literature, mathematics, science and geography. The programmes are closely linked to material circulated to schools or to existing textbooks. The service has done much to help teachers in poor areas and to further the government's aim of narrowing the gap between the middle class and less privileged groups. There is also experimental work being done on educational technology, notably at the Educational Technology Centre. In the main, however, educational technology in Israel still has a long way to go, though many of the better-off schools are well equipped with hardware.

Religious Schools

When the State education system was established in 1948, the religious schools were not fully integrated into the State system. The ruling party (MAPAI) required the support of the religious parties in the coalition government, and the latter made the continued existence of religious schools a condition of their support. There is, therefore, a separate structure of religious education within the State system. The religious schools are under the direction of the Religious Education Department in the Ministry of Education. They offer basically the same curriculum as the State schools but with a higher proportion of religious subjects (6-11 hours per week at elementary level). The number of children attending religious schools, both elementary and secondary and including the autonomous Agudat Yisrael network is about 30% of the total.

Kibbutz Schools

The four *kibbutz* movements developed their own education system during the time of the Mandate. When the State was established the *kibbutz* schools became part of the State system. In practice, however, they have maintained many distinctive features. In the first place, all *kibbutz* children are expected to remain at school until the age of 18. For the first six years of their education, they attend residential primary schools in the individual *kibbutz* and some later transfer to regional *kibbutz* secondary day or boarding schools.

Arab Schools

While Arabs enjoy equality in Israel it is, nevertheless, necessary to consider Arab education as a separate part of the system. This is because the language used in the schools is Arabic rather than Hebrew and because the curriculum in Arab schools is different from that of other State schools in that it does not include Bible studies and Hebrew literature, which bulk large in the normal Jewish education. Apart from this the basic curriculum is similar. Now almost all Arab boys and about 80% of Arab girls attend full time education. But included in the statistics for Arab education is the Druze community of 35,000. Very few Druze girls complete secondary school studies. A significant role in Arab education is played by secondary schools financed by Christian religious orders in Nazareth, Haifa and elsewhere. These schools are subject to inspection by the Ministry of Education but operate as private schools on a fee paying basis.

Teacher Training

Teachers are trained either in teacher training colleges or in university faculties of education.

College

There are 58 teacher training colleges in Israel. The majority of students take a three-year course but some colleges have been given academic status and now offer a four-year BEd course.

University

Six universities offer first degrees in education, four offer post-graduate courses. The Ministry of Education's long term aim is for all secondary school teachers to be university graduates. There are two possible ways of qualifying through university study - either by obtaining a BEd degree (over four years) or by obtaining a degree in some other subject and following this with a teaching qualification (the more usual method). The basic admission requirement for university teacher training is the full matriculation certificate, and this applies even to graduates of teacher training colleges. However, experienced teachers may be accepted, and some students are admitted to preparatory courses.

In-Service

There is an elaborate programme of in-service teacher training in operation in Israel. The amount spent on this is, relatively speaking, larger than in Britain. Refresher courses of all kinds are arranged by the inspectorate, sometimes in cooperation with the universities, and financial inducements are offered to teachers who attend them. There are also full time courses leading to certification for unqualified employed teachers. Teachers wishing to acquire further knowledge and information are helped by a network of so-called 'pedagogic centres'. They are not fully developed teachers' centres but do provide an opportunity for teachers to look at new books and teaching aids.

Higher

There are eight university institutions in Israel. Seven of them have under-graduate students; the eighth, the Weizmann Institute, is a research institution where only post-graduate teaching is undertaken. The number of students at the seven institutions is 70,000. More than one fifth of the students are post-graduates. It is currently the policy in all the universities to increase the number of post-graduate students while attempting to maintain under-graduate numbers at something like their present size.

The universities are as follows:

University	*Founded*	*Students*	*Staff*
Technion-Israel Institute of Technology	1913	9,600	1,500
Hebrew University of Jerusalem	1925	16,000	2,000
Weizmann Institute of Science	1934	480	2,450
Tel Aviv University	1955	17,550	3,000
Bar-Ilan University (religious)	1957	7,600	1,000
University of Haifa	1963	7,000	800
Ben-Gurion University of the Negev	1967	5,000	1,960
Everyman's University (Open University)	1974	8,000	–

Universities in Israel have been distinguished by their rapid growth in the last 15 years. Until 1965 university education was the monopoly of the Hebrew University of Jerusalem, and the Technion in Haifa. The Weizmann Institute being entirely concerned with research, did not properly count as a teaching university. Both the Technion and the Hebrew University resisted the establishment of new universities but, in the end, pressures from those demanding more higher education were too strong for them. The University of Tel Aviv, established in 1955, has expanded very rapidly; so too have the other recent foundations. Though this rapid expansion has led to certain problems, the creation of a system of higher education at so rapid a rate, while still maintaining standards, has been a major achievement of the State of Israel. There are some 1,000 Arab students at Israeli universities. The largest number of 500 is at Haifa University - 400 at the Hebrew University, Jerusalem, and 120 at the orthodox Jewish religious university at Bar Ilan.

Admission

The basic admission requirement for university is the matriculation certificate based on the *Bagrut* examination. Exceptions may be made for graduates of *kibbutz* schools or vocational institutions but usually these students have to spend a year in a preparatory course before final acceptance. By law the matriculation certificate qualifies a student for admission without further examinations. In practice now a *numerus clausus* operates and candidates must also meet departmental requirements e.g. stated grades in examinations, successful completion of certain tests, etc. However, the Israeli university authorities are very anxious to encourage Arabs and they are sometimes admitted with lower qualifications than their Jewish contemporaries. This may lead to trouble when these students find their studies difficult at a later stage.

Courses

The basic first degree is the bachelor's degree, which usually takes three years but in some subjects such as engineering, architecture and law, four years' study is required. Medical and dental programmes last six years. The master's degree requires one or two years' study, and may or may not entail a thesis. The PhD consists of three years or more of course work and research, with research as the more important element of the two. Until recently students could not proceed direct from a bachelor's degree to a PhD but had to take a master's first. However, it has now become common for students to proceed by what is called the direct route to the doctorate, so that if their academic results in the first degree are sufficiently good they are exempt from the master's. Most PhD students are, however, in their late 20s before they get their doctorate. Degree programmes are organised on the credit system and most first degrees require students to take two subjects.

Other Institutions

Other degree-granting institutions in Israel include the Bezalel Academy of Arts and Design, and the Rubin Academy of Music. Higher vocational schools include the College of Economics and Social Studies, the College for Educational/Social Workers, and Israel Institute of Productivity, the Ruppin Institute (*kibbutz* training) and the School of Journalism.

Non-Formal and Adult Education

There is an extensive system of further education organised partly by the Ministry of Education, partly by the *Histadrut* (Trades Union Congress), and partly by the local authorities. There are six colleges *(Miklalot)* and evening classes are held in all centres of population. Some of these are vocational, others recreational. The Jewish Agency and other bodies organise residential and non-residential courses in Hebrew for new immigrants.

7 EDUCATIONAL ADMINISTRATION
Centralised Control

The Israeli system is essentially a centralised one based on European models rather than on the British. The Ministry of Education is responsible for pre-primary education, primary/elementary education, for almost all secondary education and for teacher training colleges. What happens inside schools is determined by the State. The Ministry of Education prescribes detailed curricula, syllabi and even, in some cases, timetables for schools. Textbooks are subject to scrutiny by ministerial committees and the use of non-approved textbooks is frowned upon, although it sometimes takes place. On the other hand, parental groups may influence up to 25% of the curriculum in each school. The Ministry also has some say in the internal conditions of the school; for example it fixes a maximum proportion of pupils in any one class allowed to repeat a year. The Ministry is responsible for educational experiments, administers examinations and has considerable power over teachers. Appointment of teachers to elementary schools has to be approved centrally and the Ministry selects headmasters (although in the larger cities this is done in consultation with local authorities).

Local Authorities

The role of the local authorities in Israeli education is not a very significant one. Under the compulsory education law of 1949, State and local authorities are jointly responsible for pre-primary and primary/elementary education. However, the responsibility of local authorities is, in fact, restricted to construction and maintenance of buildings, supply of furniture and equipment and the provision of auxiliary services. The local educational authorities are also responsible for pupil registration.

Headmasters

The role of the headmaster in the administration of Israeli education is a significant one. Indeed, headmasters tend to be very greatly preoccupied with administration. They have less contol over what is taught in their schools than headmasters in Britain, and also do a great deal of bureaucratic work in connection with the finances of the school and the administration of staff.

Administrative Structure - Education System

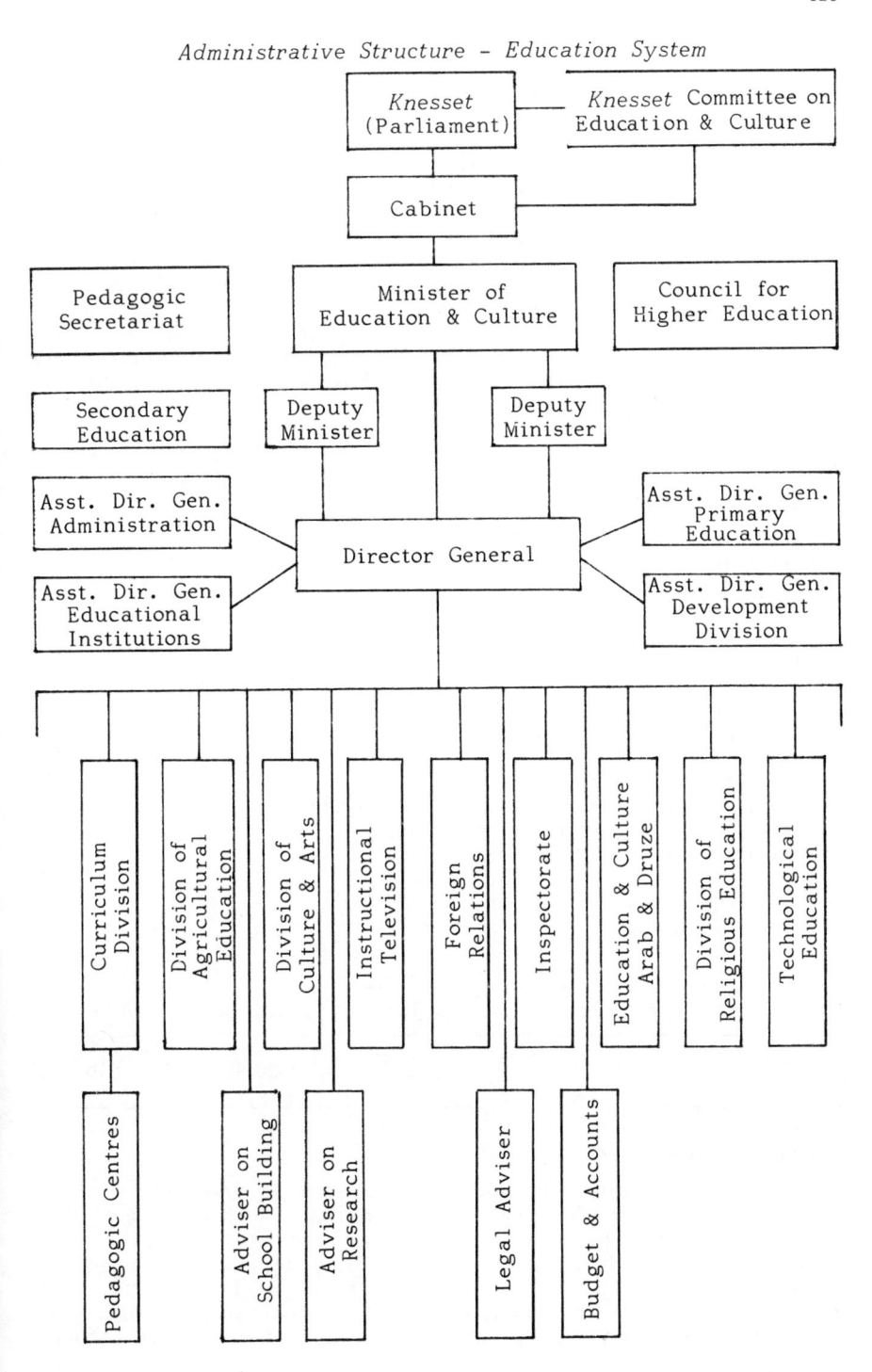

```
                    ┌──────────────┐   ┌──────────────────┐
                    │   Knesset    │───│ Knesset Committee on│
                    │ (Parliament) │   │ Education & Culture │
                    └──────┬───────┘   └──────────┬───────┘
                           │                      │
                    ┌──────┴──────┐               │
                    │   Cabinet   │───────────────┘
                    └──────┬──────┘
                           │
┌──────────────┐    ┌──────┴───────┐    ┌─────────────────┐
│  Pedagogic   │    │  Minister of │    │   Council for   │
│ Secretariat  │    │Education &   │    │ Higher Education│
└──────────────┘    │   Culture    │    └─────────────────┘
                    └──┬────────┬──┘
┌──────────────┐  ┌────┴───┐ ┌──┴─────┐
│  Secondary   │  │ Deputy │ │ Deputy │
│  Education   │  │Minister│ │Minister│
└──────────────┘  └────────┘ └────────┘
```

(Asst. Dir. Gen. Administration · Asst. Dir. Gen. Educational Institutions · Director General · Asst. Dir. Gen. Primary Education · Asst. Dir. Gen. Development Division)

Divisions under Director General:
- Curriculum Division — Pedagogic Centres
- Division of Agricultural Education — Adviser on School Building
- Division of Culture & Arts — Adviser on Research
- Instructional Television
- Foreign Relations — Legal Adviser
- Inspectorate — Budget & Accounts
- Education & Culture Arab & Druze
- Division of Religious Education
- Technological Education

Inspectorate

For inspection purposes, the country is divided into seven regions, each region coming under a regional director. For general inspection, each regional director has two regional inspectors for State schools and one for State religious schools. Under the regional inspectors there are about 300 area inspectors over the country as a whole. In addition to the general inspectors, there are chief inspectors for each subject who are based in the Ministry. Some subjects, but not all, have local inspectors who are Ministry officers working to the chief inspector. Recently a system of teacher counsellors (visiting teachers) was introduced. These counsellors work to the local subject inspector where there is one and direct to the chief inspector where there is not. Inspectors have more power than their opposite numbers in Britain. In addition to giving advice to teachers and helping plan the curricula, they are also administrators armed with power to insist that a teacher should be removed from a school (though their power to expel him from the ranks of the profession is limited by the Teachers Union).

8 EDUCATIONAL FINANCE

Education Budget

More money is spent on education in Israel than any other area save defence; the total amounts to 8.5% of the total Ordinary Budget. More than two thirds of this money is provided by the Treasury to the Ministry of Education and the rest comes from local authorities and private sources. More than half the money provided by the Treasury is, in its turn, raised by the Jewish Agency from the Jewish communities abroad. Proportionately speaking, more money is invested in elementary than in secondary education. The decision on how money is to be spent rests with the Ministry of Education.

Allocation of Funds
Expenditure on Education: Distribution by Level
Percentage of Expenditure

Pre-school	First Level	Second Level	Third Level	Other
6.1	32.7	25.5	30.1	5.6

Overseas Support

One special feature of Israeli education is the fact that its development relies in part on financial contributions from diaspora Jewry. This money is handed over to the Ministry of Education to be spent as it wishes. However, smaller sums are raised by 'friends' of various institutions in Israel. These are paid direct to schools, such as the ORT vocational schools which are splendidly equipped, or the group of religious schools financed by the middle-of-the-road Mizrachi movements in America. Formally speaking, the Ministry exercises some control on how these diaspora funds should be spent but, in practice, their existence enables schools which receive money to secure better equipment and more favourable conditions for the students. In university education the importance of outside funds is even more marked. The individual fund raising activities of the various universities in the diaspora bring in large sums each year amounting to about 35% of the total amount spent. The new Everyman's University will be entirely financed by the Rothschild Foundation for the first seven years of its operation. Thereafter, if successful, if will become the responsibility of the Ministry.

Administration of Finance

State and State religious schools are financed jointly by the Ministry and local authorities. The Ministry pays all teachers' salaries with the local authorities covering costs of maintenance and sharing in the construction of new buildings. Local authorities may impose an education tax for special reasons. The Ministry provides about 80% of the funds for higher education.

9 DEVELOPMENT AND PLANNING OF THE EDUCATION SYSTEM

Development

Traditionally, Jewish society in the diaspora was passionately interested in education. In order to maintain their standing in societies which were often hostile, the Jewish communities made every effort to educate their members. This emphasis was maintained in Palestine. One of the first preoccupations of the pioneering settlers of the late nineteenth and early twentieth centuries was education and, given the very small resources of the Jewish community in Palestine at that time, an astonishingly high percentage of their funds was spent on it.

The period of the Mandate saw considerable economic growth and the provision of education developed considerably. At an early stage, the Jewish community chose to build up its own system while the Arab system was developed by the Mandatory authorities. The Jewish community was not homogeneous and as a result, created several distinct groups of schools: left wing, centre and religious. Each 'trend' as it was known, enjoyed its own separate existence and was financed by its own supporters in Palestine and in the diaspora. In addition to the school system, the Jewish community established the first university in Palestine, the Hebrew University of Jerusalem. The Hebrew language was revived (until the nineteenth century its use had been largely liturgical) and its use in Palestine by Jews from all over the world provided a unifying factor of the first importance.

Arab Systems

The Arab education system developed more slowly. A network of elementary schools was established but when the British left still only about 60% of boys and 20% of girls attended them.

Arab exodus after 1947 included most of the intellectuals and teachers and this made things extremely difficult when the Israeli government sought to develop Arab education in the 1950s. An Arab Teacher Training College was established and many Arab schools were constructed. In the late 1950s the first schools for Bedouin were constructed.

Educational Objectives

Today, in the State of Israel, education is regarded as of the highest importance. The aims of the State education system were defined in the State Education Law of August 1953: "State education is to be based on the values of Jewish culture and the achievements of science, on love of the homeland and loyalty to the State and the Jewish people, on practice in agricultural work and handicraft, on pioneer *(halutzic)* training, and on striving for a society built on freedom, equality, tolerance, mutual assistance, and love of mankind". The emphasis in this formal statement on what may be loosely called the pioneering virtues, mirrors the original preoccupation of the Jewish settlers in Palestine but does not fully reflect reality. There are, in effect, two principal aims in the minds of most Israeli educators. They are: firstly to integrate into one society the Jews from many different backgrounds; and secondly to produce a population of well educated and technically competent people. This latter is the more important as Israel has few natural resources of her own.

These are the aims of the majority. There is, however, a substantial minority of religious Jews for whom a third aim is of great importance, perhaps taking priority in some senses over the other two. For the orthodox minority the maintenance of Jewish religious standards and the education of children and young people in the Jewish religion is of prime importance. This is not to say that in religious schools the other aims are ignored, but they take a less prominent place. The religious stream within the State educational system is self-contained and its curricula and the motivation of its students and teachers differ from those of the rest of the system.

Educational Planning

Educational plans for all except higher education originate from the Ministry of Education. Within the Ministry there is a pedagogic secretariat which draws up long term plans. The local authorities are expected to adapt themselves to these. Recently, the Ministry has been calling increasingly on advice from academics. The ambitions of various institutions and local pressures mean that, in practice, the execution of educational decisions is less authoritarian and rigid than might at first appear likely.

It is generally recognised that in higher education there is too little planning. The National Council for Higher Education retains the right to approve the establishment of new university departments but until fairly recently this was a formality. In practice, each university developed as far and as fast as it could, subject only to financial limitations. The Ministry allocated funds rather in accordance with the degree of pressure which the individual institution could bring to bear than with any preconceived plan. In recent years, however, the Ministry has taken a much more positive line. The National Council has become more vigorous and a body, similar to the British University Grants Committee, has been established which will make possible more rational development.

Current Trends

There is a good deal of creative thinking to be found amongst those concerned with education in Israel. However, the resources available are not always sufficient for the implementation of policies which everybody agrees are desirable. Thus it is recognised that higher education is, on the whole, better developed than either primary or secondary education, but the improvement of school buildings and teaching methods in schools proceeds somewhat slowly. This is in great part due to the absence of funds, though the conservatism of officials and teachers also plays its part. But problems are being tackled; among the new policies can be noted:

(i) integration and social equalisation by means of the reform of the secondary school system, particularly the introduction of junior high schools and the large increase in budgets for programmes for the disadvantaged pupils

(ii) reform of the curricula as a result of work by teams of university and school teachers

(iii) use of educational television and to a lesser extent of educational technology

(iv) reform of methods in primary schools with more emphasis on 'open' teaching

(v) greater emphasis on the study of Jewish history and tradition throughout the school system

(vi) introduction of planning in the universities and of more rigorous selection at under-graduate level to prevent unlimited expansion

(vii) improvements in teacher training with the ultimate aim of making an all-graduate profession.

Someone returning to Israel in 1988 may reasonably expect to find a system in which the content of curricula has more or less kept pace with modern developments; in which education in schools has improved as it has received more attention than in the past; in which methods of instruction have changed very much for the better; and in which standards in higher education have been maintained.

REFERENCES AND FURTHER READING

Avidor, Moshe (1976). 'Education for a Growing Nation', *Israel Digest*, (fifth edition).
Avidor, Moshe (1974). *Education and Science*. (Compiled from material originally published in *Encyclopaedia Judaica*). Keter Books.
Central Bureau of Statistics (1978). *Schools and Kindergartens 1977/78*.
Council for Higher Education (1977). *Higher Education in Israel. Statistical Abstract*, Planning and Grants Committee.
Dicks, Brian (1975). *The Israelis, How They Live and Work*. David & Charles, London.
Eisenstadt, Samuel N. (1970). *Integration and Development in Israel*. Pall Mall Press, London.
Elon, Amos (1971). *The Israelis: Founders and Sons*. Weidenfeld & Nicolson, London.
Israeli Society (1974). Institute Symposia No. 2, Institute of Jewish Affairs.
Katz, Elihu (1976). *The Secularisation of Leisure: Culture and Communication in Israel*. Faber, London.
Lucas, Noah (1974). *The Modern History of Israel*. Weidenfeld & Nicolson, London.
Michman, Joseph (1973). *Cultural Policy in Israel*. UNESCO, Paris.
Segre, V. D. (1971). *Israel: a Society in Transition*. Oxford University Press.
Smilansky, Moshe (1971). *School Reform as an Approach in Macro Development*. (An unpublished paper prepared at Ohio State University, College of Education, Urban Leadership Programme, Faculty of Educational Development.)
UNESCO (annual). *Statistical Yearbook*. UNESCO, Paris.

Structure of the Education System in Israel

Age	3	4	5	6	7	8	9	10	11	12	13	14	15	16	17	18	19	20	21	22	23	24
Level				I						II					III					IV		
Stage				1						2				3				4				
Compulsory																						
School type				Primary						Junior high			Senior high General & vocational			Vocational technical education / Teachers colleges / General & technical universities						

▨ Education preceding the first level
Examinations: Vocational certificates at end of stage 3

Kibbutz movement schools

Source: UNESCO/IBE International Yearbook of Education
Compulsory Education: Age Limits 5–15   Duration (years) 11
Entrance age to pre-school education: 3

421

ISRAEL BASIC STATISTICS		1970	1975	1976	1977
1	Total population (000)	2,974	3,455	3,554	3,648
2	Population 6-17 (000)	750	814	831	852
	% female	49	49	49	49
3	Enrolment, all levels	696,958			
	% female	48			
	First level	478,951	535,320	549,413	567,915
	% female	48	49	49	49
	Second level*	142,521	170,168	173,188	176,886
	% female	51	52	52	52
	Third level	55,486		85,081	83,671
	% female	44		46	47
4	Teachers, all levels	51,111			
	% female				
	First level	27,780	32,657	34,579	35,838
	% female			76	77
	Second level	14,031			
	% female				
	Third level	9,300			
	% female				
5	Public expenditure on education				
	Total (000) pound	1,061,000	5,511,000		
	As % of GNP	5.5	6.8		
6	% enrolment (MF) by level	100			
	First level	71			
	Second level	21			
	Third level	8			
	% enrolment (F) by level	100			
	First level	70			
	Second level	22			
	Third level	8			
7	Entrance age: Duration of				
	First level education	6:8	6:8	6:8	6:8
	Second level education	14:4	14:4	14:4	14:4
8	Enrolment ratios (MF)				
	First level	96	97	96	97
	Second level	57			
	Third level	19.92		25.29	24.73
	Enrolment ratios (F)				
	First level	95	97	97	97
	Second level	60			
	Third level	18.20		23.77	23.59

* From 1975, data do not include second level teacher-training.

Italy

CONTENTS

1 Geography 424
2 Population 426
3 Society and Culture 427
4 History and Politics 428
5 The Economy 431
6 The Education System 433
7 Educational Administration 443
8 Educational Finance 447
9 Development and Planning of the
  Education System 448
10 The System in Operation 450

In Italy, a nation with long traditions but a relatively short history as a sovereign state, there was no popular education before 1870. According to the census of 1951 some 25% of the population was officially illiterate, in 1961 the figure was 9.9% but by 1971 there were still 2.5 million 'official' illiterates. The Constitution lays down that education shall be compulsory and free of charge for at least eight years, but each political party has its own proposals for educational reform. The permanence of the bureaucracy, and instability of parliamentary government government and the problems of reconciling political and social interests have combined to constrain change. Highly centralised control exercised by the Ministry of Public Instruction and the Ministry for Culture and Cultural Assets and, for planning, by the Technical Committee for Educational Planning has not prevented sectional interests from defending their position with success. Among the important interest groups are the Roman Catholic authorities and in recent years members of the university student body.

Regional differences are considerable and substantial repetition at all levels and quite high drop-out rates, except at the first level, reflect a situation which suggests that the aims of legislation have not yet been fully realised.

Uniformity throughout the system is due to the fact that examinations are set centrally, thus ensuring that the same curriculum is followed in comparable schools. Examinations are used to measure academic achievement, determine which pupils are promoted or repeat a year of study, and how pupils are selected for streams in the upper stage of second level education. The system shows the same kinds of unequal provision and selectivity found in other Western European nations.

Since 1952 attempts have been made to reform the first and second stages of second level education to provide greater equality. In 1968 the Communist Party proposed to reorganise the upper school system along comprehensive lines. In 1972 the Minister of Public Instruction produced plans but they were not discussed in Parliament. In 1975 the Socialist Party, the Christian Democrats, the Social Democratic Party and the Republican Party all put forward proposals. An attempt was made to see what common ground could be found. A ministry plan, under Minister Malfatti, in 1976 recommended the abolition of the various kinds of academic secondary schools in favour of a kind of comprehensive school. Large scale curriculum reform has not taken place but the expansion of secondary education along traditional lines has created serious problems in the universities, whose enrolments trebled between 1960 and 1969.

Student unrest in 1968 forced the concession that there should be free access to higher education. Anyone over 25 can enrol without a secondary school diploma. More than a million students were unevenly distributed between the Humanities 20%, Social Sciences 14%, Education 7.5% and the natural sciences and engineering just over 10.0% each. The expansion of university enrolments has resulted in high wastage rates, failure to complete courses by registered students who enjoy many privileges. Conditions of study are poor and the expansion of university numbers contrasts sharply with the uneven provision of first level education and the rigidity of secondary school curricula.

The Editor

1 GEOGRAPHY

Topography

Italy, with a land area of 297,000 square kilometres (116,000 square miles), is the third largest country of the European Economic Community. About five sixths of its area is peninsular Italy, the rest consisting of Sardinia and Sicily and a number of much smaller islands. Much of the terrain is mountainous, the principal chain, the Appenines, effectively splitting the peninsula along its major axis. To the north the Alps make a natural frontier with France, Switzerland, Austria and Yugoslavia and enclose the great alluvial plain of northern Italy in which the main industrial cities are situated. There are other areas of plain along the west coast, roughly between Pisa and Naples, and in the south east (or 'heel') of the country. Both the main islands are largely mountainous.

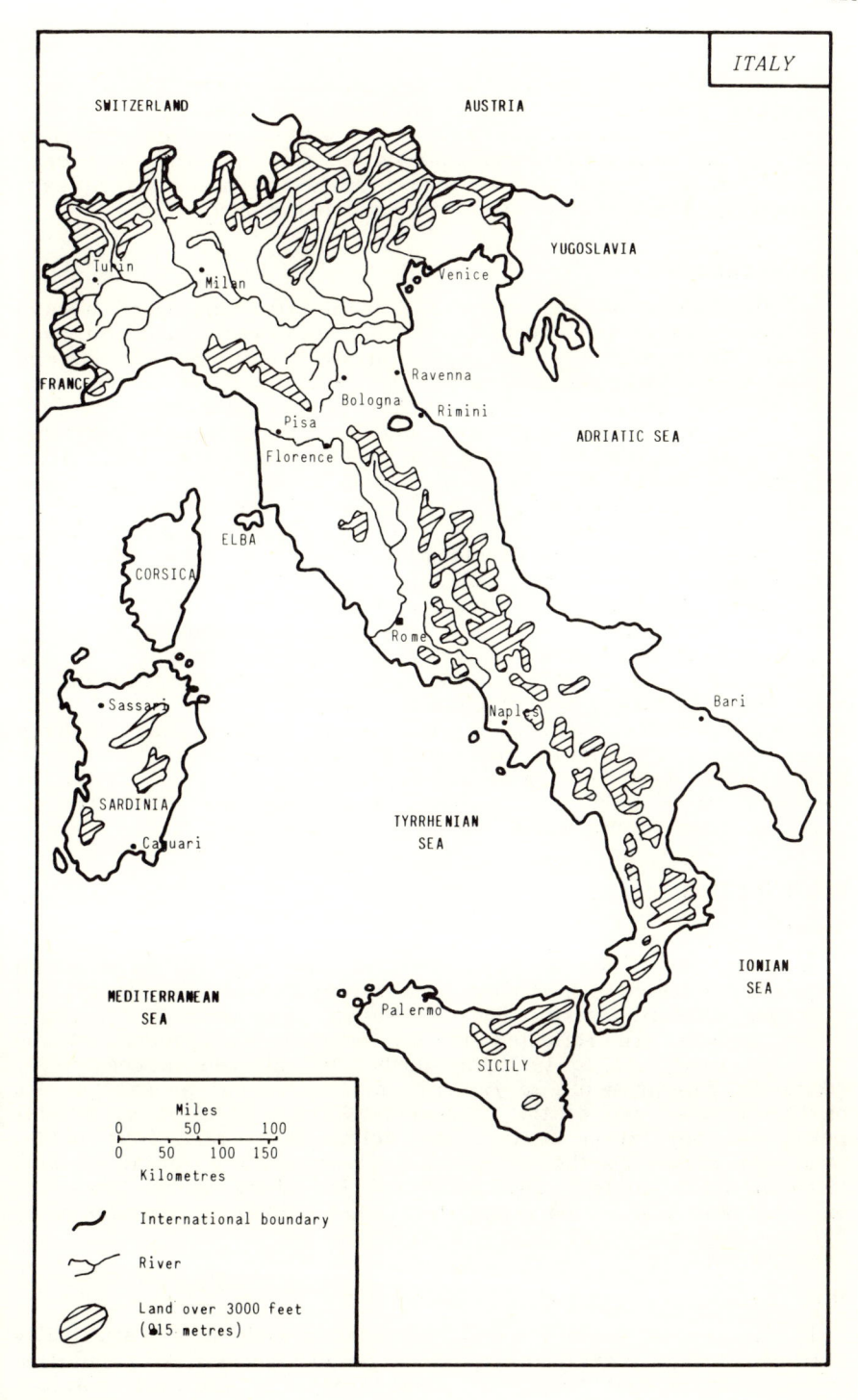

ITALY

Climate

The usual description – 'hot dry summers, warm wet winters' – applies generally to Italy but there are climatic variations nonetheless. In mountainous areas the winters can be extremely cold; in the south the summers may be very hot and very dry. In the central region the weather is mild for most of the year, the average summer temperature in Rome being 24°C (75°F).

Communications

In the north of the peninsula, communications were always relatively easy, but north/south and east/west movement was difficult because of the country's physical features. The islands tended to be isolated. Following the development of an effective rail network during the latter part of the nineteenth century there was some breaking down of the communication barriers, at any rate on the mainland. But problems persisted until after the end of World War Two, when the development of a system of internal airways and ferries and more recently the creation of more motorways *(autostrade)* has finally made many areas, accessible and open to development. There are now 16,218 km of railway track, nearly half of which is electrified. In 1974 there were 284,736 km of road and 5,262 km of motorway (and there will be 6,146 km when the programme is completed).

External communications have been improved recently by the construction of a number of rail and road tunnels through the Alps thus creating better contacts between Italy and central and north western Europe. The traditional maritime links between Italy and the Balkans, the eastern Mediterranean and North Africa have been strengthened in the last 20 years with the improvement of harbour facilities. Italy has the ninth largest merchant fleet in the world (10 million gross tons).

2 POPULATION

Growth

In 1975 Italy had a population of just over 56 million, an increase of nearly 3.5 million on the previous decade. Emigration averages something like 2,000 per annum. The problems of population growth are reflected in the educational problems of the country: from 1961 to 1971 the number of children in compulsory education rose from 6.5 to 7.5 million. The annual average excess of live births over deaths is nearly 400,000. There is no official policy on population control but active pressure groups within what are known as the lay parties advocate more liberal legislation on birth control and abortion. But there is no concensus on what the legislation should be. Family planning services vary between regions.

Distribution

In the last 50 years the balance of population has dramatically shifted. In 50 years the percentage of the active population in agriculture and living in rural areas has declined from 60%

to 20%. The most densely populated areas are now those with intensive industrial activity. In some parts of Liguria and Lombardy the average density per square kilometre is 300. Italy has always had an under-developed south and a developed (industrialised) north. After the collapse of Italy's overseas empire migration from the south which hitherto had gone to the United States or to the colonies turned increasingly to the north.

3 SOCIETY AND CULTURE

Social Patterns

Italian society is traditionally conservative and stable, based on the strength of the family and on loyalty to a close-knit local community. Until the comparatively recent growth of very large cities, urban dwellers were still fairly close to rural life and could feel an affinity with it. The south of Italy retained elements of eastern attitudes, particularly in the treatment of women, and generally remained more feudal. But with increased social mobility over the past 25 years (for change of domicile was restricted under Fascist legislation) the structure of society has begun to break down. The relative wealth of urban dwellers has encouraged a 'flight from the land' to Italian cities and beyond and Italians have formed a sizeable proportion of the *gast-arbeiter* phenomenon of northern Europe. Some five million Italians now work abroad and remit money to relatives at home. The social consequences of this migration, both within and outside Italy, have been catastrophic. Families have been sundered, a disastrous strain has been placed on urban housing, new slums have been created and the problems of rootless urban semi- or unemployed have led to much petty theft and to considerable organised crime, creating a serious and unsolved educational problem.

Language

Italians are a single national group speaking one language. In some border areas a second language is spoken, but only in the Alto Adige (South Tyrol) is a first language, German, recognised and protected by constitutional provision, where in 1971 39,000 children were educated in German language schools and 18,000 in Italian language schools.

Religion

The official religion of Italy (recognised by the 1929 Lateran Pact) is the Catholic Apostolic Roman Religion. Under the treaty Roman Catholic doctrine is compulsory in Italian schools, but parents have the right of withdrawal on grounds of conscience. Recently a parent of a seven-year-old girl has challenged before the courts the concept of religious instruction in schools, claiming that non-religious education is a right guaranteed by the Constitution. Lay parties are urging the removal of all religious education from the State system. The government introduced a Religious Education Bill designed to remove anomalies existing between the 1929 Concordat and the 1948 Constitution, by reinforcing the parents' right of withdrawal. Nominally the population is predominantly Roman Catholic, but Italy was united by anti-clericals and a strong lay opinion has informed social development since World War Two, culminating in the legislation of divorce (1974) and abortion under restricted circumstances (1977). A movement for the renegotiation of the Concordat gathered momentum during 1975/76 and the Church was inclined to accept the increasing secularisation of society as long as its moral rights were protected in a pluralist State. The Church provides a fair proportion of pre-school education and some 7% of primary and secondary school children are in Church Schools.

4 HISTORY AND POLITICS
Historical Development

The Italian peninsula enjoyed political unity under the Roman Empire, but this ended in the fifth century when the seat of Empire was transferred to Constantinople. During the next 14 centuries the country was fragmented and suffered attack and invasion from many quarters. By the early nineteenth century most of Italy was under despotic rule, based on the power of the French, Austrians, Spanish and the Church. However, nationalism was reborn and liberal revolutionaries, allied to the Piedmontese House of Savoy, succeeded in over-throwing the governments in one state after another, so that after a decade of struggle Rome became the capital of a unified and independent kingdom of Italy in 1870. The State and the Papacy were estranged.

After 1970

However, the new kingdom failed to evolve a viable form of constitutional government. Instead of a bi-partisan parliamentary system there developed a rule of parliamentary expediency and of government by manipulation, both by the granting of favours and by the exertion of pressures. After World War One the country was seriously disturbed by industrial and social unrest among left wing groups, which the government was powerless to control. The newly formed Fascist Party undertook violent, direct retaliatory action against the socialists, with the tacit approval of the government. In the outcome the better organised and unified Fascists won the struggle and in 1922 began their 20 years of dictatorship in Italy. Fascist rule emphasised the supremacy of the State in every department of national life, with the suppression of opposition and with an attempt to create a second Roman Empire. Formal relations were finally re-established between the State and the Vatican. Italy entered World War Two on the German side, but in 1943, following the fall of the dictator Mussolini, the successor government signed an armistice with the Allies and then became a co-belligerent against Germany. Mussolini and many Fascists, however, continued to fight with the Germans and during two years of general conflict in Italy there also raged a bitter and brutal political civil war.

Post-War Politics

Italy has had many changes of administration since the first post-war general election of 1948; the twenty-fourth administration took office in July 1976. There are a large number of political groups fostered partly by the system of proportional representation employed in Italian elections. In terms of the popular vote, the two largest parties are the Christian Democrats (DC - essentially right wing and Catholic, though embracing a range of views from centre to far right and subject to faction) and the Communists (PCI). The rest of the left is considerably fragmented and there are various other groups including Republicans, Monarchists, Liberals and Neo-Fascists. The DC has been at the heart of every government but one since 1948, by alliances with parts of the left in the 1950s, with the right (including the Neo-Fascists) in the early 1960s, and then with the centre-left again. In parliament the concessions which such compromise requires can lead to emasculation or withdrawal of proposed legislation. Negotiation of coalition loses parliamentary time and agreed draft legislation of lower political priority may simple be lost in the welter of parliamentary business.

Coalition has proved more difficult and the increasing polarisation of Italian political life was reflected in the general election results of the 1976 when the DC with 38% of the vote was only able to form an administration which was in effect a coalition of abstention with the Communists who had obtained some 34% of the total vote. Polarisation has introduced into all spheres of Italian life and not least into education a whole series of political imperatives for reform requiring the sort of action which in other societies is frequently undertaken by select committees, parliamentary commissions or by the institutions themselves. In Italy parliamentary discussion and legislation is generally the only form of action available.

Constitutional Structure

By a referendum of 1946 the monarchy was abolished and a republic established. The present structure of the Italian State is based on the Constitutional Charter of 1 January 1948 which provided Italy with an altogether new system following the collapse of the Fascist state. Government is by a Council of Ministers, supported by an elected assembly. (There is also a Council of State but this is a juridical, advisory organ to safeguard justice in the administration.) The Head of State is a President, elected by secret ballot of members of the assembly; he serves for seven years, is elegible for re-election and has the powers of a constitutional monarch. The Italian parliament is bi-cameral, consisting of a Chamber of Deputies and a Senate.

Deputies are elected by universal suffrage of citizens over 18 years, senators by citizens over 25 years. A certain number of senators sit by right (e.g. former presidents) or by nomination by the president for distinguished service to the State. Legislation is normally initiated in one of the two chambers or in both together. Senators and deputies may initiate legislation and so may an individual elector who can amass more than 50,000 signatures in support. A referendum may be held to ascertain the electorate's wishes on legislation (e.g. the referendum on divorce in 1974).

The President appoints ministers. They have the right and sometimes the obligation to attend sittings of both chambers. Each minister is usually head of a ministry but a minister without portfolio may attend the Council of Ministers. Each ministry has one or more under-secretaries who are not part of the government and do not attend the Council of Ministers. They are the delegates of the minister in the assembly and are most invariably either deputies or senators. As soon as a Prime Minister feels that his administration no longer commands the requisite majority in either chamber he resigns. The President consults and appoints a Prime Minister-designate with full powers and that Prime Minister either forms or fails to form an administration.

Regional Government

The republic is divided into *regioni*, *provincie*, and *comuni*. There are 20 *regioni* each with governments performing certain legislative functions. Five of these *regioni* for political and economic reasons have more functional autonomy than the rest (e.g. the *regione* of Sicily). Generally regional assemblies have power to legislate on matters of regional concern, particularly the organisation of regional departments and administration, communal and provincial boundaries, police, medicine, museums and libraries, town planning, tourism, transport, public works and professional training. The *regioni*, while receiving contributions from central government, also have certain fund raising powers with the more autonomous *regioni* administering some of the revenue from taxes and levies raised within the region.

Provincie

These are districts of State and regional decentralisation. The provincial finance department and its educational inspectorate, for example, are branch organs of the State with a sphere of competence within the province. Each province has a council, *junta*, and president, all elective and all honorary. The provinces are responsible for public works, public health and public education.

Comuni

These are the smallest autonomous units whose districts are fixed by law. A commune is responsible for local police, health and hygiene, public welfare and public works of local interest and for this purpose may levy local communal taxes. The mayor (sindaco) presides over municipal and communal councils and in addition to being head of the communal administration he is a government official responsible for those functions delegated by the State (e.g. registration of births, deaths and marriages and public law and order).

International Relations

In foreign policy Italy has been consistent in allying herself with the western bloc, through membership of NATO, OECD and other organisations. Italy has also strongly favoured the European concept from its inception and the right of employment in all EEC countries is undoubtedly attractive and important to Italy with its surplus not only of workers but also of graduates and professionals. The emergence of the PCI as the second party in voting strength has obliged it to make certain affirmations about the future. Its current dedication to the concept of Eurocommunism has been accompanied by promises that if the party were to form a government it would be a loyal partner in NATO and member of the EEC. However, Italy has established some significant trading relationships with the Eastern bloc (for example plant for the assembly of FIAT cars in the USSR). She has willingly provided hospitality to institutions of European and international standing - EURATOM, ESRO, UNESCO, FAO, etc. - and has thereby gained politically and financially.

5 THE ECONOMY

Agriculture

Agriculture still represents an important element in the Italian economy but its importance has decreased. It accounted for 9.5% of GNP in 1974 and in that year 16.2% of the working population was engaged in agriculture (30% in the south). Difficult terrain, sparse rainfall and small farms limit the efficiency of agriculture as most farms are too small for mechanisation. The 'flight from the land' is also raising the average age of farm workers. Successive plans have been put into operation to modernise the agricultural sector and increase productivity; on larger and more modern farms there has been some improvement. The chief crops are wheat, maize, grapes and olives.

Industry

Natural methane gas and oil have been discovered in the Po Basin and offshore in the Adriatic and Italy is now self-sufficient in natural gas which is widely used as fuel. There are also plans to exploit hydroelectric power. However, Italy is generally poor in mineral resources to support heavy industry though there is some iron ore and pyrites, lead, zinc and aluminium. Her real strength lies in manufacturing industries producing cars, textiles and office machinery. Industrial development since World War Two has led to what is now called the 'second industrial revolution'. In 1974 industry employed 31% of the labour force and accounted for 29% of GDP. Much of the industrial development has been in the north, particularly in the Po valley, exacerbating the traditional north/south imbalance in living standards. The steel industry has expanded rapidly and the motor vehicle industry is especially important. FIAT has 83% of Italian automobile production and 12% of total European production. The engineering and food processing industries have suffered from fragmentation with many small firms competing with large State-owned organisations. State-owned industry accounts for about half of total industrial investment especially in shipbuilding, petrochemicals, power and natural gas. The automobile, electrical and textile industries are still in private hands. Tourism makes a very important contribution to the country's wealth.

Employment

Over the ten year period from 1961 to 1971 there was a significant fall in the numbers employed in textiles and mining. By far the highest numbers of workers are employed in commerce and engineering. The post-1974 industrial recession has led to widespread unemployment and unemployment figures remain high.

Economic Development

Italy has a mixed economy based on government financing and widespread social security, the comparatively favourable conditions of which have been negotiated by unions organised into four main groups: *Confederazione Generale Italiana del Lavoro* (CGIL and Communist dominated); *Confederazione Italiana Sindacati Lavoratori* (CISL and Roman Catholic); *Unione Italiana del Lavoro* (UIL); and *Confederazione Italiana Sindacati Nationali Lavoratori* (CISNL). The economy developed fast in the 1950s and early 1960s with an average annual increase in the gross national output of about 7%. The result was a widespread redistribution of wealth which has affected even the more backward areas of the country economically (though perhaps less thoroughly than was hoped). Along with the redistribution of wealth there has been a slow erosion of what was thought of as a specifically Italian way of life and a steady approximation to the urban standards of expectation common to the other members of the EEC. For example, in the EEC Consumers' 'League Table' (in December 1976) Italy came fifth in the number of motor cars per 1,000 of the population. Only Germany had more miles of motorway and Italy had twice the mileage of the next in line, France. All other EEC countries except France and Ireland had more telephones per 1,000 head of population and Italy came last but one in the TV list. But no country spent more than the Italians on going to the cinema, which remains a very live industry.

Economic Situation

Nevertheless, the Italian economy differs in important respects from those of many other western European countries. The average per capita income is appreciably below that in other EEC countries. The average income in the south is just over half that of the whole country and the wide differences in economic and social development between the south and the north represent a long term economic problem as yet unsolved despite increased investment in the south. In 1969 the rapid expansion of the economy was interrupted by labour unrest but the economy was recovering before the energy crises of 1973/74. Measures taken to stimulate growth accelerated inflation. The years 1973 and 1974 saw a budgetary deficit and a worsening balance of payments. Though the balance of payments deficit was reversed in 1975 and inflation contained, this was at the price of underinvestment, stagnation in industry and increasing unemployment.

In August 1975 reflationary measures boosted industrial production but adversely affected the balance of payments and the rate of inflation (running at 16%). By the end of 1976 inflation was running at something like 20% per annum and the level of unemployment was over a million and a quarter. The lira continued to float downwards in relation to the dollar and other hard currencies, and the Italian economy seriously preoccupied not only the richer members of the EEC but the rest of the North Atlantic community. In 1979 while imports and exports were considerably up on 1978 figures the former rose by 35% and the latter by 26%.

6 THE EDUCATION SYSTEM

Academic Year

The school year extends from early September to the end of June and is divided into three terms. Pupils attend for approximately 200 days each year. Classes are in attendance six days with an average of four hours classwork daily.

Pre-School

In 1968 State nursery schools for children from 3 to 6 years were established by legislation, absorbing previously existing kindergartens (attached to primary teacher training schools) and nursery schools (attached to training schools for nursery school teachers). Attendance is optional and free. Pre-primary schools aim to develop the child's personality and to prepare for primary education. Where numbers and situations allow the schools are divided into sections by age. Legislation provides for the establishment of new schools, with priority for areas of special need, since it was one of the intentions of the legislation to help compensate for 'inadequate family backgrounds which give rise to situations whereby there may be a rapid fall in the social scale'. There are also many communal, religious and other private pre-primary establishments (78% of pre-primary provision in 1973) which are fee paying and of varying educational character. Services offered range from pure child-minding to character development activities and even to attempts at formal education.

The outsider might expect to find the Montessori methods widely developed within the Italian pre-primary and early primary system specially in view of Maria Montessori's first success in enabling backward children from slum areas in Rome to pass the State reading and writing tests of the time. Montessori methods, however, are generally found within the private sector only, although a few State schools have 'Montessori' added to their names. Generally, however, methods have been revised back to a much more teacher centred, carefully controlled and structured style than Montessori practised or than is nowadays found in nursery schools in other developed countries.

First Level Schools *(scuola elementare)*

At age 6 children are obliged to go to primary school which is free to all and lasts until age 11. The five-year period is divided into two cycles of two years and three years respectively. In the first cycle there is a general curriculum but in the second there is the beginning of subject learning: religious instruction, moral and civil education, physical education, history, geography, science, arithmetic, geometry, Italian, drawing, writing, singing and handicraft. The examination at the end of the fifth year is for the Primary School Certificate *(licenza Elementare)* which qualifies the child for admission to the middle school *(scuola media)*. In 1977 the Ministry of Public Instruction decided to launch a pilot scheme to introduce the learning of foreign languages (English/French) into the primary school curriculum, and asked for help from the British Council and the Service Culturelle Française.

Second Level (Middle) Schools *(scuola media)*

At age 11 a child passes from primary to middle school where a free and compulsory course of education is followed for a further three years. The curriculum includes both compulsory and optional subjects (with compulsory subjects occupying a maximum of 26 hours per week). Among these compulsory subjects are: religious instruction, Italian, history, civics and geography, mathematics, nature study and elementary science, a foreign language, art education and physical education. Handicraft and music are compulsory in the first year and become optional thereafter. In June 1977 Latin was abolished as a required subject in the second and third years of *scuola media* and musical and craft education occupy the hours previously spent on Latin. In the teaching of Italian language 'due reference will be made to its Latin origin and its historical evolution'. In each school year the pupils have an opportunity to take up one more option. In some cases where local conditions permit, an optional additional period of ten or more hours per week *(doposcuola)* covering subsidiary studies and out of school activities may be offered.

The *scuola media* is intended to assist the formative development of the child through a teaching programme of a general nature to give his guidance for either further education or professional job orientation. At 14 the child takes the Middle School Certificate *(Licenza di Scuola Media)* which admits him to the upper secondary school.

Upper Second Level Schools *(scuola secondaria superiore)*

Upper secondary school is not compulsory and caters for students from age 15 to 19. While the middle school aimed essentially at developing the child's personality and attitudes, upper school, organised within a complex and rigid structure, had traditionally aimed at providing a profounder cultural, vocational and sometimes specialist preparation. The upper school system includes various forms of teaching carried out in different types of institutions and schools as follows:

(i) classical/scientific/art high schools aiming to prepare students for higher studies in arts or sciences

(ii) technical institutes preparing students intending to hold technical and administrative jobs at intermediate level

(iii) vocational institutes for the training of skilled workers

(iv) art institutes and schools for the practice of find arts, performing arts and crafts

(v) teacher training institutes *(magistrale)* for the training of pre-primary and primary school teachers (see **Teacher Training** later).

Classical Upper School (liceo classico o liceo ginnasio)

This type of school has existed virtually throughout the history of State education in Italy. It prepared students for entrance to university and other higher education. The five-year course is divided into two cycles of two and three years and the curriculum is humanistic. Subjects taught in the two-year cycle are Italian, Latin, Greek, a modern foreign language, history and civics, geography, mathematics, religious instruction and physical education. In the three-year cycle, pupils study Italian, Latin, Greek, history and civics, philosophy, natural sciences, chemistry, geography, mathematics, physics, history of art, religious instruction, and physical education. Greek and Latin still represent an important part of the course. At the end of the fifth year students sit for the certificate of secondary education *(Diploma di Maturità Classica)* which qualifies for admission to all faculties of the university.

Scientific Upper School (liceo scientifico)

This provides more specialised preparation for those intending to study science at university. The course also lasts five years of which the first is intended to be a bridging year between *scuola media* and *scuola superiore*. Subjects studied in the first year are Italian, Latin, history, civics and geography, a foreign language and literature, mathematics, drawing, religious instruction and physical education. In subsequent years the subjects are Italian, Latin, a foreign language and literature, history and civics, philosophy, natural sciences, chemistry, geography, physics, mathematics, drawing, religious instruction and physical education. The leaving certificate *(Diploma di Maturità Scientifica)* qualifies for admission to all university faculties. The examination at both classical and scientific schools consists of written examinations and an oral 'defence' though with pressure of numbers the oral can be perfunctory.

Arts High School *(liceo artistico)*

This school is intended to give a thorough grounding in the arts and is often attached to the tertiary level academies of fine art. The course lasts four years, divided into two cycles of two years. The first cycle includes literary, scientific and artistic subjects while the second offers two alternatives – preparation either for an advanced course in art at the academies or for entrance to a university school of architecture. The final certificate is the artistic diploma *(Diploma di Maturità Artistica)*. Students may enter the State examination for art teachers in middle and secondary schools to enter the academy of fine arts. A further one-year supplementary course qualifies the holder to enter all university faculties.

Technical Institute *(istituto tecnico)*

This gives secondary education with a vocational bias for the training of technicians and supervisory staff. Subjects covered include: aeronautics; agriculture; business and commerce; surveying; domestic science, industrial studies; nautical studies; tourism. Courses generally last five years (six for agriculture) and training is both theoretical and practical. A two-year general preparatory course, common to all institutes (which postpones the need to choose a definite specialisation) is followed by a three-year technical course with emphasis on practical studies. The final certificate is the technical school certificate *(Diploma di Maturità Tecnica)* which qualifies for admission to a university course. (The sixth year at an *istituto tecnico agrario* is optional and qualifies the student as *perito agrario*, a useful qualification to enter the profession.)

Vocational Institute *(istituto professionale)*

This exists for the training of skilled workers in particular fields of importance to the economy. Training is given in six subject areas: agriculture; nautical studies; commerce; industrial studies and handicrafts; hotel management, domestic science. Admission is by the Middle School Certificate or by entrance examination for those who have completed their compulsory education without obtaining a certificate. Courses are generally of two or three years' duration (three years for agriculture) and are more practical than those of the technical secondary schools. Curricula are to some extent still experimental, in an attempt to define the most satisfactory way of meeting the needs of the economy. The diploma awarded at the end of the course *(Diploma di Qualifica Professionale)* has employment value, but it also enables the student to sit an examination to enter the final years of the technical secondary schools *(istituti tecnici)*. Since 1969 there has been an experimental post-vocational diploma integration course of two or more years' duration leading to a vocational leaving certificate *(Diploma di Maturità Professionale)* which qualifies for admission to higher education.

Art Institute (istituto d'arte)

In this type of institution training is usually related to a local art or craft tradition and the course consists of woodwork, ceramics or some other applied art. Admission to the course is by Middle School Certificate or by entrance examination. The course is of three years' duration, leading to a diploma in art *(Diploma di Maestro d'Arte)* which qualifies a student to sit the examination for secondary school art teachers or to take a further two-year advanced course in art leading to the *Diploma di Maturità d'Arte Applicata* which qualifies for admission to an academy of fine arts or a university.

Conservatory of Music

Entrance is normally by examination but most conservatories have their own middle school annexes and students with the Middle School Certificate from these are exempted from the entrance examination. Students are given formal musical training (piano, singing, composition, etc.) plus complementary general studies. Courses are usually divided into three stages, with a certificate at the end of each, the final certificate being the Diploma of the Conservatory. The length of the course depends on the musical training followed and may be from five to ten years in all.

National Academy of Dance

This institution offers a variety of courses for dancers, instructors and choreographers, including updating and specialist classes. The diploma awarded to dancing instructors is the *Diploma Abilitante all'Insegnamento della Danza*.

Third Level (Higher) Institutions

Education at tertiary level is obtained at universities and institutes of higher education, both State run and independent. University teaching is offered through faculties which generally offer several degree courses, the duration of which varies from four to six years and which lead to the conferment of an academic title known as *diploma di laurea* (or first degree). In addition to the degree courses there are also shorter two to three year courses for a diploma, some of which follow on from the degree and some of which are taken instead of degree courses.

Admission

Admission to a State university depends on the possession of the appropriate secondary school leaving certificate or diploma and there is no limitation on numbers. Private universities of which there are a number, both secular and religious, must have the same entrance standards but may apply selective criteria and restrict intake. The number of students in 35 State and 14 private institutions approaches one million.

Courses

Examinations, written and oral, are held at the end of each year and the results of each particular course are shown on the degree certificate. After the satisfactory completion of all courses the student submits a thesis and is finally examined orally on the subject of the thesis by a board consisting of 11 members of the faculty, each of whom marks a candidate out of a total of 10 marks. The final standard of degree is shown as the sum of the individual marks out of the total 110. An exceptional student with marks 110/110 may be awarded honours *(cum laude)* on the unanimous recommendation of the board. Sometimes the recommendation *cum laude* is accompanied by an undertaking on behalf of the university to publish the thesis. A student emerges from university with the title of Doctor. But apart from the occasional diplomas mentioned above there are no post-graduate degree courses. As courses may be repeated and as there is no fixed time for the preparation of the thesis degrees are rarely awarded after the minimum period of study.

University Organisation

The organisation of the university is in faculties and each faculty is composed of a number of institutes each headed by a full professor *(professore ordinario)*. The directors of the institutes compose the faculty board and elect their Dean for a limited term. All *professori ordinari* participate in the election from their number of the Rector *(Rettore Magnifico)*, also for a limited term. The academic secretary *(segretario)* is similar to the post of registrar in a British university and is a permanent official. There is no equivalent to a British university Chancellor. A *professore ordinario* is appointed after the vacant post has been advertised and candidates have been examined by a jury of *professori ordinari* from the same or related discipline not necessarily drawn from the university in which the vacancy arises. The jury generally selects its candidates on the record of research and teaching ability and candidates are expected to give a demonstration lecture. A short list of three candidates is put forward from which the appointment is made and subsequently confirmed by the minister.

Under the *professore ordinario* who is either the holder of the chair or a titled and thus permanent professor, are a bewildering number of appointments. Most of these are temporary, the most senior being the *professore incaricato*, appointed for a limited term after competitive selection. Lower down the scale are assistant professors *(assistenti)* junior lecturers *(contrattisti, assegnisti* or *borsisti)* junior research assistants *(esercitatori)*, all temporary, some paid for their services and some voluntary. the unpaid departmental assistant often has an alternative job, working on the fringes of university life with the expectation that he may be in line for a paid temporary appointment. The *borsista* or *assegnista* is in receipt of a research scholarship usually lasting for three years; he may be invited to assist with third and fourth year student guidance and thesis preparation. *Contrattisti, borsisti* and *esercitatori* are appointed by the faculty.

Other Institutions

Among other non-university tertiary institutions are the academies of fine arts *(accademia di belle arti)* which prepare students for a professional career in the arts. Entrance is by the *diploma di maturità artistica, diploma di maestro d'arte* or by examination. There are four branches of study: painting, sculpture, decorative arts and stage design. The course lasts four years from roughly age 18/19 to 22/23, with an examination each year. The final diploma is academic, not vocational. The National Academy of Dramatic Art *'Silvio d'Amico'*, prepares theatrical producers and actors in three-year courses. Entrance is limited in number by examination and public competition.

Teacher Training

The teacher qualifications required for the various levels of education are as follows:

(i) pre-schools: *diploma di abilitazione all' insegnamento nelle scuole di grado preparatorio*

(ii) primary schools: *diploma di abilitazione magistrale*

(iii) middle schools: degree from a faculty of education *(magistero)* or other university degree + qualifying certificate for this level *(abilitazione)*

(iv) secondary high schools: degree from a faculty of education (for literary subjects only) or other university degree + qualifying certificate for this level *(abilitazione)*.

Teachers in pre-school and primary schools will mostly have been trained at the *instituti magistrali* (teacher training colleges at upper secondary level) though by no means all *magistrali* pupils go on to teach (there is a high proportion of girls to boys in these schools).

Pre-School

Prospective nursery school teachers follow a three-year course which covers Italian methods of education, history, hygiene and child care, music and group singing, domestic science and needlework, plastic arts and drawing, teaching practice and religion. Teaching practice is held in pre-primary schools attached to many of the *magistrali*. At the end of the third year at age 17 the students sit the State examination leading to the pre-school teaching diploma.

First Level

A student proposing to be a primary teacher follows a four-year course of which the first is a bridging year. In subsequent years his studies include Italian, Latin, history, civics and geography, philosophy and methods of education, psychology, natural sciences, chemistry, mathematics and physics, drawing and art, group singing, physical education and a musical instrument. Each subject studied at the *magistrale* includes an element of teacher training. Firmly in the centre of the study programme are psychology, pedagogics and philosophy and there is a rigorous philosophy course. The course is pretty comprehensive and does not allow much specialisation. In the third year pupils visit an elementary school and make a careful study of the organisation, timetable preparation and delivery of lessons, textbooks, teaching aids, games, library, arrangements for homework, etc. In the fourth year pupils pay further visits and study the organisation of education generally. Teaching practice is held in local primary schools and students are divided among classes in order not to disturb the normal working of the school. They have the help either of a primary school teacher or of a special director assigned by the local education office. At the end of the fourth year students sit the diploma examination and on the strength of this may apply for a teaching post or join the education faculty of a university. Some universities also accept this diploma for admission to degree courses in foreign languages and literature. Holders of the diploma may also attend a one-year supplementary course *(corso integrativo)* and if successful are qualified for admission to all faculties of the university.

Second Level

Secondary school teachers come almost entirely from universities but those who have followed a course in the *facoltà di magistero* should have done some teacher training and teaching practice. How much seems to depend on the individual. In any case it is likely to be small. Secondary school teachers of mathematics and science will be graduates of science faculties since the *magistero* does not provide a scientific preparation. The only formal professional teacher training received by graduates of academic faculties is a short 'methods course' *(corso d'abilitazione)* lasting a few months. In 1971 a government decree announced the addition of a fifth teacher training year to the university degree course, which was to precede a period of teacher training practice. This provision was in accordance with an Act of 1968 which proposed training courses to promote interest in fundamental educational problems, to develop professional aptitudes and ability, and to favour a more detailed knowledge both of the subject to be taught and of relative teaching methods. Despite the legislative provision for the fifth post-*laurea* teacher training year, most candidates for posts in middle and upper secondary schools have only the basic degree.

Appointments

Admission to the lists of permanent staff in all levels of school is by competition, known as the *concorso*. In 1973 a government decree established the basic criteria and regulations for public competitions, and appointments must be made either on the basis of qualifications or as a result of qualifying competitions and examinations. Pre-school teachers are recruited by competitions within each province and there is no examination. Primary school teachers are selected either by qualifications or as a result of examination; upper school teachers by qualifications and by their performance in an examination. Middle and upper school teachers, in addition to holding a specific qualifying certificate must have been in service for at least two years after obtaining that certificate; consequently frequent movements are usual before established service is obtained. In addition graduates usually begin their teaching careers as unqualified supply teachers *(supplenti)*.

Non-Formal and Adult

According to the census of 1951, 25% of the population was 'officially' illiterate; this figure had sunk to 9% by 1961 and by 1971 there were 2.5 million 'official' illiterates. A steadily increasing percentage of the work force has more than elementary education. In the year 1970 the national work force consisted of 19.5 million workers of whom 2.7 million had no educational qualifications at all, 10.6 million had a primary leaving certificate, 1.5 million a secondary school leaving certificate and 0.6 million a university degree. In 1975 3% of the work force had more than the primary qualification and the same percentage had a degree, while 53.5% had the primary certificate only.

Educational qualifications are required not only for entry to the various training opportunities and to employment itself, but also for the enjoyment of certain civic rights and duties: for examle, one must hold the primary certificate in order to be accepted as a candidate for election to the voluntary local magistrates' court. The trade unions are thus very interested in the development of the education system to enable more workers to achieve higher qualifications and for the school curriculum to be brought closer into line with industrial and other needs.

Range of Classes

In 1972 professional and adult education was made a responsibility of the regions and each *regione* has assigned a different priority to its efforts. Courses exist for professional updating, cultural enrichment, and for adults to acquire a school leaving certificate. Social centres of permanent education established in 1961 to replace the old reading centres are intended to act as focal points for spontaneous adult education activity and for the development of defined courses.

For a young person between 15 and 19 the choice of courses is limited and confusing. Day release schemes for working people are not generally available so that further study is undertaken either at night or as a registered apprentice. The Apprenticeship Law of 1965 laid down courses of study which apprentices were obliged to follow; (employers with apprentices in training do not have to pay the heavy social insurance contributions otherwise obligatory for all employees). The government has also agreed that working people may have a number of paid hours of work to sit examinations and a work timetable to enable them to attend night school. Night school is usually a repeat performance of the day school programme. Students study for the appropriate *diploma di maturità* and are thus following a heavily loaded timetable requiring four hours attendance/study on five nights a week and Saturday mornings for up to six years. There is a high drop-out rate from night school study as a result either of fatigue or of the inappropriate curriculum. The qualification obtained at night school was recognised in 1971 as equivalent to the *diploma di maturità*. Night students, many of them national servicemen, attend a special session for the *maturità* which qualifies them for admission to university.

Workers' Education

In 1972 the Metal Workers' Union won the right for a percentage of its members to be released for general technical education courses for 150 working hours in every three years. In July 1976 the allowance was increased to 250 hours. All the hours may be taken in one year but no more than 50% of the time required for any course can be taken from working hours. Not more than 2% of the work force of any particular firm may offer itself for study purposes at the same time, and the total number of hours to be conceded by any one firm in a year is limited to 30 hours multiplied by the number of workers on the payroll. At the time of the original concession only an estimated 20% of industrial workers had completed *scuola media* and, in 1972, 2,200 young people were released onto the labour market without the *Licenza di Scuola Media*. The unions decided, therefore, to concentrate on rendering illiterate workrs literate and on allowing older workers to complete their middle school education. The result of this was that in February 1976 under 10% of the participants were below age 20 and only 160,000 working 15 to 19 year olds were attending vocational or scholastic courses. In 1974, the first year of the programme, 14,237 workers were enrolled (9,327 from the north, 2,819 from the centre and 2,091 from the south). In 1975 enrolment went up to 38,790 (19,665/10,177/8,949). In 1976 enrolments were about 74,000 and this number had risen to over 100,000. A high percentage of student workers (more than 20%) drop out before completing the course.

7 EDUCATIONAL ADMINISTRATION
Ministerial Control

The ministries have responsibility for different aspects of education and educational provision in Italy. The Ministry of Public Instruction (*Ministero della Pubblica Istruzione*, or MPI) and the Ministry for Culture and Cultural Assets (*Ministero dei Beni Culturali ed Ambientali*, or MBC). All primary, secondary and tertiary formal education is administered centrally by the Ministry of Public Instruction, although other ministries, notably the Ministry of Labour, have responsibility for some vocational training. All syllabi are organised centrally. Universities are governed by a highly authoritative Fascist law (1933) which, while leaving them in theory autonomous, vests a great deal of control in the MPI. All teachers and educational administrators at all levels of State education are State servants in the direct employ of the Ministry of Public Instruction. Private institutions exist at all levels but must satisfy the norms and requirements of the MPI if their students are to have legally valid qualifications.

Ministry of Public Instruction

The Minister of Public Instruction is supported by three Ministers of State *(Sottosegretari)* each senators, one with special responsibility for primary, one for technical and professional and the third for secondary and higher education. The minister has his own private office *(gabinetto)* with a head (principal private secretary) and staff who fulfil some of the roles played in Britain by the permanent and deputy secretaries who coordinate the work of the ministry and advise the minister. The ministry is divided into 11 directorates-general covering the various educational levels from primary education upwards and also personnel and administration, cultural exchange, private education, popular education and buildings and equipment. Directors-General are appointed by the President on the advice of the Council of Ministers. They are always members of the ministry and may be appointed from outside the civil service. There are also four inspectorates for arts education, school health, physical education and sport and pensions and a section responsible for pre-primary education. One office within the ministry is of special interest: the *Ufficio Studi, Documentazione e Programmazione*, a kind of research and intelligence branch. Among its responsibilities is the study of the education systems of other countries. It brings important developments overseas to the notice of the relevant departments and arranges two colloquia at Villa Falconieri, Frascati, on educational topics.

444

ADMINISTRATION

ORGANISATION OF THE MINISTRY OF PUBLIC INSTRUCTION

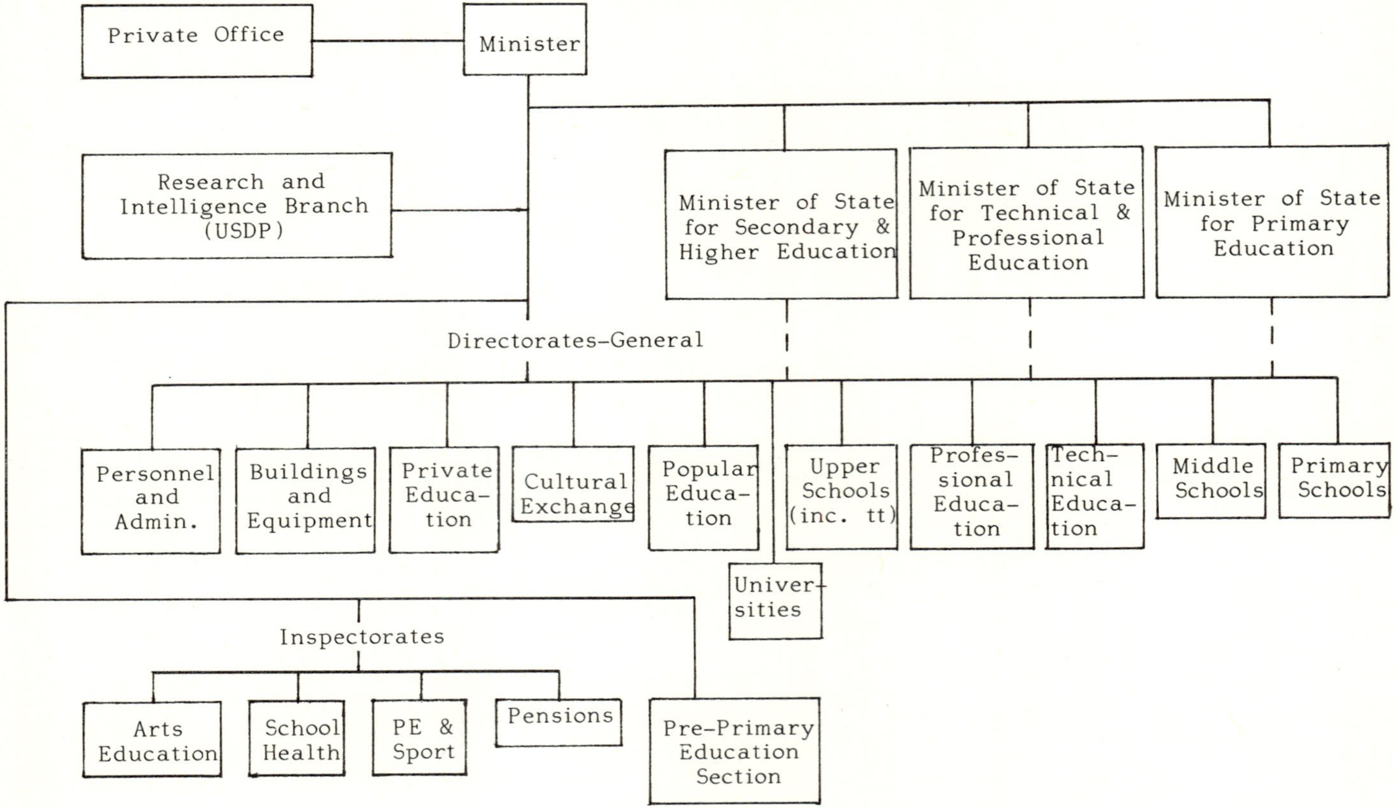

```
┌───────────────┐    ┌──────────┐
│ Private Office│────│ Minister │
└───────────────┘    └──────────┘
                          │
           ┌──────────────┼──────────────┬──────────────┐
           │              │              │              │
    ┌──────────────┐ ┌──────────────┐ ┌──────────────┐
    │ Minister of  │ │ Minister of  │ │ Minister of  │
    │ State for    │ │ State for    │ │ State for    │
    │ Secondary &  │ │ Technical &  │ │ Primary      │
    │ Higher Ed.   │ │ Professional │ │ Education    │
    │              │ │ Education    │ │              │
    └──────────────┘ └──────────────┘ └──────────────┘

┌──────────────────┐
│ Research and     │
│ Intelligence     │
│ Branch (USDP)    │
└──────────────────┘

Directorates-General:
  Personnel and Admin.
  Buildings and Equipment
  Private Education
  Cultural Exchange
  Popular Education
  Upper Schools (inc. tt)    — Universities
  Professional Education
  Technical Education
  Middle Schools
  Primary Schools

Inspectorates:
  Pre-Primary Education Section
  Arts Education
  School Health
  PE & Sport
  Pensions
```

The Minister of Public Instruction is also President of the National Council for Public Instruction *(Consiglio Nazionale della Pubblica Istruzione)*, the highest consultative organ in the land for all educational matters below tertiary level. It functions through five committees responsible respectively for pre-primary, primary, lower secondary, upper secondary and arts education. Apart from its function of evaluating scholastic activity and services and formulating teaching programmes, the council also elects councillors responsible for teaching discipline. Members of the council are not necessarily members of the ministry but are educationists and others elected by school headmasters, teachers, non-teaching staff, central and outposted administrators of the MPI. For the 1977 election 17,000 electoral centres were set up in schools, ministries and outposts. The National Council holds office for five years and meets at least once every three months or when a meeting is requested by one third of its members.

The fundamental aims of the Ministry of Public Instruction are as follows:

(i) to promote public education, establish schools, guarantee the freedom of the teachers, supervise State and non-State institutions

(ii) to guarantee the education supply

(iii) to promote and coordinate the supervision of education

(iv) to promote higher education and research respecting the autonomy of universities

(v) to spread Italian culture abroad

(vi) to coordinate regional programmes and the point of view of regional, national, international and financial interest.

Ministry for Culture

The Ministry for Culture and Cultural Assets was hived off from the Ministry of Public Instruction in 1974. The minister is president of three advisory councils: for antiquities and fine arts, for academies and libraries, and for archives. The Directorate-General of Antiquities and Fine Arts operates through superintendencies for antiquities, for monuments, for galleries, in the main historical centres. Sometimes in smaller centres monuments and galleries form one superintendency. The Directorate General for Academies, Libraries and the Diffusion of Culture is responsible for all State libraries and cultural centres, and the Directorate-General of the Archives of State is responsible for the central State archives and the State archive in each minor historical centre. The ministry also controls the National Recorded Sound Library.

Regional Responsibilities

Regional school boards (soprintendenza, each with a soprintendente) are ministerial delagacies in the major centres with responsibility for school buildings and for qualifying courses for secondary school teachers. The soprintendenza provides the central interface with regional governments who find funds for building and educational provision to supplement the national budget. However, regional governments are asking with increasing insistence for a greater part in determining regional priorities in educational provision and the development of regional centres of education has been much talked about. In the next five years it will be seen how much power the central ministry is prepared to devolve on what are at present consultative bodies.

Lower education offices (provveditorati agii studi) are responsible for the functioning of State schools in each province, for staff in all matters not reserved to the central ministry, for the inspection of non-State schools and adult education. The Provveditore or Director of Education, is the local agent of the Ministry of Public Instruction and presides over the Provincial Schools Council on which sit representatives of the teachers, parents and district authorities to discuss and approve the schooling provision in the province. Examination results are assessed by local teachers but the MPI nominates to each local panel of teacher examiners other teachers from outside the particular provveditorato.

School Districts

In 1974 a new law required the *regioni* to organise school districts *(distretti scolastici)* in an ambitious attempt to decentralise and humanise school administration. The objective of the legislation is 'to achieve the democratic participation of the local community and of social forces in the life and activity of the school . . . with the intention of developing the potential of scholastic institutions both in actual education and all activities connected with education. Its aim will be the full enjoyment of the right to study, the cultural and civil growth of the local community and the better functioning of the educational services'. *Distretti scolastici* will enjoy administrative autonomy and will be able to raise funds for this purpose. Districts will consist of rural and urban zones sharing common social and economic features.

The local community elects up to 50 representatives to the school district council and the first elections took place in November 1977. Each 100,000 inhabitants (and in densely populated conurbations 200,000) are served by such a council. Boundaries are determined by the regional governments. The councils have a life of three years and will meet quarterly or as often as one third of the members may request. Each of the councils are composed of at least:

3 head teachers and other directorial staff elected by the teaching personnel

5 teachers elected by their peers

7 parents (one of whom should be a parent of a child in a non-State school)

3 representatives elected by trade unions, neither teachers, nor administrative personnel

2 representatives of self-employed workers designated by union bodies which represent this class of worker

3 representatives of 'social forces' in the district, one being designated by the Chamber of Commerce, Industry, Agriculture and Arts and Crafts, the other two appointed by the Provincial Council

7 members elected by the *commune*.

The scope of the council includes all types and grades of school but excludes universities, academies of fine art and conservatories. Its main brief is to discuss the schooling needs of the district and advise on the closer integration of school and community. But within the general ambit of government directives on education, its functions also cover the arrangement of educational guidance, school medical and psychological services, adult education courses, and sporting and cultural activities for the pupils. The council may recommend a course of action or programme to the competent authorities. It may recommend to the *provveditore agli studi* organisational and structural reforms which may result in the better use of teachers' time or school organisation and buildings; it may ask the ministry to approve studies which lead to a better understanding of the locale. If the regional government so desires it may also be the channel for financial and other assistance to schools, or students following adult education courses.

8 EDUCATIONAL FINANCE

Education Budget

Public expenditure on education more than doubled between 1959/65 but thereafter the rate of increase was slow and there was an actual decline between 1967/69. In terms of gross national income and of total government expenditure, public expenditure on education has not increased much since 1965 though the MPI's share of the education budget has fluctuated in both directions. In 1974 ministerial funds represented 15.2% of total State funds and 7.8% of Gross National Income. In addition to expenditure by the Ministry of Public Instruction, other government departments also contribute to education, to the extent of about one sixth of the total spent by the MPI, whilst regional governments, provinces and communes contribute upwards of 25% of the amount spent by central government. Demand from all sections of the system for additional finance is now so great that the government could only meet them by severe cutting of public expenditure in other sectors.

Allocation of Funds
Expenditure on Education: Distribution by Level
Percentage of Expenditure 1976

Pre-school	First level	Second Level	Third Level	Other
5.0	29.3	46.7	12.0	7.0

9 DEVELOPMENT AND PLANNING OF THE EDUCATION SYSTEM

Origins

Italy's strong tradition of education and scholarship has been based since the Middle Ages on the universities and the private academies. The first university in Europe was at Bologna, one of the first medical faculties at Salerno, and Italian universities produced the classical triad: priests, doctors and lawyers. The academies, which were formed mainly in the sixteenth, seventeenth and eighteenth centuries in most princely states, including the Papal States, were learned societies which met to discuss their members' research and to facilitate publication. Some like the *Accademias dei Lincei* and *della Crusca* were every bit as distinguished as the Royal Society. But despite educational traditions there was no popular education before 1870 and the new nation therefore had two immediate aims: to introduce mass primary education and to develop higher education along lines that were being exploited in the rest of western Europe. The development of industry from the turn of the century onwards revealed the need for vocational training at school level and for technical and scientific courses at the university. Only after World War Two could it be claimed that the battle for literacy had been won, that five years of compulsory primary education was making the new generation literate and that illiterates as such were a legacy from the past.

Present Position

The Constitution lays down that education shall be compulsory and free of charge for at least eight years, that State schools shall be open to all, and that all capable and deserving persons shall have the right to continue their studies up to the highest level. Mandatory education begins at age 6 and continues until age 14. Institutions and individuals have the right to open schools and educational establishments provided that they are not a charge on the State in the first instance. If they are to have parity with State counterparts they must guarantee educational provision equivalent to that in State institutions. Where the State is unable to meet its constitutional obligations for primary and secondary education it can subsidise private schools to carry out these obligations.

Planning and Reform

Since 1970 responsibility for educational planning has been vested in the Technical Committee for Educational Planning, appointed by the minister to advise him. Before any significant reforms can be implemented they must have parliamentary approval. Implementation of planning legislation is the responsibility of the ministry, subject to legal and financial inspection by the audit department *(corte dei conti)*.

Educational reform has traditionally been the result of social and economic pressures, particularly the shift of population from rural occupations to the production and service industries which need a more highly educated work force. In the last decade the expected challenge from the left to the elitist concept of higher education has led to a general acceptance, by educationists at least, that the curriculum should be more broadly based. Each political party engages in producing its own plan for educational reform (usually piecemeal, sector by sector) but the problems of reconciling all political and social interests have until now proved too great for the attentions of a government beset by economic crises. Every part of the educational system is under challenge for renewal and reform and each part of it is strongly defended by sectional interests. In common with most other European countries the student body itself has entered the debate. The basic problems facing Italian educationists are to decide on which of the various blueprints for reform the nation wishes to follow, and how finance is to be provided. There is, however, a sense of helplessness before the dimensions of the problem and the inability of the nation's administrative infrastructure to cope, and an extreme suspicion among the 'consumers' of education itself that much educational reform has been produced from standard political stances and is concerned as much with the reform of society on certain lines as of education itself.

University Reform

In April 1977 the Council of Ministers approved a draft law. Its main proposals included:

(i) rationalisation of university titles, academic years, examination times, etc.

(ii) institution of a four-year post-graduate degree by research *(dottorato di ricerca)*

(iii) abolition of the present faculty arrangements and the duplication of courses involved, and the setting up of departments under elected directors

(iv) rationalisation of courses under the guidance of the government with special reference to 'the effective requirements of the production economy and the different level of technical and professional preparation such requirements demand'; courses of little relevance or utility will be suppressed

(v) establishment of a network of councils within the university with specific responsibilities including academic course councils *(consigli di corsi di laurea o di diplomi)*

(vi) establishment of a National University Council under the chairmanship of the minister including representatives of teaching and non-teaching staff, the students, the National Council for Economy and Labour, the National Council for Public Instruction, etc.

(vii) reduction of the categories of university staff to two main organised groups: *professori ordinari* and *professori associati* who will have the same functions and be represented equally on university governing bodies; introduction of regulations governing the number of working hours and outside activities.

These proposals are not greatly different from the Communist Party's plans and the reform has some consensus support among the main political parties. The PCI would like to decentralise the grants system and to set up a national body which would oversee university policy and funding. It is remarkable how far the British model is reflected in both the DC and PCI policies for reform, particularly in the departmental system, the introduction of the research doctorate and the concept, formally enunciated by the PCI, that university policy should be taken out of the hands of politicians. The ministry and the unions were virtually in agreement on the rationalisation of categories of teaching staff. *Contrattisti* and *borsisti* will be phased out and in the transitory period no more *contrattisti* and *assegnisti* were recruited. The number of graduates admitted to research doctorate courses (now intended to be the qualification for a university teaching career) will be roughly equal to the number of vacant posts for associate professors. However, staff reorganisation was attacked by student extremists and associations of university staff who feel that the provisions for the many fringe teachers in the universities are not generous enough.

10 THE SYSTEM IN OPERATION

Secondary School Reform

Root and branch reform of the secondary school cycle has been discussed for the last 25 years and in 1952 a ministerial working party was established to reorganise the system 'urgently'. In 1963 the reform of the *scuola media* with the abolition of the *scuola di avviamento* (second class *scuola media* for less able children) rendered even more urgent the reform of upper schooling. Another ministerial working party decided that this should be done within three years. In 1968 the Communist Party for the first time formally suggested the comprehensivation of the upper school system. The following year a mini-reform of the *diploma di maturità* was undertaken in the expectation that there would soon be a major reform. In 1970 the main lines upon which upper schooling should be reformed were prescribed by a commission under the presidency of the republican deputy

Biasini on the basis of suggestions made by experts at a special conference at the Villa Falconieri, Frascati. In 1972 the then Minister of Public Instruction and the PCI both produced plans for reform but no parliamentary time was found to discuss them. During the summer of 1975 the Socialist Party of Italy, the Christian Democrats, the Social Democratic Party and the Republican Party all put forward their proposals and a parliamentary committee was formed to see if there was enough common ground for a single platform of reform.

Malfatti Plan

Towards the end of 1976 the MPI under Minister Malfatti issued its plan for reform. It contained 23 articles on the new organisation of the *scuola secondaria superiore*. But there were features of this governmental project which differed markedly from those submitted by the political parties. The main and most far reaching proposition was that the *licei classici*, *licei scientifici*, *magistrali*, *istituti tecnici* and *istituti professionali* should all be abolished. The two- and three-year cycles would be replaced by an obligatory first year which would constitute 'consolidation and orientation' immediately after age 14 and the school leaving age would be raised to 15. After this preliminary year there would be four years in which the syllabus would cover common and optional subjects. Thus the first year of the new upper secondary school would become obligatory for all children. Those not proposing to continue in formal education beyond age 15 would in that year be introduced to technology and practical manual work. The remaining four years of instruction would be a comprehensive system providing for five streams, viz.:

(i)   languages, letters, arts

(ii) logic, mathematics

(iii) history, philosophy and social science

(iv) sciences

(v)   technology.

The intention in each stream would be to give basic preparation for professional higher education. The government proposed a special commission to decide how the five main streams of upper schooling will be constructed. The minister was chairman and of the 50 or so members, 10 were senators, 10 deputies and 23 were experts nominated by the National Research Council, the Ministry of Public Instruction, the Council of the Economy, and the Council of Work. There were also representatives of school teachers' unions.

Another important feature of the plan was the abolition of the end of year examintion which the student had to pass before he was promoted. Students were henceforth to move upwards after promotion tests and were to be able to move freely between one stream of study and others. The *diploma di maturità* was to show that the student had a competence in at least three subjects and an oral examination was to be given in all subjects studied in the last year. The diploma was to show what studies had been followed and give the comprehensive marks scored in the examination. Along with the structural reform was a plan for the *aggiornamento* of teachers. There was talk of 750 training centres, one for each large town 'as in England'. The reference was to teacher resource centres, which were studied at one of the 1975 Anglo-Italian colloquia.

For those students who do not wish to go on to a university the government proposed to create post-secondary institutes *(istituti superiori)* intended to give a qualification between the *diploma di maturità* and a degree, in order to give young people a technical/professional preparation matching the requirements of employment in the economic, social and productive sectors. These 'super-courses' were to last two years in length and the institutes be administered by councils composed of representatives of the teaching body, of the *regione* of the chamber of commerce, of non-teaching personnel and of the students. The *istituti superiori* was to approximate to further education colleges, following an investigation of the systems of other countries, including the British.

The Malfatti Plan incorporated a good deal of thinking during the seventies and observation of overseas practice, including a wide ranging view of British comprehensive education that was undertaken in 1975 at Villa Falconieri. In general most people welcomed the overall objective of bringing all the educational institutions into one general system, but there was disappointment from the left that the school leaving age was not to be raised at the same time to age 16. However, some feared that the Malfatti reforms would lead to a massive enrolment on university courses. The creation of a further education cycle was not primarily intended to reduce pressure on the universities since this could only be achieved by limiting numbers. It was seen more as providing an opportunity for in-service professional education for secondary school leavers who would otherwise have gone straight into business or industry. Nevertheless the plan was to limit access to university faculties to those who have finished a relevant course of studies for the *diploma di maturità* Those who wished to follow a course for which the *maturità* had not prepared them would have to take an initial preparation course. The promise to institute the *aggiornamento* of teachers was an important condition of the plan in which the assistance of foreign agencies, particularly in language and science education, was requested.

Adult Education Reform

A bill before parliament proposed that the regions would be responsible for artisan and professional instruction. Despite the projected secondary school reform, students still leave higher education without any professional preparation so that the following was to be provided:

(i) taught preparatory courses 'to give socio-economic information to those marginal students who are having difficulty in finding work, to enable them to choose the kind of work they might be able to do'

(ii) initial qualificatory courses, for those who have completed their compulsory schooling at age 15

(iii) training courses for intermediate levels of professionalism

(iv) specialist courses or updating for workers

(v) professional reconversion courses (recycling), to facilitate job mobility

(vi) courses for invalids, sub-normal and educationally retarded

(vii) artisan courses.

The regions were to have a free hand in enabling private organisations, firms, etc. to organise such courses under their aegis. The Ministry of Public Instruction, however, was to remain responsible for 'super-courses' foreseen in the Malfatti Plan.

REFERENCES AND FURTHER READING

Borrelli, Mario (1972). *The School and Capitalist Development*. Nuffield Teacher Enquiry, University of York.
Buoro, Sandro (1978). *La Nuova scuola a tempo pieno.* Editori Riuniti, Rome.
Clark, Burton R. (1977). *Academic Power in Italy: bureaucracy and oligarchy in a national university system.* University of Chicago.
Cosenza, Catello (1980). 'Italy: imbalance between higher education and employment in higher education', *Europe,* 5, no.2, April/June.
European Journal of Education (1980). 15, no.2 (reform in upper secondary education).
Italian National Commission for Unesco (1971). *Cultural Policy in Italy.* Unesco, Paris.
Kloskowska, A. and Martinotti, G. (1977). *Education in a changing society.* Sage, London.
Minio-Paluello, L. (1946). *Education in Fascist Italy.* OUP, London.
OECD (1969). *Reviews of national policies for education: Italy* OECD, Paris.
OECD (1973). *Classification of educational systems in OECD member countries: Austria, Ireland, Italy.* OECD, Paris.
Reguzzini, Mario (1976). *Innovation in in-service education and training of teachers: Italy.* OECD, Paris.
Trivellato, Ugo (1979). *The determinants of student achievement in Italy: an exploratory analysis of the causal patterns of achievement in the IEA Six Subject Survey.* Almqvist & Weksell.
UNESCO/IBE (1980). *International Yearbook of Education,* **XXXII**. Unesco, Paris.

Structure of the Education System in Italy

Age	3	4	5	6	7	8	9	10	11	12	13	14	15	16	17	18	19	20	21	22	23	24
Level				I						II						III					IV	
Stage				1		2			3			4										
Compulsory																						
School type	Scuole materne	Scuole elementari 1st / 2nd	Scuole medie	Scuole secondarie superiori — Licei: (a)classici (b)scientifici (c)tecnici; Istituti tecnici; Istituti magistrali; Scuole magistr.; Istituti prof.	2-year univ.; University faculties and Higher Institutes																	

▨ Education preceding the first level

Examinations: compulsory at end of stage 3 and stage 4 (*Maturita*)

Source: UNESCO/IBE International Yearbook of Education

Compulsory Education: Age Limits 6-14 Duration (years) 8
Entrance age to pre-school education: 3

ITALY BASIC STATISTICS		1960	1970	1975	1978 (approx.)
1	Total population (000) % female	50,223 51	53,565 51	55,023 51	56,697 51
2	% population 0-14 years % female	25.0 49	24.4 49	49	23.0 49
3	Enrolment, all levels % female	6,958,214 45	9,352,077 46	10,685,306 47	10,909,571 47
	First level % female	4,493,540 40	4,841,279 44	4,833,415 46	4,648,504 47
	Second level % female	2,194,829 40	3,823,556 44	4,875,179 46	5,208,725 47
	Third level % female	269,845 27	687,242 38	976,712 39	1,052,342 40
4	Teachers, all levels % female	405,062 59	600,923	729,958	796,565
	First level % female	200,185 74	224,646 77	255,267 83	271,747 85
	Second level % female	187,706 48	332,106	432,867	481,698 56
	Third level % female	17,171 6	44,171	41,824	43,120
5	Public expenditure on education Total (000) Liras As % of GNP As % of public expenditure	708,936 3.6	2,500,061 4.3	5,675,784 5.0	7,346,892 5.1 9.3
6	% enrolment (MF) by level First level Second level Third level	100 65 32 4	100 52 41 7	100 45 46 9	100 43 48 9
	% enrolment (F) by level First level Second level Third level	100 70 28 2	100 54 40 6	100 47 45 8	100 45 47 8
7	Entrance age: Duration of First level education Second level education	6:5 11:8	6:5 11:8	6:5 11:8	6:5 11:8
8	Enrolment ratios (MF) First level Second level Third level	111 34 6.61	110 61 16.69	107 71 25.48	105 74 25.58
	Enrolment ratios (F) First level Second level Third level	109 28 3.61	109 55 12.85	106 67 20.13	22.68

Luxembourg

CONTENTS

1	Geography	458
2	Population	460
3	Society and Culture	461
4	History and Politics	462
5	The Economy	463
6	The Education System	464
7	Educational Administration	471
8	Educational Finance	473
9	Development and Planning of the Education System	473
10	The System in Operation	475

The size and geographical location of the Grand Duchy of Luxembourg account for the fact that its schools reflect features of three of its near neighbours, particularly France and Germany and for the fact that in the absence of a university in Luxembourg students attend foreign universities, mainly in Belgium, France, Germany, Switzerland and the United Kingdom. A law passed on 18 June 1969 authorised the Luxembourg government to recognise officially educational diplomas and certificates obtained abroad.

The general structure of the school system resembles a traditional European model. First level education starts at the age of six and lasts six years. Some pupils follow courses in three supplementary grades up to the school leaving age of 15. To be admitted to a secondary school pupils must have successfully completed the six primary school grades and must have passed an entrance examination in French, German and arithmetic. Secondary education lasts seven years and starts with a year of orientation. The programme of studies in private and State secondary schools is the same for boys and girls.

As in France and the Federal Republic of Germany, middle and technical schools provide opportunities for pupils who do not find a place in a secondary school after the sixth grade. Schools with comprehensive seventh grades enable pupils who successfully complete this year to transfer to a range of technical and vocational schools or to the second year of a secondary school. It is therefore a year of orientation made possible by the abolition of Latin and English in the first year of secondary education. This differentiation of the first stage of second level education and the postponement of final selection for academic secondary schools is reminiscent of traditional features of the French and Federal Republic of Germany systems.

The law of June 1969 authorised the creation in Luxembourg of a university centre which offers two types of university level course. The *cours universitaires*, offered in a wide range of sections, are equivalent to a first year of university studies. The *cours complementaires* provide instruction in professional fields specific to Luxembourg. Attendance is required to qualify for such professions as lawyer, teacher, doctor of medicine and so on.

The first European school was founded in Luxembourg in 1953 to offer the children of European officials a complete schooling from nursery school up to university level. It is divided into four linguistic sections based on German, French, Italian and Dutch languages. The first *baccaleuréat européen* (university entrance examination) took place in 1959. After 1962 other European schools were opened.

The presence of an international community helps to account for the existence of study centres in European affairs, language courses, evening classes and courses for adults organised all over the country either by the Ministry of Education or by international friendship societies.

The Editor

1 GEOGRAPHY

Topography

The Grand Duchy of Luxembourg has a total surface area of only 999 square miles (2,586 square kilometres): the maximum distance from north to south is 51 miles (81 km) and from east to west 35 miles (56 km). This makes it one of the smallest states in Europe and far smaller than any of its partners in the European Communities.

The Grand Duchy lies at the heart of Western Europe and finds itself sandwiched between two very different cultural areas: while it is bounded to the south by French Lorraine and to the west and the north by the French speaking Belgian provinces of Luxembourg and Liège, to the east lie two German *Länder*, the Rhineland Palatine and the Saar. This location has had a profound influence on the country's institutions, its language policy and its education system and has made it a focal point in recent years for several international organisations.

Geographically the Grand Duchy falls into two distinct regions. The northern third consists of the sparsely populated *Osling*, an eastern continuation of the Belgian Ardennes. To the south lies the *Gutland* or *Bon Pays*, an area of rich farmland including on the eastern frontier the vineyards of the Moselle. In the centre of the *Gutland* lies Luxembourg City, occupying a

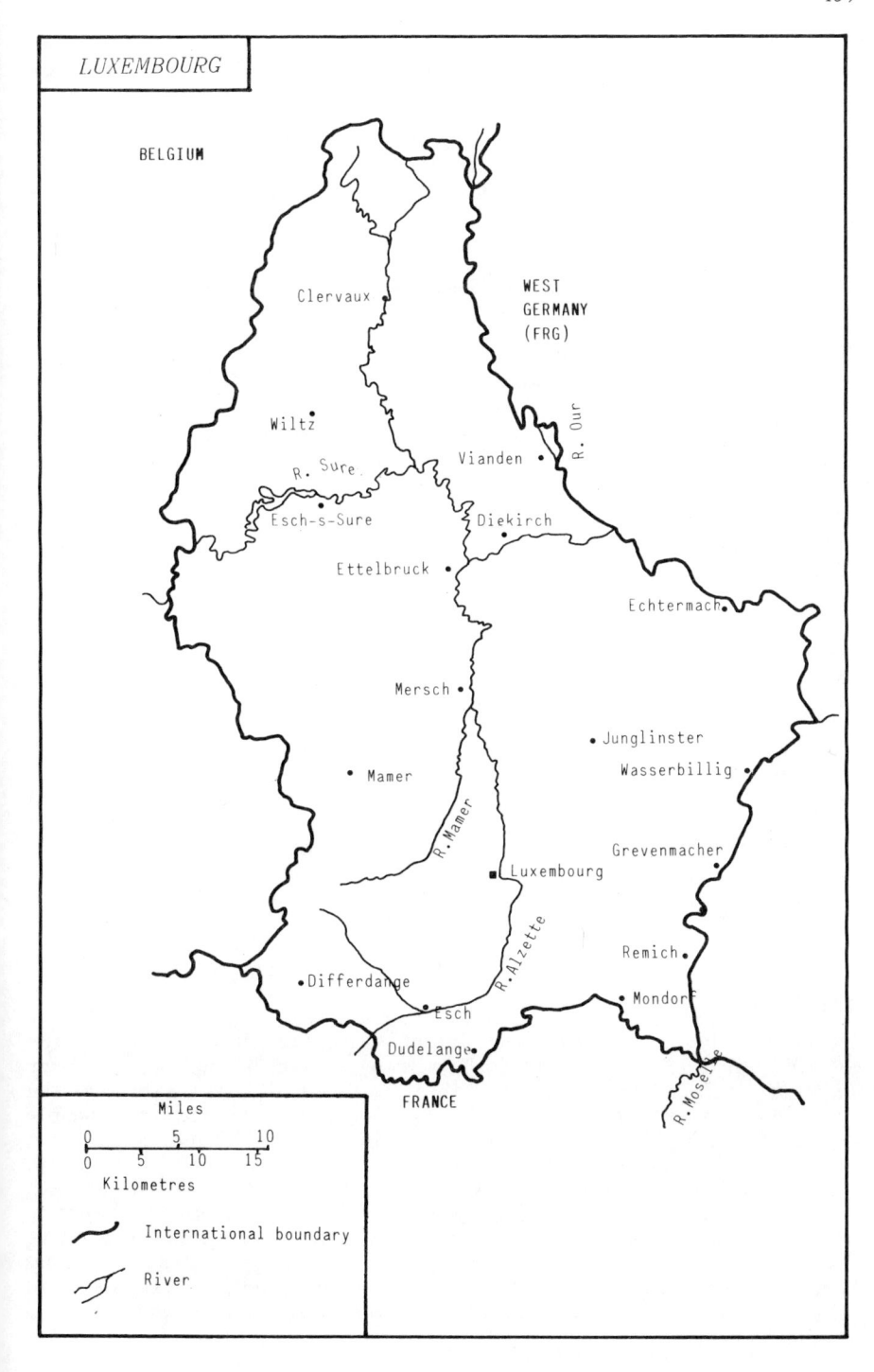

LUXEMBOURG

commanding site and formerly one of the strongest fortresses in Europe: it has given its name (which means 'small stronghold') to the whole country. In the extreme south west near the French border is the industrial area, centred on Esch-sur-Alzette and based on the mining of iron ore; this tiny district has brought prosperity to Luxembourg and made it the world's highest per capita producer of steel.

Climate and Communications

Climatically the country lies between the maritime climate of North West Europe and the more extreme, semi-continental régime of Central Europe. As a result winters are relatively cold, especially in the *Osling*. Road and rail communications within the country and with neighbouring countries are excellent. In 1964 the Moselle was canalised between Thionville in France and Koblenz in Germany; this provided Luxembourg with a valuable means of access to the Rhine and the Ruhr.

2 POPULATION

Growth

The total population of the Grand Duchy in 1979 was 363,700 having risen from the 1947 census figure of 290,000 inhabitants. The average growth rate between 1966 and 1970 was 0.19% per annum. With an average of 335 inhabitants per square mile (132 per square kilometre) population densities are higher than in the Belgian province of Luxembourg (49 per square kilometre) but rather lower than in the neighbouring parts of France and Germany. The population is very unequally distributed, however, between north and south: the sparsely populated *Osling* and the northern part of the *Gutland* continue to lose population to the southern part of the *Gutland*, which accounts for three quarters of the total population. The only relatively dense urban settlements are in Luxembourg City (79,300 in 1979) and the industrial towns near the French border (e.g. Esch-sur-Alzette), but even here people have not lost contact with the countryside.

Distribution

Ethnically the population is of Germanic descent. Until the second half of the nineteenth century Luxembourg was a poor agricultural country hardly able to feed itself. Many of the people were forced to emigrate; as a result there are more people of Luxembourg origin in the USA than in the Grand Duchy and more in the Chicago area than in Luxembourg City. This trend changed dramatically with the discovery in the late nineteenth century that fine steel could be made from the iron ore deposits in the south of the country. Emigration dwindled and more recently the country's booming economy has attracted many foreign workers. Large numbers of Portuguese, Italians and Spaniards, as well as Yugoslavs, Belgians, French and Germans work in the steel and construction industries. The government's policy of encouraging foreign workers to bring their wives and families with them has gone a long way in dispelling their anxieties.

3 SOCIETY AND CULTURE
Language

Since the population is of Germanic descent, their mother tongue (Letzeburgesch) is a Mosell dialect of German. But although Letzeburgesch is widely used in everyday speech by people of all social classes, it is scarcely ever written nor is it used beyond Luxembourg's frontiers. In view of the Grand Duchy's geographical position, French and German are equally important means of communication. This fact was recognised in the 1868 Constitution which made both French and German official languages. French tends to be the language of diplomacy and cultural exchange and official texts are usually in French, while German is the language of commerce and of the people. In October 1939 Letzeburgesch was made the third official language of the country.

The education system aims to make all pupils trilingual by giving them a thorough grounding in German and French. Most children arrive at school speaking only Letzeburgesch: this language is taught as a subject at primary level and may be used as the working language for other activities at first, but German is taught from the beginning and becomes the working language for all activities as early as possible. French is taught as a foreign language from the middle of the second year. At secondary level Letzeburgesch disappears from the timetable after the first year, but German and French are taught throughout the course. At this stage French is the medium of instruction for some subjects, German for others. As for other languages, English, Italian or Spanish (and sometimes Russian or Dutch) may be taken at secondary level.

Religion and Social Patterns

There are no major social divisions among the population. As a result of the economic prosperity there is very little poverty and with some 98% of the inhabitants at least nominally Roman Catholic, society is not divided along religious lines. Freedom of worship is an old tradition and the few Protestant ministers and Jewish rabbis are paid by the State in the same way as the priests. The national motto of the Luxembourgers: *'Wir wellen bleiven wat mir sin'*, ('We want to stay as we are') accurately depicts a stable, affluent, bourgeois, conservative society. But there is another side to the Luxembourger: the smallness of his country has forced him to look beyond its borders. The modern Luxembourger still has a strong sense of nationality but is at the same time cosmopolitan, outward looking, a lover of travel and conscious of the need for close cooperation between neighbouring states.

4 HISTORY AND POLITICS

Origins

The present tiny Grand Duchy, with its prosperous modern economy, is a creation of the last hundred years. In the course of previous centuries the country experienced greater changes in its geographical area and its political influence than any of its neighbours.

Following the withdrawal of the Romans in the fifth century the area became firmly Frankish, and in the tenth century Luxembourg began to exist as a separate entity: on 12 April 963 the Abbey of St Maximin in Trier granted Siegfroi, Count of the Ardennes, certain lands which included the ruins of a Roman fort called Castellum Lucilinburhuc. The strategic position of the fortress contributed to the town's prosperity and by the fourteenth century the House of Luxembourg was making a bid to dominate all Europe: at this period the area of Luxembourg was four times its present size and its influence stretched from the North Sea to the borders of Russia and from the Baltic to the Alps. In 1354 the Counts assumed the title of Dukes. By 1443, however, the country had lost its independence and became a mere province under Philip the Good, Duke of Burgundy. Henceforth, like Belgium, Luxembourg became an integral part of the Spanish (and later the Austrian) Netherlands. After the French Revolution the country became a French province (*le département des forêts*) until 1815 when, together with Belgium, it became part of the Kingdom of the United Netherlands. In 1839, soon after Belgian independence, the western half of Luxembourg was ceded to Belgium (the present Belgian province of Luxembourg). The eastern part (the territory of the modern Grand Duchy) remained the property of the Orange family, and the Prussian garrison, which had occupied Luxembourg City since 1815, remained. It did not leave until 1867 when the European powers finally guaranteed the independence of the (now much reduced) Grand Duchy, on condition that the fortress be dismantled.

Government and Politics

The form of government is a constitutional monarch with a hereditary Grand Duke (or Duchess) as Head of State. The present Luxembourg dynasty was founded in 1890 when union with the crown of the Netherlands ended. The Constitution is modelled on that of Belgium and was proclaimed in 1868. The Grand Duke is not simply a symbolic ruler: he has the right to initiate legislation. He appoints a *Council of Government* consisting of the Prime Minister and five other ministers. This constitutes the administration, but in practice it is based upon the support of the *Chamber of Deputies*. The 59 Deputies in the Chamber are elected by universal suffrage for a period of six years on the basis of one member for just over 6,000 inhabitants. Debates are mainly held in French. The main political parties are: the Christian Socialists; the Workers Socialist Party; the

Democratic Party; the Communist Party; and the Social Democrat Party. Governments in the late seventies were coalitions, in 1980 of Christian Socialists and Democrats.

As in Belgium the basic unit of local government is the *commune*. The 126 *communes* enjoy a large measure of independence and are grouped into *cantons* and these in turn into administrative districts, each of which is administered by a government representative who is appointed by the Grand Duke.

International Relations

For a country as small as Luxembourg total economic independence is impossible. Between 1842 and 1918 the country formed part of the German *Zollverein;* consequently its economic and social legislation closely parallels that of Germany. This link was dissolved at the end of World War One, and in 1922 (after France had rejected the Luxembourgers' desire for economic union) the Belgium-Luxembourg Economic Union was formed, since when the Belgian and Luxembourg economies have been closely linked. In 1948, the Benelux Customs Union (between Belgium-Luxembourg and the Netherlands) came into operation; it was extended in 1958 by the treaty setting up the Benelux Economic Union, which aims to coordinate the economic, social and financial policies of the three countries. There are no customs formalities between Belgium and Luxembourg, and a decree of 14 October 1944 made the Luxembourg franc of the same denominations and exchange value as the Belgian franc. Belgian money circulates freely in the Grand Duchy and French money is also readily accepted, but the Luxembourg franc may only be exchanged at banks in Belgium.

In international affairs, Luxembourg is an active member of the main international organisations, including the United Nations and its agencies, OECD, the Council of Europe, the EEC, the Western European Union and NATO. The location of Luxembourg City at the heart of Western Europe made it an obvious choice as the headquarters of European organisations, and from 1952 onwards it was the seat of the European Coal and Steel Community. The European Centre Building now houses the Secretariat of the European Parliament and serves for three months of the year as the meeting place of the Council of Ministers of the European Communities. Luxembourg City also houses the Court of Justice of the European Communities, the Community Statistical Office and the headquarters of the European Investment Bank, emphasising the country's growing importance as an international financial centre. After steel and tourism international banking is now the country's third major source of foreign income.

5 THE ECONOMY

The historical development of Luxembourg since independence is virtually synonymous with the rapid economic development of the country. In less than a hundred years it was transformed from a poor, feudal, agricultural backwater into a prosperous modern state. The basis of the transformation was the steel industry, whose development was only possible after the discovery in 1875 of the Gilchrist-Thomas method of smelting. In addition, the wastes from the smelting process turned out to provide exactly the fertilisers needed to make the soils of the northern and central farmlands commercially productive. Thereafter the economic prosperity of the country was assured, and the industrial importance of the Grand Duchy is now out of all proportion to its size. Steel is still the main industry, but during the 1960s the government, recognising the dangers of an over-dependence on one product, encouraged foreign investment by offering financial incentives to small and medium sized firms. Some 50 firms (many American) took up the offer with the result that chemicals, engineering, tyres, plastics and textiles are all now represented in the economy. Agriculture is highly mechanised and intensive, but it continues to lose workers to the steel industry (and increasingly to other industries) as well as suffering from the division of the land into small plots, little progress having been made with redistribution. In 1971 10.2% of the labour force was employed in agriculture compared with 47.3% in industry.

6 THE EDUCATION SYSTEM

The law passed on 5 August 1963 fixed compulsory education at nine years, starting in the calendar year in which the child reaches the age of 6. This means that at the beginning of the school year in September some of the new entrants are only 5 years $8\frac{1}{2}$ months old.

Academic Year

There are three terms in the school year, which runs from 1 September to 16 July with holidays lasting two weeks at Christmas and Easter.

Pre-School Education *(L'éducation préscolaire)*

This is not compulsory but is available for children from the age of 5, usually in pre-school classes attached to primary schools. Attendance for 5 year olds is compulsory. The Law of 5 August 1963 required the *communes* to set up *jardins d'enfants* (with financial support from the State) if there was an average of 20 children in the appropriate age range three years running. There has been a marked increase in such classes since the Law came into effect. The number of classes were doubled. Only 1% of the classes are privately run; they are subject to the authorisation of the Ministry of Education. All teaching is in Letzeburgesch and all the teachers are women. The teachers seek to foster the physical, intellectual and moral development of the children and to prepare them for entry to the primary school.

First Level Education *(L'enseignement primaire)*

Primary education is confined to the first 6 years of compulsory education (children aged 6-12). It is split into three cycles each of two years. Tuition is free in State and communal schools (any travelling costs incurred by pupils are also paid). Fees are charged in private schools, but only a very small percentage of all pupils enrolled in primary schools attend private establishments. Schools may be coeducational or single sex: coeducational schools are particularly common in the rural northern part of the country.

The curriculum is the same for all children and includes religious instruction, Letzeburgesch (half an hour per week), German (7-9 hours per week in the first and second years, 5-6 hours thereafter), French (6-8 hours per week beginning during the second year), arithmetic (5-6 hours per week), national history, study of the local environment, geography, natural history, art, crafts, music, writing, physical education and education in road sense. The working language is at first Letzeburgesch, but this role is quickly assumed by German. French is taught as a foreign language throughout the course. Out of school the language used between teachers and pupils continues to be Letzeburgesch. The decision as to whether a pupil should be promoted from one class to the next is made by the teacher on the basis of the marks earned during the preceding three terms.

The teacher-pupil ratio aimed at is 1:20 and classes of over 30 are becoming rare. A high proportion of teachers are women.

Also included in the primary system are an institute for the mentally handicapped, an institute for the blind, an institute for deaf mutes, a school for children with speech defects, schools for sick or very delicate children and schools for children from broken homes.

Pupils who have completed six years at primary school but do not wish to transfer to some kind of secondary course spend their last three years of compulsory education (12-15) either in *classes complémentaires* or in the *école primaire supérieure*. Both of these are part of the primary system. Pupils are admitted to the former without an examination, and the course prepares them for a career. In addition to general subjects the curriculum includes metalwork and woodwork for boys and home economics for girls. On completion of the course pupils are given a *certificat de fin d'études primaires*. These classes are usually given in single sex schools, and in rural areas pupils from several communes are grouped in district schools. The *école primaire supérieure* used to offer a more academic course than the *classes complémentaires*, and the pupil was required to pass an entrance examination.

Intermediate Education *(L'enseignement moyen)*

The *collèges d'enseignement moyen* were created by the law of 16 August 1965 with the aim of providing a general course lasting five years, which would prepare pupils for junior and middle level positions in the Civil Service and the private sector. Teaching is less theoretical than in secondary schools. These schools are thus similar to the *Realschulen* in Germany. Certain classes are also available in technical schools, in the State vocational school at Esch-sur-Alzette and in a private girls' school.

The five-year course is divided into two cycles, a lower cycle of three years and an upper cycle of two years. During the lower cycle the curriculum is the same for all pupils. It consists of religious instruction (or a course of ethics), German, French, English (from the beginning of the second year), arithmetic, algebra, geometry, history and geography, natural science, civics, commercial practice, art, music, physical education, and home economics for girls. In the upper cycle pupils choose one of three sections: the biological and social science section (which includes courses in biology, anatomy and chemistry), the commercial section (book-keeping, data processing and typing) or the technical section (mathematics, physics and technical drawing). If they pass the examination at the end of the course (in all subjects studied), they receive the *certificat de fin d'études moyennes*. This enables them to go on to other types of training if they wish (e.g. nursing).

Secondary Level Education *(L'enseignement secondaire)*

At the age of 12, after completing six years of primary education, the majority of pupils take entrance examinations in German, French and arithmetic which give access to second level, intermediate and technical schools. The length and type of course followed varies depending on the type of school attended.

Academic Secondary Level Education

Before 1968 academic secondary education was given in three different kinds of *lycée:* classical *lycées*, *lycées* for boys and *lycées* for girls. The law of 10 May 1968 abolished these distinctions, but the aim of the *lycée* remains the same: to give pupils a general education which will prepare them for university studies. It may thus be compared with the German *Gymnasium*.

Second level education is given in State or private *lycées:* the 1968 law envisaged the creation of communal secondary schools. Schools may be coeducational or single sex. The private schools are all girls' schools run by the Catholic Church. Only two of them offer a full secondary course. Private schools used to cater for 45% of girls' secondary education, but the proportion has dropped with the opening of coeducational schools. Fees are charged in private schools, but State secondary education is free, and bursaries and government subsidies are available for children from poor families.

The course lasts seven years, divided into a lower cycle of three years (classes 7-5, the classes being numbered in descending order), and an upper cycle of four years (classes 4-1). At the end of the lower cycle the pupil must pass an *examen de passage* before being allowed to proceed to the upper cycle.

In the seventh class (i.e. first year), which is known as the *classe d'orientation*, the curriculum is identical for all pupils and also identical to the curriculum of the first year of the intermediate and technical schools. This helps to ease pupils gently into the strange environment of the *lycée* and makes transfers between *lycée*, intermediate school and technical school easier. At the beginning of the sixth class the pupil must choose between the classical branch (in which case he starts Latin) and the modern branch (in which case he starts English). If he chooses the classical branch, English is added to the timetable in the fifth class, but in the fourth class he must choose to study either English or Greek for the remainder of the course. From the beginning of the fourth class the degree of specialisation increases: the classical branch splits into two sections - a Latin languages section and a Latin sciences section (with the option of taking mathematics or sciences or economics). The modern branch is similarly split into a modern languages section and a modern languages sciences section (with the same options as in the Latin sciences section).

At the end of the first class pupils take the *examen de fin d'études secondaire*, an examination organised by the Ministry of Education which decides on the nature of the tests at the start of the school year. The language to be used for each subject is that prescribed for the teaching of the subject in the first class (almost all subjects are taught in French in the upper cycle of secondary education). Most pupils must take French, German, English and philosophy in the examination although those who choose to specialise in mathematics or sciences are required to take only two modern languages. In addition, pupils take between three and five of the following subjects (depending on the option chosen): Greek, Latin, history, political economy, a fourth modern language, mathematics, physics, chemistry, biology and economic science. Pupils who fail are only allowed to retake the examination twice. Those who pass are awarded the *diplôme de fin d'études secondaires*, which gives access to higher education both in Luxembourg and in neighbouring countries.

Technical and Vocational Education
(L'enseignement technique et professionnel)

The technical schools provide a five-year post-primary course for those who wish to become skilled workers or technicians. The course consists of a two-year orientation cycle followed by three years of specialisation. The diploma awarded at the end of the course is equivalent to the CAP *(certificat d'aptitude professionnel)* awarded by the vocational schools. Since 1970/71 pupils have also been able to stay at technical school for an extra two years in order to obtain the *diplôme de technicien*. Pupils wishing to study commercial subjects usually take a four-year course at a vocational school followed by one year's practical training. If successful, they receive the CAP in commercial subjects. This course has been less popular since the intermediate schools introduced an option in commercial subjects.

Vocational Training

Apart from the five-year post-primary courses in technical and commercial subjects described above, several other types of training are available.

The *Ecole Technique de Luxembourg* runs four-year courses leading to the qualification of *ingeniéur-technicien*. Students who have completed five years in a *lycée*, an intermediate school or a technical school are admitted without an examination; those who hold only the CAP must take an entrance examination. After the first year (which is preparatory), students specialise in one of three sections: mechanical, engineering, civil engineering or electrotechnology. Those who obtain a 'good' in the final examination are qualified to take an engineering degree abroad if they wish.

At a lower level, full time courses are available in business management, secretarial training, salesmanship, training for the hotel trades, agricultural training, and training for the paramedical professions. Most courses start at 14 and last two or three years (but five years for the paramedical professions).

Apprenticeships usually last between $2\frac{1}{2}$ and 4 years depending on the trade. During this period the apprentices must attend classes (8-16 hours per week). The qualification he obtains is the CAP or the CCP *(certificat de capacité pratique)* if he is not able to master the theoretical component in the course for the CAP.

Third Level (Higher) Education

Before the advent of modern industry, Luxembourg was a thinly populated country with a system of education which was highly selective. As a result the number of students proceeding to university was very small. There neither existed nor was there any real demand for an independent national university. Students prefer to study in the universities of neighbouring countries. Anxious, however, to maintain some kind of control over the type of qualifications obtained by those intending to enter the country's Civil Service, teaching, legal and medical professions, the Luxembourg authorities insisted that students who had obtained foreign degrees should on their return take supplementary examinations before nationally appointed examining bodies. However, such a system led in time to a lack of coordination between the studies proper and the ensuing examinations.

On 18 June, 1969, therefore, a new law was introduced to resolve this problem and others in the field of higher education. The keynotes of this law were as follows:

(i) all national degree examinations should be abolished after 1974. (During the interim period 1969-74 students were to be allowed to opt for either system.)

(ii) foreign degrees should be automatically recognised subject to ratification by the Minister of Education on the advice of the ad hoc committee

(iii) a University Centre *(Centre Universitaire de Luxembourg)* should be created which would offer two types of university level courses: *Cours Universitaires* and *Cours Complémentaires*.

The *Cours Universitaires* provide the first year of a university course and are open to all holders of the secondary school leaving certificate: there is no *numerus clausus*. There are departments of law and economics (providing two different courses, for students who want to go on to universities in France and Belgium respectively), letters and humanities (providing courses in philosophy and psychology, classics, French and Italian, German, English and history and geography) and science (providing courses in medicine, pharmacy, mathematics, physics, chemistry and biology). The year is divided into two semesters; at the end of each the student takes written and oral examinations. On the basis of these and of his work during the year, he is awarded a *certificat d'études* in the appropriate subject. As for the *Cours Complémentaires*, these are post-graduate courses designed primarily to give further training to those students who want to enter the professions.

The University Centre is governed by an administrative council made up of the administrators of the university who are selected for a period of four years. The Council designates a president from among its members. Members of the teaching staff at the Centre are appointed by the Minister of Education on the recommendation of the Council and the department concerned. Many of the staff are part time and frequently come from the nearest universities in neighbouring countries (e.g. from Liège, Nancy, Strasbourg and Saarbrücken).

Article 23 of the Luxembourg Constitution allows students complete freedom in their choice of a university abroad. In practice the majority of students go to universities in France, Germany, Belgium and Switzerland with a few in Austria, USA and Britain. Except in England they are admitted to the second year of the course. They may if they choose, of course, go straight into the first year at a foreign university without attending the *Cours Universitaires*.

The *Université Internationale de Sciences Comparées* was founded in 1957 on private initiative, but with moral and financial support from the State; it runs post-university courses on the European Communities and in comparative law and economics and is part of the *Centre Universitaire*.

Adult Education

The first official courses for adults were started in 1965/66, but have proved very popular. Courses available are vocational; they prepare participants for the secondary school leaving certificate, the technical school leaving certificate or for the examination for the *ingénieur-technicien* qualification.

Several communes and private organisations also run courses, usually in languages, technical or commercial subjects or art. These courses are normally subsidised by the State. In addition, the *Ecole Supérieure du Travail* runs courses for workers in law, economics, politics and social sciences.

Teacher Training

Until 1972 nursery school teachers received a three-year training in private colleges which qualified for State support. For admission they were required to have completed four years of secondary education; the qualification they obtained was the *brevet de maîtresse de jardin d'enfants*. Since 1972 these courses have begun to be integrated with those for primary teachers at the *Institut Pédagogique;* in future all courses will be post-secondary.

Primary school teachers take a two-year course at the *Institut Pédagogique* in Walferdang, north of Luxembourg City. The institute is coeducational. Applicants must hold the *diplôme de fin d'études secondaires;* entry to the institute is selective. Students receive a monthly allowance throughout the two-year course; the qualification awarded is the *brevet d'aptitude pédagogique*. Students who wish to teach handicapped children must spend a third year at the institute.

Teachers for the lower cycle (first three years) of the intermediate school are required to possess the *brevet d'enseignement moyen* and to spend two years at a university abroad followed by a two-year period of professional training in Luxembourg. Primary school inspectors qualify by taking a one-year course of professional training. Teachers in the upper cycle (last two years) of the intermediate school are usually university graduates (see below).

Teaching staff for second level and technical schools must take the full secondary school course, which is usually followed by a year at the *Cours Universitaires*. The remainder of their degree course (usually three or four years) is taken at a foreign university. As a result of the Act of 18 June 1969 the French *maîtrise*, the Belgian *licence* and the German *Staatsexamen* are all now recognised in Luxembourg. Those who wish to teach a foreign language are required to take their degree in a country where the language concerned is spoken. On returning to Luxembourg students must take a two-year professional course at the *Cours Complémentaires* at the end of which they are awarded the *certificat d'aptitude aux fonctions de professeur de l'enseignement secondaire*. Following this there is a one-year probationary period. Secondary school teachers are known as *professeurs-docteurs*.

In-service training courses for primary teachers are held regularly at the *Institut Pédagogique*. Such courses are voluntary but have proved popular; of the total primary teaching force about a third attend courses each year. There are no in-service facilities for secondary teachers, but they are sometimes able to attend vacation courses in neighbouring countries.

7 EDUCATIONAL ADMINISTRATION

All sectors of education are governed by regulations and directives drawn up by the Minister of Education and executed by the relevant bodies (the *communes*, the inspectors or the directors of second level schools). The population is, however, so small that educational administration developed slowly and empirically and no homogeneous structure has yet evolved. When the need arises, teachers (usually selected from the staff of secondary schools) are given posts in the Ministry of National Education either as Government Counsellors (and later as civil servants) or as seconded teachers. Below the head of the administration (the Minister of Education) there are, therefore, counsellors or seconded teachers heading the sections charged with responsibility for the various levels of education, the Foreign Cultural Relations Service and the National Youth Service. The chief inspectors and the remaining staff of the Ministry are civil servants.

The responsibility for providing education does not, however, lie exclusively with the Ministry. At primary level responsibility is divided between the Ministry and the *commune* the latter having the right to appoint teachers, create new classes and supply school buildings and equipment. In vocational and technical education responsibility is shared between the Ministries of Education, Labour and Economic Affairs and the Trade Councils and at secondary level between the Ministries of Education and Public Works (which provides the buildings) and sometimes the *commune* in which the school is situated.

Inspection is carried out by inspectors at the primary level and by the heads of schools in secondary, vocational and technical education. The functions of the primary school inspectorate include both the educational and administrative aspects. There is one inspector to approximately 200 teachers. Inspectors are either secondary school teachers who have taken an ad hoc course or primary school teachers who have taken a three-year university course in psychology, education and a special subject and have passed the examination for the primary school inspector's certificate. The inspector has no authority over curricula which are prepared by the Ministry although teachers may submit their observations. Textbooks are also prescribed by the Ministry after consultation with teachers. At primary level they are written by Luxembourg teachers and published in Luxembourg, but at other levels very few Luxembourg texts exist except in geography, geology and civics. In other subjects French, German or Belgian textbooks have to be used and adopted where necessary. Despite the apparent control of both curricula and textbooks by the Ministry, teachers are encouraged to experiment, to devise their own courses and to suggest other textbooks provided they do not deviate too violently from Ministry directives. With the exception of primary school teachers all staff are appointed by the Grand Duke.

There are many private (mostly Catholic) schools, especially secondary level schools for girls and for the physically handicapped. Although the State does not subsidise private education, it exercises the right of inspection over all schools, so private

ADMINISTRATION

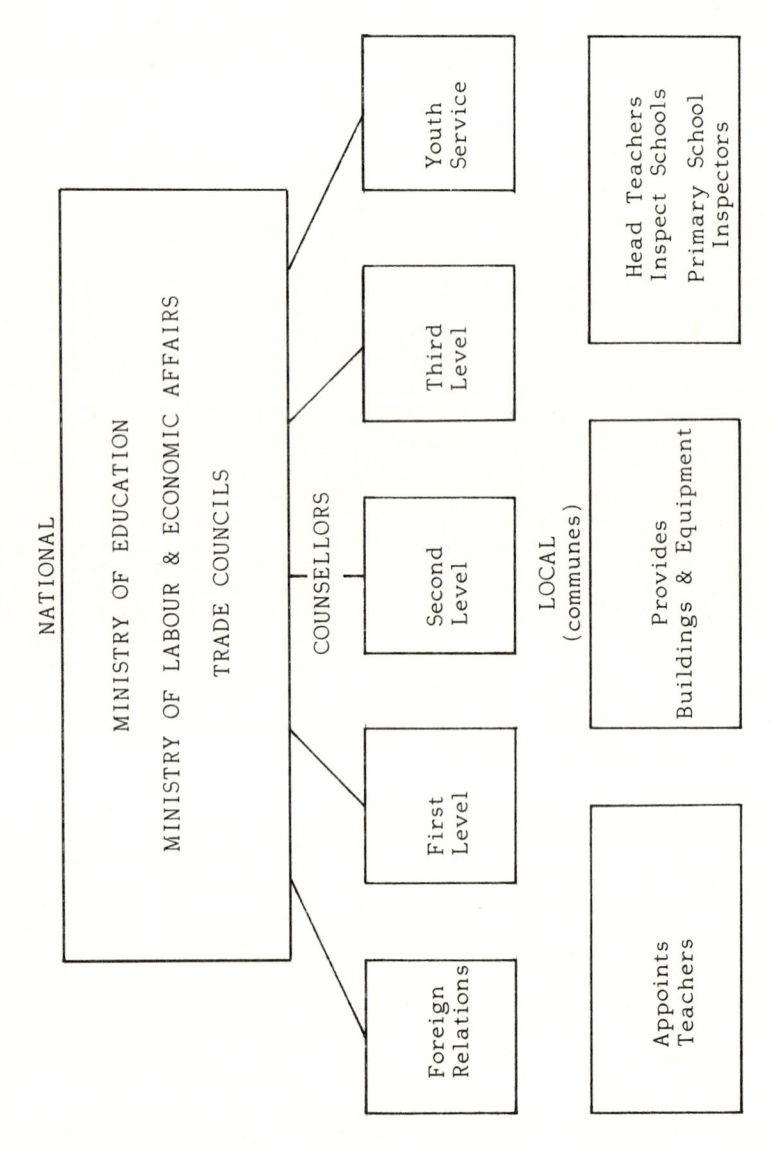

NATIONAL

MINISTRY OF EDUCATION
MINISTRY OF LABOUR & ECONOMIC AFFAIRS
TRADE COUNCILS

- Foreign Relations
- First Level
- Second Level
- Third Level
- Youth Service

COUNSELLORS

LOCAL (communes)

- Appoints Teachers
- Provides Buildings & Equipment
- Head Teachers Inspect Schools
  Primary School Inspectors

schools must follow the official syllabi, use the prescribed textbooks and enter their pupils for the State examinations.

8 EDUCATIONAL FINANCE

Source of Funds

Between 1960 and 1965 public expenditure on education almost doubled. After 1965 expenditure has continued to rise rapidly. The swift increase was due mainly to the rapid rise in enrolments during the 1960s and to the opening of intermediate schools. Education accounts for one sixth of the national budget. The percentage of GNP allocated to education rose from 1.7 in 1961 to 4.4 in 1971. At the first level the government provides subventions to the *communes* for the construction of schools, the operating and maintenance costs and for teachers' salaries. At other levels the *communes* share only in the cost of erecting buidings and maintaining them. Teachers' salaries account for more than 60% of recurrent expenditure.

Allocation of Funds
Expenditure on Education: Distribution by Level
Percentage of Expenditure 1977

Pre-school	First Level	Second Level	Third Level	Other
-	41.5	41.1	1.8	15.6

9 DEVELOPMENT AND PLANNING OF THE EDUCATION SYSTEM

Development

As in neighbouring countries, the traditional educational pattern in Luxembourg consisted of two systems: one for a small elite from the middle and upper classes and the other for the working classes. The former was first embodied in the monastic schools at Echternach (founded in 698) and Luxembourg City (founded in 1083) to which a number of other monastic schools were added in the eleventh and twelfth centuries, many opened at the instigation of Countess Ermiesinde who ruled the country between 1196 and 1247 and realised that the future of Luxembourg depended on the intellectual and moral development of the nation. These schools aimed to provide a classical education, concentrating on Greek and Latin, but not neglecting the teaching of French and German. Their tradition was perpetuated by the Jesuits who opened a college in Luxembourg city in 1603. The Jesuit order was suppressed in 1773 but the school remained in existence and is now the Athénée Grand-Ducal, the oldest *lycée* in the Grand Duchy. The first communal schools for the working classes were established towards the end of the Middle Ages (e.g. in 1480 in Luxembourg City), but even in the nineteenth century attendance in rural areas was very irregular in winter, and the schools were usually closed during the summer.

They provided only very basic instruction in the three Rs.

The first Education Law of 26 July 1843 provided, among other things, for the opening of a normal school to train teachers for the communal schools. The general principles of education in the Grand Duchy were laid down later in Article 23 of the 1868 Constitution (subsequently revised on 21 May 1948). The Constitution declares that the State is responsible for seeing that all Luxembourg children receive primary education, which is free and compulsory. (The duration of compulsory education has changed over the years: it is now fixed at nine years.) Private schools are permitted but they are not subsidised by the State. The State also assumed responsibility for opening the necessary secondary and vocational schools and the colleges required at post-secondary level.

Since the 1950s there has been an increasing realisation of the need to 'democratise' education and to provide a wider choice of courses at the secondary level, which was still based on the two-pronged system of an academic school for the élite and upper primary classes for the majority. As a result a succession of Acts were passed during the 1960s affecting almost every branch of the education system. The main ones are as follows: the Act of 5 August 1963 reforming pre-first level and first level education; the Act of 16 August 1965 instituting a five-year intermediate school (école moyenne) to replace the upper primary course; the Act of 10 May 1968 reorganised secondary education and the Act of 18 June 1969 reorganised post-secondary education. This Act also provided for the recognition of degrees and diplomas obtained at foreign universities. Vocational and technical education has been reformed.

Planning

Educational policy is drawn up by the Minister of Education. Those consulted during its preparation include the special advisers to the Ministry, the teachers' association, the *Conseil Supérieur de l'Education Nationale* (the consultative body on general educational problems), the College of Inspectors (for primary education) and the College of Directors and general or sectional teachers' conferences (for secondary and technical education). There is thus an active and constructive partnership between government and teaching circles over the consideration of future policy.

A notable feature of planning is the statistical and school map service, which resembles the French *Carte scolaire*. It provides the basic data for determining and forecasting the evolution of school populations and future requirements in terms of premises, staff and teaching resources.

The stimulation of educational research is in the hands of the Ministry and especially of its Advisory Committee for the Promotion of Educational Research. The research is undertaken by the Pedagogical Institute with students helping in the breakdown of the surveys made by the advisory committee. The results are published in the *Courrier de l'Education Nationale*. Consideration has been given to the teaching of foreign languages, the transition from primary to post-primary education and the question of the *maturité scolaire*.

10 THE SYSTEM IN OPERATION
Current Problems and Trends

In education, as in other fields, Luxembourg is in a unique situation: the country is so small that it is bound to take account of conditions beyond its frontiers and adapt its own institutions accordingly. In the educational sphere this entails adapting to several quite different systems, principally those of France, Germany and Belgium. The need for flexibility and adaptation is most marked in higher education, but it is not absent from other levels of the system. This explains to a large extent the degree of detailed central control over syllabus planning, which leaves little room for the personality and initiative of the teacher.

The major problem in primary education stems directly from the smallness and geographical location of Luxembourg: it is the necessity to teach, from the beginning of the course, two languages, neither of which is the pupil's mother tongue. As a result, a large part of the week must be devoted to language learning, and some other subjects (e.g. science) are either omitted or are taught only occasionally. Given the linguistic situation in the country it is difficult to see how this dilemma can be resolved.

At the post-primary level the most notable feature has been the rapid increase in numbers. Between 1960 and 1969 enrolments in *lycées* (both State and private schools) increased by 46.7%. The increase for girls (58.6%) was considerably greater than that for boys (38.6%). In technical and vocational education the overall increase (69.6%) was even greater, but in this case the increase for girls was quite spectacular compared with that for boys (132.1% compared with 41.6%). Enrolments in intermediate education have also increased. Several reasons have been put forward for this *explosion scolaire*. The main ones are that more pupils (and particularly girls) have chosen to stay at school beyond the minimum leaving age of 15; that improved counselling arrangements have redirected into other courses pupils who would previously have left; and that new courses started in some sectors have atracted additional pupils and that the children of foreign workers have swelled the numbers considerably.

Apart from its implications for the curriculum, the rapid expansion in the numbers of post-primary pupils has created problems as regards the provision of buildings and equipment and in the supply of teachers. The quality of most school buildings is good, but some schools had to be housed in temporary premises erected at short notice. Large sums have also had to be spent on equipping the new schools. The standard of equipment is high.

The rapid increase in pupil numbers has also caused an acute shortage of teachers, especially of language teachers, but the situation improved except in mathematics and science subjects.

Primary school teachers have the social status of the middle grades of the Civil Service; others that of the senior grades. It is notable that at both primary and secondary levels teachers must be Luxembourgers. Their average teaching load is 22 hours per week at secondary level and 27 hours at primary level.

As more pupils decided to stay on at school, swelling the numbers of the already overcrowded *lycées*, it became increasingly apparent that the upper primary schools did not constitute a suitable alternative. In 1965, therefore, the intermediate schools were created to provide vocational instruction of a mainly academic nature as a preparation for commercial, administrative, scientific and technical careers. These schools expanded rapidly since their inception and may parallel the success story of the *Realschulen* in Germany, which serve a similar purpose. The second level system remains a tripartite one, however. The only concession to the comprehensive idea has been the attempt to delay specialisation and make it easier for pupils to transfer from one type of school to another. This has been done by instituting *classes d'orientation* in the *lycée* course and in intermediate, technical and vocational schools and by lengthening the period of orientation. At a higher level attempts are being made to remove blind alleys; those who wish to specialise further after completing the intermediate school course, for example, can now go either to the *Ecole Technique* or to the School of Commerce and Management, which trains middle grade executives.

In the past there was little contact between schools and parents. The parents are represented on various *commissions scolaires* and *commissions d'enseignement*, and some teachers and heads involve parents in activities. Pupils, like their peer groups abroad, have set up committees and organised demonstrations and strikes in recent years, but their action has been completely non-violent. Some of their grievances in 1968 were acknowledged to be justified by the Ministry of Education: for example, their doubts about the future of the then *Cours Supérieurs*, about their chances of studying abroad and about the thorny problem of the value which would be accorded abroad to their Luxembourg qualifications. Since then students at the *Cours Universitaires*, the *Institut Pédagogique* and the *Ecole Technique*, and even pupils at the *lycées*, have been consulted when the syllabus is to be modified, and their views have usually been taken into account.

In the field of higher education, discussion has often centred on the question of whether Luxembourg should have a complete university of its own. The suggestion has been made for reasons of national prestige and because it is thought that intellectual work and scientific research would increase if there were libraries, laboratories and university professors on the spot. Proponents of the idea point to Luxembourg's central position in Europe and consider it the mission of a university in Luxembourg to effect a reconciliation between the Germanic and Latin civilisations. In the past, however, the disadvantages always outweighed these arguments: Luxembourg is very small, it does not have its own language or distinctive civilisation and it is essential for the well being of the country that its young people should be given the motivation to study abroad. Enrolments at foreign universities are rising so rapidly that the universities may be unable to continue to admit Luxembourg students. It is becoming increasingly difficult for courses at the *Cours Universitaires* to keep in step with the constantly changing structure of degree courses in some neighbouring countries (e.g. France), especially since courses in the various countries to which Luxembourg students go may not all be changing in the same direction. It is possible that Luxembourg may find itself forced in future to establish a second year course at the *Cours Universitaires*, or even a complete first degree course.

There is the problem of providing adequate facilities for pupils in the rural areas of the north. Until recently there were only two State *lycées* for girls with the result that private schools (nearly always run by the Catholic church) had to shoulder much of the responsibility for providing academic second level education for girls. Now *lycées* which were formerly boys' schools are allowed to accept girls. It is less easy to ensure that children from rural areas are given equality of opportunity compared with their peers in urban areas. The usual solution is to transport them without charge to district schools where *classes complémentaires* technical and vocational courses are provided. State intermediate schools have opened in the *Osling*, but State secondary education is still available only in Diekirch, Echternach and areas further south. A travelling library created by the National Youth Service is for use in the isolated villages of the *Osling*.

In summary the problems with which Luxembourgers are concerned may be summarised as follows:

(i) an imbalance between subjects in the first level school curriculum, caused by the necessity to teach children two foreign languages in addition to their mother tongue

(ii) a shortage of teachers of mathematics and science subjects

(iii) the need to delay specialisation at secondary level and to make transfers between different types of school easier

(iv) finding ways of actively involving parents in the work of the schools

(v) adapting courses at every level (but particularly at the *Cours Universitaires*) so that they are in step with those of neighbouring countries

(vi) ensuring that qualifications obtained in Luxembourg are given due recognition abroad (especially in the case of students who hold the *certificat d'étude* from the *Cours Universitaires*)

(vii) providing adequate facilities in the rural areas, particularly at the more advanced levels.

Trends

A few years ago educationalists became discontented and impatient with the traditional system. The result of this change of attitude has been a series of rapid changes affecting almost every aspect of the system.

In addition to structural changes all State education is free (including the *Cours Universitaires* and the courses for adults), and at the primary level the State pays, as far as possible, for books, materials and the cost of transport. Private bursaries and government subsidies are available to support able students from poor homes who wish to prolong their education beyond the compulsory nine-year period. Loans are also provided for students who go abroad to study; in principle, they are repayable, but they may be converted into grants, provided the students complete their studies successfully.

The Law of 16 August 1965 provided the framework for the establishment of a *Centre de Psychologie et d'Orientation*. As a first step the *Département d'Orientation Scolaire et Services Sociaux* was established and a counselling service for grade 7 pupils was planned (those in the *classe d'orientation* and the *septièmes communes*) and careers guidance for older pupils. Pupils receive the guidance they require and the country's training facilities are fully exploited. The task of coordinating these courses is assumed by a *Service d'Orientation* within the Ministry of Education.

Pre-primary level has been restyled in accordance with the latest research findings on child development with a view to giving all children an equal start. In the field of secondary education common courses for all students in the 12-15 age range (the so-called *tronc commun*) should delay specialisation for as long as possible. The third main issue concerns the future of private schools within the education system. Here private schools which provide an education in parallel to the State should be able to ask for full or partial integration into the State system.

REFERENCES AND FURTHER READING

Committee for General and Technical Education (1972). *The Education of the 16 to 19 Age-Group.* Country Report: Luxembourg. Council of Europe, Strasbourg.

Council for Cultural Co-operation (1970). *School Systems: A Guide* (revised edition. Council of Europe, Strasbourg.

Council of Europe (various dates). *Newsletter.* Council of Europe, Strasbourg.

Courrier de l'Education Nationale (various dates). 'Plan d'Etudes for different types of schools and colleges'.

Grand Duché de Luxembourg, Ministère de l'Education Nationale (1974). *L'Education Nationale au Luxembourg.* (Cartes et Graphiques 1960-71), Luxembourg.

Ludovicy, E. (1971). *L'enseignement au Grand-duché de Luxembourg.* Luxembourg: Ministère d'Etat, Service Information et Presse, Série 'Connaissance du Luxembourg', No. 4.

Neumeister, H. (1973). *Modern Languages in School.* II, Country Reports. Council of Europe, Strasbourg.
OECD (1973). *Economic Surveys: BLEU.* OECD, Paris.
Schultze, Walter (Ed.) (1968-70). *Schools in Europe.* Julius Beltz Verlag, Weinheim & Berlin.
Secretariat of the CME (1973). *Problems and Pressures in Education Policy.* (Country reports prepared for the eighth session of the Standing Conference of European Ministers of Education, held in Berne, 4-7 June 1973). Secretariat of the CME, Strasbourg.
Tussler, A. J. B. and Alden, A. J. L. (1970). *A Map Book of the Benelux Countries.* Macmillan & Co. Ltd., London.
UNESCO (1971). *World Survey of Education.* V: Educational policy, legislation and administration. UNESCO, Paris.
UNESCO (1981). *Statistical Yearbook 1980.* UNESCO, Paris.
UNESCO/IBE (1980). *International Yearbook of Education,* **XXXII**. Unesco, Paris.

Structure of the Education System in Luxembourg

Age	3	4	5	6	7	8	9	10	11	12	13	14	15	16	17	18	19	20	21	22	23	24
Level				I									II					III				IV
Stage				1						2				3	4	5	6					
Compulsory																						
School type																						

School types: Jardin d'enfants; Ecole primaire; Classes complémentaires; Enseignement moyen 1st cycle; Enseignement secondaire; Enseignement moyen 2nd cycle; Enseignement secondaire technique; Observation; Moyen; Formation professionnelle; Institut pedagog; University; Other higher institutions; Abroad

Education preceding the first level

Examinations: Compulsory at end of stages 2 to 6

Source: UNESCO/IBE International Yearbook of Education

Compulsory Education: Age Limits 6-15 Duration (years) 9
Entrance age to pre-school education: 4

LUXEMBOURG BASIC STATISTICS	1960	1970	1975	1978 (approx.)
1 Total Population (000)	314	339	342	356
% female	51	51	51	51
2 % population 0-14 years	21.4	22.0		20
% female	49	44	44	45
3 Enrolment, all levels	39,967	51,323	52,618	51,868
% female	48	48	49	49
First level	31,582	34,530	33,123	27,510
% female	50	49	49	49
Second level	8,238	16,430	19,012	24,056
% female	39	47	49	49
Third level	147	363	483	302
% female	31	42	42	42
4 Teachers, all levels		3,323		
% female		39		
First level	1,197	1,750		1,449
% female		53		
Second level	529	1,451		
% female		25		
Third level	51	122	137	172
% female		11	8	11
5 Public expenditure on education				
Total (000) francs	846,700	2,244,400	3,641,300	6,520,200
As % of GNP	3.6	4.4	5.2	5.2
As % of public expenditure				14.1
6 % Enrolment (MF) by level	100	100	100	100
First level	79	67	63	53
Second level	21	32	36	46
Third level		1	1	1
% enrolment (F) by level	100	100	100	100
First level	83	68	63	53
Second level	17	31	36	46
Third level		1	1	1
7 Entrance age: Duration of				
First level education	6:6	6:6	6:6	6:6
Second level education	12:7	12:7	12:7	12:7
8 Enrolment ratios (MF)				
First level	125	112	101	102
Second level	29	48	63	67
Third level	0.70	1.56	2.00	1.23
Enrolment ratios (F)				
First level	125	112	102	103
Second level	23	46	63	66
Third level	0.46	1.33	1.72	1.06

Malta

CONTENTS

1	Geography	484
2	Population	486
3	Society and Culture	486
4	History and Politics	487
5	The Economy	489
6	The Education System	489
7	Educational Administration	493
8	Educational Finance	495
9	Development and Planning of the Educational System	495
10	The System in Operation	499

The Maltese have been united by their Semitic language and the Roman Catholic Church. Until the end of the Second World War from 1814 when Malta was incorporated into the British Empire, foreign influences and the country's economic dependence on the British Royal Navy helped to shape an educational system which in several respects is similar to that found in the UK. For example, first level schooling begins at the age of five and lasts for six years. Second level school pupils prepare for the UK General Certificate of Education examinations at 'O' level or its Maltese equivalent. Advanced level examination syllabi are followed in government, private and university secondary schools or colleges. On the other hand curricula in second level schools are more broadly based than in England and for the first two years all pupils take the same 13 subjects with little choice except that Italian, French or German can be taken as a second foreign language and boys take music and craft while girls study home economics. At the upper stage of secondary education as well as following a general core of subjects pupils opt for one of three specialised courses in either arts subjects, science subjects, or practical subjects.

The provision of craft and technician training in government trade schools, technical institutes and in other centres also represents a break with English tradition. On the other hand university provision and teacher training reflect the influence of English models on this level of education.

Politics have played an important role in the evolution of education. Between the world wars Maltese was not used officially for purposes of instruction but political groups associated with the Church tried to foster Italian at the expense of English as a language of instruction. Under Mussolini considerable efforts were indeed made to increase the impact of Italian culture.

Independence in 1964 when finance and defence agreements were concluded with Britain permitted the introduction of internal politics into education discussion and debate. When in 1970 the Nationalist Party formed a government it proposed to introduce secondary education for all in a way that was unacceptable to the Labour Government which came to power in 1972. It proposed to establish comprehensive second level schools. Advisory international committees have helped to formulate policies for second and third level education.

A bone of contention, with party political implications, has certainly been the historical position and power of the clergy in the conduct of Maltese education.

The Editor

1 GEOGRAPHY

Topography

The Maltese islands are a small, rocky archipelago of three main islands - Malta, Gozo and Comino - situated in the Mediterranean 58 miles south of Sicily and 180 miles north of Africa. The total area is 122 square miles. The longest distance in Malta itself from south east to north west is 17 miles and the widest is 9 miles from east to west. The corresponding figures for Gozo are 9 and $4\frac{1}{2}$ miles. In other words, the combined area is comparable to that of the Isle of Wight. There are no mountains or rivers but there are some famous deep water harbours.

Climate

The typical Mediterranean climate made Malta a major tourist centre during the 1970s. It never snows and average mean temperatures are 80°F (27°C) in summer and 60°F (16°C) in in winter. High winds are common in winter and the sirocco often blows in late summer.

Communications

There is an extensive network of macadamised roads on the island and a car ferry between Malta and Gozo ($4\frac{1}{2}$ miles distant). Since 1930 there have been no railways. Air Malta began independent operations in 1974 and there are regular flights by them and other airlines from Luqa airport to London, Rome and other European cities. There is a thrice weekly car ferry which runs between Malta and Sicily. Cargo and small cruise ships also call at Malta.

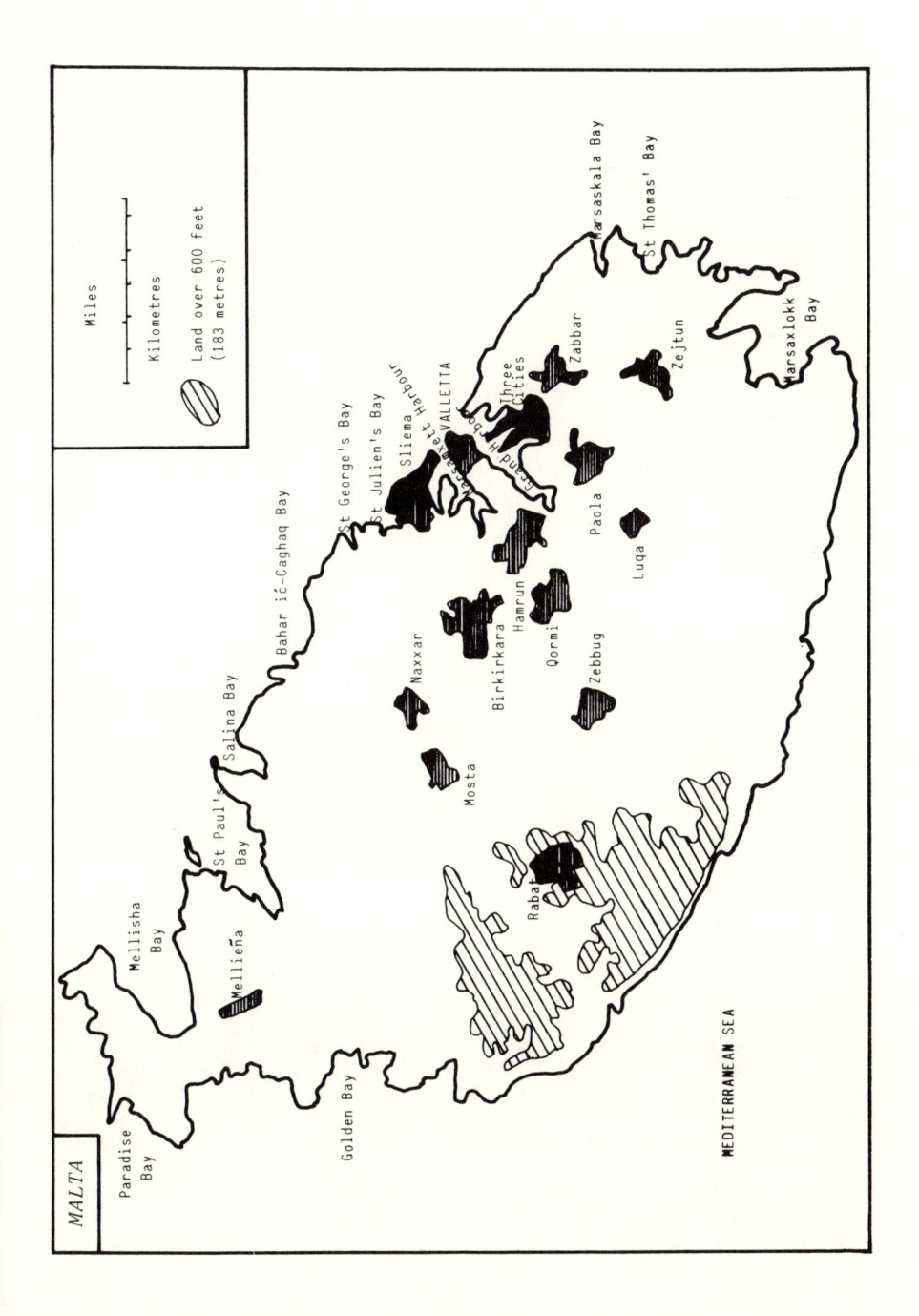

MALTA

Paradise Bay
Mellisha Bay
Mellieña
St Paul's Bay
Salina Bay
Golden Bay
Bahar ić-Caghaq Bay
St George's Bay
St Julien's Bay
Sliema
Grand Harbour
Marsamxett Harbour
VALLETTA
Three Cities
Zabbar
Marsaskala Bay
St Thomas' Bay
Zejtun
Marsaxlokk Bay
Paola
Luqa
Naxxar
Birkirkara
Hamrun
Qormi
Zebbug
Mosta
Rabat

MEDITERRANEAN SEA

Miles
Kilometres
Land over 600 feet (183 metres)

2 POPULATION

Growth

In the 90 years after the first census of 115,000 in 1842 the population roughly doubled but since the Second World War it has remained almost static at just under one-third of a million. In fact with emigration to Australia, Britain, USA and Canada and a falling birth rate in the 1960s, the population is expected to decline gradually. Although infant mortality rates have dropped sharply since the war, the overall falling birth rate is the determining factor.

Distribution

Although Gozo with its 25,000 population is practically all rural, Malta itself has a high density of population. Although one-third of the population is technically rural, most people live in townships which merge into each other rather as London 'villages' did in the nineteenth century. To a visitor arriving by sea the island appears thickly built up with the capital Valletta leading on to a host of further fortifications and stone built terrace houses. Further modern developments with hotels, restaurants and offices along the coast add to this impression.

Immigration Groups

Although human habitation dates from about BC 4000, the written history of Malta begins with the Phoenicians who were followed by the Carthaginians. During the Second Punic War Malta became part of the Roman Empire (St Paul was shipwrecked there in AD 60) and the vicissitudes of history have lead to occupation over the centuries by the Arabs, the Normans, the Aragonese, the Knights of St John, the French and the British. The population has therefore suffered the incursions of many national strains but the generality of the people is typically Mediterranean, i.e. small and dark haired and volatile in character.

3 SOCIETY AND CULTURE

Language

Historically the two unifying forces in the culture of the Maltese nation have been their Semitic language and the Roman Catholic church. Clearly its century and a half of British occupation meant that the armed forces and especially the Royal Navy were the main providers of employment and English became widely used as a commercial language.

Between the two world wars there were serious constitutional differences between the colonial governors and the local political parties with Mussolini openly offering support to the Nationalist Party. This political struggle split the country culturally over the language question. In schools, while Maltese was ignored or even forbidden, the children had to speak Italian in the morning and English in the afternoon. Italian was used in the law courts and favoured by the Church and it is still a *sine qua non* in educated society. However, the Second World War led to its loss of official status so that English and Maltese are now the two official languages of administration. Maltese is used in courts of law and is the language of general use in the islands.

Religion

Practically the whole native population of Malta is Roman Catholic, although there is an Anglican cathedral and churches of other denominations. Although the first Bishop of Malta, St Publius, was installed shortly after St Paul's shipwreck in AD 60, historians doubt whether Christianity flourished much during the Arab occupation. Only in 1831 did Malta become separate from the Archdiocese of Palermo. British Government policy was not to interfere in Church affairs but between the wars the Church was implicated in local politics and openly opposed Lord Strickland's Constitutional party. In more recent times it opposed the Labour Party during elections and was much concerned over proposals to amend the 1964 Constitution which guaranteed its status and gave it certain basic rights.

The Church has always been an important force in education where it still controls the private schools which account for 20% of all pupils on the island. Until 1973 the men's and women's residential Teacher Training Colleges were run by religious bodies but have now been amalgamated into the government-run College of Education.

Social Patterns

There are a number of Sovereign Orders of Knights, including that of St John of Jerusalem, centred in Malta. The titles of some of the noble Maltese families date from the fourteenth century, although the great majority of them were granted by Grand Masters and are eighteenth century creations.

The introduction of free secondary education for all in 1972, the increases in taxation on the one hand, and basic food subsidies and the recent introduction of family allowances on the other, and industrialisation has made the social structure more egalitarian. This is a common phenomenon in Europe and with an increase in industrialisation the same pattern is likely to be repeated in Malta.

4 HISTORY AND POLITICS

Origins

For the past two millenia Malta has been the football of the Mediterranean. As the influence of various imperial powers swept to and fro across the Middle Sea none of the naval commanders could afford to ignore the strategic position and deep water harbours of the Maltese islands. Phoenicians, Carthaginians, Romans, Byzantines, Arabs, Normans and Aragonese held it in turn but it was really the coming of the Knights of St John in 1530 which set its stamp on Maltese history. In 1565 the Great Siege led to the defeat of the Turks and the following two centuries of knightly rule under the Grand Masters gave Malta most of the architectural marvels which have made her famous - the Auberges of the Langues, the Manoel Theatre and the great sea-girt fortresses. The landing of Napoleon in 1798 broke the rule of the Knights. Then, after two unhappy years of French misrule, Malta became a main base for the British Royal Navy and in 1814 they asked to be incorporated into the British Empire. The islands spent an uneventful century under the Pax Britannica and the colony gained its first self-governing constitution in 1921.

Between the two world wars, in 1930 the constitution was suspended for two years and the pro-Italian Nationalist Party gained a decisive lead over Lord Strickland's Constitutional Party. The Second World War brought an end to the luxury of internal political manoeuvres but self-government was once again restored in 1947. Broadly speaking, since then Maltese politics have been dominated by the rivalry between the Labour Party and the Nationalist Party. In 1955 a proposal was made to integrate Malta's representation in the British House of Commons. In the event this came to nothing and the Nationalist Government which came to power in 1962 accepted Independence in 1964 when financial and defence agreements were concluded with Britain. In 1974 Malta became an independent republic in the Commonwealth.

Government

The Constitution of 1964 under which Malta became an Independent state within the Commonwealth, provided for a Governor-General who was appointed by HM Queen Elizabeth II. Parliament consisted of Her Majesty and a single chamber House of Representatives consisting of 55 members elected by ten electoral divisions. The Governor-General appointed ministers on the advice of the Prime Minister. He also appointed judges and magistrates to the Superior and Inferior Courts where they held office *quam diu se bene gesserit*.

This Constitution was revoked when, at the instigation of the Prime Minister and as a result of talks between the two main political parties, Malta opted to become a Republic on December 13, 1974. However, the country has remained within the Commonwealth. Under the Constitution the Church lost some of its formerly privileged position.

Besides the office of the Prime Minister there are 12 government ministries and independent statutory bodies such as the Public Service Commission, Malta Broadcasting Authority, and other government boards, e.g. National Assistance Board.

In 1976 the Malta Labour Party was returned to office. In 1980 it had 34 seats while the main opposition party, the Nationalist Party, had 31 seats.

International Relations

Malta is officially an unaligned country and maintains diplomatic relations with the Western world and also with the Communist Bloc and the Third World powers.

5 THE ECONOMY
Agriculture

Agriculture plays a significant role in the economy. Potatoes, tomatoes, onions, cabbages and cauliflowers are exported.

Industry

The Government's development plans aim at industrialising Malta to get away from the previous 'siege economy'. Foreign investment is sought for light industry and the Chinese Government has actively supported the new dry dock with exports and technical aid. Growing unemployment has caused concern – two parastatal bodies – the Pioneer Corps and Dirghaja-il-Malten – were founded by the Government to ameliorate the situation.

Economic Situation

Malta's economy, though not large, experienced rapid growth in the 1970s. Between 1968 and 1973 its gross domestic product increased by 60%. Total exports rose by 40% in one year (1972-73). The people of Malta have become used to a relatively high standard of living but the rundown in British military personnel had an effect on their balance of payments. On the other hand, tourism is becoming increasingly important and tourists numbered more than half a million annually in the late seventies compared with 38,000 in 1964.

6 THE EDUCATION SYSTEM
General

The Education Act of 1974 makes education compulsory for all children from the ages of 6 to 16 years and is free in all government schools.

The Academic Year

The school year in Malta normally runs from October to June. Primary schools open on 15 September and end on 15 July. Secondary schools open on 1 October and end in the first week of July. Institutions of higher education start on 1 October and end in June. Trade schools work from 1 September to 31 July.

There are Summer, Christmas, Easter and Carnival vacations as well as a number of public holidays. These vary in length with the type of school but generally the Christmas break lasts for ten days to two weeks and Easter lasts one week. Carnival lasts two days and other public holidays amount to nine if they all fall on weekdays.

All government schools, including the university, work from Mondays to Fridays. Primary schools work $5\frac{1}{2}$ hours a day whereas secondary schools work 6 hours a day, their timetable being based on 40 periods of 35 minutes each week.

Pre-School

There are government and private kindergartens and nursery schools for 4 and 5 year olds.

First-Level Schools

Children are admitted into government primary schools at the age of five. The first year is pre-primary or kindergarten.

The primary school course (including the pre-primary year 1) lasts six years. The curriculum includes English, Maltese, religion, physical education, mathematics, nature study and elements of science, geography, history, civics, art, music and (for girls) needlework. English and Maltese are both used as languages of instruction. Promotion is by age and a system of continuous assessment is used. Remedial and special education are provided where necessary. There are 107 government primary schools in the Maltese islands.

There are private nursery schools, kindergartens and primary schools. They are mostly run by religious orders and are fee paying. The curriculum consists of Maltese, English, mathematics, religion, physical education, civics, history, geography, environmental studies, nature study and science, art and handwork, singing and music, and (for girls) needlework. Emphasis is placed on activity methods and individual interests.

Second-Level Schools - Lower and Upper Stages

Second level education is open to all students who have finished the primary school course. It is organised on an area basis in government schools and there are no entrance tests or examinations. The course lasts five years (forms 1 - 5), average ages 11 to 16 years and leads to the General Certificate of Education at ordinary level or its Maltese equivalent. After the second year of second level education, promotion is by merit. A system of continuous assessment, which includes annual examinations, is used. Students may opt to transfer to craft courses in the trade schools and technical institutes during the course. At the end of the five-year course students may sit for the GCE examination at 'Ordinary' level.

Upper stage second level education is open to students with at least six passes in the General Certificate of Education ('O' level). The course lasts two years. Up to 1972/3 studies for the Advanced level were carried out in one government secondary school, private schools' sixth forms (6a and 6b) and also at the university's Junior College, where they were divided under Arts and Science. With effect from 1973/74, the university's Junior College and the government schools' sixth forms merged to form the current upper secondary school (774 students in October 1979). Four private schools/colleges also run sixth forms.

The curriculum for secondary level is general and comprehensive and is divided in two cycles. In the first two years all students take the same subjects: English, Maltese, Arabic, physical education, religion, mathematics, science, geography, history, civics, art, music and craft (for boys) and home economics (for girls), and one other foreign language (Italian, French or German).

From the third year the curriculum is divided into a common core for all students and a choice of specified option groups of subjects.

In the last three years students continue to study Maltese, English, religion, physical education, civics, one foreign language, general science and, in the case of girls, home economics. They are also asked to choose one of five groups of subjects for specialisation according to their interests and abilities. There are three groups of 'options'; arts, science and practical which comprise:

(i) one additional foreign language (French, Italian, German, Latin or Arabic)
(ii) history or geography
(iii) physics, chemistry and biology and pure and applied mathematics
(iv) technical drawing and craft (for boys) and home economics (for girls)
(v) the basic subjects plus European history and either art or music.

Students are asked to choose three main subjects according to the course they follow. There are also subsidiary subjects and enrichment courses to support the main subjects.

There are also private secondary schools which cater for those pupils who do not want to enrol in government secondary schools. Some schools have boarding facilities and cater for expatriate students as well. Entry is by selective examination, each school holding its own tests. Their curriculum largely follows that of grammar schools. They also prepare students for GCE examinations in sixth forms for 'A' levels, when the course lasts two years.

Special Education

Government provides special education for handicapped children and students, including blind adults. There are schools for the physically handicapped, educational subnormal and emotionally disturbed, hospital classes and peripatetic teaching. Certain private organisations run residential institutions for the severely physically and mentally handicapped.

Technical and Vocational Education

Technical education at craft and technician levels is provided in government trade schools, technical institutes and other centres.

Trade schools, entered after the third year of second level education, offer vocational training in a number of trades such as mechanical engineering, plumbing, electrical installation, carpentry, building construction, agriculture, arts and crafts, etc. and (for girls) dressmaking, millinery and allied trades. These schools first opened in 1971 and taken on a full time basis offer courses of three year duration and lead to a Trade Certificate.

Technical education is provided by three technical institutes. They run craft and technician level courses in mechanical, electrical and automobile engineering, carpentry, joinery, tailoring, telecommunications, including radio and TV servicing and radio for marine officers. The courses lead to a City and Guilds of London Institute Examination. Entry for craft level courses is at the same age and similar to that of trade schools whereas a full secondary or craft level course with suitable GCE or craft certificates is required for the technicians' course. The final year of a full technician course is usually taken at the Malta College of Arts, Science and Technology (MCAST).

Courses at technical institutes are run on a full time, part time or sandwich basis. They also train apprentices.

There are also, apart from the technical institutes, a Centre for Industrial Electronics (opened in October 1974), a School of Art, which up to now has catered for the teaching of design and history of art on an evening basis, and a School of Music opened in April 1975.

Commercial and secretarial courses are also run by private organisations such as the Malta Society of Arts, Manufacture and Commerce.

Third Level Education - Higher Education and Teacher Training

Higher education in Malta is available in three institutions, i.e.:

> The Royal University of Malta
> The New University
> The Malta College of Arts, Science and Technology.

The Royal University of Malta is a statutory body and the oldest establishment of higher education in the island, dating from 1592. It provides courses leading to the degrees of Bachelor (general or honours), Master (or licentiate) and Doctor in the following faculties: Theology, Laws, Medicine and Surgery, Engineering and Architecture, Dental Surgery, Arts and Science.

Degree courses usually last four or five years. Doctorates in Laws and Medicine take up to seven years. The university is administered by a council appointed by the Prime Minister. The executive head is the Rector. There is also a senate and faculty boards to run academic affairs. The institution is non-residential.

The Malta College of Education was founded in 1973 to replace the two teacher training colleges which were closed down at the end of 1972/73, and it provided pre-service and in-service courses for teachers in Malta. Now training for the first and second levels and for technical teaching is run by the Department of Educational Studies at the New University. All teachers in government employment have to be trained, the normal course lasting four years. Entry is based on qualifications (a minimum of seven passes at GCE 'O' level, one of which must be in the English language, and three at 'A' level), age (minimum 17) and selection by interview. The course is organised on the basis of six months of study and six months of work and could lead to a BA in Education. This type of course is intended for teachers up to the third year of second-level education.

For university graduates a one year course concentrating on teaching methods and educational theory leads to a certificate to teach. In-service and refresher courses are provided for teachers. The university is mixed, non-residential and lay.

The Malta College of Arts, Science and Technology has the following departments; mechanical engineering, electrical engineering, business studies, hotel management and food technology and a servicing department. Various courses are run in each department and some of these lead to degrees of the Royal University of Malta and to associateships of professional institutes. Courses are held on a full time, part time, sandwich and evening basis. Entry requirements depend on the nature and level of the course.

7 EDUCATIONAL ADMINISTRATION

In the main, government, through the Cabinet of Ministers and the Department of Education, formulates policy for all primary, secondary and trade schools, technical institutes and the schools of art, navigation, music and evening classes. Schools are established either by the Ministry of Education or by individuals licensed by the Minister. An Education Department within the Ministry implements policy, except for the university, by using governmental and non-governmental bodies. It provides specialised services such as guidance and counselling and testing.

An advisory Council of Education and a Commission for the Development of Higher Education work through standing committees.

Some educational institutions and welfare services are run and administered by government departments other than the Education Department. These include:

ADMINISTRATION

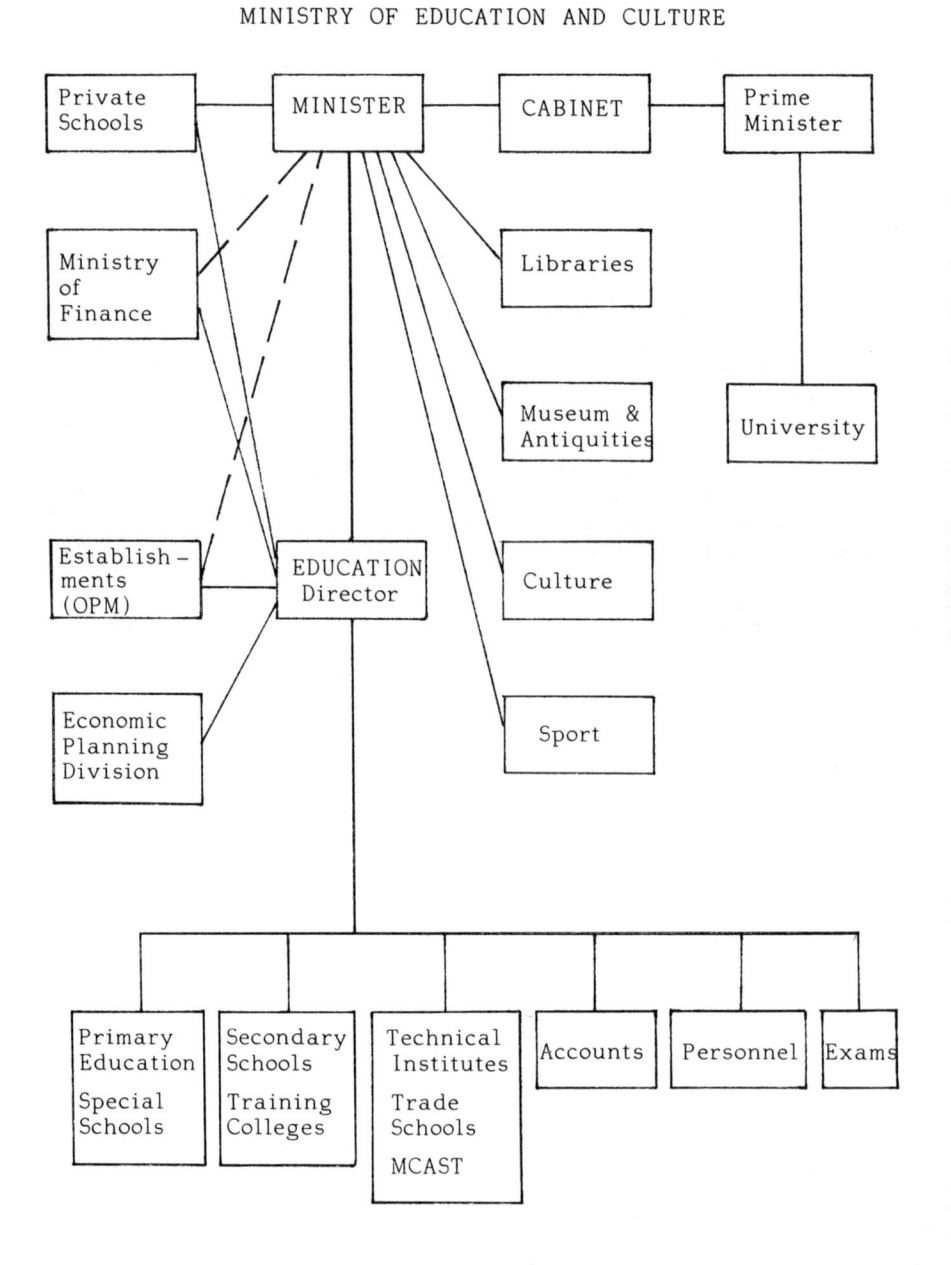

MINISTRY OF EDUCATION AND CULTURE

| Private Schools | MINISTER | CABINET | Prime Minister |

Libraries

Museum & Antiquities

University

| Ministry of Finance |

| Establishments (OPM) | EDUCATION Director | Culture |

| Economic Planning Division |

Sport

| Primary Education / Special Schools | Secondary Schools / Training Colleges | Technical Institutes / Trade Schools / MCAST | Accounts | Personnel | Exams |

The School of Nursing } run by the Medical and
The School of Hospital Catering } Health Department

The Approved School
Orphan Institutions
Family Welfare and Probation Services } run by the Department of Labour and Social Services
Apprenticeships

The Royal University of Malta enjoys autonomous status. A number of private schools, both primary and secondary, offer more or less the same facilities that exist in State schools. Private schools are largely academic and fee paying and offer no facilities in technical education.

8 EDUCATIONAL FINANCE
Budget

Government expenditure on education is provided from central funds. The Education Department submits annual estimates to the Ministry of Finance for vetting and approval before presentation to Parliament. These include:

(i) government recurrent and capital expenditure on education
(ii) annual block grants to the Royal University of Malta
(iii) grants to private schools.

In the late seventies government expenditure on education was in the order of 6% of the GNP.

Allocation of Funds
Expenditure on Education: Distribution by Level
Percentage of Expenditure 1976

Pre-School	First level	Second level	Third level	Other
–	23.7	51.0	11.7	15.6

9 DEVELOPMENT AND PLANNING OF THE EDUCATIONAL SYSTEM
Educational Objectives and decrees

Formal education in Malta can be traced to the fifteenth century when religious schools and schools of the Commune are known to have existed.

Higher education goes back to the founding of the Collegium Melitense by the Jesuits in 1592. In 1727 it was raised to the status of Academy with the power to grant degrees and in 1768 when the Grand Master banished the Jesuits it was raised to the status of university. In 1798 Napoleon suppressed it and changed it into an *Ecole Centrale* but in 1800 the first British Commissioner reopened the University, since when it has been financed by Government funds. In 1937 it became the Royal University of Malta and ten years later it became fully autonomous.

The first elementary schools were opened in 1819 and a Royal Commission of 1836 recommended that these should be taken over by the government. From then onwards the government expanded the number of free primary schools which grew alongside the existing private (i.e. religious) schools. In 1924 a Compulsory Attendance Act obliged parents to register their children for education up to the age of 12.

In the inter-war period the national language, Maltese, was not used for purposes of instruction, at least officially, but certain politically and clerically inspired forces tried to foster Italian at the expense of the English language. Mussolini was spending large sums of money on 'cultural' propaganda and the Roman Catholic Public School, St Edward's, was founded by the Strickland family at this time to counter the spread of Italian influence in education.

Following World War Two the government passed the Education Act of 1946 and by the Royal University of Malta Constitution Ordinance of 1946 the University gained a large measure of administrative and academic autonomy. A large primary and second school building programme was undertaken for the increasing numbers of pupils. Pre-service training for teachers had been introduced in 1944 and in the 1950s two Teacher Training Colleges for men and women were built.

In 1956 education was made completely free in government primary and secondary schools while Industrial Training Centres and Technical Institutes were started for technical education. In higher education 1961 saw the founding of the Polytechnic (MCAST) with Commonwealth Development and Welfare Funds and UNESCO assistance and in 1964 the foundation stone for the new campus at the Royal University of Malta was laid by HRH Prince Charles.

Education became a bone of contention between the two main political parties. In 1970 the Nationalist party, then forming the Government, introduced 'Secondary Education for all' but this was countered in 1972 by the Labour Government turning the previous Grammar and Secondary General schools into comprehensive type Area Schools. Selective examinations of the eleven-plus sort were abolished and a middle school examination was imposed after the first two years of common second level studies.

In 1974 a new Education Act appeared based on the recommendations of the International Committee on Education under the chairmanship of Professor H A Ree (University of York). By this an Advisory Council for Education was set up to advise the

Minister. The main changes under the 1974 Act have been:

(i) the extension of the minimum school leaving age to 16
(ii) a compromise on the provision of religious instruction and the possibility of 'opting out'
(iii) the registration of private schools
(iv) the ban on employment of children of school age.

The section on tertiary education was based on the XIV and XV Reports of the Dahrendorf Commission. These aimed at the setting up of a Commission for the Development of Higher Education and in particular the need for university reform.

Planning

Until recently 'planning' would have been rather a misnomer for the running of education policy in Malta. In colonial days a great deal of education was left in the hands of the Church, while the government provided general education on the British model, but there was a time lag in the matter of systems. For example the changes in Maltese secondary education in 1970 were based on the British Education Act of 1944 and the 1972 drive for comprehensivisation resulted from previous experiments in the UK.

Planning proper may be said to have begun in 1972 when the Government set up a Commission for the Royal University of Malta and a European Committee of Education for Malta. The Government objectives for the latter as agreed with the Minister were given as:

(i) equality of educational opportunity
(ii) to improve the status of manual labour and at the same time to increase (a) the personal competence of individuals, and (b) awareness of their potential contribution to society
(iii) to encourage the economic self-sufficiency of Malta
(iv) to move away from the British system of education towards a system based on the needs and culture of Malta, always taking into consideration the importance of harmonising this system with that of Western Europe
(v) to develop independence of thought and a sense of responsibility among individuals.

Both these bodies were international in character. The result of the recommendations of the International Committee on Education regarding reforms in the school sector were seen in the 1974 Education Act.

The work of the Statutory Commission of the Royal University of Malta, which was appointed by the Prime Minister on July 4, 1972, was much more controversial. The Commission was not only entrusted with the powers and duties envisaged in Section 13 of the Royal University of Malta (Constitution) Ordinance 1947 but 'specifically charged with the responsibility of advising the Government on how best its social and economic policies could be achieved through a liberal and free University'.

In the XIVth report (the interim report) submitted in March 1973 the Commission dealt with the immediate problems of the university and made recommendations with regard to the provision of finance for the financial year 1973-74 and covering the academic year ending in September 1974.

The XVth report was divided into two parts. The first dealt with the legislative and organisational changes necessary to make the university more responsive to the requirements of the country and to create better coordination with other institutions of higher learning. The second dealt with changes in the academic field which the Commission considered important and capable of achievement in the medium term.

Part I dealt with the role of the university in Maltese society and suggested the structural changes. It contained recommendations for certain legislative changes aimed at integrating the university more closely into the national educational framework, while leaving it with that degree of academic and administrative freedom required in an institution of higher learning. Part II advised on the grant for the academic year 1974/75 and indicated the general direction of desirable future developments. This included finance and academic reforms with particular comments on the various faculties in the university.

The government's underlying polity for education in its 'Development Plan 1973-80' could be described as follows:

(i) to provide equality and improvement of educational opportunity
(ii) to promote a greater awareness of the dignity, status and potential contribution to society of her citizens
(iii) to move toward a system based on Malta's needs and culture, bearing in mind the importance of harmonising this system with that of Western Europe
(iv) to develop independence of thought and a sense of responsibility among individuals.

It is with these in view that the following have already been implemented:

(i) compulsory education from 6 to 16 years of age
(ii) the introduction of a comprehensive system of free primary and secondary education leading up to the General Certificate of Education
(iii) the introduction of vocational trade schools for students who, having finished at least Form III of second level education, wish to take up a craft course
(iv) the closer integration of private and state schools
(v) the introduction of nursery classes and kindergartens

(vi) for children between the ages of 4 and 6 as circumstances permit
(vi) the consolidation and expansion of technical education
(vii) the reform of higher education brought about by the setting up of the Commission for the Development of Higher Education.

10 THE SYSTEM IN OPERATION
Current Trends

The introduction of 'secondary education for all' led to a number of problems.

Examinations

After examinations were abolished, the public outcry and falling standards in schools led to the re-introduction of an annual national examination. Transfer to trade and technical institutes is based on either an entrance examination or on continuous assessment and vocational choice. Admission to upper second level schools is based on success in 'O' level examinations.

Curricula

The Education Department establishes curricula for first and second level schools. Schools, however, are encouraged to devise special curricula for slow learners and the non-academic. The Department maintains a staff of inspectors and other specialists to prepare studies in curricula changes and examinations. GCE examinations are prepared in the United Kingdom and taken in Malta.

The quality of teachers and the number of well qualified inspectors place constraints on the realisation in practice of curriculum reforms.

Schools and Equipment

If new methods of teaching and more flexible curricula are to be introduced school buildings will have to be improved, modern teaching aids provided and libraries improved.

Teachers

Efforts are being made to keep teachers up to date and to redeploy them when and where necessary. Refresher courses for first and second level teachers and for those in trade and technical schools are provided with this in view. Demographic trends make long term plans to bring the demand for and supply of teachers into balance difficult to formulate, let alone achieve in practice.

Industrialisation

Government plans to industrialise the country are reflected in the emphasis placed on trade schools and domestic/craft options in general second level schools. Teachers' attitudes towards 'good' students suggest that to redress the balance between general academic studies and practical courses will be difficult.

General Expectations

Policy is directed towards the cultivation through education of the moral, cultural and intellectual potential of the personality and the all round development of individuals. Education should promote a respect for manual labour, technical and vocational education so as to contribute to the satisfactory evolution of society.

Structure of the Education System in Malta

Age	3	4	5	6	7	8	9	10	11	12	13	14	15	16	17	18	19	20	21	22	23	24
Level				I							II					III					IV	
Stage				1						2			3		4		5					
Compulsory																						
School type				Primary						Secondary					Upper Second							

Trade schools / Technical institutes

Teacher training

Malta College of Arts, science & Technology

University
Institutes of higher educ.

▨ Education preceding the first level

Examinations: compulsory at end of stage 2 (GCE 'O' level)

Source: UNESCO/IBE International Yearbook of Education

Compulsory Education: Age Limits 5–16   Duration (years) 8
Entrance age to pre-school education: 3

MALTA BASIC STATISTICS	1960	1970	1975	1978 (approx.)
1 Total population (000)	329	325	329	340
% female	52	52	52	52
2 % population 0-14 years	86	74	63	
% female	45	46	46	
3 Enrolment, all levels	72,563	66,248	63,668	61,938
% female	47		47	
First level	61,643	40,021	29,834	31,363
% female	49	48	48	49
Second level	10,391	24,388	32,409	28,921
% female	39		46	45
Third level	529	1,839	1,425	1,674
% female	38	34	28	25
4 Teachers, all levels		3,373	4,155	4,666
% female			46	46
First Level	2,238	1,391	1,421	1,931
% female		72	69	67
Second level	341	1,662	2,498	2,511
% female	30		37	35
Third level	98	320	236	224
% female	15	11	6	6
5 Public expenditure on education:				
Total (000) pounds	1,983	6,436	7,105	9,063
As % of GNP	3.9	6.3	4.4	3.5
As % of public expenditure				9.7
6 % enrolment (MF) by level	100	100	100	100
First level	85	60	47	51
Second level	14	37	51	47
Third level	1	3	2	2
% enrolment (F) by level	100	100	100	100
First level	88		49	53
Second level	12		50	45.5
Third level	1		1	1.5
7 Entrance age: Duration of				
First level education			5:6	5:6
Second level education			11:7	11:7
8 Enrolment ratios (MF)				
First level	126	108	101	110
Second level	21	50	75	71
Third level	2.30	5.59	4.60	5.47
Enrolment ratios (F)				
First level	127	108	101	111
Second level	16		70	66
Third level	1.54	3.61	2.53	2.73

Netherlands

CONTENTS

1 Geography	504
2 Population	506
3 Society and Culture	507
4 History and Politics	508
5 The Economy	510
6 The Education System	511
7 Educational Administration	524
8 Educational Finance	526
9 Development and Planning of the Education System	528
10 The System in Operation	531

The fact that the Netherlands is a small flat country with a population of 14 million people helps to explain how, in spite of religious differences, it is possible to identify what may be described as a Dutch national character. One of its main constituents is a respect for liberty which allows virtually any group of parents to set up a primary school with full State financial support, or for a larger group of parents to set up a secondary school with substantial State support. Consequently, in education as in other walks of life, there are three large systems of education; one meets the needs of Roman Catholics, a second the needs of Protestants and a third the needs of the non-sectarian humanists. Many other private schools exist, such as those run by the Montessorians.

The Dutch systems of education are regulated by legislation initiated by the Minister of Education and Sciences. Hence while municipal and district council have a good deal of responsibility for the conduct of schools under their purview, there is, in terms of standards, textbooks, curricula and examinations, more uniformity than might be expected. Within the Ministry of Education and Science there is a Directorate of Research and Planning which has responsibilities for the whole education system.

Until recently this system was complex. Tradition ensured that Greek, Latin and Mathematics dominated academic secondary school curricula and were used as the core of subjects which formed the base of the curriculum for the several kinds of academic secondary school. They were central to selective processes leading to admission to the university. Alongside the several academic schools and the general school which did not prepare pupils for university, there were several types of vocational and technical schools in which the length of the courses (short or long) were related to the skills needed in the occupation for which pupils were rather specifically trained. Thus on a common primary school base had been created a highly differentiated second level of education and a third level of education which included humanistic and technological universities.

Reformers have paid attention to the age of transfer from first to second level schools - it now takes place at the age of $12\frac{1}{2}$. They have also worked towards reducing differentiation at the second level of education by integrating the various types of secondary education so that as a guideline for policy the idea that there should be one type of education for the 12-15 year olds has been accepted. Attempts have been made to reduce, particularly in the *gymnasia*, the position of the classical languages and emphasise modern languages as was traditional in the *atheneum*. Officially neither the *gymnasium* nor the *atheneum* exist, having been combined in the *lyceum* which offers a common first year course for those entering this type of second level education at the age of $12\frac{1}{2}$.

As in most countries the universities were the scene of considerable student unrest and the pressures brought to bear on the administration have resulted in a sharing of power by students and professors.

The Editor

1 GEOGRAPHY

Topography

The Netherlands is small - 36,758 square kilometres or 14,358 square miles - of which 2,819 sq km consists of rivers, canals, lakes and other uninhabitable areas. But it is both densely populated and highly developed. Situated on the North Sea, it contains the estuaries of three great rivers (the Rhine, Maas and Scheldt). Consequently the Netherlands has come to seek its livelihood in shipping, commerce and the transit trade, the latter consisting in the transport of goods to the other densely populated, highly developed and industrialised countries lying further inland. More than half the country lies beneath the high water level of sea and rivers, so the many dykes and pumping installations are essential for keeping the land dry. Land reclamation is still in progress.

Climate

The country has a marine climate, with cool summers and mild winters.

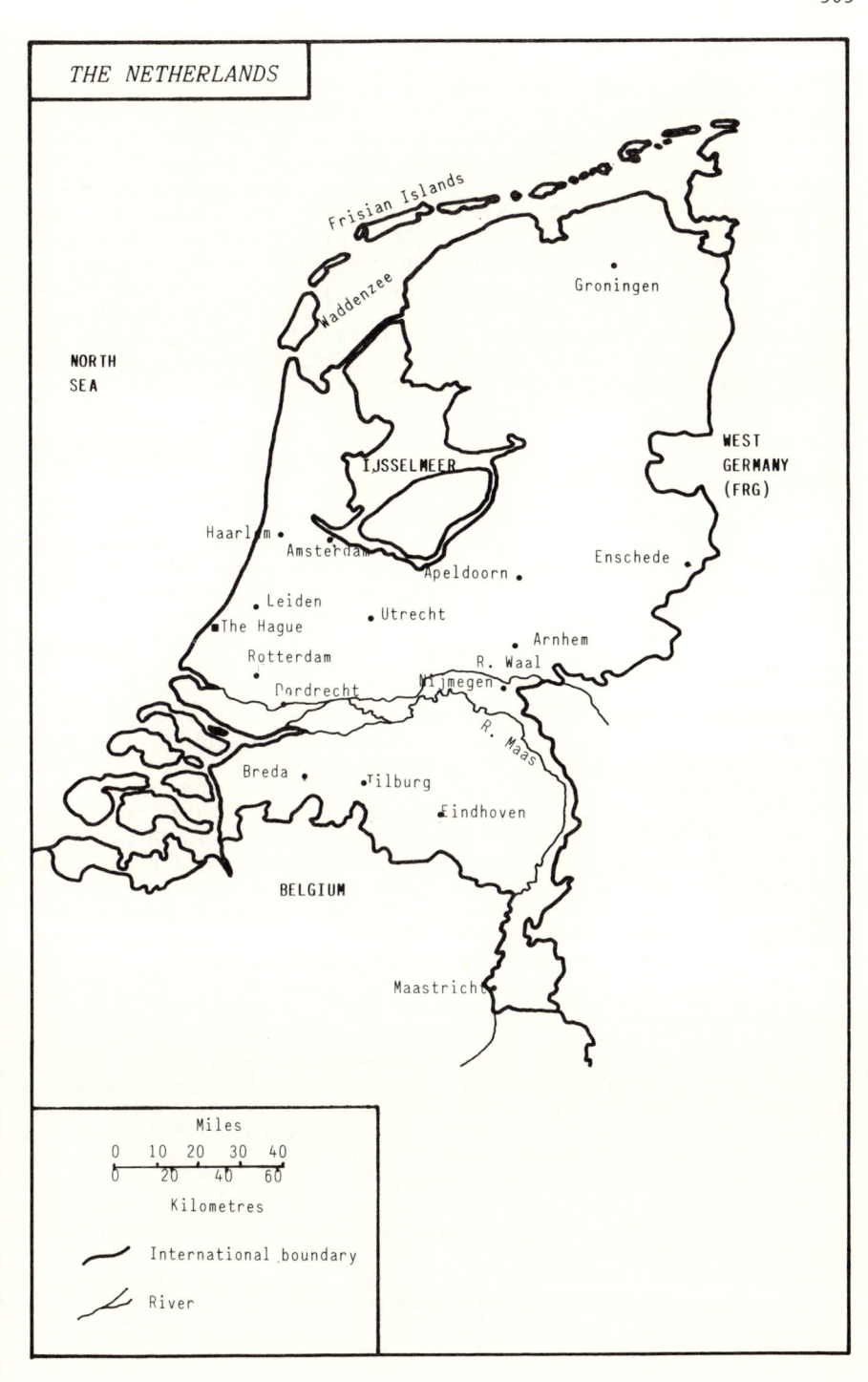

THE NETHERLANDS

Frisian Islands

Waddenzee

Groningen

NORTH SEA

IJSSELMEER

WEST GERMANY (FRG)

Haarlem
Amsterdam
Apeldoorn
Enschede
Leiden
Utrecht
The Hague
Arnhem
Rotterdam
R. Waal
Dordrecht
Nijmegen

R. Maas

Breda
Tilburg
Eindhoven

BELGIUM

Maastricht

Miles
0 10 20 30 40
0   20   40   60
Kilometres

⁓ International boundary
⌇ River

Communications

The already highly developed transit trade has assumed even greater importance within the EEC, and Rotterdam is now the busiest port in the world. Of all seaborne goods that are loaded or unloaded in the EEC countries, 30% pass through Dutch sea ports. To maintain their leading position Netherlands ports are modernising intensively. Road, rail and air links are well developed and it is as quick to travel by road or rail to Brussels as it is to Groningen in the north of the country or Maastricht in the south. In under two hours from Amsterdam or The Hague it is possible to be in the Federal Republic of Germany, while Heathrow is only 45 minutes away. There are 86,345 km (53,966 miles) of road (including 1,800 km [1,125 miles] of motorway) with 2,832 km (1,770 miles) of railway track.

2 POPULATION

Growth

The Netherlands has a population of nearly 14 million, which is very large for such a small country. On average 390 Dutchmen have to share each square kilometre. The birth rate was 12.5 live births per thousand in 1977, having fallen from 18.3 in 1970; at that time it was still above average for Western Europe.

Distribution

One third of the population is concentrated in two of the 11 provinces, namely North Holland and South Holland. In the most densely populated part of the country – that is to say the conurbation in the west of the country formed by Amsterdam, Rotterdam, The Hague and Utrecht and known as the 'Randstad' – there are almost 900 people to every square kilometre. There are no really large cities but Amsterdam, Rotterdam and The Hague are by far the largest towns. The other 14 towns with more than 100,000 inhabitants are: Utrecht, Eindhoven, Haarlem, Groningen, Tilburg, Nijmegen, Enschede, Zaanstad, Arnhem, Breda, Apeldoorn, Dordrecht, Maastricht and Leiden.

Immigrant Groups

After links with Indonesia were broken in 1956, large numbers of Indonesians were integrated, with relative success, into Dutch society. This might be attributed to the fact that these immigrants were as Dutch in outlook and culture as those born in the Netherlands. Churches and other welfare organisations have played a large part in the integration of immigrants, although success has been less marked in the case of those from the Netherlands Antilles and Surinam, and more recently with other immigrants such as Turks. In recent years the south Moluccan community have been pressing their claims for independence in some cases by means of terrorist attacks on civilian and strategic targets.

3 SOCIETY AND CULTURE

Language

Dutch is related to English and Low German and the variant spoken in the province of Friesland has marked similarities to English. It is necessary for all immigrant groups in the Netherlands, including European immigrants (for example Turkish, Spanish and Portuguese), to master the Dutch language if they wish to be integrated into the society. The better educated Dutch, by virtue of the country's geographical situation, history and commerce, have long applied themselves to learning foreign languages, and one can expect to find proficiency in English, German and French, in that order. Many of those living near the borders of the Federal Republic of Germany and Belgium/Luxembourg respectively will probably be proficient in their neighbour's language.

English

From January 1970, the previous pre-university school leaving requirements of passes in English, German and French were modified, and only one foreign language was required of all secondary school pupils. More than 40% chose English. International courses run in the Netherlands and aimed particularly at Third World countries are generally conducted in English. Three of the main centres for such courses are The Institute of Social Studies in The Hague, The Building Centre in Rotterdam, and the important University of Agriculture in Wageningen.

Religion

According to the provisional results of the 1971 census, 39% of the population belong to the Roman Catholic Church, 23% to the Dutch Reformed Church (Protestant) and 7% to the other – more orthodox – Protestant Churches. A further 8% of the population belong to churches other than those mentioned above, while 23% have no connection with any church. The Constitution guarantees freedom of religion. In recent years there has been a clear tendency in the Netherlands for the various churches to cooperate and engage in innovation. The innovating zeal of the Dutch Roman Catholic bishops and young clerics has attracted special attention both at home and abroad.

Social Patterns

Calvinism has struck deep into the Dutch character, whether Protestant or Catholic, and this manifests itself in an earnestness which has its outlet traditionally through a strict ethical religious code or an outstanding instinct for business. There is a fine balance maintained between tolerance and intolerance which is reflected in one of the most elaborate bureaucracies in the world on the one hand, and an often anarchic approach to the law on the other. Recently the young have tended to dissociate themselves from established social and political values, generally accepting greater permissiveness in relationships, and showing a more casual approach to life. The counter reaction to this permissive trend is not particularly vociferous. There is an acceptance of the individual's right to determine his own way of living, although the ambivalent attitude which arises from the clash of tolerance and Calvinism gives rise to a situation where minor social deviations are unlikely to be legally punished, though the deviation will probably be officially noted. A good example of ambivalence is the manner of recruitment for, and administration of, the armed forces. On the one hand, conscription for 16 months is still the rule, and is likely to remain so. On the other, the conscripts are allowed to wear their hair and beards as they please, saluting is not obligatory, and as many as 40% of those eligible for call-up obtain exemption for medical, psychiatric and other reasons.

Family ties are strong, but familial and other relationships are based on the acceptance of people as they are, rather than on how they wish to appear. Old city centres tend to remain intact and rings of later development encircle the towns with the most modern (and sometimes high rise) buildings on the outer ring. In the new parts, there is the familiar problem of dormitory areas where there is still little community or social activity. Some of the larger towns, and Amsterdam in particular, are in the forefront of the social changes which are sweeping European and other societies, while there is social legislation affecting old age, widows' and orphans' pensions, child allowances, sickness benefits, health insurance and unemployment benefits. People with incomes in excess of Dfl.33,650 a year are not covered by national health insurance but will insure privately.

4 HISTORY AND POLITICS

Origins

The Dutch are descendants in remote times of Germans, Friesians, Saxons and Franks, and did not aspire to nationhood until 1581 when the various bishoprics, provinces and towns rejected the fanatic intolerance of the sovereignty of the King of Spain and formed a republic. The federal government was aristocratic; within the sea-linked towns the citizens were happy to leave administration to the bourgeois regents while they concentrated on trade and industry; trade was becoming worldwide, and a colonial empire was being founded. In 1806 Napoleon imposed his rule, first through his brother and later directly as part of the empire. The House of Orange was restored in 1813 when the French retreated and Prince William landed from England, pledging a constitution defining the rights of the monarch and people. The Netherlands became a kingdom. This constitution, dividing the country into nine provinces, was short-lived because the congress of Vienna united the northern and southern Netherlands with Liège and Luxembourg. When the Belgians seceded in 1830, the Netherlands was reconstituted with 11 provinces as today.

Since World War Two

During World War Two the Netherlands was occupied by Germany and following liberation in 1945 chose to abandon neutrality. In the post-war period the Netherlands has been involved in the process of decolonisation. Like the French, the Dutch used to regard their colonies as part of one big country with a centralised government in the homeland, as opposed to the British concept of as much self-rule as external forces allowed. Indonesia gained independence in 1946, and in 1963 was given responsibility for Dutch New Guinea. Surinam gained independence in 1975, leaving Netherlands Antilles as the only remaining possession.

Government and Politics

The Netherlands is a constitutional monarchy. By accident of birth, women have been monarchs or regents since 1890 - the Queens Emma, Wilhelmina and Juliana. In January 1980 Queen Juliana announced her intention of abdicating in favour of her daughter, Crown Princess Beatrix. Queen Beatrix herself has broken the dynastic pattern by having three sons. There is very little republican feeling and the Dutch without fuss respect their democratic monarchy, which is to some extent involved in government. The monarch has a hand in the formation of governments and is titular president of the Council of State - the highest appeal court in administrative matters. The popular public relations image has been to show the former Queen Juliana riding a bicycle.

There are two parliamentary chambers. Election to the 75-member first chamber is for six years and is made by the provincial councils. Election to the 150-member second chamber is for four years by proportional representation, which results in numerous small parties representing a variety of electoral interests. Two Protestant parties and one Catholic party still share a large part of the central vote and this blurs the line between right and left in political terms. Government and bureaucracy have been strongly centralised in the Netherlands since Napoleonic times and a side effect of this is that many laws relating to education are an integral part of the Dutch constitution, jealously preserved on all sides. The link between government and the academic world is extremely close and there are always some professors in the cabinet.

International Relations

For geographical and economic reasons the Netherlands has succeeded in reconciling national and international interests to a greater degree than most countries. The Netherlands was a founded member of the Council of Europe, NATO, Western European Union, OEEC and its successor OECD, the European communities, and the United Nations Organisation and its agencies. The Customs Union of the Benelux countries, mooted during the war and started in 1960, is likely to have far reaching importance for the rest of Europe and to prove a model of its kind. The Dutch are anxious to keep Europe as open as possible and much of the credit for the Netherlands' splendid record in international relations and in the EEC must be attributed to Dr Joseph Luns who till 1971 was foreign minister for 18 years. The man in the street enjoys the fruits of the Common Market, but jealously safeguards his national identity.

5 THE ECONOMY

Agriculture

Dense population, costly ground, and a high level of technical development are three factors that have led to the intensive cultivation of high quality agricultural and horticultural products. Of the total land area, 77% (almost 2.2 million hectares) is under cultivation, 63% being grassland, 31% arable land and 6% horticultural land. The measures taken by the EEC are designed to achieve an agricultural structure in which only profitable undertakings can survive. This has meant that many small firms in the Netherlands have disappeared (with the encouragement and support of the Agricultural Development and Rationalisation Fund) and large holdings have developed that are strongly capital intensive and not very labour intensive. Thanks to mechanisation, they now achieve a high production level. Only 7% of the working population is employed in agriculture and fisheries.

Industry

Industry employs about 40% of the labour force and contributes about 40% to national income. The industrial strength of the country is spearheaded by shipping, shipbuilding, the oil industry and chemicals. These last two, plus natural gas production, have grown especially rapidly. The Netherlands is the chief gas producer and exporter in the EEC; natural gas meets about 55% of present energy requirements but reserves are now declining.

Economic Situation

The Netherlands economic structure has been based for centuries on banking, commerce and transport. Fifty three percent of the working population is employed in the services sector. An acute eye for business, mixed with natural geographical advantages, has produced in the Netherlands one of the most favourable economic climates in the world. The economy benefits from the highest rate of overseas investment of any EEC country. The inflow of capital is mainly directed to high technology sectors and has to be matched by a corresponding supply of skills from the Dutch population. The government attempts to regulate the economy in a sophisticated way. Certain wage rises are linked automatically to the cost of living index, as are rents. The relationship between employers and trade unions is productive.

The two problems of the late 1970s were inflation (5% in 1978 though it had been higher) and unemployment (200,000 in 1978). In 1978 the government announced a plan to promote exports, reduce unemployment and keep inflation low by cutting public expenditure, encouraging private industry and restraining wages.

6 THE EDUCATION SYSTEM
General

Compulsory education begins on 1 August in the year in which a child reaches the age of 6 years 8 months, and ends at the end of the school year after 10 years' attendance, or at the end of the school year in which a child reaches the age of 16. Compulsory education is free. For children wishing to continue beyond the age of 16 there are further educational opportunities, assisted by scholarships or interest-free loans.

Efforts are being made to turn the entire education system from nursery school to university into one coherent whole. The Secondary Education Act, which came into force in 1968, was a first step in this direction. One of the main purposes of the Act was to integrate the various types of secondary education. High priority has been accorded to curriculum development in an endeavour to achieve this reform. Integration of education for 4-12 year olds is in preparation, and is to be carried out by stages, in order to do full justice to the continuity of the growing and learning process in young children.

Academic Year

The school year begins in late August or early September and ends in late June. Schools work five days per week, including either Saturday morning or Wednesday afternoon. In higher education, the academic year extends from September to June.

Pre-School

Under the Pre-Primary Education Act of 1955, the State encourages and assists pre-primary schools, both public and private. These schools cater for children between the ages of 4 and 7. As education is not compulsory for the pre-primary age group, coverage is not universal with 80% of the age group at 4+ attending and 90% at 5+. To qualify for a grant, the pre-primary school must be open from 8.30 to 11.30 and 2.30 to 4.30 on Mondays, Tuesdays, Thursdays and Fridays, and on Wednesdays from 8.30 to 11.30 only. The schools have a common timetable for work and play, which includes games, physical activities, the handling of teaching aids, modelling, drawing and painting, music, story-telling, and learning nursery rhymes.

The gradual merging of pre-primary and primary schools is envisaged. At the same time the question of making education compulsory, possibly part time, for 4 or 5 year olds, is under consideration, as is the possibility of lowering the age of admission (to 3 years 9 months).

First Level

This is a six-year course covering an age range of pupils of roughly $6\frac{1}{2}$ to $12\frac{1}{2}$. There is a common timetable, and by law there must be 1,040 lessons of 60 minutes. The traditional syllabus includes the following subjects: Dutch language and literature, history, geography, physics, biology, arithmetic, writing, road safety, speech training, music, art, handicrafts and physical education.

The 1920 Primary Education Act has been gradually modified under a Primary Education Bill of 1970. One of the earliest developments was for teachers to abandon narrow subject teaching and treat their subjects as coming within the broader fields of the three Rs. Other developments supported by the Bill are the elimination of divisions into classes by years, the introduction of English in the upper classes, and the smoothing of the transition from pre-primary to primary school. English is the favoured second language because it is regarded as the most useful international language, because it is taught in the transitional class in secondary schools, and because it is taught as the first language in neighbouring countries. At this level learning is fully programmed, and work books are used throughout the schools. Materials and apparatus are bought by the school from approved shops. Teachers may buy what they like in the way of textbooks and materials from lists officially approved by the Inspectorate, subject of course to the grant available. In State schools, class teachers rarely give religious teaching, but a visiting teacher deals with Bible history.

In the primary school, record cards are kept and the pupils are continuously assessed. The practice of having to repeat a year has almost been eliminated. There is intelligence and attainment testing in the top three classes of the primary school for selection purposes. It is widely recognised that intellectual and social differences between children of the same age will make it necessary to provide physical conditions and methods of work which will take account of each child's individuality and different rate of progress. It is hoped in this way to eradicate backwardness, to apply efficient diagnostic testing and remedial teaching and to eliminate the repetition of classes, which in the primary schools today is tolerated only in the sixth grade. A number of experiments have taken place in this area.

The Enschede experiments, which have been continuous since 1954, are directed towards the elimination of poor performance in the primary school, and already improvements have been made in the individual teaching of reading. Special activities to compensate for home deficiencies led to the abandonment of grading in classes. The teaching of arithmetic and social subjects is now being tackled. The experiments are run by a schools advisory service in which psychologists, social workers, and educationists collaborate. The Amsterdam 'Flos' (flexible organisation of the school) project deals with 5-11 year olds, and is preparing and using teaching and learning packages which are not bound to a given space of time, and which ensure that each child moves at his own pace. The school curriculum is divided into three parts: basic skills (reading, writing and arithmetic), exploration of the world, and creative work. The Rotterdam project is a ten-year experiment concentrated on deprived areas and relating educational innovation to social environment, seeking full parental cooperation. The six-year class system has been replaced by dividing subject-matter into units, and children work through the units at their own pace. Groups of up to ten children are taught Dutch, reading and arithmetic, and other subjects may be taught in groups of 50 or so with the use of audio-visual aids.

Special

Since 1949 12 types of special school have been recognised for children with mental and sensory handicaps (for example the mentally and physically handicapped, deaf, blind and partially-sighted, delicate, epileptics, seriously maladjusted) and four types of school for children who are not handicapped, but are unable to attend an ordinary primary school because their parents are itinerant (bargees, gypsies, fairground operators). A Royal Decree in 1967 recognised four additional types of special primary school, special secondary education and nursery departments at certain special schools. Since August 1977 it has been possible to establish schools for children with multiple handicaps.

Second Level Schools

Excluding the technical or vocational secondary sector (*Beroepsonderwijs* - BO) there are basically four types of secondary school, each having $12\frac{1}{2}$ as their usual age of entry:

LAVO   *Lager Algemeen Voortgezet Onderwijs*
        - lower general secondary education, for years 1 and 2

MAVO   *Middelbaar Algemeen Voortgezet Onderwijs*
        - intermediate general secondary education, for years 1-4

HAVO   *Hoger Algemeen Voortgezet Onderwijs*
        - higher general secondary education, for years 1-5

VWO   *Voorbereidend Wetenschappelijk Onderwijs*
        - pre-university secondary education, for years 1-6

The letters AVO stand for Dutch words meaning general further education; the prefixes L, M and H signify lower, medium and higher. The letters VWO stand for Dutch words indicating that this type of school prepares students for higher education.

Since the compulsory school leaving age has been raised to 16 (in 1975) practically 100% of all pupils go on to full secondary education. About 60% go to a VWO, HAVO of MAVO school and 40% to a vocational school. Primary school headmasters advise parents on the choice of type of secondary school, though parents decide, but there is also selection for HAVO and VWO. These schools are legally obliged to select on the basis of the certificate given by the primary school headmaster, and either an entrance examination, achievement test, psychological test or trial period. In most cases an achievement test or psychological test is chosen. One of the available achievement tests is that produced by CITO, the National Institute for Educational Measurement of the Netherlands. But in spite of the requirement by law of two means of selection, there are no universal criteria for assessment of pupils' performance levels, no uniform cut-off points or national grading procedure. During the first (or bridge) year in the chosen secondary school there is further assessment and guidance, after which the misfits are directed to a more appropriate school or stream.

The idea of one type of education for 12 to 15 year olds has been accepted in principle as a guideline for policy. The Secondary Education Act introduced the first step in this direction in the form of a common transition or bridge year (from primary to secondary school) and made it legally possible for combined schools *(scholengemeenschappen)* to be formed. These are not comprehensive schools in the true sense, but do combine two or more types of school (occasionally including vocational schools) under one management. A few combined schools extended the transition year to a two- or three-year transition period. In preparation for the complete integration of all schools for 12 to 15 year olds, controlled experiments are to be undertaken which will break through the existing educational structure. Integration experiments are restricted to the first three years of secondary schools.

Changes in the lower classes of pre-university schools (VWO) and higher general secondary schools (HAVO) and within the universities and higher vocational training institutes, (including amendments to their admission procedures), will make it necessary to review the teaching in the higher classes of VWO and HAVO schools. The problems of the transition between senior secondary and post-secondary education are being studied in the light of this.

LAVO

Under the old system children could take a 7th or 8th class in the primary school or a one or two-year course in a school for continued primary education, paying special attention to social and manual subjects. These options are now taken in LAVO schools. Sometimes they are combined with schools for secondary technical and vocational training at lower level, the LAVO course being given in the first two years. In 1970 there were 105 LAVO schools. While there are LAVO courses within other schools, now only 16 LAVO schools remain, 40 having been absorbed into the community schools. The remainder will be phased out completely, some being taken into the lower secondary vocational sector.

MAVO

Many more children used to follow a ULO (*Uitgebreid Lager Onderwijs* - extended primary) course lasting either three or four years, and offering a choice between languages, sciences, mathematics and commercial studies in addition to the basic curriculum. The extended primary school certificate was a standard recognised by all employers and opened the way to technical school or teacher training. The ULO course was finally phased out in 1972 and was replaced by MAVO (intermediate general secondary education). A four-year MAVO certificate can admit to the fourth year of HAVO schools, or to intermediate technical and vocational schools, or through a preparatory year, to certain types of higher level technical and vocational training. The MAVO school covers the last four years of compulsory education.

HAVO

HAVO schools were introduced in 1968 and offer a five-year course. The aim is to provide a good general secondary education to prepare for study at institutions of higher education other than univesities. In the first three years the course is common to all; in the fourth and fifth years there is a choice of subjects, with a leaving examination in six subjects which admits holders to the tertiary level technical and vocational schools. The Inspectorate is promoting the idea that upper HAVO pupils who can manage seven subjects should be allowed to take them, though they should only be examined in six. The HAVO course may also be taken in special departments of VWO and MAVO schools. Such departments offer the fourth and fifth year of HAVO and begin after three years of VWO or four years of MAVO. Similar two-year departments are also attached to academies for primary school teacher training.

VWO

There were three types, *gymnasium*, *atheneum* and *lyceum*, each offering a six-year course straight on from the primary school. The school leaving certificate of passes in seven subjects, which must include Dutch and one foreign language, gives admission to the universities. The *gymnasia* taught Latin and Greek throughout, while from the fourth or fifth year onwards the school divided into an A-stream concentrating on the classics and a B-stream concentrating on mathematics and science, B having equal status with A. There was no Latin or Greek in the *atheneum*, but there was greater emphasis on modern languages, history, geography, law and economics. The *atheneum* also divided from the fourth or fifth year into an A-stream concentrating on economics and social science and a B-stream concentrating on mathematics and science. Officially *gymnasium* and *atheneum* no longer exist, being combined in the *lyceum*, which offers a common first year. Since 1973 all fifth and sixth years have been known as the VWO course. Already there are instances of VWO schools in large towns administratively combining their fifth and sixth years after computerising choice of subjects, timetables and facilities.

Examinations

Secondary school examinations for the terminal certificate are in two parts - a school examination and a public examination. The first enables the schools to assess the value of their work and the second offers guarantees of standards to the next sector in education or to employers and society at large as to the value of the certificate. Multiple choice questions and 30-minute oral examinations have been introduced, but the schools now conduct their own orals. The school leaving examination is a certificate of education in all subjects. Failure in one subject may be compensated by a high mark in another, but for failure in two there is no compensation, and the pupil is expected to repeat his examination year and re-sit.

Technical and Vocational

About 40% of the children of compulsory secondary school age opt for vocational training: this is therefore an important sector. There are vocational schools at junior, senior and higher levels covering technical, economic/administrative, agricultural education and others.

Junior

Junior vocational schools (LBO) attempt to provide young people from the ages of 12 to 16 with a general education in a more practical teaching and learning situation and to give them an initial idea of careers and professions as well as further study and training in senior or higher vocational schools. The LBO course lasts four years; the first year is a general one. In the second year there are 20 periods per week in general subjects, so that the course is still fairly general. Subsequently there is a vocational phase lasting two years. The first year is usually regarded as a transition year, and the first two years together comprise the lower school. In the lower school the general aim on the one hand is to assist students to get bearings in the new situation by using suitable educational and didactic aids and methods and on the other hand to give them some idea of their capabilities in terms of further study and the choice of careers available to them.

Senior

The aim of senior technical and vocational schools is to prepare young people from the ages of 16 to 20 for middle grade executive positions in society, for independently practising a profession or further education and training, for example in higher vocational education. Pupils from general secondary schools are normally admitted to these schools, and pupils from junior vocational education, depending on the level they have reached there, may also be admitted. Senior technical and vocational schools (MTS) provide general preparation for middle grade technical positions. The accent is placed on good insight into the practical problems by providing students with a good deal of theoretical and technical knowledge. The main courses given in the senior technical schools are in building, mechanical engineering, electrical engineering, and civil engineering. The courses last four years, one of which is a practical year. The senior technical school certificate entitles a student to be admitted to post-secondary vocational establishments and to the teacher training course for junior and senior vocational school teachers. The certificates of a number of schools and departments qualify one to set up as an independent contractor. There are a number of special senior vocational schools which teach particular subjects. Follow-up courses are also held.

Higher

Higher vocational education and university education together comprise post-secondary education. Higher vocational education in general is intended to give the student a theoretical and practical training at such a level that he is equipped, after having acquired some experience, to occupy a managerial or senior position. It is obtained in higher vocational institutes (HBO). Numerous arguments favour a close link between higher vocational education and the universities. A number of committees have been set up to examine in the various sectors how this cooperation can be brought about. There have been steps towards regulating both types of education in one act. Admission to higher vocational institutes is in general possible with a HAVO certificate or certificate from a senior vocational course. Higher technical education (HTO) is given in technical colleges and courses last four years. The third year is spent in industry under the supervision of the school. With an HTO certificate it is possible in certain instances to go on to further study at a university.

Apprenticeship

Apprentices sign an agreement with their employers by which they receive practical training in the firm, and general and vocational training in a school. This agreement is a legal contract and apprenticeship agreements are monitored nationally. The normal admission requirement to apprenticeship is the junior vocational school certificate, or evidence of completion of equivalent education. In most cases apprentices attend school for one day a week for a full school year. The practical training is divided into elementary and advanced courses with the elementary stage lasting at least one year. At the end of the practical training apprentices take an examination which is organised nationally. The demand for apprenticeship schemes has been declining of late.

Participation Education

In 1970, the government produced a policy document entitled 'Measures for the Education and Employment of Early School Leavers'; this was followed in 1975 by a memorandum entitled 'Towards Participation in Education'. Participation education was started as a national educational reform project in a joint venture undertaken by the apprenticeship training institutes and the institutes for early school leavers. The latter provide informal training and educational guidance for young people up to the age of 18 who have not participated significantly in secondary education. Both oganisations chose as their point of departure early school leavers in the situation in which they live and work, although with a clear difference of emphasis. The apprenticeship training institutes have always given priority to teaching young people a trade, while the institutes for early school leavers have been more interested in helping them to develop as human beings. All of the participation education projects are different; they start from different points of departure and develop in different ways. Their main point of resemblance is that they are all forms of full time education for 16-18 year olds. Moreover, a lot of work undertaken in all the projects is located outside the schools.

Participation education has a wider range of teaching aims than traditional school subjects. Roughly, these aims can be divided into three categories:

(i) the development of general personal and social skills which includes increasing pupils' ability to view themselves, their own situation and potential, values and norms, needs, etc., and their capacity to deal with them; social skills include learning to communicate, to solve problems, to make plans, to make decisions, etc.

(ii) the development of basis skills in arithmetic, mathematics, language and other relevant school subjects

(iii) the preparation of young people for entry into work which includes introducing them to various trades, teaching them how to deal with labour situations and giving them a command of the various skills they need to become part of the labour process; finally, it includes enabling them to choose a trade and helping them to plan a career.

Under this system the learning process is based on three principles:

(i) broader teaching aims
(ii) individual programmes
(iii) locating the teaching inside and outside school.

These principles can be worked out in different ways depending on the respective importance of intramural and extramural school activities and the extent to which they relate to one another.

Third Level (Higher) Institutions

Higher education is given in 21 institutions of university standard. Of these, six are full universities within the meaning of the University Education Act of 1971, that is they have seven or eight faculties. They are:

University	Founded	
Leiden	1575	
Groningen	1614	
Utrecht	1636	
Amsterdam	1632	(university status 1876)
Free University of Amsterdam	1880	
Catholic University of Nijmegen	1923	

There are two universities of only three faculties, namely Tilburg (a Catholic foundation), and Erasmus University in Rotterdam. The Agricultural University at Wageningen (1917), and the technological universities at Delft (1905), Eindhoven (1957), and Twente (1961) have departments rather than faculties, Delft being most comprehensive with general science, mechanical, electrical, chemical and civil engineering. The most recently founded university in the State University of Limburg at Maastricht (1975), and this began as a medical school. A few of the institutions of university status have religious affiliations. The Free University of Amsterdam is Calvinist in origin and still answerable to a private - though not necessarily Calvinist - foundation. The Catholic University of Nijmegen retains a link with the Church, and while not subject to the Church's authority, sets out to serve the Catholic community. The University of Tilburg is Catholic in origin only, but serves a predominantly Catholic area. The new University of Limburg is a State university, though similarly serving an almost totally Catholic area. The Theological College of the Reformed Churches has university status. Tilburg University and Eindhoven University of Technology agreed in 1970 to work together when suitable new disciplines were proposed, as not only is each institution limited in its range of subjects, but they are only 30 km apart. There is a possibility that they may eventually join or federate to become the University of Brabant. Students normally live at home or in lodgings. Of late, to meet shortages of accommodation, blocks of flats for students have been built. With the exception of Twente, largely residential on a campus, this approaches the collegiate system, though there are usually large cafeterias open to all students.

Entrance

Admission to a university is open to anyone who has obtained a leaving certificate - based on examination in seven subjects including Dutch and one foreign language - from the appropriate form of six-year pre-university secondary education. Because of an increase in the numbers qualifying for admission it became necessary in 1972 to impose admission limits in medicine, dentistry, biology, veterinary science, social geography and history. For these subjects selection is literally by lottery, conducted by the Government Central Office for Admissions at Groningen. This unpopular act restricts the traditional freedom of choice of study, e.g. a would-be student of history may be offered a place to study an alternative subject. Bad luck in the lottery may be compensated by automatic admission in the following year. However, there are increasing indications that for certain disciplines admission is only granted to those who have the right subject combination and good grading in the pre-university examination. Grades run from 10 (excellent) to 1 (very poor). It could be argued that the real selection for university takes place at the end of primary schooling.

Degrees

The university course lasts five to seven years, but changes are proposed. The first examination - *kandidaats*, is usually taken after two or three years. The final *doctoraal* examination, taken three years later, entitles a student to the degree of *doctorandus*, or in law *meester* or in technology *ingenieur*. (The abbreviations 'drs', 'mr' and 'ir' are used as titles before one's name.) It is now proposed to initiate a four-year university course to the first degree of *doctorandus*. The first year will be an introductory or orientation year with an examination at the end which will provide an opportunity for re-orientation. Students who fail will be allowed a second introductory year in another field of studies. The technological universities consider that four years is insufficient time in which to train a professional engineer, and that any qualification obtained after this shorter period of study could not be accepted as equivalent to the present 'ir'. In consequence, the universities hope to introduce a new higher degree obtainable after one or two more years of study, in addition to the first four years.

Until recently students could delay or resit any of their examinations, but in the early 1970s universities laid down the maximum time that could be taken to complete the various courses. In most courses the *kandidaats* examination was to be passed within four years (2½ for law) and the *doctoraal* in seven years (six for law and social science, eight for dentistry, nine for pharmacy and medicine). Under the new system students will only be allowed to extend their four-year university course by a year if they fail their final examination, in order to re-sit. Some form of time limit on the use of laboratories and equipment is also envisaged.

The highest academic award is the doctorate, for which substantial research is necessary, taking at least three and often many more years. The printed thesis has to be defended in public before a board of professors. It has been proposed that postgraduate students be introduced to research methods in a one-year research diploma course. Some may be appointed as research assistants for a maximum of three years at a research institute not necessarily within the university, in order to prepare for a doctorate. Others will be given opportunities for professional or vocational training.

Teacher Training

Teacher training in the Netherlands is well developed and students train in different institutions and at different levels depending on the kind of school in which they propose to work.

Pre-Primary

Admission to pre-primary teacher training may be at age 15-16 for those who have a four-year MAVO certificate or have completed the first three years of a pre-university or HAVO school. Part 1 takes three years, and those who pass may proceed to the one-year Part 2 for a headteacher's certificate or qualify for primary teacher training.

Primary

This training takes place in *pedagogische akademies* (teacher training academies or colleges of education) of which in 1970 there were 98 distributed as follows:

State and municipal	24
Protestant	27
Roman Catholic	44
Others	3

The course, until 1970, was in two parts, Part 1 lasting 2 years and Part 2 one year. Since then Part 2, which was optional and conferred eligibility for appointment as headteacher, has been made compulsory and there is only one final examination taken at the end of Part 2. Besides qualifying for primary teaching the final certificate allows teachers to offer certain subjects such as Dutch, arithmetic, geography, history, and biology at general secondary schools. The requirement for admission to a teacher training academy is a HAVO leaving certificate or the leaving certificate of a pre-university school or a full pre-primary teachers' certificate. Some academies admit students for a preliminary two years during which they take the fourth and fifth years of the HAVO course.

The curriculum of the teacher training academies is closely related to the primary school curriculum. It prescribes for Part I:

Subject	Number of Lectures
Pedagogy, educational and child psychology General methodology and subject teaching methods	280
Dutch language and literature	280
Aspects of cultural and social life	120
Music	240
Art	100
Handicrafts	160
Physical education	160
History	80
Geography	80
Physics	80
Biology	80
Arithmetic	80
Writing	160
Road Safety	20
Speech improvement	10

Other subjects may be added to the list. There are also 240 hours teaching practice in primary schools.

Secondary (non-university)

This experiment, begun in 1970, is based on the interim report of a State commission under the chairmanship of Dr J B Drewes, a senior official of the Ministry of Education and Sciences. The commission's terms of reference were to produce recommendations regarding the organisation and curriculum of a new teacher training course. The report was published in 1966, but caused such an upheaval in education circles that it took four years to get the principal recommendations implented in the form of cautious experiments. The proposals of Dr Drewes and his fellow members — which do not apply to the universities — centred on the following points:

    (i)   teachers should be divided into three grades: the 1st (the highest), the 2nd and the 3rd grades

    (ii)   every student teacher should study two subjects to

a level corresponding to one of these grades

(iii) practical professional training must form a substantial and compulsory part of the training of teachers.

This last proposal was worked on by a special sub-committee, known as COLOV (Committee on Secondary Teacher Training in Educational Principles and Practice) which began work in 1970 and produced its interim report in 1972. It is based on a cyclical model with five stages, namely objectives, content, learning activities, methods and evaluation. Sub-committees to define the consequences of the proposals for the various school subjects began work in 1969; a supplementary report appeared for 1970.

These proposals were extremely important as for the first time in the history of Dutch education a fully integrated, academic and professional training course was offered for secondary school teachers. The first experimental training began in 1970. Training takes place in teacher training institutes, and it is planned that eventually there will be one in every university town. Although each institute is linked to a university, the institutes are financed directly by the Ministry of Education and Sciences. So far the institutes are training third grade teachers for the MAVO schools, and second grade teachers for the HAVO schools. First grade teachers for VWO schools are still the province of the universities which prepare them for degrees.

The minimum qualification for admission to the secondary teacher training institute is a certificate of five years general secondary education (HAVO). During the course two teaching subjects are studied and teaching practice runs concurrently. For the Third Grade Certificate the course is to last three years with an extra half year's practical, and for the Second Grade four years with an extra half year's practical, and it is intended that those in the Second Grade Course who wish to qualify for the First Grade shall be able to do so by a further two years at a university, i.e. they will be admitted as *kandidaats* and will only have another two years to study to reach doctorandus level.

Secondary (University)

All under-graduates are regarded as potential teachers, and a very high proportion do become teachers. The universities therefore require all students during the two years before their doctorandus degree to follow lectures organised by the University Department of Education in pedagogics, the psychology of adolescents, general methodology and the methodology of the degree subject. Each university department offering a subject taught in the pre-univrsity schools has a section which is called upon by the Education Departments to lecture on methodology. Students must also spend 60 hours sitting in at lessons in pre-university schools, when they may occasionally be invited to teach. However, the stimulus provided by the new non-university courses will probably mean changes within university teacher training.

Non-Formal and Adult

Each of the larger towns supports a social-cultural centre called a *'Volksuniversiteit'* - a kind of people's college, offering facilities for the non-vocational pursuit of knowledge and culture. These centres tend to be most popular with the middle income groups. In smaller towns there are privately sponsored cultural societies, sometimes subsidised by the municipality, which may meet in hotel halls or in municipal centres.

Evening Classes

Evening classes are available either through the municipal *Volksuniversiteit* (see above) or through private institutes, and are very popular. Those at the private institutes offer a second chance or an alternative route to State examinations for various school leaving certificates, including technical or vocational certificates. Anyone willing to study in this way would tend to be dealing with theory as the private institutes would not have technical or engineering workshops.

Distance Learning

Correspondence courses have existed since about 1890, and are now well established. They meet an increasing demand for refresher training and for the study of new subjects either for improving job prospects or for leisure. The Recognition of Correspondence Course Institutes Act of 1973 introduced State inspection of institutes providing correspondence courses, and put an end to the work of the private Correspondence Course Inspectorate.

The Open University idea has been examined by a government commission and it is likely that correspondence courses, radio, television, tutorials, etc. will be used to offer education at all levels to the public at large. The government has set up a working group to keep under review educational and other problems in this field.

7 EDUCATIONAL ADMINISTRATION

Local Control

The administration of education is largely decentralised. The municipalities and district councils have their own directors of education whose role is largely financial. The largest municipalities have professional educators on their staffs who are able to influence the content of education and recommend to the municipality the approval of books and materials additional to those subsidised and approved by the central government. But even in Amsterdam the powers of the City Education Department are limited. The universities are self-governing with governing body representation consisting of one third academic staff, one third technical and administrative staff, and one third students.

525

ADMINISTRATION OF THE EDUCATION SYSTEM IN THE NETHERLANDS

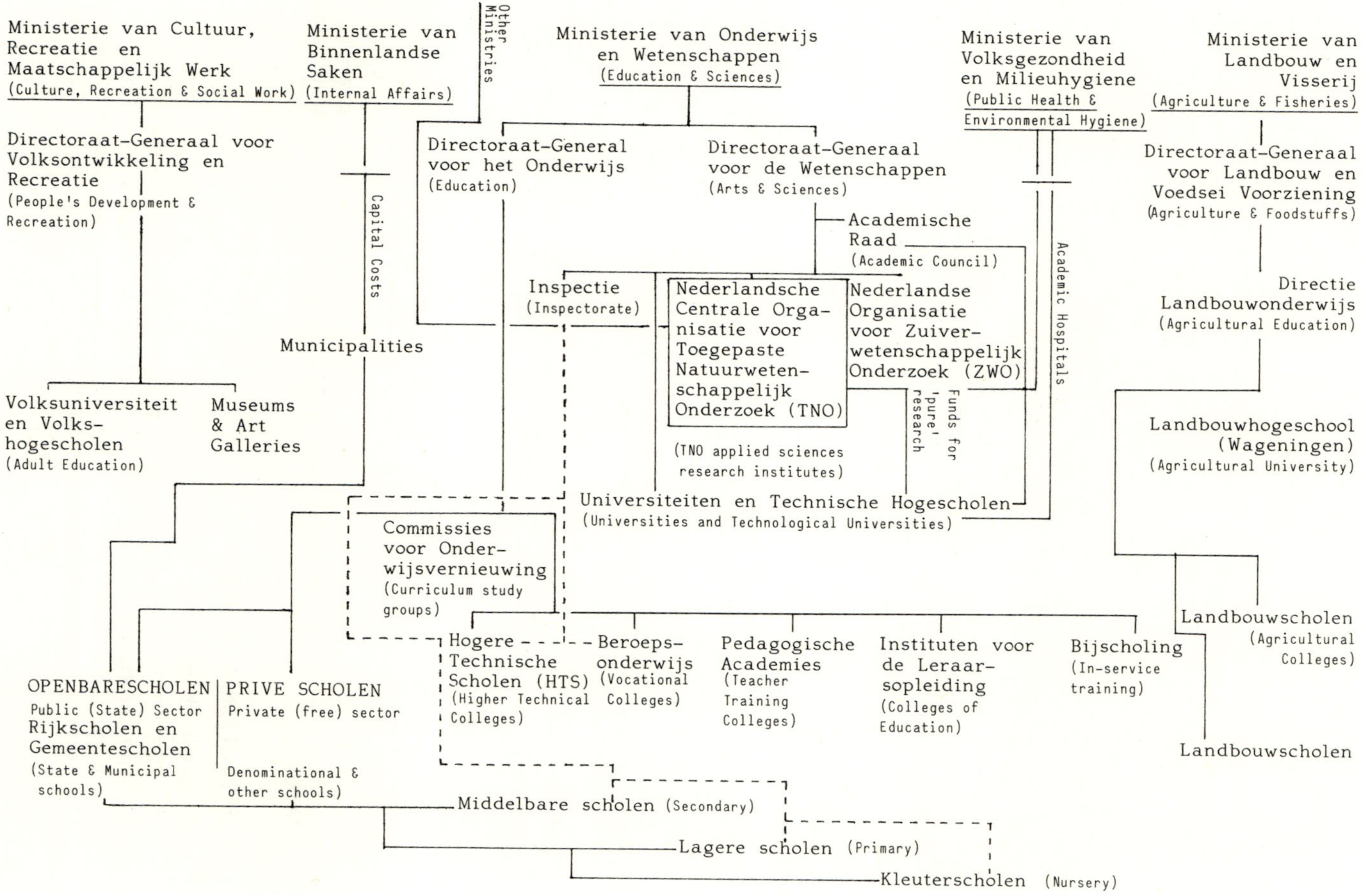

Ministerie van Cultuur, Recreatie en Maatschappelijk Werk (Culture, Recreation & Social Work)
- Directoraat-Generaal voor Volksontwikkeling en Recreatie (People's Development & Recreation)
  - Volksuniversiteit en Volkshogescholen (Adult Education)
  - Museums & Art Galleries

Other Ministries

Ministerie van Binnenlandse Saken (Internal Affairs)
- Capital Costs
- Municipalities

Ministerie van Onderwijs en Wetenschappen (Education & Sciences)
- Directoraat-Generaal voor het Onderwijs (Education)
- Directoraat-Generaal voor de Wetenschappen (Arts & Sciences)
  - Academische Raad (Academic Council)
  - Nederlandse Organisatie voor Zuiver-wetenschappelijk Onderzoek (ZWO) — Funds for 'pure' research
  - Nederlandsche Centrale Organisatie voor Toegepaste Natuurwetenschappelijk Onderzoek (TNO) (TNO applied sciences research institutes)
- Inspectie (Inspectorate)

Ministerie van Volksgezondheid en Milieuhygiene (Public Health & Environmental Hygiene)
- Academic Hospitals

Ministerie van Landbouw en Visserij (Agriculture & Fisheries)
- Directoraat-Generaal voor Landbouw en Voedsel Voorziening (Agriculture & Foodstuffs)
  - Directie Landbouwonderwijs (Agricultural Education)
    - Landbouwhogeschool (Wageningen) (Agricultural University)
    - Landbouwscholen (Agricultural Colleges)
    - Landbouwscholen
    - Bijscholing (In-service training)

Universiteiten en Technische Hogescholen (Universities and Technological Universities)

Beroepsonderwijs (Vocational Colleges)
- Hogere Technische Scholen (HTS) (Higher Technical Colleges)

Commissies voor Onderwijsvernieuwing (Curriculum study groups)

Pedagogische Academies (Teacher Training Colleges)

Instituten voor de Leraaropleiding (Colleges of Education)

OPENBARESCHOLEN Public (State) Sector Rijkscholen en Gemeentescholen (State & Municipal schools)

PRIVE SCHOLEN Private (free) sector Denominational & other schools

Middelbare scholen (Secondary)

Lagere scholen (Primary)

Kleuterscholen (Nursery)

Responsible Ministries

The Minister of Education and Sciences is responsible for legislation in education and for its enforcement. For the schools, the Education Council advises the Minister on parliamentary bills, problems connected with curricula, the reorganisation and improvement of education, and the enforcement of the various acts. For the universities the Minister is advised by the Academic Council. He is assisted by one or more State Secretaries who are, like himself, politically responsible to parliament, and by a permanent staff consisting of a secretary-general, who is responsible for the day-to-day running of the Ministry, two directors-general, one inspector-general, and other advisers, and departmental and divisional heads.

The arts (plastic and performing), museums (which here include art galleries), adult education, youth and community work, physical training, sports recreation, leisure pursuits, social welfare, film, radio and television, are the ultimate responsibility of the Ministry of Cultural Affairs, Recreation and Social Welfare, although in all except film, radio and television the municipalities share some of the responsibilities.

Inspectorate

The schools belong to private societies - the various religious and humanist denominations - and the municipalities or the State. Because there is such in-built divisiveness in educational provision, the Central Government Inspectorate plays an important role in coordination, administration, the setting of standards and the approval of basic books, educational aids, and other materials. It is significant that in practice the government refrains from approving or rejecting the curricula of private primary schools, which are in the majority, though what they do has to be notified to the Government Inspectorate which is expected to ensure common standards. For pre-primary education the country is divided into 28 districts, each with an inspector, the whole supervised by two chief inspectors and an assistant. For primary education there are four regions, each under a chief inspector and fairly evenly divided between 69 inspectors. Pre-university secondary education is divided between six teams each of four inspectors, and general secondary education between 17 inspectors. There are also inspectors for every branch of technical and vocational education and each kind of special education.

8 EDUCATIONAL FINANCE

Education Budget

In 1978 gross central and local government expenditure on education amounted to 8.79% of the Gross National Product; this fell slightly in 1980. As a percentage of the total central government budget, expenditure on education in 1979 was 23.3% and this fell to 21.3% in 1980. It contrasts with 27.4% in 1974.

Allocation of Funds
Expenditure on Education: Distribution by Level
Percentage of Expenditure 1977

Pre-school	First Level	Second Level	Third Level	Other
5.6	19.7	34.6	28.0	12.1

Primary

Ordinary primary education, as governed by the 1920 Elementary Act (now known as Primary) and its regulations, whether public or private, is paid for by the State: teachers' salaries, including social security and other insurance premiums for the statutory number of teachers, and any supernumeraries engaged with the permission of the Minister of Education and Sciences are paid by the Ministry, while the capital and recurrent costs of building, maintaining and equipping schools are met by the municipalities, which are in turn reimbursed by the Ministry of Home Affairs. Pre-primary education is financed in much the same way, though some of the costs are covered by fees, for which there is a means test.

Secondary

Under the Secondary Education Act the Minister determines normally before 1 October what new or projected schools are to qualify for the defrayment of expenses over the next three years. By expenses are understood: salaries, allowances and superannuation contributions of all school personnel; cost of buildings, furniture and equipment; recurrent costs; the costs of religious education or of instruction by representatives of the Humanists' Union. Once a subvention has been made to a school, continuation of financial support depends on the school's conforming to the numerical and other standards laid down by the central government. If, however, a school fails to measure up to these standards, the Ministry of Education and Sciences will refuse its subvention, and the municipality itself will have to bear the cost.

Higher

Whether public or private, all institutions of higher education are required to draw up a development plan every few years for a period to be stipulated by the Minister, as well as an annual budget, to be submitted through the Academic Council to the Minister of Education and Sciences. After receiving the various financial plans the Minister and his colleague, the Minister of Finance, draw up a consolidated plan which is submitted to the Secretary General and is also communicated to each institution for the budget to be considered by its governors.

After the government's contribution has been determined, the Minister approves the budget, possibly with the exception of specific items. Where approval has been withheld, the governors have the right to appeal to the Crown.

The government accepts responsibility for the full approved costs of the State universities, but withholds $1\frac{1}{2}$% of the cost of private universities. Whether State or private, the university must not exceed the accepted norm for equipping and maintaining a university. All State universities have corporate status which allows them control of capital and revenue, though most of it consists of grants from the public treasury. Provisions for students in the way of residences, etc. are fully reimbursed by the government.

Grants

Students may receive a government grant determined according to the student's and parents' means. This is adjusted annually by reference to the cost of living index. Of the grant, 60% is an award and 40% an interest free loan. Parents also have handsome increases in their children's allowances and a reduction in their income tax when they maintain a full time student. One student living at home counts as two children, and one student living away from home counts as three children for children's allowances, which are paid to all parents irrespective of their income. For income tax purposes one student is considered as equal to three children. There are full scholarships for very gifted students. Post-graduate students may receive a government loan if they are doing approved research. Medical students are given loans only, because of their earning potential.

9 DEVELOPMENT AND PLANNING OF THE EDUCATION SYSTEM

Development

In the early days education was sponsored by the Churches, with an emphasis on Latin, and was largely for the wealthier upper and middle classes. The early sixteenth century brought the full force of the Reformation, and the northern Dutch readily became Lutherans or Calvinists. After the Synod of Dordrecht (1618-19), the *Gereformeerde Kerk* (Calvinist) took charge of education, a responsibility not relinquished till 1795, and all teachers were required to signify their allegiance to the new religion. Only in the south were Catholics able to continue to teach without permission. In the eighteenth century, apart from the classical gymnasium leading on to a university for the wealthy, there were ordinary fee-paying schools in the main towns for those destined to work in trade and industry. The larger provinces also started free schools for poor children. From 1863 the gymnasia were supplemented by *hogereburgerscholen* (higher citizen = modern grammar schools). By the end of the century there were also extended elementary schools.

The Napoleonic Education Act of 1806 established religiously neutral State schools, but during the next 100 years there was first a struggle for the right to found confessional private schools, granted in 1857, and then over the question of grants for private schools, resolved in 1917 with the equal financial treatment of State and private schools. Although distorted by confessional conflicts, Dutch schools have traditionally aimed at providing pre-university courses for the nation's leaders and, from the nineteenth century, an elementary education for the lower classes, leading to vocational training in agricultural, maritime, commercial and industrial activities. Since the 1939-45 war the country's twentieth century industrial revolution has been greatly accelerated and has been accompanied by a social revolution. Against this background the need for an all round improvement in education and educational opportunities became apparent to the Dutch.

Educational Objectives and Decrees

The government accepts that the purpose of education is to prepare young people for active participation in the type of society to which it is thought they will belong on reaching maturity. Education must therefore provide opportunities for everyone to realise as fully as possible his intellectual abilities, artistic gifts, and social potential.

The nation's Constitution declares the duty of the government to give constant care to education, and guarantees the freedom of education in respect of both teaching and learning. In prescribing that private schools shall be as well maintained as publicly maintained schools, the Constitution requires that parents shall be given the opportunity of providing their children with the kind of education that conforms to their religious beliefs, their philosophy, their way of life, or the method of education they prefer - exemplified by the proliferation of Dalton, Montessori and Jena schools in the larger towns.

The present school system is based on the following post-war Education Acts:

(i)   Teacher Training College Act 1952

(ii) Pre-Primary Education Act 1955 (in force 1956)

(iii) University Education Act 1961 (replacing the Higher Education Act of 1876)

(iv) Secondary Education Act 1963 (not fully implemented till 1968; an act so comprehensive in its scope that it was popularly referred to as the 'Mammoth Act')

(v)   Apprenticeship Training Act 1966

(vi) Special Education Decree 1967

(vii) Compulsory Education Act 1969 (replacing the Act of 1900)

(viii) Primary Education Bill 1970 (to replace the Elementary Education Act of 1920 and being gradually enacted).

There are also Administrative Orders and Decrees.

Planning and Policy Making

Within the Ministry of Education and Sciences there is the Directorate of Research and Planning which is charged with the task of replanning the whole education system and keeping it under constant review so as to match the changing needs of a progressive society. Since its installation in 1919 the Education Council has been the main advisory body, in the form of a permanent board. The Council now has 80 members, divided into seven sections corresponding to the various branches of education. The members are appointed on a personal basis. The Council advises the Minister of Education and Sciences and – in matters of agricultural education – the Ministry of Agriculture and Fisheries, either at his request or on its own initiative, on problems of a general nature concerning the education that is the responsibility of the ministries concerned.

Consultation

Consultation on education policy takes various forms:

(i) *Organised Consultations*
These take place in the Special Advisory Committee on the Legal Status of Those Engaged in Education (Teaching and Non-teaching Staff). The committee is responsible to the Minister of Education and Sciences and is sub-divided into six departments

(ii) *Lochern Consultations* (named after the town where they take place)
The function of these consultations is a dual one. Firstly, measures for the organisation of education are discussed at various levels with those in the field and secondly the consultations constitute a source of information when it comes to policy making. The consultations are led by the Inspector-general of Education and are in the form of working groups, composed of representatives of the appropriate departments of the Ministry, the inspectorate of the sector concerned, the head teachers' associations, federations of school managements, teachers' organisations, and educational advisory centres. Students in higher vocational education are also included in the working groups for this field. Elementary, secondary and higher agricultural education have their own working groups under the Department of Agricultural Education, whose membership is determined in a similar way to those under the Ministry of Education and Sciences. Representatives of the Ministry of Agriculture and Fisheries also serve on working groups with a coordinating function. The groups work for the various sectors of education. In a few cases they have been replaced by steering committees for secondary and higher vocational education. The committees act as a link between the institutions and the Ministry

(iii)   *Central Consultative Committee*
This committee is composed of 24 representatives of the teaching organisations. Consultation is primarily concerned with plans for the solution of the major problems in education such as the training of secondary teachers, integrated education for the 12 to 15 year olds, etc.

Reform

The didactive reform of education is largely entrusted to teacher advisory centres which deal with the content of education and teaching method. There were many such centres after 1945, tending to specialise and pulling in different directions but, following new grant regulations, three national teacher advisory centres were created in 1966 - Protestant, Catholic and State - and each has its regional or location sub-centres, while there is coordination between the three national centres. Teachers' subject associations also initiate and cooperate in educational improvement. Syllabus revision is being gradually undertaken through permanent commissions set up by the government, such commissions being linked for convenience with a university educational research centre. An important instrument for educational reform is the in-service retraining of teachers and the provision of refresher courses. A special branch of the Ministry has been set up to organise such courses, and is headed by the Director of the Department of Teacher Retraining.

Research

A government-established Educational Research Institute opened in 1966. The Institute funds commissions, coordinates and supports educational research but undertakes none directly. The Institute established the central test-devising institute, the Development Centre for Educational Technology, and various units for curriculum development. Since the founding in 1963 of the first educational research centre at the Eindhoven University of Technology, similar centres have been developed at all universities. The main fields of research are concerned with syllabi, the democratisation of education, achievement testing, teacher guidance, pupil guidance, and educational technology.

10 THE SYSTEM IN OPERATION
Current Trends

Examinations

It is thought that following reforms now in progress - such as child centred learning at the primary stage, integrated teaching, compulsory and optional subjects at the secondary stage, and the abolition of repeating a class - it will prove necessary to revise the whole system of examinations. Examinations have already been abandoned at the end of the primary school in favour of testing and guidance based on school records and recommendations.

Curriculum

Units for secondary curriculum and syllabus reform have been officially established, and work is in progress towards the harmonisation of curricula and examinations through experiments in integrated and differentiated education. There are so many difficulties in devising suitably integrated curricula and in satisfying so many equally earnest educational reformers that change is likely to be very gradual.

Research

Because of the increased number of students and the rising costs and complexity of equipment, the government has been re-appraising the value of research within the universities and is likely to bring about a transfer to research institutes and industry. For cost effectiveness, priorities will have to be determined, inter-university cooperation will be required, and the avoidance of duplication of cost and effort by sharing of research tasks between the universities themselves, and between the universities and research institutes. There is likely to be a call for greater cooperation in expensive research between the Netherlands and other EEC countries, notably Britain.

Universities

The second oldest university, Franeker in Friesland, was closed by Napoleon. The nearest university for the Friesians is Groningen. There is now a move afoot to establish a Friesian University in Leeuwarden, the provincial capital, where there is already a nucleus in the form of a college of adult education, a faculty of social science opened in 1972, and a teacher training institute shared with Groningen since 1971.

REFERENCES AND FURTHER READING

Much of the information in this summary has been drawn from the latest available publications of the Documentation Department of the Ministry of Education and Sciences. These are not as up-to-date as we would wish but wherever possible the information has been considered in relation to the current situation.

Date	Title	Docinform
7.1968	Democratisation of education in the Netherlands	226
3.1969	Apprenticeship training	234
3.1969	Nautical training in the Netherlands	242
6.1969	School system in the Netherlands	245
10.1969	The educational institutes for early school leavers in the Netherlands	250

Date	Title	Docinform
9.1970	Educational development in the Netherlands in 1968-1969-1970	265
7.1971	Training teachers and head teachers for pre-primary schools in the Netherlands	281E
10.1972	Primary school teacher training	288
10.1973-2.1974	Outline of vocational education policy in the Netherlands	296E
1973/4	The education of the 16-19 age group in the Netherlands school system	299E
3.1974	Secondary school teacher training in the Netherlands	300E
5.1974	Expenditure on vocational education in the Netherlands	301E
3.1975	Basic documentary material covring education in the Netherlands	304
4.1975	Educational development in the Netherlands	302E
11.1975	Commercial education in the Netherlands	309E
1.1976	The development and position of vocational training in the Netherlands	308E
1.1976	Education and training for migrants in the Netherlands	301E
3.1976	The Secondary School, first stage ("Middenschool") in the Netherlands	311E
1977	Bibliography of non-Dutch publications on education and science policy in the Netherlands 1965/75	313E
1.1978	Student-trainee schemes consultative document	1E
1.1978	Teaching migrants with a special reference to language teaching	2E
7.1978	Special Education Memorandum	3E
9.1978	Special education in the Netherlands	317E
6.1979	Apprenticeship training in the Netherlands	321E

Structure of the Education System in Netherlands

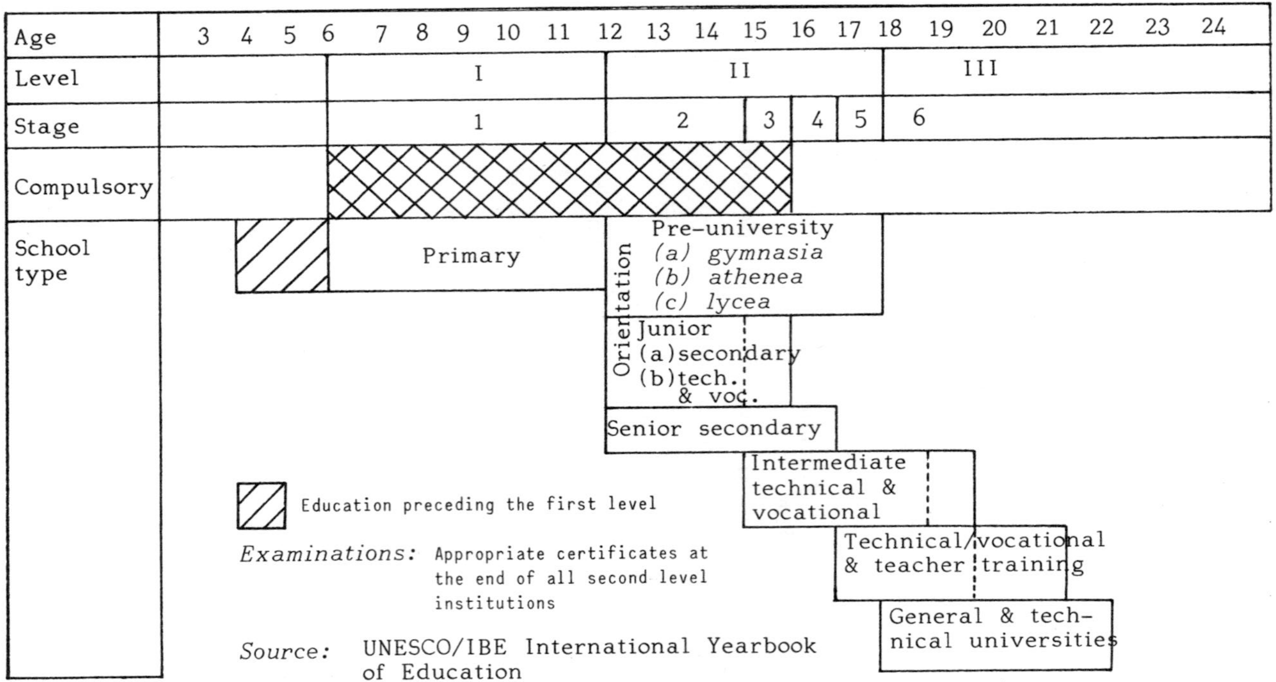

Age	3	4	5	6	7	8	9	10	11	12	13	14	15	16	17	18	19	20	21	22	23	24
Level						I						II					III					
Stage						1					2		3	4	5	6						
Compulsory																						
School type																						

School types:
- Primary
- Pre-university (a) gymnasia (b) athenea (c) lycea
- Junior (a) secondary (b) tech. & voc.
- Orientation
- Senior secondary
- Intermediate technical & vocational
- Technical/vocational & teacher training
- General & technical universities

Education preceding the first level

Examinations: Appropriate certificates at the end of all second level institutions

Source: UNESCO/IBE International Yearbook of Education

Compulsory Education: Age Limits 6-16 Duration (years) 10
Entrance age to pre-school education: 4

THE NETHERLANDS BASIC STATISTICS	1960	1970	1975	1978 (approx.)
1 Total population (000)	11,480	13,032	13,598	13,936
% female	50	50	50	50
2 % population 0-14 years	30.1	27.3	...	24.0
% female	49	49	49	49
3 Enrolment, all levels	2,271,578	2,699,870	3,025,078	3,101,118
% female	47	46	47	47
First level	1,415,703	1,462,376	1,453,467	1,413,277
% female	48	49	49	49
Second level	749,646	1,006,327	1,283,585	1,367,340
% female	47	45	47	47
Third level	106,229	231,167	288,026	320,501
% female	26	28	33	35
4 Teachers, all levels	...	...	...	...
% female	...	...	...	...
First level	41,633	39,243	52,700	55,362
% female	52	49	46	45
Second level	...	...	...	...
% female	...	...	...	...
Third level	...	...	...	...
% female	...	...	...	...
5 Public expenditure on education				
Total (000) Guilders	2,006,000	8,874,000	18,096,000	21,968,000
As % of GNP	4.7	7.7	8.7	8.4
As % of public expenditure				25.4
6 % enrolment (MF) by level	100	100	100	100
First level	62	54	48	45
Second level	33	37	42	44
Third level	5	9	10	11
% enrolment (F) by level	100	100	100	100
First level	65	58	51	48
Second level	33	37	43	44
Third level	3	5	7	8
7 Entrance age: Duration of				
First level education	6:6	6:6	6:6	6:6
Second level education	12:6	12:6	12:6	12:6
8 Enrolment ratios (MF)				
First level	105	102	101	101
Second level	58	75	90	92
Third level	13.18	19.51	25.93	28.84
Enrolment ratios (F)				
First level	104	102	101	102
Second level	56	69	86	89
Third level	6.88	11.12	17.34	20.47

Norway

CONTENTS

1	Geography	538
2	Population	540
3	Society and Culture	541
4	History and Politics	542
5	The Economy	544
6	The Education System	546
7	Educational Administration	555
8	Educational Finance	558
9	Development and Planning of the Education System	559
10	The System in Operation	559

Norway is a social democracy but a Labour government has been in office with brief interludes during World War Two and more recently. Nevertheless the reform of second level education along comprehensive lines reflects the social egalitarian objectives of the Labour party and has taken place without highly politicised debate. A feature of the system is that compulsory education lasts for nine years and is provided in a basic unified comprehensive school *(grunnskole)*. This form of comprehensive school has emerged, as in most European countries, from a selective system of second level education. Selection was for some time restricted to the second stage of second level schools which enjoyed very different reputations. Alongside the *gymnasium* were vocational, commercial and technical schools. There was dissatisfaction with the differential esteem accorded to the various types of school - with the *gymnasium* preparing pupils for university entrance enjoying the highest status. Between 1976 and 1979 a comprehensive reorganisation of second stage, second level schools (upper secondary schools) was designed to integrate provision across the academic/vocational range of schools. Differentiation is maintained through a curriculum organised into eight study courses of which the general studies option *(allmonnfag)* most closely resembles the former academic *(gymnasium)* curriculum. Most courses include a one or two year basic course followed by one or two more years of specialised studies geared either to entrance to higher education or to specific jobs. The possibility of offering all these options depends to some extent on the size of the school. The nature of the country and general principles help to explain why an optimum maximum school size is set at 450.

The fact that large numbers of people live in isolated rural areas indeed helps to explain the emergence of a highly centralised system of administration designed to ensure as much equality of provision as possible. The historically close connections between Church and State remain symbolised in a Ministry of Church and Education, which lays down minimum standards for buildings, equipment and class size. Other ministries are responsible for some of the vocational schools and the administration of the system is being devolved to regional and local authorities. How this will affect equality of provision remains to be seen in spite of the growing sums of money allocated by the central government to education.

In the interests of promoting the maximum opportunity for children regardless of their socio-economic background or geographical location, pre-school opportunities have been expanded, research concentrates on curricula and methods of teaching and to integrate children with special needs into the normal schools. Teachers are given incentives to stay in the rural and northern areas. These trends show attention to the socio-economic and geographical differences rather than linguistic and religious differences that influence equality in the Norwegian system.

The Editor

1 GEOGRAPHY

Topography

Of those countries whose history, economic development and moulding of national character have been shaped by their geography, Norway must lay claim to being one of the best examples. It covers an area of 324,000 square kilometres (125,000 square miles) - 193,000 sq km if Spitsbergen and Bear Island are also included - and spreads over 1,760 km from north to south between latitudes 57°N and 71°N. It has a coastline of 21,000 km because of the west coast fjords and islands. Nearly three quarters of the landmass is made up of barren rocks, mountain ranges and arctic tundra, 24% is covered by forests and barely 4% is suitable for tilled arable land. Norway's educational organisation and the way of life of her people can only be seen in the light of these physical characteristics.

Climate

Climate undoubtedly affects the people and their occupations. Although one third of the country is above the Arctic Circle, Norway has the largest positive temperature anomaly on the surface of the globe with temperatures in the Arctic Circle often higher than those further east or south. The east of Norway, including Oslo, has a more continental climate ranging from -18°C (0°F) in winter to about 29°C (84°F) in summer.

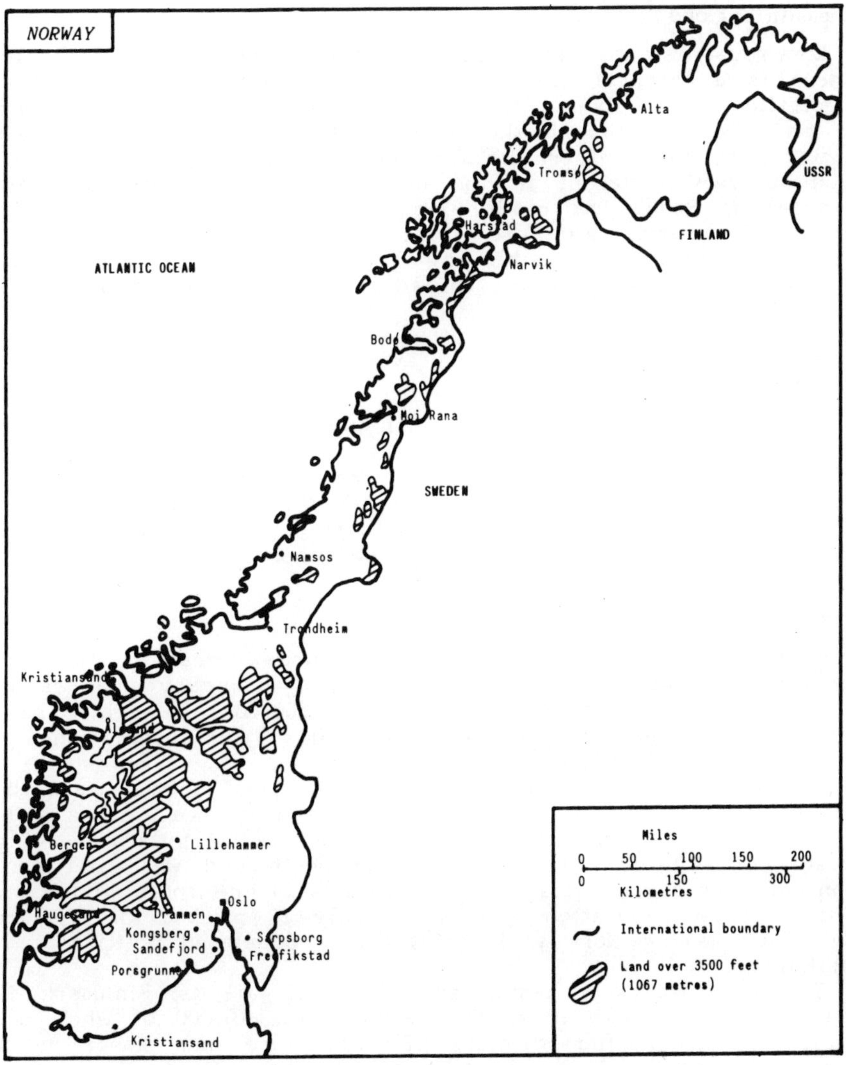

NORWAY
ATLANTIC OCEAN
Alta
Tromsø
USSR
Harstad
FINLAND
Narvik
Bodø
Moi Rana
SWEDEN
Namsos
Trondheim
Kristiansund
Ålesund
Bergen
Lillehammer
Haugesund
Drammen
Oslo
Kongsberg
Sandefjord
Sarpsborg
Fredrikstad
Porsgrunn
Kristiansand
Miles
0 50 100 150 200
0 150 300
Kilometres
International boundary
Land over 3500 feet (1067 metres)

Nevertheless, everywhere winter means snow, long nights, a few hours twilight and little sunshine for several months; in the summer the reverse is the case. Rainfall is greatest in the west, with 200 cm or more in Bergen.

Communications

Enormous distances make transport and communications difficult. There is a total of 4,257 km of railway, more than half of it electrified, and about 78,000 km of road, of which 25,000 km is main road. Although the network of roads, railways and air services in the southern half of the country is good, the situation is very different in the north. The railway network terminates at Bodø. The roads along the west coast are frequently broken by fjords and are linked by ferries. Certain regions are only easily accessible by plane; others by boat. Such obstacles have hampered the spread of post-secondary education.

2 POPULATION

Growth

The population in 1801 was just under one million. Although there was a steady increase in the nineteenth century much of this was offset by emigration to the USA. By 1930 the population had reached 2.8 million and by 1970 it was 3.8 million. In 1979 it was estimated at just over 4 million. The average increase in recent years has been just under 1% per annum.

Distribution

Of the present population 45% live in urban areas. Oslo, which expanded rapidly partly as a result of boundary changes in 1948, had a population of almost 500,000 in 1980 while only two other towns, Bergen and Trondheim, have populations of over 200,000 and 100,000 respectively.

By far the majority of people live in small communities. The difficulties of communication and the relatively small areas suitable for habitation have led to a scattered population living mostly in isolated communities in the north and west and more concentrated communities in the lowlands of the south and east. The average population density is only 12 per sq km (32 per sq mile) making Norway the most thinly populated political unit in Europe.

The most sparsely populated region of all is Finnmark in the north where about 79,000 people live, 20,000 of whom are Lapps. Although the majority of Lapps are now fishermen or farmers, several thousand still live nomadic lives. It is from this region that depopulation has been most acute in post-war years, as people have moved southwards, towards large communities. A reaction to this migration, and the problems of centralisation and urbanisation in the southern cities, has recently set in and the government, faced with the prospect of neglecting the north or of developing it, is now committed to developing it. Educational policy in recent years has been designed to reinforce this commitment.

3 SOCIETY AND CULTURE

Patterns of Living

One of the most impressive aspects of society in Norway is the apparent lack of class distinction. This has partly been brought about by taxation aimed at social levelling, but generally results from a common sense of sharing and togetherness, and a determination to make democracy and democratic sharing really work. This sense of democratic sharing is greatly encouraged in schools and women have complete equality with men. Nevertheless, the Norwegians are hardy, independent, home-loving and conservative. There are generation conflicts, mostly commonly revealed in the urban areas, as in all Western societies. To a lesser extent there are urban/rural disparities - progressive versus conservative views. The most important recent manifestation of these differing views was the referendum held in 1972 on the possibility of future membership of the EEC. the recent immigration to Norway of Asians has set up some tensions which have come as a surprise to a country proud of its record of tolerance and commitment to Third World development.

Social Development

Norway has a highly developed system of social security - encompassing help to unmarried mothers, illegitimate children, children from broken homes, the aged, the mentally and physically handicapped, and the unemployed. State legislation regulates working conditions by setting maximum working hours, stipulating safeguards against accidents and disease, and guaranteeing minimum paid holidays, though the foreign workers employed in offshore oil exploration and development complain of their 'second class citizen' status. Unions are industrial rather than craft based, with a consequent reduction of inter-union disputes, and collective wage agreements are frequently negotiated for two-year periods, with built-in cost of living adjustments and safeguards on negotiation and arbitration. If any dispute breaks out that cannot be settled mutually it must be brought before the Labour Court, established in 1925. One result of this cooperation between government, employers and workers is relative harmony and stability in industrial relations.

Language

Norwegian has two distinct and rival forms - *bokmål* (book language - a derivative of Danish) and *nynorsk* (new Norwegian). They are sometimes referred to as *riksmål* (national language) and *landsmål* (countrywide language). Although both languages are legally equal and both are taught in schools, 75% of all children use *bokmål* as their main language. In addition there are urban and rural dialects. Whereas *nynorsk* has its greatest strength in the west it is really an artificial development that grew up in the last century as an attempt to create a purely 'Norwegian' language independent of all Danish influence. So far all attempts to blend the two languages into *samnorsk*, a common language, have met with vigorous opposition.

English is the main foreign language in Norway, easily surpassing German and French, and is the language used by Norwegians in diplomacy and trade. It is introduced as a compulsory language in all schools from the fourth year. At the second level it is second only in importance to Norwegian.

Religion

Christianity was introduced into Norway during the eleventh century by the kings Olav Trygvasson and Olav Haraldsson, who had come into contact with it during Viking raids in Western Europe. Only gradually, however, did it replace the Norse deities and become the accepted religion of the country. There were frequent clashes between the Roman Catholic Church and the monarchy in the following centuries and at the time of the Reformation (1536) the Lutheran brand of Protestantism became the State religion.

Today the Evangelical Lutheran Church of Norway is the State church, though religious freedom and tolerance are enacted in the Constitution. As much as 95% of the population belong to it, though the number of practising Christians is declining. Even so, 75% of all marriages are still performed by the Church. By law the King must be a member of the Church of Norway of which he is head. With the advice of the Minister of Church and Education he appoints all members of the clergy of the Established Church. Their salaries and pensions are paid by the State. Since 1956 women have been given equal status in the Church and the first woman minister was appointed in 1961. Administratively the Church is divided into bishoprics (9), deaneries (91), parishes (567) and congregational districts (1,053). Far from being an insignificant influence in Norwegian life, the Church still has a vital role to play. Norway boasts the highest number of missionaries per head of population and the close links between the Church and educational provision can be seen in the common administration of the Ministry of Church and Education.

4 HISTORY AND POLITICS

Origins

Norway has been inhabited for 14,000 years. By the beginning of the Christian era there were already elements from central and eastern Europe intermingled in small agrarian communities. These began to merge into small kingdoms during the eighth and ninth centuries and were united into one kingdom under Harald Haarfagre in 872. Even so, because of mixed marriages between the rulers of Denmark, Sweden and Norway, and in the face of constant Danish attacks, it was difficult to maintain any sense of unity. During the fourteenth century the kingdoms of Sweden and Norway were united and by the end of the century Denmark was added, through Queen Margaret, wife of Haakon VI (1355-80). Because she herself was Danish it was natural that all important offices should be allocated to Danes. In spite of uprisings in both Norway and Sweden, Norway became, to all intents and purposes, a part of Denmark from 1442 to 1814.

Nineteenth and Twentieth Centuries

The union of Norway and Denmark came to an end in 1814 but from then until 1905 Norway was controlled by Swedish monarchs. The dissolution of this Union in 1905 after increasing tensions, was unanimously endorsed by a national plebiscite: Norway regained its independence under a popularly elected constitutional monarch, Prince Charles of Denmark (Haakon VII), whose wife, Maud, was the youngest daughter of Edward VII of England. (On his death in 1957 King Haakon was succeeded by the present King, Olav V.) During World War One Norway remained neutral, though her merchant fleet proved of inestimable value to Britain, and in the immediate post-war years she was bogged down by political stalemate and economic depression. With the outbreak of World War Two Norway again stated a policy of strict neutrality but this was ignored by Hitler and in April 1940 German forces invaded the country. The royal family took refuge in Britain where they established a government in exile, the Germans appointed a Norwegian collaborator, Quisling, as Prime Minister of Norway and the people, though unprepared for war and occupation, took to underground resistance on a large scale.

Political Development

A Labour government has been in office since 1935, with a break of five years during World War Two and two brief interludes subsequently. The referendum on whether Norway was to join the EEC, held in September 1972, gave rise to much discussion and cut across party and social divisions. A strong feeling of nationalism mixed with an anxiety over possible economic domination by the United States, Germany and multi-national companies influenced the vote, but one of the major effects was the fragmentation of hitherto traditional political parties. The (traditional) Labour Party was returned to power in September 1973 with a reduced vote, and formed a minority government. In 1977 a general election gave the Labour Party and its ally, the Socialist Left Party, an aggregate majority of just one seat enabling the minority Labour government to continue in office. The Conservative Party formed a new government in 1981.

Government Organisation

Norway is a constitutional and hereditary monarchy based on the laws of 1814. Executive power is vested in the King and is exercised through a Council of State, consisting of the Prime Minister and seven other Councillors, all of whom are members of parliament (the *Storting*) but have no voting rights. Parliament meets for four years and cannot be dissolved by the King. Its 155 members are elected on the basis of proportional representation and divide themselves into two, the *Lagting* (38 members – roughly equivalent to an upper house) and the *Odelsting* (the rest). Legislation is generally initiated in the *Odelsting*. The country is subdivided into 19 counties (*fylker*) and about 50 urban and 400 rural districts each with an elected authority in control. Considerable scope is given to these authorities whose revenue comes from local income tax, municipal trading profits and State grants.

International Relations

In international affairs Norway has shown considerable zeal in promoting the United Nations, of which she was a founder member (and for which she provided the first Secretary-General, Trygve Lie) and in providing aid to the developing world. She joined NATO in 1949 after plans for a Nordic military alliance had collapsed, and was a founder member of the Nordic Council (1952) which is designed to develop close social, economic and cultural links between the Nordic countries, allowing for free movement of trade and persons. Norway was also a founder member of EFTA (1959) and after a popular rejection of its membership of the EEC in 1972 established a harmonious relationship with the Community.

5 THE ECONOMY

Economic Development

From the mid-1850s the Norwegian economy began to change considerably. subsistence farming began to give way to a freer market economy. The railways and steamships began to link different parts of the country more closely together; the urban population increased by 200% between 1850 and 1905 and the number of industrial workers rose from 12,000 to 80,000. The restoration of Norwegian independence coincided with fundamental changes in the economic life of the country: the harnessing of hydroelectric power and the beginning of an industrial revolution; the growth of organised labour, industrial disputes and the establishment of a political Labour Party. Labour governments have gradually initiated complete or partial State control of mines, transport, and some industries. A system of licences, quotas, price controls and subsidies is used to influence the national economy. Under their mixed economy the Norwegians' standard of living has soared to one of the highest in the world. Between 1950 and 1964 the GNP rose by 173%. Investment has in the past been mainly in hydroelectric evelopment, industry, the mining of mineral resources and shipbuilding. By 1960 Norway had the fourth largest merchant fleet in the world and shipping has continued to be one of the country's main sources of income. However, in recent years considerable investment has been made in offshore oil and gas extraction and in the petroleum industry. Norway is now a net exporter of oil and the expectation of oil revenues has enabled her to borrow heavily partly to maintain high employment at a time of world economic recession which has affected the traditional shipping and shipbuilding industries.

A corollary has been the steady inflation of manufacturing costs which has seriously hampered Norway's ability to compete in export markets.

Agriculture

Less than 3% of the land area is farmed and the geographical structure and climate both make farming difficult. Under these conditions farming can only be undertaken by a few, and other traditional occupations, notably fishing, forestry and the merchant navy, still absorb quite large numbers. In 1976 agriculture and forestry employed 8.5% of the workforce and contributed about 5% of GNP. Farms are generally small holdings and dairy farming and fodder production are important. Agriculture is heavily protected and imports are strictly controlled. Forestry products are a major export and the industry is becoming increasingly mechanised. Fishing has declined in importance. However, it is still the main livelihood for the people of many of the coastal villages and the quantity of fish caught by Norwegian fishing vessels is greater than any other European country except the USSR.

Industry

Industry and commerce have steadily gained in importance and now employ 26% and 13% of the labour force respectively. Between them they account for well over half of the GNP. Major developments have taken place in the electrochemical and electrometallurgical industries, in the mining of iron ores, copper and zinc, the processing of aluminium, and the expansion of paper and pulping industry. Manufacturing and mining contributed over 28% of GNP in 1976 and industry employed nearly two million workers in 1979. Because of the successful exploitation of large scale hydroelectric power schemes, Norway has been able to develop power-intensive industries. Food processing, engineering and shipbuilding are also important. Paper making has experienced setbacks owing to a reduction of world demand. However, the exploitation of North Sea oil should expand petrochemical and oil based industries. Norway's reserves have been estimated as 3,000 to 4,000 million tons, but the government is controlling the pace at which this is developed. It is suspected that large reserves of crude oil might be under the sea bed west of Tromsø and exploration in the far north, despite opposition from environmental lobbies, is just beginning.

Economic Situation

The Norwegian economy has remained very stable amid recent recessions and booms everywhere else and this situation seems likely to continue, as she benefits from her resources of oil, gas, and hydroelectric power. However, because Norway has to import most of her raw materials and many manufacturing products, she constantly has a balance of trade deficit (though this is to some extent offset by 'invisible' earnings in the form of shipping and insurance). It is hoped that development of the regions, especially in the north, may to some extent help generate economic growth, particularly if new mineral resources are discovered but, like many other countries, Norway's real strength lies in utilising her manpower to the full, and the education system, particularly in the vocational/technical fields, is designed to do exactly that. the declining numbers of people living in small communities and remote areas tend to rely very heavily on their own resources and a large percentage are self-employed. Nevertheless, without State aid and helpful cooperation between government and private enterprise in such ventures as road building and hydroelectric power schemes, many Norwegians would find it hard to survive economically.

6 THE EDUCATION SYSTEM

Academic Year

The academic year runs from August to June (35 to 38 weeks) divided into two semesters, 'autumn' and 'spring', separated by Christmas and the long summer break. In addition, short holidays are taken in the autumn, mid-February and Easter (somewhat longer).

Pre-School

Pre-school education for the under-7s is voluntary and is provided in the main by kindergartens *(barnehager)*. In addition there are supervised outdoor playgrounds *(barneparker)* as well as in some municipalities in-schooling programmes for 6-year old children *(førskole klasser)*. The number of kindergartens expanded considerably in the 1970s and something over 12% of children between 0 and 7 years, or 25% of the 6-year age group taken separately are in attendance, mostly in urban areas. the aim of the government as expressed in the 1975 Act on Kindergartens was to step up the provision to double the places by the end of 1981, i.e. making provision for 25% of the 0 to 7-year old age range. The 1975 Act charged the local authorities with the responsibility for planning the expansion of kindergartens but also for deciding the rate at which expansion should take place. Clearly the danger is that the poorer rural communities will continue to lag behind affluent centres like Oslo.

A 'typical' kindergarten consists of about 16 children aged 3 to 7, presided over (ideally) by a qualified pre-school teacher assisted by two to three adults. Kindergartens may be owned either by the local authority or privately (though in the latter case are usually in receipt of substantial official funding). In either case they are managed by a committee which includes representatives of the parents, the staff and the local authority. The Act defines the purpose of kindergartens as being the provision of a structured environment for children with an emphasis upon play and social contact with other children and adults with a view to developing tolerance and self-expression. The supervised playground *(barnepark)* is for the children who would otherwise have few opportunities for outdoor play in the company of other children.

Basic (Compulsory)

Compulsory education lasts for nine years (age 7-16) and is provided by the basic (unified comprehensive) school *(grunnskole)*. This is divided into two stages; the junior *(barnetrinnet)* for classes 1 to 6 and the youth *(ungdomstrinnet)* for classes 7 to 9 (with an optional tenth class in some cases) which is roughly comparable to the British junior comprehensive school. The normal pattern then is six years at a *barneskole* followed by three years at an *ungdomsskole*. Schools are coeducational and 75% of them use the *bokmål* version of Norwegian. The proportion of pupils in private *grunnskoler* is tiny.

Teaching hours are normally from 0830 to 1400 hours for five days a week - divided into 45 minute periods separated by short play breaks and a longer 'sandwich' break at around 1100. Seven-year old children are in school for just 15 periods a week though this builds up to a maximum of 30 in the sixth grade. Teachers in the *barneskole* for the most part are trained in colleges of education *(laererskoler* or *pedagogiske høgskoler)* and in the *ungdomsskole* they often have additional studies on top of their teaching qualification (or may have received all of their higher education at a university).

The work of the *grunnskole* is regulated by the 'model plan' *(mønsterplan)* produced by a committee appointed by the Ministry of Education in 1971/72. The 1974 edition contains nearly 400 pages and is divided into: a general part outlining the basic school's duties and modus operandi; and a specific part which deals with the various school subjects and topics. The general part is based upon the social purposes which basic schooling, as defined in the 1969 Education Act, is designed to promote, viz:

> "to make pupils good members of the community . . . to help give pupils a Christian and moral upbringing; to develop their mental and physical abilities; and to give them a good general knowledge so that they may become useful and self-reliant human beings both at home and in the community."

The social egalitarian objectives of the Norwegian State underpin the organisation of schools along comprehensive lines and emphasise the concomitant commitment to mixed ability teaching ('individualised learning') and to the 'common core' approach to the curriculum. Thus all pupils follow the same timetable throughout the first seven years of *grunnskole* with limited subject options in grades 8 (five periods) and 9 (ten periods). The subjects in the curriculum are: religion, Norwegian, mathematics, music, art and craft, physical education, local studies (grade 1-3), housecraft (grade 7) and English, science and social studies (from grade 4 onwards). In the *ungdomsskole* one period a week is set aside for pupil participation in the class council. In addition to these obligatory subjects there are certain obligatory topics which must be covered (traffic training, alcohol, drugs, tobacco, environment, careers, school councils, family life, consumer education, nutrition, first aid, dental health, and sex education), together with certain non-obligatory topics (drama, gardening and plant care). The optional subjects which may be taken in grades 8 and 9 cover amongst others extra foreign languages, music, art, office work, typing, fishing and seamanship and agriculture.

At the end of basic schooling pupils sit written examinations in some subjets (usually two from among Norwegian, mathematics, english and science). These, together with oral examinations and teachers' assessments in the remaining subjects *(standpunkt karakterer)*, produce a final mark. Recently there has been keen controversy between those who wish for social and pedagogic reasons to abolish assessment and the system of awarding marks (not just at 16 but throughout the school system) and those who wish to retain them.

Special

In 1976 the regulations concerning special education for the handicapped were incorporated into the *Grunnskole* Act. As a result the municipalities became responsible for ensuring proper instruction for handicapped children by arranging remedial instruction on an individual or class basis within the normal day schools or by providing separate schools. As far as possible the aim is to integrate handicapped children into the regular *grunnskole*.

Upper Second Level Schools

Upper secondary education *(videregående opplaering)* is defined as post-basic schooling principally for the 16 to 19 age range. In 1975 over 140,000 pupils in this category were receiving full time education in 'grammar' *(gymnasium)*, vocational, commercial and technical schools. The 1974 Law (effective from 1976) on *videregående opplaering* reflected the dissatisfaction felt with a system which conferred unequal status on different types of schools, caused undue specialisation, and was felt to be too rigid. Between 1976 and 1979, therefore, a 'comprehensive reorganisation' of upper secondary schools took place to integrate educational provision across the academic-vocational spectrum. The main objective was to give everyone who had completed compulsory schooling the right and opportunity to follow courses for three years (or four in some cases) at the upper second level stage and to allow pupils increased flexibility both in combining subjects and choosing courses (though the entitlement to upper secondary schooling need not be taken in three consecutive years nor immediately after leaving basic school).

The curriculum is organised into eight study courses of which the general studies option *(allmennfag)* most nearly resembles the former *gymnasium* curriculum. The remaining seven are vocational courses in aesthetics, fishing and maritime subjects, trade and office work, handicraft and industry, physical education, home economics and health and social subjects. Most study courses consist of a one- or two-year basic course *(grunnkurs)* and a one- or two-year further education course *(videregående-kurs)*. The vocational courses are job oriented and practical in their nature whilst the general studies course *(allmennfag)* is followed by the majority of pupils wishing to proceed to higher education. The *allmennfag* course consists of obligatory subjects (Norwegian, modern languages, social sciences, mathematics, natural science and physical education) which form the bulk of the one-year *grunnkurs*. In the second and third years whilst up to 50% of the timetable continues to be filled by the compulsory subjects (with the exception of mathematics and natural sciences) candidates elect to specialise along one of four branches or lines *(linjer)*. The subjects of the four lines are:

(a) *natural sciences:*
physics, chemistry, biology and mathematics

(b) *social sciences:*
history, geography, social and business economics, law and mathematics

(c) *languages:*
English, French, German or a new language not previously studied in the basic school

(d) *music:*
followed by very few students.

An alternative pattern consists of a two-year basic course followed by either a one-year supplementary course, a transfer into the second year of the general studies course or a transfer into the second year of a vocational studies course. The two-year basic course covers substantially the same ground as the first years of the general studies course and a vocational course though with rather more scope for selection of subjects. About a quarter of the age group may opt for this pattern.

The need to utilise existing premises coupled with an optimum maximum size for a *videregående skole* of 450 makes it impossible for any single school to offer all ten study courses. Entry to *videregående skole* is determined by criteria decided on by the Ministry and the county authorities and may include the assessment mark obtained in the basic school, relevant experience, teacher recommendation and the pupil's motivation. It is expected that up to 85% of the age range will be entering the *videregående skoler* (two thirds of them on vocational courses) though not all will be able to follow the study courses of their first choice.

Examinations in *videregående skoler* are based on 'study guides' produced, or being produced, by the *Radet for Videregående Opplaering* (the Council for Upper Secondary Education). The general studies course currently terminates with examinations for the *examen artium*, which consists of between three and five written papers which are externally marked with oral examinations and internal teacher assessments. It is due to be replaced and one canvassed possibility is that all written examinations will be abolished in favour of internal assessment with external moderation.

Higher

Higher education in Norway is provided in what can be characterised as national and regional institutions. The former consist of the universities and university level national colleges and the latter of the 'regional colleges' viz *distriktshøgskoler* (district colleges), *pedagogiske høgskoler* (teacher training colleges) and advanced vocational institutions (of engineering, social services, music and advanced nursing). Entrance to higher education is based on the *examen artium* or its equivalent though relevant experience is taken into account whilst certain university faculties which are heavily over-subscribed (such as medicine and technology) operate a *numerus clausus* and insist upon additional qualifications.

Universities and University Level Institutions

There are four multi-faculty universities together with specialised institutions, viz:

>University of Oslo
>University of Bergen
>University of Trondheim
>University of Tromsø
>Agricultural University of Norway *(Norges Landbrukshøgskole)*
>Free Faculty of Theology *(Menighetsfakultet)*
>State Veterinary College *(Norges Veterinaerhøgskole)*
>School of Architecture *(Arkitekthøgskolen)*
>Norwegian College of Physical Education and Sports *(Norges Idrettshøgskole)*
>State Academy of Music *(Musikkhøgskolen)*
>National Academy of Arts *(Statens Kunstakademi)*
>Norwegian School of Economics and Business Administration *(Norges Handelshøgskole)*
>Norwegian College of Fishing *(Norges Fiskerihøgskole)*

The University of Trondheim came into existence in 1969 as a result of the amalgamation of the Norwegian Institute of Technology *(Norges Tekniske Høgskole)*, the State College for Teachers *(Norges Laererhøgskole)* and the Royal Norwegian Society for Sciences *(Kongelige Norske Vitenskaplige Selskab)*. Oslo University dates back to 1811, Bergen to 1948 while Tromsø is the newest, being founded in 1972 as an attempt to provide an infrastructure of higher learning north of the Arctic Circle. In 1978/79 there were over 41,000 students in these institutions of whom around 20,000 were in the University of Oslo and over 7,000 in each of Bergen and Trondheim universities.

Students at the universities and university level institutions follow courses leading to a wide variety of degrees up to doctoral level. Two characteristics of the universities are that no strict time limit is set for the completion of studies for a degree and that all students (except at *Norges Tekniske Høgskole*) must first complete a preliminary course leading to the examination *examen philosophicum* (which normally takes six months). In the liberal arts, social and natural sciences and in some other fields, subjects are taken at subsidiary *(grunnfag)*, minor *(mellomfag)*, and major levels *(hovedfag)*. The average length of study for Norwegian degrees is between five and seven years and they are acquired by accumulating subjects at the subsidiary and minor levels for a lower degree with a major level subject added for a higher degree. Candidates in the liberal arts, social sciences and natural sciences usually read for a cand.mag. *(candidatus magisterii)*, roughly a bachelor's degree. Higher degrees, awarded after usually two years of further study and/or research at *hovedfag* level, lead to degrees like the cand.philol. *(candidatus philologiae)* and cand.real. *(candidatus realium)* which roughly correspond to a Master's degree in the humanities and sciences respectively. Graduates of *Norges Tekniske Høgskole* obtain the degree *Sivil Ingeniør* after 4½ years. In some fields of study a *licentiat* degree is offered on the basis of research to those already possessing one of the regular higher degrees. There are a few courses preparing for the doctor's degree such as that for the *doctor ingeniør* of Trondheim which is designed to represent the academic level of a PhD. All other doctorates are awarded after dissertations of original research have been examined by a committee of specialists and after the candidate has publicly defended his work in two public lectures.

Regional Colleges

The supervision of regional higher education which in its emphasis upon 'regional' reflects the strong trend in recent years to decentralise control of education, is the responsibility of regional college councils *(regionale høgskole styrene)*. District colleges *(distriktshøgskoler)* are the 'flag ships' of the regional system and their purpose is to provide post-school education at tertiary level, but unlike the universities by offering much shorter courses (of between one and three years), often vocationally orientated or based upon the particular needs of the region and built on an interdisciplinary approach. In addition the regional colleges are given a wide responsibility for adult education at tertiary level within their region. Some courses are organised therefore on a part time basis and orientated towards practical problems found in private and public administration. Graduates from district colleges are awarded the degree of 'high school candidate' *(høgskole Kandidat)* after two years. There are nine district colleges (for Finnmark, Nordland, Oppland, Østfold, Sogn and Fjordane, Telemark, Møre and Romsdal, Rogaland and Agder). A new district high school in Hedmark opened in 1979. The government's aim is to expand this sector faster than any other to provide both for the marked growth in qualified school leavers (from 5,770 in 1960 to 16,431 in 1973) and for those of 25 years or over who are not formally qualified but have five years' vocational experience and aspire to a higher education.

The decision to establish the first district colleges in 1969 was taken because of the growth in demand for a sort of higher education which would be less 'ivory tower' than the universities but broader, and more innovative than that of the non-university colleges (of engineering, social work, etc.). The district colleges have attempted to develop a distinctive profile and to resist the academic drift to the universities. This they have done by providing study courses in fields where the universities have not yet been able or willing to take an initiative (e.g. tourism, mass communications, maritime transport, ecology, youth problems) as well as by devising new courses around traditional university subjects. Even so courses at *grunnfag* or *mellomfag* level are often offered which usually provide the basis for a transfer to university without loss of credit for completed studies.

Research

Research in Norway outside industry is shared by the universities (and regional colleges) and specialist institutes of which one of the most important is SINTEF *(Selskapet for Industriell og Teknisk Forskning ved NTH* - The Foundation for Scientific and Industrial Research at the University of Trondheim) which is an independent institution employing over 700 people undertaking research for industry on a shared facility basis with Trondheim University. Research funds are distributed by sponsoring bodies of which the two most important are the Norwegian Research Council for Science and the Humanities *(Norges Almenvitenskapelige Forskningsråd - NAVF)* and the Norwegian Research Council for Science and Technology *(Norges Teknisk-Naturvitenskapelige Forskningsråd - NTNF)*.

Overseas Study

Over 300 Norwegian students follow courses of higher education overseas, particularly in the fields of medicine and engineering. In March 1979 the principal venues were Britain and the Republic of Ireland (656), Federal Republic of Germany (591), Sweden (533), US/Canada (418) and Denmark (402).

Teacher Training

Teacher training is coordinated by the Council for Teacher Education *(Laererutdanningsrådet)* though in line with the policy of decentralisation more and more responsibility will be devolved upon the *regionale høgskolestyrene*. The two main routes into teaching are through the colleges of education and the universities and training is offered at three levels - *laerer, adjunkt* and *lektor*.

The majority of teachers at *barneskole* are *laerer*. Prior to

1973 they were trained at *laererskoler* for two years (after *examen artium)* or four years (without *artium*). The new law on teacher education (1973) changed the name of the *laererskoler* to *pedagogiskehøgskoler* (literally 'pedagogical high schools') and stipulated a basic three-year training based upon *examen artium* or equivalent. It includes education theory, teaching practice, pedagogical studies in the majority of subjects taught in the basic schools and 'academic' study of selected main subjects. *Adjunkt* status is obtained either by a further one year's approved study in the case of a *laerer* or, in the case of university graduates holding a lower degree (e.g. cand.mag.) by completing a six-month course covering educational theory and teaching practice at a *pedagogisk seminar*. *Lektors*, the majority of whom work in *videregående skoler* have either obtained a higher university degree and taken the six-month course at the *pedagogisk seminar* or have completed approved studies at *hovedfag* level lasting for a minimum of two years after *adjunkt* and three years on top of *laerer* status.

Vocational Tertiary

A variety of high schools provide advanced courses of vocationally orientated study in the fields of engineering, social work, nursing education, business administration, and medical and paramedical programmes. In all some 12,000 students are involved of whom about 5,000 are in colleges of engineering. The 12 colleges of engineering *(ingeniørhøgskoler)* offer two- and three-year full time courses. Entrance requirements are usually *examen artium* or successful completion of two years of study at the *videregående* level in an appropriate study course.

Non-Formal and Adult

The Norwegian Adult Education Act of 1976 has as its objective "to contribute to providing adult persons with equal opportunities to acquire knowledge, understanding and skill, which will improve the individual's sense of value and personal development and strengthen the basis for independent achievement and cooperation with others in working and social life". The promotion of a more equal society which has underpinned the reforms in basic and *videregående skoler* can thus be seen to be paramount at the adult level. Adult education is provided by a variety of sources both public and voluntary. The former, which include schools, colleges and universities, receive 100% public funding for the courses for adults which they arrange whilst the remainder are subsidised at the rate of 80% of the total approved costs. The major principle in the demarcation of courses is that public institutions will be responsible for 'fundamental' education (the normal school and college subjects) leaving shorter courses which are not restricted by examinations and are more closely linked to the personal or professional requirements of the individual participants to the voluntary organisations. These are run in part by political organisations, and in part by groups representing special interests. The best known examples from the first category are the *Arbeidernes Opplysningsforbund* (Workers' Educational Association) linked with the Labour Party and *Aftenskolen* (the Evening School) connected to the Conservative Party. In the second category are voluntary organisations such as the *Folkeakademienes Landsforbund* (Association of People's Academies) and the *Norges Husmorforbund* (the Norwegian Housewives Association).

In a category on its own is the *Folkeuniversitet* (Folk University) which is the national body into which the *Studentersamfundets Fri Undervisning* (Students' Free Teaching) are grouped. The oldest of these SFU was founded in Oslo in 1864 to encourage university students to five free teaching to working class adults. Although the courses for the most part are now no longer free, its operations are heavily subsidised by the Ministry of Education and local authorities. There are over 300 local branches of the *Folkeuniversitet* which between them offer both academic and vocational courses.

A special feature of the Scandinavian countries are the folk high schools *(Folkehøgskoler)*. In Norway the 88 schools are regulated by an Act of 1949 but are independent of all but minimum State control. They are essentially residential schools offering one- and two-year courses to young adults over the age of 17. For the most part the education provided is not related to examinations and great emphasis is placed upon personality development. Many students who pass through the *Folkehøgskole* before going on to higher education see it as a respite from the academic 'rat race'.

A major provider of education are the correspondence schools which are regulated by an Act of Parliament. Many are grouped into the Norwegian Association of Correspondence Schools *(Norsk Brevskole Forbund)*. Correspondence schools must receive Ministry approval regarding the subject matter and educational content of their courses which span a very broad spectrum. Potentially one of the most important new developments in adult education is the establishment of the Norwegian Institute of Distance Education *(Norsk Fjernundervisning)*. Notwithstanding the very considerable provision of adult and non-formal education in Norway already (in 1975, for example, over 50,000 different study courses were conducted involving nearly 700,000 students) there is felt to be a need for programmes of individualised learning through distance teaching techniques. Initially the target will probably be groups such as the handicapped or the unemployed in need of re-training and NFU's task will be to arrange for the appropriate courses through cooperation with the existing adult education organisations. Of particular importance in making this possible are the Norwegian Broadcasting Corporation *(Norks Rikskringkasting)* and the National Film Board of Norway *(Statens Filmsentralen)*. Unlike the British Open University, NFU will not, at least initially, be concerned with the provision of degree level courses.

7 EDUCATIONAL ADMINISTRATION
Central - The Ministry of Education

As a result of the geographical and social circumstances of the country with significant numbers dwelling in remote rural areas, Norway's educational system came to be highly centralised in order that as much equality of opportunity as possible might be made available for all children irrespective of where they lived. The Ministry of Church and Education lays down minimum standards for hours of work, equipment, buildings, teaching aids, floor space, the size of classes, etc. At school level it approves all textbooks and controls the curriculum and syllabi. (It should, however, be noted that certain vocational schools come under the control of other Ministries, e.g. the schools and colleges of agriculture and the veterinary college are administered by the Ministry of Agriculture while kindergartens are supervised by the Ministry of Family and Consumer Affairs.)

The Ministry of Church and Education is divided into eight departments plus a special unit for Nordic cooperation. The work of the departments is further subdivided amongst 28 sections some of which are serviced by advisory councils (which include, besides those shown on the organisation chart, councils for pupil affairs, engineering education, the education of Lapps, the provision of in-service courses for teachers and liaison with the folk high schools). These advisory councils are usually composed of successful practising teachers who are seconded for four-year terms of office. In addition there are a number of permanent special consultants, e.g. in English, music and remedial Education.

Regional

The administration of the educational system is being increasingly devolved to regional and local authorities. The non-university higher education sector will be supervised by the 16 regional college boards *(regionale høgskolestyrene)* which are composed of elected representatives and a full time director. Schools are administered by the counties *(fylke)*, each with its school director *(skoledirektør)* who is a State official responsible to the Minister. He is also chairman and coordinator of regional policy through the county school boards *(fylkeskolestyrer)* which consist of a minimum of five members elected by the county council. Their main responsibility is the direct supervision of the upper secondary schools and the supervision of elected local *(kommune)* school boards which are in their turn responsible for the basic schools. Each local school board is assisted by a full time official *(skolesjef)* of the *kommune* who keeps in close touch with headmasters and benefits from the advice of area teacher councils.

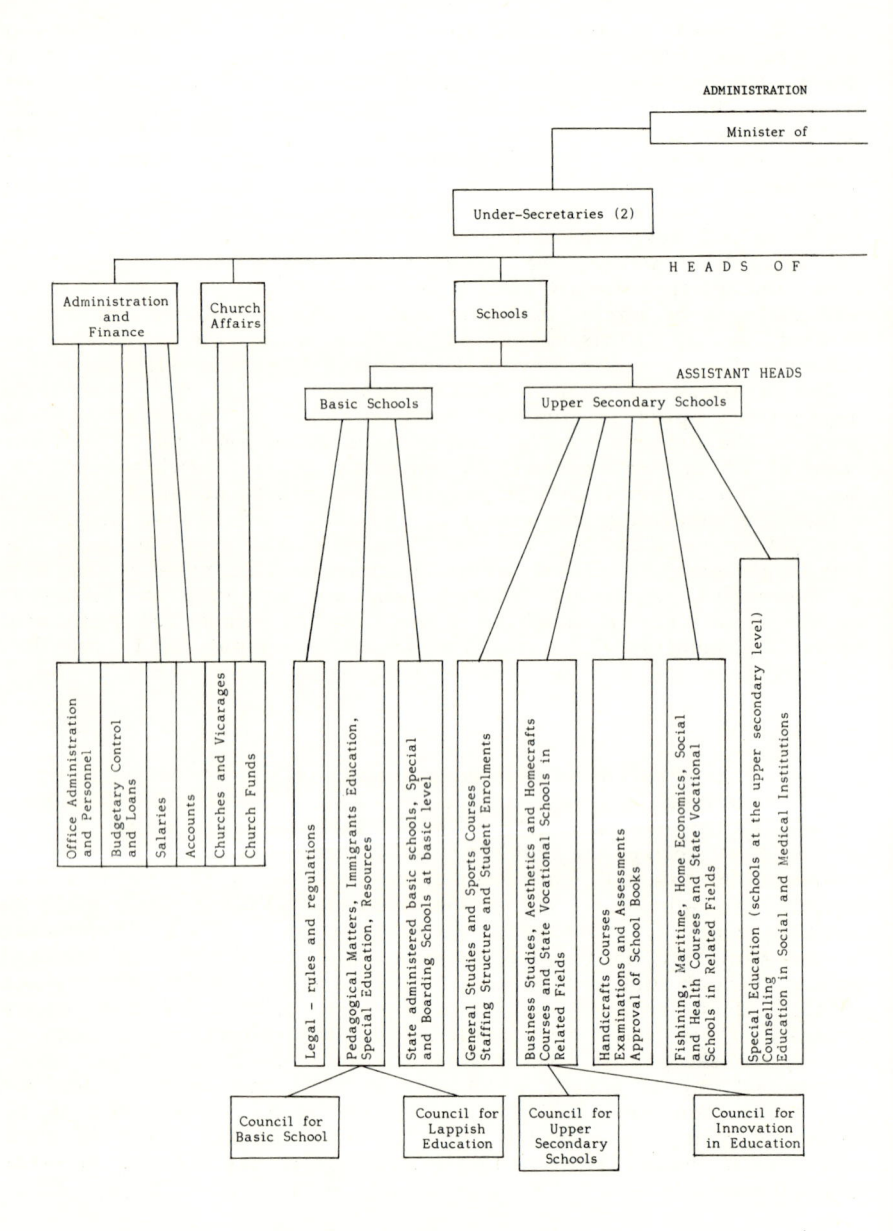

THE NORWEGIAN MINISTRY OF EDUCATION

ADMINISTRATION
- Minister of
- Under-Secretaries (2)

HEADS OF
- Administration and Finance
- Church Affairs
- Schools

ASSISTANT HEADS
- Basic Schools
- Upper Secondary Schools

Administration and Finance:
- Office Administration and Personnel
- Budgetary Control and Loans
- Salaries
- Accounts

Church Affairs:
- Churches and Vicarages
- Church Funds

Basic Schools:
- Legal – rules and regulations
- Pedagogical Matters, Immigrants Education, Special Education, Resources
- State administered basic schools, Special and Boarding Schools at basic level

Upper Secondary Schools:
- General Studies and Sports Courses Staffing Structure and Student Enrolments
- Business Studies, Aesthetics and Homecrafts Courses and State Vocational Schools in Related Fields
- Handicrafts Courses Examinations and Assessments Approval of School Books
- Fishining, Maritime, Home Economics, Social and Health Courses and State Vocational Schools in Related Fields
- Special Education (schools at the upper secondary level) Counselling Education in Social and Medical Institutions

Councils:
- Council for Basic School
- Council for Lappish Education
- Council for Upper Secondary Schools
- Council for Innovation in Education

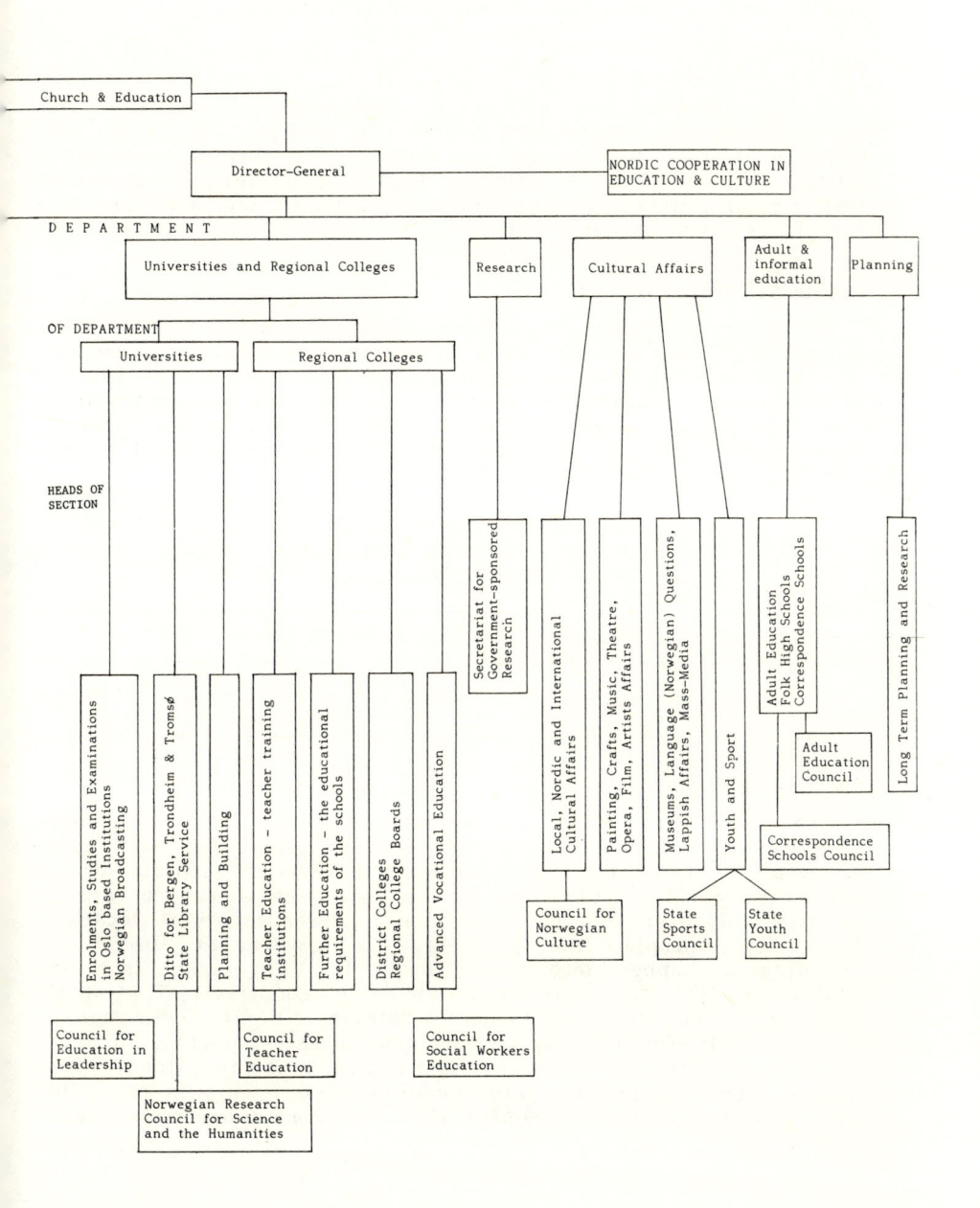

Church & Education

Director-General — NORDIC COOPERATION IN EDUCATION & CULTURE

DEPARTMENT

- Universities and Regional Colleges
- Research
- Cultural Affairs
- Adult & informal education
- Planning

OF DEPARTMENT

Universities | Regional Colleges

HEADS OF SECTION

Universities:
- Enrolments, Studies and Examinations in Oslo based Institutions, Norwegian Broadcasting
  - Council for Education in Leadership
- Ditto for Bergen, Trondheim & Tromsø, State Library Service
  - Norwegian Research Council for Science and the Humanities
- Planning and Building

Regional Colleges:
- Teacher Education – teacher training institutions
  - Council for Teacher Education
- Further Education – the educational requirements of the schools
- District Colleges, Regional College Boards
- Advanced Vocational Education
  - Council for Social Workers Education

Research:
- Secretariat for Government-sponsored Research

Cultural Affairs:
- Local, Nordic and International Cultural Affairs
  - Council for Norwegian Culture
- Painting, Crafts, Music, Theatre, Opera, Film, Artists Affairs
- Museums, Language (Norwegian) Questions, Lappish Affairs, Mass-Media
- Youth and Sport
  - State Sports Council
  - State Youth Council

Adult & informal education:
- Adult Education, Folk High Schools, Correspondence Schools
  - Adult Education Council
  - Correspondence Schools Council

Planning:
- Long Term Planning and Research

Internal

Norwegian educational institutions are characterised by a high degree of internal participatory government via staff, student and (at basic school level) parent councils.

Private Schools

Private schools are relatively unimportant in Norway and their numbers have declined rapidly in the past 20 years. The majority of those that remain are either kindergartens, commercial schools *(handelskoler)* offering basic commercial or secretarial training or Steiner schools (nine in all). A few are language schools or correspondence schools.

8 EDUCATIONAL FINANCE

Increasingly large sums have been allocated to education since World War Two reflecting both the expansion of the education service and the increased proportion of resources devoted to it - e.g. education's share of national income expenditure rose from 3.2% in 1950 to 6.3% in 1969. In 1978 central government expenditure on education was 14.4% of the national budget and 7.6% of the GNP.

Allocation of Funds
Expenditure on Education: Distribution by Level
Percentage of Expenditure 1977

Pre-school	First Level	Second Level	Third Level	Other
-	48.5	26.7	14.1	10.7

Sources of Funds

Expenditure on schools is shared with the local authorities who collectively raise about 45% of the costs. The exact ratio of local to central government contributions to schools varies with the economic resources of the localities since the aim is to offer education of the same quality irrespective of location. thus, for example, the percentage of government subsidy to spending on upper secondary schools in 1979 varies from 38% (Oslo) to 75% (the four most northerly counties). The single most expensive item is teachers' salaries. Higher education is almost totally financed by central government. Students, in addition to receiving grants, usually require to borrow money from *Statens Lånekassen* (the State Lending Fund). This is repayable over a period of years, usually after employment has commenced.

9 DEVELOPMENT AND PLANNING OF THE EDUCATION SYSTEM
Development

Until relatively recent times the influence of the Church on education in Norway has been considerable and its continued association is reflected in the name of the administering ministry viz *Kirke- og Undervisnings Departementet* (the Ministry of Church and Education). Before the nineteenth century most schools were ecclesiastical foundations whose primary aim was the cultivation of the skills necessary to an understanding of the sacrament of confirmation and of Church litany. The surge of nationalism associated with the break-up of the union with Denmark led to the founding of the University of Oslo in 1813 and to the first Primary School Act of 1827 (though primary schooling did not become complsory until 1889). Two developments of the nineteenth century have continued to influence the modern educational system. They were the establishment of Folk High Schools and the beginning of free adult education through the *Studentersamfundets Fri Undervisning* (now incorporated into the present day 'folk university'). It was the impact of World War Two which acted as a catalyst for the very considerable changes which have occurred in the educational system in the last quarter of a century, beginning with the Experiment in Education Act of 1954 which empowered the Ministry of Education to carry out experimental work in most types of school. The first result of this innovatory activity was the Primary Schools Act of 1959 which authorised local education authorities to provide a basic education for all children stretching over nine years (a process which was ended by the 1971 Act ratifying the nine-year compulsory basic school).

Objectives

The underlying principles behind the development of basic schooling were to promote maximum equality of opportunity for children irrespective of their socio-economic background or geographical location, together with the need to "train people for democracy". The expansion of basic schooling has produced pressure at the upper levels and has resulted in the reorganisation of the grammar and vocational schools into combined *videregående* (upper secondary) schools which aim to provide a three-year education on demand to all requiring it. The expansion of higher and continuing education likewise stems from the realisation that a country with a population of just 4 million people can maintain a high standard of living only if its human resources and abilities are fully exploited.

10 THE SYSTEM IN OPERATION
Current Trends

The following educational trends may be identified:

(i)   an expansion of pre-school education reflecting both the tendency of mothers of young children to go out to work and the increased importance attached to organised early childhood education

(ii) an increased emphasis upon what happens inside educational institutions now that the structure of the system is more or less delineated. The National Council for Innovation in Education *(Forsøksrådet for Skoleverket)* and the other advisory councils of the Ministry of Education, together with sponsored research in the *pedagogiske høgskoler, distriktshøgskoler* and universities are focussing upon the curriculum and teaching methods. The *leit motiv* of the education system is designed to be 'learning how to learn' instead of learning information per se. This has implied increasing emphasis upon individualised learning, deferred specialisation, experimentation with open plan and increased involvement of students in the decisions affecting their education. In this last respect mention can be made of the expansion in the number of qualified counsellors and of the involvement of school and college students in the governing bodies of their respective institutions

(iii) the commitment to the equalisation of life opportunities has led to determined efforts being made to reduce divisive factors. Thus, wherever possible the handicapped are integrated into normal learning institutions; attention is being directed to the special learning difficulties of immigrants; opportunities are being increased to enable adults to make good a disadvantaged childhood education and various endeavours are being made to correct the imbalance in amenities existing between town and country and north and south. With respect to the last point the drift to the towns of the south has caused the authorities to introduce special inducements to professionals such as teachers to stay in rural and northern areas which have teacher shortages and a high turnover rate, whilst the educational infrastructure of the far north has been strengthened by the establishment of a university at Tromsø and a *distriktshøgskole* at Alta

(iv) recent years have seen a marked tendency toward a decentralisation of educational administration at every level reflecting the importance laid upon making education socially and regionally relevant. Considerable centralised control nevertheless continues to be exercised in the interests of ensuring uniformity of provision in a country characterised by great disparities of economic resources as well as enabling the government to integrate education planning into its macro-economic strategies

(v) considerable importance is being attached to the integration and development of the regional college system.

REFERENCES AND FURTHER READING

Aftenposten (published annually). *Facts about Norway*.
Bates, T. (1979). *Appropriate Media and Methods for Distance Education in Norway*. Elab, Trondheim.
Central Bureau of Statistics. *Educational Statistics*. Oslo.
1. Survey, 1 October 1975
2. Primary Schools, 1 October 1976
3. Upper Secondary Schools, 1 October 1975
4. Education of Persons 16 Years and Over, 1 October 1975
5. Universities and Colleges, 1 October 1976.

Council of Europe (1972). *The Regional Colleges* (Distriktshøgskole) *in Norway*. Council of Europe Secretariat, Information Note of the Working Party on Diversification of Tertiary Education.
Dalin, Åke (1977). *(The Norwegian Adult Education Act.* Royal Norwegian Ministry of Church and Education.
Haywood, R. (1978). *Recent Reforms in the Organisation and the Curriculum of Norwegian Secondary Schools*. Unpublished paper, School of Education, University of Newcastle upon Tyne.
Hove, Olav (1968). *The System of Education in Norway*. Royal Norwegian Ministry of Church and Education and Grundt Tanum.
Høyem, I. (1975). 'The Norwegian System of Education'. Included in *16-20: Current Developments in Europe*. The Further Education Staff College (Study Conference 75/37).
Instilling fra Felles Nordisk Utvalg for å Utrede Kravene til Laererutdanning i Dagens Skole (1977). *Laererutdanning ved Universitet/Høgskole i Norden*.
National Council for Innovation in Education (1974). *Reform of Upper Secondary Education in Norway*.
Nordahl-Olsen, G. (Ed.) (1975). *University Studies in Norway - a guidebook for foreign students*. Universitetsforlaget.
Norwegian Petroleum Consultants A/S (1978). *Engineering Education in Norway*.
Popperwell, R. G. (1972). *Norway*. Ernest Benn.
Royal Norwegian Ministry of Church and Education. *Act of 13 June 1969 No.24 (concerning the basic school) and supplementary Act of 13 June 1975*. Fellestrykk A/S, Oslo.
Royal Norwegian Ministry of Church and Education (1973). *Ingeniør Utdanning i Norge*.
Royal Norwegian Ministry of Church and Education (1975). *Mønsterplan for Grunnskolen*.
Royal Norwegian Ministry of Church and Education (1976). *Laereplan for den Videregående Skole*.
Royal Norwegian Ministry of Church and Education (1979). *St. Prp. Nr. I (1978-79) for Budsjetterminen*.
Royal Norwegian Ministry of Consumer Affairs and Government Administration (1977). *Kindergartens in Norway*.
Royal Norwegian Ministry of Consumer Affairs and Government Administration (1978). *Family and Child Policy in Norway*.
Royal Norwegian Ministry of Foreign Affairs (1977). *The Norwegian Education System*.
Salmon, M. J. (Ed.) (1976). *Situation of and Trends in Tertiary Education in Europe*. Council of Europe and North East London Polytechnic.

Structure of the Education System in Norway

Age	3 4 5 6 7	8 9 10 11 12 13	14 15 16	17 18	19 20 21	22 23 24
Level		I	II		III	IV
Stage		1	2	3	4	
Compulsory						
School type	(a) day care (b) kinder-garten	Unified comprehensive		Secondary	Academic state colleges / Junior colleges / Universities / Folk high schools	

Education preceding the first level

Examinations: Final written examination at end of stage 1

Source: UNESCO/IBE International Yearbook of Education

Compulsory Education: Age Limits 7-16 Duration (years) 9
Entrance age to pre-school education: 5

NORWAY BASIC STATISTICS	1960	1970	1975	1978 (approx.)
1 Total population (000)	3,581	3,877	4,006	4,059
% female	50	50	50	50
2 % population 0-14 years	25.9	24.5		23
% female	48	49	49	49
3 Enrolment, all levels	631,018	738,467	783,397	806,230
% female	48	49	48	48
First level	429,675	385,628	390,129	396,672
% female	49	51	49	49
Second level	187,055	302,792	326,640	336,559
% female	48	49	49	49
Third level	14,288	50,047	66,628	72,999
% female	34	30	38	44
4 Teachers, all levels	39,547	56,290		
% female	39	41		
First level	18,500	19,713	46,901	43,971
% female	52	61	51	55
Second level	19,146	31,459		
% female	29	33		
Third level	1,901	5,118	6,650	6,697
% female	15	17	16	16
5 Public expenditure on education				
Total (000) Kroner	1,344,300	4,771,600	10,456,000	11,484,000
As % of GNP	4.1	5.9	7.1	7.6
As % of public expenditure				14.4
6 % enrolment (MF) by level	100	100	100	100
First level	68	52	50	49
Second level	30	41	42	42
Third level	2	7	9	9
% enrolment (F) by level	100	100	100	100
First level	69	55	51	50
Second level	30	41	43	42
Third level	2	4	7	8
7 Entrance age: Duration of				
First level education	7:6	7:6	7:6	7:6
Second level	13:6	13:6	13:6	13:6
8 Enrolment ratios (MF)				
First level	118	104	102	100
Second level	53	84	88	90
Third level	6.87	15.91	22.15	24.28
Enrolment ratios (F)				
First level	118	109	102	100
Second level	53	83	88	91
Third level	4.77	9.94	17.08	21.47

Poland

CONTENTS

1 Geography 566
2 Population 568
3 Society and Culture 569
4 History and Politics 570
5 The Economy 571
6 The Education System 572
7 Educational Administration 580
8 Educational Finance 581
9 Development and Planning of
 the Education System 582
10 The System in Operation 584

Poland is a nation state, the Polish People's Republic, which came into being in 1945. The troubled history of Poland dates from the middle of the tenth century when it became a State; subsequent partitions left the Poles without a State until 1918 and after 1945 facing the task of recreating a viable and unified political entity.

The numerous political forces which have shaped Poland's history cannot disguise the strength of Catholicism and the permanent cultural and educational influences of France. Thus, when the communist and socialist parties merged in 1948 the task of educationists and government was to transform a selective system of education which benefitted the middle and upper classes to the disadvantage of people living in the rural areas and the industrial workers and to repair the devastation of the war years when the whole education system was virtually destroyed.

Since 1945 reconstruction and reforms have been designed to provide greater equality of provision to solve the illiteracy problem represented in 1945 by a figure of 18% of people over the age of nine. Planning has been centralised under the control of national ministries but a departure from normal procedures took place in 1973 when a non-Party commission was asked to pronounce on future educational developments. Predictably the practical recommendations followed a Soviet model and the one adopted in the German Democratic Republic. Reform proposals include the expansion of pre-school education, the extension of compulsory education to ten years of basic unified schooling of a polytechnical nature, the creation of specialist schools for students who have completed basic education and wish to enter higher academic or professional studies, the establishment of technical schools for graduates from the ten year schools, and provision for 17-year olds to enter higher education by means of special entrance examinations.

The success of these reforms will have to be judged in the light of the immediate past. Seven-year basic education was not made compulsory until 1956. Differentiation between second level school types was reduced slowly while at the same time the diversification of higher education, necessitated by expansion and national needs was a product of plans made in 1950 to reorganise the faculties and bring them together in autonomous institutions of higher education. The successful development of specialised technical secondary education, at the expense of the arts and sciences is revealed in the fact that in 1977/78 some 149,000 students matriculated at the end of the ten year school while over 216,000 matriculated in technical and professional subjects. It should be remembered, however, that in the Continental European tradition the Polish second level curriculum includes a large compulsory core. Optional subjects are divided into languages, biological sciences, technology, mathematics, economic history and aesthetics.

Resistance to reform is non-political and reflects a general unwillingness on the part of educationists to change this practice even if they are prepared to revise their rhetoric and ideology. The strength of Catholic feeling also represents an obstacle to the total secularisation and universalisation of a system which until recently catered for a Catholic population and was elitist.

The Editor

1 GEOGRAPHY

Topography

Poland is situated in eastern Europe, bounded in the north by the Baltic Sea, in the east by the USSR, in the south by Czechoslovakia and in the west by the German Democratic Public. The area of the country is 309,056 sq km (119,327 square miles) and the length of the border is 3,536 km (2,210 miles) of which 696 km (435 miles) are coastline.

Most of Poland consists of lowlands, which form part of the great European plain. However, towards the southern border the land becomes more mountainous to form the Sudeten and Carpathian mountains, the latter rising to 2,400 metres (8,000 ft). The major rivers are the Vistula, which follows a meandering course through the cenral part of the country, and the Oder which forms a large part of the western boundary. About one fifth of the country is forested.

Climate

The climate is the continental type with long cold winters, during which heavy snowfalls occur, and warm dry summers.

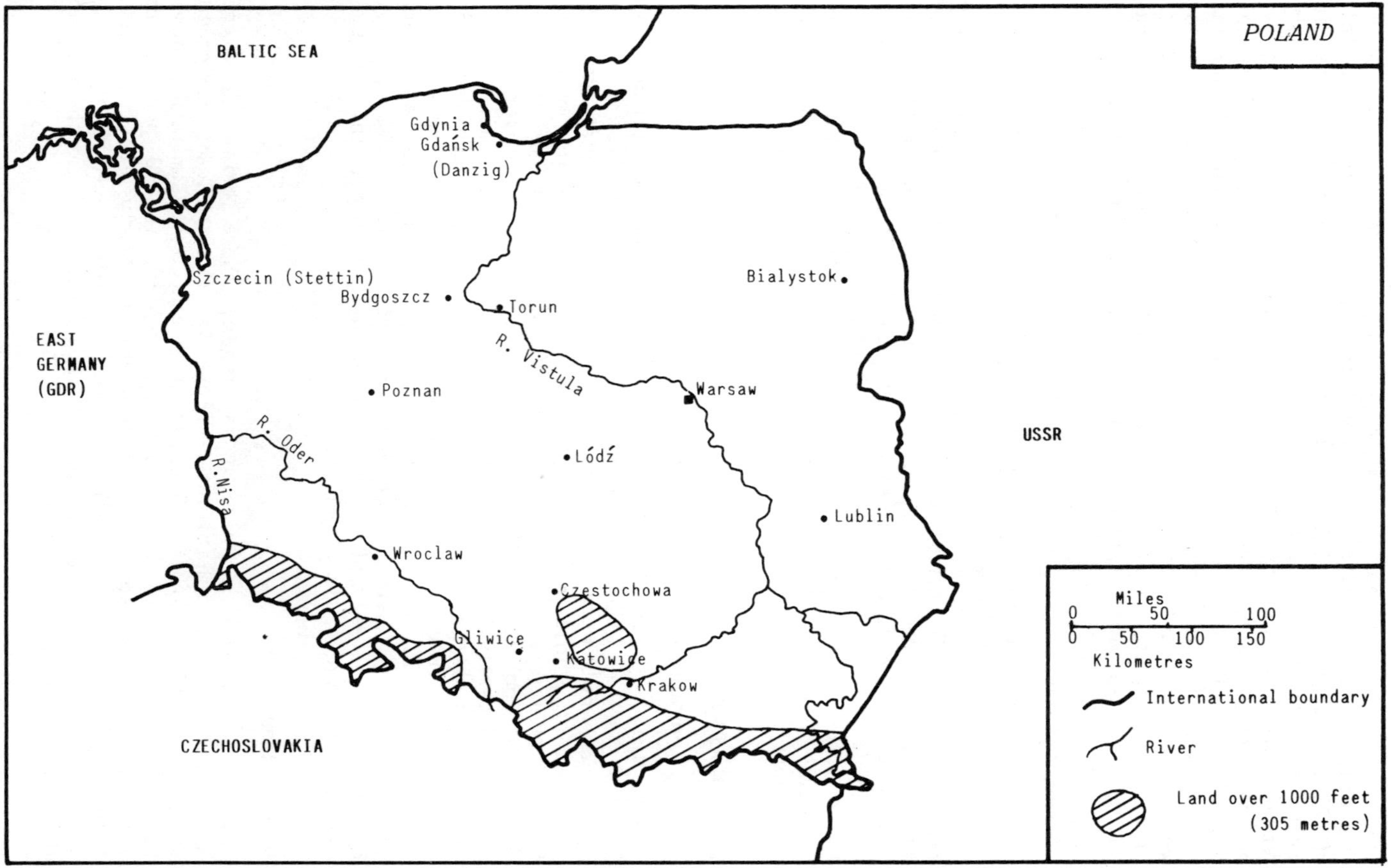
POLAND
BALTIC SEA
Gdynia
Gdańsk
(Danzig)
Szczecin (Stettin)
Bydgoszcz
Torun
Bialystok
EAST
GERMANY
(GDR)
R. Vistula
Poznan
Warsaw
USSR
R. Oder
Lódź
R.Nisa
Lublin
Wroclaw
Czestochowa
Gliwice
Katowice
Krakow
CZECHOSLOVAKIA
Miles
0
50
100
0
50
100
150
Kilometres
International boundary
River
Land over 1000 feet
(305 metres)

The Baltic region has an average temperature of -1°C (30°F) in January, 18°C (64°F) in July, and a mean annual rainfall of 23.6 inches. The lake district in the north east has an average January temperature of -4°C to -2°C (25-28°F), July temperatures of 16-18°C (61-66°F) and a mean annual rainfall of over 23.6 inches. The region of valleys, extending from the Baltic Lake District to the Carpathian and Sudeten Mountains has a somewhat harsher winter in the eastern part than in the west. The Sudeten, Carpathian and Tatra Mountains have a colder and longer winter, and relatively short summer, with a comparatively high annual rainfall of over 150 cm (59 inches).

Communications

The country has well developed road, rail and inland waterway systems, and plans are at present being put into operation for extensive improvements and modernisation. There are nearly 27,000 km (16,777 miles) of railway line, both standard and narrow gauge, 99,442 km (61,793 miles) of major roads, and nearly 4,572 km (2,841 miles) of navigable waterways. The Polish airline (LOT) maintains extensive internal and external services. Three major ports on the Baltic coast, Gdynia, Gdansk, and Szczecin, handle a total of 18.6 million tons of cargo annually. Transport links with all the neighbouring countries are excellent.

2 POPULATION

Composition and Growth

According to the 1970 official census the population was 32,805,000. In 1980 it was estimated at 35 million, of which more than half were under 20 years of age. Only just over 1% consisted of ethnic minorities. The annual increase in population is approximately 0.9%, having declined from 1.95% in 1955. Government policy in the past was actively to support birth control. Recently, however, due to the continual fall in the birth rate and the high probability of a net population reduction in the near future, this policy has been changed. Propaganda is increasing in an attempt to encourage parents to have more children, three being regarded as the ideal. Unfortunately, due to wage rates and an acute housing shortage, this propaganda may have little effect.

Distribution

Some 52% of the population is urban, there being 24 towns with over 100,000 inhabitants. There is a significant movement from countryside to town but no problems of assimilation have been evident. The average population density is 270 per square mile. Outside the towns the population is fairly evenly distributed in small towns, villages and isolated settlements. The major urban concentration is in the south and southwest, in the Silesian industrial region.

Emigration

Poland has undergone large emigration movements, particularly during the latter half of the nineteenth century and, more recently, as a result of World War Two. Between 10 and 11 million Poles live abroad, some 60% of them in the United States. In 1971 there were 1,700 immigrants and 30,200 emigrants. There have also been considerable internal migratory movements, particularly after World War Two when large numbers of the population left those eastern parts of Poland which now form part of the Soviet Union.

3 SOCIETY AND CULTURE

Social Patterns

Despite migratory movements, the family unit in Poland is still strong and the extended family has been preserved as a coherent group. There are also the vestiges of a hierarchical class structure, though there is no evidence of any class conflict. Party membership gives considerable social advantages. In general, Polish society is moving in the same direction as societies in other developed countries. Fashions in clothes, music and so on are almost indistinguishable from those in Western Europe and there is the same concern for equal opportunity and the improvement of the quality of life.

There is an extremely strong demand for education, which is seen as a necessary prerequisite for employment carrying high status and/or financial reward. The possession of the highest educational qualifications still carries considerable status. Differences in salary between different types of employment are not great, but they are still sufficiently different for incentives for advancement to exist.

Culture

Historically Poland has been linked to most major European cultural movements, to which she has made her own distinctive contribution despite frequent and radical alterations of frontiers. Perhaps to a greater extent than in most countries significant emphasis is placed on the improvement of the general cultural standards of the whole population, as is evidenced by the large subsidies given to all branches of the arts and the important place the arts have assumed in society, as exemplified in the cultural content of radio and television programmes.

Religion

Freedom of religion is guaranteed under the constitution. The population of the country is predominantly (95%) Roman Catholic, and the estimated proportion of regular churchgoers is as high as 80%. Other religious groups include the Polish Orthodox Church (527,000 members) and protestant sects (140,000 members). Jews now account for only some 30,000 of the population, compared with $3\frac{1}{2}$ million before World War Two.

Recent events point to a greater understanding between Church and State, probably as a result of new and more realistic Vatican policies. Formal agreements regulate Church/State relations. Religion is not taught as a separate subject in schools, and apart from the Catholic University of Lublin and its own theological colleges, etc., the Church has little direct influence on education.

4 HISTORY AND POLITICS

Historical Development

Poland celebrated the 1,000th anniversary of her foundation in 1966. However, modern Poland dates only from 1944 with the foundation of the Polish People's Republic.

Government Organisation

Poland has a centralised system of government based on the Soviet model and operated in accordance with the 1952 constitution. The supreme legislative body is *Sejm*, or parliament, elected for a period of four years by all citizens over 18 years of age. The *Sejm* elects a 15-man Council of State, presided over by the Head of State. The *Sejm* also elects the supreme executive body, the Council of Ministers. Despite all this machinery, supreme power lies, in fact, with the *Politburo* of the main political party, the Polish United Workers' Party (PZPR). In addition to the PZPR there are two other smaller parties, the Polish Peasants Party and the Democratic Party. All three parties share the same objectives and present a united front in the *Sejm*. Party representation in the *Sejm* has remained fairly constant, averaging: PZPR 55%; UPP 25%; DP 9%, and non-party deputies 11%. Elections were held 1961, 1965, 1972, 1976 and 1980. Martial law was imposed in 1981.

Local government is organised on a three-tier basis. The country is divided into 22 administrative provinces or *voivodships* of which 5 are cities. Each *voivodship* is divided into *powiats*, and there are 390 of these divided in turn into 2365 *gminas*. This system came into being as a result of the local government reforms carried out in 1973, giving more responsibility at local level, but to larger areas.

International Relations

Poland is a member of the east European military alliance, the Warsaw Pact, and also of the east European economic union. She is thus closely linked with her immediate neighbours USSR, East Germany and Czechoslovakia, as well as with the other countries of the eastern bloc. In recent years Poland's relations with the West have shown a distinct improvement. A number of loans have been negotiated for the purchase of the capital equipment required to meet the needs of Poland's developing industries.

A major factor in Poland's foreign policy has been her relationship with the two Germanies. There are strong links with

East Germany which in some way is seen as less responsible than West Germany for Nazi misdeeds. However, relations with West Germany have shown a distinct improvement during the past few years. West Germany's 1971 acceptance of Poland's western frontier on the Oder/Neisse line has led to the establishment of diplomatic relations and a more friendly attitude between the two countries. Understandably, Poland is much concerned with the inviolability of her present frontiers and statements respecting this appear in all her major international agreements.

Cultural/scientific relations and exchanges with eastern Europe are governed by cultural agreements which support a large amount of interchange, particularly with the USSR. Cultural links with the major western countries (Great Britain and the USA excepted), are also governed by agreement. These are in operation with Belgium, Italy, Austria, Scandinavia and particularly France with whom Poland has traditionally strong ties.

5 THE ECONOMY

Agriculture

Poland is one of the world's major agricultural nations. Paradoxically, although a socialist country, 86% of all agricultural land remains in private hands, with an average holding of 5 hectares. Some 30% of the population earn their living by agriculture. Animal production is very important - ham, bacon and sausage making a significant contribution to Polish exports. The principal crops are rye, wheat, oats, sugar beet and potatoes. Agriculture is still rather under-developed; in 1971 2.5 million horses were used on farms compared with 300,000 tractors and there is little sign of sophisticated farm machinery.

Industry

Poland operates a socialist economy with State control of industry and means of distribution. She entered an intensive phase of industrialisation. Her industrial growth rate was among the ten fastest in the world, and there is an accelerating movement of workers from the land into industrial and other non-agricultural employment. Major natural resources include coal, copper ores, iron ores and zinc/lead ores. Important industries are shipbuilding, textiles, engineering, steel, cement, chemicals and foodstuffs. The main exports are coal, ships, steel and clothing. Some 60% of Poland's trade is with the countries of the Council for Mutual Economic Assistance (CMEA) of which she is a member.

Five Year Plan

The 1971-75 Five Year Plan aimed at increasing exports and satisfying a growing demand for consumer goods on the home market. It was planned to increase industrial production by 50% and real incomes by 18%. These targets were exceeded. Total agricultural production rose from 305,476 million zloties in 1970 to 464,497 million in 1974; industrial production increased from

1,079,345 million zloties to 1,596,450 million over the same period. National income increased by 32.9% in the first three years of the Plan which envisaged a 40% increase over the five-year period. From 1970 to 1973 all food prices were nominally frozen, and prices remained in fact fairly stable. This freeze was lifted late in 1973 on all but basic foodstuffs, i.e. bread, milk and potatoes, with the effect of an immediate price rise for many products and services. In 1980 workers and farmers pressed the government to negotiate a number of improvements with the trade unions.

6 THE EDUCATION SYSTEM
Academic Year

The academic year runs from October to June and is divided into two semesters, October to February, and February to June.

Reforms

Under a resolution adopted by the *Sejm* in 13 October 1973, radical changes in the educational system were to be introduced and the changeover is expected to be compulsory in the 1980s. The central change is the extension of free compulsory education to ten years of unified primary/secondary schooling (leaving age 17), preceded by one to three years of mandatory kindergarten, and followed by a two-year optional college-type course offering specialised curricula for those wishing to enrol in institutes of higher education.

Pre-School

Babies and young children from the age of a few weeks to three years can be accommodated in nursery schools. Such schools are for the benefit of working mothers (most mothers work), and hence accommodate children throughout the working day. Parents must pay a proportion of the cost of sending their children to such schools, the proportion depending upon their income.

Pre-primary schools are available for children from 2 to 7 years of age. These are voluntary schools, again intended for the children of working mothers, to whom priority is given. They are normally open from 7.30 a.m. to 3.30 p.m. and meals are provided. Demand for these schools far exceeds supply, but the pre-school educational system is being expanded from 78% to all 6-year old children in 1974 so that all children receive at least one year's schooling before starting at the primary school at the age of 7. A draft infant school curriculum was drawn up which forms the lead in to the entire new ten-year cycle of compulsory schooling, and it is now being tried out in a number of infant schools.

First Level (Old System)

Under the 'old' system children enter primary school at the age of 7 for an eight-year compulsory course. The curriculum is a general basic one with a second language – normally Russian – introduced in the fifth year. A third language – English, French or German – is available from the sixth year. In the fifth to eighth years some 38% of the pupils' time is spent studying the humanities, while 49% of the time is spent in studying mathematics and science based subjects. In the final year all pupils sit an examination covering the subjects taught in the primary school, on the results of which the school leaving certificate is awarded. In addition to normal free primary schools run by the Ministry of Education, there are also schools attached to, and run on behalf of, industrial and agricultural undertakings. The latter are often run on a seasonal basis, during harvest time. One hundred percent of the 7-14 age group receive education and nearly 20% of the age cohort attend higher education.

Second Level (Old System)

Secondary education is optional and free and is entered at the age of 15 or 16 years. It is open to candidates successful in the entrance examination and more than 90% of pupils continue their studies at secondary level. There are two main types of school: General Secondary and Vocational Secondary.

General

A four-year course is offered, generally leading to college or university entrance. A broad-based general education is given in the first three years, during which the student's time is divided as follows:

humanities, i.e. languages (Polish, Russian and one other), history and sociology	42%
sciences, i.e. mathematics, physics, chemistry, biology, hygiene and geology	35%
practical subjects, i.e. woodwork, metalwork	9.5%
art, physical and paramilitary training	13.5%

Students in the final year can choose one of four main options: biology/chemistry; mathematics/physics; humanities; geography/economics.

For particularly gifted children there are 13 secondary schools at which specific emphasis is placed on the teaching of mathematics; and some 40 schools where at least part of the instruction is carried out in a foreign language, e.g. English, Russian, French or German. Part time and evening courses are also available for students who wish to complete secondary education but cannot attend full time. In 1972 out of a total of 2,373,722 students in secondary education, 609,397 were studying in general secondary schools and 76% of these were working full time. Seventy percent of the pupils were girls.

Vocational

These schools provide a four- or five-year general vocational course, entry being direct from primary school after an entrance examination. There is a tendency for individual schools to specialise in specific subjects or groups of related subjects, though this is not always so. In addition to full time courses, evening and part time courses are available.

Examinations

These are held regularly, up to four times a year to assess the students' progress. A student who completes his secondary education has the right to sit the school leaving examination, the *Matura* but is not obliged to do so. Students are examined in two compulsory subjects, Polish and mathematics, and in three other subjects of their own choice. Those wishing to go on to higher education must be examined in the two or three subjects in which they will be examined for entrance into an institution of higher education. Those not intending to proceed to further study may select any additional subjects. The range of options is quite wide and includes foreign languages, social science, biology, geography, chemistry, astronomy, technology, art and music. Students at vocational schools may take the *matura* on completion of the fifth year of study. However, the majority do not choose to proceed to higher education and leave to follow their trade or profession without taking the examination.

Somewhat more pupils take the *matura* in vocational secondary rather than general secondary schools. A high proportion of the full time general secondary school candidates pass, nearly half the part time pupils fail. Overall about half the vocational secondary school candidates fail the *matura*, the percentage of part time candidates being particularly high.

First and Second Level Education (Reformed)

After at least one year's pre-school education entry to primary school takes place at the age of 7 years. The old system is being replaced by a compulsory ten-year course of general education. The curriculum is changing from a concentric system (where a subject is taught less intensively in the pupils' earlier years, and repeated later but with the provision of a larger number of facts), to a linear type of system (where something new is added every year). Pupils who cannot cope with the course and have poor results in the middle grades will be directed to vocationally oriented classes so that they can continue their work without difficulty.

Course Structure

The course is divided into two parts: *initial* (grades 1-3, ages 7-9) and *systematic* (grades 4-10, ages 10-17).

The *initial* stage will attend to the child's development in learning and also in physical fitness and manual skills. The latter should be acquired through classes which will introduce him to rudimentary notions of modern technology. Also included in the syllabus are art and music for the purpose of cultivating his powers of expression and sensibility. Throughout this period, a basic place will be occupied by such subjects as Polish and mathematics. The new curriculum for the initial stage was put into practice in 1978/9 and textbooks and teaching aids had already been prepared. Teacher training for this age range is being expanded.

In grade 4 (at the age of 11) pupils begin to receive a solid grounding in particular subjects (hence the term 'systematic'). Compulsory classes in grade 4 amount to 29 hours a week, including two hours each of technical and manual activities and one hour each of art and music. Beginning with grade 6, there are additionally two hours of optional classes on special subjects, increasing in grade 8 to four, though the total number of classes is to be reduced so as to keep them at a level of no more than 36 hours a week. On reaching the ninth grade, the pupil will be 15, that is, the age of the present primary school leaver, and will still have two years of learning. Instruction now takes on an inter-disciplinary character, regard being given to other educational needs such as family life and sexual guidance and sets of subjects will be embarked upon integrating knowledge from different disciplines. In this way the traditional 17-item curriculum - modernised in its substance - will be offered in logically uniform groups: humanities and social sciences on the one hand, mathematical and natural sciences on the other, founded on the two basic subjects - Polish and mathematics. The new curriculum for the systematic stage is being phased in over the years 1980-86.

An ancillary role in this extension of the teaching process is to be performed by extra-syllabus classes - compulsory in principle but chosen according to individual capacities and interests. Apart from these, other kinds of optional activities will be offered in the form of societies and sports. Periods devoted to socially useful work practices (ranging now from three to six hours a month) are to be retained.

Examinations

The ten-year school leavers will be entitled either to sit for university entrance examinations or choose from a wide variety of vocational schools. Changes in the examination system mark a departure. The first step is a new system for the secondary school diploma. Every young person who wants to obtain this diploma must pass an examination in Polish and in mathematics (which differs depending on whether he is following a scientific or humanistic programme). Afterwards, he has a choice of two paths. The first is traditional: he passes an examination in fixed subjects before an examining board. The second consists of independent work, with the aim of promoting independence, encouraging a broadening of knowledge, and preparing students for study in institutes of higher education.

Post-Compulsory

The ten-year course will be followed by a two-year optional college-type course offering specialised curricula for those wishing to enrol in institutes of higher learning. Exceptionally talented graduates from the ten-year course will be permitted to by-pass the 'specialisation' schools and proceed directly into higher education. Alternatively, vocational training, a job, or military service will aim to facilitate further study by giving the 17-year old a couple of years of preparation for life.

Vocational

Vocational training is, of course, currently available in vocational secondary schools but it is also offered by at least two other kinds of institution.

Basic Trade Schools

These provide full or part time two- or three-year post-primary school courses leading to the diploma of a skilled worker. Separate schools are available for training in agricultural subjects. Training is available in all basic manual skills. In 1972 there were nearly 5,000 such schools with about one million students, producing some 300,000 graduates annually.

Post-Secondary Vocational Schools

These offer full or part time courses from one and a half to two years in length to graduates of the general secondary schools. Professional subjects such as librarianship, nursing and other paramedical subjects are taught.

Third Level (Higher) Institutions

There are 85 institutions of higher education in Poland, all of which are under State control except for one Catholic university and two theological colleges. The universities and technical universities enrol more than 50% of the 400,000 students. The rest study in higher engineering colleges, agricultural academies, higher schools of economics and medical academies. Relatively few enrol in maritime colleges, art, music and drama schools and theological colleges. Except for admissions to higher engineering colleges a very high proportion of pupils entering institutions of higher learning come from the general secondary schools.

Evening, part time and external students make up approximately 10%, 39% and 0.7% of the total. Evening and part time studies are available in most types of institution, the major exception being the medical academies.

Of the 20 universities and technical universities, with one or two exceptions, most of the latter are post-1945 creations, but enrolments in them are high.

University	Founded	Students (1972)
University of Gdansk	1970	–
Jagiellonian University Krakow	1347	9,320
University of Lodz	1945	11,300
Catholic University of Lublin (private)	1918	2,300
Marie Curie-Sklodowska University, Lublin	1944	9,812
Adam Mickiewicz University, Poznan	1919	7,000
Nicholas Copernicus University, Torun	1945	5,057
Silesian University, Katowice	1968	7,500
Warsaw University	1913	19,538
Boleslav Beirut University, Wroclaw	1945	11,326
Czestochowa Technical University	1949	3,600
Gdansk Technical University	1945	8,850
Krakow Technical University	1945	7,432
Lodz Technical University	1945	10,175
Poznan Technical University	1918	7,143
Silesian Technical University, Gliwice	1945	17,625
Szczecin Technical University	1955	5,587
Warsaw Technical University	1898	22,556
Wroclaw Technical University	1945	11,500
Krakow Academy of Mining and Metallurgy	1919	14,650

Entrance

Entrance to higher education is by means of competitive entrance examinations set by each university or college. These examinations are marked on a points basis. Extra points are given to specific groups, for example children of peasants or workers and those applying for less popular subjects. (Male applicants to medical schools receive extra points as part of an attempt to encourage more men to join a predominantly female profession.) Students must apply to the university covering their own *voivodship* or town. Standards at all universities are substantially similar. However, should a student wish to follow a course not available at his local university, he may apply elsewhere.

Financial Assistance

Higher education is free and government and industrial maintenance grants are available. These grants are assessed on parents' income and, to a lesser extent, on academic performance. Grants are awarded to students in whose families the per capita income is less than a stated minimum per month. If the per capita income rises above this level there is a pro rata reduction in the grant. Grants are on a scale in favour of students who achieve the best results, but extra financial assistance is available where students are forced to live away from home or where there is particular hardship. A substantial majority of students receive government help in the form of grants and prizes. The rules governing the making of grants are continually updated. For instance, in the academic year 1974/75 family allowances were introduced and also supplements for those renting apartments.

Courses

Arts, languages and humanities are taught at the universities and engineering and scientific subjects at the technical universities. Universities have departments of mathematics and pure science but no applied science is taught and the approach is mainly academic.

The first degree *(Magisterium)* takes between four and five years to complete, depending on the subject (medical degrees take $6\frac{1}{2}$ years). The length of degree courses has recently been slightly reduced with the abolition of the compulsory military training element. Courses are built on a system of 'credits'. Generalised basic studies constitute the first two years and students specialise in their last two or three years. Part of the final year is spent writing a thesis based on an experimental project or, more usually, on a survey of published material.

There are two types of doctoral degrees. A conventional doctoral degree takes three or four years of full time study and is awarded on the basis of a publicly defended thesis. Grants are available for doctoral students, though over 50% of degrees are awarded to those working part time. In 1972, 2,801 doctoral degrees were awarded. The advanced doctoral degree *(Doktor Habilitowany)* is awarded on the basis of advanced post-doctoral study and published research. In 1972, 518 such degrees were awarded. The advanced doctoral degree is necessary to any member of a university staff wishing to advance beyond the level of lecturer.

Universities and technical universities also run post-graduate courses, normally lasting two semesters, designed primarily to update the academic training of graduates who have been in employment for some time.

Examinations

Examinations in universities are held twice a year, in February and June. Not all subjects which the student has studied are examined but only those considered essential to his further progress. The function of most university examinations is to assess the student's capabilities. However, institutes of higher education tend to accept more students on to the first year of the courses than they can accommodate in subsequent years. There is a relatively high dropout rate at the end of the first year of university study.

University Organisation

Although the organisation of universities is not always the same, in general the responsibility for research and teaching is split between institutes and departments. The university is divided into a number of faculties responsible for teaching, and a number of institutes, each responsible for research in a specific subject area. Although faculties, headed by a Dean, run the teaching side of the university, their function is primarily administrative, the actual teaching being carried out by members of the institutes.

Teacher Training

Except for the training of pre-primary teachers, all teacher education in Poland is at post-secondary level and courses contain a strongly vocational element.

Pre-School

A five-year post-primary school course is available at special training colleges for students who enter direct from the basic school. This course includes teaching practice, educational theory, psychology and general education up to the standard of *Matura*.

First Level

Students follow a three-year post-general secondary school course at a teacher training college. In 1970 there were 16 such colleges, 6 automonous and 10 attached to universities but the numbers have been increased considerably since then. These colleges also provide further part time training ($1\frac{1}{2}$ or 2 years) for the graduates of two-year crash courses, designed as part of the post-war teacher training programmes, which were phased out in 1968. These courses are designed to bring the crash-course graduates up to the level reached by the present teacher training colleges, and to assist with their special needs, a Radio and Television Teachers' University (NURT) has been created.

Secondary

Students follow a five-year post-secondary education course at either a higher school of education or a university department of education.

Technical

Following the successful completion of a post-primary basic trade school course and the passing of an entrance examination, the student follows a three- or four-year course at a technical teacher training college. The course includes a pedagogical element and a continuation of the student's own education up to the standard of the vocational secondary school graduate. Two-year courses in technical teaching are available for graduates of secondary vocational schools.

Adult and Non-Formal

The concept of *education permanente* has received much publicity and public discussion and many factories and professional organisations operate active and popular updating and retraining programmes for their employees and/or members. The Central Technical Organisation (NOT) and the Polish Economic Society have been active in this field. The system is likely to expand on a national basis.

There are also the so-called 'Folk Universities', which offer courses in social, educational and cultural subjects; and 'rural' universities designed to encourage 18-25 year olds in country districts to continue their general education and to develop their interest in artistic and cultural pursuits. Television is being used increasingly as a tool of adult education, offering formal training courses for farmers, teachers and students taking university entrance examinations. It is planned to expand the scope of these programmes to cover a much wider range of activities than at present, and to make television an integral part of the adult education system. Primary and secondary level courses are still run on an evening and part time basis for adults who have not had the opportunity of completing their primary education. But these courses are being phased out as the need for them decreases.

7 EDUCATIONAL ADMINISTRATION

Centralised Control

Nationalised education administration is under the control of the Ministry of Science, Higher Education and Technology and the Ministry of Education and Schooling. All major decisions relating to educational policy, expenditure and curricula are taken by one or other of these bodies. At all levels right up to the universities syllabi are planned centrally by the ministries and must be followed. The Ministry of Education and Schooling is responsible for the writing and printing of school textbooks and maintains a printing and publishing organisation, the largest in Poland, for this purpose.

Local Responsibilities

Matura examinations are set at *voivodship* level but are approved by the Ministry.

ADMINISTRATION

MINISTRY OF SCIENCE, HIGHER EDUCATION AND TECHNOLOGY	MINISTRY OF EDUCATION AND SCHOOLING
	LOCAL AUTHORITIES *(VOIVODSHIP)*
	DISTRICTS

8 EDUCATIONAL FINANCE

Education Budget

The budgetary allocation for education is approved by the *Sejm* as part of the annual finance bill. In 1970 16.5% of the national budget was spent on education; in 1971 the figure was 13.4% and in 1972 is was 16.4%. During these years the percentage of total public recurrent expenditure spent on education was respectively 8.6% and 9.1%.

Allocation of Funds
Expenditure on Education: Distribution by Level
Percentage of Expenditure 1978

Pre-school	First Level	Second Level	Third Level	Other
7.1	27.4	22.1	25.8	17.6

Distribution

Financial allocations for education are made for each *voivodship* with general instructions as to how the budget is to be spent. Each *voivodship* then allocates an education budget to the *powiats* within its boundaries. The *powiats* are responsible for the actual spending of money, for example, on school buildings and renovation, staff salaries, and equipment. Although the general areas of budgetary allocation are laid down centrally at both *voivodship* and *powiatship* level some flexibility is allowed within these limits.

9 DEVELOPMENT AND PLANNING OF THE EDUCATION SYSTEM

Origins

Before World Two educational facilities in Poland were extremely limited, particularly in rural areas. Secondary and higher education was almost exclusively the privilege of the middle and upper classes. In 1945 some 18% of the population over 9 years of age were illiterate. During the German occupation the whole education system, including schools, teaching staff and equipment, was virtually completely destroyed. However, very courageously some universities and schools continued their teaching activities underground. The major post-war educational priority, in addition to that of restoring a system largely destroyed during the war, was to correct the educational imbalance in the population, and to solve the illiteracy problem, by a massive programme of school construction, and reconstruction, and teacher training. The principle of uniform, free and compulsory education was also established.

National Education Congress

The present educational system is based on the principles evolved at the 1945 'National Education Congress'. This Congress laid down the following principles which, in 1952, were incorporated into the Polish Constitution:

(i)   elementary schooling should be free and complsory

(ii) there should be constant development of secondary schools to provide general or vocational education, and of universities

(iii) the assistance of the State should be available to raise the skills of all working citizens in both town and country

(iv) there should be a system of scholarships, hostels and other forms of material assistance for students.

It was not until 1956 that seven-year elementary education was made compulsory. Between 1961 and 1966 a universal system of eight-year primary education was introduced and a new phase was entered, aimed at extending the period of compulsory schooling and adapting the education system to the needs of the modern, scientifically based industrial society into which Poland is developing.

Planning Institutions

National education policy is under the control of the ministries. There are Party members working within them and the Party's approval must be obtained before any major decisions are taken. The Party thus retains overall control of planning, policy and decision making. There are also a number of research institutes attached to the ministries, which have an advisory function and assist with planning decisions. These institutes are:

Institute of School Programmes - teaching methods and development of school curricula

Institute of Youth Research - the effects of the educational system on the development of young people and their integration into the socio-economic life of the country

Institute of Teacher Training and Professional Development - teacher training techniques and the socio-economic and pedagogical problems of teachers

Institute of Pedagogical Research - the theory and practice of education.

1973 Report

A major departure from the normal planning procedure occurred in 1972 when a non-Party commission, under the chairmanship of Professor Szczepanski (Director of the Institute of Philosophy and Sociology of the Polish Academy of Sciences), was set up to examine the current educational system and to make recommendations on its future development. The Commission's report was published in the autumn of 1973 and the radical changes proposed were adopted by the *Sejm* on 13 October 1973. Briefly they involve:

(i) expansion of pre-primary education

(ii) extension of compulsory education to ten years of unified primary/secondary schooling

(iii) foundation of 'specialisation' schools offering two-year courses to students wishing to pursue higher academic or professional studies; (exceptionally talented students to be allowed to bypass these schools)

(iv) foundation of vocational training schools offering technician training over six months to two years for graduates of the ten-year schools

(v) provision for those who left school at 17 and have been employed for two years to enter higher education by means of special entrance examinations.

10 THE SYSTEM IN OPERATION

Provision

Attendance at primary school is universal, and secondary and tertiary education are available to all who are adequately qualified. The well developed and extensive system of adult education ensures that education at all levels is available to every citizen. The urgent post-war requirement for trained personnel, and the need rapidly to satisfy demands for skilled workers as they arose, resulted in a complicated and perhaps rather unwieldy system of further education and teacher training.

Within the limits imposed by the availability of finance and equipment, vocational training is adequate and there is a reasonable balance between vocational and academic graduate outputs. The total number of places in all institutes of higher education is fixed by the Ministry of Science, Higher Education and Technology. The number is determined by the projected pattern of demand for graduates and other trained personnel. This close planning and control of the whole educational system results in an even balance being maintained between the various levels of the system, and ensures the supply of trained personnel to meet national employment needs.

One of the main post-war aims of the scheme to rebuild education was that no child of primary school age should be more than three kilometres from a school, no mean target in a country whose population is as widely and evenly distributed as that of Poland. This aim was largely achieved, though at some cost to the quality of schools and equipment. Most pupils live at home and there is a bus service to take children to and from school in country districts. However, some primary age children and rather more of secondary school age are too far from the nearest school to attend as day pupils. In such cases boarding facilities are provided and the children go home for the weekends. With the passage of the post-war population bulge, the demand for primary school places has decreased and a number of such schools in country places have been amalgamated with a resulting concentration of resources. These comprehensive community schools in villages now cater for 81.3% of rural pupils.

The specific distribution of the school network in both towns and villages, matching the economic and demographic prospects of different regions is being entrusted to special *voivodship* committees. Their estimates show how many more classrooms are needed for the ten-year schools including those in villages. Over the 1970-1980 decade 900 new schools were proposed and 770 others had to be expanded. The answer to this problem was found in standard designs for a unit system, which also places under one roof pre-school and ten-year school facilities. But other solutions, too, have been produced by a competition organised by the Ministry of Education and Schooling and the Association of Polish Architects. Twenty-two accepted designs dealt with what are called educational units covering a whole set of schools (not only the ten-year schools).

Buildings and Equipment

Immediately after the war the rebuilding and rapid expansion of the school system resulted in a lowering of the standards of school building and equipment, especially in rural areas. The system of rationalising and amalgamating primary schools, now that the post-war bulge has passed, has facilitated an improvement in standards. In general the standard of school building is now higher, though schools still tend to look rather dull and monotonous. However, the interiors are brightened up by the extensive use of posters and wall displays. Equipment, though good, is often in rather short supply, limiting the range of experimental work possible. Plans for refurbishing or building new schools are often subject to extremely long delays due to the considerable labour and equipment shortages in the building industry. A policy of 'self-help' is often resorted to.

Teachers

There was an acute shortage of trained teachers after World War Two which was temporariy relieved by the setting up of 'crash' training programmes. All except a very small number of teachers, by now probably less than 1%, are regarded as being qualified. The two-year 'crash' post-war teacher training programme has been wound up and teachers so trained are being given part time courses to bring their training up to the required minimum standard. Part time training courses will eventually result in all teachers being fully trained. Perhaps because of the shortage of trained teachers methods have tended to be traditional, but in recent years there has been a movement to break away from passive learning and the traditional teacher/class relationship. New primary syllabi, introduced from 1968/69, have placed greater emphasis on practical equipment, self-teaching techniques and the encouragement of individual creativity. Teacher training is a key matter in the current educational reforms and the government is spending many millions of zloty on this.

At the primary and general secondary levels, a large majority of the teachers are women. In vocational and technical training establishments, most are men. The social status of all teachers is high, reflecting the high status given to learning and academic achievement in the country as a whole. Despite the set curricula and textbooks, teachers are given a considerable amount of professional freedom in the way they teach, the order in which programmes are covered and the amount of time given to any one section and to practical work. However, high social and professional status is not reflected in the teachers' rates of pay. Until 1973 teachers' pay lagged behind that of the other professions. However, a large pay increase brought their salary up to its present level, slightly higher than the national average. The minimum teachers' pay is less than most teachers in primary schools earn and not much more than half that earned by secondary school teachers. Headmasters earn a good deal more, up to twice the salary of a secondary school teacher. Another major government priority is the improvement of teachers' living and working conditions.

Wastage and Repetition

Dropout and repeater rates cannot be regarded as excessive at any level. The average dropout rate at primary level in 1971/2 was a mere 0.6%, rising to 2.2% and 3.0% in general and vocational secondary schools. At trade schools the rate was 6% and in higher education among full time students it was 8.9%. Throughout the system the percentage figure for those repeating years is around 6%. What wastage there is can be ascribed mainly to failure to make the grade academically and to social factors such as the need to contribute to the family income. Adequate part time facilities are available to enable this group to complete their education.

REFERENCES AND FURTHER READING

Barnett, Clifford R. (1958). *Poland: its People, its Society, its Culture.* HRAF Press, New Haven, Conn.
Huszcz, Miroslav (1979). *Education in the Polish People's Republic.* Wydawnictva Szkolnei Pedagogiczne, Warsaw.
Kliskowska, A. and Martinotti, G. (1977). *Education in a Changing Society.* Sage, London.
Liberska, Barbara (1974). *Education and Youth Employment in Poland.* Carnegie Commission on Policy Studies in Higher Education, Berkeley, California.
Pachocinski, Ryszand et al. (1974). *Adult Education in People's Poland.* European Centre for Leisure and Education, Prague.
Okon, Wincenty (1973). *The School Readiness Project.* Unesco/IBE, Paris.
Sanyal, Bikas C. et al. (1978). *Graduate Employment and Planning of Higher Education in Poland.* IIEP, Paris.
Simon, Brian (1954). *Education in the New Poland.* Lawrence and Wishard, London.
Slomszynski, Kazimiorz (Ed.) (1978). *Class Structure and Social Mobility in Poland.* Sharpe, White Plains.
Szcepanski, Jan (1978). *Systems of Higher Education: Poland.* New York International Council for Educational Development.
UNESCO (1979). *Educational Reforms: Experiences and Prospects.* Unesco, Paris.
Ziernsky, Maria (1978). *Early Child Care in Poland.* Gordon and Breach, London.

Structure of the Education System in Poland

Age	3 4 5 6 7 8 9 10 11 12 13 14 15 16 17 18 19 20 21 22 23 24
Level	I · II · III · IV
Stage	1 · 2 · 3 · 4 · 5
Compulsory	
School type	Nursery schools · Primary · Vocational classes · Secondary · Vocational schools · Technical schools · Universities and institutions of higher education

▨ Education preceding the first level

Examinations: Final examinations at end of stage 3

Source: UNESCO/IBE International Yearbook of Education

Special schools for delicate and physically and mentally handicapped

Compulsory Education: Age Limits 7–15   Duration (years) 8
Entrance age to pre-school education: 3

POLAND BASIC STATISTICS	1960	1970	1975	1978 (approx.)
1 Total population (000)	29,561	32,472	33,840	35,010
% female	52	51	51	51
2 % population 0-14 years	33.5	26.9		23
% female	49	49	49	49
3 Enrolment, all levels	5,881,261	7,016,210	6,326,118	6,405,079
% female	48	50	50	50
First level	4,841,157	5,256,970	4,309,823	4,105,404
% female	48	48	48	48
Second level	836,724	1,361,343	1,440,796	1,677,044
% female	50	57	55	48
Third level	203,380	397,897	575,499	622,631
% female	40	47	54	55
4 Teachers, all levels				
% female				
First level	147,863	228,743	208,173	199,982
% female	71	80	81	82
Second level	44,878	164,353	171,610	
% female		39		
Third level	19,098	33.695	50,272	53,808(Univ.)
% female	26			34
5 Public expenditure on education				
Total (000) Zlotys	17,410	36,974	50,449	
As % of GNP	4.6	4.9	3.7	3.1
As % of public expenditure				7.3
6 % enrolment (MF) by level	100	100	100	100
First level	82	75	68	64
Second level	14	19	23	26
Third level	3	6	9	10
% enrolment (F) by level	100	100	100	100
First level	83	72	65	61
Second level	15	22	25	28
Third level	3	5	10	11
7 Entrance age: Duration of				
First level education	7:7	7:8	7:8	7:8
Second level education	14:4	15:4	15:4	15:4
8 Enrolment ratios (MF)				
First level	109	102	100	100
Second level	50	49	53	67
Third level	9.16	14.12	16.87	17.77
Enrolment ratios (F)				
First level	107	100	99	99
Second level	50	57	60	75
Third level	7.34	13.55	18.60	19.93

Spain

CONTENTS

1 Geography 590
2 Population 592
3 Society and Culture 593
4 History and Politics 594
5 The Economy 596
6 The Education System 599
7 Educational Administration . . . 606
8 Educational Finance 608
9 Development and Planning of
 the Education System 609
10 The System in Operation 611

It has been said that there are seven Spains, not one. Certainly in rural parts of the country, which is strongly Catholic, regional loyalties, sometimes finding expression in separatist movements, exist. These loyalties are a legacy of the independent mediaeval kingdoms and of invasions at the hands of Roman, Arab and other invaders. Language plays an important role in mobilising regional sentiments. Thus the Basques, Catalans, Galicians and Asturians claim the right to retain and indeed develop their own identities. The régime established under General Franco in 1939 managed to contain political movements based on cultural differences and ensured peace and stability at the expense of individual liberties. After his death under a constitutional monarch, King Juan Carlos, separatist movements have re-emerged, political parties number 200 and in the 1977 elections the Communist Party took part and the Socialist Party gained 115 seats.

While this political and cultural diversity is, among European countries, a rather unique feature of Spain, the fact that the educational system has been dominated by the Church has ensured a measure of unity as far as education is concerned and that unity reflected elements common to European systems of education rather than to a distinctive Spanish tradition. Since 1970 the Church has revised its position *vis à vis* its involvement in the control of education and indeed faces, as in France, fierce opposition from anti-clerical right wingers.

Features of the development of Spanish education similar to those found elsewhere in Europe include an expansion of voluntary pre-school provision in State and private centres; an integrated basic general education period of schooling from 6 to 13. This reorganisation was introduced through the Education Act of 1970, was designed to replace the former selective system and was completed in 1974/75. It has made possible a massive increase in the number of pupils receiving free basic education. This level of education is now divided into two four-year stages but evaluation in both of them are by continuous assessment. The severity of the previous selection procedures has been reduced and now the post-basic education course (EGB) will be followed by a three-year course leading to a single school leaving and university entrance examination for students aged about 17 or 18. As in many countries these reforms were designed to improve equality of opportunity in and access to the second and third levels of education and to provide an integrated system of schooling which can be adapted to the abilities of individual pupils.

Vocational schools have been extensively developed since 1945 and it is now possible for a large section of Spanish pupils to enter one of the several kinds of vocational/technical schools or centres after they have completed the eight-year basic education course. A majority of pupils, in fact, continue their education and training in these schools, having been unable to gain admission to a general secondary school which prepares pupils for the *Bachillerato Unificado y Polivalente* (BUP) and thus for entrance to the university.

University enrolments, as elsewhere, have risen dramatically since 1950 when the figure was about 54,000. In 1976 it had reached a total of some 458,000. Teacher education has been incorporated into the university structure although pre-school and first level teachers are still trained in institutions which were formerly secondary schools for teachers *(escuelas normales)*. They have been renamed *(escuelas universitarias de formación de profesorado de EGB)*, incorporated into the universities and train teachers for the new basic schools.

Over the last thirty years illiteracy rates, at 20% in 1950, which were high for Europe, have been reduced considerably. There are a number of ways in which adult students can improve their qualifications including a national university of distance education *(Universidad Nacional de Educación a Distance (UNED)*.

The Editor

1 GEOGRAPHY

Topography

Mainland Spain, with an area of 486,272 sq km (189,950 square miles) and a coastline of 2,080 km (1,300 miles), is more than twice the size of Britain and occupies five sixths of the Iberian peninsula. It is extremely mountainous and in altitude is second only to Switzerland in the whole of Europe; the average altitude

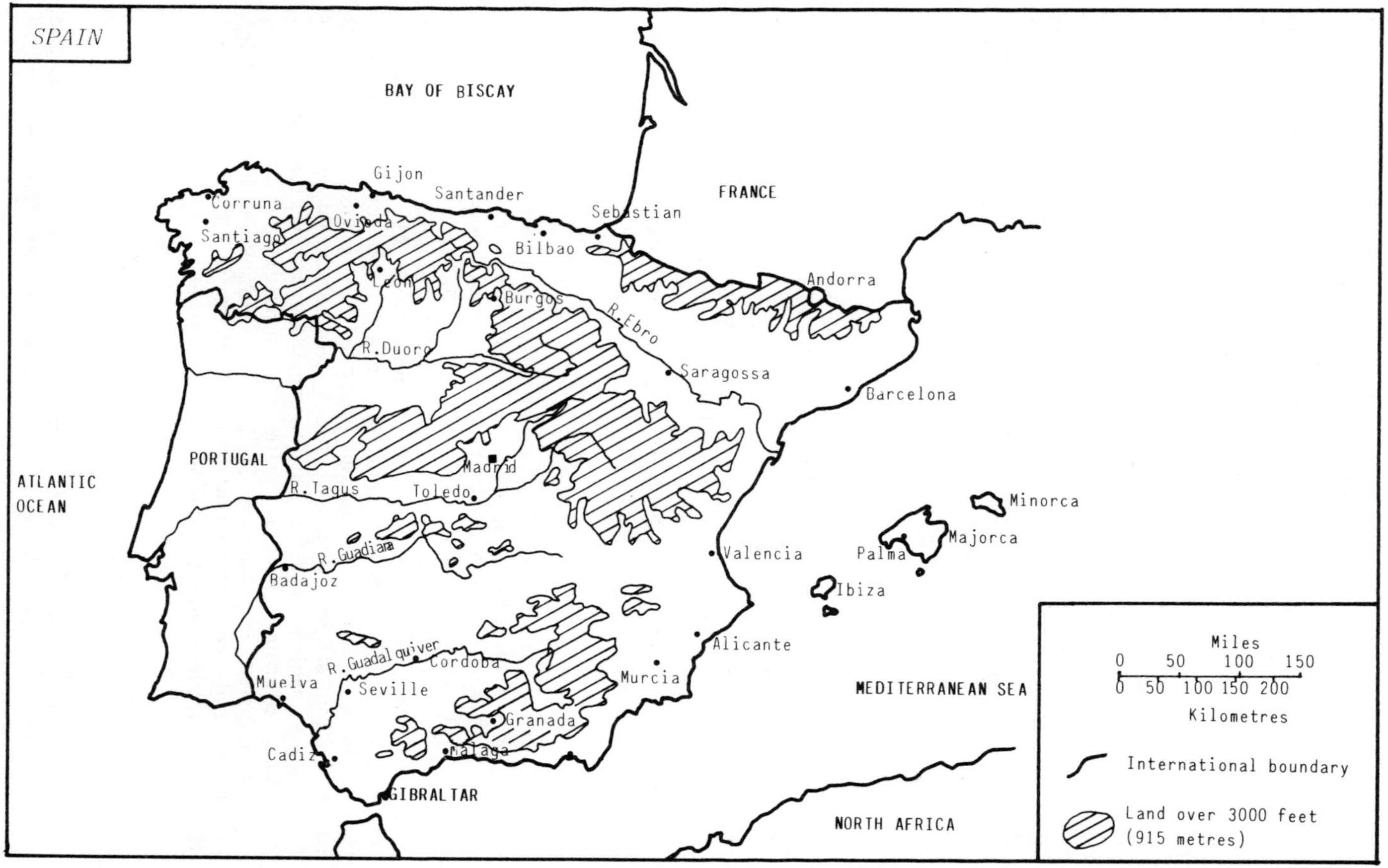
SPAIN
BAY OF BISCAY
FRANCE
ATLANTIC
OCEAN
PORTUGAL
MEDITERRANEAN SEA
NORTH AFRICA
GIBRALTAR
Corruna
Santiago
Gijon
Oviedo
Santander
Bilbao
Sebastian
Andorra
Leon
Burgos
R.Ebro
R.Duoro
Saragossa
Barcelona
Madrid
R.Tagus
Toledo
Minorca
Majorca
Palma
Ibiza
Valencia
R.Guadiana
Badajoz
Alicante
R.Guadalquiver
Cordoba
Murcia
Muelva
Seville
Granada
Cadiz
Malaga
Miles
0 50 100 150
0 50 100 150 200
Kilometres
International boundary
Land over 3000 feet
(915 metres)

is 670 metres (2,263 feet) and almost 20% of the land is over 1,000 metres high. It is crossed by five great mountain chains running roughly east to west and one in the south west running in a southerly direction. The centre of the country is occupied by a great tableland *(meseta)*. The complicated geographical structure of Spain has been of great importance in its historical and economic development.

Two sets of offshore islands are administered as part of Spain. The Balearic Islands, an archipelago off the east coast of mainland Spain covering an area of 4,954 sq km (1,935 square miles), consist of 11 islands of which Majorca is the largest. The Canary Islands are a group of 7 islands and 6 islets with an area of 8,517 sq km (3,327 square miles) situated in the Atlantic Ocean to the south west of Morocco and about 160 km off the coast of the former Spanish Sahara. There are also two enclaves on the North African coast, Ceuta and Mellila, which have areas of only a few square kilometres each.

Climate

Reinforcing the regionalism encouraged by the mountains is the variety of climatic types. The north has an Atlantic climate with cool winters, mild summers and heavy annual rainfall. The dry Mediterranean south and east are separated from the north by the *meseta* which is also dry but subject to continental extremes of temperature in winter and summer. In several areas, for example the province of Estremadura, problems caused by lack of rainfall in the past are being dealt with by a system of dams and reservoirs which is rapidly making Spain a country of inland lakes.

Communications

The mountains have always hindered communication and few rivers are navigable. Roads and railways radiate from the centrally placed capital, Madrid. The roads have been greatly improved in recent years, mainly as a response to the enormous increase in traffic, and a far greater volume of commercial goods is not transported by road than rail. At the end of 1976 Spain had 145,328 km of road including 1,091 km of motorway. The railway system is being improved by means of a large modernisation scheme which includes electrification of many lines. Topography makes air transport very suitable for Spain and the State airline, Iberia, with its subsidiary, is the second biggest carrier in Europe. It has an extensive internal flight schedule and runs international flights to North and South America, northern Africa and all over europe.

2 POPULATION

Growth

For its size, Spain has a very small population – 35.8 million (1976 estimate). The density per square kilometre (68) is low for Europe, and less than one third of that of Britain, but there is great variation across the country. Although hardly phenomenal, the annual rate of increase during the 1960s was, at 1.1%, one of the highest in Europe and almost three times that of Britain; improved medicine and hygiene have greatly reduced infant mortality and the overall death rate since the turn of the century. By 1980 there were 5.4 million children in a population of 37.7 million.

Movements

Emigration since 1960 has totalled over 4 million but many of these people have been and are temporary migrants to Europe who return after three or four years. A more permanent feature has been the movement of some 4-5 million peasants to the cities since the late 1950s. Twenty-three of the 50 provinces have actually lost population, although their capitals have all gained, with the sole exception of Toledo. The shift is from the marginal agricultural regions of Andalusia, Estremadura, Galicia and parts of Castille to the industrial centres of Madrid, Barcelona, Valencia, Bilbao, Sevilla and to the tourist zones including the Canaries and the Balearics. Madrid now has a population of some 4.4 million people, Barcelona 2 million, Valencia 1 million, and Bilbao 950,000.

3 SOCIETY AND CULTURE

Social Patterns

Rapid industrial growth, urban development, a swift rise in the material standard of living, the influence of tourists from the north and the Americas, the experiences of workers returning from northern Europe, the number of Spaniards who now travel extensively, the onset of television; all have contributed to a change in traditional Spanish attitudes and customs. Gone are the parochial attitudes of the 1940s and 1950s; dress, behaviour and censorship too are rapidly relaxing. While the family continues to be a closely knit group, most Spaniards have ceased to be inward looking and see themselves firmly as Europeans, though independence and individualism are still strong. In some parts, however, an intensely regional outlook prevails, a legacy of the independent mediaeval kingdoms and of Roman, Arab and other invaders. Groups with their own language and cultural traditions include the Basques, Catalans, Galicians, and Asturians, all vociferous in proclaiming their separate identities.

Religion

Spain is a Catholic country and the Church dominated education until recently not only because historically it had been an integral part of the culture and character of Spain but also because in a relatively poor and isolated country it had no serious competition. However, since 1970 when free basic education for all was advocated and in the face of far-reaching economic and social change the Church has begun to revise its outlook. Of late it has shown a desire to free itself from its close involvement and identification with Francoism and to concern itself increasingly with major social problems. (The most fierce anti-clericals now are right wingers.) The rigid, dogmatic attitudes of the 1940s and 1950s are fast disappearing though still retained by the older churchmen; there is in fact something of a generation gap between those who are socially motivated and liberal in their outlook and those who are more traditionally conservative. However, officially the Spanish Church is still opposed to contraception, abortion and divorce.

4 HISTORY AND POLITICS

The Nineteenth Century

Following its great period of wealth, political influence and culture during the sixteenth and seventeenth centuries, Spain gradually became a backwater of Europe. The period of 1814-1931 following the Peninsular War (War of Independence) and the restoration of the Bourbons was politically chaotic. The monarchy was briefly replaced by a republic in 1873 and in 1931 King Alfonso XIII was deposed having increasingly sought to undermine parliamentary government by misusing his constitutional powers. The main developments during this period were the growing polarisation between liberals and revolutionaries on the one side and conservatives, traditionalists and reactionaries on the other and the emergence of the soldier-politician, an important figure in Spanish politics for with a weakened monarchy, the army was one of the few institutions capable of maintaining unity in the country.

The Civil War

The Second Republic lasted five years (1931-36). In February 1936 an electoral alliance of the left assumed power in succession to the right wing régime which had ruled for the previous three years. However, the alliance was split and not strong enough to govern effectively. Inexorably the political situation was hardening into irreconcilable extremes as each party recruited squads of thugs who clashed openly with rival groups. The assassination of Calvo Sotelo, the most forceful figure on the right, finally precipitated outright war in July 1936. Initially in two thirds of the country the right wing rising failed; three of its four leaders were killed leaving Francisco Franco y Bahamonde *generalissimo* and supreme politial leader. He proved a clever and tenacious war leader and with some assistance from fascist régimes in Europe led a victorious campaign which ended with the capitulation of Madrid in April 1939. During the war between 700,000 and 1 million Spaniards were killed and about 350,000 left the country.

Franco Régime

General Franco established in 1939 an authoritarian rule which gave Spain peace and stability while severely restricting individual liberties. By dint of political acumen, clever and thorough planning and sheer ruthlessness, he succeeded in holding power, keeping the various factions which supported him in balance with one another and crushing any attempt at a united opposition. All decisions were taken centrally by Franco presiding over his chosen ministers. After World War Two, in which Spain remained neutral, Franco announced in 1947 that the monarchy would be restored on his death or retirement. In 1969 he nominated Prince Juan Carlos, grandson of King Alfonso XIII, as his successor. During Franco's rule overt opposition to the régime gradually faded though the Basque Separatist movement (ETA) continued to pursue its aims by guerilla methods. However, in January 1974 Carlos Arias Navarro became Prime Minister and promised reforms. These promises combined with increased freedom of the press, an apparent weakening of Franco's health and the Portuguese revolution in 1974 led to increased left wing political activity.

Since Franco

In November 1975 General Franco died and was immediately succeeded by King Juan Carlos. In December a more liberal cabinet was formed but the reform programme it announced the following April was widely condemned for not moving sufficiently quickly towards complete democracy. In July 1976 the King appointed Adolfo Suárez Gonzalez Prime Minister in succession to Arias. In December a popular referendum approved the government's proposal for the establishment of a two-chamber elected legislature. General elections were held in June 1977 in which the Communist Party took part having been legalised earlier in the year; (other political associations had been permitted since April 1976). There are now over 200 political parties in Spain but at the elections five main groups emerged: right wing conservatives; centrists (led by Sr Suárez); socialists; communists and separatist groups. During his 11 months as Prime Minister Sr Suárez gained widespread respect for his success in introducing reforms without incurring the serious hostility of any major political group. In the elections his Centrist Alliance was the most successful party though with 165 out of 350 seats in the lower house his government did not achieve an overall majority without coalition. The Socialist Party gained 115 seats. In 1981 associated with the fall of Suárez there was an unsuccessful military coup. In 1982 a Socialist government was elected for the first time since the 1930s.

Government Organisation

Since 1975 Spain has been a hereditary monarchy. The King is Head of State and has considerable powers including the appointment of the Prime Minister (President of the Government) and on his recommendation the Council of Ministers. He also has a power of veto over legislation and the right to call referenda on important national issues regardless of parliament. The King is advised by two councils - a Council of State and a Council of the Realm (both of which consist partly of elected and partly of nominated members). The Council of Ministers initiates legislation which is discussed by the legislative assembly (Cortes). Spain is divided into 50 provinces (47 on the mainland, two on the Canary Islands and the province of the Balearics). Each has its own assembly (diputación provincial) and an appointed civil governor. In September 1977, a measure of autonomy was given to Catalonia, and the regional government (Generalidad) was provisionally re-established. A similar measure of autonomy for the Basque country seems likely to be approved shortly.

The constitutional reforms approved in December 1976 provide for a two-chamber legislature with a lower house consisting of 350 elected deputies and an upper house with 207 members elected regionally, four from each mainland province, one from each insular province, plus two each from Ceuta and Melilla, and 41 members appointed by the King. Each of the houses will have a four-year life. Elections are by a system of proportional representation. The presidents of each of the two houses are elected by members but the King appoints an overall President of the Legislature, and the President of the Council of the Realm. It is likely that the King's powers will be gradually reduced as Spain moves further towards complete democracy.

International Relations

Until the late 1940s the régime was ostracised on account of its previous connections with the Nazi and Fascist dictatorships and its own policy. Then in the 1950s it progressed to an agreement with the USA for the establishment of bases in Spain and to membership of UNO and UNESCO. Since then Spanish diplomacy has been particularly active in the Arab world, where it has maintained good relationships throughout successive Arab/Israeli conflicts, and in Latin America where it seeks to strengthen ties through *hispanidad;* for example, an important trade agreement has been concluded with Cuba. It has also had some success with its overtures to East European states for increased economic and cultural cooperation; the Russian Atlantic trawler fleet is now based at Tenerife and regular flights to and from Moscow carrying relief crews were established in 1973. Relations with France are particularly strong in the cultural as well as in the commercial, industrial and defence spheres. In 1977 Spain made formal application to accede to the EEC.

5 THE ECONOMY

Natural Resources

Spain is relatively well off in mineral resources but does not have sufficient quantities of hydrocarbons and metallic ores to cover the needs of the industrial sector. Minerals include coal, iron ore, copper, tin, zinc, lead, nickel, phosphates, potash.

Economic Situation

Spain is now the fifth largest industrial nation of Europe and its 1972 growth rate of 7.5% was second only to Japan's in the OECD area. This 'economic miracle' has gained momentum since the early 1960s through three successive development plans and the stimulus of an EEC boom across the frontier. Between 1963 and 1974 national income per capita increased from less than US$500 to US$2,000 though there are still considerable regional variations; the per capita income in Barcelona is about three times that of Galicia or the poorer parts of Andalusia. The economic boom carried Spain through 1974 despite the worldwide recession but in 1975 the annual growth rate was only 0.8%. Investment fell by 9% and unemployment rose to 6% as migrant workers returned from abroad. In February 1976 the peseta was devalued by 10% and this contributed to an increase in the inflation rate which was running at 20% in the months up to May 1976. In October of that year emergency measures were introduced including wage restraint, import controls and sales incentives. During the first half of 1977, inflation was running at a rate of 25%, and was expected to rise. In July 1977 the peseta was further devalued by 25% and urgent discussions were held between all political parties about the necessity for further economic measures. These measures were made law on 14 November and included an additional property tax, and increased taxes on luxury goods.

Agriculture

Out of a total surface area of 50.5 million hectares, 46.9 million are cultivable; in 1975 23.9 million hectares were under cultivation. The total value of agricultural production in 1975 was 897,698 million pesetas. For various reasons agriculture has traditionally been one of the economic sectors most closely tied up with politics. But in spite of the emphasis which has been given to agrarian policy, especially latterly, what is certain is that it has always been more theoretical than practical; that is, declarations have tended to be ahead of concrete action, partly owing to difficulties caused by the Spanish climate and partly owing to the structural deficiency of the farms. On the other hand recent agrarian policy has suffered from some disorder, the profound change in demand not having been foreseen with sufficient anticipation, leading to a serious imbalance on the commercial side, and exacerbating many of the problems arising from difficulties in exporting agricultural products. Agricultural policy for the future will have to be geared to Spain's possible entry to the EEC, rejecting any closed policy and if necessary reorienting Spanish agriculture so that it can serve as a complement to the agriculture of the EEC countries. Duplication will have to be avoided, at least as long as productivity in those commodities most affected by competition is not increased.

Agricultural products still represent a high proportion of exports but industrial products now account for more than 70%

in addition to some mineral products. During the 1960s with the industrial boom there was a dramatic increase in the export of manufactured goods - particularly ships, motor vehicles, electrical machines, shoes and rubber goods. The USA has traditionally taken a large proportion of Spanish exports but in 1975 took only 10% behind France (14%) and the Federal Republic of Germany. Nearly half of Spain's exports go to EEC countries. The annual trade deficit has been enormous for some years but until 1974 earnings from tourism and migrant workers abroad more than compensated for this. In 1974 oil prices and reduced export opportunities coupled with stagnation in the tourism industry and a decline in foreign earnings doubled the trade deficit.

Industry

Spanish industry is largely a post-1940 phenomenon, initiated and greatly aided by American investment and military expenditure. It is now able to satisfy local demand over a wide range of consumer goods and durables. In particular heavy industry has expanded rapidly, especially shipbuilding, steel, chemicals, plastics, electricity and gas. However, Spanish industry is still characterised by extremes with mammoth national firms contrasting with great numbers of tiny factories that are technically backward. Most manufacturers purchase foreign patents; for example, there is no Spanish-designed car although Spain is in the top five European motor manufacturing countries. Research and technology are largely lacking and consequently Spain can be expected to invest more money in the development of higher technical institutes.

The State participates in industry through the *Instituto Nacional de Industria*, created in 1941 to develop basic industries. The INI can be regarded as a holding company which covers different sectors; energy, steel production, mining and transport; it can also be regarded as a multinational company. Of the 58 companies in which the INI participates directly, 32 have more than 1,000 employees and seven more than 10,000. Over 50% of naval construction, steel production and mining is controlled by INI companies. Participation in other basic sectors (oil, chemicals and electricity) is, however, far less. The INI's role has developed since its formation when it concentrated on only two sectors; later it passed through a phase in the 1960s of giving financial assistance in low rentability sectors where private enterprise is reluctant to participate, and in more recent years it has assumed a complementary and even competitive character, being represented on innumerable Boards of Directors. With almost 87% of the total gross product the INI is the most important organism in public enterprise. The private banks have also had an enormous influence on industrial development, though the independent commercial organisations, while participating in 68.1% of industrial activity, account for only 3.2% of the total gross product.

6 THE EDUCATION SYSTEM
General

The new Education Act came into force in 1970 and was intended to replace the old system within ten years. The following description attempts to cover both the new system and remaining parts of the old.

Academic Year

The academic year runs from October to July with the long vacation in the summer. At school level it lasts 220 school days.

Pre-School

Pre-primary education is voluntary. It is offered both in State centres where it is free and in private centres. The cycle is divided into two stages: *jardines de infancia* for the 2-3 year age group and *escuelas de parvulos* for 4-5 year olds. In 1974/75 there were 853,322 pupils in pre-school education (322,685 in State centres). About 25% of all centres were in Madrid, Barcelona and Valencia.

Basic *(Educación General Basica)*

The period of schooling for the 6-13 age group is now called *educatión general basica* (EGB). EGB was instituted by the 1970 Education Act to achieve the objectives of integrated schooling, equal opportunities for all and a system which can be adapted to the abilities of each pupil. Substitution of EGB for the former system of primary education (*enseñanza primaria* - ages 6-9) and lower secondary education (*bachillerato elemental* - ages 10-13) began in 1971/72 and the changeover was completed in the academic year 1974/75.

This cycle of education is compulsory and is now free. Some primary and secondary schools are still privately run. The State had increasingly extended its aid to families in low income groups so that the number of students receiving free education rose from 260,400 in 1972/73 to 810,640 in 1973/74. In 1974/75 the total number of pupils at primary level was 5,361,771 of whom 3,229,863 were in State centres. Schools work a five-day week with voluntary attendance on Saturdays for extra-curricular activities. The language of learning is Spanish but regional languages may be studied if circumstances permit. English replaced French as the first foreign language following the 1970 Education Act and it is now in great demand as Spain moves towards membership of the EEC.

The EGB is divided into two cycles covering eight years of school life. The first cycle serves the 6-10 age group and consists of grades 1-5; the second cycle serves the 11-13 age group and consists of grades 6-8. Subjects taught in the first cycle are divided into two main groupings as follows:

(i) 'areas of expression' which include Spanish, a foreign language, mathematics, arts and crafts, music and sports

(ii) 'areas of experience' which include the social and natural sciences and religion.

Evaluation is by continuous assessment made by the school staff and noted in the pupil's academic record (*extracto del registro personal del alumno* - ERPA). The areas taught in the second cycle are:

(i) languages - Spanish, English or French and the vernacular (e.g. Basque and Catalan) where the local situation demands it

(ii) social studies - the interdisciplinary study of geography and history, anthropology, law, sociology, etc.

(iii) mathematics

(iv) natural sciences

(v) artistic expression (music, art, drama and handicrafts)

(vi) religious education

(vii) physical education and sport.

Pupils at this level are also judged by a process of continuous assessment which usually involves regular tests. If the pupil fails to make the grade at the end of one year he can go on to the next but has further coaching to help him recover lost ground. The second cycle leads to the qualification *Graduado Escolar* for the more able, and *Certificado de Escolaridad* for the less able.

Second Level Schools

Under the old system those who passed the examination on completion of primary studies and obtained the *Certificado Estudios Primarios* were admitted to a four-year junior secondary course *(bachillerato elemental)* leading to the examination of that name taken at the age of 13. After this they could continue studying for a further two years for the *Bachillerato Superior* examination or take a three-year course for the *Bachillerato Técnico Superior*. In 1974/75 the last grade of the *Bachillerato Elemental* course became stage of EGB, and by the end of the academic year 1977/78 the *Bachillerato Superior* and *Bachillerato Técnico Superior* courses were completely replaced by a three-year course leading to the *Bachillerato Unificade y Polivalente* (BUP).

Compulsory subjects taught in the *Bachillerato Unificado y Polivalente* (BUP) course are Spanish and a foreign language, social sciences, science, mathematics, art and music, religion, physical education and sports. In addition the pupil chooses one of the following: industrial technology, agriculture, commerce and home economics. The aim is to give the pupils some idea of Spanish economic development at a local level. The BUP certificate given by the Ministry of Education and Science at the end of the course enables the holder to enter either vocational education or a university preparatory course.

Vocational

Vocational schools have been more extensively developed since 1945 than any other branch of second level education. Vocational education has been available at several different kinds of institution training skilled and specialist workers.

Vocational High Schools

These schools (variously called *centros de enseñanza media y profesional, institutos laborales* and *escuelas medias laborales)* combined vocational courses with general education and were originally designed for the large section of the Spanish school-age population excluded from traditional secondary studies. Students could transfer to the vocational school at any time before or after completing the primary course. Specialisation was in one of four areas: agriculture, industrial studies, fisheries or administration and commerce. A five-year course culminated in the *Bachillerato Laboral Elemental*, followed by a two-year course for the *Bachillerato Laboral Superior*. The higher diploma might in some cases be substituted for the general *Bachillerato Superior* as a prerequisite for admission to university.

Technical Secondary Schools

To enter a school of this kind *(escuelas técnicas de grado medio)* pupils would have attained the age of 12 years and obtained a certificate equivalent to the *Bachillerato Elemental*. The first two years of the five-year course were devoted to academic studies and introduction to the trade to be followed; the remaining three years were almost entirely vocational in nature. Completion of the course entitled the student to the qualification *perito* or *aparejador* (expert) and he could if he wished apply on the strength of it for admission to a university.

Professional Trade Schools
(centros de formación profesional industrial)

The courses in these institutions have been changed as part of the educational reform. The new FP is in three stages, each of two years' duration; it consists of:

(i)   Grade I, for those students who have completed their basic education but do not go on to study for the *Bachillerato Unificado y Polivalente* (BUP). It is now compulsory and free

(ii) Grade II, for those who have successfully completed their BUP and those who have done further complementary courses after doing Grade I

(iii) Grade III, for those who have done the first cycle of a university course or have completed a complementary course after finishing Grade II successfully.

The first stage (Grade I) of FP consists of a six-month period called 'Introduction to the World of Work' followed by specialisation in a trade such as metalwork, catering and agriculture. Each first stage technical school offers facilities for at least two main trades. The courses (Grades II and III) for secondary and university (first cycle) leavers were introduced in 1976/77. There will be adaptation courses at all stages. Separate schools exist for maritime studies, agriculture, applied arts and crafts, fine arts, commercial education, medical auxiliary and welfare officers' training.

Workers' Universities (universidades laborales)

These were founded in the 1950s with funds provided by *sindicatos* (workers' associations) and offer courses for working class children over the age of 11. They offered mainly practical technical courses but have adapted to changing circumstances and are now running more general education courses (including EGB and BUP) for entry to Higher National Certificate type courses at the higher technical institutes. They are lavishly equipped and are the responsibility not of the Ministry of Education but the Ministry of Labour though some are run by religious organisations on behalf of the Ministry. The radical wing of the *Falange* movement was identified with these institutions and the very generosity of their endowments has aroused the criticism and envy of more orthodox academic establishments.

Pre-University

Attendance at a one-year pre-university course has traditionally been required of all students applying for admission to a Spanish university. The preparatory course (*curso de orientación universitaria* - COU), nominally part of the university course, was established in 1971/72 on an experimental basis to replace the old *preuniversitario* (PREU). The specific goals of COU are to deepen the student's knowledge of basic sciences, to help him determine the course of his career, and to equip him with the intellectual processes and techniques for a higher education. The course includes three compulsory subjects: Spanish, a foreign language, and mathematics. The student can also study three optional subjects from a list of five. This list may include another foreign language. Additionally there are a number of compulsory classes to attend in religion, civics, careers guidance and study techniques. Evaluation at present is by continuous assessment but a recent innovation adopted to control numbers is a 'selective test' to be set by individual faculties. Staff teaching the COU are graduates.

Third Level (Higher) Institutions

In 1980 there were eighteen State universities and some private ones. In that year student numbers (including those enrolled at higher technical institutes) had reached over 200,000 compared with 54,605 in 1950. Between 15,000 and 20,000 foreign students study at Spanish universities, the majority of them from North and South America.

Entrance

University education is cheap, and available in theory to anyone who has passed the COU year and also to people aged over 25 who are without secondary schooling but pass the appropriate examinations. In 1975 the government introduced a small element of selectivity by testing for aptitude and assessing motivation for higher studies, but this met with sustained opposition. Later attempts have also been violently opposed. The faculties of science and pharmacy require students to follow a selective course *(curso selectivo)* which they must pass before going on to the first year proper. In all the higher technical institutes the first year of study is considered selective *(tiene cáracter selectivo)*.

Courses

The licentiate *(título de licenciado* or *licenciatura)* is traditionally the first university degree and requires five years of study (six for pharmacy, medicine and veterinary medicine). The doctorate, the highest degree offered in Spain *(título de doctorado)* requires a minimum of one years' additional study (two in the faculty of medicine). It involves course work, the completion of a thesis under professional direction, and rigorous examinations. Doctorates are seldom completed in one year. University and higher technical education is now divided into three levels: a first cycle for basic study (three years); a second cycle for specialised study (two years); and a third cycle for further specialisation and research. The larger universities offer nine fields of study: sciences, politial sciences and sociology, economic and management sciences, law, pharmacy, arts, medicine, veterinary science and information science. In the higher technical institutes *(escuelas técnicas superiores* - ETS) architecture, aeronautical engineering, agronomics, civil engineering, industrial engineering, mining, forestry, naval engineering, and telecommunications are studied.

Study Patterns

University studies may be pursued officially *(oficial)* or as an external student *(no-oficial)*. The external students do not usually attend university classes and must be examined by a university board in order to validate their studies and receive grades. Official students matriculated for the degree are required to attend classes and follow a full course of study.

Teacher Training

Teachers for the various levels of education are trained as follows:

(i) class teachers for EGB education enter a three-year course after completiong the pre-university year (COU). these courses were formerly offered in *escuelas normales*, now renamed *escuelas universitarias de formacion de profesorado de EGB* and incorporated into the universities. At the end of the course, the students obtain the title of *Diplomado en Profesorado de EGB* in their own speciality which will permit them to work in State or private schools at the *pre-escolar* and EGB levels. The students then obtain a vocational qualification by following the *curso de pedagógicas* (CAP) which is a one-year teacher training course

(ii) teachers at BUP level take the CAP after a full five-year degree course.

Institutes of Education

These institutions *(institutos de ciencias de la education)* are incorporated into the local university. The Directors of the ICEs usually hold chairs in the university and are appointed by the Ministry of Education on the proposal forwarded by the Rector; they receive the salary and status of the dean of a faculty. Most members of the ICE are carried on the university payroll, with other university responsibilities, except in the case of the assistant director and the four heads of department who work full time for the ICE itself and are paid direct by the Ministry. The four departments are administration, research, teacher training, guidance and counselling and courses. Extra staff for short courses run by the ICE are contracted ad hoc. As the body responsible for teacher training, each ICE supervises the studies of the EGB teachers at the local *escuela universitaria* and directly runs the CAP courses followed by graduates. ICEs also direct and supervise COU courses in the university district and those schools which are declared *centros pilotos* where experimental research may be carried on.

The chief advisory body on teacher-training as well as the coordinator of the ICEs and their research programmes is the INCIE (formerly CENIDE). It concentrates mainly on long term problems and organises seminars for ICE teachers. It also runs the scholarship scheme for training future ICE teachers abroad. Superbly equipped by UNESCO, it has as yet lacked sufficient finance to plan programmes on the scale required.

Training for Language Teaching

The Ministry of Education runs certain official language schools *(escuelas oficiales de idiomas)* in Madrid, Barcelona, Valencia, La Coruña, Bilbao, Malaga, and Alicante. These schools are paid for by the Ministry of Education. Students attend evening classes of one hour, five days a week. Teachers are on part time contracts. Students who complete a course and pass a final examination receive a certificate which entitles them to teach in officially recognised schools at intermediate level. In practice, however, preference at these schools is always given to graduates. These official language schools should not be confused with the *escuelas de idiomas* which are university language schools supervised by the relevant university language department and catering for students of all faculties.

Adult and Non-Formal

By a decree of 10 March 1950 a National Literacy Board was established to coordinate efforts to combat illiteracy. In that year the illiteracy rate was 20%; by 1970 the figure had dropped to 8.9%.

There are a number of methods by which adult students can supplement a lack of formal secondary education. Many schools offer *bachillerato* courses in the evenings, and there is also a system of secondary education by radio and television. Students who cannot attend an official centre for classes are tutored by correspondence courses organised by *El Instituto Nacional de Enseñanza Media e Distancia* (INBAD). This is a national teaching centre which caters both for Spanish students and foreigners living abroad. Those registered are classified as official students and the qualifications they receive are as valid as those issued by formal institutions. BUP and COU syllabi are taught according to the present system. When the INBAD began its activities during 1975/76 there was a total registration of 6,824 students following the first year of BUP, within a year registration had risen to 11,562.

The *Universidad Nacional de Educación a Distancia* (UNED) was included in the Third Development Plan covering the years 1972-75; it was established on 18 August 1972, and commenced operation in January 1973. It has the same status as the conventional universities. The main centre is in Madrid and there are 11 regional centres spread over the whole country giving access to university education in the remoter areas. The UNED seeks to:

(i) further the idea of equality of opportunity in higher education particularly in the more inaccessible districts

(ii) take the pressure off other universities

(iii) provide new courses, methods and techniques with the aid of the most sophisticated up-to-date equipment

(iv) reinforce traditional education and recover those who had to leave higher studies before completion

(v) raise the general cultural level of the country and contribute substantially to *educación permanente*.

In 1976, the UNED had 27,500 students enrolled in ten courses with an additional course for students over 25 years of age. There were also 7,300 students following a course on updating of teaching methods for teachers at EGB level. No less than 90% of UNED students have other employment. There are 790 tutors (including those at regional centres).

7 EDUCATIONAL ADMINISTRATION
Organisation of the Ministry

The administrative structure of the Ministry of Education and Science was promulgated in March 1971. It offered a more logical administrative response to the new educational structure. The Ministry is made up of the Minister of Education, an Under-Secretary, eight Directors-General and the Provincial Delegations. The Minister of Education is a member of the Council of Ministers, is selected by the Prime Minister and approved by the Head of State. An Executive Council assists the Minister in the elaboration of policy. The Minister is President of this Council, the Under-Secretary is Vice-President and all Directors-General are members. The Ministry also has a number of consultative bodies to which it may refer to advice. The two main ones are the National Council for Education and the National Universities Council. Both are widely representative of the bodies concerned with education, but not necessarily of all shades of opinion in the country.

Centralised Control

The administration of the Spanish education system is highly centralised and the government controls all aspects of planning and organisation. Responsibility for the planning and forecasting of growth in education, budgeting policy, the drawing-up of programmes of needs, investments and their financing, proposals for the creation or suppression of teaching centres, and the construction and installation work carried out by the Ministry is in the hands of the Director-General of Programming and Investment. The Director-General for Educational Guidance and Policy is responsible for the drafting of study plans and syllabi for the different levels and kinds of education, the recognition of equivalent studies, research and assessment of teaching methods, the drafting of teacher training programmes and the coordination of the work of the provincial inspectorates. The Ministry of Education is responsible for the appointment of heads of State schools (on the recommendation of the previous head and/or the senior teachers), directors of the *Institutos de Ciencias de Educatión*, and rectors of universities. Ministerial approval is required for other senior university appointments.

Attempts to Decentralise

Attempts have been made to decentralise through the Provincial Delegations and by increasing university autonomy, but progress

ADMINISTRATION
THE STRUCTURE OF THE MINISTRY OF EDUCATION

```
                              MINISTER
                                 │
        ┌────────────────────────┼────────────────────────┐
   Executive                                         Private Office
   Council                                          (Gabinete Tecnico)
                                 │
                        Office of Under Secretary
                                 │
   ┌─────────────────┬───────────┼───────────┬─────────────────┐
   │                 │                       │                 │
Office of the   Director General    Director General    Director General of
Secretary       of Personnel        of Programming      Archives and Libraries
General for                         and Investment
Technical and
Administrative
Affairs
   │                 │                       │                 │
Director General  Director General   Director General    Director General
of Vocational     of Educational     of Universities     of Fine Arts
Training          Guidance & Policy  and Research
& Adult
Education

Consultative Bodies        Provincial Delegates       Autonomous State Entities
```

has been slow. Most universities now have their own statutes but the autonomy vested in them is nugatory. An interesting innovation in university administration has been the creation of the post of Manager (gerente) who is not a professional civil servant, and is appointed by the Ministry from a proposal by the Rector. This post represents the beginning of a university administrative staff and a loosening up of economic and administrative management.

8 EDUCATIONAL FINANCE

Education Budget

State spending on education in 1972 represented 2.7% of GNP and the budget of the Ministry of Education was 18.9% of the State budget. Projects in education involved a doubling of this expenditure by 1980 (at 1972 prices).

Allocation of Funds

The percentage distribution of the 1976 education budget between the various branches of the Ministry was as follows:

	%
Office of the Under Secretary	2.8
Secretary General for Technical & Administrative Affairs	0.3
Director-General of Vocational & Adult Education	2.7
Director-General of Personnel	56.5
Director-General of Educational Guidance and Policy	19.1
Director-General of Universities & Research	10.8
Director-General of Fine Arts	1.5
Equal Opportunities Fund	6.2
Other	0.1
	100.0

Expenditure on Education: Distribution by Level
Percentage of Expenditure 1977

Pre-School	First Level	Second Level	Third Level	Other
–	61.2	17.5	15.1	6.2

The State subsidises school transport where necessary, school meals and the purchase of educational materials. Money is made available from the Ministry to the *Instituto Nacional de Ciencias de la Educatión* which distributes it between the different universities. The ICEs are funded through the university budget. Wherever possible, universities try to draw on other sources of funds besides the Ministry of Education, for ICE work as well as research, (e.g. *cajas de ahorros* [local savings banks], local firms, etc.).

Foreign Aid

Capital expenditure has been augmented by two major loans from the International Bank for Reconstruction and Development (IBRD). The first loan of US$12 million was to finance 50% of the first capital programme under the 1970 Education Act (including the founding of 19 primary schools, 20 comprehensive secondary schools and 8 ICEs). The second IBRD loan signed in 1972 was for US$50 million and was part of a US$152 million scheme to achieve the objectives of the educational reform by (i) extending the coverage of the reform in general secondary education to major population centres, thereby ensuring an adequate foundation of pre-vocational education on which to build up-to-date technical education; and (ii) introducing a new concept of vocational, technical and engineering education along with the related teacher training. While the principal purpose of the project was to improve the quality of education by advancing the reform, it will also increase the output of trained or trainable manpower in needed areas. The project included 39 secondary schools, 37 primary grade and secondary grade technical schools, an agricultural institute, a technological university and institutes of education. It emphasised the need for providing more sophisticated skills for the next stage of Spain's industrial development programme.

9 DEVELOPMENT AND PLANNING OF THE EDUCATION SYSTEM

Origins

As in most European countries the history of education in Spain is a history of the conflict between Church, State and liberal opinion. One event which was to have considerable influence on twentieth century Spain was the founding of the *Institución Libre de Enseñanza* in 1895 by a group of professors who had been dismissed by the State authorities. This was a free university dedicated to the idea of non-official, non-dogmatic education and produced most of the leading figures in Spanish intellectual and political life in the 1920s and 1930s. Its ideas came to be closely associated with the educational reforms of the 1930s to which the nationalist victory in the civil war put an end.

After the civil war, education was placed more firmly than ever in the hands of the Church. There were a few bright spots, however, notably an incipient primary school building programme, an attempt in the *Bachillerato Técnico* to deal with the lack of technical education, an effort to tackle the problem of adult illiteracy, and the foundation of the *universidades laborales* (workers' universities).

1970 Education Act

The new Act was formulated by Spanish experts with the aid of three UNESCO advisers. The motive force came from the educational and technological needs of economic progress and social change. It was an important step towards greater integration in the country and the breaking down of economic and social barriers which had derived from the narrow and elitist system of education. Many of the educational ideas put forward earlier as a result of the pioneer work of the *Institución Libre de Enseñanza* were revived, although the contribution was not acknowledged.

The Act reflects a compromise over major issues - the tension between government and private schools; the rights of the State, the Church and the consumer; the struggle against illiteracy and discrimination; and fundamental questions of ideology. It inevitably antagonised people of all shades of opinion. Conservatives saw it as a return to the disastrous anarchy of the 1930s, the Church as the end of an age long hegemony in education, and the liberals as a cynical use of principles to cover the real intention of serving the needs of big business and self-perpetuation of the régime. The reforms led to rioting in the universities and discontent among teachers; the provision of universal free primary education and primary technical education means that, at the best, Church schools will be able to work on 'voluntary aided' principles; and it does seem that the main objective of these reforms was to provide the technological infrastructure for the next stage of Spain's economic progress.

The main principles underlying the Act were:

(i) a recognition of the right of every citizen regardless of his social class or economic circumstances to receive education

(ii) that education was to be a permanent, continuous process not limited by institutions or scholastic levels

(iii) the need to establish a close relationship between the hopes of the nation in education on the one hand and the social and economic requirements of the country on the other

(iv) the creation of a unified, flexible structure which would guarantee a complex network of relationships between the different levels and cater for individual needs

(v) the establishing of a period of vocational training after *educación general basica* (EGB) to help the individual make a more effective contribution to the community.

Plans for University Sector

The objectives of the universities as defined by the Education Act were as follows:

(i) to complete the training of young people; to train students for the occupations necessary to the country; and to provide refresher courses and permanent education for them

(ii) to encourage cultural progress, promote scientific research at all levels and train scientists and teachers

(iii) to contribute to the improvement of the national education system and to the social and economic development of the country.

Detailed plans involved increased autonomy for the universities, reform of administration, entrance procedures, courses, teacher status, research and financial affairs. In particular the government sought to encourage an extension of the range of university courses to include subjects such as engineering, teacher training, commerce and journalism. The *Institutos de Ciencias de Educación* were incorporated into the university system. An advisory board was set up, the *Junta Nacional de Universidades* (National Universities Board) whose standing executive committee is the Council of Rectors.

10 THE SYSTEM IN OPERATION

Trends

Spain is fully participating in the educational debate that is being carried out all over Western Europe, and some aims will probably be achieved. Greater use will inevitably be made of new media, through the example of UNED. A greater flexibility of curricula, syllabi and qualifications is already apparent, and hardly a day passes without some important person making a criticism of the present system; for example, that 80% of the useful information that children acquire is acquired out of school, and 80% of what they are given in school is useless. What is already quite clear is that Spanish educationists are anxious to see for themselves what is happening in other countries, particularly Germany, France, Great Britain and the USA. Already there is a great interest in Nuffield materials and the practical approach to the teaching of science. The distance education programmes are well established and it is reasonable to conclude that the Spaniards will show ingenuity in using modern technology to make their education system more effective and economical.

REFERENCES AND FURTHER READING

Benavent, José (1980). "Spanish education during the 1980s". *Comparative Education*, **16**, No.3.

Castillejo, José (1937). *Wars of Ideas in Spain: Philosophy, Politics and Education*. Murray, London.

Hochleitner, Ricordo Diez et al., (1978). *The Spanish Educational Reform and Lifelong Education*. Unesco, Paris.

Maravall, José V. (1978). *Dictatorship and Political Dissent: Workers and Students in Franco's Spain*. Tavistock, London.

Moricada, Alberto (1976). *Sociologia de la educación*. Cuadernos para el Dialogo, Madrid.

OECD (CERI) (1972). *Developments in Recurrent Education: Case Study Spain* by Pablo Guzman. Centre for Educational Research and Innovation, Paris.

OECD (1972). *Classification of Educational Systems in OECD Member Countries: France, Norway, Spain*. OECD, Paris.

Structure of the Education System in Spain

Age	3	4	5	6	7	8	9	10	11	12	13	14	15	16	17	18	19	20	21	22	23	24
Level				I								II			III							IV
Stage				1					2			3			4		5			6	
Compulsory																						
School type				*Educación básica general* 1st stage					2nd stage			*bachillerato*			*Formación profesional* Primer — Tercer		COU		*Facultades y escuelas superiores* / *Escuelas universitarias*			

Education preceding the first level

Examinations: (a) leaving certificate at end of stage 2
(b) technical certificates at end of stages 3 and 4

Source: UNESCO/IBE International Yearbook of Education

Compulsory Education: Age Limits 6–15 Duration (years) 10
Entrance age to pre-school education: 2

SPAIN BASIC STATISTICS		1960	1970	1975	1978 (approx.)
1	Total population (000)	30,303	33,778	35,433	36,775
	% female	51	51	51	51
2	% population 0-14 years	27.0	27.8		26.0
	% female	49	49	49	49
3	Enrolment, all levels		6,104,969	7,382,177	7,586,877
	% female		46	48	48
	First level	3,387,350	3,929,569	3,653,320	3,624,136
	% female	51	50	49	49
	Second level	728,363	1,950,496	3,188,619	3,381,677
	% female		42	48	48
	Third level	87,388	224,904	540,238	581,064
	% female	23	27	36	38
4	Teachers, all levels				
	% female				
	First level		115,607	172,122	197,706
	% female		58	58	57
	Second level	40,095	90,770		
	% female				
	Third level	4,193		29,701	34,100
	% female			19	20
5	Public expenditure on education				
	Total (000) pesetas	7,864	53,156	83,090	154,003
	As % of GNP	1.1	2.1	1.7	2.2
	As % of public expenditure				16.8
6	% enrolment (MF) by level		100	100	100
	First level		64	49	48
	Second level		32	43	45
	Third level		4	7	7
	% enrolment (F) by level		100	100	100
	First level		69	51	46
	Second level		29	44	48
	Third level		2	6	6
7	Entrance age: Duration of				
	First level education	6:5	6:5	6:5	6:5
	Second level education	11:6	11:6	11:7	11:7
8	Enrolment ratios (MF)				
	First level	110	123	115	110
	Second level	23	56	73	76
	Third level	3.95	8.91	20.77	21.54
	Enrolment ratios (F)				
	First level	116	125	115	110
	Second level		48	71	7
	Third level	1.87	4.83	15.02	16.39

Sweden

CONTENTS

1	Geography	616
2	Population	618
3	Society and Culture	619
4	History and Politics	621
5	The Economy	622
6	The Education System	624
7	Educational Administration	630
8	Educational Finance	634
9	Development and Planning of the Education System	635
10	The System in Operation	636

Amongst the best known achievements of Sweden, noted for its recent enviable high standard of living, is the 'rolling reform' of the educational system. Under a Social Democratic government which remained in power for more than 40 years a commission was set up to report on the reorganisation of secondary education along comprehensive lines. Recommendations by the commission were suported by a mass of empirical evidence and over a period of 20 years changes were introduced which transformed the system from a typically selective organisation to one in which a compulsory nine-year comprehensive school *(Grundskola)* is followed by a three-year upper secondary school *(Gymnasium)*. Differentiation is provided in the 22 different courses or 'lines' offered in these upper secondary schools. In two-, three- and four-year courses they are grouped into arts and social subjects, economics and commercial subjects and scientific and technical subjects. There is some overlap between the sectors through the provision of jointly taken subjects and courses. Theoretical studies are provided in some two-year courses and dominate the three- and four-year courses.

Post-war expansion of university and higher education has been considerable so that in a population of just over eight million more than 130,000 students attend universities, far surpassing even France's high proportion of students per head of population. A commission which spent five years on its deliberations went further by recommending in its report U 68 that to redress the distorted pattern of admission to universities in favour of the top socio-economic group a system of recurrent education accessible to all should be developed. This scheme was designed to alternate periods of study with periods of occupational activity.

Whether the reorganisation of second level education and the expansion of third level education will equalise opportunity and provision to the extent desired by the social democratic reformers in this culturally very homogenous country depends on how far rural and urban children can be provided with the same opportunities. A well developed system of adult education has historically helped to equalise learning opportunities. A recent issue is whether the immigrant workers who intend to settle permanently can be absorbed. The children of immigrants may receive instruction in their mother tongue but otherwise follow the same curriculum. While the Swedish Lutheran Church maintains its pre-eminent position other religious minorities are so small as to be negligible, secularism is growing.

Economic change in the form of industrialisation in Sweden has been recent and, comparatively speaking, rapid. Superficially the culture has also changed in many respects. The same can be said about aspects of education. To the foreign observer the many traditional features which remain appear paradoxical.

The Editor

1 GEOGRAPHY

Topography

Sweden is easily the largest, both in size and in population, of the Scandinavian countries. Between its southernmost town, Trelleborg, on latitude 55°20'N and the Three Nations Marker where Finland, Norway and Sweden come together at latitude 69°04'N lies a distance of 1,574 km (977 miles) - about the same as that between Trelleborg and Naples. The mountain range on the west lies mainly in Norway, and Sweden is a relatively flat country, heavily forested and covered with lakes. The average width between the Norwegian frontier and the Gulf of Bothnia is about 300 km (188 miles). The area is 449,793 sq km (173,654 square miles), which makes it the fourth largest country in Europe. Only Russia, France and Spain are larger.

The characteristic topography of Sweden, with its dense coniferous forests, thinning out a little towards the south, and its tens of thousands of lakes, is due to the relatively recent melting of the last glaciers (12000-8000 BC). There are extensive archipelagos on both the east and west coasts, which make inshore navigation difficult but which provide splendid recreation areas during the summer months. The long coastline has no fjords of the Norwegian type, but there are deep inlets which make good harbours. Off the south east coast there are two large islands, Gotland and Öland. The latter has recently been joined to the mainland by a bridge, said to be the longest in Europe. For Sweden Öland is suprisingly treeless, due to the occurrence of chalk outcrops.

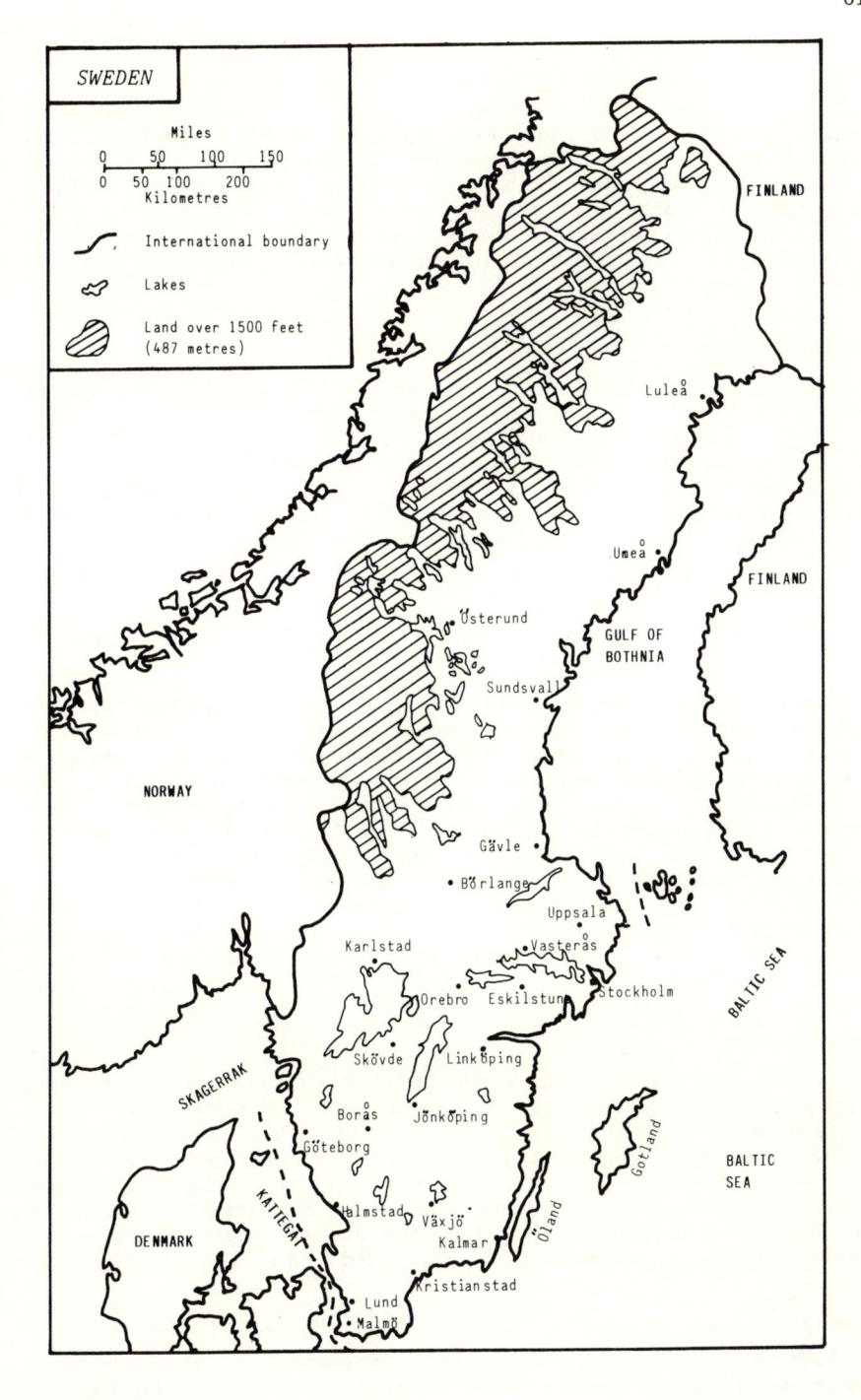

SWEDEN

Miles
0 50 100 150
0 50 100 200
Kilometres

— International boundary
⌒ Lakes
▨ Land over 1500 feet
   (487 metres)

FINLAND

Luleå

Umeå

FINLAND

Östersund

GULF OF
BOTHNIA

Sundsvall

NORWAY

Gävle

Borlänge

Uppsala

Karlstad

Västerås

BALTIC SEA

Örebro Eskilstuna Stockholm

Skövde Linköping

Borås Jönköping

SKAGERRAK

Göteborg

Gotland

BALTIC
SEA

KATTEGAT

Halmstad

Växjö Öland

DENMARK

Kalmar

Lund Kristianstad
Malmö

Climate

The climate is affected by the Gulf Stream and is relatively mild, at least in the southern third of the country *(Götaland)*. Central Sweden *(Svealand)* and Northern Sweden *(Norrland)* are usually under snow from November to April, but rainfall and humidity are both lower than in Britain. The Gulf of Bothnia is generally frozen over for the same period. Summers are short (June to August) but are warm and sunny, with temperatures rising to over 21°C (70°F). In summer, too, the hours of daylight are very long.

Communications

Sweden has a very good railway system with 11,360 km of track (in 1976), of which about 7,500 km is electrified. There are about 98,000 km of road, and good local bus services (most of which connect with railway services and are operated by the Swedish State Railways). The State Railway also operates ferry services to Denmark and the GDR. International air transport is provided by SAS (in which Sweden has a substantial share).

2 POPULATION

Growth

The total population of Sweden is just over 8.3 million. Between 1850 - when industrialisation began - and 1950, the population doubled from 3.5 million to 7 million, despite the fact that over one million Swedes emigrated to the United States during the same period. By the 1965 census, however, the increase had slowed down almost to a standstill, and with the current birth rate (about 13 per 1,000 per year) only just exceeding the mortality rate, it is expected that the future trend will be one of very slow growth and an ageing population. The number of the population over 65 is around 15%, and approximately half of the country's annual population growth is accounted for by net immigration.

Distribution

Sweden has one of the lowest population densities in Europe. There are 20 inhabitants to the square kilometre (52 to the square mile) but the spread is uneven. Over 90% live in the southern half of the country, and the average population density in *Norrland* is only 3 per square kilometre. There is an urban drift in Sweden as elsewhere, but the only serious problem is to prevent a southward drift from the extreme north, which would leave *Norrland* even more under-populated than it is at present.

Groups

Part of *Norrland* is Swedish Lappland, in which live one quarter of Scandinavia's total population of 15,000 Lapps. The

Lapps, of course, have their own language and culture. The Swedish government keeps a paternal eye on them, but does not much interfere with their traditional way of life. Those who wish to become assimilated find it easy to do so and a number have taken this step. Apart from the Lapps the population of Sweden is remarkably homogeneous. It is a country in which 95% of the people share the same language, the same religion and the same culture.

Immigration

Since World War Two Sweden has admitted political refugees and foreign workers from the poorer countries of Europe. There are now some 500,000 immigrants living in Sweden, but of those 50% are from Finland or the other Nordic countries and many of the remainder do not intend to settle permanently. Moreover, of the 190,000 Finnish immigrants many are of Swedish stock and have Swedish as their mother tongue. Immigrants from the Nordic countries do not need work or residence permits, and can apply for citizenship after three years, whereas other nationals must wait for seven years. The impact of this immigration on the education system is growing, though at present confined principally to Stockholm and a few of the larger towns. The children of immigrants are given special instruction in Swedish for a transitional period, and may also receive instruction in their native language, but otherwise they follow the same course of education as Swedish children, and have the same rights and obligations.

3 SOCIETY AND CULTURE

Social Development

The dominant facts about Swedish society are that it has not been involved in war for the last five generations (since 1815, in fact) and that the transformation from a poor, backward state on the eastern edge of Europe to a modern industrial society is of very recent origin. The really major changes have all occurred during the last 50 years, under the aegis (until September 1976) of successive Social Democratic governments. The result is that Sweden today has a surprisingly new look about it. There is none of the debris of early industrial development. The new or newish factories are often built in quite small urban areas (in Sweden an area is classed as urban if it has a mere 200 inhabitants), and every Swede has easy access to the countryside.

Planned industrial development has been accompanied by a comprehensive series of measures in the field of social welfare, which was a major part of the political philosophy of the Social Democratic Party and was continued as far as the economic downturn allowed, by the coalition government. The Swede today is protected from the cradle to the grave, though he pays for it in high taxation and fairly rigid bureaucratic control. The old nobility and the bourgeoisie have given way more readily in Sweden than in other countries to pressures from below for a more equitable sharing of the national wealth. This has resulted in a remarkable absence of industrial strife and a high all-round standard of living. No doubt other factors have played their part, such as the low population and absence of land pressure, the generally disciplined national character, and freedom from external influences.

Living Patterns

The younger generation of Swedes is experimenting with new forms of living, tacitly backed by a government which believes in social engineering, as a means of creating a smooth-working, frictionless society. Cohabitation instead of marriage, households in which the wife is the breadwinner and the husband looks after the children, single mothers, easy divorce and complete sexual freedom from an early age are commonplaces in today's society, and no social stigma appears to be attached to them. It should be noted in passing that a large number of Swedish women stay in employment after marriage and/or childbearing in order to maintain the expected standard of living, and lack of parental discipline can be a problem.

Culture

The foregoing trends apart, the cultural and artistic values of Sweden are firmly those of Western Europe. In music, painting, opera, ballet, theatre and film, State patronage is paramount but standards are high and there is no dearth of native talent. Special State organisations are entrusted with the task of ensuring that the provinces are not deprived of the chance to see and hear good theatre and music. The public libraries are first class, and so too are the museums.

Religion

Christianity came late to Sweden — as late as the twelfth century, and was followed by the Reformation only three centuries later. The part played by the Swedish King Gustavus Adolphus in the Thirty Years War determined both the political and religious balance of power for the rest of the seventeenth century. Since then Lutheranism has been firmly established in Sweden and is the only religious force that need be taken into account. The Church is controlled by the State, and Swedish clergymen, who are paid by the State, perform some of the functions of minor civil servants. Modern Sweden is very much a secular State and a very tolerant one. Religious belief is declining, as it is elsewhere, and the power of the Swedish Lutheran Church has changed. Of the 60,000 Catholics in the country less than 10,000 are native-born Swedes. Other religious minorities are so small as to be negligible. Religious instruction still appears on the school timetable but means nowadays a study of comparative religion and other philosophies, including Marxism.

4 HISTORY AND POLITICS

Origins

Sweden can be said to have entered history with the early Viking trading expeditions and warlike forays between the seventh and ninth centuries AD. While Danish and Norwegian Vikings sailed westwards to Britain, Greenland and even the North American continent, the Swedish Vikings crossed the Baltic and then sailed down the Russian rivers as far as the Black and Caspian seas. When Sweden began to emerge as a separate country in the twelfth century, it included what is now Finland, and though during the fifteenth century all four Nordic countries were united in the so-called Kalmar Union, thereafter there was one long series of bitter conflicts between Sweden-Finland on the one side and Denmark-Norway on the other.

Seventeenth Century Onwards

The seventeenth century was Sweden's age of imperial glory, when Gustavus Adolphus and his successors captured a string of provinces round the eastern and southern shores of the Baltic Sea. But in the early eighteenth century Sweden overreached herself, Charles XII was defeated by the Russians at Poltava, and Swedish power declined rapidly. A century after Poltava Finland was lost, as a result of Napoleon's short lived treaty with Russia, but at the Congress of Vienna Sweden received compensation in the cession of Denmark from Norway. (The union with Norway lasted another 100 years, being finally dissolved, at Norway's request, in 1905.) The period of Napoleon's hegemony in Europe coincided with the arrival on the throne of a weak and ineffective king, which together produced a short period of internal strife, a constitutional revolution and a change of dynasty. The form of government adopted in 1809, based upon the separation of powers, is still the basis of the Swedish constitution. In 1810 a French Marshal, Jean Baptiste Bernadotte, was chosen to be Crown Prince, and succeeded to the throne in 1818 as Karl XIV Johan. The nineteenth century was in general a period of peaceful, liberalising reforms, and after 1850 of increasingly rapid industrialisation. Sweden successfully maintained her neutrality through the two world wars of the present century, and has now become a highly industrialised country with an impressive record of achievement in most fields, and a standard of living comparable to that of the United States.

Government and Politics

Sweden is a democracy and a constitutional monarchy. The King is the formal Head of State, but has no political power. The idea of introducing a republic has often been discussed but seems to enjoy little support among the people, a fact which was amply proved when King Carl XVI Gustaf succeeded his grandfather in November 1973. There is universal suffrage for all Swedish citizens over the age of 18 who vote every three years to elect a unicameral parliament *(Riksdag)* of 349 members. All elections are by proportional representation, which is designed to ensure a distribution of seats between the political parties in proportion to the votes cast for them nationally. (A party must score at least 4% of the total vote to qualify for representation.) There are five major political parties: Social Democrat, Conservative, Liberal, Centre (formerly Farmers) and Communist. In the September 1976 general election (in which 90% of the electorate voted) a Conservative-Liberal-Centre coalition ended the 44-year rule of the Social Democrats, gaining 180 seats in the *Riksdag* compared with the Social Democrats' 152 and the Communists' 17. In October 1978 the coalition collapsed as a result of a disagreement over nuclear policy and the Liberal leader (who had not taken part in the coalition) was invited to form a minority Liberal government. Elections held in 1979 resulted in the formation of a coalition government. Swedish governments are stable. Important legislation is generally only undertaken after lengthy and earnest attempts to reach a consensus or middle-of-the-road decision; a process which begins with a Commission of Enquiry whose terms of reference are set out by the ministry concerned and approved by the government. The usual democratic freedoms obtain, but there is growing evidence of political pressure being exerted both on and by the mass media (in particular television), the trade unions and even the teachers.

International Relations

The cornerstone of Swedish foreign policy is neutrality. She has no military alliances of any sort, and has even built up an independent armaments industry. Some of the characteristic features of Swedish society - and the flourishing state of her trade balance up to 1976 - are due to her having missed the common European experiences of the twentieth century; and even her close neighbours in Scandinavia tend to regard her with some envy. She has refused to consider joining the EEC and sticks staunchly to her neutral posture between East and West, though her trade is mostly with the West. Within Scandinavia she is, of course, the dominant partner in the Nordic Cooperation Council, whose work covers many different fields, including education. Here Sweden is generally thought to be too progressive. Besides maintaining her neutrality, Sweden aims at the liberalisation of world trade, at strengthening the United Nations, at disarmament, and at assistance to developing and newly emerging nations. Through the Swedish International Development Authority (SIDA) she has established a position as one of the leading aid-giving nations.

5 THE ECONOMY

Agriculture

Swedish agriculture is highly mechanised and efficient, but relatively small scale. Some 5% of the total working population of 4 million is employed in agriculture, and only 7% of the total land is arable. There are very few large estates and the total number of farmers (i.e. farm owners) is about 130,000. Cattle products are more significant than grain crops (wheat, oats and barley), providing some 80% of farming income, and there is a marked tendency towards specialisation in one or two crops and/or cattle products. Marketing is cooperative, and government policy has three main aims: to rationalise farming; to provide price protection; and to maintain a minimum self-sufficiency in food (about 80% - enough at least for emergencies). At present food imports represent 8% of the total.

Industry

Sweden is basically an industrial country. Its GNP grew from 1950 to 1970 at an average annual rate of 4%. Since 1970 it has levelled off at about 1.5%, with one year of zero growth. In 1900 only 30% of the population lived in towns; now it is at least 80% and by 2000 this figure is expected to rise to over 90%. The main natural resources, on which the industrial prosperity of the country is based, are wood and iron ore. Snow-fed rivers, running mainly south east from the frontier mountains to the Baltic, provide ample hydro-electric power. The main industries are metalworking and engineering, and timber, pulp and paper. Much lower down the scale are textiles (including leather and furs), food processing, mining, motor car manufacture, shipbuilding and chemicals (including fertilisers and pharmaceuticals). Wood is the basis of the timber paper, pulp and furniture industries; iron ore of the steel, motor car and shipbuilding industries. Over 90% of industry is privately owned, and apart from the public utility services the only considerable section of industry which is publicly owned is the mining of iron ore. Engineering products, fuel, chemical products and raw materials are imported.

Economic Situation

The Swedish economy is firmly directed towards exports, with nearly three quarters going to the European market. Since 1977 Sweden's balance of trade has entered into deficit, partly as a result of world recession, and partly because high unit labour costs have impaired the competitiveness of the country's exports. The devaluation of the Krona by nearly 20% in 1977 did bring about some improvement in trade figures, but inflation rose in 1980, to a peak of 14%. Unemployment is at a nominal 2%, but this relatively low figure is partly due to the generous, but essentially uneconomic, government-funded support programmes which have in effect subsidised employment in a number of industries - particularly in those most vulnerable, such as iron and steel, shipbuilding, pulp and textiles. However, in addition to these work-support programmes, extensive and successful re-training schemes have been set up in an attempt to divert unproductive labour from work-intensive industries, but despite the success of these and other job schemes, unemployment - particularly within the 16 to 24 age range - continues to rise.

As a result of the recession, which has had a very sobering effect on Swedish expectations of ever increasing prosperity, priority has been given to improved export marketing and technological research and innovation, particularly in the energy field, where the debate on the need for nuclear power development has been a political and social preoccupation ever since the coalition government came to power in 1976. The Centre Party has become increasingly isolated in its resistance to any increase in present sources of nuclear energy.

Living Standards

In spite of recent setbacks, Sweden continues to enjoy an enviably affluent standard of living, with 345 cars and 370 TV sets per 1,000 inhabitants, and an extremely high per capita consumption of electricity. Salaries and wages are high and though rates of taxation are among the highest in the world the government is generous in its provision of social benefits, which include index-related State pensions from the age of 65. Although the recession has imposed some strain on labour relations, wage agreements between the Swedish Employers' Federation (SAF) and the two powerful trade union organisations have been reached with a high degree of responsibility on both sides, and comparatively few work days are lost through industrial action. This is largely attributable to the fact that labour and management have a traditional resistance to government intervention in wage negotiations, and are therefore anxious if at all possible to avoid conflict in their centralised collective bargaining.

6 THE EDUCATION SYSTEM

Academic Year

At school level the academic year extends from mid-August to the end of May. It is divided into three terms. There are short holidays for Christmas/New Year and Easter, and a week's winter holiday in February.

Pre-School

In accordance with the 1973 Act legislating for pre-school education, all municipalities must provide facilities for children below age 7, but attendance is optional. Working parents may send their children to day nurseries from the age of six months, on a full or part time basis, and all children (irrespective of whether both parents are working) are entitled to places at the age of 6 years; however, the pressure on places for the latter group is heavy owing to lack of adequately trained staff. The emphasis throughout pre-schooling is on play activity and social training, to ensure that all children, whatever their background and capacities, reach the starting point of compulsory education together. Formal instruction is not given.

Basic *(grundskola)*

Compulsory education begins at age 7 and continues for nine years. It is divided into three stages or cycles of three years each, as follows:

(i) junior level *(Lågstadium)* corresponding to primary school for ages 7 to 10

(ii) middle level *(Mellanstadium)* for ages 10 to 13

(iii) senior level *(Högstadium)* for ages 13 to 16.

Not all stages are necessarily available in one and the same school building, particularly in the sparsely populated areas, but the system is uniform throughout the country, and is often called the 'comprehensive school'.

In the first two stages the children are taught by class teachers (trained, but usually non-graduates); in the third stage they are taught by subject teachers (graduates). A teaching period lasts for 40 minutes, and at junior level these are often divided into two lessons of 20 minutes each. There are 20 periods per week in grade 1, 22 in grade 2, 30 in grade 3, 34 in grade 4 and 35 thereafter. The school day usually lasts from 8.00 a.m. to 3.00 p.m.

Curriculum

From a common curriculum an increasing number of options are progressively introduced. At junior level subjects studied include: Swedish, mathematics, music, physical education, religious instruction and local studies, with English and handicraft introduced in grade 3 (at age 9). At middle level drawing, civics, history, geography and nature study are added. In grades 7-9 (senior level) pupils take physics, chemistry and biology instead of nature study with compulsory home economics in grades 8 and 9. At this level, too, there is an optional subject chosen from German, French, economics, art and technology, and further options are proposed. Until recently pupils could opt for 'general' or 'advanced' courses at senior level in foreign languages and mathematics but this has now been abandoned.

Assessment

In accordance with the prevailing *social* philosophy, formal external examinations have been discarded in favour of continuous assessment, based partly on frequent standardised tests, centrally prepared and locally marked. The system of assessment is based on the scale 1 to 5 (with 5 as the maximum). This is intended to be related to average performance throughout the country. A proposal to abolish grading was fiercely opposed in some quarters. Less successful pupils may be asked to repeat a year, but in practice this rarely happens. Throughout school remedial or special instruction *(specialundeervisning)* is available for individual pupils in need of it.

Special

The system provides admirably for minority groups. All schools are obliged to offer the children of non-Swedish parents mother tongue tuition as well as additional instruction in Swedish. Present policy is to assimilate handicapped children whenever possible within ordinary schools. In July 1978 the special allocation of resources to remedial teaching was replaced by a 'reinforcement resource' fund giving the schools and the municipalities greater flexibility and freedom in providing for special local needs. School staffs include student welfare work teams, some with specially trained supervisors and psychologists, and everything possible is done to provide individual care and guidance.

Second Level Schools *(Gymnasium)*

It is estimated that up to 80% of 16-year olds go on directly to study for two, three or four years in the integrated upper secondary school *(gymnasium)*. In 1964 the corresponding figure was 30% and entrance was clearly selective: the number of places in particular courses is still limited and therefore when demand exceeds places preference is given to students on the basis of marks awarded in their comprehensive school leaving certificate and other qualifications such as job experience.

The secondary school offers 22 courses or 'lines' organised in sectors as follows:

ARTS AND SOCIAL* SUBJECTS	ECONOMICS AND* COMMERCIAL SUBJECTS	SCIENTIFIC AND TECHNICAL SUBJECTS
Two-year courses	*Two-year courses*	*Two-year courses*
consumer course	distribution & clerical course	see below ¶
nursing course †	economics course§	*Three-year courses§*
social course§		natural sciences course
music course (experimental)§	*Three-year courses* §	
Three-year courses§	economics	*Four-year courses§*
liberal arts course		technical course
social sciences course		
Special courses	*Special courses*	*Special courses*

* The arts-social subjects sector and the economics-commercial subjects sector tend to be coordinated, for instance through provision of a large number of jointly taken subjects and courses

† The courses are organised in whole or in part only by schools under the jurisdiction of county councils. This also holds for special courses in the fields of agriculture, forestry and medical-nursing-social work

§ Mainly theoretical studies

¶ Clothing manufacturing course, building and construction course, electro-technical course, motor engineering course, agricultural course*, food manufacturing course, processing techniques course, forestry course*, woodwork course, workshop course, technical course§.

(Source: *Swedish Institute Fact Sheet 1977*)

In 1978 the largest numbers of places (over 9,000) were found in the two-year social course; the three-year natural sciences course had some 9,000 places; the two-year distribution and clerical course had over 8,000 and the two-year nursing course approximately 8,000. Trends are for the number of places in the various two-year vocational courses to increase, and for those in the two-year theoretical course to decline.

All the upper secondary school courses (provided pupils have done two years of English and two of Swedish at this level) are designed to qualify for admission to higher education, though for a few higher education courses extra qualifications may be necessary. As in the comprehensive school there is no school leaving examination: in their last term pupils are given a leaving certificate *(slutbetyg)* stating their average mark per subject, on the scale 1 to 5. Scholastic performance is controlled by the National Board of Education in the form of a more or less continuous series of centrally administered tests, but pupils are automatically promoted annually to the next grade - though there is provision for 'voluntary non-promotion'.

Third Level (Higher) Institutions

In Sweden this is generally referred to as post-secondary, rather than higher or tertiary; the collective term now applied to it is *högskola* and includes vocational education and teacher training as well as university studies. The universities comprise Uppsala, Lund, Stockholm, Gothenburg, Umeå and Linköping, though research is also carried on at a college of technological education in Luleå. Uppsala (founded in 1477) and Lund are the most venerable universities, though now a little different from the others. The largest of the six is Stockholm with over 26,300 students and the smallest are Umeå and Linköping with 7,200 each. There are three university affiliates at Örebro, Växjö and Karlstad, linked with the universities of Uppsala, Lund and Gothenburg respectively. They teach only up to first degree level, for the most part in the humanities and social sciences. In addition there are three large and prestigious institutes with full university status: the Caroline Institute (medicine and dentistry), the Royal Institute of Technology in Stockholm and Chalmers Technical Institute in Gothenburg (engineering and technology), with a total of over 11,000 students in all.

The number of university students in 1977 was 132,000. University admission is restricted in some faculties, especially medicine, dentistry, pharmacy, engineering and technology (where a so-called *numerus clausus* operates) and unrestricted in others. A normal first degree course *(Fil.kand)* takes three years, and is built up on a credit point system at the uniform rate of 40 points per year. Facilities exist for students to earn a number of points, then go out into working life and subsequently return – at intervals if they so wish – to increase their points total. Moreover, mature students, of literally any age, can enter the unrestricted faculties if they can provide evidence of having had a secondary education, of possessing adequate competence in both Swedish and English, and of having had a minimum of four years' certified job experience. As a result of this, there is a tendency for the number of full time students in the age range 18-24 to go down, while the enrolment of older students in the age range 25-47 steadily increases. At the University of Linköping a considerable majority of the annual intake were part time students in 1979.

Virtually all basic research is conducted at the universities, or in partnership with them. The money for research is distributed by the national research councils in cooperation with the Ministry of Education, and post-graduate students who are working for a doctorate can apply for special stipends. A doctorate is normally obtained after four years of post-graduate studies plus practical research experience. The intermediate degree of *Fil.lic (Filosofie Licentiat)* has been abolished, together with the variant of the *Fil.kand* known as *Fil.mag (Filosofie Magister)*, which until 1970 was taken mostly, but not exclusively, by students intending to become graduate teachers. Two more specialised degrees, *Fil.pol.mag* (political science and economics) and *Jur.pol.mag.* (political science and law), have also disappeared.

Outside the university system there are a number of specialist colleges, notably those of Social Work and Public Administration, of Journalism, Veterinary Medicine, Agriculture and Forestry. The College of Economics and Business Studies *(Handelshögskola)* in Stockholm is a special case because it is still a private foundation, the only one of its kind left in Sweden. It enjoys a very high reputation. There is also a College of Librarianship in Borås.

Teacher Training

Teacher training was, from July 1977, integrated with the universities in the regional *högskola* units, and became (with the exception of in-service training) the responsibility of the National Board of Universities and colleges instead of the National Board of Education.

The basic qualification for teachers of general subjects in the junior and middle levels of the comprehensive school is a three-year training course. There are 32 teacher training institutions, many of which are small and cater only for specific fields such as nursing, handicrafts, physical education, etc., and of these nine provide a one-year post-graduate course for specialist or subject teachers going on to teach in the third stage of comprehensive school or in the integrated upper secondary school. One term of the one-year course is devoted to supervised practice teaching.

Teaching is a relatively well paid profession. Because of this, and the good social standing of the profession, there is some pressure on places in the training institutions. Since 1975 there has been a cutback in training places for class teachers, but quite a steep rise in provision for pre-school teachers and staff responsible for recreational activities. The 'output' of subject teachers remains relatively steady.

Five 'study days' are set aside for in-service training during the academic year: attendance is compulsory and teachers are relieved of their normal duties in order to be present. Longer in-service courses are rare in Sweden, but modern language teachers are given generous financial support to attend appropriate courses overseas.

Non-Formal and Adult

Because the spread of education has taken place comparatively recently there are many middle-aged and older people who have had only six years of formal schooling. Extensive efforts to remedy this, and to enable the educationally under-privileged to continue their education, are made in a variety of ways.

The major sources of adult education are the folk high schools, the municipal adult schools and the study circles. There are now 110 folk high schools, with boarding facilities, and with a total annual enrolment of 150,000 students attending courses of two days to over 30 weeks in length. The intake now includes a growing number of immigrants and handicapped persons, and emphasis is put on student participation in both the planning and the implementation of study programmes. Municipal adult schools, run by the local authorities, offer day and evening full time and part time courses corresponding to those in the basic and upper secondary schools, and have a total enrolment of about 210,000 students, a number of whom follow non-academic vocational training programmes in fields such as handicrafts and commercial subjects. Among the 'school' courses offered, English, mathematics, Swedish and German are said to be the most popular. Adult education organisations sponsored both by trade unions and university extra-mural departments, offer a wide range of part time courses, usually in the form of study circles. In 1977, over 2,600,000 participants are said to have attended some 290,000 such study circles – an impressive figure even if one takes account of the fact that an individual may enrol in two or more. A small proportion of participants, approximately 1%, attend study circles at university level, but for the vast majority the level corresponded to is the third stage of comprehensive school, and it is estimated that at least one-third of the places is taken by 'priority groups' such as union members, immigrants and the handicapped.

Labour market training has developed rapidly, mainly in response to relatively high unemployment in certain industries, and includes special courses organised by the National Board of Education and held at many different centres. These courses, which are run on a continuous admission basis, are clearly successful in that 85% of those having taken the courses obtain jobs within three months of completion of their training.

In distance learning, educational programmes on radio and television are produced by the Swedish Educational Broadcasting Corporation, a subsidiary to the Swedish Broadcasting Corporation, which is funded by government. The programmes are designed for adults as well as schoolchildren, and are prepared in collaboration with adult education organisations. Many eminent academics, among them the former rector of Uppsala, believe that the need for recurrent education would have been better catered for by developing distance learning based on the universities, rather than by setting up new institutions. Correspondence colleges such as Hermods offer courses up to degree level; while another organisation, *Brevskolan*, caters principally to the needs of certain special-interest groups.

7 EDUCATIONAL ADMINISTRATION

Ministry of Education

Education falls within the purview of the Ministry of Education and Cultural Affairs. It is a characteristic, however, of the Swedish Civil Service to vest important duties of both an executive and planning nature in central administration agencies, of which two are concerned wholly with education. These are the National Board of Education *(Skolöverstyrelsen)* dealing with primary and secondary education, and in-service teacher training; and the National Board of Universities and Colleges (UHÄ) dealing with higher education and research. The Ministry itself has a staff of less than 200 and deals mainly with questions of budgeting and policy making, and of course the framing of government bills for consideration by the Swedish *Riksdag* or parliament, whereas the National Board of Education had an establishment of 775 in 1978.

National Board of Education

The National Board of Education lays down curricula and teaching methods, plans and coordinates the overall capacity and location of schools, promotes pedagogical research and ensures that the available resources are effectively used. Influence is also exerted on choice of materials (which are listed and recommended, if not actually prescribed, in catalogues distributed by the State Institute for Information on Teaching Materials, established in 1974). In effect the National Board runs the State school system. It has a 12-member governing board, all of whom are appointed by the King-in-Council, and is organised in seven divisions under a Director-General and a Deputy Director-General.

Local Administration

At local level there are both county school boards and municipal school boards, the members of which are politically elected. County School Boards are assisted by a permanent secretariat with usually three school inspectors. The Municipal School Boards have a permanent Director of Schools, with one or more assistant directors and appropriate staff, depending on size. County School Boards have regional planning responsibilities and exercise control over State grants for education. They also appoint teachers and promote in-service training. The inspectorate operates on a subject basis, and consists of 26 full time inspectors and five part time, covering the whole country and responsible to the National Board of Education, which also appoints specialist school consultants who are often former inspectors. As in further and higher education, attempts are being made to increase the decision making powers conferred upon the local authorities in such matters as the adaptation of comprehensive school curricular options to community needs: in 1976, for example, the municipalities received a block grant equivalent to approximately one quarter of teachers' salaries, with considerable allocatory powers.

School Councils

Within each school there is a teaching staff council, a subjects conference and a class conference for every class. The latter body, made up of those teachers who work in a class plus the headmaster, decides which pupils move up to a higher class and which, if any, must stay down. In the upper secondary schools there is in addition a so-called cooperation council, consisting of the headmaster, plus teacher and pupil representation, and experiments with such councils are now also being conducted in the compulsory comprehensive schools.

University Administration

This pattern is repeated at university level. With the exception of the College of Agriculture, which is under the aegis of the Ministry of Agriculture, all State institutions of further and higher education now come under the Ministry of Education and its administrative agency, the National Board of Universities and Colleges (which has the same function at post-secondary level as the National Board of Education has vis-à-vis the schools). The National Board of Universities and Colleges has a permanent staff of 235, an operational budget and a fund for educational research and development. It is headed by a Director-General who, as Chancellor of the six universities, chairs meetings of the Board, and it is organised into seven divisions, plus an auditing and an information office whose responsibilities include international contacts: in addition, there are five permanent planning commissions (each consisting of 15 members appointed by government) acting as advisory bodies. It is true to say that further and higher education are

THE NATIONAL BOARD OF EDUCATION

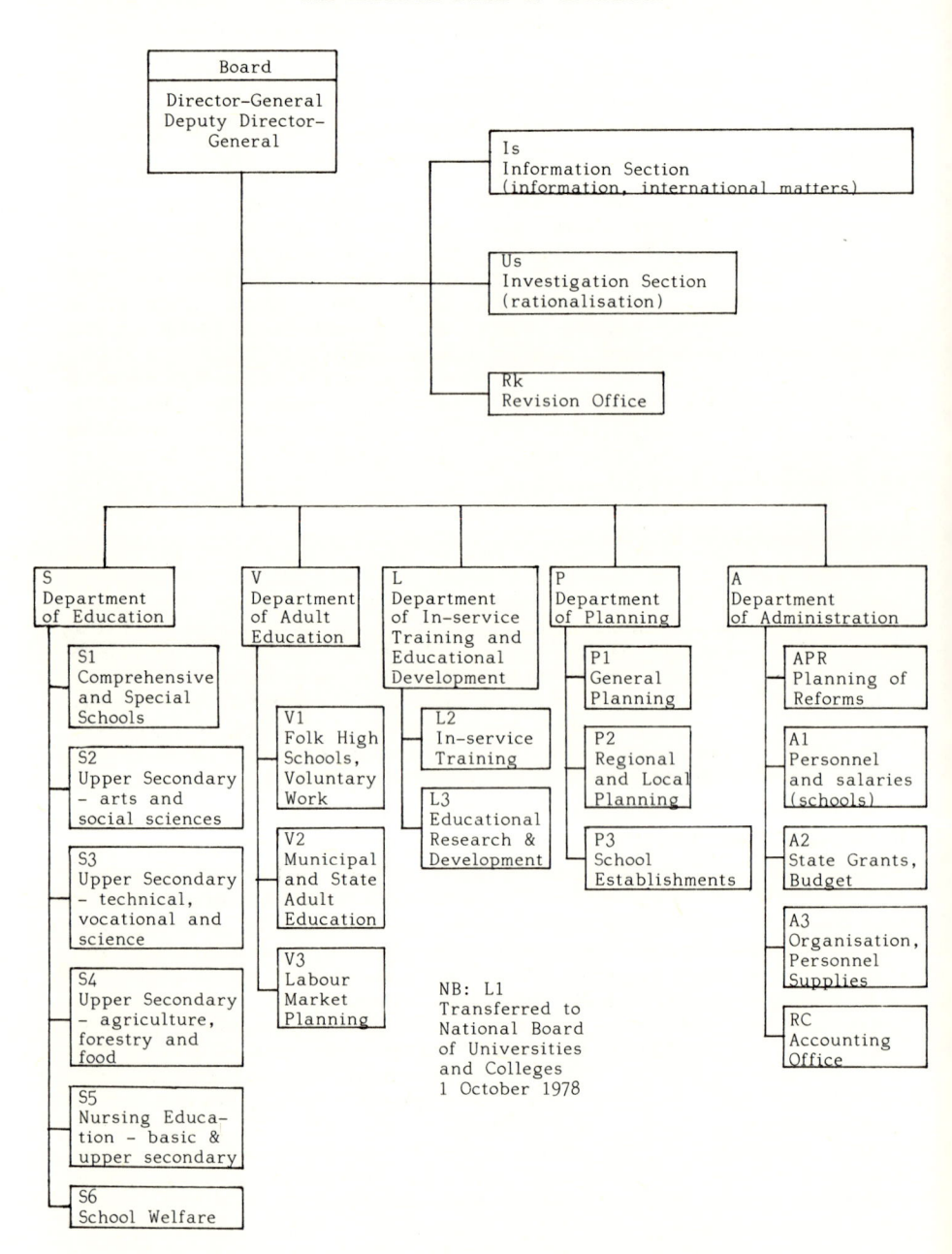

Board
Director-General
Deputy Director-General

- **Is** Information Section (information, international matters)
- **Us** Investigation Section (rationalisation)
- **Rk** Revision Office

S — Department of Education
- S1 Comprehensive and Special Schools
- S2 Upper Secondary – arts and social sciences
- S3 Upper Secondary – technical, vocational and science
- S4 Upper Secondary – agriculture, forestry and food
- S5 Nursing Education – basic & upper secondary
- S6 School Welfare

V — Department of Adult Education
- V1 Folk High Schools, Voluntary Work
- V2 Municipal and State Adult Education
- V3 Labour Market Planning

L — Department of In-service Training and Educational Development
- L2 In-service Training
- L3 Educational Research & Development

NB: L1 Transferred to National Board of Universities and Colleges 1 October 1978

P — Department of Planning
- P1 General Planning
- P2 Regional and Local Planning
- P3 School Establishments

A — Department of Administration
- APR Planning of Reforms
- A1 Personnel and salaries (schools)
- A2 State Grants, Budget
- A3 Organisation, Personnel Supplies
- RC Accounting Office

Source: *National Swedish Board of Education*

ADMINISTRATION
THE NATIONAL BOARD OF UNIVERSITIES AND COLLEGES

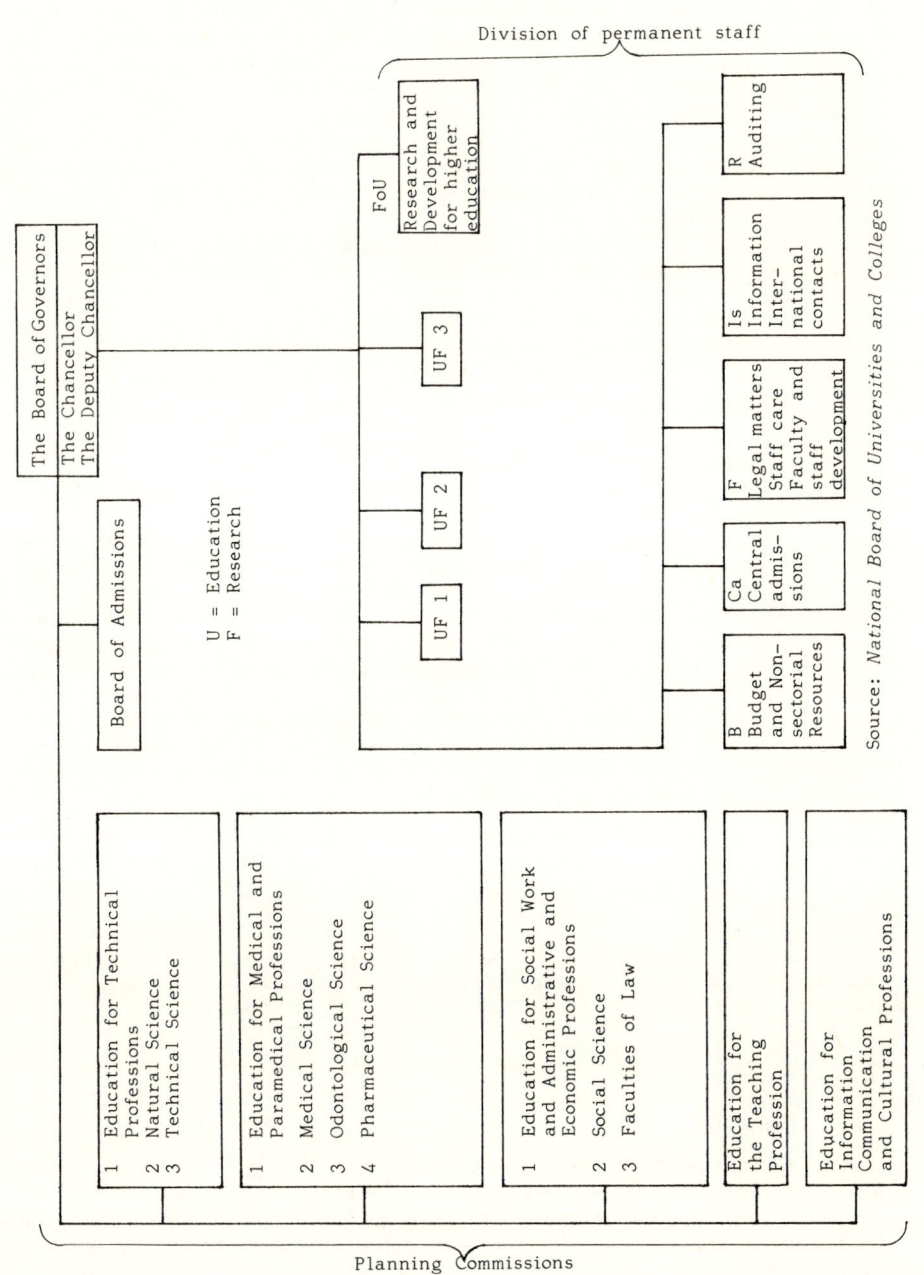

Division of permanent staff

The Board of Governors

The Chancellor
The Deputy Chancellor

Board of Admissions

U = Education
F = Research

FoU — Research and Development for higher education

UF 1   UF 2   UF 3

B — Budget and Non-sectorial Resources

Ca — Central admissions

F — Legal matters Staff care Faculty and staff development

Is — Information International contacts

R — Auditing

Source: *National Board of Universities and Colleges*

Planning Commissions

- 1 Education for Technical Professions
- 2 Natural Science
- 3 Technical Science

- 1 Education for Medical and Paramedical Professions
- 2 Medical Science
- 3 Odontological Science
- 4 Pharmaceutical Science

- 1 Education for Social Work and Administrative and Economic Professions
- 2 Social Science
- 3 Faculties of Law

Education for the Teaching Profession

Education for Information Communication and Cultural Professions centralised in the same way as school education: degree courses are largely uniform throughout the country.

The country is divided into six regions for administrative purposes, each containing one of the universities. Each has a regional board, with responsibility for resource allocation to the institutions in the region. The board consists of 21 members appointed by the government, with one third of the members representing educational interests and two thirds 'public' interests (i.e. the trade unions, the political parties and business). Within each region there are local boards (24 in all) representing the different educational institutions in their area, but with one third of their members acting on behalf of public interests.

The individual rectors (vice-chancellors) of the universities, though of course they come from the academic world, are appointed by the UHÄ, as are all holders of professional chairs. But the Chancellor of the Universities (and chairman of the National Board) himself is not an academic; he is an administrator, and one of them was previously the Director-General of the National Board of Education.

8 EDUCATIONAL FINANCE

Education Budget

Education is financed almost entirely from public funds, and State contributions are approximately 11% of the national budget (7.5% of GNP) as regards comprehensive, upper secondary and municipal adult education: and some 2.5% for further and higher education. The cost of primary and secondary education is shared by the municipalities and the central government. State subsidies for current expenditures are based on teacher salaries and average half the total local costs incurred for operating both types of schools. Higher education is paid for by the State alone. the municipalities' share of school costs amounts to as much as 20% of their budgetary resources.

Allocation of Funds
Expenditure on Education: Distribution by Level
Percentage of Expenditure 1977

Pre-school	First Level	Second Level	Third Level	Other
–	37.7	12.3	11.0	39.0

Social Benefits

All education is free of charge, including textbooks, and an excellent school meals service provides free lunches for all pupils, the week's menus being published in advance in the local newspapers. All pupils going on to the upper secondary school receive a flat rate study grant, with a supplement in accordance with parental income, in addition to which they may be granted study loans, and travel or accommodation supplements according to need. Students in higher education get both an outright grant at a fixed rate, and a loan which is based on the student's academic performance, financial situation, number of dependents, etc. The loan is interest free but tied to the cost of living index and has to be repaid in instalments up to the age of 50. The guiding principle behind such measures is that the individual's right to education is guaranteed by law and no one need go without for financial reasons.

9 DEVELOPMENT AND PLANNING OF THE EDUCATION SYSTEM
Development

Compulsory primary education lasting for six years was first introduced in Sweden in 1842 when it was still very much an agrarian society. There were a few secondary schools, but the percentage of each age group that attended them was very small. In 1904 the secondary schools were split into two sections, a six-year *realskola* or junior secondary school and a four-year *gymnasium*, or upper secondary school. Until 1927 there were State schools for boys only, girls being educated in private schools. The instruction offered was largely academic, leading to a final examination *(studentexamen)* which qualified students to enter the universities. It was similar to the German pattern, for up to World War Two Sweden was much under German influence and German was the first foreign language taught.

Educational Objectives

Since 1945 Swedish education has been subjected to considerable change, and the final revised pattern began to emerge in the 1970s. Until 1976 the Social Democrats were the ruling party in government and they imposed their views. The purpose of education today is clearly seen as social engineering, to produce a society in which all are equal, and which is as free as possible from all forms of friction and envy. During the last decade extensive educational reforms have been carried out to ensure that every child has a precisely equal start in life. The new system is universal and monolithic with only one type of school for every child, and every effort is made to remove handicaps, whether the latter result from parental problems, poor home backgrounds or physical or mental disabilities. Private schools have almost entirely disappeared. There are a few which still call themselves private and charge fees, though they are subject to State control with regard to syllabi and could not exist without State subsidies. (The International School in Stockholm, which caters for children of non-Swedish families and is fee-paying, is an exception.)

It is not surprising that, in a country dedicated to the principle of social engineering and the benefits of a comprehensive welfare system, education should be highly centralised, and that it should reflect both social and economic needs – for example, in the emphasis placed upon provision for pre-schooling, vocational training, and the necessity to abolish conventional sex-roles in such subjects as crafts and home economics. At secondary level - and to a considerable extent at tertiary level also - specialisation has been dropped in favour of a more broadly based general education plus vocational training.

In the Council of Europe Sweden is active in promoting her educational ideas and theories, some of which find ready support from the educational planners of other Council members. Within the Nordic Council working parties try to establish common school syllabi for the Scandinavian countries, but this is a slow process. Sweden is a pace setter and her neighbours do not always find her ideas palatable.

Planning Institutions

Government planning is initiated through commissions of enquiry *(utredningar)*. A high-powered committee is appointed to investigate a problem and issue a report. Everyone concerned then has a chance to read the report and submit suggestions or amendments. A consensus is reached before enacting legislation is passed through parliament.

10 THE SYSTEM IN OPERATION

Current Plans

Recently attention has focussed on pre-school and post-secondary education. There are plans to increase the provision of nursery and infant schools and to train more nursery and infant school teachers, so that there will be places available for all children at age 6. A Commission working on a plan for the future of post-secondary education issued its report in 1973 - an 800 page book which took five years to produce. This Commission is known as U68.

U68

The aims of U68 are best shown by quotation:

"The present organisation, with its emphasis on consecutive education, tends to assign a decisive importance to choices made by school children. There is strong evidence that this is an essential factor underlying the distorted social distribution of the upper secondary school, with its over-representation of the first socio-economic group in the lines that most directly prepare pupils for the types of higher education most in demand . . . U68 recommends that planning be directed at the development of an organisation which will stimulate recurrent studies . . . In this way, periods of study will alternate with periods of occupational activity . . . The intention should be to offer every individual a suitable pattern of education."

In July 1977 the coalition government effected legislation which, though modifying certain of the U68 proposals, considerably revised the administrative organisation of post-secondary organisation of post-secondary education and introduced both curricular reforms and changes in selection and admission requirements designed to facilitate increased enrolment of mature students – opening up a wide range of courses (with the exception of some special courses such as medicine) to those over 25 with a minimum of four years' work experience and adequate study atptitude assessed by means of a voluntary test. A large number of 'general' courses, catering for a majority of students in further and higher education and based on national 'core' syllabi, was planned for the following vocational areas: administration, economics and social sciences; welfare and medicine (to provide basic medical qualifications for nurses), thus enabling them to qualify as doctors after a shorter than normal period of special medical training); culture and information; technology; and teacher training in fields such as pre-schooling and social counselling. The quota of foreign students admissible to any course was fixed at a maximum of 10%. The major administrative effect of the 1977 legislation was the comprehensive unification of all full time post-secondary education under the National Board of Universities and Colleges (UHÄ).

REFERENCES AND FURTHER READING

The main sources of information about Swedish education are the occasional papers published by the relevant Swedish authorities: the Ministry of Education, the National Board of Education, and the National Board of Universities and Colleges. Other documents include the reports of the Commissions of Enquiry and various publications of the Swedish Institute.

Andersson, Inger and Sundgren, Lars (1976). *The Internationalising of Education in Sweden.* SIDA.
Berg, B. and Ostergren, B.(1977). *Innovations and Innovation Processes in Higher Education.* National Board of Universities and Colleges.
Bergendal, Gunnar (1977). *Higher Education and Manpower Planning in Sweden.* National Board of Universities and Colleges.
Bowman, Sohlman and Ysander (1978). *Leaving and earning.* National Board of Universities and Colleges.
Boucher, L. (1982). *Tradition and Change in Swedish Education.* Pergamon, Oxford.
Higher Education – Proposals by the Swedish 1968 Education Commission (1973). Allmänna Förlaget.
Huntford, Roland (1971). *The New Totalitarians.* Allen Lane.
Husén, Torsten (1971). *Education in the Year 2000.* Swedish National Board of Education.
Johansson, Sven-Akê (1977). *School Finance in Sweden.* (Part of an OECD study of primary school finance).
Karlsson, J.-S. and Rudhe, C. (1973). *Forms of Governance for the Educational System in Sweden.* Swedish Ministry of Education.
Kumm, Bjorn (1977). *Ever Heard of Sweden?* Swedish Institute.

Marklund, S. and Soderberg, P. (1967). *The Swedish Comprehensive School*. Longmans.
National Board of Education (1976). *School in Sweden*. Information for Immigrants.
Oakley, Stewart (1966). *The Story of Sweden*. Faber and Faber.
Orring, Jonas (1967). *School in Sweden.* SÖ Förlaget. (English edition 1969).
Östergren, Bertil (1975). *Planning for Change in Higher Education.* Office of the Chancellor of Swedish Universities.
Secretariat for Nordic Cultural Cooperation (1977). *Environmental Education in the Nordic Countries.*
Stenholm, Britta (1970). *Education in Sweden.* Swedish Institute.
Swedish Institute. Various fact sheets, booklets and stencils.

Structure of the Education System in Sweden

Age	3 4 5 6	7 8 9 10 11 12 13 14	15 16 17	18 19 20 21 22 23 24
Level		I	II	III	IV
Stage		1	2	3	4	5	
Compulsory		////XXXXXXXXXX		
School Type		Comprehensive Junior ǀ Intermediate ǀ Senior	Upper Secondary a. theoretical b. vocational c. integrated	Universities and regional centres — Teacher training colleges — Adult education – study circles — Folk high schools, radio, TV

▨ Education preceding the first level

Source: UNESCO/IBE International Yearbook of Education

Compulsory Education: Age Limits 7-16 Duration (years) 9
Entrance age to pre-school education: 3

SWEDEN BASIC STATISTICS	1960	1970	1974	1978 (approx.)
1 Total population (000)	7,480	8,042	8,257	8,278
% female	50	50	50	50
2 % population 0-14 years	22.0	20.8		21.0
% female	49	48	49	49
3 Enrolment, all levels	1,157,334	1,311,029	1,349,279	1,455,188
% female	49	48	49	49
First level	650,066	615,331	688,806	689,893
% female	49	49	49	49
Second level	465,244	554,480	531,594	575,190
% female	50	48	49	51
Third level	42,024	141,218	128,879	190,105
% female	36	42	46	
4 Teachers, all levels				
% female				
First level		30,800	42,958	38,689
% female		83	80	81
Second level		54,970	54,656	61,759
% female		44	45	47
Third level				
% female				
5 Public expenditure on education				
Total (000) Kronor	3,086,700	13,150,000	18,451,100	29,407,300
As % of GNP	4.6	7.7	7.5	7.7
As % of public expenditure				13.4
6 % enrolment (MF) by level	100	100	100	100
First level	56	47	51	47
Second level	40	42	39	40
Third level	4	11	10	13
% enrolment (F) by level	100	100	100	100
First level	56	48	51	47
Second level	41	42	40	41
Third level	3	10	9	12
7 Entrance age: Duration of				
First level education	7:6	7:6	7:6	7:6
Second level education	13:7	13:7	13:7	13:6
8 Enrolment ratios (MF)				
First level	96	97	97	96
Second level	55	72	70	69
Third level	9.04	21.34	21.81	
Enrolment ratios (F)				
First level	96	97	98	97
Second level	56	71	70	72
Third level	6.59	18.51	20.43	

Switzerland

CONTENTS

1 Geography	642
2 Population	644
3 Society and Culture	645
4 History and Politics	646
5 The Economy	649
6 The Education System	650
7 Educational Administration	656
8 Educational Finance	658
9 Development and Planning of the Education System	659
10 The System in Operation	662

Switzerland is now a Confederation of 25 Cantons. Since the sixteenth century, when the last bonds of dependence on the Austrian House of Hapsburg were broken, Switzerland has adopted a policy of neutrality. Within the country there are cultural differences which belie the outsiders' view of a middle class, prosperous, completely unified nation.

There are several mother tongues and four national languages. Sixty-five percent of the population speaks German, 18% French, 12% Italian and 1% Raeto-Romansch. The rest have a different mother tongue. Local dialects are spoken but each of the main linguistic groups live in a distinct geographical area. Thus, while German, French and Italian are official languages and at least two of the three must be taught in schools, few Swiss are bilingual.

Again, while since 1848 complete religious tolerance has been accepted, and while Geneva is the site of Calvinism, the proportions of Protestants (48%) and Catholics (50%) in the population are very similar. Cantonal schools took over from the Churches in the nineteenth century, but many schools are virtually confessional and the Churches can maintain their own schools.

This diversity helps, no doubt, to account for the strength of feeling associated with the maintenance of communal administration of educational provision. Doubtless the physical terrain reinforces the persistence of local control. Each of the Cantons is responsible for public education. Power is usually delegated to local school boards. Moves to unify the system by introducing Federal legislation have been made, with some success, but it remains the case that local pride and cultural differences ensure that communal participation in the running of schools remains, compared with many countries, at a substantial level.

Aims are not, for example, laid down in Federal or Cantonal Constitutions and the administration of schools is very decentralised. Planning is, however, carried out at the Federal level but tends to emphasise the needs of science, research and vocational/technical education in the interests of the economy.

Cantonal reforms tend to follow the pattern of language-related national systems. Moves to raise the age at which children transfer from a common or comprehensive school have been fairly widespread and in 1974 Geneva, Vaud and Valais introduced a *cycle d'orientation* covering for all pupils a three-year period from ages 12-15 during which they are all taught the same basic subjects. This scheme reflects moves made in France to introduce a period of orientation. Differentiation and selection increases as pupils move up through the system. Five types of school leaving certificate, for example, are recognised by the Confederation. In type A there is specialisation in Latin and Greek; in type B in Latin and modern languages; in type C in mathematics and science; in type D in modern languages and commercial subjects; and in type E in economics. Some 80% of children, however, opt for vocational education at the end of the compulsory school – frequently under apprenticeship schemes. The relatively sharp division between general education and vocational training is traditional and has been subjected recently, as elsewhere, to criticism by those who wish to see a comprehensive reform of secondary education. Cantonal variation in the period of compulsory education, curricula, textbooks, make comprehensive reforms desired but, in practice, place constraints on change.

The Editor

1 GEOGRAPHY

Topography

Switzerland lies in the heart of Europe between 45°50'-47°45' N.lat and 5°58'-10°3' E.long., surrounded by (in descending order of frontier lengths) Italy, France, Germany, Austria and Liechtenstein, with which it has the closest links. Its 16,000 square miles are divided into three natural regions – the Alps (60%) in the west and southwest, the Jura Mountains (10%) in the northwest and the Central Plateau (30%) on which the majority of the Swiss live. The country is 218 miles from west to east and 136 miles from north to south. Five percent of its total surface is covered by lakes, and its mountain streams are the sources of four of Europe's largest rivers – the Rhine, the Rhone, the Inn and the Ticino. Altitudes vary from 15,217 feet at Pointe Dufour on Monte Rosa to 633 feet above sea level on the shores of Lake Maggiore.

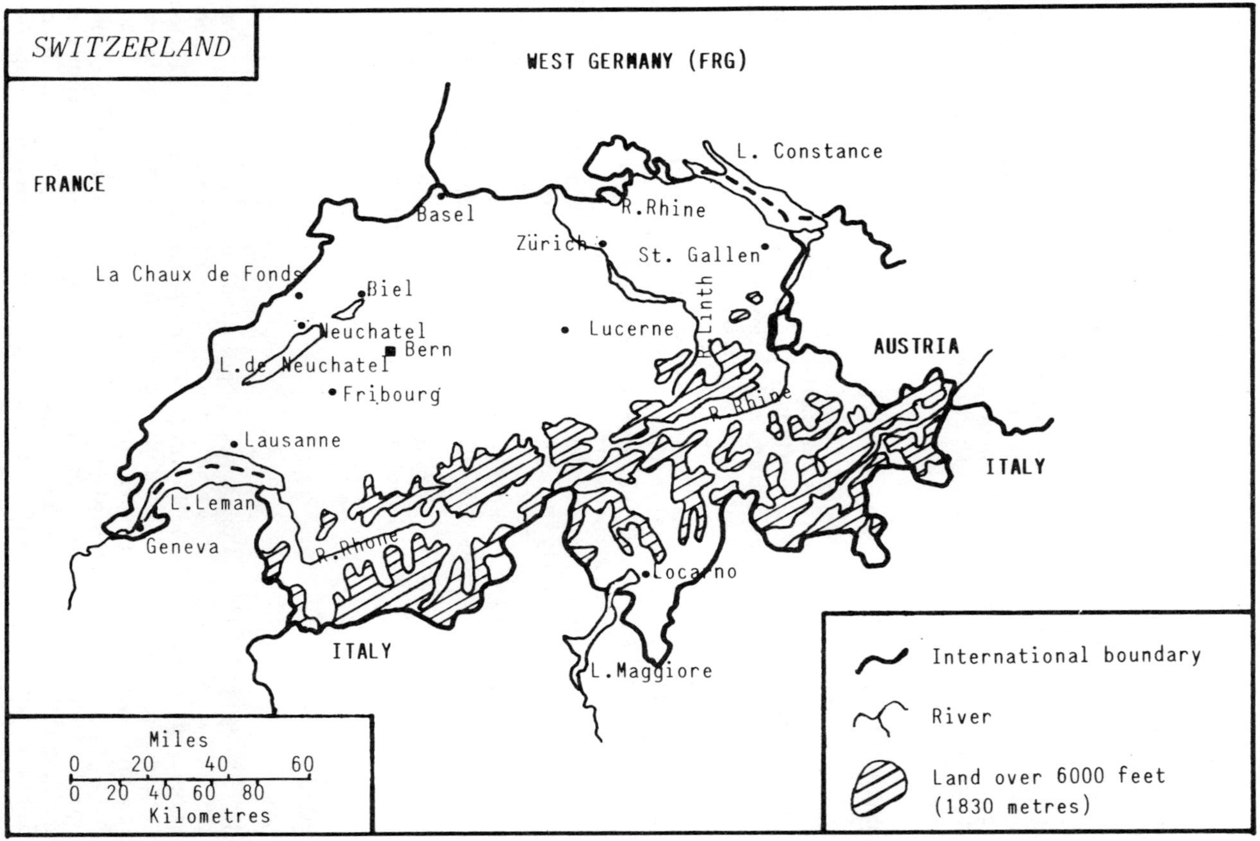
SWITZERLAND
WEST GERMANY (FRG)
FRANCE
L. Constance
Basel
R.Rhine
Zürich
St. Gallen
La Chaux de Fonds
Biel
R.Linth
Neuchatel
Lucerne
Bern
L.de Neuchatel
AUSTRIA
Fribourg
R.Rhine
Lausanne
ITALY
L.Leman
Geneva
R.Rhone
Locarno
ITALY
L.Maggiore
Miles
0 20 40 60
0 20 40 60 80
Kilometres
International boundary
River
Land over 6000 feet
(1830 metres)

The rugged terrain contains few mineral deposits and severely limits agricultural production, except for animal husbandry and dairying. Centres for various Swiss industries are: machinery - Zürich and Geneva; watches - Geneva, La Chaux-de-Fonds, Le Locle and Bienne; clothing - Zürich and St Gallen; textiles - the entire northeast; metal processing - the Jura Mountains and the Cantons of Solothurn, Zürich and Schaffhausen.

Climate

A temperate climate prevails throughout most of the country, with an average temperature of about 49°F in the Plateau cities. However, wide and sudden variations in weather may occur frequently, resulting from spectacular differences of altitude and gradient. The snow line fluctuates between 2,000 and 10,000 feet.

Communications

Switzerland is often called 'The Crossroads of Europe' and, as such, prides itself on its excellent transport facilities. The railways are considered the finest on the continent: there are 3,560 miles of track (including 428 miles of surface and aerial mountain lines) 98% of which are electrified. Forty-seven percent are privately owned. Swiss railways carry over 320 million passengers and move 60 million tons of freight each year. Rail transportation is generally preferred to lorry, although the nation's 37,620 miles (60,192 km) of road are in good condition and well maintained. There is transport on the larger lakes and the ships are being modernised. While Switzerland has no ocean ports, it is easily accessible by ship. Basel on the Rhine has direct waterway connections to Strasbourg, the Ruhr, Rotterdam and Antwerp. Basel handles about 40% of all Swiss foreign trade and annually dispatches some 8 million tons of freight down river.

For historical and administrative reasons the country is divided into 25 units called cantons. The federal capital is Bern.

2 POPULATION

Growth

In December 1978, the total population of Switzerland was 6,268,000 inhabitants, of whom about 16% were foreign. The percentage of foreigners is falling. Overall the total population decreased during the 1970s and the proportion of the population below the age of 25 years declined slightly.

With an average population density of 152 inhabitants per square kilometre, Switzerland is a densely populated country. The distribution of population is very uneven owing to topographical and economic factors. Sixty percent of the total population live in urban areas. According to a 1980 estimate the largest cities are: Zürich (376,400); Basel (183,000); Geneva (150,000); Bern (142,400); and Lausanne (131,400).

Groups

The Swiss nation is made up of two main, closely related groups: those of Latin and those of Alemannic origin. There are three linguistic divisions in the former. The mother tongue of the Swiss people is thus divided between four national languages, approximately as follows: German 65%; French 18%; Italian 12%; Raeto-Romansch 1%. The remaining 4% of Swiss have a different mother tongue. While using 'high German' as the occasion requires, the German speaking Swiss also preserve their local dialect which is used almost exclusively as a spoken language. The national language groups represent distinct geographical areas: the three main groups being situated in the east, west and south respectively and the Romansch in the northeast of the Alps. There is a language problem at the civic and social level since communications to the people as a whole must be in the three main languages and relatively few Swiss are truly bilingual. English, on the other hand, is continually gaining ground as the most widely used foreign language in Switzerland and to a considerable extent tends to oust the use of a second national language in practice. German, French and Italian are regarded as the official languages of the Confederation and are used as such by the authorities and Federal Civil Service. At least two of these three are taught compulsorily in schools. Since 1938 Romansch has been recognised as the fourth national language.

3 SOCIETY AND CULTURE

Language and Social Class

Swiss society is essentially middle class, displaying all the characteristics implicit in this description – conservatism, stolidity, prosperity. A large proportion of its citizens are business and professional people; only a minority can be described as working class (although there is a fairly large peasantry or agricultural working class) and a smaller minority still is in the highest income bracket.

This class structure has developed largely as a result of the country's special economic characteristics. Switzerland seems to have had the good fortune to gain most of the advantages of the industrial revolution and yet avoid most of its troubles. By virtue of the nature of the industry it has developed (which is largely precision-based), no large *Lumpenproletariat* has been formed (imported foreign labour has filled this role) and consequently the demand for social and economic reform has not been as great as that which has faced other European nations during the past 50 years. Also it has been possible until recently to deal with internal problems of this nature in an atmosphere unclouded by sharp ideological conflict.

There are few major divisions among the population – either social or ethnic. The distinct geographical and national characteristics of the three main linguistic groups create, however, a social barrier and sense of rivalry between them. This finds expression in demands for Cantonal autonomy. As in other

European countries, there has developed a certain degree of conflict between youth and older age groups, but actual clashes, for example at university level, are few and relatively mild.

The family unit continues to play an important role in society and because of this and the relatively late starting age of compulsory education the family has a strong and generally restraining influence on young people. Indeed, parents play a considerable part in school administration through representation on local School Councils, in some cases by Cantonal regulation.

Religion

Geneva has been called the Protestant Rome. It was the site of John Calvin's epochal Protestant community and today harbours the headquarters of the World Council of Churches, a prominent ecumenical body. Switzerland once saw conflict between her Protestant and Catholic citizens - as well as between Christians and such colourful non-believers as Rousseau and Voltaire - but since 1848 complete tolerance has been the rule. Confessional freedom is laid down in the Federal Constitution but confessional schools are permitted provided that no child of a different faith is made to attend unwillingly.

4 HISTORY AND POLITICS

Historical Developments

The Swiss nation as we known it today has developed over a period of nearly 700 years. Its origins lie in the Founding Pact of 1 August 1291; this was a pact of mutual assistance signed by the representatives of three communities which categorically rejected any administrative and judicial system imposed from without - in other words the jurisdiction of the Austrian House of Hapsburg, rulers of the Holy Roman Empire of which Swiss territory was then a part. This pact is regarded by the Swiss as the birth certificate of the Confederation.

The struggle against the Austrian Hapsburgs continued into the fourteenth and fifteenth centuries. During this period the Confederation grew in size (to 13 cantons in all) as it was joined by further communities and towns and as rich territorial concessions were made in payment for services rendered by Swiss contingents called to fight with other nations' armies. These became much in demand as Swiss military prestige increased as a result of the confederate army's repeated triumphs against the Hapsburgs. The over-ambitious anti-French policy of Cardinal Schiner led, however, to defeat of the Swiss at Marignano (northern Italy) in 1515 and one year later a perpetual alliance was signed with François I. Thus the last bonds of dependence on the Empire were broken, and henceforth Switzerland vowed to adopt a policy of perpetual neutrality, though it continued to furnish the courts of Europe with picked troops.

The Reformation preached by Zwingli and Calvin at the beginning of the sixteenth century found fruitful soil for expansion in Switzerland, thanks to the critical works of humanists like Erasmus. The spread of Protestantism did not, however, go unchallenged by Swiss Catholics and indeed even led to brief civil wars in 1529 and 1531. It was on account of religious schisms in their ranks that the Confederate army took care to refrain from the religious wars taking place in neighbouring states in the mid-sixteenth century (Wars of Religion and Thirty Years War). This gave substance to the Swiss tradition of neutrality, which was fortified by the formal recognition of Swiss sovereignty by the signatories of the Treaty of Westphalia (1648).

The Napoleonic era saw the occupation of three cantons by the French army and the subsequent collapse of the old Confederation. This was replaced by a unitary constitution (the 'Helvetian Republic') which was totally unsuited to the temperament of the Swiss people. Switzerland then became a battlefield for the French against their allied enemies. More serious still, internal disorder and factions were rife in the country as a result of disputes between 'unitarians' and 'federalists'. This situation was brought to an end in 1803 by Napoleon's Act of Mediation which returned Switzerland to a federal state. The Act also added to the 13 old cantons six new ones, former associated or dependent regions. (The number was eventually increased to 22 after the fall of Napoleon by the accession of three new territories.) At the Congress of Vienna in 1815 the great European powers proclaimed the perpetual neutrality of Switzerland.

Religious issues which had divided the nation since the advent of Protestantism came to a head in 1846 when a separatist movement was formed by the Roman Catholic cantons known as the Sonderbund. The Confederate Army put an end to the movement very quickly, however, thereby opening the way to a general reconciliation. The Constitution of 1848 which was established after these events and revised in 1874 defined the political organisation which is still in force today.

Government and Politics

Switzerland is one of the world's oldest democracies, a federal republic marked by a high degree of decentralised authority and an unusual amount of direct citizen participation. The nation is divided into 22 Cantons, three of which are divided into half-Cantons; each of the 25 Cantons and half-Cantons controls its own system of education, public works, social welfare and police protection. The Federal government retains only those powers specifically delegated to it by the Constitution of 1874 and exercises them primarily through legislative rather than executive decision. The national legislature sitting at Bern is composed of two houses. A National Council, now containing 200 members, is popularly elected and includes one representative for each 24,000 citizens. The Council of State has 46 members (19 Cantons and two representatives each and the six half-Cantons one each); the members may be either chosen by direct election or appointed by the Cantonal legislature. Both houses, known as the Federal Assembly, together choose a seven-man Federal Council to act as the nation's executive branch for a four-year term, each of the seven Councillors being made responsible for a Federal Department. The office of President of the Confederation is rotated annually among the Council members, but all real power is held by the Council itself.

The most distinctive feature of Swiss democracy is its provision for direct citizen participation in lawmaking. Not only must amendments to the Constitution be submitted to the voters for majority approval, but *all* federal legislation is referred to popular referendum if requested by 30,000 voters or the governments of eight Cantons. Further, 50,000 petitioners can force an original Constitutional amendment to be placed on the ballot, and it will become law if a majority approves. Of Switzerland's seven major political organisations, the Social Democrats, who advocate stronger social legislation and wider government participation in industry, are perhaps the strongest. But politics at the national level is seldom partisan, and party loyalty is not nearly so significant a factor in Switzerland as it is in other countries.

The Swiss legal system is relatively uncomplicated and contains both Federal and Cantonal trial and appeals courts, which hear civil and criminal cases. Where the Federal Government or a Canton is a party to a lawsuit, and in some cases where private individuals are the litigants, the Federal Tribunal in Lausanne has both original and appellate jurisdiction.

The system and policy of government are reflected in the education system, which is strongly Cantonal, with only minor Federal participation and control.

International Relations

Political neutrality is the keynote of Switzerland's foreign policy, and the country belongs to no international organisations of a political character. It adheres only to those of strictly economic, general or social character. While it therefore eschews *membership* of e.g. the United Nations and its agencies, the World Bank and IMF, it nevertheless cooperates with them actively and makes contributions to their programmes. In practice, therefore, Switzerland's trade, development and society are considerably influenced by international organisations and agreements of the kind mentioned above, largely by dint of its geographical position and industrial ties. In addition, and again arising out of its policy of neutrality, Switzerland is home to various worldwide bodies such as ILO, IBE, ITH, the Red Cross, the UN office, UPU, WATA, World Council of Churches, World Wildlife Fund, etc., which tend to operate in relative isolation from, and without influence on, the Swiss environment.

Contemporary Switzerland continues firmly to maintain its neutrality, and has used it to develop humanitarian functions. The International Red Cross was founded thanks to the efforts of Henri Durant in 1863 and since the beginning of this century Geneva has been chosen as the seat of many international organisations.

5 THE ECONOMY

Natural Resources

Landlocked, largely mountainous with a damp climate and few useful mineral resources, Switzerland was endowed by nature with no more than the basis of a meagre pastoral economy. It has, however, developed into one of the most highly industrialised and prosperous countries of the world. The reasons for this are many, of which the most important are the country's favourable geographical position in Europe, its principle of armed neutrality, the determination and hard work of its people, and a judicious use of skilled foreign labour at all levels.

To compensate for their country's paucity of mineral wealth, the Swiss have specialised in manufactures that require a high degree of skill and a minimum of raw materials (e.g. watches, electrical engineering machinery, embroidery and silks). Their products are thus renowned worldwide for their excellent quality and high unit value relative to their weight.

Manufacturing Industry

Half the economically active population is now employed in manufacturing, building and handicrafts; of these the vast majority work in industrial establishments employing 50 people and under. Giant industrial concerns are not a feature of the Swiss economy; of the 11,423 industrial establishments in operation in 1973, only 2% of these employed up to 500 people and only 0.25% employed over 2,000; conversely 65% employed fewer than 50 workers.

In numbers of workers and total product value, the machinery industry is clearly Switzerland's giant. Much of its output is made to order and over 70% of all production is exported. Products include industrial, electrical and power equipment; scientific, industrial and technical instruments; electronic equipment; diesel engines and locomotives; and agricultural and printing machinery. Second in importance after machinery is the chemical industry followed by watches, textiles and foodstuffs. Farm production, 75% of which involves animal husbandry and dairying, supplies only half of domestic food requirements; for this reason, on a per capita basis, Switzerland is one of the world's largest importers of agricultural products. Given, however, the high proportion of non-productive land (23.6%) represented by lakes, glaciers and barren rocky slopes, agricultural production is surprisingly high. As in other European countries, there has been a continuous drift of agricultural workers to other occupations with the result that barely 7% of the labour force is employed in agriculture. In the tertiary sector of the economy, tourism, banking and insurance are the main sources of foreign currency.

Trade

Because such a high percentage of the country's national income is earned abroad, the one weakness of the Swiss economy is its dependence on world economic conditions. Until 1974 these conditions were highly favourable; since then, however, signs of a minor recession have developed in the building, watch and clockmaking industries. Unemployment figures are relatively low but in the Swiss context the general employment index rarely fell below 100%. Unemployment is controlled to a considerable extent in the Swiss economy by reducing the number of residence permits issued to foreign workers. Thus Switzerland is able to 'export' a major part of its unemployment.

The high parity of the Swiss Franc may price some Swiss exports out of world markets and there is a possibility of an electrical power shortage. Almost all sources of water power which can economically be harnessed have already been exploited and there are strong objections from local pressure groups on ecological and safety grounds to the construction of atomic power stations.

6 THE EDUCATION SYSTEM
Pre-School

Pre-school education is available for children between the ages of 3 and 6. Except in Geneva where compulsory education begins with a year of semi-infant school for 6-year olds equated with the first year of primary school, education at this level is not obligatory. Many schools are run by the Communities (or as in the case of Geneva and Basel city, by the Cantonal authorities) and are virtually free; others are private schools which charge fees, often at a modest rate, thanks to Cantonal subsidies. The number of pre-primary schools in urban and rural areas and attendance of them is growing constantly.

In German Switzerland the influence of Froebel is most noticeable and there is often no actual instruction. In French and Italian Switzerland the prevailing theories are those of Claparède, Ferrière and Montessori, and those of Decroly. There are English medium private pre-primary schools, and primary schools taking children from the age of 4+.

First and Second Levels - General

By virtue of her system of Cantonal government, Switzerland has traditionally displayed considerable variety in her education system at the first and second levels. Not only have there existed differences between Cantons in the structure of their education system, but there have also been discrepancies as regards the length of compulsory schooling and the starting date of the academic year. In recent years, however, various steps have been taken to achieve greater coordination and uniformity at the national level. Thus in 1970 the Conference of Cantonal Directors of Education and the Federal Council approved the Concordat on School coordination. The latter was instituted in 1971 with the approval of ten Cantons. Two years later, it had been endorsed by a further ten Cantons. The Concordat bound its members to uniformity as regards the age of entry to school (6 years), the duration of compulsory schooling (9 years), the length of study to school leaving examinations (minimum 12 years, maximum 13) and the start of the school year (between 15 August and 15 October).

There is considerable educational activity in Switzerland outside the national system. Throughout the country but especially in the French speaking sector there are several international schools including English medium boarding schools, often coeducational. These schools prepare their pupils for GCE 'O' and 'A' level examinations. There are also English medium day schools in Bern and Zürich which terminate at 'O' level.

First Level (Primary)

In the majority of Cantons primary education starts at the age of 6. In the remainder, the starting age is 7. Tuition is free; it is compulsory and in its lower grades it is based on a common curriculum which includes reading, writing, study of the environment and pupil's mother tongue, arithmetic, PT and singing. Some Cantons also include traffic instruction. After the third, fourth, fifth or sixth school year, pupils enter the upper primary school for the second stage of their compulsory education. Here they are graded into two, three or four groups, (depending on the numbers involved) according to ability and career intention. The different types of instruction offered are arranged either in parallel courses between which there exists, in certain circumstances, the possibility of transfer, or in grouped courses. They may have different names from one Canton to another, but they all have one and the same object: to prepare the pupils for the different types of secondary education. There are, therefore, practical sections, sections having a more or less commercial or technical character, and classical sections preparing for the *gymnasium*.

These varying types of instruction are intended to facilitate not only the needs of vocational guidance, but also assessment of abilities. The programme of the final classes - practical or pre-vocational sections - has been amplified by the introduction of optional subjects (modern languages, technical drawing). In the other sections of the upper grades of compulsory education the teaching of a second modern language, i.e. a second national language, is compulsory for all pupils; in German speaking Switzerland it is French, in French speaking Switzerland it is German, in Italian speaking Switzerland French or German and in Romansch speaking regions it is German. For children in the classical section, it is also usual to begin the study of Latin and, in some cases, Greek also. This system evidently prejudges later courses of study and for this reason some educationists, with the interests of late developers in mind, have been campaigning to reform it. Geneva, Vaud and Valais introduced in 1974 the *cycle d'orientation* which merges all sections of lower second level education in one integrated comprehensive school. This covers a period of three years from the age of 12 to 15 during which period pupils are all taught the same basic subjects: history, geography, French, the mother tongue, natural history and drawing. For German and mathematics, pupils are taught at three different levels according to aptitude. Latin, technical subjects and extra foreign languages are all optional. The advantages of this system are obvious in that it avoids the heartburnings and injustices of a decision at the age of 11 or 12. This scheme was subsequently extended to other Cantons.

Special education is provided for handicapped (mentally retarded, abnormal, maladjusted) children, either in special classes belonging to the public schools or in specialised institutions, public or private. Private, fee-paying schools exist for all levels but no more than 5% of all children attend private primary schools and in the Canton of Solothurn they are forbidden altogether.

Second Level Education (General)

A high proportion of children continue their general education after completion of their compulsory schooling at the age of 16. For those who decide to abandon their studies altogether, it is compulsory in 17 Cantons and half-Cantons to attend 'non-vocational continuation' schools which last (according to the Canton) from half a year to four years. During this period pupils receive further general education (mother tongue, book-keeping, civics and general knowledge) and in rural areas boys are given additional instruction in agricultural techniques while girls learn homecrafts. For those who decide to stay on, however, there is broadly speaking a choice between pursuing their general education at upper second level or embarking upon vocational training of some kind.

Upper Second Level Education

There are two categories of course available in the field of upper second level education.

The first is a short course which is intended mainly for girls; this is a broadly based course leading to a diploma which enables them to bridge the gap between the end of their compulsory education and their entry to those vocational schools which have a minimum entrance age of 17 or 18 (e.g. schools of social work, training schools for kindergarten teachers). The second is an extended course (four or five years) preparing for the Federal or (less frequently) Cantonal Maturity (school leaving) certificates and qualifying for admission to a university. The Federal leaving certificate is a general admission qualification and a Cantonal leaving certificate is more limited. There are five types of school leaving certificate recognised by the Confederation between which students may choose: type A specialising in Latin and Greek; type B in Latin and modern languages; type C in mathematics and science; type D in modern languages and commercial subjects; and type E in economics. The last two types were only introduced in December 1972 and replaced corresponding Cantonal certificates. Maturity examinations must include the first and second national languages, mathematics and one of the special subjects for each type as an absolute minimum. It is obligatory for pupils to study these subjects and history to the end of their schooling; other subjects taken in common by all students in the second cycle of secondary education (geography, physics, chemistry, natural sciences, drawing or music) can be abandoned in the last two years.

Further general education of this type is given generally in higher secondary schools or *Gymnasia*. The majority of these schools are public ones, run either by Cantons or municipalities. Independent schools, particularly denominational schools, do however play an important part in upper secondary education - they are attended by no less than one third of all pupils at this level. Students over 20 years of age who wish to qualify for university admission may prepare for Maturity examinations either in Cantonal Maturity schools for adults or in private evening schools.

Vocational Education

As about 80% of children opt for vocational education at the end of compulsory school attendance. Vocational education can be obtained either in an apprenticeship combined with attendance at a 'vocational continuation school' or in vocational schools of different types.

Apprenticeship training is the option most commonly followed by school leavers. It is governed by Federal regulations (Federal Law on Vocational Training and Education of September 1963) which determine the designation of the profession, the length of the apprenticeship, the teaching programme, organisation of examinations, etc. - these apply to over 280 professions. During the full duration of the apprenticeship (which varies from between two and four years, depending on the profession) students must attend vocational continuation schools for one day or two half-days a week where they are given a more general, theoretical type of instruction. Once the apprenticeship is completed, students are obliged to take a final examination (conducted by the Cantonal authority) which leads, if they are successful, to the Federal Certificate of Capability.

For those who do not wish to enter an apprenticeship, there are several different types of vocational institution to choose between - commercial schools, technical schools, agricultural schools, arts and administration schools, etc. Some of these schools prepare for higher studies, otherwise they usually lead after three years to a diploma qualifying for the Federal Certificate of Capability. Administration schools and sections of commercial schools prepare for employment in federal administration (railways, posts, customs) for which the minimum entry age is 17. Agricultural schools provide only winter courses in the main, their diplomas admitting to the Agricultural and Horticultural Technicum and to high schools of viticulture, conology and arboriculture.

Teacher Training Schools

Primary teachers are trained in teacher training schools. With the exception of Geneva and Basel City, these schools admit pupils at the age of 15 or 16 and given them four or five years' training to the 'Primary Teachers' Training Certificate'. At Basel and Geneva, however, this education is obtained at the university is a two- or three-year course after acquiring the school leaving certificate. In certain cases students from teacher training schools can enter a university faculty.

College of Technology

These institutions admit students who have completed a trade apprenticeship and give them an advanced vocational training of three or four years' duration. They may be compared to the engineering schools of France and Germany.

Third Level (Higher) Educational Institutions

While in most countries some of the schools included in the secondary sector would normally come under the classification of higher education, in Switzerland this term embraces the following institutions only:

THE FEDERAL INSTITUTES OF TECHNOLOGY in Zürich and Lausanne. These are of university level and as their title implies, they offer courses primarily in engineering and science.

THE CANTONAL UNIVERSITIES. There are seven of these and they are situated in the following places: Basel, Bern, Frigbourg, Geneva, Lausanne, Neuchatel and Zürich.

PRIVATE INSTITUTIONS AT POST-GRADUATE LEVEL, e.g. Jung Institute Zürich, Management Colleges in Geneva and Lausanne.

Admission to these institutions is on the basis of the Federal Maturity certificate or its equivalent from abroad. A Cantonal Maturity certificate is also acceptable for entry to certain university faculties. Latin is an additional requirement for admission to some faculties. Applicants for courses offered by the Federal Institutes of Technology must pass an entrance examination before then can be admitted.

The universities are autonomous and thus vary. Those in the German speaking zones grant doctorate degrees; the universities in the French speaking areas award licentiate and doctor degrees. The length of study at university varies between 7-8 semesters (13 for medicine), diplomas generally being awarded after four years of study. For students studying technical subjects, the emphasis is on oral examinations and the final thesis. Modern language students are normally required to spend at least three months in the country of their main language. Finally, students intending to enter the professions (law, medicine, teaching, etc.) must pass Federal examinations before they are allowed to practise.

The academic year consists of two semesters. The winter semester lasts from mid-October to the beginning of March; the summer session from mid-April to mid-July. With the exception of the Catholic University of Fribourg which is bilingual (French and German), the language of instruction is either French or German according to the area in which the institution is situated. No student accommodation is provided, although private hostels exist.

Teacher Training

Regulations governing the award of teachers certificates vary greatly from Canton to Canton except for professional and technical teachers for whom Federal regulations ensure a more common practice.

The training of pre-school teachers, after entry examinations, is provided in sections of Canton, Communal or Private Teacher Training Schools. The age of entry and length of course vary according to linguistic areas.

The duration of training courses for first level teachers varies according to the age of the student (between 15 and 18). Basel and Geneva offer university courses only, leading to the 'Primary Teachers Training Certificate' after 2-3 years. Applicants must have acquired the Maturity Certificate before they can be considered for entry. There are 53 Teacher Training Schools in total; of these 17 are private or communal (municipal) and the remainder Cantonal. The latter are confessionally neutral excepting six of the private schools which are all confessional, four being Protestant and the remainder Catholic.

Normally the minimum qualification for admission to second level teacher education is the Maturity Certificate or Primary Teachers Training Certificate plus experience. For those who wish to teach in the first cycle of second level schooling, the Secondary Teacher's Diploma is required. This can be obtained after 2-4 years' study either at a university or at a special Cantonal pedagogic institute. The curriculum of these courses lays stress on the mother tongue and a foreign language on one hand and pedagogical subjects on the other. For those who want to teach in a *Gymnasium*, a Diploma of a specialised *Gymnasium* teacher must be obtained. To acquire this, students must study for a degree for at least four years at either a Federal Institute of Technology or a University. This must be followed by 1-2 years' pedagogical study, which may also take place at special Cantonal institutes responsible for this training.

Teachers in higher technical and commercial schools must also have the Gymnasium Teacher's Diploma and in vocational schools the Secondary Teacher's Diploma is essential. In both cases this training must be followed by theoretical and practical courses in Bern organised by the Federal office of Industry, Trade and Labour.

Non-Formal

Schools run by industry, and other private schools at all levels have been mentioned. There are also some special pre-primary schools, private or Canton-aided, for the children of foreign, (mainly Italian and Spanish) workers, for whom introductory and supplementary integration classes in the school system at pre-school and first level, and out of school crèches are provided in several Cantons. Many private schools enable adolescents and adults to resume or start general studies leading to Federal Maturity examinations or commercial or other specialised studies. Some run correspondence courses or use television, e.g. collaborating with the Bavarian *Telekolleg*. The Evening Schools and Higher Technical Evening Schools accept adults who left full time schools prematurely. Their Maturity Certificates and Diplomas respectively can, since 1968, be recognised by the Federal authorities. Most big firms run training and promotion courses for their staff, and institutes for initiation into modern methods of administration have been established by industrial, commercial and banking circles. The National Swiss Library and the various Municipal and Cantonal Libraries offer extended facilities for study material.

Adult and Further Education

This is not mentioned in the Federal Constitution, though attempts have been made to establish the "principles applicable to the organisation and development of adult education and youth training out of school" by the Confederation. Several Cantons have legislated either for adult education itself or for the creation of appropriate bodies to deal with it. The Swiss Federation for Adult Education (FSEA) set up a working party in 1973 to study model laws for proposal to the Cantonal authorities and Geneva decided in March 1974 to set up a Council for Further Education for Adults.

Adult and further education proper on the widest scale with no minimum entry requirements from second level is provided by private institutions with financial help from the Confederation or more substantially from the Cantons and Communes. Bodies affiliated to the FSEA aim to provide varied social, cultural and civic activities rather than professional training or promotion courses.

7 EDUCATIONAL ADMINISTRATION

There is no Ministry or Federal office for education, and a projected 'Federal Secretariat' for questions relating to schooling has thrice been rejected by popular vote. The supreme Federal authority in education, as in all other spheres, is the Federal council of seven members. This is elected by the National Assemblies for four years' service and is re-eligible for the same period. The supreme Federal officials concerned primarily with educational matters are the two members of the federal Council to whom is entrusted control of the Department of Public Economy (vocational training), and the Department of the Interior (other educational matters). The Department of Public Economy collaborates with the Cantons and the professional associations over the administration of the vocational (non-arts) and agricultural schools. The Department of the Interior is responsible for the two Federal Institutes of Technology in Zürich and Lausanne: for educational grants and other matters affecting the Cantonal non-vocational education institutions, and the Swiss schools abroad. With these major exceptions, administration is decentralised and undertaken separately in each of the 25 Cantons (including six half-Cantons) with full powers (jealously guarded) subject only to the Federal Laws and Orders.

In all Cantons the vocational schools, except those for arts, commercial and higher technical education, are administered by the Canton in collaboration with the Federal Department of Public Economy. In nine Cantons the schools are the responsibility of the Department of the Public Economy of the Cantonal Government; in the other 16, they are administered by the Cantonal education authorities.

The administration of the other non-Federal public educational institutions is varied. In nearly all Cantons the chief authority (in theory at least) is a Director of Education, member of the Council of Government, and head of a (relatively small) Education Department.

Additionally, in each Canton and half-Canton, there is a supervisory body, usually an Education Council under the chairmanship of the Director of Education, with 5-11 other members usually appointed by the Cantonal Parliament. The amount of influence which this body wields varies from Canton to Canton; in some areas it is almost exclusively an advisory body; in the majority it is an influential decision-making authority.

In most Cantons all public education is controlled by the Cantonal authorities, with the exceptions mentioned earlier, but the administration of schools at the pre-primary (except in Basel City), primary and secondary levels are delegated to local school boards of the self-governing city, town and village communities. The members of the boards are not professional educationalists and include teachers; some have a permanent secretariat. In the larger Cantons these boards are represented on regional boards. In the largest cities (excepting Geneva) there are boards for each district, which are represented on a central board, and for the administration of municipal schools there is also a Municipal Education Department under a Municipal Director of Education. In Canton Zürich, for example, there are about 200 such communal school boards.

In six Cantons (Appenzell-Innerrhoden, Glarus, Nidwalden, Thurgau [usually], Zürich, St Gallen) there are boards of an autonomous School Community, whose members are elected by the People. In the remainder they are boárds set up by the Political Community, which usually appoints their members, with varying degrees of direct participation by the People.

These boards have full local authority and are responsible for carrying out a wide range of duties including inspection of schools, maintenance of buildings and equipment; appointment of teachers; admission, attendance and discharge of pupils; supervision of health service; preparation or approval of timetable drawn up with or by the teachers; supervision of teachers; disciplinary questions; preparation of reports for the Cantonal authorities. The Cantonal bodies' role is often that of a coordinating rather than controlling body. This is not to say they have no real power - by their control of subsidies to the Communities and by participating in the administration of their schools, the Cantonal authorities exercise a significant degree of influence over the local school boards.

This administrative pattern, while promoting close contact between the people and the schools, naturally results in great diversity and sometimes inequality of education. Together with the linguistic divisions of the country, it tends to foster regionalism and resistance to change and coordination. Present policies are designed to remove some of the worst discrepancies between Cantons and to introduce a measure of uniformity between them.

The internal administration of puplic primary and lower second level schools is carried out by a headmaster or headmistress assisted by teachers entrusted with special duties in the schools: at the upper second level a committee of teachers rather than the head is responsible for internal administration, although the head has a coordinating role. Inspection of schools is carried out at Communal and Cantonal level. In the case of the former the Inspectors are nearly always lay people, in the latter lay inspectors frequently join forces with professional inspectors. At the third level the Federal Institutes of Technology in Zürich and Lausanne are administered jointly by an Academic Council appointed by the Federal Council, a President (who is a member of the council) and by administrative staff. The Zürich Institute is furthermore governed by a Rector chosen by the professors for a term of two years and a permanent Rectorate. The Cantonal universities are administered in collaboration with the Cantonal education authority by a Rector chosen by the Senate and approved by the government Council.

Inter-university matters are the responsibility of the University Conference, the Rectors' Conference, or the Universities Central Office in Zürich, which also deals with international matters. Inter-Cantonal school matters are dealt with by the Conference and Regional Conferences of Cantonal Directors of Education and those of the Vocational Training Offices by the Cantonal Departments of Public Economy.

8 EDUCATIONAL FINANCE

Sources of finance for education are as follows:

(i) The Communities: Community schools are pre-school, first and second levels; Graduate School, St Gallen (equal share with Canton)

(ii) The Cantons: Cantonal educational institutions at all levels; grants to Communities, and subsidies for non-profit-making private schools

(iii) The Confederation: The three Federal educational institutions; training courses for vocational school teachers; subsidies for Cantonal expenditure at primary, secondary and tertiary levels, for private schools for children of Federal employees and of French speaking foreign diplomats in Bern, for inter-Cantonal and private schools for handicapped children, for private vocational schools, for adult education and Swiss schools abroad; grants for research (National Fund for Scientific Research)

(iv) Large Firms: apprenticeship schools, grants for higher technical schools, doctoral students and research in higher education

(v) Other Private Organisations: educational institutions at all levels

(vi) Fees: public educational institutions at tertiary level, private schools at all levels.

In almost all communities and Cantons the budget of the Education Department, including construction, is larger than that of any other Department. Approximately a quarter of all public expenditure by the Communities, the Cantons and the Confederation is devoted to education. Over 5% of the GNP is spent on education.

Allocation of Funds
Expenditure on Education: Distribution by Level
Percentage of Expenditure 1977

Pre-school	First Level	Second Level	Third Level	Other
3.1	-	77.3	16.5	3.1

9 DEVELOPMENT AND PLANNING OF THE EDUCATION SYSTEM

Origins

The aims of education are not defined in the Federal Constitution and subsequent laws, except for the principles of compulsory primary education and the freedom of conscience and belief. Nor are they for the most part defined in the Cantonal Constitutions, although nearly all Cantonal school laws contain a prefatory declaration of principle.

The original purpose of primary schooling in the Cantons was to educate citizens for democracy; its main aims, therefore, were the formation of character and temperament, the acquisition of knowledge and the development of ability and physical fitness. The twentieth century has witnessed a change of emphasis from these objectives to the pursuit of scientific and technological knowledge. Today, however, efforts are being made to revive civic and political education and to educate youth for responsibility in society.

Planning

There is no one body which has responsibility for the planning and coordination of education in Switzerland. Planning at Federal level is carried out by a special Coordination Committee appointed by the Federal Council, and by:

> Science and Research Division, Department of the Interior
> Pedagogical Institute for Vocational Training
> Department of Public Economy
> The Science Council
> Special Institutes of the two Technical Institutes
> Research and Teaching Division, Federal School of Gymnastics and Sport
> Federal Commissions

These bodies are all responsible to the Federal Council. Their influence on Federal policy is strong, but limited in practice by the referendum system and the autonomy of the Cantons.

At inter-Cantonal level planning is carried out by the Conference of Cantonal Directors of Education, an autonomous advisory body which submits proposals to the Federal Council and the nation, and the Regional Conferences of Directors of Education. At the end of 1973 the Conference of Directors of Education of NW Switzerland agreed to submit to the Regional Conference of their Cantonal Governments a proposal for a Regional Schools Agreement between them providing inter alia for cooperation over the planning of schools and school types, especially in border areas. The reports of the Conference were studied at Federal and Cantonal level as the basis for referenda and new Federal laws. The Cantonal Departments of Education are also planning bodies for the Cantons. The creation of a planning unit for school experiments in the Pedagogy Section of the Education Department in Zürich was approved in November 1973.

Educational Reform

Unlike most other countries in western Europe, Switzerland has not undertaken any critical reappraisals or reforms of its education system in recent years, or indeed in this century. By virtue of its dependence on its human skills, however, the country has traditionally maintained a strong interest in education and over the past ten years it has increased its financial commitment to the area fairly considerably. The increased resources have been devoted in the main to study grants and construction, university expansion and Federal aid to universities. Other trends in Swiss education in recent years have been greater school coordination, as indicated, in increased use of audio-visual teaching methods; development of orientation, information, medical welfare and research services; curriculum and organisational reforms. The latter will (or has already) affected all sectors of the system to a greater or lesser extent.

First Level

Deliberate attempts have been made to reduce class numbers to an average of between 25 and 30.

Curriculum reforms at this level include the introduction of modern mathematics and the commencement of a second national language at an earlier stage than hitherto. Special provision is made for the children of migrant workers to facilitate the learning of the language of their place of residence and to provide their integration into the Swiss education system.

Second Level

Some innovations in the field of secondary education have been mentioned - for example the introduction of the '*cycle d'orientation*' in some French Cantons and the addition of Federal Maturity Certificates Types D and E. Other changes are the diversification of the 1st Cycle in German speaking Cantons, the introduction of traffic, first aid and sex education and a modification of mathematics teaching.

In a report entitled 'The Middle School of Tomorrow' (Committee of the Conference of Cantonal Directors of Education, 1972), proposals were put forward for a far more general and comprehensive reform of second level education. The most important was the suggestion that an observation and orientation stage should be established covering the fifth to the ninth school year (i.e. the last five years of compulsory education) leading to the division of post-compulsory education into three parallel stages:

(i) Maturity stage of two cycles of two years as preparation for universities

(ii) Diploma stage of three years maximum, as preparation for special vocational schools

(iii) Vocational stage for apprenticeships.

The idea of an orientation stage is favoured in several Cantons. This reform was badly needed to make the system fairer for late developers as was the report's second major proposal that there should be greater permeability of the education structure.

Third Level (Higher) Education

In higher education the Universities Law, first passed in 1968 and modified in 1972, inaugurated a new era in Swiss university policy since its main objective was to secure greater Federal control of university policy in exchange for increased financial help. The general aim of the revision was the greater coordination and rationalisation of university policy and the ultimate establishment of the 'Swiss University' in the country.

One of the spearhead proposals was full Federal responsibility for Medical (non-clinical) and Science faculties. As the negative outcome in March 1973 of the popular vote on the revision of the education articles in the Constitution made it impossible to revise the principles of the law, an advance project was prepared and submitted to the Cantons, universities and other interested bodies later that year. Its reception was fairly mixed but on balance, unfavourable.

Meanwhile university expansion has slowed down considerably due to the difficult financial climate. Indeed, current university budgets came close to zero growth. Since the numbers of students leaving school with Maturity Certificates is rising continuously and the university is virtually the only regular outlet for holders of such certificates, even if admission requirements are raised, the Federal authorities will have to make a choice between increasing the capacity of universities or providing some other study arrangements for holders of upper secondary school leaving certificates.

10 THE SYSTEM IN OPERATION
Problems

To the external observer the main problems facing Swiss educators are:

(i) the need for greater coordination of educational policy at national level to standardise educational opportunities between Cantons

(ii) the need still further to reduce the sharp divisions between the different levels and sectors and increase the permeability between them, and to reduce the large number of small establishments in certain areas

(iii) the need to make more adequate educational provision for the children of foreign workers, although their numbers are declining

(iv) the need to improve teacher education

(v) the need to improve the quality and increase the status of vocational training

(vi) the need to reduce the rate of repeaters, failures and drop-outs.

Manpower

On the whole the education system is relatively well geared to the needs of the labour market. The Swiss economy is heavily dependent on its human skills and these are competently taught in its vocational and technical schools. Up to mid-1974 the general employment index had for many years never fallen below 100%. Consequently there has for a long time been a strong demand for personnel of all qualifications. With the advent of a minor recession, however, this is unlikely to continue to be the case. In the long term, however, various prospective studies tend to show a chronic shortage of specially qualified personnel, implying the need for an education policy favouring the expansion of higher education and the reinforcement of the system at middle levels of training.

Policies and Outcomes

On the whole the system, or rather the 26 different systems, works well in the Swiss context. This is not to say, however, that there are no problems. The delegation of administrative responsibility to the Communities can cause complexity of procedure in some cities, where changes may involve several Cantonal and Communal bodies and in the case of vocational schools the Federal body as well.

The great decentralisation of education has produced wide and satisfactory distribution of educational establishments generally, except at pre-school level. Since 1950 second level education has been decentralised, firstly of the 1st Cycle, later of the 2nd Cycle. The large number of small establishments, one-teacher schools or schools with only two or three teachers for all classes, are an obstacle to structural reform and the best use of teaching methods. At the same time, the rise in school population, accentuated by the large numbers of children of foreign workers, made provision inadequate, even in some important towns. It also entailed difficulties of organisation and the threat of the introduction of 'numerus clausus' at university level, already virtually existing in Medical Faculties. The need for more pre-schools increased as more mothers went out to work. A high proportion of the age group 4-6 were foreigners, many of whom wished to stay in the country and required language study before entering first level schools. Swiss legislation makes it possible to send foreign workers home in times of economic recession.

The incidence of students repeating courses is fairly high. this and total failures can be attributed partly to the structural rigidity at post-first level which limits transfer possibilities and the insufficient amount of individual attention given to pupils, and to a failure to elicit parents' wishes regarding the choice of post-first level school types.

There are annual first and second level 2nd Cycle school assessment tests. At the end of the primary period, examinations or tests play a part in weeding out and determining the type of further schooling to be followed. Thereafter examinations within compulsory education tend to disappear in favour of a complex procedure of judgement and orientation and/or a formal period of observation and orientation. The Maturity examination at the end of the second level period, though subject to Federal norms, is not organised by the Federal authorities. The schools recognised for the purpose are themselves responsible for the examination, important attention being paid to the results in the previous year. The university is virtually the only regular outlet for holders of the Maturity Certificate. The incidence and the difficulty of university examinations vary according to the structure of studies in the faculties; by and large a relatively large number of drop-outs occur during the first semesters, due to examination failures or wrong choice of study or type of education.

Teachers are on the whole adequately qualified. Formal qualifications may be waived in favour of personal interview at times of shortage. A shortage of qualified teachers which was severe at primary level and in rural areas resulted in a partial lowering of the otherwise satisfactory competence level of teachers and the standard of teaching methods. Teacher training tends to be short, with an imbalance between general and pedagogic study and is little developed at the pre-school level. The training of first and second level teachers is not fully integrated.

School teachers are generally well paid, particularly in the wealthier Cantons. The percentage of women teachers in primary education is about 60%, in second level education at the first stage about 20% and at the second stage about 10%. The relatively low percentages of women teachers no doubt helps to explain the satisfactory socio-economic status enjoyed by teachers generally.

School curricula are laid down by the Cantonal authorities, following recommendations, in the case of communal schools, by the School Boards in collaboration with the teachers. Though tending to rigidity and overloading, they are subject to constant revision and improvement. Programmes vary greatly throughout the country, ranging from the summary, allowing teachers an important margin of liberty, to (in rare cases) clear cut, detailed plans of study. In general, teachers have full freedom of methods and at second 2nd cycle level also a wide choice of textbooks. Variations in curricula and textbooks, as well as in the date of school entry date and structure, handicap those pupils, particularly in compulsory education, who have to transfer from one Canton to another. University and Higher Technical Institute curricula are drawn up the Professors subject to the approval of the Rector/Cantonal authorities, and the President/Academic Council respectively. Revisions thus involve a lengthy procedure, which nowadays also includes the agreement of the student representatives.

The prestige pattern after first level school is direct entry to *Gymnasium* for Federal Maturity Certificate Classics Type A or B, or failing that, entry via second level schools for types B-E - and admission to University or Federal Technical Institute. The predominant branch/subject favoured by pupils in general secondary education is the *Gymnasium* for Maturity type B with English, and in higher education the University Faculties of Law, Economy, Letters or Medicine, or (in Zürich) the Federal Technical Institute Departments of Architecture and Civil Engineering.

The structural separation (after compulsory schooling) of general, professional and technical education is accentuated by the diversity of administrative responsibility, and there is virtually no permeability between the different sectors. There is a need to develop further a second level education leading to specialised vocational schools and at the same time to raise the prestige of vocational training and extend apprenticeship training. In third level technical education, the division between the Higher Technical Schools and the two Federal Institutes of Technology makes passage from one type to the other difficult.

REFERENCES AND FURTHER READING

Blanc, Emile et al. (1970). *Educational innovation in Switzerland: Traits and Trends*. Unesco, Paris.
Bottani, N. et al. (1976). *Recurrent Education: Policy & development in OECD Member Countries: Switzerland*. OECD, Paris.
Committee of the Conference of Cantonal Directors of Education (1972). *The Middle School of Tomorrow*.
Egger, Eugen et al. (1974). *Education in Switzerland*. Swiss Education Documentation Centre, Geneva.
OECD (1971). *Classification of Educational Systems in OECD Member Countries, Austria, Luxembourg, Switzerland*. OECD, Paris.
Tripet, Edgar (1970). *Cultural Policy in Switzerland*. Council of Europe, Strasbourg.

Turkey

CONTENTS

1 Geography	668
2 Population	670
3 Society and Culture	671
4 History and Politics	673
5 The Economy	676
6 The Education System	678
7 Educational Administration	686
8 Educational Finance	687
9 Development and Planning of the Education System	690
10 The System in Operation	690

Turkey's geographical position helps to explain the diversity found in the country. A small proportion of the country is in Europe; the rest (to the east) borders the Soviet Union, Iran, Iraq and Syria. Of the total population of 40 million, 35 million live in the non-European part (Anatolia) of the country. Cultural traditions reflect this division and a major attempt was made in the 1920s by Kamal Atatürk to westernise the country when the Turkish Republic was founded in 1925. Western institutions and a formal education system were introduced. Many features of this system reflect the influences of France. Despite changes the framework of education remains much the same as when it was created.

Against attempts to modernise its political and cultural institutions should be weighed the persistence of traditional beliefs and ways of life. Almost all Turkish citizens are Moslems. Small Armenian, Greek Orthodox and Jewish minorities are found in Istanbul. Atatürk attacked eastern customs and adopted the Latin script. In fact Moslem practices, particularly in the villages, are maintained. Family traditions, attitudes to women, arranged marriages, and the persistence of linguistic loyalties have made modernisation a slow process. Attempts to create a Turkish national consciousness through the elimination of foreign, including Arabic and Persian works, has discouraged the study of foreign languages and the continued use, from Ottoman days, of English and French for commercial and diplomatic purposes. The need, however, for an international language is reflected in the use of English as the medium of instruction in the two Turkish universities and in the extensive teaching of English in many private and government secondary schools.

These tensions are typical of countries striving to modernise themselves politically, culturally and educationally in the face of diverse and powerful cultural traditions and, as a consequence of recent economic developments, in the face of polarisation created by urbanisation.

Education in Turkey should, in short, be viewed against a background of religious unity, linguistic and cultural diversity and in the light of differences between the many rural areas and the few large urban centres.

Some indications of the level of provision made under these circumstances are that most pre-primary schools are private, compulsory education lasts only five years, there is a high drop-out of pupils between the first and second stages of the basic schools at the age of 12 and there is a sharp differentiation at the upper secondary stage of education between academic general education and technical and vocational training. Modernisation is reflected in the existence of 19 universities, most of which were established along the lines of earlier French and German institutions. At the same time there is a great need for adult education to meet the needs of a population of whom only 61% are literate in towns and far fewer are literate in villages and for those who need vocational training.

At the crossroads of Europe Turkey has educational problems which are similar to those found in Europe and those experienced in the developing countries of the world.

The Editor

1 GEOGRAPHY

Topography

Turkey consists of Turkey in Europe, a small territory of 14,400 sq km (9,000 square miles) including the important cities of Istanbul and Edirne, bordered by Greece and Bulgaria, and divided by the straits of the Bosphorus and Dardanelles from Anatolia, a vast area, stretching some 2,000 km (1,230 miles) east to west and 960 km (600 miles) from north to south, bordered by the Soviet Union, Iran, Iraq and Syria. For about half its length east to west, Anatolia forms a blunt peninsula, surrounded by the Eastern Mediterranean, Aegean and Black Seas. However, half the total area of the country lies east of a line drawn from Iskenderun at the far end of the Mediterranean to Samsun, due north of it on the Black Sea. Turkey has a total area of 780,576 sq km (487,860 square miles). The main problem posed for Turkey by her own geography is the huge distance between the relatively rich west and the eastern provinces.

Anatolia consists mainly of upland, in the west comparatively level and fertile, in the east mountainous and arid; around the edges, there are areas of less climatic severity, such as the very fertile Aegean coast, the Çukurova region around Adana

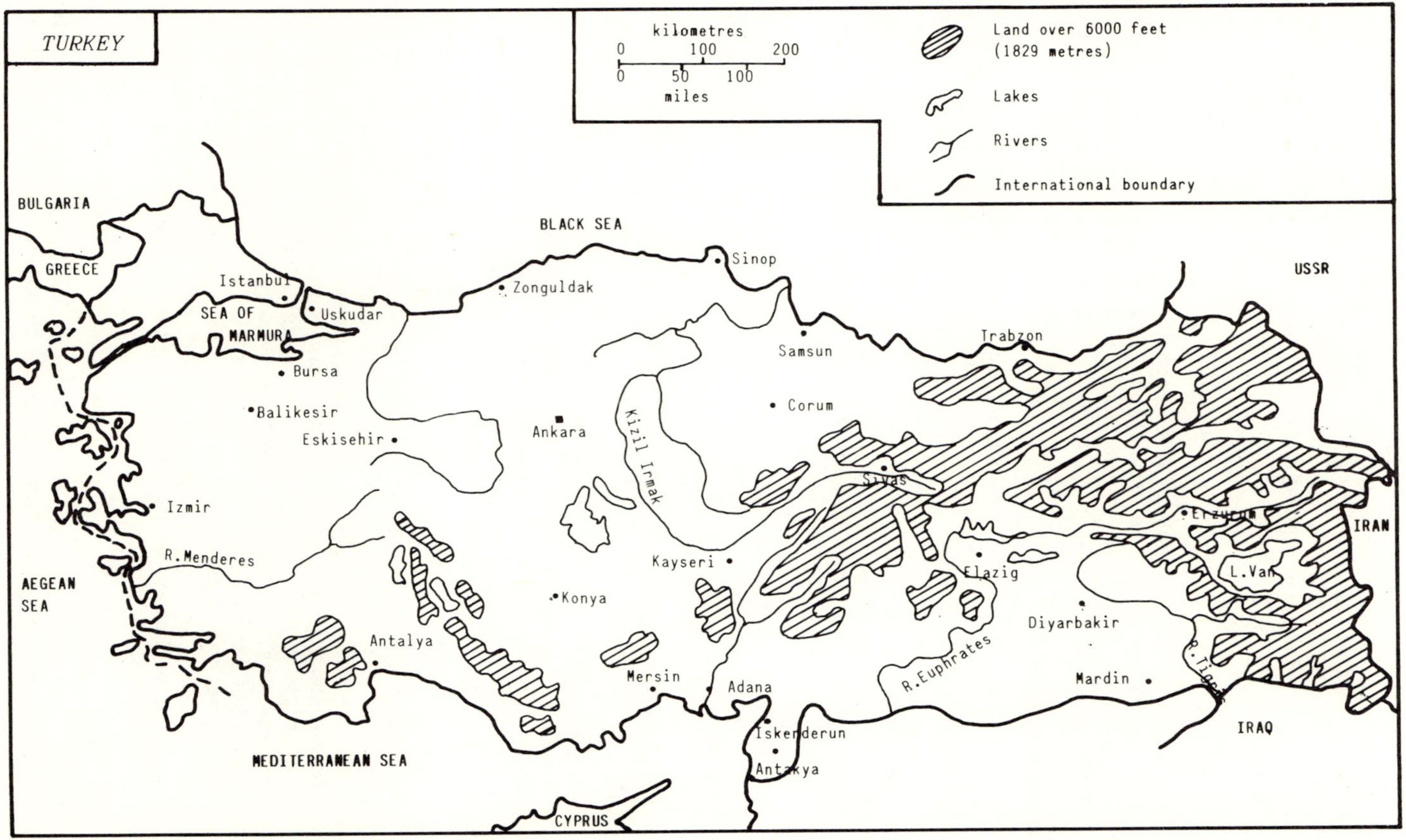
TURKEY
kilometres
0 100 200
0 50 100
miles
Land over 6000 feet
(1829 metres)
Lakes
Rivers
International boundary
BULGARIA
GREECE
BLACK SEA
USSR
IRAN
IRAQ
AEGEAN
SEA
MEDITERRANEAN SEA
CYPRUS
SEA OF
MARMURA
Istanbul
Uskudar
Bursa
Balikesir
Eskisehir
Izmir
R.Menderes
Antalya
Zonguldak
Ankara
Konya
Sinop
Kizil Irmak
Samsun
Corum
Kayseri
Mersin
Adana
Iskenderun
Antakya
Sivas
Trabzon
Elazig
R.Euphrates
Diyarbakir
Mardin
L.Van

in the central south, and the moist forested Black Sea coast. In the east, Turkey contains the headwaters of the Tigris and Euphrates, whose capability for irrigation and power is only beginning to be utilised. In other parts of the plateau, rivers such as the Sakarya and Kizilirmak meander about sluggishly, leaving considerable areas as useless saline desert.

Climate

The climate in Turkey varies considerably between regions. In the Asian interior the climate is one of great extremes with severe winters and hot summers. On the Mediterranean coast the climate is more equable with mild winters and warm summers.

Communications

Communications over the whole country have been hard to establish, and although bus and rail systems and internal airways now link all the main towns satisfactorily, small towns and villages are still very isolated places, even in areas which are generally well off. Nevertheless, travel in Turkey, though sometimes uncomfortable, is remarkably reliable. There is 9,870 km of railway track and in 1976 the road network totalled 140,000 km. There is a large private tanker and cargo fleet and a State corporation, Turkish Maritime Lines, operates passenger and cargo traffic with a fleet of 19 ships and 68 ferries. Regular steamship services run between Istanbul and all the large coastal towns.

2 POPULATION

Growth

The estimated population of Turkey in 1980 was 45,000,000, of whom over 36,000,000 lived in Anatolia. Turkey has an annual population growth rate of around 2.5% (5.3% in towns and 1.8% in rural areas) and the population increased by one third between 1960 and 1970. Exact figures for the school age population are not available, but an estimate is that almost a third of the population is between the ages of 6 and 17. There is a government-sponsored birth control programme which operates actively, but it has so far not had much real effect. Apart from traditional attitudes, the programme has had to reverse the official policy of the first 40 years of the Turkish Republic, when a high birth rate was encouraged for nationalistic and security reasons. The main effect of Turkey's demographic situation and her education is, of course, its sheer pressure of numbers, and the demands of a scattered population for education to be extended to them. Large cities are also faced with the consequences of heavy immigration into their poorer areas.

Distribution

In 1970, only five of the 67 provinces had population densities of over 100 per sq km, and 19 had densities of 30 per sq km or less. Of these provinces, 14 lie in the eastern half of the country, where only Tabzon has over 100 per sq km. Half of the total population lives west of Ankara. Between 1960 and 1970, the number of towns with over 100,000 people increased from 9 to 32, while the percentage of the total population living in outside provincial and sub-provincial capitals fell from 67.8% to 61.5%, indicating a heavy migration to the large towns; (Istanbul now has a population of about 2.6 million, Ankara (the capital) 1.9 million and Izmir 900,575). This migration from country districts, and particularly from the east, continues, as does emigration, to Western Europe by *gastarbeiter*. It is estimated that there are now over 1,500,000 Turks living aborad. The population is settled, except for gradually diminishing tribes in the east, but considerable numbers migrate temporarily from their land to find seasonal work in such places as the cotton plains around Adana.

3 SOCIETY AND CULTURE

Westernisation

The founder of the Turkish Republic, Kemal Atatürk, believed that Turkey's only choice was to adopt European institutions of government, and also European modes of personal behaviour. He ruthlessly cut away any trait which spoiled this vision. Attempts made since Atatürk's death to adopt a more lenient view of 'eastern' customs, such as unofficial polygamy, withholding of education from village girls, and semi-compulsory religious practice, have always brought strong reactions from both the intellectual classes and the military, a combination which ultimately carries the day in Turkey.

Social Patterns

Families are closely-knit, and a fierce masculinity can destroy good intentions towards women and their place as independent individuals. Marriages are normally arranged for village people, and in higher levels of society a certain amount of arrangement takes place, if only because young people feel unsure of their own ability to choose. At all levels, there is a very practical attitude to marriage, as a necessity for a settled life. Divisions in Turkish society are more evident between members of the same generation than between generations. In many ways, the generation which came to power with Atatürk was more radical than that which immediately followed it and today's radical youth finds inspiration among those who then helped Atatürk to accomplish his reforms. The main split in Turkey today is that between city and country, and latterly, employer and worker. Among educated people, the split goes from left to right, with both sides claiming to represent the true spirit of Atatürk and of Turkish nationalism and culture.

Education and Culture

Attitudes to education in Turkey are generally positive. Only in remote parts, especially in the east, is it common for fathers to prevent their daughters from attending school. In such places, teachers have to tread warily. Times of political stress also throw up feelings of antipathy against universities, which are accused of corrupting youth and neglecting nationalist education (by which is usually meant religion). Since the days when Atatürk forbade performances of classical Turkish music because it did not fit his idea of 'civilised music' attitudes have softened, and there is now a lively interest in promoting traditional arts, particularly music and folk-dancing. At the same time, Turkey produces artists of high quality in the Western tradition, and the theatre, opera and ballet enjoy substantial State subsidies.

Language

In the south-east there is a large Kurdish speaking element, and a smaller Arabic speaking one. These are all regarded as Turks. Since the establishment of the Turkish Republic, it has been a primary aim of all governments to foster the spirit of Turkish national consciousness, language and culture, all of which had been somewhat overwhelmed within the multi-cultural Ottoman Empire, where only a peasant would describe himself as a Turk. One of the continuing manifestations of this has been the language reform movement, led by the Turkish Language Commission, which systematically removes all foreign words, especially those of Arabic and Persian origin, and substitutes 'real Turkish' equivalents, often by invention. The first big step was taken in 1928 with the adoption of the Latin script, which at once cut off the younger generation from all earlier written works. The progressive purification of the language since then has meant that even works written in the 1930s, in Latin script, are now barely intelligible. This process has been accepted remarkably easily, especially by successive younger generations. At the same time, there is a great sense of pride in the unique features of the Turkish language, and of its extension over large parts of Central Asia.

This linguistic nationalism has sometimes had the effect of discouraging the learning of foreign languages, through the compulsory use of Turkish in areas (commercial, religious, cultural) where Western European languages were often used in Ottoman days. On the other hand, the new language has allowed access to a vigorous new literature and press to the great mass of the literate population. English is used as the medium of instruction in two Turkish universities: Middle East Technical and Boğaziçi (formerly Robert College). There are quite a large number of private and government secondary schools where English is taught intensively, and used as a medium in some subjects. The existence of these institutions has undoubtedly helped to produce an elite of English speaking technologists and other specialists for whom the doors of foreign institutions are open. However, English is also needed and used by Turks connected with the numerous foreign cultural, developmental and military aid programmes which operate here. Commercial needs are expanding, and the tourist industry is an obvious customer.

Religion

A very large proportion (98.9%) of all Turkish citizens are Moslems, and the great majority of these belong to the Sunni sect. The small Armenian, Greek Orthodox and Jewish minorities are significant only in Istanbul, since the exchange of population and other disturbances during the two World Wars and the War of Independence. There is a group of Nestorian Assyrian Christians in the south east. The non-Sunni Moslems, usually known at 'Alevi' are also to be found mainly in the east, predominating among Kurdish speakers, but Alevi villages are to be found scattered all over the country.

Religious activity received the full force of Atatürk's attack on 'eastern' customs. The Turkish Republic is an officially secular state, without a state religion, and in which equal rights are guaranteed to the followers of all religions. This is in direct opposition not only to Ottoman practice but to the express requirements of the *Seriat* (Islamic Law), under which non-Moslems are allowed to co-exist with Moslems only on certain specific terms, which imply permanent inferiority. Atatürk also abolished dervish orders, forbade ministers of religion to wear special clothes in the street and made prayer difficult by making Moslems wear hats with brims. The adoption of Latin script, and the consequent cutting of easy access to the Koran and other Islamic precepts, was the most devastating act of all. Since then, this fierce onslaught has not been maintained, but the principle of secularism is always strongly defended against the attacks made on it from time to time by religious movements. In the villages, religion and customs such as polygamy continue without much practical interference from the law. This serves to reinforce among educated people the belief that religion is a reactionary influence on Turkey.

4 HISTORY AND POLITICS

Origins

When the Roman Empire was divided in 395 AD Turkey came under the jurisdiction of the Byzantine Empire sited at Byzantium (Istanbul). In the following centuries it was attacked by both Persians and Arabs, conquered by the Turks (who opposed Islam, restored to Byzantine rule by the Crusaders and then regained by the Turks. The Ottoman Empire, founded in 1299, gained control of Anatolia in the mid-fourteenth century, and later of Istanbul. It reached its zenith in the seventeenth century when it stretched from Hungary across the Aegean to North Africa and east to Palestine. By 1918 only what is now Turkey was left. The official Turkish attitude to the Ottoman

Empire is that, at least in its latter years, it was a dying and oppressive institution, weighing equally unfairly on all its component nationalities. There is no doubt that, in practice, the Turks consider that the Empire was their Empire, and feel all the pride or shame for its achievements.

Political Development

Modern Turkey dates from the victory of Atatürk's forces over the Greek invaders in 1922, and the establishment of the Republic in 1923. There followed 15 years of direct rule by Atatürk and the Republican People's Party (*Cumhuriyet Halk Partisi*). This period, which can be called the revolutionary phase of modern Turkish history, saw the forcible abolition of the old socio-political system based on Islamic Law, and the establishment of a system with the usual organs of a Western state. After Atatürk's death in 1938, Turkey entered upon a much less dramatic period. An important development was the establishment of a multi-party parliamentary system in 1946. Unsuccessfully attempted by Atatürk, it led in 1950 to the dismissal from power of the Republican People's Party. Since then, parliamentary democracy has survived, despite various setbacks. The Turkish press, which is free from government control and representative of the whole political spectrum, has played an important role despite persecutions of its more left wing elements in the 1950s and 1960s.

Recent Events

After years of bureaucratic government by the RPP, the Democrat Party régime of Bayar and Menderes appeared at first sight to offer a welcome breath of fresh air. But economic mismanagement and the unpopularity of links with the USA led to opposition and the régime responded by repressing leftward movements, especially among university students and staff. This, and the remarkable personal following acquired by Menderes himself, led to the army coup of 1960, in which he was deposed, later being executed. The Turkish armed forces, following their old personal allegiance to their commander, Atatürk, have traditionally acted as watchdogs against attacks on his reforms, and there has been no danger that they might permanently take over the government. Nevertheless, the 1960s were a period when the military always had to be taken account of, and the presidency of the Republic until recently was always held by a military man. Between 1961 and 1965 Ismet Inönü of the RPP led a succession of coalition governments but in the 1965 elections the Justice Party (Conservative) came to power with Süleyman Demiral as Prime Minister. Despite a position right of centre is was again the military who stepped in to depose him in 1971 when it was clear that his government would not accomplish essential reforms in the face of widespread unrest. For the next two years there was government under military supervision but elections were held in 1973 and as no party had an overall majority Bülent Ecevit (leader of the RPP) formed a coalition government with the NSP (National Salvation Party), an avowedly religious group.

This unlikely alignment lasted until late 1974 when an election called by Mr Ecevit resulted in the formation in March 1975 of a new government led by Mr Demirel's JP in coalition with the NSP and two smaller parties of the right. Following further inconclusive elections in the summer of 1977 Mr Ecevit was unable to form a new government, and Mr Demirel's National Coalition remained in office until the turn of the year, when it was defeated following a series of defections by JP deputies to the RPP. Still without a majority in parliament, the RPP government formed by Mr Ecevit at the beginning of 1978 depended for its survival on the support of a group of independent deputies, most of whom were rewarded with government posts. Over the following 22 months this fragile basis was gradually eroded as more and more RPP and independent deputies defected to the opposition, dispirited by the government's failure to overcome the twin problems of a crippled economy and burgeoning political violence. Following a disastrous series of by-election results in October 1979, Mr Ecevit's parliamentary support finally collapsed, and the following month Mr Demirel established a new minority JP government dependent upon promises of support from various small parties of the extreme right. An army coup in September 1980 resulted in the appointment of General Kenan Evron as President and Bulent Ulasu as Prime Minister of a civilian Cabinet.

Government Organisation

Turkey is a democratic republic with a bicameral Grand National Assembly, consisting of a Senate with 183 members (150 elected by universal suffrage, with staggered six-year terms) and a National Assembly with 450 members elected by universal adult suffrage every four years. The GNA elects one of its members to be President of the Republic for seven years. The President appoints the Prime Minister from the members of the majority party in the legislature and the PM appoints the Council of Ministers. The President has the power of veto but can be over-ruled by a majority decision of the GNA. There are 67 provinces but the Turkish system of government is a centralised one, with only limited powers delegated to the provincial administrations (headed by governors) and the city councils.

International Relations

Turkey's relations with the outside world are dominated by the strategic importance of her location, and by the prolonged crisis in her economy. She is a member of NATO, though her role in it has been adversely affected by her difficult relations with Greece. Turkey also gives political and economic support to the Turkish Cypriots, on whose behalf she intervened in Cyprus in 1974. She is increasingly interested in regional questions. Involvement in events in neighbouring Iran has been scrupulously avoided. There is little sign of an Islamic revival in Turkish domestic politics. Diplomatic relations with Israel have been maintained.

Turkey is a member of OECD and the Council of Europe, and an associate member of the European Community. An important factor in the relationship with the EEC is the presence within the Community of well over one million Turkish migrant workers. The most pressing need on the international front in 1980 was for the successful negotiation of massive economic assistance from western countries. Difficulties in these negotiations probably contributed to a growing emphasis on relations with Arab countries (including Iraq and Libya) and with the Soviet Union (particularly over the supply of energy). However, the Soviet invasion of Afghanistan in January 1980 injected a new sense of urgency into Western attitudes towards economic and other aid to Turkey.

5 THE ECONOMY

Natural Resources

Minerals are, so far, not abundant, probably due to limited exploration. Mining accounted for only 1.3% of GNP in 1974. Chromite and boracite are important exports. For fuel, Turkey relies mainly on her rather low grade coal, mined in the western Black Sea region, but she also supplies about 20% of her own oil requirements from wells in the south east. Latterly, exploration in European Turkey and in the Western plateau has given hopeful results, and prospecting also goes on in the Black Sea and Aegean. More lignite is being used for electricity production, and although only 4% of hydroelectric power potential is used, it already supplies 25% of electricity requirements.

Pattern of the Economy

The new republic came into being with a huge burden of debts, after a general flight of capital and confidence, along with the Levantines and foreigners who had provided most of both, not to mention the loss of economically rich territories. Under Atatürk, a system of state capitalism (etatism) was propounded as the best method of encouraging European-style development and industrialisation. Specially created banks set up and managed such enterprises as textiles, mining, and various agricultural industries. These enterprises are often criticised both from within and from outside Turkey, and they have not been spectacularly efficient. Nevertheless, the performance of the Turkish economy in the two decades up to 1977 was good, with real output growing, on average, by more than 6% per annum.

Agriculture

The variety of Turkish climates gives the possibility of a very varied agricultural industry and the country could certainly become a leading food exporter. The western plateau is good for cereals, and the western and southern coasts for fruit. Meat production, especially mutton, is already of high quality, and could be expanded greatly in the east. Forestry could also be a major industry in the Black Sea area. However, so far most of these activities are underdeveloped. Wheat is the most important food crop with sugar beet, barley and potatoes; cotton is the most important industrial crop. Up to now most government investment has concentrated on the industrial crops, cotton and tobacco.

Industry

Industry has been the most rapidly expanding sector with textiles and chemicals representing major areas of growth. The Five Year Plan 1973-77 allocated 45% of investment to mining and manufacturing industry in an attempt to create a modern heavy industry base to promote export opportunities and import substitution. In 1974 industrial production increased by 9.1% and accounted for about 23% of GNP and 39% of exports with over 50% of industrial production consisting of capital goods (mostly State owned). Consumer goods production was mostly financed from the private sector. Most industrial development has been in the west, for East Turkey is less capable of supporting industry and therefore has not gained from industrial expansion. The objective of the fourth Five Year Plan (1979-83) is to achieve an average growth rate of 8% and to control inflation.

Foreign Cooperation

Turkey has received considerable overseas aid, largely multilateral, and most from an OECD consortium with the World Bank and European Investment Bank established in 1962. The EIB is also involved in the Turkish economy through Turkey's Association Agreement with the EEC which dates from 1963. So far, the benefits to her have been regarded as disappointing, and while there is probably no alternative to her reaching some such accommodation with EEC, whe will no doubt continue to press for better terms, and for the right to full participation in Community decisions, so far denied. In 1975 Turkey concluded bilateral agreements with Iran and the Soviet Union and by June 1979 capital aid received from the World Bank amounted to US$1,814 million in 54 projects. Most Turkish trade is with Europe and the USA with the Federal Republic of Germany taking most exports and providing most imports and Britain and Italy also represented.

1977 Economic Crisis and Recent Developments

The remarkable period of sustained economic growth which began in the mid-1950s came to an abrupt end with the major financial crisis of 1977, from which the economy had yet to recover by 1982. Among the causes of the crisis were:

(i)   massive increases in imports which, as a proportion of GNP, doubled between 1970 and 1977

(ii) decline of remittances from Turkish workers abroad, due to immigration restrictions in Western Europe, and an unrealistic exchange rate for the Turkish Lira

(iii) inflation, partly fuelled by a rapidly increasing Public Sector Borrowing Requirement

(iv) world increases in oil prices

(v) neglect of the agricultural sector

(vi) stagnation of exports

(vii) concentration on sophisticated capital-intensive forms of industrial development which raised costs and called for imported components and plant.

Tough and unpopular measures taken during 1978 to combat the effects of this crisis included several devaluations of the currency, wide ranging import restrictions, massive increases in prices of the products of State economic enterprises and large tax increases. The effect of these measures on the overall financial position was disappointingly small, but their effect on domestic inflation was painfully large. The year 1978 ended with inflation at about 50% and on a steeply rising trend which was to take it towards 100% by the end of 1979.

It was clear that Turkey's economic crisis could not be overcome without massive financial assistance from outside. In December 1978 Turkey entered into discussions with the International Monetary Fund, in an effort to agree substantial standby credits. These discussions broke down because of the domestic political unacceptability of certain of the IMF's conditions, but were resumed in April 1979. They were adjourned again in mid-May without agreement. On 31 May 1979 OECD member governments pledged special aid to Turkey, in addition to special export credit aid. Disbursement of the OECD aid package, however, was made conditional on Turkey reaching agreement with the IMF. Similarly conditional was a fresh package of commercial bank loans. Agreement with the IMF was therefore important not only in its own right, but also as a trigger for other financial aid. Substantive discussions could not be held in the summer or autumn of 1979, however, because by this time Turkey had reached political crisis. It was not until December 1979 that the IMF team was able to come to Ankara for discussions with the new government of Mr Süleyman Demirel.

6 THE EDUCATION SYSTEM

General

The basic structure of the formal education system was determined more than 50 years ago at the beginning of the Turkish Republic. Although the system has grown in new directions and undergone several changes, this basic framework has remained essentially the same. It has three main phases: basic education (ages 7 to 14); secondary level education (15-18); and third level education (18+). For a very few children, this three-phase system is preceded by a pre-school phase from ages 3 to 6.

Pre-School

Pre-primary education is considered an adjunct to the public education system rather than an integral part of it. Most pre-primary schools are privately operated, though some are attached to State primary schools. They are concentrated in the larger towns and cities, where they meet a need arising from the rapidly rising number of working mothers.

Basic - First Level Schools

The first five years of basic education are provided in primary schools, attendance at which is compulsory and free of charge for all children between the ages of 7 and 11. Primary school term dates are determined by local authorities. Primary schools may be established jointly with or separately from middle schools as dictated by local resources and conditions. National policy was to have 100% enrolment by 1978, but this is not yet fully attained.

The Ministry of National Education determines the number of hours spent each week on each subject in primary schools as follows:

Subject	I	II	Year III	IV	V
Turkish	10	10	10	6	6
Mathematics	5	5	5	4	4
Science	-	-	-	4	4
Social Studies	-	-	-	3	3
Introduction to Science & Social Studies	5	5	5	-	-
Drawing and Handicrafts	1	1	1	2	2
Music	1	1	1	1	1
Physical Education	1	1	1	1	1
Religion (optional)	-	-	-	(1)	(1)
Extra-curricular activities	2	2	2	2	2
Moral Education	-	-	-	1	1
TOTAL	25	25	25	25	25

Children who fail to reach the required standard at the end of any year may repeat it, and by this process it is possible for a child to remain in primary school until the age of 14. Normally, however, the primary phase of basic education ends at age 11 with the award of a Primary School Learning Certificate.

Basic – Middle Schools

The formal position is that the holder of a Primary School Learning Certificate has automatic right of entry into middle school. In practice, however, there is a high drop-out rate at the transition stage between primary and middle schools, and middle school enrolments constitute less than 50% of the age cohort.

The Ministry of Education's curriculum coverage for Middle Schools is as follows:

Subject	Year I	Year II	Year III
Turkish	5	5	5
Mathematics	4	4	4
Social Sciences	4	4	4
Sciences	4	4	4
Foreign Languages (English, French or German)	3	3	3
Drawing	1	1	1
Music	1	1	1
Physical Education	2	2	2
Moral Education	1	1	1
Compulsory Options	4	4	4
Religion (optional)	(1)	(1)	(1)
TOTAL	30	30	30

The 'compulsory options' referred to are studies of subjects of special interest to the region in which the school lies – e.g. local history or geography, or studies of the local economy, industry or agriculture.

In addition to normal middle schools, there are also evening middle schools, which usually operate in the same buildings. These are designed to allow those who take up employment after primary school to continue their formal education. If middle school education is done at evening middle school, it takes one year longer than at day school, but it provides exactly the same right of access to secondary education. Stipulated curriculum coverage in hours per week is as follows:

Subject	Year I	Year II	Year III	Year IV
Turkish	4	4	4	3
Social Sciences	3	3	3	3
Mathematics	4	4	4	4
Sciences	2	3	3	4
Foreign Language	2	2	2	3
Morals	1	1	1	–
Religion (optional)	(1)	(1)	(1)	–
Optional Subjects: commerce; handicraft; home economics; music; agriculture	2	2	2	2
TOTAL	19	19	19	19

Second Level Schools (upper stage)

Secondary schools (age group 15-18) fall into two types:

(i) General *Lises*
(ii) Technical and Vocational *Lises*.

General Lises

These are the academic schools which form the core of secondary education in Turkey. They offer middle school graduates a three-year course leading to the State *Lise* Diploma, which enables them to apply for admission to higher education institutions. The programme consists of 11 to 13 courses per year, including at least one foreign language. The first year is common to all pupils and the curriculum comprises: Turkish language and literature, history, geography, natural science, a foreign language (English, French or German), physical education, religion (optional) and minor elective subjects. In the second year pupils must make a choice between science or arts, according to their abilities and interests. In the science branch, mathematics, physics and chemistry are emphasised, while in the arts branch the stress is on Turkish language and literature, philosophy, sociology, history, geography and foreign languages. As in the case of middle schools, it is possible to complete *lise* education by attendance at evening *lises*. The course takes one year longer (four years) and successful graduates receive the full State *Lise* Diploma.

Assessment in general *lises* is by combination of annual examinations and continuous assessment. In the final State *Lise* Diploma examination, pupils achieving 70% are unconditionally successful, while those achieving 45-69% may or may not receive their diploma, according to the grades they have received in continuous assessment.

Certain 'special' *lises* are worthy of particular note. Twelve *anadolu lises* cover both the middle and secondary phases, and their distinguishing characteristic is that some subjects (particularly science and mathematics) are taught in a foreign language. Entry to these schools, which have an average of about 1,000 pupils each, is highly competitive. Even more competitive is entry to the Ankara Science *Lise*, which caters for children showing outstanding ability in science. This highly prestigious school, which has 34 teachers for under 300 pupils, serves as a centre for pilot studies in science teaching methodology and curriculum development, for wider application in the secondary system. A total of 12 minority *lises* are operated by and for religious and ethnic minority groups, such as Greeks, Armenians and Jews. There are also 12 *foreign lises* operated by non-Turkish citizens, though a majority of their pupils are Turkish.

Technical and Vocational Lises

Although the general *lises* described above remain the core of the secondary sector in Turkey, there has recently been a growing emphasis on expanding the number and capacity of technical and vocational *lises*.

Technical Lises: These are specialised institutions and include the following specialised types:

>   electricity
>   electronics
>   chemistry
>   machinery
>   motors
>   building

Courses in technical *lises* are designed to prepare students either for professional life or for a further three years, with growing emphasis on the specialist subject of the particular school, though with coverage also of the general subjects taught in academic *lises*. Technical *lise* graduates have the same rights of application to institutions of higher education as do graduates of general *lises*.

Vocational Lises: These fall into eight main types as follows:

>   industrial vocational *lises*
>   girls' vocational *lises* (home economics, etc.)
>   public health vocational *lises*
>   commercial vocational *lises*
>   agricultural vocational *lises*
>   meteorology vocational *lise*
>   animal husbandry vocational *lise*
>   land registration and cadastre vocational *lise*

Courses in these *lises* are designed to prepare students for working life in their particular fields, though successful graduates are also permitted to apply for admission to higher education courses in their specialist fields only. Courses last for two years after the common first year, and stress practical as well as theoretical aspects of the subject concerned.

Third Level (Higher) Institutions

Institutions of higher education providing a minimum of two years education after secondary level, can be divided into three categories:

>   (i)   universities
>   (ii)   academies
>   (iii)   schools of higher learning.

As with all other levels of education beyond the compulsory attendance period, students who can do so pay towards their studies, but scholarships and residential facilities enable those of limited financial means to study at a higher level, in accord with the policy of equal opportunities for all. In addition, there are *hazirlik*, or preparatory classes designed to bring graduates of technical or vocational *lises* up to the standard of entry to university education.

Admission to higher education is open to all graduates of the secondary system who are successful in the centrally organised Inter-University Student Selection Examination. This examination is highly competitive. In 1978/79, for example, there were some 375,000 candidates of whom less than 10% scored sufficiently highly to gain admittance to higher education. The grades required for admittance to particular faculties reflect supply and demand for higher education in the subjects concerned. In recent years it has been faculties of medicine and engineering which have been able to demand the very highest grades for admittance.

Universities

At present there are 19 universities in Turkey, ranging from the well established, multi-faculty establishments in the major cities to the less developed fledgling institutions in remoter towns. Many of the smaller universities depend on visiting staff from the more established ones. Most courses take four years, though in medicine, agriculture, veterinary science etc., they can be longer than this. The universities are listed as follows:

(i) Istanbul University
(ii) Istanbul Technical University
(iii) Boğaziçi University (Istanbul)
(iv) Ankara University
(v) Middle East Technical University (Ankara)
(vi) Hacettepe University (Ankara)
(vii) Atatürk University (Erzurum)
(viii) Ege University (İzmir)
(ix) Karadeniz Technical University (Trabzon)
(x) Bursa University
(xi) Çukorova University (Adana)
(xii) Diyarbakir University
(xiii) Firat University (Elaziğ)
(xiv) Selçuk University (Konya)
(xv) Anadolu University (Eskişehir)
(xvi) Cumhuriyet University (Sivas)
(xvii) İnönü University (Malatya)
(xviii) 19 Mayis University (Samsun)
(xix) Antalya University.

Most Turkish Universities were established in the French or German tradition, with separate faculties enjoying a high degree of autonomy, subject to the overall control of the Rector. Exceptions to this general pattern are Hacettepe, Boğaziçi and Middle

East Technical Universities, which are organised on more 'departmental' lines. Boğaziçi and Middle East Technical University conduct all teaching through the medium of English, and have substantial English language preparatory schools to prepare under-graduate students for English medium instruction. PhD is the minimum qualification required for teaching in a university and promotion for university staff is on academic merit, as measured by highly formalised systems of examinations and theses.

Academies

During the 1960s and 1970s the major growth centres in the Turkish higher education system have been the academies and schools of higher learning, rather than the universities themselves. Student enrolment in academies increased three-fold between 1960/61 and 1975/76. Entry to academies is open to secondary school leavers who achieve an appropriate grade in the Inter-University Entrance Examination, and the curricula provide for two years of general academic education, followed by two years (or three in the case of the Fine Arts Academy) study in the particular field of study of the academy concerned. for almost all purposes, academy diplomas are regarded as equivalent to university degrees. The five types of academy are listed below with the duration of their courses, and the number of institutions of each type.

	Duration of course	Number of Institutions
State Academy of Fine Arts	5 years	1
Academies of economic & commercial sciences	4 years	5
Academies of Engineering & architecture	4 years	13
Academies of Social Services	4 years	1
Academies of youth and sports	4 years	3

Schools of Higher Learning

These are post-secondary professional training institutions open to students who achieve an appropriate grade in the Inter-University Entrance Examination. Courses last between two and four years. There are 90 such institutions, of which all but 14 are concerned with teacher training either for the general education system or for specialised fields such as technical education, industrial training, commerce and tourism, etc. The 14 non-teacher training schools of higher learning are: 7 higher institutes for Islamic studies; 2 State conservatoires; the Higher Marine School; the Higher School for Applied Fine Arts; the Police Institute; the Higher School for Tobacco Experts; and the Higher School for Health Administration.

Teacher Training

The system of training teachers for Turkish schools is in a state of flux, changing from the traditional pattern in which teachers were trained at 'one step above' the level at which they were going to teach, to a more professionalised, higher level system. Elements of both systems were running concurrently, but the new system described here is just coming into use.

All would-be teachers must be graduates of the secondary system and must pass the Inter-University Entrance Examination at a level sufficiently high to enable them to enter a pedagogical institute, a higher teacher training school or a university or academy. Intending primary school teachers follow a two- or three-year course at one of 67 pedagogical institutes. Intending teachers in middle schools or *lises* must complete a four-year course in either a higher teacher training school or a university or academy. Training of teachers for specialised *lises* is carried out through four-year courses in the Higher Technical Teacher Training School for Girls, the two higher technical teacher training schools, and the higher teacher training school for industrial arts and commerce and commerce and tourism.

Non-Formal and Adult

Non-formal education consists of two main subdivisions: general education and technical and vocational education. Several directorates of the Ministry of Education, Ministries of Agriculture, Village Affairs, Public Works, Industry, Labour, National Defence, Health and Social Welfare, Directorate of Religious Affairs and others have responsibilities for carrying out adult education programmes. It is the job of the General Directorate of Adult Education to provide coordination and cooperation between these various agencies. As well as the opportunities noted in previous sections for adults to complete their formal education in evening *lises*, commercial *lises*, etc., there is a large non-formal adult education programme in existence aimed at increasing literacy and providing training and education in various subjects where there is a demand. It is hoped to organise all aspects of non-formal education in closer cooperation with formal education, in order to help people acquire corresponding qualifications and to make effective use of each other's resources.

Literacy is as high as 65% in towns but much lower in villages. Literacy courses are organised for a duration of four months each year with six hours' study per week, and aim to teach reading, writing, citizenship, history, geography and science to illiterate adults. Training programmes for women stressing health and family planning operate largely through mobile courses touring the villages, although regional schools are often used for these activities. Vocational, technical and cultural education are provided in adult education centres through evening courses. Cultural activities are also arranged by these centres.

Vocational education is offered in practical trade schools, which train people who would like to acquire a trade in a short time, and vocational training centres which train skilled workers.

Applicants to practical trade schools should have completed at least primary school. Vocational centres train skilled workers and instructors for on-the-job training programmes. Courses are organised both in the institutions, in factories and on sites. On-the-job training in all sectors of employment is being given increasing importance as a part of non-formal education. In the villages, there are also vocational courses for men in carpentry, building, blacksmith work, etc.

7 EDUCATIONAL ADMINISTRATION

Centralised Control

As with the overall administration of the country, educational administration is firmly centralised under the Minister of Education. Only the autonomous universities are free from direct government control. The Ministry is responsible for drawing up curricula, coordinating the work of official, private and voluntary organisations, designing and building schools, developing educational materials and so on. The Supreme Council of National Education discusses and decides on curricula, regulations etc. prepared by the Ministry. However, its decisions can only be finalised after approval by the Minister himself.

Organisation of the Ministry

Below the Minister in the hierarchy come the two under-secretaries, who are civil servants, but are appointed personally by the Minister and not promoted from within the Ministry. (This means that the Minister retains a high degree of personal control and his policies are quickly reflected in appointments throughout the education system.) One of the under-secretaries is responsible for technical and vocational education and the other for all other matters. Each of the under-secretaries has working for him a number of general directorates and departments with central directorates serving both wings of the Ministry. The two most important of these central departments are the Board of Education and the Board of Inspection. The Board of Education is the Ministry's research, consultation and decision making body responsible for planning, legislation regulations, and drawing up curricula. The Board of Inspection supervises all educational institutions, carries out research projects and is responsible for personnel training.

Regional Organisation

Educational affairs in the provinces are organised by the Directors of National Education appointed by the Minister. However, they work under the direction of the provincial governor. Primary school inspectors are attached to the provincial directorates of education though they are answerable to the Board of Inspection. They are responsible not only for the supervision of pre-primary and primary schools but also adult education institutions, children's libraries and all kinds of privately organised courses and lessons.

8 EDUCATIONAL FINANCE

Education Budget

In the 1970s (in the years for which figures are available) the proportion of total public spending allocated to education increased from 11.98% in 1969 to 13.23% in 1972, and 15.06% in 1975. The 1979/80 education budget was 75,398 million Turkish Lira, of which some 55% was allocated to the primary sector, 17% to the middle school sector, and 11% to technical and vocational education.

Allocation of Funds
Expenditure on Education: Distribution by Level
Percentage of Expenditure 1977

Pre-school	First Level	Second Level	Third Level	Other
-	46.2	36.5	14.5	2.8

Foreign Assistance

The Turkish education system receives substantial technical assistance, both from multilateral agencies and from bilateral programmes. Among multilaterally funded projects in 1978, the following were of particular note:

(i) UNDP/UNESCO assistance to the development of Karadeniz Technical University

(ii) UNDP/UNESCO assistance to new Turkish universities

(iii) UNDP/UNESCO assistance to adult education

(iv) UNDP/UNESCO assistance to Marine Sciences Department, Middle East Technical University

(v) OECD assistance to Middle East Technical University, Bogaziçi University and the Ministry of Education (US$264,600).

Major bilateral donors were:

(i) Austria, which spent over US$3.5 million on more than 600 fellowships, and on other educational projects

(ii) Federal Republic of Germany, which spent over US$2 million on asistance to ETV, Turco-German university partnerships, and 122 fellowships

(iii) France, which spent over US$1 million on staff and equipment for two French medium secondary schools, US$400,000 on assistance to the teaching of French in universities and teacher training colleges, and US$350,000 on applied science teaching and research in four Turkish universities

ADMINISTRATION

ORGANISATION OF THE MINISTRY OF NATIONAL EDUCATION

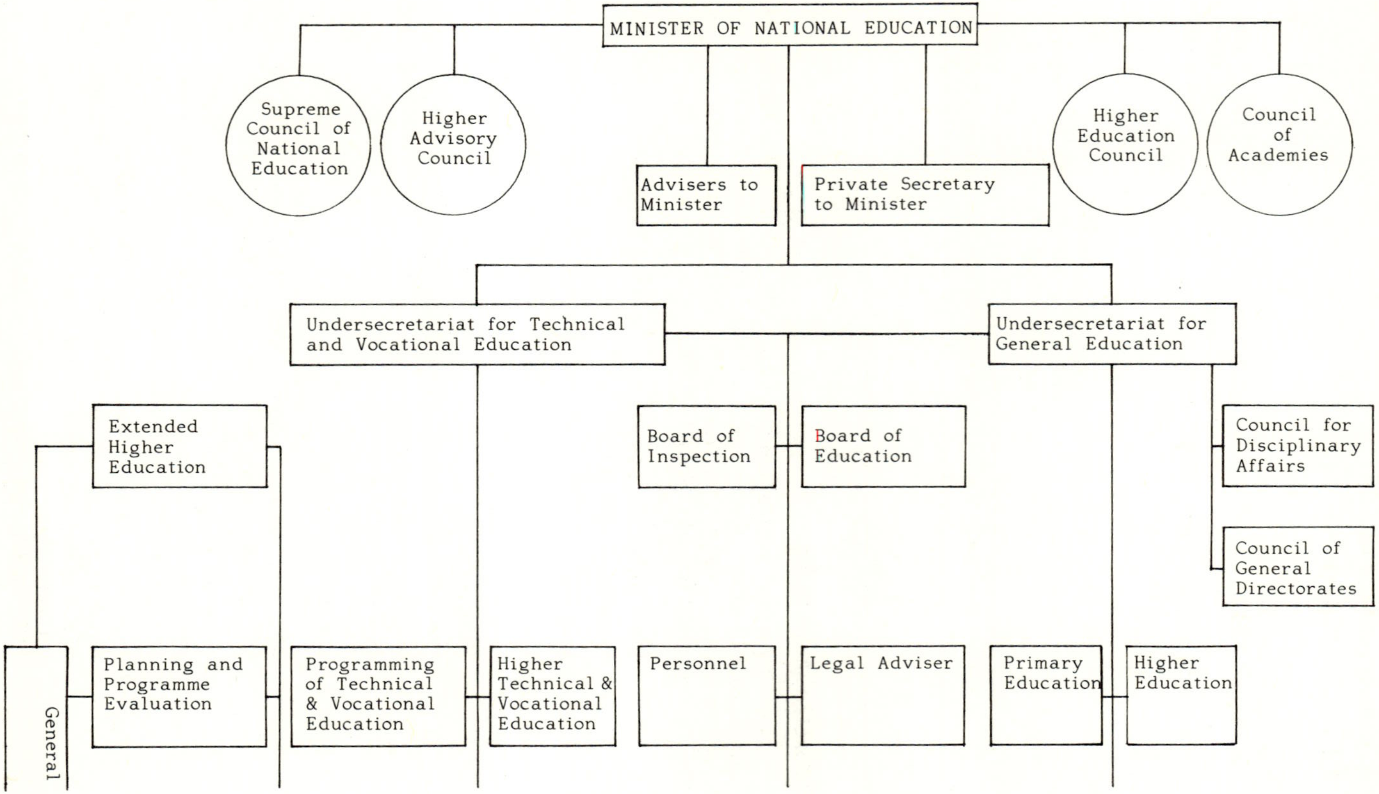

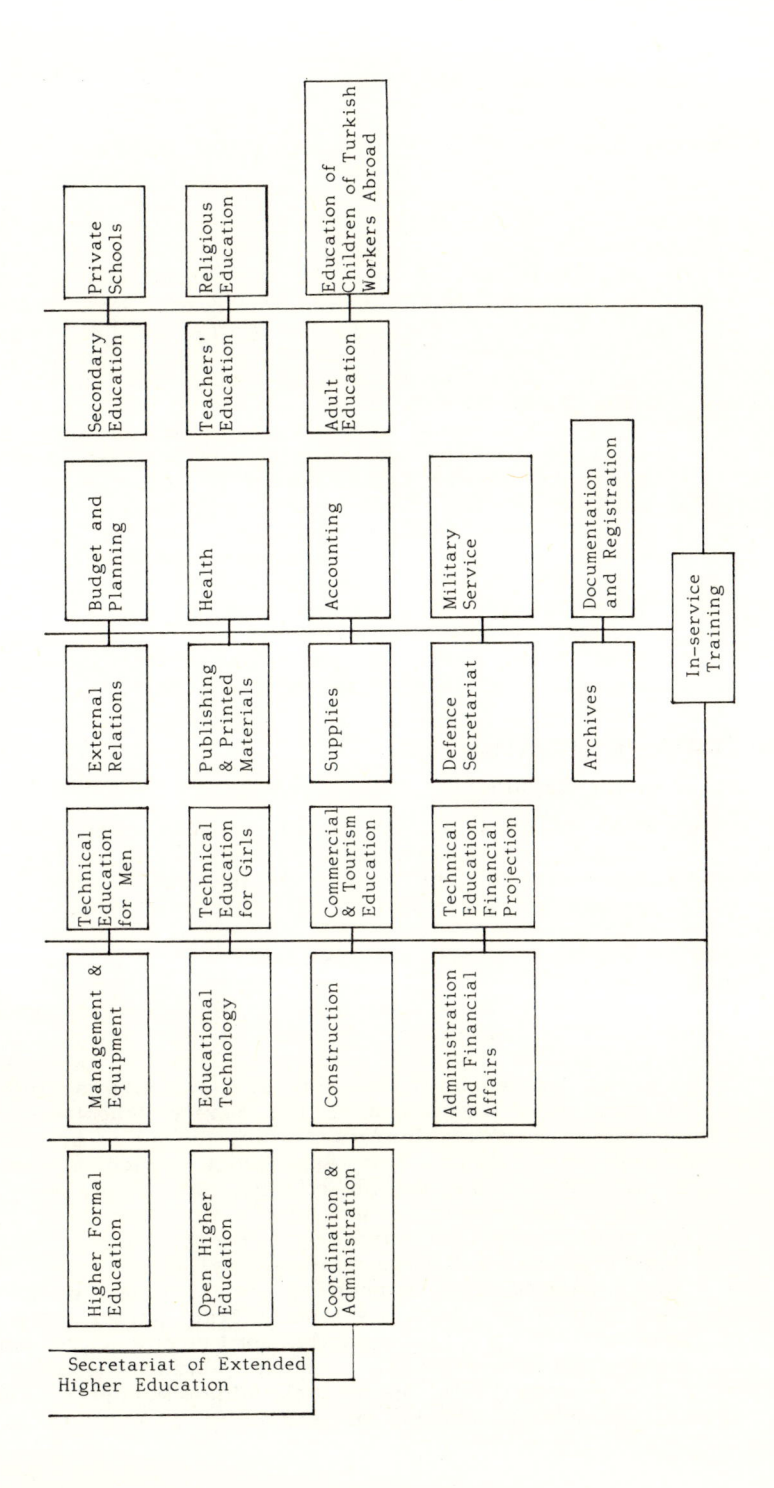

Higher Formal Education	Management & Equipment	Technical Education for Men	External Relations	Budget and Planning	Secondary Education	Private Schools
Open Higher Education	Educational Technology	Technical Education for Girls	Publishing & Printed Materials	Health	Teachers' Education	Religious Education
Coordination & Administration	Construction	Commercial & Tourism Education	Supplies	Accounting	Adult Education	Education of Children of Turkish Workers Abroad
	Administration and Financial Affairs	Technical Education Financial Projection	Defence Secretariat	Military Service		
			Archives	Documentation and Registration		
				In-service Training		

Secretariat of Extended Higher Education

(iv) Britain's bilateral education aid in the same year amounted to some US$450,000.

9 DEVELOPMENT AND PLANNING OF THE EDUCATION SYSTEM
Origins

Early attempts at westernisation, by nineteenth century sultans and politicians, were always piecemeal affairs, never challenging the framework of the Islamic State. Like everything else, education was finally taken out of the hands of the religious authorities, and the influence of the old system is in that respect negligible. The new system, based on the French, has in fact historical roots in the nineteenth and even late eighteenth centuries, starting with the institution of French style military colleges. Slowly the reforming parties established schools and colleges in the belief that by westernising its leading soldiers and administrators the Empire could regain its superiority over the Christian states. On the other hand, there was no attempt to bring into existence, through education, classes equipped with either the skill in agricultural techniques which had become general even in remote areas of Western Europe, or with the technical knowledge to provide a workforce for industrial expansion. Thus, the Empire acquired an often highly sophisticated elite, without the substructure of basically skilled masses to allow material or social advance on the Western model.

10 THE SYSTEM IN OPERATION
Developments in the Republic

The educational policies of the early republic were rather different, but Turkey has nevertheless tended to shy away from establishing programmes of instruction in the skills which are in practice required by the majority of her people, that is the peasant and urban working classes. On the other hand, institutions following academic programmes familiar to Western European eyes, have expanded rapidly. The most famous example of this is the history of the village institutes, a *cause célèbre* among Turkish educationists. These were founded in the early 1940s, with the explicit aim of training village children in the skills and crafts required in peasant life, and with the express intention that the graduates would become not merely schoolteachers in villages, but community leaders, able to give practical guidance on any local issue. This experiment, which attracted international attention, was killed off by the fundamentally conservative İnönü government after World War Two, and the institutes converted into primary teacher training colleges following a much less practical and more academic syllabus.

Atatürk was particularly concerned to remove religious influences from education, but his successors, partly from a spirit of greater tolerance and partly for electoral reasons, have gone back from his rigorous position. During the rule of the Democrat Party under Celal Bayar and Adnan Menderes (1950-1960), special secondary schools for intending men of religion were opened (*imam-hatip okullari*), and these have continued, providing an alternative scheme of education to higher level, where students can 'graduate' from the Higher Institute of Islam, qualified to teach religion and become *imams* (priests). The Institute does not have university status, though there is a Faculty of Theology in Ankara University. Various private schools, started by Christian missionary bodies, survived the advent of the republic, but have no actual religious influence on the Turkish scene. Perhaps the best example is that of Robert College, founded in the last century by American missionaries, and until 1960 the only English medium institution of higher education in Turkey. Over the years it produced a remarkable array of public figures, including the previous Prime Minister and opposition leader, Bülent Ecevit. The nationalisation of the university level section of this college a few years ago probably indicates the ultimate fate of all foreign educational institutions, whether of religious origin or not. Robert College is now at Boğaziçi University.

Planning Institutions

The Ministry of Education contains a small Planning, Research and Coordination Department. However, it has neither the resources nor the authority of the State Planning Organisation *(Devlet Planama Teşkilati)* responsible to the Prime Minister's Office, which produces Five Year Plans for the overall development of the country, and vets proposals for development investment against the objectives of these Plans. The organisation has a great deal to do with foreign agencies, as all technical assistance proposals, whether whole programmes or individual requests for training awards from State organisations, must be approved by it. This should ensure that foreign input of Turkish education accords with Plan objectives. However, the SPO cannot, of course, ensure that the Ministry of Education can keep up the rate of investment needed from local sources.

REFERENCES AND FURTHER READING

Kazamias, Andreas M. (1966). *Education and the Quest for Modernity in Turkey.* Allen & Unwin, London.
OECD (1977). *Decision-making in Educational Systems: the experience in Three OECD Countries.* OECD, Paris.
OECD (1972). *Classification of Educational Systems in OECD Member countries: Netherlands, Sweden, Turkey.* OECD, Paris.
OECD. *Mediterranean Regional Project Country Reports: Turkey.* OECD, Paris.
Stone, Frank A. (1973). *The Rub of Cultures in Modern Turkey: Literary View of Education.* Indiana University, Bloomington.

Structure of the Education System in Turkey

Age	3 4 5 6 7 8 9 10 11 12 13 14 15 16 17 18 19 20 21 22 23 24
Level	I　　　　　　II　　　　III
Stage	1　　　2　　3
Compulsory	
School type	Primary　Middle　Lycée (a) general (b) vocational (c) technical ／ Higher teacher training institute ／ Academies and higher learning institutions ／ Universities

Basic

▨ Education preceding the first level

▨ (shaded) Examinations: (a) primary school diploma at end of stage 1
    (b) middle school diploma at end of stage 2
    (c) Inter-Universities Selection Examination for university entrance

Source: UNESCO/IBE International Yearbook of Education

Compulsory Education: Age Limits 7-12   Duration (years) 5
Entrance age to pre-school education: 3

TURKEY BASIC STATISTICS	1960	1970	1974	1978 (approx.)
1 Total population (000)	27,509	35,231	38,901	43,210
% female	49	49	50	50
2 % population 0-14 years	41.4	41.7		41.0
% female	47	49	49	49
3 Enrolment, all levels	3,413,426	6,490,498		
% female	35	39		
First level	2,866,501	5,011,926	5,377,708	
% female	37	42	44	
Second level	481,628	1,308,779		
% female	26	29		
Third level	65,297	169,793	218,934	
% female	20	19	21	
4 Teachers, all levels	91,560	189,258		
% female	26	34		
First level	62,526	132,577	160,271	
% female	22	34	38	
Second level	24,963	47,452		
% female	34	37		
Third level	4,071	9,229	13,778	
% female	19	23	24	
5 Public expenditure on education				
Total (000) Liras	1,211,600	4,269,835		
As % of GNP	2.6	2.9		
6 % enrolment (MF) by level	100	100	100	
First level	84	77		
Second level	14	20		
Third level	2	3		
% enrolment (F) by level	100	100	100	
First level	89	84		
Second level	10	15		
Third level	1	1		
7 Entrance age: Duration of				
First level education	6:5	7:5	6:5	
Second level education	11:6	12:6	11:6	
8 Enrolment ratios (MF)				
First level	75	109	104	105
Second level	14	28		41
Third level	2.86	6.09	6.59	8.0
Enrolment ratios (F)				
First level	58	94	94	95
Second level	8	16		26
Third level	1.16	2.42	2.87	4.04

Yugoslavia

CONTENTS

1	Geography	698
2	Population	698
3	Society and Culture	700
4	History and Politics	701
5	The Economy	705
6	The Education System	708
7	Educational Administration	719
8	Educational Finance	723
9	Development and Planning of the Education System	724
10	The System in Operation	725

Yugoslavia's educational system is particularly interesting because of the diversity found within the country and the extent to which, since the end of World War Two, socialist solutions have been offered to the problems that differences of language, religion and ethnicity create. The six republics that constitute Yugoslavia are indeed countries with distinct characteristics. Most of the people are of Slavic origin but there are also many Italians, Austrians, Turks, Hungarians, Albanians, Czechs, Romanians and Bulgarians. To this diversity is added that associated with religion and language. Nearly half the population is Orthodox Christian, and a high proportion of the rest are Roman Catholics. More than 10% of the population is Muslim and there is a tiny number of Jews. The major religious groups are, however, concentrated in one or other of the six republics. Similarly members of the major language groups live together in different republics. The three main spoken languages are Serbo-Croat, Slovene and Macedonian. The Latin and Cyrillic scripts are used in Croatia and Serbia respectively.

The terrain of the country, moreover, tends to isolate certain groups of people. Most of the country is mountainous and Montenegro in particular is barren and difficult for travel. The roads along the Adriatic are steep and winding and the coast is indented and strung with islands. There are, however, fertile plains in the northern central regions near the Hungarian border. Bordered as it is by Italy, Austria, Hungary, Romania, Bulgaria, Greece and Albania, and subject as it has been to many invasions, Yugoslavia was and is a land of many cultures. Unification came only after the First World War when the country received its present name but before and during the Second World War relationships between the nationalities and religious groups were uneasy or violent. The role of Josep Broz Tito and his Partisans was important in the creation in 1963 of the Socialist Federal Republic of Yugoslavia.

Since then educational policy, influenced by Soviet practices in the first instance, has had to take account of diversity, the distribution of the population and the relative isolation of some groups. A feature of the system has been the decentralisation of decision making so that republics, provinces and communes have a major say in decision making. Parents and workers are encouraged to participate in the development of education within guidelines established by the Inter-Republican Provincial Commission on Educational Reform.

On major issues of policy it is for the individual republic to determine how far a common language should be taught within its boundaries. While no religious instruction is permitted in schools, freedom of worship is guaranteed and schools for the training of priests are permitted. Socialist policies inform other aspects of development. For example: the expansion of pre-school institutions has received increasing attention; the creation of a compulsory eight year school for everyone has received high priority; equality of access to all levels of education regardless of race, nationality, sex and social background has been a principal objective; co-education has been promoted; permanent education has been advocated; the self-management of educational institutions has received great attention; the need to meet diversity while promoting unity has been regarded as a major issue; and attempts to strengthen the ties between work and education have been central to policy throughout the post-war period. These general lines of policy have found expression in the details of development at all levels and stages of education. They represent within the Yugoslav context an adaptation of Marxist educational policies.

The Editor

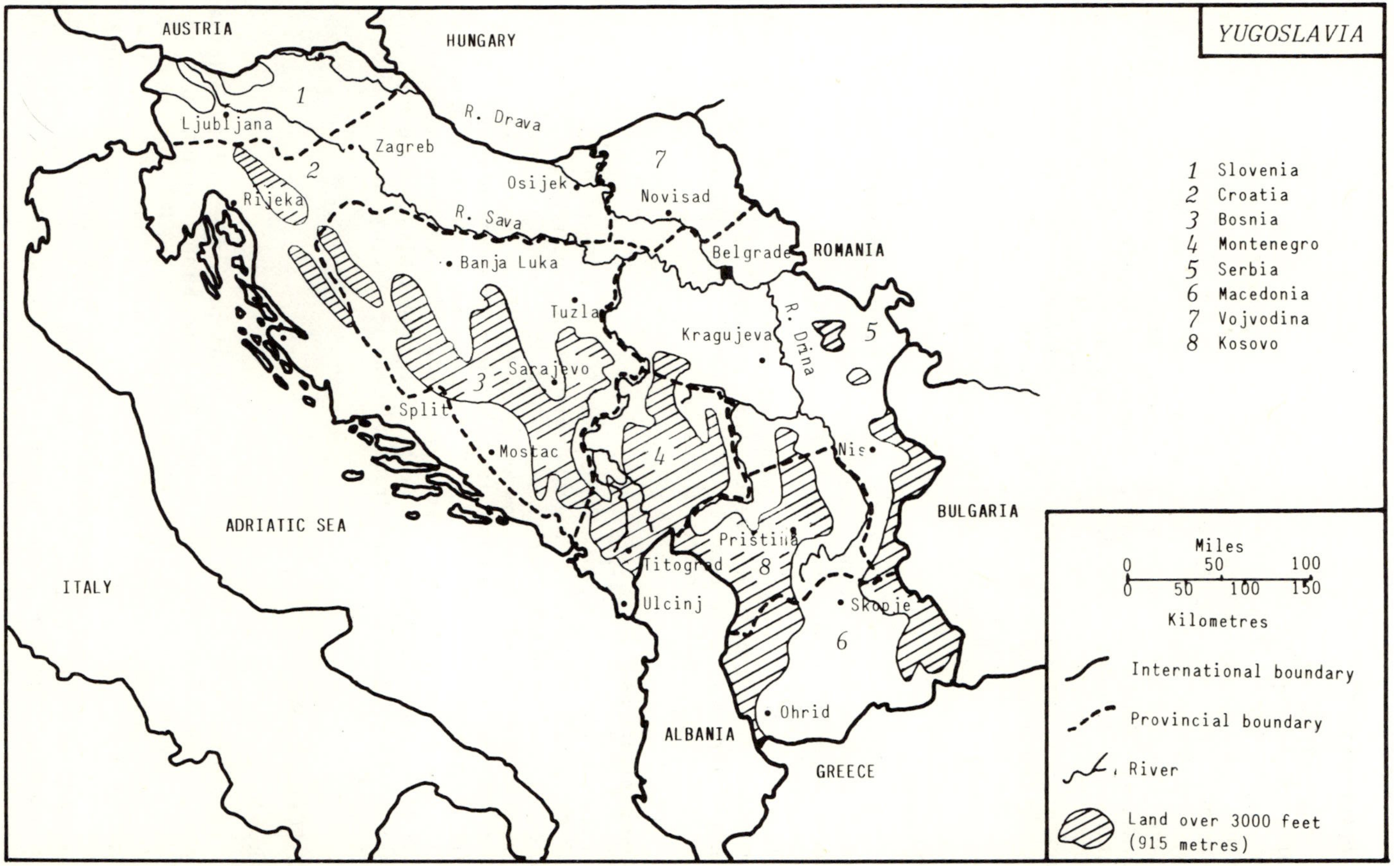

YUGOSLAVIA

1 Slovenia
2 Croatia
3 Bosnia
4 Montenegro
5 Serbia
6 Macedonia
7 Vojvodina
8 Kosovo

Miles
0 50 100
0 50 100 150
Kilometres

— International boundary
--- Provincial boundary
⌇ River
▧ Land over 3000 feet (915 metres)

1 GEOGRAPHY

Topography

Yugoslavia is the largest country in the Balkans with an area of nearly 256,000 sq km (98,841 square miles). Its coastline of 2,000 km (1,250 miles) running approximately north west to south east from Istria to Ulcinj, extends along most of the eastern side of the Adriatic and is much indented and strung with islands, eight of them being over 100 sq km in area. By land Yugoslavia borders on seven other countries - Italy, Austria, Hungary, Romania, Bulgaria, Greece and Albania - and it includes considerable topographical variety, ranging from the fertile plains near the Hungarian border to the barren terrain of Montenegro. Most of the country is mountainous, some of it densely forested, but the northern central part, bordered by the Danube, Sava, Drava and Tisa, is in effect a southern extension of the Hungarian Plain.

Climate

The Adriatic coastal strip has a Mediterranean climate with mild winters and warm summers; most of the mountain ranges have an alpine climate with long cold winters and shorter cooler summers, while the rest of the country has a central European climate with cold winters and hot summers. There is steady rainfall throughout the year. The average mean daily summer temperature in Belgrade is 71°F (22°C) and the winter mean is 32°F (0°C), but variations can be very great.

Communications

Yugoslavia has about 9,762 km (6,101 miles) of railway of which 2,911 km (1,819 miles) have been electrified. There are regular rail and air services linking the principal towns. Great improvements have been made in the major roads which join the main cities and further large scale works are planned. There are currently 112,200 km (70,125 miles) of road in Yugoslavia; the two main arterial roads run from the western frontier to Salonica via Ljubljana, Zagreb, Belgrade, Nis and Skopje and along the Adriatic coast from Rijeka to Ulcinj and inland to Titograd.

2 POPULATION

Growth

According to the 1971 census, the total population of Yugoslavia was 20,523,000. Estimates based on demographic trends put the 1975 figures at 21,352,000 and forecast 22,352,000 for the end of the decade. Birth and death rates have both been falling since the 1950s. For the whole of Yugoslavia live births per 1,000 of population have dropped from about 27 in 1955 to 17.2 in 1978. Deaths have fallen from just over 10 per 1,000 to about 7 for the same period. It is expected that from 1970 to 2000 there will be an increase of 82% in people over the age of 65, with the exception of Kosovo where there will be a rise in the working population.

Distribution

	1971 census (000)	1975 estimate (000)	1980 projection (000)
Yugoslavia	20,523	21,322	22,299
Bosnia-Herzegovina	3,746	3,966	4,240
Macedonia	1,647	1,767	1,913
Slovenia	1,717	1,771	1,825
Croatia	4,426	4,496	4,584
Montenegro	530	556	593
Serbia (total)	8,447	8,765	9,144
- Restricted Territory	5,250	5,393	5,540
- Vojvodina	1,953	1,982	2,012
- Kosovo	1,244	1,390	1,592

Sources: Statisticki Kalendar Jugoslavije 1980, Belgrade 1980, p.33, adapted.
Projection of the Yugoslav Population for 1970-2000, Yugoslav Survey (1975)

In the two areas with the highest but falling birth rates (Macedonia and Kosovo) the death rates are still falling. the poulations of Bosnia-Herzegovina, Montenegro and macedonia will soon become ageing ones, while that of Kosovo is expected to be young at the end of this century. It was predicted that the total population of Yugoslavia would grow at an even slower rate post-1970 than before. The number of school age children (7-14 years) will slowly decrease overall but it is expected to rise slowly in Slovenia and Macedonia and fast in Kosovo. another characteristic of the Yugoslav population is large scale migration to towns away from agricultural activity. The ageing process in the agricultural poulation is greater than in the total population. There are also significant numbers of Yugoslavs working temporarily abroad.

Groups

Yugoslavia means literally 'the land of the South Slavs', a rather more accurate term than the original title of the composite state that emerged after World War I, the 'Kingdom of Serbs, Croats, and Slovenes'. The six republics that constitute Yugoslavia are indeed countries of more or less distinct Slav peoples. There are also many non-Slav nationalities, some in substantial numbers and others at least numerically significant in specific areas like Italians in Istria, Austrians in Slovenia and Turks in their own villages scattered over much of southern Yugoslavia. The most significant non-Slav groups are the Albanians, who make up most of the population of Kosovo and are also well represented in Macedonia, and the Hungarians who, with smaller numbers of Romanians, live in Vojvodina. Also represented, though in much smaller numbers, are Bulgarians, Czechs, Slovaks, Vlachs (a people akin to the Romanians), Germans, Poles, Russians, Ukrainians, Ruthenians (closely akin to the Ukrainians), Romany-gypsies and Jews. In the 1971 census, the numbers declaring themselves to belong to one of the South Slav nationalities were: Serbs 39.7%; Croats 22.1%; Muslims 8.4% (almost certainly Bosnians in the great majority of cases); Slovenes 8.2%; Macedonians 5.8%; and Montenegrins 2.5%. The principal non-Slav nationalities were: Albanian 6.4%; Hungarians 2.3%; and Turks 0.6%. A further 0.3% declined to declare any nationality at all, and 1.3% described themselves simply as Yugoslav.

2 SOCIETY AND CULTURE

Language

Three main languages are spoken in Yugoslavia: Serbo-Croat, Slovene and Macedonian. In language the Serbs and Croats are not identical but close; it is quite possible to speak of a single Serbo-Croatian language with certain dialectal differences. Croatian is always written in the Latin alphabet; Serbian is written usually in Cyrillic (both scripts are learnt in school and Serbs use both). Whether they should be regarded as distinct languages is a political rather than a linguistic matter; they are in any case mutually comprehensible without much difficulty. The same cannot be said for the other two main Slavonic languages of Yugoslavia, Slovene and Macedonian. The Slovenes share with the Croats much of their historical and religious background but their language, though related, is different enough to preclude easy understanding. The Macedonians are different again; historically they are akin to the Serbs but linguistically closer to the Bulgarians, who are given to describing Macedonian as a Bulgarian dialect. The remaining South Slav nationalities rest their identity on factors other than linguistic, for both the Bosnians and the Montenegrins speak Serbian. Widespread though the use of Serbo-Croat may be, there is no official language for the whole of Yugoslavia; all the languages, Slav or other, have equal status in law. It is for the individual republic to determine how far a common language should be taught within its own boundaries.

Religion

The religious picture in Yugoslavia is extremely complex, largely due to the various peoples having been subjects of different empires in the past, and having responded to them differently. Shortly after the last war the percentage of the population adhering to the various religions were as follows: Orthodox 49.53%; Roman Catholic 36.7%; Muslim 12.52%; other Christian (e.g. Protestant and Uniate) 1.14%; Jewish 0.04%. The distribution, however, was and is very uneven. Slovenia is almost entirely Catholic with a tiny Protestant minority; Croatia is predominantly Catholic but has significant numbers of Orthodox round much of the border with Bosnia. Vojvodina, now part of Serbia but formerly Hungarian, is mixed. Montenegro is overwhelmingly Orthodox though there are Muslims (mainly Albanians) on the borders with Albania and Serbia. Serbia, although long under Turkish rule, was not pressed into conversion (Ottoman policy being generally tolerant of religion) so that the vast majority of Serbs remained Orthodox; the substantial numbers of Muslims in Serbia are accounted for almost entirely by the Albanian population. Macedonia, likewise, is predominantly Orthodox but includes substantial Albanian and Turkish Muslim populations. Bosnia-Herzegovina was not under Austrian rule long enough for its religious composition to be much affected and the Catholic population there is mainly overspill from Croatia. However, Turkish rule was long-standing and large numbers in Bosnia were converted to Islam, particularly landowners; their descendants make up the large concentration of Serbian speaking Muslims who describe themselves in census returns as Muslims rather than Bosnians. The remainder of the population is Orthodox.

No religious instruction is permitted in schools, though the Yugoslav variant of Marxism is. The post-war constitution (Article 25) separated Church from State but guaranteed freedom of worship, allowed schools for the training of priests and permitted the State to give financial aid to any religious community. In the immediate post-war period relations were bad with all three communities, though accommodation was eventually reached with the Orthodox and then the Muslims. Relations with the Catholic Church remained bitter for much longer, mainly due to the role ascribed to the clergy during the war. By 1953 a new law had clarified the principles of the 1945 constitution, including clergy and their families in the State insurance system and making financial aid available to all the major religious communities. The churches have been shorn of any temporal power and political associations based on religious affiliation are still forbidden; otherwise the Churches seem to be active and well supported without much interference from the secular authorities, although during compulsory national service it is not possible to practise one's religion.

4 HISTORY AND POLITICS

Early Separation

Yugoslavia is a relatively young country with ancient roots. The South Slavs were never politically united until modern times, an early division between the Latin and Greek Churches ensuring that they went their separate ways throughout most of their history, whether as independent states or, more commonly, under the rule of one of the major powers. From the fourteenth to nineteenth centuries Serbia was subject to the Ottoman Empire though Montenegro was never totally subdued. In the north, Slovenia remained part of Austria while most of Croatia became, with Hungary, a dependency of the Habsburg Empire in the seventeenth century. Neither Croatia nor Slovenia was content with its role and relationships with Austria and Hungary fluctuated considerably, but the central fact of Habsburg domination left a tendency to identify with central Europe rather than the Balkans, which remains to some extent even today.

Unification

During the nineteenth century Habsburg power continued to grow while the Ottoman Empire declined. Serbia attained effective autonomy as early as 1817, and was fully independent (and larger) by 1878. By the end of the Second Balkan War of 1913 Serbia had defeated Bulgaria, absorbed Macedonia, and achieved a common frontier with Montenegro. Bosnia, on the other hand, had been annexed in 1878 by Austria, worried by the closing of further avenues to expansion in the Balkans and by the effect of Serbian victories on the Slav populations of the Habsburg dominions. The assassination of the heir to the Habsburg throne at Sarajevo in 1914 was seized as a pretext for war, with consequences to Europe and the world that are well known. Serbia was over-run but preserved most of its army, and when the Central Powers collapsed in 1918 Serbia re-emerged as the most powerful component of the new state established by the Treaty of Versailles. The Kingdom of Serbs, Croats and Slovenes, with a Serbian king, was renamed Yugoslavia in 1929.

After 1929

However, relations between the nationalities, particularly between Serbs and Croats, remained uneasy and often broke into violence. The Royal dictatorship of 1929 was, in part, an attempt to check social unrest. It did not work; King Alexander was assassinated by Croat nationalists and the problems remained unresolved. Attempts to reach an accommodation with Nazi Germany were no more successful; subservience to Hitler by the Yugoslav authorities led to a coup d'état in 1941 and the formation of a broad based government determined to resist Nazi demands. This was followed in short order by invasion and rapid conquest by the Axis powers, though their control was never complete. As a result Yugoslavia was dismembered. Large tracts of territory were taken by Germany, Italy, Italian-occupied Albania, Hungary, Romania and Bulgaria, and a puppet Croatian state (excluding Dalmatia but including Bosnia) was set up. A savage civil war followed in which the protagonists were a variety of fascist and royalist groups, as well as the mainly communist Partisans.

The Partisans

The Partisans, under Josep Broz Tito, had the advantage of being the only Yugoslav resistance force, and pursued a policy of concentrating on national liberation rather than (at this stage) social revolution. They gained considerable support from the civilian population who often paid dearly for it; the fate of Kragujevac, where every male over 15 was shot, was an extreme but not unique example of the occupying power's policy of systematic reprisal for guerilla activities. As the only effective anti-Nazi force the Partisans also received support (eventually) from the Western Allies, although Soviet support was lukewarm. By the end of the war the Partisans had liberated almost the entire country by their own efforts (though Soviet help was given to take Belgrade). The Yugoslav Communist Party, with a substantial degree of popular support, thus found itself in complete control. There had been great destruction and loss of life, over 10% of the Yugoslav population having been killed. Although in one sense the Liberation War had done much to unify the country, much suspicion and bitterness was bound to linger below the surface. The establishment of a federal rather than a unitary state was an attempt to mitigate some of these tensions. In spite of some internal crises, the régime has managed to remain stable and to liberalise itself considerably since World War Two, greatly helped by its origins in the Liberation War and by the dominant personality of President Tito.

Federal Organisation

The Socialist Federal Republic of Yugoslavia (SFRY), so named by the 1963 constitution, consists of the six Socialist Republics and the two Socialist Autonomous Provinces within Serbia. Serbia (capital Belgrade) is the largest republic with an area of 88,000 sq km (33,976 square miles), followed by Croatia (capital Zagreb) with 57,000 sq km (22,007 square miles), and Bosnia-Herzegovina (capital Sarajevo) with 51,000 sq km (19,691 square miles); the others are substantially smaller, Macedonia (capital Skopje) has 26,000 sq km (10,038 square miles), Slovenia (capital Ljubljana) has 20,000 sq km (7,722 square miles), Montenegro (capital Titograd) 14,000 sq km (5,405 square miles). The two autonomous provinces in Serbia are Vojvodina (capital Novi Sad) with 22,000 sq km (8,494 square miles), and Kosovo (capital Pristina) with 11,000 sq km (4,247 square miles). The rest of Serbia is often referred to as the Restricted Territory.

Government in Yugoslavia, substantially centralised until 1948, is now highly complex, reflecting the complexity of the country itself and the policy, developed since the 1950s, of decentralising authority in economic and social affairs. In Belgrade there is the SFRY Assembly which consists of a Federal Chamber with 220 members and a Chamber of Republics and Provinces with 88 members. Its concern is now largely with military and external affairs and only broadly with internal matters, these being substantially decentralised to the SRs and further down to local level. The republics and autonomous provinces have their own assemblies, consisting of Chambers of Associations of Labour, Chambers of Communes and Socio-Political Chambers, the first of these being consistently the largest. The unit of local government is the Commune, of which there are 515 with their own assemblies and at the 'grass roots' there are the local communities or districts with their own elected councils. The self-management pattern is repeated, essentially, in industry and in institutions of all kinds (including schools) with the delegation of considerable responsibility to the workers' councils. In practice there is far more participation at local level than is normal in communist countries. There may be both advantages and disadvantages to this system but any other solution would seem to be incompatible with the continued unity of the country.

Political Power

Even though governmental machinery and even economic management are decentralised, political power is not. Since World War Two this has remained firmly in the hands of the League of Communists of Yugoslavia (SKJ). The League has about 1,885,000 members and is backed by a cluster of non-party but supportive organisations such as the Socialist Alliance of the Working People of Yugoslavia (14,850,000 members) and the Confederation of Trade Unions of Yugoslavia (3,710,000).

International Relations

Yugoslavia has constantly been the exception to the rule among the communist countries of Europe. It was the only one where the régime came to power almost entirely as a result of home-made revolution. Having had little help from Stalin during the war it managed to defy his attempts to impose policies to his own liking; and, having been expelled from the Cominform in 1948, managed to survive the 'cold war' period without being drawn into the western orbit either. Yugoslavia had perforce to establish links with the West, political as well as economic, and has maintained these; it has also re-established links with the East, but on independent terms and has steered clear to involvement with either NATO or the Warsaw Pact. Since the 1950s Yugoslavia has pursued a policy of non alignment and played host to the first Conference of Non-Aligned Nations in Belgrade in 1961. This policy has been maintained to the present, though relations with neighbours have often been uneasy (as witness the reluctant acceptance of Soviet intervention in Hungary in 1956 and condemnation of it in Czechoslovakia in 1968); but there now appears to be an assurance of non-intervention from the USSR following Brezhnev's visit to Belgrade in 1976, although events in Afghanistan have caused grave anxiety and Yugoslavs may still be worried from time to time.

5 THE ECONOMY

Economic Development

The economic development of Yugoslavia over the past two decades has been impressive, characterised by rapid economic growth and structural transformation. Gross Domestic Product between 1954-75 grew at an average annual rate of about 7% in real terms, but fell to 6% by 1979. Per capita GNP in 1978 is estimated to be US$2,390 at 1978 market prices. The social sector, in particular industry, has been the driving force of the economy. The share of industry in GDP has increased to about 49% while agriculture has declined to about 14%, paving the way for the development of a modern industry/service oriented urban society. Yugoslavia's high growth rate has, however, led to a large visible trade deficit, only partly offset by invisible earning from tourism and workers' remittances. Yugoslavia is now entering a period of consolidation when growth rates will be held down to more manageable levels and when it is hoped investment and inflation will also be controlled.

Figures from Britain's trade with Yugoslavia are:

	1976	1977	1978	1979
Imports from Britain	£128m	£175m	£160m	£174m
Exports to Britain	£34m	£40m	£38m	£51m

Mineral Production and Energy

Yugoslavia has important mineral resources including oil, natural gas, coal (mostly lignite and brown coal), iron ore, non-ferrous metal ores (including lead, zinc, chrome, nickel, copper, bauxite and manganese), building stone and a large hydroelectric power potential. It also has domestic resources of gold, silver, platignum and other rare metals. With the exception of the USSR, Yugoslavia is Europe's principal producer of copper and a major supplier of lead, zinc and bauxite.

Industry

Yugoslavia produces a wide range of industrial goods, including ships, locomotives, lorries, cars, machinery, electronic equipment, textiles, chemicals, petrochemicals, plastics, fertilisers and a wide range of consumer goods. Other rapidly expanding industries include food-processing, construction and telecommunications. Industrial production rose by 8.9% in 1978 (one of the highest growth rates in the world), but was accompanied as in 1977 by unrestrained investment of around 11%. This pace of industrial activity, while helping to alleviate the high unemployment rate, has also created a balance of payments problem and has highlighted weaknesses in the productive infrastructure. The rapid growth rate has relied on technology imported from the West and very often on imported raw materials, both creating long term difficulties. Heavy investments are being made in energy and basic raw materials and affording those industries higher tariff protection, in order to reduce dependence on imports and boost exports. As part of the government's overall policy of restricting economic growth during the next planning period, industrial production for 1980 was expected to expand by around 7%, with particular emphasis to be placed on engineering, ferrous metallurgy, electrical machinery, chemicals and rubber products.

Agriculture

The rapid growth of industry over the past 30 years has reduced the proportion of the working population employed in agriculture from around 80% to 30% in 1978. Despite this decline, agriculture has one of the highest priorities within the country's long term development plans with an emphasis on linking the sector with industrial production. More than 80% of the agriculture is in private hands and a significant proportion is conducted on a part time basis by men and women. The major food crops are wheat, maize, sugar beet, rye and potatoes, with grapes, plums, apples, soya and sunflower seeds also of importance. The major industrial crops are hemp, flax, cotton, tobacco, hops and opium poppies. Livestock production is important and beef and pork are among the principal exports. There are also large resources of timber, with around 35% of the land area under forest. The largest forests are in Bosnia, in the centre of the country, with smaller forests in Slovenia, in the north. A large investment programme is under way to exploit substantial timber reserves and increase exports. There is also a sizeable fishing industry. The salt water catch consists mostly of sardines, sprats, anchovies and mackerel and the fresh water catch mainly of carp.

Employment

Estimates for 1979 put the number of employed persons at 5,612,000 compared with 4,513,000 in 1974, the great majority being in the 'social' as opposed to the private sector (5,503,000 in 1979, 4,422,000 in 1974). Of the 1979 figure, 4,555,000 were involved in 'economic activities' (e.g. manufacture, State agriculture, forestry, construction, transport and communications, trade and catering, arts and crafts, public utilities, the increasingly important tourist industry being subsumed under appropriate heads); by contrast, 948,000 were employed in education, culture and social welfare, social and State agencies. Trends in the employment of women are of particular interest: in 1970, 1,207,000 were employed (1,169,000 in the social sector, 38,000 in the private); by 1979 there were 1,982,000 (1,940,000 social and 42,000 private). Most women in urban centres are employed (46% of the workforce in Zagreb). The employment of women is concentrated in the 'non-economic' sector (education, culture, health and social welfare). In 1979, 3,168,000 men were employed in the economic sector and 395,000 in non-economic activities, whilst for the women the figures are 1,387,000 and 553,000 respectively, giving a ratio of 8:1 for men and 2.5:1 for women respectively in economic:non-economic activities.

The Structure of Employment
(000s)

	1970	1975	1976	1977	1978	1979
Total population	20,371	21,365	21,573	21,775	21,968	22,107
Employment						
Socialised sector	3,765	4,667	4,833	5,065	5,280	5,503
of which: female	1,169	1,586	1,663	1,751	1,840	1,940
economic activities[1]	3,059	3,869	3,999	4,182	4,363	4,555
of which: industry[2]	1,418	1,802	1,872	1,961	2,022	2,100
non-economic activities[3]	706	798	834	870	916	948
Private sector employed abroad[4]	783	940	870	825	815	800

Key:

[1] All activities except non-economic activities

[2] Excluding construction

[3] Social welfare and cultural activities (including health and scientific activities) social organisations, economic chambers, banks, finance and insurance, social security, government, education

[4] The peak was reached in 1973 when 1,100,000 Yugoslavs were working abroad

Sources: Statistical Kalendar Jugoslavije, 1980 and OECD Economic Survey, May 1980.

The extent of unemployment in Yugoslavia is difficult to determine, but on the basis of those people registered as seeking jobs, there were 762,000 unemployed at the end of 1979 representing about 14% of those in paid domestic employment. The problem of unemployment is compounded by pronounced regional disparities, a high number of school leavers and the return of Yugoslav workers from abroad, particularly West Germany, where economies have been hit by recession. Per capita GNP in Slovenia, Croatia and Vojvodina is far higher than that in Montenegro, Macedonia and Kosovo and the Yugoslav authorities face considerable political and economic problems in switching resources from rich to poor regions. Since the Second World War the massive shift of population from rural to urban areas has created problems of housing shortages and inadequate structural facilities and, although the proportion of the population remaining in rural areas has been reduced to about one third of the total, pressures from those wanting to move to the towns are still strong.

6 THE EDUCATION SYSTEM
Academic Year

The school year normally begins on 1 September. It is divided into two semesters, normally September to mid-January and early February to 10 June (secondary schools), 20 June (elementary schools) and 20 May for the highest grades of elementary and secondary schools. Examinations are held in June and may be retaken in September. Higher education classes start in October preceded by entrance examinations. All schools are required to have between 180 and 210 working days in the year. Most schools operate a shift system so that one school building can handle a double quantity of pupils. Education takes place in the language of each nation (i.e. Croatian or Serbian, Slovene and Macedonian). Education in the language of minority nationalities is organised in pre-school, elementary and secondary education and, if there is a sufficient number of students - in higher education as well. Textbooks have to be purchased by parents.

Reforms in Progress

The reform of the system of secondary education was announced in 1974 and at the time of writing there is still incomplete introduction of the new structure and curricula in the different republics. Statistical data showing progress of the reform are still incomplete. The development and reform of the higher education system started earlier, from a Joint Commission in 1957 initiating reforms from 1958-1967, the current reforms in education stem from resolutions taken at the Third Conference of the League of Communists of Yugoslavia in December 1972. Comparison of the 'old' and reformed systems may be made by following the basic direction of the reform, which was agreed by an Inter-Republican Commission (comprising representatives of the republics and autonomous provinces) but there are disparities in the number of teaching hours, timing and implementation of new courses, emphasis on curriculum content etc. between the republics, according to their differing needs as seen by the Republican Committees for Education.

The most important part of the current reform is the realisation of a first phase 'common core' curriculum for the first two years of post-elementary education (starting at age 15). While implementation of the reforms has moved rapidly in Vojvodina and Croatia, statistics published in 1980 show that Bosnia-Herzegovina, Macedonia and Slovenia have not yet started to implement either phase of the reform. In some regions (Serbia,

Kosovo and Vojvodina) it is reported that some changes have also been introduced in elementary education. At all levels of education the reforms are directed primarily to intensifying work related and polytechnical education and to the establishment of close links between education and work. The aim is also to increase attendance, particularly of children in areas of low development and of low income families, and to increase the successful completion of each level.

Pre-School

Although not compulsory, this is becoming an increasingly important component of the educational system. It is carried out in half-day nursery schools for six half-days a week (with the exception of Slovenia), in all-day nursery schools as well as pre-school classes and groups attached to elementary schools or other institutions. In Slovenia, children not attending kindergarten are required to attend a 'small school' for a year before entering elementary education. Formal lessons are not given, but children are divided by age levels (3-4, 4-5, 5-7) in groups of between ten and 25, and involved in activities designed to promote physical fitness and development, hygiene, a basic understanding of the physical and social environment, development of spoken language and fundamental understanding of numbers; extensive use is made of games, music, singing and visual art. The programmes are similar throughout the country and aim to improve attendance, especially of children from low income families, to provide opportunity for development and education from the earliest stage. It is the intention, wherever possible, to link pre-school institutions to elementary schools, to strengthen both their social and educational functions and to intensify parental cooperation with pre-school and elementary institutions.

First Level and Lower Second Level Schools

This level of education is compulsory. In some republics, children may be admitted at 6 (although 7 is the norm) and it is also possible under exceptional circumstances to continue until 17 (although 14/15 is the norm). This level of education is organised in two stages which are generally quite distinct and may be called 'primary' (teaching by one general class teacher) for the first four years, and 'secondary' (i.e. teaching by subject specialists) in the second four years. The balance of curricula may vary a little from one republic to another but the samples given will serve to give an impression of subject balance for compulsory courses. Time is also to be provided for optional courses (up to one hour per week), supplementary courses (two hours per week) and free activities covering sport, art (one hour per week in the first four years, two hours per week in the second four years).

Unreformed Secondary

Pupils continuing after compulsory elementary education from 14/15 to 18/19 years had a number of alternatives in type of school available. Under the reform this range is being reduced but as distinctions still exist in a number of areas they are briefly described below.

Secondary Schools ('Gymnasia' or Grammar Schools)

These are to be phased out under the reform. Attendance ends with the examination required for entry to higher education or for employment.

(i) General Secondary – four years' general education, with an option at the end of the first year to specialise in social studies and languages or natural sciences and mathematics

(ii) Classical Gymnasia – emphasis on social studies and language from the beginning of the four years

(iii) Teacher Training Gymnasia – four years as above emphasising training of prospective teachers.

Art Schools

These are comparable in status and level to the gymnasia, with four-year courses in music, ballet, theatre and the industrial arts with the option of proceeding to higher education.

Technical and Vocational Training Schools

Admission may be by competitive examination, depending on the number of places available. The courses are of four years and provide technician training for specific occupations (industry, mining, forestry, architecture) and general education is also included. Skilled workers may also complete special two-year programmes in these schools. Students may continue into higher education at two- or four-year schools of higher learning.

Trade Training or Skilled Workers' Schools

The courses are usually of three years and practical training in school workshops or outside enterprises is included. For some trades, these schools will accept pupils who did not complete primary schooling.

Other

This category includes schools which are not of secondary level but are being incorporated into the secondary system in some republics and provinces.

(i) General Technical Schools – two-year courses providing specific training for particular trades but including general education. Graduates either go into work or continue into another phase of technical school

(ii) Trade Schools, Professional Training Schools, General (Joint) Secondary – two-year courses

(iii) In some areas there are schools for highly skilled workers (two-year course after skilled workers' school) or the same preparation is effected at two-year college level schools for worker education.

Reformed Secondary or Directed

Under the reform, secondary education, covering ages 14/15 to 18/19, is divided into two phases, a first 'common base' or 'core' (also called general or common secondary) of two years, and a second phase also of two years. Pupils will be able to follow the first phase only or both phases either in different institutions enrolling in any stream of the second phase irrespective of optional or special courses taken in the first phase, or both phases in continuity in the same institution.

First Phase

This provides a two-year common general and polytechnical education combined with general preparation for work. It allows for pupils to decide on an orientation for their future occupation. The compulsory part of the curriculum over the two years will contain: mother tongue and literature (plus majority language in the given republic), a foreign language, arts, Marxism and self-management, geography, mathematics, physics, chemistry, biology, physical and medical education, defence and protection, and initiation in production and technology, general practical work. Optional subjects may be taken for interest, but also to give opportunity for professional and educational orientation.

Second Phase

Admission to this phase is by open competition. This will be normally of two-year duration but may be less (minimum of six months) and has a dual role. The first is to qualify workers of fourth grade for employment (i.e. at the end of secondary education, successful completion of examinations) in a specific subject (e.g. civil engineering, shipbuilding, mining, geology, agriculture and food technology, forestry, economics, etc.). The second is to prepare candidates for continuing into higher education. This phase will be provided in 'educational centres' which were formed by the amalgamation of specific trade schools to provide training in one or more vocations. It is envisaged that independent secondary level schools for specific occupations may also be opened. Most syllabi for the second phase do not envisage the continued existence of grammar schools in their present form. These are expected to be transformed to allow for preparation for work as well as for further education. Three groups of compulsory subjects are envisaged within a total of 30 teaching hours a week:

(i) subjects for all pupils – mother tongue and literature, Marxism and socialist self-management, physical and medical education

(ii) general vocational subjects – generally a foreign language plus general culture and technology with emphasis on a particular profession

(iii) professional and practical courses – oriented to training for an occupation or completion of the fourth grade examination. Practical or productive work is compulsory for 10-15 days a year.

In addition, facilities will be provided for optional courses. The second phase is completed by examination, practical successes leading to professional qualifications and theoretical leading to further/higher education: there is considerable regional diversity in proportions of fourth graders entering employment – the intention of the reform is to involve the bulk of this level in employment. This phase can also be provided within a higher education centre as a preparatory course for study (e.g. teachers).

Third Level (Higher) Educational Institutions

Entry to post-secondary education requires successful completion of secondary education. Some candidates may be admitted automatically if exceptional marks are gained at secondary school or specific competitions won. Entrants are normally graded according to their performance at the end of secondary school and, depending on the demand for places, are normally required to take further tests. Before the reform, higher education was organised in three stages or degrees, each of which was a qualification in itself and lead to the next stage. Under the reform these degrees have been eliminated and replaced with a grade system continuing from the fourth grade, reached on successful completion of secondary education, to the tenth grade which is achieved after completing a doctorate. The eighth grade is usually achieved by education and employment.

Four main types of higher education institution can be recognised: two-year schools of higher learning, four-year schools of higher learning, art academies and faculties (associated into universities).

Before 1980 *vise skole* were literally translated as 'higher schools' but were, confusingly, lower than the *visoke skole* (literally 'high schools'). This confusion has now been resolved in the official 1980 statistics by using 'high' for the two-year schools and 'higher' for the four-year schools. For clarity this document uses 'two-year school of higher learning' and 'four-year school of higher learning' respectively.

Two-Year Schools of Higher Learning (Vise Skole)

These schools provide basic training for entry into the professions and may be followed by employment or further study. The schools include teacher training schools (see below) and 'technical colleges' (engineering, agriculture, traffic and communications, medical auxiliaries). In the new grading structure, completion of the course is grade VI, which may be considered as half-way to British degree standard, and a two-year Diploma of Higher Learning may be issued. The graduate acquires the title of her or his profession (e.g. Engineer) without the attribute 'with diploma' which is given on successful completion of the four-year school (see below).

Four-Year Schools of Higher Learning (Visoke Skole)

These are of equal rank and of similar function to faculties, with the difference that little or no post-graduate work is organised. In several republics, schools and faculties are being transformed into research institutes in particular fields. It is likely that the title of these four-year schools will be changed to faculty. The schools provide four-year, and sometimes five-year, courses in aspects of commerce, economics and engineering as well as music and physical culture. Completion of the course leads to grade VIII, with the title, according to professions, of (for example) Engineer 'with diploma'. This may be considered as British degree level.

Art Academies

There are four kinds of art academy – for music, dramatic art, fine arts and applied arts. In certain subjects advanced training is also provided for primary and secondary school teachers. Courses are of four years' duration (although study may extend to five years) and on completion eighth grade is achieved.

Faculties

These provide four- or five-year courses to eighth grade (university first degree level), ninth grade (master's degree) and tenth grade (doctoral level). Before the 1980 Act, the university was a compulsory association of faculties and every faculty had to belong to a university. Subsequently the role of the university was reduced by making it a voluntary association of faculties and other institutions. The implementation of this, however, varies according to the decisions made at republican level. In Serbia, faculties and colleges have to be university members – academies being associated separately, while elsewhere the universities are voluntary associations open to all higher education institutions (so that, for example, the Split faculty of law has not joined the University of Zagreb). There are 19 university communities of various faculties (Belgrade [2], Zagreb, Ljubljana, Sarajevo, Titograd, Skopje, Pristina, Novi Sad, Nis,

Kragujevac, Tuzla, Banja Luka, Mostar, Split, Rijeka, Osijek and Maribor) and a special University of Arts in Belgrade.

Post-Graduate Studies

These are organised by the faculties, academies and four-year high schools. The master's degree (mr) takes 1-2 years with presentation of a thesis. A doctorate is acquired after a master's and may exceptionally, with or without an oral examination, be acquired on the basis of a number of prominent scientific publications and a successful thesis presentation. Post-graduate students are often part time and theses related to an employer's research requirements.

Grading

In elementary and secondary schools marks are on the scale 1 to 5 (1 = fail, 2-5 = pass). Descriptive assessment may be made and general behaviour is also marked. In most university level schools, marks are either from 1-5 or 1-10 (5 = fail; 6 up = pass). Examinations are held very frequently throughout the educational system and the marks obtained are recorded in pupils' examination results books which they use throughout their education.

Teacher Training

The system of teacher training has been undergoing continual change since the mid-1960s. Secondary level (4-5 years) teacher training remains only in some republics, and is being phased out. Applicants who have completed elementary education (at 15 years old) may be accepted into secondary level forms of the pedagogical academies and the remainder have to complete secondary education before applying to pedagogical academies. It is envisaged under the reform that training preparatory to a two-year or four-year higher education will take place in the final phase of the directed secondary system. Increasingly, all teaching personnel are required to have four years of professional training at pedagogical high schools or pedagogical academies. All teachers must pass a professional examination after they have been teaching some time. Teachers who have already entered the profession without four years of higher education are required to take in-service training. A teacher may teach several subjects and in 1976 nearly 50% of subject teachers taught more than one subject in several schools. The largest number of teachers working in several schools were, however, working within one education centre. Changes in supply and demand for particular teachers resulting from curriculum changes under the reform are being met by providing retraining or additional training. The reform also encourages the use of experts from industry to teach certain subjects with pedagogic assistance. Social workers (with two or four years' education) and school psychologists (with four-year school of higher learning) are employed as expert assistants for certain posts in pre-school, elementary and secondary schools.

Summary of Teachers' Qualifications

Pre-School Teachers	Secondary school diplomas with in-service training

Elementary School Teachers
  first stage - 4 years:
    general teachers	

second stage: subject teachers	+ subject teachers first stage: two-year intermediate post-secondary at pedagogic academies or teacher training schools, or higher education
Secondary School Teachers	Teacher training within faculties plus teaching practice
teaching associates	with secondary, intermediate or higher education assist teachers in practical aspects
practical instruction teachers	for production-related work within school; they have intermediate, higher or skilled worker examinations
specialist associates	intermediate or higher education social workers, psychologists etc. in schools
University Teachers lecturers, assistant professors and professors	hold doctorates (exceptionally only master's) and are bound to be active in scientific work as well as teaching
assistant lecturers, trainees	assist university teachers in practical work
researchers	no teaching, pure researchers are research associates or senior research associates.

Technical Teaching

Teachers of specialised subjects teaching at secondary level will have completed the corresponding university faculty and also received additional teacher training. For practical subjects in education centres (photographic and printing, woodworking and furniture making, construction etc.) instructors may have worked in appropriate enterprises as well as possessing the appropriate diploma from a school for highly skilled workers.

In-Service Training

All teacher trainees must take an examination after the initial two years' teaching practice - this gives the title of *ucitelj* ('educator'), *nastavnik* ('teacher'), *profesor* ('professor'). In some republics this examination has been eliminated because of the introduction of compulsory in-service training (Slovenia, Bosnia-Herzegovina) arranged in schools, pedagogical schools, adult education centres, trade unions, etc. In some republics all teachers must complete an appropriate in-service course within five years.

Special and Other Education

Schools for Children with Disabilities

Children with physical or mental disabilities are educated in special pre-school, elementary and secondary school institutions or in special classes in regular schools. The education reforms aim at increasing the provision for all children with disabilities.

Ethnic Minorities

For children who belong to ethnic groups, the communities in which they live organise pre-school, elementary and secondary education - and if there are sufficient candidates, post-secondary education in their native language. These children also learn the language of the republic in which they live and are taught classes in Yugoslav culture and history. Teaching may be bilingual in nationally mixed environments. At the end of the 1977-78 school year there were 1,547 elementary schools, or sections within schools, for minority nationalities, with 466,478 pupils. The summary on the next page gives schools and pupils for ethnic groups.

Adult Education

Provision for adult education is made in special schools for adult education covering elementary and secondary education and vocational skills, classes at regular schools and at educational centres linked to their employment. At the beginning of the 1978/79 school year there were 373 and 423 schools for adult education at elementary and secondary level respectively, with a total of 89,796 students, two thirds of whom were male. By law, certificates awarded are equally as acceptable as those obtained in regular schooling, but there are differences of content and organisation. Courses last for four years instead of eight, by the reduction of elements of the elementary school curriculum, and they may be taken by correspondence. The courses emphasise work-linked subjects and adult students are not required to take a foreign language, art, music, technical training or physical education although many do so voluntarily. At post-secondary level, part time study is the norm.

Schools of Ethnic Nationalities in 1977-78 End of School Year

	Elementary[1] education		Secondary[1] education		Primary and Secondary	
	schools[2]	pupils	schools[2]	pupils	special[3] education pupils	adult[3] education pupils
TOTAL	1,547	466,478	343	70,289	991	4,636
Albanian	1,145	411,718	207	58,777	212	3,359
Bulgarian	68	3,323	1	12	–	–
Czech	12	657	–	–	–	–
Hungarian[4]	172	33,187	86	8,962	726	1,167
Italian	29	1,218	13	457	–	–
Romanian	31	2,801	12	429	–	40
Ruthenian	4	969	3	216	17	–
Slovak	23	5,706	9	661	27	70
Turkish	63	6,899	12	775	9	–

[1] Regular schooling
[2] A school having classes with instruction in languages of nationalities is taken as a unit
[3] Primary and secondary education
[4] Including bilingual schools

Illiteracy figures based on the 1971 census give a total of 2,550,000 or 15.1% of the population broken down as follows:

Age:	10-19	20-34	35-64	65 and over
%:	3.1	5.2	21.6	42.8

There is considerable variation between the regions and the sexes, but there has been a gradual fall since the census. Courses for adults are organised by local communes, industries, trade unions, etc.

Non-Formal

Apart from courses run by industrial enterprises and trade unions, much continuing education is provided by Workers and People's Universities. These are forms of adult education centres and not to be confused with the higher education universities conferring academic degrees. Course length varies from two weeks to two years. While some courses lead to vocational qualifications, others are social in emphasis designed to raise the level of general education.

Military Schools

The Yugoslav Army trains commissioned and non-commissioned officers in its own institutions, from secondary level to postgraduate studies. As a rule these schools undertake training which cannot be provided in civilian schools, but the system is essentially similar to the civilian educational system with entry by open competition. Efforts are made to ensure even distribution of members of all nationalities of Yugoslavia. all nationals are eligible for admission subject to general eligibility on grounds of successful completion of primary or secondary school, medical and social fitness, and approval of their family. In addition to curricula based on educational requirements for the Services, general education in military schools corresponds to that in civilian schools and comprises about 50% of the courses in military secondary schools and 40% in military academies. All higher military schools organise two-year MA courses, one-year specialisation courses and confer Doctorates of Military Science upon passing an oral examination and defence of a thesis.

Religious Secondary and Higher Learning Schools

These schools prepare pupils aspiring to the clergy and are directed and managed by the corresponding religious communities. In 1977/78 there were 18 religious secondary schools (1,652 pupils : 244 teachers) and ten religious schools of higher learning (1,110 students : 72 teachers).

7 EDUCATIONAL ADMINISTRATION

Decentralisation

As befits such a complex country, the mechanism of educational management and administration in Yugoslavia is highly complex. In brief, legal responsibility resides principally with the republics and provinces with a substantial degree of decentralisation within the republics. Organisations at every level are involved including the schools themselves and the local community.

Republican and Communal Responsibilities

Legislation is a matter for the republican or provincial assemblies; the amount of detail laid down varies from one region to another, but the responsibility is clear enough. Carrying out the laws is overseen by a republican secretariat for education and culture, which also maintains an inspectorate for the republic as a whole. Republican education councils, appointed by the assemblies or their executive councils, are responsible for drawing up plans, curricula, syllabi, etc., though again the degree of detailed prescription varies. There is also a variety of specialist committees or institutions for the promotion of education, publishing of textbooks, journals on education, diverting additional funds to poorer regions, etc. At the level of the commune, the assembly has responsibility for setting up schools, changing and developing their functions, and through its specialist bodies is responsible for finance, inspection, professional supervision. Thus the commune is responsible for the general provision of educational services in its area.

Self-Management

Detailed running of the schools is left to the schools themselves and each individual institution has its own self-management organisation, the Assembly of Workers (i.e. all those employed in the school) and the School Council, an elected body with representatives of the teachers, parents, socio-political organisations and, in the case of secondary and higher institutions, the students as well. In the case of school centres there is normally one self-management organisation for the whole centre, plus a committee for each component school. There are also professional bodies responsible for educational policy and practice - teachers' councils (chaired by the school directors) and form councils (chaired by the appropriate form teachers). School directors are normally appointed for a four-year period by the school council (though in Slovenia this is done by the commune assembly). In addition to this, teachers elect delegates to the commune assembly, and also to the increasingly important 'self-managing community of interest' for education in the area. Teachers at all levels are likely to be involved in a great many committees. Institutions of higher education are organised on similar lines but with students participating in the self-managing committees.

Scheme of Military Schools by Level and Service Situation in the 1974/75 Academic Year

Military schools	JNA Services	Field Army (FA)	Air Force and Anti-Aircraft Schools Defence (AAD)	Navy (N)	Schools for JNA Services
SECONDARY SCHOOLS	Military gymnasia 4 years	Bratstvo-jedinstvo Military gymnasium Belgrade; Ivo Lola Ribar Military gymnasium Zagreb; Franc Rozman Stane Military Gymnasium Ljubljana	Marsal Tito Air Force military gymnasium Mostar		
	Secondary military schools 4 years	Secondary military school - FA Sarajevo; Secondary technical military school - FA Zagreb	Air Force technical military school Sajlovac	Naval technical secondary military school Split	Secondary service corps military school Sarajevo; Secondary musical military school Zemum
HIGHER	Advanced military school - 2 years	Military academy - FA Belgrade	Air Force military academy Zadar	Naval military academy Split	Military Academy of economics Belgrade

	Military academies 4-5 years	Technical military academy – FA Zagreb	Air Force technical military academy Rajlovac		Military medical academy Belgrade
M I L I T A R Y	Command-staff academies 1 year	Command-staff academy – FA Belgrade	AF and AAD academy Belgrade	Naval Command-staff academy Split	JNA Military political college Belgrade
S C H O O L S	National defence schools				National defence school Belgrade

Source: Yugoslav Survey, 1975

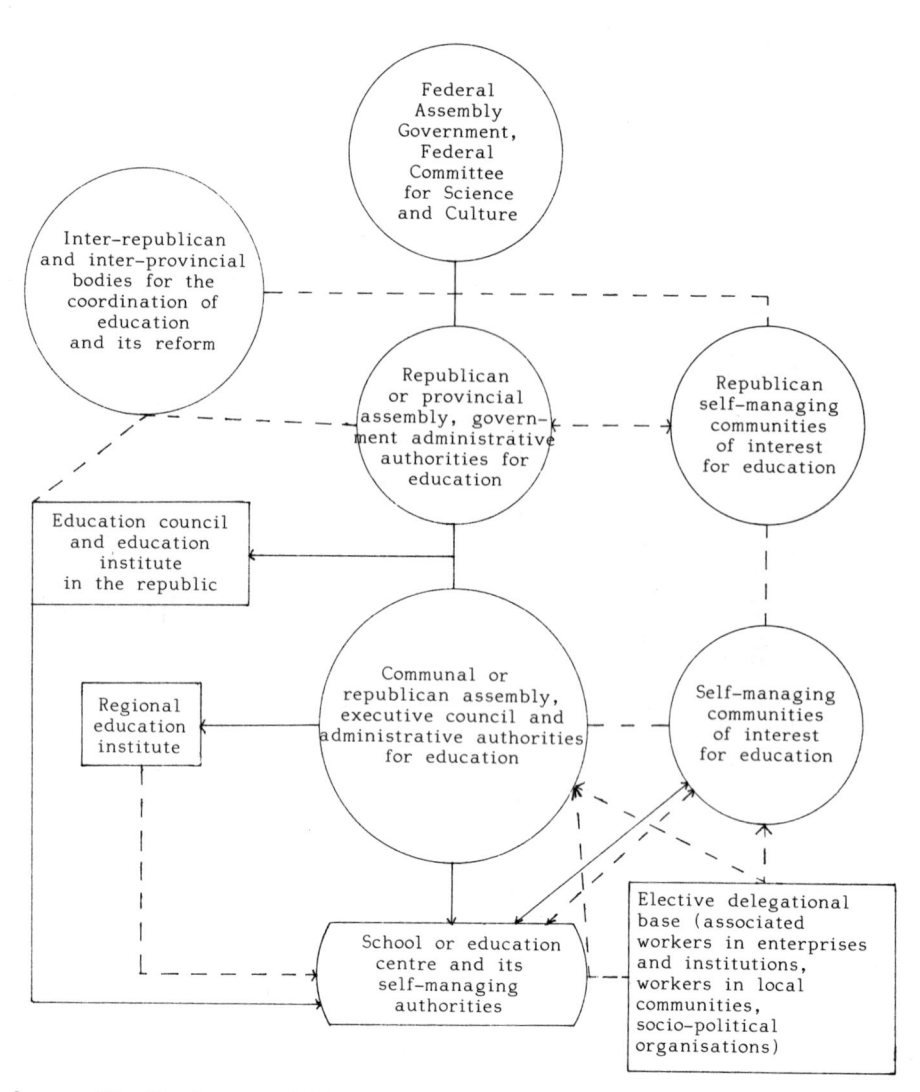

Educational Administration

```
                    ┌─────────────┐
                    │   Federal   │
                    │  Assembly   │
                    │ Government, │
                    │   Federal   │
                    │  Committee  │
                    │ for Science │
                    │ and Culture │
                    └─────────────┘
```

- Inter-republican and inter-provincial bodies for the coordination of education and its reform
- Republican or provincial assembly, government administrative authorities for education
- Republican self-managing communities of interest for education
- Education council and education institute in the republic
- Regional education institute
- Communal or republican assembly, executive council and administrative authorities for education
- Self-managing communities of interest for education
- School or education centre and its self-managing authorities
- Elective delegational base (associated workers in enterprises and institutions, workers in local communities, socio-political organisations)

Source: 'The Development of Education in Yugoslavia 1974-76': Yugoslav Commission for Cooperation with UNESCO and Republican Institute for the Advancement of Training and Education, Belgrade, July 1977.

Organisation of Reforms

Most important from the point of view of the present reforms, an Inter-Republican Provincial Commission on Educational Reform was established in 1975. This brings together the republican representatives of the school systems including the secretaries for education (roughly, the ministers), representatives of the appointed education councils, and the directors of planning organisations called Institutes for the Promotion of the School Systems (or their equivalents). Thus, although the details and the timing of the reforms vary considerably from one republic to another, there is a substantial degree of similarity in their direction and principles, and indeed in the institutional pattern through which they are interpreted.

Education Information and Documentation

All republics and provinces have bodies responsible for provision of information on the educational system and educational policies. The various organisations (educational institutes, centres, faculties) cooperate in the exchange and provision of information and are developing their educational information systems to form a network. At federal level it is proposed to set up an inter republican/provincial education information centre for providing information not easily available at republican or provincial levels and this centre will form part of international networks of educational information. With the reforms in the education system concomitant information systems are being set up.

8 EDUCATIONAL FINANCE

Financial Administration

The financing of educational institutions is also decentralised being based on a system of agreements between the schools themselves and the communes: the money comes from taxation raised by the appropriate 'communities of interest'. (In some cases this function may be exercised by communities of interest covering more than one commune but the principle is essentially the same.) The detailed internal distribution of funds is a matter for the school itself, though the criteria generally have to be approved by the commune or even republican assembly. Some schools also receive funds directly from republican sources, from industrial enterprises and many, especially those with a technical bias, raise money externally through producing and selling goods, servicing equipment or training personnel for outside commercial enterprise.

Distribution of Resources

A system of purely local financing would perpetuate the inequalities between richer and poorer areas; all republics therefore use a system of supplementary financing, whereby additional funds are channelled by the republican authorities to areas of particular need with a view to equalising standards of school provision. This has not yet been fully realised even within republics, and the republics themselves are far from equal in resources. Some inter-republican differences are likely to remain for some time, but within each republic the trend is towards greater equality, while leaving responsibility for raising and managing funds as far as possible with the local communities.

Education Budget and Allocation of Funds

Given this decentralisation of financing it is obviously difficult to produce overall figures for educational expenditure. However, the figure for total educational expenditure in 1978 was 44.5 billion dinars, representing 5.5% of the national income. The percentage breakdown of current expenditure by levels was as follows:

	%
Pre-school and primary	49.2
Secondary	25.6
Tertiary	15.2
Other types	1.8
Not allocated by level	8.2

9 DEVELOPMENT AND PLANNING OF THE EDUCATIONAL SYSTEM

Federal Influence

There is no single body at federal level analogous to a Ministry of Education, but there are a number of mechanisms to ensure a considerable degree of coordination, especially in planning. In 1972, a standing conference of republican and provincial institutions for the promotion of education was set up in Ljubljana (chiefly for the harmonisation of policy and strategy) and an institute responsible for educational information and documentation exists in Belgrade. The Federal Institute for International Educational, Cultural and Scientific Cooperation coordinates international links, though republican bodies are largely responsible for this.

Political Involvement

While in the final analysis control of basic policies in education, as in other areas, may be seen to be in the hands of the League of Communists of Yugoslavia, the self-management system not only secures participation at all levels but also provides a check on the exercise of power. Education in Yugoslavia is intended to further the development of a socialist society by teaching Marxist ideology and providing the necessary skills and attitudes to enable people to work towards this end.

Basic Principles of Educational Policy

These may be listed as follows:

- expanding pre-school institutions and increasing enrolment
- compulsory eight-year elementary schooling for all
- open access to all levels of education, and equality without regard to race, nationality, sex, social background or means
- coeducation: joint education of boys and girls on all levels
- socialist orientation of the system: decreasing role of State and engaging working people and citizens in management of education
- equality of institutionalised and extra-mural forms
- education as a permanent process
- continuity and integration with the needs of society while ensuring the maximum degree of democracy
- free instruction
- self-management organisation of all educational institutions and linking with other organisations of associated labour
- right to instruction in the student's own tongue
- special provision for pupils with disabilities and with exceptional abilities
- a balanced programme 'strengthening ties with the whole field of work, promoting general and polytechnical education, a Marxist ideological orientation and the ideas of brotherhood, unity and internationalism'
- diversity of educational forms, programmes and methods but with unity in variety and a high degree of self-management rights.

10 THE SYSTEM IN OPERATION

Within the context of these principles emphasis has been placed on reform of the system; at the 1974 Congress of the League of Communists, a major priority was seen as the continuous development and modernisation of education involving not only increased flexibility in the system, but also changes in content with a view to giving pupils the skills for further learning. Allied to this was a concentration on the promotion of education combined with work, with greater emphasis on general work education and social 'character formation', participation in socially useful and productive work and the cultivation of individual potential through optional courses. To this end the 1974 Congress called for closer links between educational and labour organisations within the framework of self-management with the aim of planning educational policy more closely in accord with the needs of labour. In addition the 1974 Congress called for greater emphasis on ideological education both in theory and practice through the study of Marxism and through a closer involvement of pupils in the management of schools in collaboration with the various relevant bodies. Major importance was also placed on the role of education in the reduction of social differences. Proposals towards the achievement of this aim include:

- special efforts to eradicate illiteracy
- development and expansion of pre-school education
- provision of universal eight-year schooling
- elimination of dualism in secondary education
- equalisation of conditions of work in schools
- expansion of remedial classes for the socially disadvantaged
- more scholarships for students
- expansion of boarding schools
- free transport and textbooks
- provision of school canteens.

Other concrete proposals were the improvement of the training and conditions of teachers and an expansion and greater use of educational research.

REFERENCES AND FURTHER READING

Barclays Bank Limited (1980). *ABECOR Country Report: Yugoslavia*. Barclays Bank Limited, May 1980.

Federal Statistical Office (1980). *Statistical Pocketbook of Yugoslavia, 1980)* (26th issue). Belgrade.

Inter-Republic Committee for Cooperation with OECD in the Field of Education (1980). 'Report on the conditions, problems and policy of education in the Socialist Federal Republic of Yugoslavia'. Federal Administration for International Scientific, Educational, Cultural and Technical Cooperation, Belgrade.

Juhas, M. (1975). 'Education and its Reform in Yugoslavia'. Institute for Studies in Education, Belgrade.

Juhas, M. (1978). 'Educational Reform in Yugoslavia'. *Yugoslav Survey* XIX, Nov. 1978, 75-98.

Juhas, M. (1979). 'Secondary Education - Trends and achievements'. *Yugoslav Survey* XX, August 1979, 83-94.

Lloyds Bank Limited (1980). *Economic Report - 'Yugoslavia'*. Lloyds Bank Limited, Overseas Division, January 1980.

OECD (1980). 'Yugoslavia'. *OECD Economic Surveys*, May 1980.

Rakic, P. (1979). 'Teaching Staff in Elementary and Secondary Schools'. *Yugoslav Survey* XX, May 1979, 149-158.

Stanic, D. (1975). 'Military Schools of the Yugoslav People's Army'. *Yugoslav Survey* **XVI**, May 1975, 89-102.
Yugoslav Commission for Cooperation with UNESCO and Republican Institute for the Advancement of Training and Education (1977). 'The Development of Education in Yugoslavia 1974-1976'. Belgrade.

Structure of the Education System in Yugoslavia

Age	3	4	5	6	7	8	9	10	11	12	13	14	15	16	17	18	19	20	21	22	23	24
Level					I									II						III		
Stage					1									2		3				4		
Compulsory					/////	XXXXXXXXXXXXXXXXXXXXX																
School type					Ecoles primaires (Poly-technique)									Ecoles secondaires base General communeVOC.				Enseignement supérieur Hautes écoles et facultés				

/// Education preceding the first level

Examinations: professional qualifications associated with each stage

Source: UNESCO/IBE International Yearbook of Education

Compulsory Education: Age Limits 7-15 Duration (years) 8
Entrance age to pre-school education: 3

YUGOSLAVIA BASIC STATISTICS	1960	1970	1975	1978 (approx.)
1 Total population (000)	18,402	20,371	21,322	21,914
% female	51	51	51	
2 % population 0-14 years	30.5	27.4		25.0
% female	49	49	49	49
3 Enrolment, all levels	3,287,858	3,822,285	4,153,918	4,281,165
% female		46		
First level	1,715,584	1,579,064	1,494,825	1,427,769
% female	48	48	49	49
Second level	1,431,700	1,982,018	2,264,101	2,413,785
% female		45		46
Third level	140,574	261,203	394,992	439,608
% female	29	39	40	39
4 Teachers, all levels		163,639		
% female		51		
First level		58,353	60,904	57,335
% female		67	67	79
Second level	68,603	88,493		127,906
% female		47		49
Third level	10,404	16,783		21,767
% female	20	21		22
5 Public expenditure on education				
Total (000) Dinars	732,940	8,739,000	28,897,000	
As % of GNP	2.3	4.9	5.2	
6 % enrolment (MF) by level	100	100	100	100
First level	52	41	36	33
Second level	44	52	55	56
Third level	4	7	10	11
% enrolment (F) by level	100	100	100	100
First level		43		35
Second level		51		56
Third level		6		9
7 Entrance age: duration of				
First level education	7:4	7:4	7:4	7:4
Second level education	11:8	11:8	11:8	11:8
8 Enrolment ratios (MF)				
First level	111	105	102	99
Second level	59	63	76	82
Third level	8.61	15.93	20.00	22.52
Enrolment ratios (F)				
First level	109	104	102	98
Second level		58		78
Third level	5.07	12.87	16.31	18.18